NELSON

CAROLA OMAN

NELSON

THE REPRINT SOCIETY
LONDON

By the Same Author

BIOGRAPHIES

ELIZABETH OF BOHEMIA
HENRIETTA MARIA

HISTORICAL NOVELS

THE EMPRESS
CROUCHBACK
MAJOR GRANT
OVER THE WATER
THE BEST OF HIS FAMILY

MODERN FICTION

NOTHING TO REPORT
SOMEWHERE IN ENGLAND

FIRST PUBLISHED 1947
THIS EDITION PUBLISHED BY THE REPRINT SOCIETY LTD.
BY ARRANGEMENT WITH HODDER AND STOUGHTON LTD.
1950

PRINTED IN ENGLAND BY
HAZELL WATSON & VINEY LTD
AYLESBURY AND LONDON

Nelson Monuments, with the exception of a few, spontaneously erected close upon the news of Trafalgar, were not much liked by his contemporaries, and are to-day revered rather for the man than the manner of commemoration. When, at last, Trafalgar Square was pronounced complete, the result was condemned by Londoners: the gentlest critics complained of sensations of disappointment, and "unworthiness". The Neo-Gothic tower dominating the Calton Hill, Edinburgh, has been several times threatened with demolition.

Something of the same fate has attended the efforts of authors. "The bibliography of Nelson", wrote Sir J. K. Laughton in 1894 "is enormous, but comparatively little of it has any real value." The first biography of Nelson was published during his lifetime, after the battles of the Nile and Copenhagen, and before Trafalgar; but John Charnock, an enthusiastic Naval volunteer, who had a rich source in Captain William Locker, Nelson's old sea-daddy, "improved" original letters and contrived to produce a work of outstanding dullness. A number of ephemeral memoirs of no authority were rushed into print to meet the popular demand upon the death of a hero. In 1809 came something solid. The Rev. James Clarke, Librarian and Chaplain to the Prince of Wales, and John M'Arthur, who had been Secretary to Lord Hood and Sir Hyde Parker, had collaborated before, in the monthly "Naval Chronicle". Both had been afloat in the Royal Service, and M'Arthur, when Purser of the Victory, had often encountered Nelson. They had been generously supplied with material, particularly by the Nelson family. Their list of "Orders received prior to publication", printed in the first of their two handsomely-produced, weighty, illustrated, calf-bound quarto volumes, contains the names of all who had known Nelson best. As a book of reference their work falls into the "difficult" category, as it is unprovided with an index; but no reviewer drew attention to this in 1809, or to a more serious omission. The biographers announced that for the last four years of their hero's life, they had preferred to devote themselves exclusively to "his more splendid public character". The authors of "The Life and Services of Horatio, Viscount Nelson, from his Lordship's MSS.," had also to contend with one more

disadvantage than is inevitable in a biography composed with a strict eye
to the susceptibilities of survivors.

The public of their own day accepted the semi-official biography with
docility. Proofs were sent to the widowed Lady Nelson, to Earl Nelson
and his sisters, and, upon her own request, to Lady Hamilton. A special
copy, upon vellum, was acquired by the British Museum. A second
edition (still un-indexed), in three volumes, followed in 1840. At a date
when no Englishman's home of any pretensions was complete without a
library, it was expected that every library should contain a copy of the
standard life of a national hero.

Meanwhile, an author who could write had unblushingly "lifted" the
undigested material of Messrs. Clarke and M'Arthur into English litera-
ture. The Poet Laureate, in 1813, added scarcely any information of value,
and some mistakes, but "Southey's Nelson" is one of the tales that hold
children from play and old men from the chimney corner. (An edition
published in 1922, with notes by Sir Geoffrey Callender, saves the modern
reader from accepting the inaccuracies of 1813.) Another contemporary,
James Harrison, stands, by general consent, lowest in esteem of Nelson
biographers. He was a man of dreadful calling, a hireling, and his duty, as
he understood it, was to produce, against time, a two-volume biography
of Nelson, designed at all costs to exalt the claims of Lady Hamilton to a
Government pension. The result, published in 1806, has been described by
David Hannay, a severe critic, as "one of the most nauseous of known books",
and it has always been so much resented for its insincerity that the fact that
it contains a little information obtainable nowhere else is usually overlooked.

In 1814, having stolen the originals from a patroness who had no more
to give, Harrison printed, anonymously, "The Letters of Lord Nelson to
Lady Hamilton", which had a succès de scandale, was denounced as a
forgery by many of the hero's admirers, and gave a tottering woman the
last shove towards a premature grave. The stolen originals passed en bloc
into the possession of Dr. Thomas Pettigrew, and were used by him in
1849 for yet another two-volume biography. As Pettigrew offered no
explanation of his ownership of these startling documents, in a book
otherwise "distressful bread", he was discredited and much abused. Other
letters from the collection which he made have drifted into the market at
intervals, the most important being the lot bought by Mr. Alfred Morrison
at Sotheby's in 1888, privately printed in 1894, and generally known as

"*The Morrison MS.*". The whereabouts and correct text of the "*Harrison*" letters remained a source of speculation for exactly a hundred years. There should, somewhere, be sixty-one of them, all in the unmistakable, foursquare, toppling, hasty but highly legible, left-handed writing of Nelson's later years. They had not been quoted from sight since Pettigrew used them. They might have been destroyed.

They were sought for in vain by Sir Harris Nicolas, who completed in 1846 his seven-volume collection of "*The Letters and Despatches of Vice-Admiral Lord Viscount Nelson*", the work which remains to-day the Bible of the Nelson student. Nicolas had full access to the essential MSS. which were inherited by Nelson's niece, Lady Bridport, and bought from her son in 1895 by a special grant of Parliament, for the Nation. The ninety-two volumes in the British Museum are catalogued as Add. MSS. 34,902–92, "Nelson Papers", and 35,191, "Bridport Papers". Sir Harris was unlucky in that the relicts of Messrs. Clarke and M'Arthur refused permission for him to inspect the material lent to these authors. He was obliged to do as he had done in the case of the "Harrison" letters, print from what had been already published, and he did so unhappily, as he had reason to believe that the collaborators had disregarded the first principles of editorship.

Much that Sir Harris Nicolas longed to see is now available, and has been consulted for the present biography. Inspection of the manuscripts collected by the late Lady Llangattock, foundress of the Nelson Museum, Monmouth, disclosed five bound volumes, labelled "Nelson Papers". Of these, the first three contain the originals of letters from Nelson to his wife, opening with his proposal of marriage following a verbal declaration, and ending with his last note before the stormy homecoming which resulted in a separation. All the letters quoted by Clarke and M'Arthur are there, and comparison of what they printed with the originals shows that they not only cut, and ran several letters into one; they altered the wording, giving false evidence which has been repeated by every succeeding Nelson biographer. There are, in addition, in these three volumes, upwards of a hundred and twenty letters in the hand of Nelson, which have never been printed; and the biographers of 1809 principally eschewed, not the trivial or repetitive, but the intimate. The remaining two volumes of "Nelson Papers" in the Llangattock collection, one labelled "Holog. Coresp." and four portfolios, include Nelson family correspondence, the "recollections" supplied by Lady Nelson to M'Arthur and Nelson's own Journals of his Calvi and Bastia campaigns, and his actions at St. Vincent.

Amongst the considerable collections at the National Maritime Museum, Greenwich, are to be seen those of Nelson's daughter (Nelson-Ward MS.). Early in 1949, the Museum acquired the Nelson collection formed by Sir Thomas Phillipps, Bart., antiquary and bibliophile (1792–1872). MS. No. 29,914, Box 3, proved to contain fifty-five letters from Nelson to Lady Hamilton, last used by a biographer in 1849. Comparison of these originals with the printed versions showed that the asterisks introduced by Harrison often signified a lost sheet, not a deletion, and where passages in the letters had been deliberately deleted, it was not by the pen of the original writer. In most cases the words, although heavily scored out, could, with care, be deciphered. That Nelson sent to Lady Hamilton love-poems of his own composition could no longer be doubted.

Harvard University Library possesses the collections bequeathed by Miss Amy Lowell, Mr. Joseph Husband and an anonymous donor.

The author wishes firstly to record her debt of gratitude to the late Sir Geoffrey Callender, Director of the National Maritime Museum, Greenwich, for assistance and advice extending over four years; she would also thank the Council of the Borough of Monmouth for permission to inspect and make transcripts from the Llangattock MS. in the Nelson Museum, Monmouth; John Eyre-Matcham, Esq., and Messrs. John Lane (publishers of "The Nelsons of Burnham Thorpe", by the late Miss Eyre-Matcham) for permission to quote from the Matcham MS.; the Hon. Mrs. Fremantle for permission to quote from "The Wynne Diaries", edited by Anne Fremantle; Brigadier Sir H. Floyd, Bart., for the loan of the Polar Journals of Thomas Floyd, R.N. (1751–78); T. A. Thorpe, Esq., for the loan of the letters of George Thorpe, R.N. (1790–97) (and the Editor of "Blackwood's Magazine" for permission to quote from Mr. T. A. Thorpe's article in Vol. 1535 "Blackwood's Magazine"); the Rev. Hugh Nelson-Ward for information kindly communicated on the subject of his grandmother, Horatia; Kenneth Pridie, Esq., for advice on the subject of Nelson's amputation; the Rector of Burnham Thorpe for local information; Miss Henrietta Tayler for the revision of proofs; and James Ross, Esq., City Librarian at the Central Municipal Library, Bristol, for bringing together many volumes.

C. O.

CONTENTS

ILLUSTRATIONS

Horatio Nelson, *ætat.* 18½, Second Lieutenant, H.M.S. *Lowestoffe.* *Frontispiece*

By *John Francis Rigaud*, R.A. (1742–1810). (49″ × 42″.) *Verso*

Nelson gave sittings for this portrait before sailing for Jamaica station, in 1777, but left it unfinished in the artist's studio until his return to England, when, in 1781, he presented it to Captain William Locker, R.N., with the words, "It will not be the least like what I am now, that is certain; but you may tell Mr. Rigaud to add beauty to it." Rigaud labelled it, when completed, "Captain Horatio Nelson, 1781", and Locker lent it to R. Shipster, of Woolwich, when the printsellers began to demand the portrait of an Admiral of growing reputation. Shipster's small stipple engraving, published August 14, 1797, was labelled, "Horatio Nelson, Esq., now Sir Horatio Nelson, K.B., Rear-Admiral of the Blue Squadron."

Portraits of His Majesty's Ships, *Agamemnon, Captain, Vanguard, Elephant* and *Victory.* (21″ × 14″.) *Frontispiece*

Painted by Nicolas Pocock, 1808, for Messrs. Clarke and M'Arthur's "Life and Services of Admiral Lord Nelson", in which an engraving by James Fittler was reproduced with the following inscription—"Mr. Pocock has happily succeeded in giving very accurate likenesses of the several ships in which Nelson distinguished himself, as Captain, Commodore and Admiral, and he has grouped them at anchor at Spithead, having their sails loose to dry. In the background there is a distant view of Portsmouth."

Sir Horatio Nelson, K.B., *ætat.* 39, Rear-Admiral of the Blue Squadron

By *Lemuel Abbott* (1760–1803). (30″ × 25″.) *Opposite*

Nelson gave sittings for this portrait (a "study" upon which a full-length could be based) in the house of the Lieutenant-Governor of the Royal Hospital, Greenwich (Captain William Locker), in October 1797, after the loss of his arm, but before the stump had healed. Abbott subsequently produced many other half-lengths, with additional decorations and with and without a hat, and several full-lengths, in the backgrounds of which Santa Cruz was altered, at appropriate dates, to Aboukir Bay and the quarter-deck of the *Victory* at Trafalgar.

This version, which has never before been reproduced in a biography, was engraved by Richard Earlom, December 7, 1798.

Lady Hamilton at Merton.   *Opposite*
By Thomas Baxter. (7″ × 5″.)

> This pencil sketch, which has never before been reproduced, represents Lady Hamilton in her later thirties, as Nelson knew her, at Merton. Only one of the famous Romney portraits was painted after her marriage, in 1791; all the remainder before she was twenty-one.

All reproduced by kind permission of the Trustees, the National Maritime Museum, Greenwich.

MAPS AND PLANS

Chapter I

1758–1778
(*ætat.* 0–20)

"NEPHEW TO CAPTAIN SUCKLING"

I

ON Friday, September 29, 1758, a fine day in an autumn described as very fair, the wife of the Rector of Burnham Thorpe, Burnham St.-Albert-with-Alp and Burnham Norton, Norfolk, gave birth to a son.

The curtain rises upon a placid scene. The auspices were propitious. The birthplace was lavishly picturesque. Burnham Thorpe Parsonage House was surrounded by gardens in which the Rector devotedly, but not always successfully, cultivated "laylocks", syringas, hyacinths and particularly roses: "Burgundy rose plants, a cluster rose, a Hundred leaf rose, moss roses and rose *de Meaux*". In September, according to him, "the air from our light gravell soil, impregnated with the sweet *Farinæ* of the field, is as healthy as any spott whatever". The child was welcome, as children are apt to be where first efforts to raise a family have been attended by tragedy. He was a sixth child and fifth son, but his two eldest brothers had died in infancy. The parents were well-matched in every respect. Both came of good stock; the lady's ancestry being slightly though unmistakably more lustrous than that of her husband, a fact which the Rector, least worldly of men, gratefully recognised. (On the death of the third Earl of Orford, in 1791, the Rev. Edmund Nelson put his household into mourning, and instructed a married daughter, "You may with great propriety do the same. If any ask why? you may say that the late Lord's grandfather, Sir R. Walpole, and your great-grandmother, were sister and brother. So stands the consanguinity.")

The name Horatio had entered the Walpole family in 1678. It was disliked by its second bearer, who wrote from Strawberry

Hill that he preferred to sign himself "Horace—an English name for an Englishman". Horatio, first Baron Walpole of Wolterton, had been sponsor and had given his name to the second of the Rev. Edmund Nelson's short-lived children. His son and successor was asked to perform the same duties on November 15, 1758. The parish register shows that Horatio Nelson had already been privately baptised on October 9, but this entry need not be taken to suggest delicacy. The same had been done eighteen months before in the case of his brother William, whose health was robust for seventy-eight years.

The public christenings of the Rector's children took place in the parish church of All Saints', Burnham Thorpe, less than a mile, as the crow flies, from the Parsonage House. The fields and hedge-rows on the route were bright in summer with poppies, daisies, cornflowers, musk thistles and mulleins. Hawthorns, chestnuts and much yew shadowed the holy ground. The simple and dignified little church has suffered restoration, but stands essentially as it did on the day that Horatio Nelson received the name which he was to bear for less than forty-eight years. Its nave is supported by round pillars dating from the middle of the thirteenth century. In the chancel, a knight who died on Christmas Eve, 1420, lies with his mailed feet on his house-dog, and the collar of the SS. on his steel corselet. A worn font of Purbeck marble, at which children of the village are still baptised, now has for company a great rood and a lectern made of wood from H.M.S. *Victory*.

2

Nelson's birthplace was pulled down three years before his death, but contemporary demand produced many likenesses, of which one of the most attractive is a sketch, painted from memory, by a member of the neighbouring family of Crowe.

The old Parsonage House was a two-storied, L-shaped building, composed of a couple of small houses, or big cottages, of different dates and sizes. The larger and taller half contained the tall, hooded front door and six square windows, and upon an end wall, which was a sun-trap, climbing fruit-trees were trained. The smaller half boasted two sash, two casement and two dormer windows, and the steep roof of both portions was covered by the red, fluted tiles still noticeable in the district.

His thirty acres were a continual source of alternate solace and dismay to the Rector, who delighted in chronicling the growth of his corn, turnips, pease and beans, and in walking forth upon his "charming openn lawns and fields" ("there Nature will meet you smiling"), but could not, in his less resilient moments, imagine how a farmer ever contrived to make a living.

Within the house there is mention of a little dressing-room with adjoining bedroom, "somewhat like a Bath lodging", and a guest-chamber which Captain Nelson and his lady, fresh from the West Indies, were brought to confess was the coldest they had ever inhabited. There were domestic quarters to which the Rector sent a present of hot punch on the birthday of his absent sailor son; the parlour was lit by candles in girandoles, and for a family that rose early and dined at 4 p.m., nine o'clock was bedtime.

That Horatio Nelson was the son of a clergyman is a statement which needs amplification. Both his grandfathers were East Anglian clergy; two of his great-uncles, eight cousins and two of his brothers took holy orders.

The Nelsons' nearest neighbours at Burnham Thorpe were the Crowes at the Hall, distant cousins but close friends, and the seven daughters and one son of Sir Mordaunt Martin, Baronet, "of a very ancient and Knightly family", once Marshal of the Vice-Admiralty Court in Jamaica, but now settled at Burnham Westgate. Bird names haunted the Nelsons, for after the Crowes and Martins followed a troop of Ravens, old-established attorneys. With the Cokes of Holkham, where everything was done "in Stile, with some ceremonious splendour", there was, during the youth of Horatio Nelson, no intimacy. Rolfe cousins from Hilborough Rectory and Canon Poyntz of North Creake were constant guests, and when Countess Spencer, mother of Georgiana, Duchess of Devonshire (and, what was more important to a sea-officer, presently mother of the First Lord of the Admiralty), visited her brother the canon, this ideal dowager was "as usual, extremely polite". Further afield lay "your titled relations", the genial Durrants of Scottow Hall, the Townshends at Raynham, the Walpoles of Wolterton, "very good people", and the Walpoles at Houghton.

The children of Burnham Thorpe Rectory were enthusiastically East Anglian, fully alive to the charms of a county rich in romance and mellifluous place-names—Cressingham, Blakeney, Costessey— rich, also, in old manor-houses, ruined abbeys and castles, in bowl- ing-greens, where nut-brown ale was drunk, and in clear-bedded lagoons, haunts of the heron and kingfisher, where windmills and wherries drowsed beneath immense quick-changing skies, and atmospheric effects were often of unearthly beauty.

Their immediate background in a county of which two-thirds is bounded by tidal water was of rolling fields and wooded hills, but within four miles of the Rectory came a low, flat coastline of muted colour, of sand and salt-marsh, and a streak of light, shifting and bright as fish-scales, on which far sails moved slowly. There was always a salt tang in the air blowing in at the oddly assorted windows of the Old Parsonage House, and on early mornings of silver frost, gulls stood on the lawns. On wild winter nights a distant roar was eternally audible, on wide summer days a ceaseless murmur. Of course such a district had produced naval heroes. Cockthorpe, in the adjacent hundred of North Greenhoe, was the birthplace of three Admirals—Myngs, Narbrough and Cloudsley Shovell. Local legends told of villages engulfed since the Conquest, whence mariners heard church bells ringing on holy days, and at Brancaster Bay, famous for its submarine forests, fishermen still dragged ashore the tusks of mammoths. The grave little churches of the north-west marshes, mostly flint-walled, guarded recumbent effigies and brasses of naïve beauty.

It could not be denied that, owing to their exposed position, the Burnhams were in winter and early spring colder than the rest of the county. On a Christmas evening the Rector returned thanks that he had been able to make his way, through deep snow, to per- form his duties at two parishes without injury; on a March day the beeches seemed to him to be making languid efforts.

The towns which loomed largest in the lives of the young Nelsons were Norwich, Lynn and Aylsham. There is cheerful mention of the Sessions Ball at Norwich, the Lynn Feast, the Aylsham Assem- bly. As they grew up, stage-coach, diligence, post-chaise, chariot and farm cart were setting down in these places gentry in velvet and powder, bagmen, abigails, rustics in hoods and smocks—all the types of Constable, Gainsborough, Downman, Wheatley and Morland. It was the date of "Farmer George", "Who'll Buy My Sweet Lavender?" and "Heart of Oak are our Ships".

3

The New Year of 1768, bleakest season amongst the parishes of the north marshes, found Burnham Thorpe Parsonage a house of mourning. The Rector's wife had died on the day after Christmas, and her mother five days later. The Rector performed both funeral services, entered both burials in the registers, and then, repairing heavily to his darkened home, faced the fact that it had fallen to his lot to be in future "double parent" to eight children, the youngest ten months old. No spinster or widowed sister on either side of the family was available to help him. He believed that he had never mixed enough in the great world to be an entertaining or valuable companion. He only hoped that if he should, hereafter, fall short in care and affection, his children would excuse him, and consider with compassion that his task had been too hard. "Insipid", "whimsical and very unfitt for society" were his unsparing descriptions of himself. He was six-and-forty, a tall man, with loosely-hung limbs, long irregular features, dark brows and shoulder-long, prematurely white hair. He never considered remarriage, and more than a quarter of a century later remembered the anniversary of "this day your poor Mother was laid in the peacefull grave". His father, although the younger son of a younger son, had been educated at Eton, and Emmanuel College, Cambridge. He, too, had been a Cambridge man; only delicacy had prevented his being sent to a public school. He foresaw now that the day of small things had come to the Parsonage House.

The children of Burnham Thorpe Parsonage were brought up by a father whose notions of discipline were so strict that he deemed it an indulgence for a back to touch the back of a chair, and held that weak eyes were no excuse for using glasses. His staff included four characters who sound Shakespearean—"Will, indoors" and "Peter, without", "Tom Stocking" and "Nurse Blackett", who, when her duties were accomplished, retired to become the spouse of Mr. High, landlord of the "Old Ship" Inn, Brancaster Bay. A succession of Dollys and Mollys from the village were glad to enter service at the Parsonage, where the children were many, and the master was absent-minded, but capable, when roused, of seizing a house-breaker by the collar and throwing him out of doors. Their fare was frugal. "Palisades of roast beef, or canals of Soup or rich Ragou" were not amongst the fortifications provided by a parent who pronounced "Air, Exercise, Warmth and Cleanliness" the first essentials for infant welfare, and "a Liberall Education the only antidote against Selfish cunning, a passion few are exempt from".

Horatio Nelson was nine years old when he lost his mother. She died at the age of forty-two, having borne eleven children in seventeen years. Her figure is shadowy; a portrait by a lesser artist shows a formal, upright lady in the costume of the days when the Young Pretender was hourly expected in London. But the theory that the mothers of heroes are women of spirit seems in this case to find some support. Her eldest daughter explained, in maturity, "Somehow, the Navy must always be interesting to me. I may say I suck'd it with my mother's milk, for she was quite a heroine for the sailors." Her sailor son's only recorded memory of her was that "she hated the French". She came of blood that had done the State some service.

The 21st day of October was always kept as a festival at Burnham Thorpe Parsonage House. On that day, in the year 1759, the *Dreadnought* (Captain Maurice Suckling), together with two other 60-gun ships, had engaged a vastly superior French squadron in West Indian waters. Captain Suckling, of Woodton Hall, Norfolk, brother of Mrs. Edmund Nelson, had used, on this occasion, the sword of his great-uncle and godparent, Captain Galfridus Walpole.

Further back, the pedigree of Horatio Nelson's mother showed names deeply rooted in the East Anglian soil—Sheltons, who bore the symbol of the escallop shell, in token of their presence at the siege of Adrianople, four hundred years before the Norman Conquest; Bullens of moated Hever Castle and the Manor of Blickling, whence Henry VIII had taken an ill-fated queen; Wodehouses of Kimberley, who had sent a standard-bearer to fall on Musselburgh Field; Jermyns of Deepden, who had given a portly Chamberlain to Henrietta Maria. The augmentation of a sprig of honeysuckle to the Suckling coat-of-arms had been bestowed by Elizabeth Tudor, after a Norfolk progress. The name Maurice, borne by the eldest brother of Horatio Nelson, had begun to appear in the family when Maurice of Nassau, the first soldier in Europe, was the hero of every Protestant household.

Maurice Nelson was the first of the children of Burnham Thorpe Parsonage House to leave home. The Sucklings had rallied to the aid of the Rector. Mr. William Suckling of Kentish Town, an official in the Customs and Navy Office, had promised to find an opening for one nephew; Captain Suckling would take another to sea. Maurice, according to his father's record, left home in the year of his mother's death, to become a clerk in London, at "the Auditor's office in the Excise, under Mr. John Fowle". He was fifteen. Boys were "brought forward" early in the eighteenth century. Even the Rector of Burnham Thorpe uses this expression, which strikes coldly on the modern ear. Writing at a later date of a midshipman grandson who had died at sea, he stoically adds, "There is another boy whom I have desired to be kept at school two years longer, and then brought forward." The ages of these boys were fourteen and ten.

Anecdotes of the young Horatio Nelson are in plentiful supply, and cannot be disregarded, as the source was his own family. Unfortunately, the Chaplain to the Prince of Wales, to whom they were entrusted as official biographer, had an ear for the histrionic. The result has been that posterity has received a chilling impression, not at all confirmed upon reference to original letters or the accounts of contemporaries who did not "improve" upon conversations or incidents.

The first story belongs to the period of tender infancy. When upon a visit to his widowed grandmother at Hilborough, he went bird-nesting in company with a cow-herd. Dinner-hour passed without his return, and alarm was felt lest a child so fair and fragile might have been carried off by gipsies. He was found, after long search, exhausted but composed, seated by the side of an impassable stream. To his grandmother's remark that she wondered fear and hunger had not driven him home, he replied, "I never saw Fear.

What is it?"; or, in another version, "Fear never came near me."
On a spring morning when he was seven, his bed was discovered
untenanted. He had spent the hours of darkness sleeping at the foot
of a tree which he had identified, just before he was forcibly removed to bed, as containing the nest of a rare bird.

His education began at the Royal Grammar School, Norwich, a
town in which a great-aunt, Mrs. Henley, and a cousin, Mrs. Berney,
were ready to nourish small boys on half-holiday. Before he passed
on, aged eleven, with his brother William, one year older, to Sir
William Paston's School, North Walsham, he was once allowed to
attend his father at the marriage of a village couple. He signed himself as witness "Horace" Nelson, but the Rector corrected the signature for a ceremonial occasion to "Horatio".

At North Walsham, a headmaster of the flogging tradition
awaited him, and an elderly French master, known by young tor-
mentors as "Jemmy Moisson". A Hamburg merchant, an Olym-
pian of North Walsham days, writing to the victor of the Nile and
Copenhagen in the year 1802 to ask for a consul's appointment,
was unctuously reminiscent.

"Your lordship, though in the second class when I was in the first, was
five years my junior, or four at least, and at that period of life such a difference in point of age is considerable. I well remember where you sat in the
schoolroom. Your station was against the wall, between the parlour door
and the chimney; the latter to the right."

What Nelson minor learned from "Classic Jones" and the thin
marbled volumes of a rather small establishment can only be
deduced from internal evidence. It would appear that certain
Shakespeare plays were either included in the curriculum or available at home. From the instruction of M. Moisson, a young patriot
emerged entirely unscathed, to his subsequent discomfiture, but
when the Commander-in-Chief of the Mediterranean Fleet quoted
Cato, Jones's pupil recognised the note.

His brother is the authority for the last glimpses of the schoolboy.
On a winter's morning, when the roads were becoming blocked by
snow, William and Horace returned gleefully to tell their father
that there was little possibility of their reaching North Walsham for
the opening of term. The Rector said that they must make one more

effort. He depended upon his sons not to give up the attempt unless they were convinced it was impossible. They set out again, and William presently thought that the time had come for retreat, but Horace insisted that they must persevere: "Remember, brother, it was left to our honour."

During the Christmas holidays of 1770–71, while their father was taking his annual "recruit" at Bath, William and Horace read in a local newspaper that the *Raisonnable*, of 64 guns, was being recommissioned in view of war with Spain. She had been captured from the French twelve years past, and, like most captured ships taken into the English service, had retained her old name. The appointment of her Captain was presented as likely to be of interest to Norfolk readers—Captain Maurice Suckling of Woodton.

To read in a newspaper that their uncle, who had been on half-pay for some time, was going to sea again, and with a prospect of active service, was naturally of intense interest to the boys of Burnham Thorpe Parsonage. To Horace the paragraph suggested something further: "Do, brother William, write to my father at Bath, and tell him I should like to go with my uncle Maurice to sea." William obediently wrote, and the Rector, who was in weak health and still had seven children to place, passed on the request, and in due time came a hearty answer from a surprised sea-officer: "What has poor Horace done, who is so weak, that he above all the rest should be sent to rough it out at sea? But let him come; and the first time we go into action, a cannon-ball may knock off his head, and provide for him at once."

Horatio Nelson was rated on the books of the *Raisonnable* as midshipman, from January 1, 1771. He was twelve years and three months old. But he had not been "brought forward". He had brought himself forward. An anticlimax followed when it appeared that the boy would have to go back to school as usual next term. The *Raisonnable*, captured in the year of his birth, was not yet ready for sea. His elder brother well remembered the dark and cold March morning when the eagerly awaited summons came, and Mr. Nelson's servant, Peter, arrived at Sir William Paston's Grammar School to escort Horatio Nelson to the Lynn diligence. Here the Rector, who regarded London as the place where "every man pays by the inch", and was not a little terrified at the prospect of a London inn, met his sailor son, and together they embarked for the capital. Fortunately there was no need for the ingenuous couple to go to a London inn. They went to Mr. William Suckling's handsome mansion in Kentish Town, which was built of brilliant new Georgian red-brick, and had fourteen very wide stone steps leading up to the entrance door, and in the ornamental grounds of about five acres a very fine avenue of elms. Within, Mr. Suckling's house exhibited equally fine furniture and *bibelots*, many oil-portraits and wax medallions depicting Pelhams, Walpoles and Townshends, and a black butler named Price. In these reassuring surroundings father and son presently parted, and the aspirant was forwarded alone on the last lap of his journey. He was put on the stage-coach for Chatham: the *Raisonnable* was lying in the Medway. (So, as it happened, was the *Victory*, ordered in the year of his birth.) At Chatham his troubles began. He was set down with the other passengers: nobody was present to meet him. He had difficulty in finding the *Raisonnable*, and when he had identified her, could not discover anyone who would take him out to her. At length an unknown officer questioned the straying child, recognised the name of Captain Suckling, and offered the chilled and forlorn figure "some refreshment" at his own house. This Good Samaritan then presumably saw to it that his guest got on board the *Raisonnable* before nightfall, for the Captain's nephew remembered pacing her decks for the remainder of that endless first day of his naval career, in solitary state and silence. Captain Suckling was not in his ship, and not expected for some days. His nephew Horatio Nelson was not expected at any date by anyone. It was not until the following day that "somebody" took compassion on him and spoke to him.

The rigours of the midshipman's berth in the eighteenth century have been often described, and there is no reason to think that Captain Suckling's nephew escaped the common lot. He never himself mentioned early miseries, but another boy, thirty years later, noticed an illuminating flash. The scene was the dinner-table of the Commander-in-Chief in the Mediterranean on the anniversary of the Battle of Cape St. Vincent, and Mr. Midshipman Parsons, much to his alarm, found himself, as the youngest guest present, set on the right side of a withered Admiral with one eye and one arm, "in all the brilliancy of stars and medals", in a stateroom filled with Mediterranean sunshine and presentation silver. He was too shy to look up during the meal; when it was over, and the cloth was removed, Lord Nelson offered the customary greeting, "A glass of wine with you, Mr. Parsons", and opened conversation with the words, "You entered the Service at a very early age to have been in the action off St. Vincent." Parsons replied, "Eleven years, my lord." The Admiral's smile vanished, and the boy heard him mutter, "Much too young."

4

The *Raisonnable* did not see action against Spain. The alarm of war died down in England, the *Raisonnable* was paid off, and Captain Suckling was given command of the *Triumph*, of 74 guns, stationed as guardship in the Thames. He considered the problem of the boy, Horace, who had served as midshipman in the *Raisonnable* for five months and one day, and the result of his reflections was something irregular, but decidedly sage.

On an early summer day of this year, an inconspicuous merchant vessel, belonging to the house of Messrs. Hibbert, Purrier and Norton, slipped down the Thames and spread her sails west. She was bound for an archipelago stretching from Florida and Yucatan to Venezuela; for the Bahamas and Greater and Lesser Antilles; for the tropics, and islands where a boy who had seen nothing but three Norfolk towns, and London from a stage-coach, might behold sugar and tobacco plantations, and reptiles and armadillos, and orchids and humming-birds, and forests of palm and Xanthoxylon, the admired and valuable satin-wood of commerce.

Captain Suckling had kept his nephew's name on the musterbook of the *Triumph*, altered his rating to "Captain's servant", and commended him to Mr. John Rathbone, now in the employ of a West India trading house, but once master's mate in the *Dreadnought*. Mr. Rathbone, an excellent seaman, could teach a sharp lad much more of mathematics, navigation and hydrographical charts than he would learn in a guardship lying in the Thames estuary, and the regulations of the Royal Navy allowed no youngster, unless he was the son of an officer, to go to sea until he was thirteen. Fourteen months later Captain Suckling again altered his nephew's rating, this time to midshipman of the *Triumph*. The boy Horace was back at Chatham again. He had returned from his first cruise improved in physique, and if not much more of a scholar, in his own opinion, at least, "a practical seaman". He had suffered another sea-change, of which his uncle may not have been aware. He had returned from his year in a trader filled with generous admiration for the men of the Merchant Service, and a better balanced view of their place in the body politic. If the defence of sea-borne commerce brought the officers of the Royal Navy most honour, the King's Service, nevertheless, still depended for work aloft on recruitment from Merchant Service personnel. Meanwhile every ship-of-the-line had attendant craft, and the ardent midshipman who desired to be a good seaman was told that if he studied his navigation conscientiously, he might be allowed to handle the cutter of the *Triumph* (used for the transport of stores from land, and of liberty men to sea) and even the decked long-boat. During the winter of 1772 he learnt to be "a good pilot", in scenes familiar to every lover of London's river-side, and doubly picturesque at this date. He got to know the Thames thoroughly, from the Pool and Tower, "Guardian of the City of London", to the difficult submerged delta. From Chatham he studied the Swin, chief avenue for traffic leading to the open sea, the North Sea and the Kentish coast, past Whitstable, Herne Bay and Margate sands to North Foreland. Only "by degrees", according to his own account, did he learn to become "confident of myself amongst rocks and sands, which has many times been of great comfort to me".

His trip to the West Indies had been arranged for him by his uncle; his next adventure was, like his choice of a profession, his own idea. The Honourable Daines Barrington, lawyer, naturalist and antiquary, brother of Captain Samuel Barrington of the Royal Navy, and author of an unsatisfactory translation of King Alfred's version of *Orosius*, had become fascinated by the subject of Arctic exploration. He had studied the records of previous explorers, interrogated the masters of whalers, and finally induced the Royal Society to approach Lord Sandwich, First Lord of the Admiralty.

Early in 1773, England learnt that the Government was commissioning two ships, under the command of a naval captain, eldest son and heir of an Irish peer, ordered to report on the possibilities of a North-East Passage into the South Seas. More than a century and a half had passed since the first epoch of English Arctic adventure had been brought to a close by the pronouncement of William Baffin that the North-West Passage to India was not a practicable proposition. The expedition of 1773 was avowedly undertaken primarily in the interests of science, but of course there was much talk throughout the country, in newspapers, magazines, at the dinner-table and in the parlour, of so romantic a project as a new voyage of discovery to the frozen regions, mentioned by Homer as having midnight sun at midsummer and no sun in midwinter, and believed by the Elizabethan heroes to contain "north of Boreas", a happy land of perpetual light. More professional interest was taken by the midshipmen of the *Triumph* guardship, lying at Blackstakes, many of whom had joined the Navy at a date of expansion owing to an alarm of war, and realised that the prospects of active service were not at present promising, and those of promotion in time of peace much less so.

The North Pole expedition became a fact, and the names of the two vessels being provisioned and strengthened against ice, at Deptford, became known. They were the *Racehorse* and *Carcass*, sloops, mounting bombardment guns, mortars and weapons of the howitzer class; ketch-rigged, mainmast and mizzen, to allow room for the guns in the bows. Captain Constantine Phipps, leader of the expedition, was going in the *Racehorse*, and Captain Skeffington Lutwidge, second-in-command, in the *Carcass*. Two masters of Greenland-men had been engaged for each ship, as pilots, and Dr. Irvine, who had installed an ingenious apparatus for distilling fresh from salt water, and understood dietetics, had advised that extra stores of butter and rice should be carried. The First Lord himself was going to pay a visit to the ships before they sailed; special clothing, suitable for Arctic weather, was being provided by the Navy Board—flannel jackets, waistcoats and breeches, and stockings and mitts of lamb's wool. Unfortunately for the young gentlemen of the midshipmen's berth, "no boys" was the order of the day;

their places were to be filled by effective men. Boys on such an
expedition would be "no use". The decision sounded final, yet a
loophole in the regulations existed. The captain of a man-of-war
might select some personal attendants without consulting the Navy
Board. When the expedition sailed from the Nore, on His Majesty's
birthday, June 4, both Captains Phipps and Lutwidge took with
them "persons under age". Horatio Nelson had used "every
interest", after an introduction to Captain Lutwidge, to obtain the
post of cockswain of the Captain's gig. Philip d'Auvergne, a member of the large Jersey branch of that family, claiming descent from
a cadet of the house of the last reigning Duc de Bouillon, had successfully approached Captain Phipps. Thomas Floyd, another midshipman of the *Racehorse*, had already begun to keep a journal
destined to show posterity Nelson's Arctic expedition from a boy's
point of view.

On June 27, their fellow-travellers, the gulls, who had accompanied the explorers in great numbers from the Shetlands, suddenly
deserted and a flock of strange birds took their place. Next day the
ships came in sight of a wedge-shaped island, possessed of many
pudding-shaped hills and long, branching fjords, and, towards the
north, bold, snow-covered peaks silhouetted against a cloudy sky.
Since they had arrived in the summer, the polar willow, the only
tree known on west Spitsbergen, was in flower, and some shrubs of
lowly habit, sorrel, ranunculi, saxifrages and scurvy grass, were
visible above melting snow. Dr. Irvine went ashore, and the boys
saw him striding up a hill accompanied by a large black dog. A
great many seals approached the ships, holding up their heads and
swimming like a pack of foxhounds, and in the distance four whales
were descried.

A week later the ships were among thick ice in slow, uneasy
motion. The heat of the sun greatly decreased, and fog descended.
The *Racehorse*, with both pilots at the masthead, fired signals every
quarter of an hour to apprise the *Carcass* of her position. Unseen ice
could be heard breaking with a noise like thunder. By July 30 the
explorers were becalmed in a large bay, with three visible openings
between the islands which formed it, all apparently ice-blocked.
Next morning the ice was fast closing in upon them: they got out

their ice-anchors, and moored alongside an ice-field. Captain Lutwidge and Mr. Cran, Master of the *Carcass*, who had gone ashore
in a four-oared boat, returned after two hours to announce that
they had ascended a height which commanded a wide view, and
been rewarded by the spectacle of ten or twelve leagues of smooth,
unbroken ice, bounded only by the horizon. Their homeward
journey had been difficult, and they had several times been obliged
to haul their boat over young ice. Both ships cast off, having a light
breeze to the eastward, and tried to force a passage, but by noon
were obliged to anchor again. During the afternoon the ice closed
in, and the *Racehorse* and *Carcass* presently lay within two lengths of
one another, moored to the same field. There was now no water to
be seen except a single hole, or lake, of about a mile and a half in
circumference.

The weather was exhilarating, and the ships' companies, as
cheerful as hounds released from kennel, filled their casks with
astonishingly soft, pure ice-water from the lake, and afterwards
enjoyed winter sports on the ice in the Christmas scenes which they
had been led to expect. Mr. Floyd noted that snowflakes, up here,
were of two varieties, some shaped like icicles, others like stars.
With nightfall, the clouds which had filled the skies by day miracu-
lously disappeared, and two eighteenth-century bomb-ketches, with
snow frozen on the rigging, were silhouetted against the translucent
green skies of summer Arctic night.

Their captains meanwhile were not so carefree. The Greenland
pilots, who had never been so far north before, were beginning to
show signs of anxiety, and pointed out that the short summer
season of these regions was already well advanced. They could only
suggest that parties should be set to saw an exit to the westward for
the imprisoned ships. Captain Phipps's best hope was for a strong E.
or N.E. wind, but the ships had driven into shoal water, and must,
if they or the field to which they were moored took the ground, be
inevitably lost, and probably overset. Captain Phipps, M.P., who
was, as his midshipmen proudly related, "an orator", sent for the
officers of both ships and warned them of his intention of making
ready the boats in preparation for quitting the ships, a business
which would occupy some days. He made an experimental trip

himself, in his launch, a week later, and got about two miles, with rather greater ease than he had dared to expect. His crew hauled the launch over the ice with a good will, and on his return to the *Racehorse*, in time for dinner, he was glad to notice that *morale* was high. Everyone in both vessels appeared to repose entire confidence in their officers and suffered no vain regrets at the prospect of having to abandon ship. Spirits, indeed, in the *Carcass* were presently too high for the peace of mind of that excellent man, Captain Lutwidge.

Between three and four o'clock of a misty morning, Captain Lutwidge observed, to his mingled wrath and dismay, a couple of small uniformed figures on the ice a considerable distance from the ship, separated only by a chasm from a large and menacing bear. Two of the "persons under age" who had used every interest to be allowed to join the Government expedition to the frozen North had taken advantage of thick fog during the middle watch to depart on a private hunting expedition. Signal for their return was instantly made, and one figure wavered. The other defiantly proceeded to discharge a musket at "the bruin". The weapon failed to fire, but the boy stood firm, apparently intent upon getting to closer quarters and stunning his seven-foot adversary with the butt of his useless piece. A bold and timely shot, fired by order of the infuriated Captain of the *Carcass*, had the desired effect of dismissing the bear and bringing both boys back to the ship. The chief offender was young Nelson, and when asked at an awful interview to explain conduct so unworthy of his office, he answered frankly, "Sir, I wished to kill the bear, that I might carry its skin to my father." Captain Lutwidge, who had not in his inward eye any picture of the dazzling effect that would be produced by a white polar-bear skin on the stone-cold floor of a study at "dear, dear Burnham", noticed idly that when this lad was agitated, the only visible sign was a thrusting-out of mobile lips. In after-years Admiral Lutwidge told his bear story with good humour, and Lord Nelson's brother-in-law entered it in a privately printed memoir, designed to amuse nieces and nephews of the hero.

On the night of August 8 orders were given for every man to hold himself in readiness to go away with the boats at 4 a.m. No extra clothing was to be carried, but every man was provided with a musket, ammunition and a bag containing thirty pounds of bread. Mr. Floyd, having attired himself in "two shirts, two waistcoats, two pairs of breeches, four pairs of socks, and my best hat", and stuck into his belt a pistol, a comb, a razor, a woollen nightcap and his precious journal, fell peacefully asleep on deck. Shortly before midnight he was awakened by a great noise. "The wind had shifted in our favour. Everyone was hard at work. Everything, as if by magick, wore a better form." Within twenty-four hours, they had got past their boats and taken them on board. Next day wind sprang up to the N.N.E., all sail was set, and they made their way, though not without damage, through heavy ice to the open sea. They anchored on August 11 in Smeerenberg Harbour, New Friesland, and reached Orfordness on September 25. The ships were paid off on October 15.

Captain Phipps's *Voyage towards the North Pole*, with engravings from sketches by Philip d'Auvergne and others, published in the following year, tells the official story of an expedition that was stopped by ice north of Hakluyt Headland, reached the Seven Islands, and discovered Walden Island. It is not a tale of success, and until the Napoleonic Wars came to an end, no further schemes of Polar research were undertaken by England.

5

Eleven days after the *Carcass* was paid off, a Mr. Bentham of the Navy Office presented his compliments to a Mr. Kee, whom he believed to be agent to Mr. Surridge, Master of the *Seahorse* frigate, and begged Mr. Kee to give a letter of introduction to the bearer, "Horatio Nelson, a young lad, nephew to Captain Suckling, who is going in that ship". He rightly supposed "the Master is a necessary man for a young lad to be introduced to".

A squadron, under Commodore Sir Edward Hughes, was fitting out for the East Indies, and Captain Suckling's nephew, who had spent the summer months in the Arctic, was keen enough on his profession not to wish to lose the chance of such a voyage.

Mr. Kee had no reason to regret his letter, for the Master of the *Seahorse*, finding during the next eighteen months that Captain Suckling's nephew was extremely attentive to his duties when stationed in the foretop at watch and ward, recommended him to Captain George Farmer, who rated him midshipman.

The *Seahorse* visited almost every part of the East Indies, from Bengal to Bushire, but only tantalising glimpses of the young Nelson in the gorgeous East are available. He thought Trincomalee "the finest harbour in the world". Ten years later, hearing that Commodore Cornwallis was going out to India with a convoy, he wrote advising him that under Mr. Surridge the midshipmen of the *Seahorse* had constantly taken lunar observations, and since her master had been a very clever man, he believed her log-book to be almost if not the best in the Navy Office. "We went the outward passage, and made the islands of St. Paul and Amsterdam before we haul'd to the northward." The only precaution which must be taken in approaching the peninsula was to be assured one was well to the eastward, for from April to June currents set so strong that ships, fancying themselves far to the eastward and northward of Ceylon, had been known to haul up westerly and get foul of the Maldives.

In his forties, amidst gay scenes in Naples, he confided to the spinster daughter of a deceased Admiral that once, when he was seventeen, he had sat one evening with a convivial East Indian party to the gaming-table. He had risen from the green cloth a winner, to the tune of £300. Reflecting next morning what would have been his situation had he lost instead of winning this sum, he had made a resolution never to play again.

At length, almost inevitably, the midshipman who had been noted by Mr. Surridge as a fine physical specimen went down with fever. In the East Indies at this date a lingering illness was something unusual, but to hear of the illness, death and burial of a friend within forty-eight hours was quite normal. Nelson's "malignant disorder", which produced temporary paralysis and "nearly baffled the power of medicine", all but terminated his career. It banished for ever the glowing colouring and tendency to outgrow his uniform, remarked with approval by Mr. Surridge. No one henceforward ever described him as anything but "light-haired". Dr. Perry, Chief Surgeon of the *Salisbury*, on being summoned to report on the case, said that a passage home was the only hope, and a patient who was to suffer from the after-effects most of his life, assisted by re-infection whenever he returned to tropical countries, was carried on board a home-bound frigate, physically a mere object of compassion. Captain James Pigot showed every kindness to a midshipman with a ghastly air, "almost a skeleton", who did not seem likely to last many days, and the *Dolphin* sailed on a passage likely to occupy six months. Gradually, and in his own opinion entirely due to the care of Captain Pigot, the boy entered upon a protracted convalescence.

At some date between March and August 1776, as he lay in his cot, listlessly conscious of nothing but ship-noises and sunset, in a 20-gun frigate bound from the mouth of the Hugli for Portsmouth, this austerely bred son of a Norfolk parsonage who had entered His Majesty's Service at the age of twelve underwent an experience which he deemed extraordinary. Struggling back to life on a broken wing, barely re-harnessed to the body, he considered his chances in this transitory life, and particularly his hopes of rising in his profession—"the difficulties I had to surmount, and the little influence I possessed". To his dismay, he began to know depression of a poignancy that had never troubled him before. He foresaw, with the cold and penetrating eye of one just returned from the Valley of the Shadow, that according to all reasonable expectation he must end a failure: the daunting arguments seemed unanswerable. The meagre figure, lying in his obscure sick-bed, "almost wished myself overboard". In later years Captain Hardy was perfectly familiar with talk of "the radiant orb" which his Admiral believed to beckon him on in his career. Its first appearance was at this moment. In the rise of spirits which followed the young Nelson's hour of darkness and desertion, "a sudden glow of patriotism was kindled within me, and presented by King and Country as my patron. My mind exulted in the idea. 'Well, then,' I exclaimed. 'I will be a hero, and confiding in Providence, I will brave every danger.'"

It seems clear that the story of the boy ended on that day.

6

He returned to find that his "influence" was better than he had known. During his absence, Captain Suckling had succeeded Sir Hugh Palliser as Comptroller of the Navy. This post was most important at a date when the Admiralty left all business of shipbuilding and repairs, and the mustering of men, to the Navy Board. The head of the Navy Office was at least as influential a person as the First Lord of the Admiralty. The Comptroller's nephew was immediately appointed by Admiral Sir James Douglas to act as Fourth Lieutenant of the *Worcester*, of 64 guns, just about to sail with a convoy for Gibraltar.

The diary of Captain Mark Robinson of the *Worcester* shows that on October 8 Mr. Horatio Nelson (whose appointment dated from September 24, the very day on which the *Dolphin* was paid off at Woolwich) joined his ship at Portsmouth, and "brought letters from his uncle". On the following day Captain Robinson introduced Mr. Nelson to Sir James Douglas, and wrote a letter to Captain Suckling. Next evening, after a very busy twenty-four hours "getting live-stock on board, and getting the Ship ready for sea", the Captain of the *Worcester* entertained two guests at dinner—the Mayor of Portsmouth and the Comptroller's nephew. To the Mayor, the Comptroller's nephew was not a negligible figure, for the Comptroller was likely to become Member of Parliament for Portsmouth. Next day, and again within the week, Captain Robinson, taking Mr. Nelson with him, dined with the Mayor, and when the *Worcester* came in sight of an unmistakable landmark in the second week of the New Year, Acting Lieutenant Nelson was sent ashore at Gibraltar with the Captain's letters for the British Consul at Cadiz. Captain Robinson, a lucky man to have found a Comptroller's nephew whom he might favour with a clear conscience, gave the Acting Lieutenant charge of a Watch, and said, more than once, that he felt as easy when Mr. Nelson was upon deck as any officer in his ship. The Comptroller's nephew, who knew that he was young for such a responsibility, was very pleased. He was at sea in the *Worcester* with convoys throughout a winter of very bad weather, but when she returned to Portsmouth to be paid off, early in April, the Captain was the person to be left in a sick-bed. Mr. Nelson sent word into Norfolk of his arrival in England, and hastened to London by a road with which he was to become very familiar. He hoped for a family reunion at Kentish Town, but first he had to face an ordeal.

On Wednesday, April 9, 1777, bearing with him the necessary proofs that he had gone to sea more than six years, together with the journals kept by him in H.M.S. *Raisonnable*, *Triumph*, *Carcass*, *Seahorse*, *Dolphin* and *Worcester*, Mr. Horatio Nelson presented himself for his examination as Lieutenant. His certificates further deposed that he appeared to be more than twenty years of age, but if this was so, the appearance was deceptive, for he was still five months short of his nineteenth birthday. The signatures of Captains Suckling, Lutwidge, Farmer, Pigot and Robinson testified "to his diligence, etcetera, and that he can splice, knot, reef a sail etcetera, and is qualified to do his duty as an Able Seaman and Midshipman". The syllabus included a *viva voce* examination.

When the candidate was shown into the room where officers of the Navy Board awaited him, "he at first appeared somewhat alarmed". The Comptroller, who by virtue of his office occupied the seat of honour, gave no sign of recognition. The Captains began to fire their questions, and the candidate, called upon to talk of business he understood, gradually gained confidence. By the time that the Captains had done with him, it was clear that here was one of the cases in which there could be no doubt. But not until that moment did the Comptroller rise from his place, and assuming the grand manner, beg leave to introduce his nephew. Several officers present expressed "their surprise at his not having informed them of this before", to which the Comptroller complacently replied, "No, I did not wish the younker to be favoured. I felt convinced he would pass a good examination, and you see, gentlemen, I have not been disappointed."

Next day the young Nelson received his commission as Second Lieutenant of the *Lowestoffe* frigate, and two days later his father arrived in town. Two sisters, "Sukey and Nancy", aged twenty-one and sixteen, were already at Kentish Town on a visit, and Maurice, not yet four-and-twenty, was entering his ninth year at a desk in the Auditor's office. It was in a cheerful humour that a young sailor in a hurry wrote from the solemn precincts of the Navy Office on the following Monday, to his brother William, aged twenty, undergraduate at Christ's College, Cambridge, and destined for holy orders.

"If it is not too troublesome, turn over," suggested the newly-appointed Lieutenant at the bottom of his first sheet, which briefly recounted the arrival of the family in London, and his commission "for a fine Frigate". "So I am now left in World to shift for myself, which I hope I shall do, so as to bring Credit to myself and Friends." He was well able to picture the domestic amenities of his new situation—the larboard cabin in the gun-room, 8 feet by 6, furnished by a cot of canvas on an oaken frame swinging from hooks, presenting the view of a flap-table purchased from a bum-boat or the last occupant, a latten candlestick, a sea-chest on a well-worn strip of matting, and a couple of metal rings enclosing a ewer and basin. . . .

This early Nelson letter, written in an hour of high spirits, on an April day, contrasts sadly with many of later date. The script is a small neat "fine Italian", and the signature of "Your Affectionate brother, Horatio Nelson" is not innocent of flourishes. He signed himself "Horatio", though in the family circle he was always "Horace", and his father, when abbreviating with more than usual passion, would allude to "yr bro: Hor:".

7

The *Lowestoffe* was fitting out at Sheerness for Jamaica station. She did not sail for another month, and her Second Lieutenant found time to sacrifice to the conventions. He called upon Mr. John Francis Rigaud, R.A., a native of Geneva settled at 74, Great Titchfield Street, and ordered his portrait in uniform. He gave some sittings, but not enough. The likeness was unfinished when he sailed, and waited thus, in the studio of an academician accustomed to a naval *clientèle*, for another four years. A less agreeable occupation, resulting in illness, had claimed the sitter. As the First Lieutenant of the *Lowestoffe* was on leave, an unpleasant duty had fallen to his lot. The lamentable, but as it was then held inevitable, business of pressing men for service in a newly commissioned frigate was in progress. No guardship lying in the estuary was available to receive the future ship's company of the *Lowestoffe*, so a *rendezvous* was opened near the Tower of London, at which genuine volunteers might enlist, and deserters, gaol-birds, vagabonds and such "able-bodied persons" as were liable to be pressed for service in the fleet might be retained. On a chilly spring night, while engaged on this distressing and sordid business on the banks of the Thames, Nelson began to feel very ill, and presently became inarticulate. A stalwart and resourceful midshipman called Bromwich arrived at the *rendezvous* bearing his ardent but frail senior on his broad shoulders. That this attack was due to a recurrence of his malaria, and that he was returning to the very worst climate for a person predisposed to this disease, was fortunately not recognised by Nelson or any other officer of the *Lowestoffe*. As usual, sea-air set him up again, and he was in good health and spirits by the time that the frigate dropped anchor in Carlisle Bay, Barbados, early in July. He had found in her Captain a character, in the fullest sense of the word, who was to become a lifelong friend. Captain William Locker (as his portraits by Gilbert Stuart, preserved amongst those of the Governors of Greenwich Hospital, bear witness) was a cheerful-looking person, with a weather-beaten countenance, apple cheeks, a benevolent brow from which powdered hair was thinning and a penetrating eye. At the date when Nelson first met him, he was six-and-thirty, limped slightly—result of boarding a French privateer under heavy fire off Alicante, in the year before Nelson's birth—and was a devoted exponent of the methods and practices of that great sea-officer and exemplary though peremptory man, Admiral Lord Hawke. Captain Locker, who came of a naval family and had married into a naval family, took a scholar's interest in naval history, and a human interest in his young officers, to whom he confided such pithy advice as "Always lay a Frenchman close, and you will beat him". There was hope of opportunities to do so, for already American privateers, and French privateers flying American colours, were dealing destruction to British trade in West Indian waters. The *Lowestoffe*, with her convoy of eighteen sail of merchantmen, arrived in Port Royal in mid-July. She took an American sloop with a rice cargo a month later, and on her second cruise from Jamaica, in foul November weather, overhauled an American letter of marque, between Cape Maize and Cape Nicola Mola. A heavy sea was running, and the First Lieutenant of the *Lowestoffe* failed to board the prize. Captain Locker came on deck, and seeing a boat still lying alongside and likely to be swamped, bawled, "Have I no officer in this ship who can board the prize?" Upon this, the Master of the *Lowestoffe* ran to the gangway, but found himself forestalled by the Second Lieutenant, who shouted, "It is my turn now, and if I come back it is yours." The prize had been carrying a heavy press of sail in hopes of escape, and was by this time almost water-logged. The *Lowestoffe's* boat went in on the decks of the American, and out again with the scud. Nelson very nearly did not come back. He succeeded in getting on board the prize, but after doing so was so long separated from the *Lowestoffe* that her Captain began to be anxious.

Captain Locker was not the man to deter a promising beginner. When the *Lowestoffe* sailed for her third cruise from Port Royal he gave Nelson command of a schooner—another prize, but renamed by the Captain, who was a proud parent. Mrs. Locker, heiress of Admiral Parry, had been christened "Lucy", and her first-born, now six years old, was her name-child. In the *Little Lucy*, Nelson, who had found that "even a frigate was not sufficiently active for my mind", but who was young enough to be "much obliged" for a gift of sweetmeats, made himself "complete pilot for all the passages through the Islands situated on the north side Hispaniola". He remained at sea when the *Lowestoffe* returned to Port Royal on the last day of the Old Year to heave down and new-sheath her bottom, and he took another prize in the small hours of February 9, 1778, off the West Corcos.

With early spring came changes. Sir Peter and Lady Parker arrived from New York station. Sir Peter had been appointed to succeed Admiral Gayton. Locker, who had been intermittently unwell since August, recommended his Second Lieutenant most warmly to the new Commander-in-Chief, and Sir Peter took the Comptroller's nephew into his own flagship, the *Bristol*, as Third Lieutenant. By September, Nelson had risen to be First. The two West Indies stations, even in times of peace, offered good prospects of promotion, and war with France had now begun. Two friends succeeded Nelson—Lieutenant Cuthbert Collingwood in the *Lowestoffe* and Lieutenant James Macnamara as Third Lieutenant in the *Bristol*.

Mid-October, the anniversary of Captain Maurice Suckling's celebrated engagement in 1759, found his nephew cruising off Cape

Francis Viego, the very scene. He had heard from England in April that his uncle was not well. On his return to Port Royal on October 24, after a cruise which he wrote down as "pretty successful", he learnt that his wealthy and childless patron had died in July. The Comptroller had left a Will, intended to be temporary, drawn up two months after his marriage, in which blanks had been left for the names of his sister's children. Every nephew got five hundred pounds legacy and every niece a thousand pounds. His last words to his brother-in-law before a paralytic seizure had been an assurance that the Rector would live to see Horace an Admiral. There were various small legacies to Walpole kin. Mr. William Suckling of Kentish Town inherited the residue of the estate, together with all lands, and was going to give the dress sword of Captain Galfridus Walpole to "poor Horace". "Poor Horace" wrote to his father that he should always remember with gratitude that his dear good uncle had not forgotten him, even in his last illness. The Comptroller had most kindly taken the trouble to mention his name to Sir Peter Parker. To Mr. William Suckling, he wrote:

"I trust I shall prove myself, by my actions, worthy of supplying that place in the service of my country which my dear uncle left me. . . . I feel myself to my country, his heir. I feel . . . had I been near him when he was removed, he would have said, 'My boy, I leave you to my country; serve her well, and she'll never desert, but will ultimately reward you.'"

1

SIR PETER PARKER, who had intended to promote the Comptroller's nephew, held to his purpose after the Comptroller's death. The young man to whom his attention had been directed by interest retained it by merit. Moreover, Lady Parker approved of Nelson, and this Admiral's lady was one of those redoubtable naval wives, reminiscent of the figurehead of an eighteenth-century ship-of-the-line, and regarded by her husband's officers with something of the mixture of awe and proprietary admiration reserved for such ornaments.

Nelson found himself, in December 1778, appointed a Commander to the *Badger* brig, and ordered to protect the settlers of the Mosquito shore and Bay of Honduras against American privateers. His first attempt to deal with people on shore was a success. "They unanimously voted me their thanks, and expressed their regret on my leaving them." A deputation waited upon him to ask him to explain to Sir Peter Parker and Governor Dalling what would be their situation should Spain declare war—a very necessary precaution, as within twelve months she did so. He was next detailed to protect the north side of Jamaica, where he captured *La Prudente*, of 80 tons—and had to wait two days until the papers of this French prize were discovered, stuffed in an old shoe. He was in his twenty-first year, and rising in the Service with record speed. A new note enters his letters. "The men you mentioned, I should be very happy to have with me, as the one is very assiduous, the other, you know, one of my favourites. . . . I wish I could give a good character of Mr. Capper; he is a drunkard; I need say no more. We shall part." "I know of no remonstrances—I never allow inferiors to dictate."

"Always at sea, but not with much success" was his bulletin to his father this month. He had not heard from Burnham for nearly a year. However, a few days later he had an opportunity of distinguishing himself, and witnessed a scene which he never forgot. While the *Badger* was lying in Montego Bay, on a June afternoon, the *Glasgow*, of 20 guns, came in and anchored. Two and a half hours later, smoke, closely followed by flames, was observed to be streaming towards the sunset skies. A steward, stealing rum out of the after-hold of the *Glasgow*, had upset a light amongst casks of liquor. Her crew were saved, mainly owing to the prompt action of the *Badger*. Nelson came up with his boats and ordered them to cast their powder overboard, and point their guns skyward, before leaping into the water. They were taken into the brig, causing overcrowding in a ship already troubled by the fever that came with the rains, and Nelson found Captain Lloyd "very melancholy indeed", as he well might be, and the First Lieutenant, whom he commended by letter to Locker, "a very good young man, I believe, and has not saved a rag but what was on his back".

The candid and helpful Locker had at last resigned his command, and was going home "to peace and plenty", in search of health. For many weeks his pupil hoped for a farewell meeting. "If you come on the North Side, and I hear of it, I will come in. . . . I lose my best friend by your going. . . . I shall always write to you." This promise, fortunately for biographers, was most faithfully kept.

On June 11, the pressing anxiety for his future, which had haunted Nelson since hearing of his naval uncle's death, was finally removed. He was promoted Post-Captain, and appointed to the *Hinchingbrooke*, a 28-gun frigate, formerly an enemy merchantman, re-named in honour of the First Lord's ancestral home. Further promotion could come by seniority only; no junior officer could now be passed over his head. He realised how much luck had to do with such moments in a career. "I got my rank by a shot killing a Post-Captain, and I most sincerely hope I shall, when I go, go out of World the same way."

The *Hinchingbrooke* was away on a cruise, and as weeks passed without her return, rumour reported her capture, but meanwhile her new Captain was very much employed. The victorious Comte

D'Estaing had arrived in Hayti with his armada and troops from Martinique. Jamaica, expecting invasion every day, was "turned upside down". Her military and naval commanders chose Captain Nelson to take charge of the battery of Fort Charles, Port Royal—key to the harbour, to Kingston and Spanish Town, "the most important post in the whole Island". The British residents of Jamaica displayed desirable spirit, even considering that they were deeply interested. Mr. Hercules Ross, another friend of Locker, offered all his vessels to Sir Peter Parker, and his negroes to Governor Dalling, to serve in the batteries. "Very public-spirited," commented Nelson, who believed that he was amongst a defending force of 7,000 opposed to invaders numbering 25,000. ("I leave you in England to judge what stand we shall make.") The only possibility which depressed him was that of having to learn the French language as a prisoner of war.

In England, the Spanish Ambassador was packing, the Dutch Ambassador was beginning to look gloomy, and His Majesty had sent a son into the Navy. While the *Prince George*, with Prince William Henry on board, took part in the August cruise of the Channel Fleet, Captain Nelson waited in Jamaican heat, in a small white fort, attended by redcoats and negroes, sweeping with his glass the bluer waters beyond a landlocked harbour, for its size the most perfect he had seen, and at present crowded with shipping. But the French Admiral sailed on, to Savannah, to meet with a repulse, after which he returned to France, and in September the *Hinchingbrooke* arrived in Port Royal, safe and sound. Her Captain gladly departed in her for a cruise, and took prizes which brought him a share of about £800. Had he stayed in the *Lowestoffe*, he would by now have found himself much richer, and have taken part in an engagement, for in the capture of a fort in the Bay of Honduras she was lucky enough to find Spanish treasure-ships lying in the harbour. Nelson, who was beginning to feel the usual effects of having been thirty months on Jamaica station—he only realised that he was "never well in Port" there—sent a casualty list to the absent Locker. "Our mess is broken up. Captain Cornwallis and myself live together. I hope I have made a friend of him." This officer was the Captain of the *Lion*, a younger son of the first Earl

Cornwallis, thirty-six years old, of middle height, but stout, and so red in the face that amongst seamen he was known as "Billy-go-tight". His complexion was an affliction, not an indication, for he was strictly temperate. He was also known as "Blue Billy", "Coachee" and "Mr. Whip". When a man has so many nicknames he is not generally unlovable, and Nelson's hopes were well-founded. A quarter of a century later he gratefully recalled that amongst the "sentiments which have greatly assisted me in my naval career", introduced to his notice by this single-hearted officer, were—"that you can always beat a Frenchman if you fight him long enough", "that the difficulty of getting at them is sometimes more fancy than fact", "that people never know what they can do until they have tried", and finally that, "when in doubt, to fight is always to err on the right side".

2

Dr. Benjamin Moseley was a fair example of what happens when an exiled professional man allows himself to become too much interested in native life. He held the post of Surgeon-General at Kingston for fifteen years, and when he had become inured to the custom of his patients to die of tetanus after his successful operations, he occupied his spare time with enquiries into negro superstitions. Some results of these, some anecdotes on the behaviour of sharks, and an account of the ill-fated San Juan expedition of 1780 were incorporated by him in his *Treatise on Tropical Diseases, and on the Climate of the West Indies*; and when his work attained a fourth edition in 1803, Lord Nelson contributed a note. Dr. Moseley did not himself accompany Captain (Brevet-Major) Polson and Captain Nelson to Nicaragua. A younger man, Dr. Thomas Dancer, who was interested in botany and held advanced views on sanitation, sailed from Port Royal on February 3, 1780, with the joint military and naval force bound for the Mosquito coast. He also afterwards reported in print on the expedition.

The force ordered on a particular service consisted of about two hundred regulars, of the 60th and 79th Regiments, one hundred of Major Dalrymple's Loyal Irish, two hundred Jamaican volunteers and a few marines. Their object was more impressive than their numbers. They were to obtain command of Lake Nicaragua, "which for the present may in some degree be looked upon as the inland Gibraltar of Spanish America", and after "that first conquest", and the capture of the rich cities of Grenada and Leon, were to force a passage to the Pacific, "thus cutting off all communication between the north and south". The scheme had originated in the brain of Governor Dalling, at Port Royal, but in London Lord George Germain, Secretary of State for the Colonies, was enthusiastic, and "the more sanguine part of the English began to dream of acquiring an empire in one part of America, more extensive than that which they were on the point of losing in another". Nelson's comment was, "How it will turn out, God knows." He added that he did not expect to return before the end of June, and that after "this trip", if he did not feel better, he should apply for home leave. Sir Peter had promised him command of the first frigate in which a vacancy should occur, and Captain Glover of the *Janus* had just sailed on a cruise which he seemed unlikely to survive. But if it came to that, Nelson had himself been twice "given over" by the physicians of Jamaica since Locker had last seen him.

The military destined for San Juan were disembarked in Honduras at Cape Gracias à Dios, and encamped upon a swamp to await the arrival of a reinforcement from the 79th Regiment. When this detachment of veterans from Black River appeared, it was soon evident that they should have been in hospital instead of preparing for active service. Another setback was caused by the fact that the natives, who were needed to supply craft and act as guides and pilots up the river, disappeared inland as soon as the *Hinchingbrooke* and transports came in view. The Indians of the Mosquito coast believed that the English came for no other reason than to carry them slaves to Jamaica. The troops were all re-embarked, and Captains Nelson and Polson took the action which appeared to them necessary, though they were far from assured of support from headquarters when it became known that they had obliged unwilling natives of the Mosquito shore to join them. "A light-haired boy came to me in a little frigate," recollected Captain Polson. "In two or three days he displayed himself, and afterwards he directed all the operations." They anchored at several places down the coast until they had collected sufficient Indians, and arrived in Greytown, at the mouth of the San Juan river, towards the end of the month. Here, Nelson's instructions ended. He had convoyed the troops successfully to the Spanish main, and was at liberty to return to Port Royal. But he had discovered that not a man amongst those whom he would be leaving had ever been up a river "which none but Spaniards since the time of the buccaneers had ever ascended", and no one had any idea of the positions of the enemy forts. About two hundred men, with ammunition and siege-train, were embarked in Mosquito shore craft, and two of the *Hinchingbrooke's* boats and Nelson went with them.

The story from this point becomes fully as nightmarish as the tropical vegetation described by Dr. Moseley. The banks of the San Juan, according to him, were at this time of year entirely composed either of unwholesome mud, submerged during the rainy season, from which, after sunset, arose death-dealing miasma, or of decaying leaves and vegetables which had never seen the full light of the sun. For overhead, in some stretches, trees grew so thickly that the scene, even at midday, was suffused by no more than an uncanny greenish light. The principal cape above Greytown was named Monkey Point for good reason. No sound but the chatter of these beasts, and the stirring of a heavy leaf as the lizard or snake slipped by, were heard by the sweating and pig-tailed marines, seamen and redcoats, as they penetrated through chequered green twilight towards unknown fortresses. Another enemy, as yet unsuspected, was already at work amongst them. "Yellow Jack", a disease peculiarly rife all round the Caribbean, was choosing his victims. It was a lamentable fact that the expedition planned at Government House, Port Royal, and approved in a stately chamber in London, had been sent three months too late. The invaders had arrived at the end of the dry season, and the river contained very little water in its lower reaches, and many shoals and sandbars over which boats had to be dragged. Men who got wet through three or four times a day complained of headache from the glare arising from the white sand of the district. Further up, currents and rapids awaited them. That they persevered, and reached a fortified island called San Bartholomew by the 9th of April, was, in the opinion of Dr.

Dancer, chiefly due to the exertions of Captain Nelson's men from the *Hinchingbrooke* and the Indians. Most of the soldiers, either from ignorance or indolence, seemed disinclined to make much effort. Nelson, whose language on land operations was still that of the sea, was the first to "board" the enemy outpost. He led an attack on the fort, at the head of a small party of his men, supported by a Captain Despard. The Spanish garrison, taken by surprise, fled without offering opposition. Only sixteen miles now lay between the expeditionary force and Fort San Juan, which Dr. Dancer invariably, and Nelson sometimes, referred to as "the castle". When they came in sight of "the castle", the sea-officer was all for another bold assault, but the military preferred to lay siege, a business which entailed eleven days' preparation. Simultaneously the dry season, having presented every encumbrance, came to an end; torrential rains set in, and amongst those to be smitten by the prevalent sickness was Nelson: nevertheless, he continued on duty—"made batteries, and fought them". A small further reinforcement of troops appeared on the scene. They had been brought to Bluefields by the corvette *Victor*, and amongst the letters which she had carried from Port Royal was one from Sir Peter Parker. Captain Glover had died. Captain Nelson was recalled to take command of the *Janus*.

Fort San Juan surrendered on April 24, but Nelson just missed hearing the news in Nicaragua. He sailed from Bluefields on the 23rd, and found on board the *Victor* an old companion who tended him zealously. Mr. Tyson had been his purser in the *Badger*. He learned at length that of the *Hinchingbrooke's* two hundred men, not more than ten survived. He had himself seen eighty-seven report sick in a single night, and a hundred and forty-five buried. Yet, neither soon after the event, nor later, did he condemn the whole project as futile and ill-judged. He always thought that if only the expedition had been sent at the proper season (in which case it might have encamped in the healthy Grenada and Leon country, and a road for stores from Bluefields might have been constructed), the end of the story would have been different. Sickness, not Spanish arms, had defeated a sterling body of men sent on a great adventure. He had taken part in a tragedy, not a failure.

When he arrived at Port Royal, he had to be carried ashore in his cot. "Cuba Cornwallis", to whose lodging-house he was first taken, had nursed him before. This negress, who had adopted the surname of the noble Captain who had obtained her freedom from slavery, was famous in the island for having saved the lives of many naval officers. Before Nelson moved to the country house of the hospitable Parkers (where he had a relapse), he saw Governor Dalling "several times", and succeeded in writing a long letter to Polson, congratulating him on his capture of Fort San Juan before the arrival of a superior officer, and telling him that there would be "no more heard" about their taking Indians from the shore upon the expedition. He sent messages, and good wishes for their recovery, to a long list of sick friends: he assured Polson that the Governor would be with them before July. His behaviour on his first expedition did not pass unremarked. Polson in due time reported officially to headquarters, "I want words to express the obligation I owe to that gentleman. He was the first on every service, whether by night or day. There was scarcely a gun but what was pointed by him or Lieut. Despard." General Dalling, for his part, wrote privately to Lord George Germain, hoping that His Majesty might be graciously pleased to manifest a satisfaction of Captain Nelson's conduct.

The Admiral's lady and her housekeeper took turns in sitting up with the fever-patient. Mrs. Yates, questioned years afterwards, distinctly remembered Captain Nelson as a most amiable sufferer. But presently the lady of the house had to depart from "Admiral's Mountain" for her town house on the humid coast, and a native staff, accustomed to having an eagle eye kept upon them, when they discovered that the English women were safely gone, took no further notice of the sick sea-officer lying abed. They became as invisible as the Indians of the Mosquito shore. "Oh! Mr. Ross!" wrote Captain Nelson from the mountains on a June day, "what would I give to be at Port Royal. Lady P. not here, and the servants letting me lay as if a log." He also sent word home that he was ill again, and his family must not be surprised to see him. His brother Maurice, who had his own troubles, and who had seen the records of invalided Post-Captains of no private means, wrote to his brother

William that he hoped Horace would manage to stay where he was. The *Janus*, of 44 guns, was a fine frigate, quite new. Maurice, who had, much to his relief, got transferred to the Navy Office shortly before the death of the Comptroller, was well-informed as to his naval brother's movements and prospects. Jamaica, to one seated at a desk in Seething Lane, sounded so desirable.

Nelson took up his duties on board the *Janus* and had another and more serious relapse. Many visits to the medical fraternity followed, and so strong was the impression produced by the agreeable personality of the Surgeon-General, that in 1797, when suffering agonies after the amputation of his right arm, Sir Horatio insisted on calling in Dr. Moseley; and in 1803 concerned friends felt themselves obliged to point out to Vice-Admiral Viscount Nelson that old Moseley, who had attended him in Jamaica in 1780, was not an eye-specialist. The inevitable end of this chapter in the history of Nelson took place on August 30, when he signed a note, addressed, "To Sir Peter Parker, Knight, Vice-Admiral of the Blue, and Commander-in-Chief at Jamaica," opening, "Sir, Having been in very bad state of health for these several months past," and ending with the miserable words, "I am therefore to request that you will be pleased to permit me to go to England."

3

Number 2, Pierrepont Street, was a neat house built of the local golden-grey stone, facing west, almost on the corner of the fashionable North Parade. From the corner of the street could be seen a typical Bath prospect, including the Abbey tower and the promenade called Orange Grove. The name commemorated the visit of a Dutch prince, but Captain Nelson, walking the streets of Bath on mild days of west wind and bright sun, hearing of cold weather elsewhere, was reminded of the West Indies. "This is like Jamaica to any other part of England."

In mid-January he had spoken of the possibility of having to move to other lodgings. Mr. Spry, apothecary, had not a single room unbooked for the season. If Locker should come from London, after his boys went back to school, he would have to be accommodated elsewhere. But Locker could not be persuaded that his was a Bath case. He forwarded a copy of the latest Navy List and stayed cooped-up in Gray's Inn. The gentle Rector of Burnham Thorpe, having unconsciously selected the comfortable Bath lodging in which he was to die in 1802, turned home. He had seen his son safely through an alarming illness, "carried to and from bed with the most excruciating tortures". Time, a Bath physician and surgeon, a full course of physic, the waters and the baths, had once more worked the boasted cure. Nelson pronounced his inside, at any rate, "a new man". He was not perfectly happy as yet about his left arm, which had a disconcerting habit of going quite dead and white from shoulder to finger-tips and coming back to life red, swollen and intensely painful: however, the inspiring Dr. Woodward seemed to view this train of symptoms with equanimity. The awkward moment had passed when a very sickly and slightly shabby officer, standing in a shadowy consulting-room, exclaiming at the smallness of a Bath physician's charge, had received an answer so much after his own heart that he treasured the stately cadences for the ear of a future wife. "Pray, Captain Nelson, allow me to follow what I consider my professional duty. Your illness, sir, was brought on by serving your King and Country, and believe me, I love both too well to be able to receive any more."

The convalescent liked Bath, which appeared, to one who had not as yet a large acquaintance in London, to possess many of the attractions without the disadvantages of the capital. The London papers arrived within ten or eleven hours of publication. At street corners, flooded with sunshine on winter days, the visitor met whole parties of unexpected West India friends. But the truth was that he did not "set very easy" under the hands of physicians and surgeons, and by March, striding the echoing grey streets at a good pace, "near perfectly restored", he was beginning to notice with regret that the wind hung so much westerboard. It must hinder the sailing of the Grand Fleet.

He left Bath in the London coach on an April day, travelling with Captain Kirke and family—a melancholy journey, for Mrs. Kirke, poor woman, had just been told by the medical men that they could do nothing for her. Nelson, who had been so glad when Kirke's sailor servant arrived at his lodgings to say that the master and family were come down, had recommended his own physician and surgeon. "Mrs. Kirke's case is *incurable*." The word looked dreadful, underlined in his letter to Locker. At Newbury he left the Kirkes. He had an invitation to stay with Captain Robert Kingsmill, at Sidmonton Place, Kingsclere, and here, "thirty miles on the other side London", he hoped to meet his "sea-daddy". He had promised Locker, who collected the likenesses of naval friends, the three-quarter-length portrait of Lieutenant Nelson ordered from Mr. Rigaud in 1777, and, to the best of his belief, still in the artist's studio. He did not think that, whatever it was like, it could in the least resemble him now.

4

On May 6, 1781, he passed from Whitehall through a small court-yard, masked from the street by an elegant stone screen designed by the brothers Adam, and hobbled into a solemn building well known to every sea-officer, the scene of many hopes fulfilled and frustrated. He was scarcely able to get about, but the news from America was bad. At the Admiralty, a personage who was, outside its walls, one of the most detested characters in London, a personage of somewhat ghastly countenance, possessed of great charm of manner, was short but not discouraging. Lord Sandwich could fix no time when Captain Nelson should be employed. He promised to employ him at the first opportunity. Another man might have felt relief, for there was no doubt that he was not yet fit for service. He had, it seemed, after all, left the country too soon. The symptoms which Dr. Woodward had hoped would pass off had returned, and in an aggravated form, involving his left thigh and leg, as well as his arm. He had consulted an eminent London surgeon of valuable connections, and Mr. Adair, brother-in-law of Lord Albemarle and Admiral Keppel, agreed with Dr. Woodward that further care and treatment should totally banish Captain Nelson's disorder. The unwilling patient relaxed again in his uncle's comfortable home at Kentish Town. As soon as possible he took the road down to Norfolk; here problems awaited him.

The Rev. Edmund Nelson, who was nothing if not methodical, began in the year of his naval son's return to keep "A Family

Historical Register", to which he added as events occurred. The entry under the name of his eldest daughter showed that he had made an experiment very unusual at the date.

"*Susanna* had a good school education, but as I could not give her a fortune equal to an independency, I thought it most for her advantage to be placed out to some female trade. Accordingly, at the age of eighteen, she was bound as an apprentice for three years to Messrs. Walters, reputable milliners at Bath, where she acquitted herself with much credit and propriety. At the expiration of that term she went assistant into a shop at Bath. In the year 1777, she had a legacy of £500 left her by John Morris Esq, our good, faithful and generous friend, and after the death of her uncle she gave up the thoughts of following her trade, being possessed of £2,000."

Susanna, after a few months at home, had bestowed herself, in her twenty-sixth year, upon a young merchant, carefully mentioned by her father as having been of good birth, "and in a prosperous way of trade in corn, malt, coals, etc." She was now, after the custom of the day, "Mrs. Bolton", even to her nearest and dearest, and happily settled in her bridegroom's small native town of Wells-next-the-Sea, surrounded by a large and sometimes noisily jovial circle of friends and relations, all very glad to see Captain Nelson, and mostly hoping that if he should ever touch at any of the wine countries, he would not forget them.

William, who was now a curate, "The Rev. Mr. Nelson, junior", also extended a hearty welcome to a man of the world. To his brother's dismay he had become fired with the idea of being appointed chaplain of a man-of-war. He was sure that Horace could see the right people to get him into so desirable a situation. In vain Horace pointed out that "fifty pounds, where you are, is much more than equal to what you can get at sea", and that if William had the bad luck to get with a disagreeable captain and inferior officers, he would find the life intolerable.

His two younger brothers were equally unsettled. Edmund, who had been placed with the Ravens to learn the profession of attorney, had gone off to Ostend to act as an assistant in his brother-in-law Bolton's accounting house. Suckling, aged sixteen, at present bound apprentice to Mr. Blavers, linen-draper at Beccles, was looking forward to spending a year in London, as journeyman. Mrs. Bolton, who had been old enough to notice her mother's decline, who was now expecting to become a mother herself, and whose taste for speaking her mind had been increased by marriage to a "downright" partner, said quite openly that her poor mother had "bred herself to death". There seemed no doubt that as the family had increased in numbers, it had, so far as the sons were concerned, deteriorated in physique and ability. Nor was the returned officer perfectly happy about his younger sisters. "*Anne*," according to her father's record, "from the time of leaving school, to the age of nineteen, lived in London, at a Capital Lace warehouse, Ludgate St, for which I gave a premium of £100. . . . She is, I apprehend, a Free-woman of the City of London, as her indentures are enrolled in the Chamberlain's Office." But upon receiving her uncle's legacy, Anne, like her elder sister, had without hesitation obtained her release and settled gratefully to the life of daughter at home. She was now twenty. Even Kate, youngest of the family, for whom the Comptroller's bounty had come in time to save her from a "female trade", was now in her fifteenth year. Their travelled brother sadly felt that they lacked scope. "Although I am very fond of Mrs. Bolton, yet I own I should not like to see my little Kate fixed in a Wells society."

In good time the best of news recalled him to London. He had been appointed to commission the *Albemarle*. The sympathetic and knowledgeable Maurice accompanied him when he went down to Woolwich on August 23 to pay his respects to the Commissioner of the Dockyard and perform, for the first time under English skies, the old and handsome ceremony of hoisting his pendant. The *Albemarle* was a French merchantman, *La Ménagère*, captured in 1780, and a glance at her would have told a cynical officer why she was being converted into a 28-gun frigate in the autumn of 1781, and why a young and insistent captain with a poor health record was being employed so promptly. When Locker set eyes upon her, he said damaging things. On the outbreak of war, the number of seaworthy ships in the British Navy had been startlingly inadequate, and now the war was not going well. Nelson, however, saw her with the eye of a lover. He was, he said, "perfectly satisfied with her as a 28-gun frigate. She is in dock alongside the *Enterprise*, and in some respects, I think, excells her. She has a bold entrance and clean run." He could not deny that although she had the same beam as the *Enterprise*, she was four inches narrower on the gun deck, and between decks very low indeed. She was having her under-water timbers re-sheathed with copper, and would not be out of dock for a fortnight at least. The Admiralty was being very civil to him, allowing him to choose all his own officers, and the faithful Bromwich was to be one of his lieutenants.

5

Since the story of the *Albemarle* is rather a sad one, it is best briefly told. She was never a good sailer, except going directly before the wind, and eventually her disillusioned Captain supposed that her first owners, the French, must have taught her the habit of running away. Being a brute to handle, she was also an unlucky ship, but the worst disaster to befall her was sheer ill-luck.

The winter of 1781-2 was one of persistent foul weather, and Nelson, who had spent the last three years, ailing, in the tropics, ruefully suggested that he was now being frozen for a season, to test his powers of survival. The *Albemarle*, with the *Argus* and *Enterprise*, reached Elsinore early in November, and there was obliged to wait for over a month, while two hundred and sixty sail of merchantmen, "laden with cargoes of the utmost National importance", gradually assembled for convoy. Undeterred by the spectacle of "a coast full of wrecks", Mr. William Nelson, still fascinated by the idea of becoming a naval chaplain, came up to Yarmouth to spend the last Sunday of the Old Year on board his brother's ship. He very nearly had to go to the Downs in her, as on the day following his call it was not possible to send a boat ashore. Unfortunately, waking to find that the *Albemarle* and convoy, which had been the leading feature of the seascape for so long, had vanished overnight as if by magic, only increased William's belief in the romance of a seafaring life. His brother was enduring the reality. After "driving from one end of the Downs to the other" for nearly a month, and twice parting from her anchors, the *Albemarle* was ordered round to Portsmouth to take in eight months' provisions. Her Captain, whose considered opinion of the North Sea in the festive season was now

one which many subsequent officers have endorsed, considered this
order with pleasure. He had feared the Admiralty asleep, and the
Downs station, "a horrid bad one", his inescapable fate. Eight
months' provisions were a sure sign of a long cruise, and he knew
that a squadron under Sir Richard Bickerton, whose acquaintance
he had cultivated last year, was fitting out to reinforce the East
India fleet. "Alas! how short-sighted are the best of us!" At 8 a.m.
on the dark and stormy morning of January 26, a large East India
store-ship, the *Brilliant*, driven from her anchor in the Downs,
fouled the bows of the *Albemarle*. The *Albemarle*, lightly constructed,
suffered heavy damage. Her Captain's first reaction was philosophic.
"All done in five minutes! We ought to be thankful we did not
founder. Such are the blessings of a sea life!" Only to Locker did he
add to a terse account of the accident the bitter words, "I was ordered
for Foreign service." Not until the middle of April was her Captain
able to get the "old *Albemarle*" out of Portsmouth, upon what he
described as "a damned voyage". He had been ordered to join
the *Dædalus* (Captain Pringle) at Cork, and escort another convoy,
this time across the Atlantic. What was worse, he believed that he
might have to winter in the Americas. Friends whose opinion was
valuable, "my Navy friends", urged him to apply to Admiral
Keppel for an exchange, which he would certainly get. His surgeon,
the eminent Mr. Adair, brother-in-law to the new First Lord, might
be prevailed upon to drop a hint. He decided, however, that it
would not be advisable to ask the new First Lord to cancel orders
given by a violently inimical predecessor.

While he waited for a wind at Portsmouth, an officer one year
his senior, who had been very lucky at last, made a happy return
attended by considerable popular enthusiasm. Charles Pole, of the
Success, another of the young men marked down by Locker as
promising, and represented in his portrait-gallery of pupils with a
future, had captured the *Santa Catalina*, the largest frigate afloat,
after an action off Cape Spartel, in which his seamanship had been,
by general consent, as conspicuous as his daring. But both, wrote his
contemporary to Locker, were surpassed by the young officer's
modesty, when called upon to give an account of the affair to Portsmouth audiences.

6

The *Albemarle* had a tedious passage of ten days from Spithead to Cork Cove, where her consort, the *Dædalus*, arrived the same morning. With their convoy of between thirty and forty vessels, they sailed on April 26, 1782, with a fair wind, for the New World. Eleven days later, at night, in a hard gale and thick weather, some 300 leagues to the westward of Cape Clear, the *Albemarle* parted from the *Dædalus*, and had not seen her or most of the convoy again when she anchored on May 27, in sight of a bleak and barren coast, with walls of brown rock, broken at frequent intervals by deep fjords and large bays. Nelson, whose view of Britain's senior colony did not extend to the interior, was not complimentary. "The entrance of this harbour is so narrow that you cannot sail unless the wind blows right out." Tantalising rumours of an action fought between Rodney's and De Grasse's fleets in West Indian waters well known to him had reached Newfoundland. He dismissed St. John's as "a disagreeable place", and fretted at being kept there without news of Pringle, whose orders had been to go upon Newfoundland station after seeing the *Albemarle* and convoy to the mouth of the St. Lawrence. However, he hoped that Pringle had gone on to the westward; and with all in his own ship he was more than satisfied. "They are all good. Indeed, I am very well off." A couple of days later he got news overland that Pringle and the rest of the fleet were in Capelin Bay, where he joined them, and on July 2 the *Albemarle* arrived safely at the Isle of Bec, in the St. Lawrence. Nelson had only forty-eight hours in which to gain a pleasant first impression of a picturesque upper and lower town of predominantly French attractions, before sailing on a cruise that lasted until late September. During these months, on a station renowned for possibilities of prize-money, he was lucky in taking several prizes, but unlucky in that not a single one reached port. One romantic and one thrilling incident took place while he cruised off Cape Cod and Boston.

On July 14 the *Albemarle* captured an American fishing schooner, whose owner was almost home, with a cargo which represented nearly all his worldly possessions. Nelson, who "imagined we are just getting into the Gulf Stream, by its being so very squally", and who had no officer on board acquainted with the shoals of Boston Bay, ordered Mr. Nathaniel Carver, Master of the *Harmony* of Plymouth, Massachusetts, to come on board the *Albemarle* and undertake the duties of pilot. The American obeyed with speed and skill, and without a change of countenance. When his task was completed, Nelson made him a short speech, announcing that it was not the custom of English seamen to be ungrateful. "I return your schooner, and with her this certificate of your good conduct." This certificate, signed "Horatio Nelson", was duly framed and long a treasured exhibit of a Boston home. A month later, when the *Albemarle* was again in Boston Bay, the coastal fog of a high summer morning parted to display, within gunshot, four French sail-of-the-line and the *Iris* frigate—"part of M. Vaudreuil's squadron, who gave us a pretty dance for between nine or ten hours". As all beat "poor *Albemarle*" in sailing, Nelson threw off the large ships by running boldly amongst the shoals of St. George's Bank. The *Iris* still followed, but when the *Albemarle* shortened sail, and hove-to in defiance, out of sight of the line-of-battle ships, the French frigate prudently retired and was seen no more.

By mid-September a new danger was threatening the *Albemarle*. Ship's company and officers alike began to be conscious of muscular pains, spongy gums, bodily lassitude and corresponding mental depression. The symptoms of scurvy were too familiar to the experienced sailor of the eighteenth century, and Nelson resignedly gave the order to stand away for Quebec. Since he had sailed again from the St. Lawrence within two days of his arrival there, without re-provisioning, his men had enjoyed their last fresh meal at Portsmouth on April 7, and for the last eight weeks he and his officers had been subsisting on salt beef. At this propitious moment, the fearless Carver, of Plymouth, Massachusetts, made an unexpected reappearance alongside. Determined not to be outdone in generosity by the English captain, he had brought off, at considerable personal risk, a present of four sheep, several crates of fowls, and a large quantity of fresh greens. A contest of courtesy took place before the New Englander would consent to accept any payment from an officer who had learnt a lesson in dietetics, which he was ever afterwards careful to impress on juniors. No subsequent letter of Nelson records that he ever again contracted scurvy.

After he had seen his men into hospital there, he was obliged to linger a month in the neighbourhood of Quebec. The season was the loveliest of the North American calendar, and much to his surprise, the bracing and inspiring climate of "Fair Canada" suited him perfectly. He wrote home that he had never before known what "Health, that greatest of blessings," could mean. Although he knew that his expectation and wish were to return as soon as he could to England, he gave himself up whole-heartedly to the entertainment offered by an exhilarating community.

The belles of the balls at the Freemasons' Hall were Captain Miles Prentice's daughter and her cousin, Mary, daughter of "Sandy" or "Saunders" Simpson, Provost-Marshal of the Garrison. Miss Simpson, hymned by the poetasters of the *Quebec Gazette* as "Diana" on account of "her noble and majestic air", was sixteen, of "heavenly charm", and to be lovelier yet. Nelson became "violently attached".

He made other great new friends amongst "Quebecers of note", not "Navy friends"—the Lymburners, the Davisons. . . . Alexander Davison was, like "Saunders" Simpson, a gentleman of Scottish ancestry, but he came from Northumberland. He was a bachelor, aged thirty-three, a merchant and shipowner in the Canada trade, cultured, a man of parts and affairs. At a house within view of the harbour, he offered much hospitality to officers from home. The season, the scene and "Diana" were combining to complete Nelson's conquest, when the voice of duty called. Suddenly, "arrives the *Drake* Sloop and *Cockatrice* cutter, with orders for the Transports to be fitted for the reception of Troops, and to be sent to New York; in consequence thereof, old Worth has given me orders to carry the Fleet to New York—a very *pretty job* at this late season of the year, for our sails are at this moment frozen to the yards". The remainder of this story has, hitherto, in biographies of Nelson, rested upon a single testimony.

On October 14, when the *Albemarle* had gone down the river from Orleans Island, ready for sea, Alexander Davison, walking on the beach, noticed her Captain returning to the harbour. He greeted his young friend at the landing-stage, and asked, with some anxiety, the reason for his reappearance. A brief and heated conversation followed, against a background of wooded heights in flaming autumn colours, dazzling skies and frosted shipping. Nelson divulged that after having made his farewells in Quebec, he had found himself irresistibly compelled to fly back to lay his heart and fortune at the feet of the lady who, for him, epitomised the charms of her country. Davison, in sharp alarm, used the strongest arguments he could against this sudden resolution. If the lady accepted Nelson's heart and fortune, it must mean the close of a promising career. The acquaintance was, as far as time was concerned, very slight. The Provost-Marshal's daughter, famed for her "accomplishments" and aloof bearing, was but sixteen. Nelson sadly listened to reason, and, accompanied by Davison, returned to the *Albemarle* in Bec roads, whence he sailed for New York six days later.

He dropped anchor near Sandy Hook lighthouse, twenty miles south of the south end of Manhattan Island, on November 11, "with all my Fleet safe", a fortunate record for the season. A single letter from him dated "New York" exists, and his comments on the English society of the station were not flattering. "Money is the great object here, nothing else is attended to." From the moment that he set eyes upon a squadron of the West India fleet lying in New York harbour, his mind was made up. This detachment of twelve sail-of-the-line had taken part in Rodney's action of April 12—the Battle of the Saints—had followed a division of the vanquished French fleet which had gone to refit in Boston, and would shortly be returning to the Antilles. The battle-scarred veterans from the south, riding at anchor off Sandy Hook, were under the command of Lord Hood.

7

On a mid-November day of 1782, when Lord Hood's flagship, the *Barfleur*, was lying in the narrows off Staten Island, the midshipman who had the watch on deck saw a barge from Admiral Digby's fleet come alongside. A moment later he perceived "the meerest boy of a captain I ever beheld". The visitor's dress also made him stare. For his call upon Lord Hood, the Captain of the *Albe-*

marle had attired himself in a full-laced uniform, and a waistcoat with flaps, of surprisingly old-fashioned cut. His lank fair hair was unpowdered, and his stiff Hessian pigtail was of extraordinary length. The midshipman, who had never before had the pleasure of encountering such a combination of youth and antiquity, could not imagine who this officer was, nor on what business he came. His curiosity was satisfied when the Admiral presently introduced him to Captain Nelson, whose pleasant manner and the enthusiasm which he displayed when speaking on professional subjects soon showed that here was "no common being"; nor did Captain Nelson neglect, on this auspicious occasion, to turn a correct phrase on his loyal attachment to the midshipman's august father. For if the name and bearing of Nelson had suggested nothing to Prince William Henry, Nelson, from the moment that he met the stare of those protuberant light-blue eyes, set in that slightly cod-like but bronzed countenance of heavy features, had very little doubt as to the identity of the midshipman. Prince William Henry, whose father was justifiably pleased with his look in the uniform of a Service described by His Majesty as "noble and most glorious", was, at the age of seventeen, unmistakably a son of the House of Hanover, and a very fine lad. He had not yet begun to put on weight, although he had already displayed the propensity for making long-winded unnecessary speeches which was an outstanding characteristic of the Duke of Clarence and William IV. He was not to prove an intelligent man, or valuable officer. His early zeal for the Service, which Nelson remarked with so much pleasure, deteriorated, in the opinion of later critics, into "morbid official activity", while Nelson's prophecy that he would be "a disciplinarian, and a strong one" was so lamentably fulfilled that lieutenants of spirit went to almost any length to avoid serving under His Royal Highness. But everyone who met the Sailor Prince as midshipman was delighted with him, and Nelson's enthusiasm never waned. To the Prince's credit it must be noted that he appreciated Nelson long before he was a man of mark, kept all his letters and told him so, and at a period when Nelson was unemployed and not smiled upon at the Admiralty, wrote to him, "Never be alarmed, I will always stand your friend."

The result of Nelson's call upon Lord Hood was of importance in his career, and there is evidence that he realised this. He had taken the bold step of coming to ask an Admiral whom he had met once, a few days previously, for something which he had long desired—"a better ship and a better station". On his arrival at Sandy Hook, Admiral Digby, Commander-in-Chief, had greeted him with the words, "You are come on a fine station for making prize-money", to meet the startling reply, "Yes, sir, but the West Indies is the station for honour." To return without delay to that "grand theatre of Actions" was Nelson's object, and Lord Hood's squadron was likely to sail within the week. Fortunately he had not mistaken his moment or his man. He presented himself with all the vigour and address he could muster, as "a candidate for a Line-of-Battle Ship", and the keen-faced, hook-nosed, self-reliant Admiral to whom he made this request did not suggest that he was being asked something impossible. He said, without hesitation, that he would write to Admiral Digby and ask for Captain Nelson and the *Albemarle*. Before parting, he promised the meagre but alert young officer of four-and-twenty, who preferred action to prize-money, "his friendship". Nelson's antecedents were not unknown to him. He had been well acquainted with the late Captain Suckling, both in the Service and as Member of Parliament for the borough of which Lady Hood's father had been Mayor. He must, also, have made his enquiries, for he presently told Prince William Henry that if he wished to ask any questions about naval tactics, the Captain of the *Albemarle* could give him as much information as any officer in the fleet—a surprising statement, since Nelson's only experience of action had been on the Nicaraguan expedition, and he had never yet served with a fleet.

Events then moved quickly, as they must. Admiral Digby was persuaded to part with an inferior frigate and a strange young officer who looked as if he needed prize-money but said he did not, and on November 22 the *Albemarle* sailed with Lord Hood's squadron. Nelson did not see the service for which he had hoped under Hood's flag. While the Admiral cruised off the west end of Hayti, ready to attack De Vaudreuil, the enemy went through the Mona passage between San Domingo and Puerto Rico, and to Nelson's disgust was next heard of off Curaçao. "Where they are,

God knows. We are all in the dark in this part of the world whether it is Peace or War." The war was indeed almost finished. Spain and America were ready for peace. In France grim internal troubles were threatening.

The *Albemarle*, with a fine present of rum and cigars for Locker on board, which her Captain hoped that the Customs House would not seize, came into Portsmouth harbour on June 26, 1783. "After all my tossing about in various climates, here at last am I arrived, safe and sound. I found orders for the *Albemarle* to be paid off at this place. On Monday next I hope to be rid of her." On July 3 he saw the last of her, and a touching scene took place after he had made his farewells. "The whole Ship's company offered, if I could get a Ship, to enter for her immediately. . . ." The scene was remarkable, as well as touching, because at Spithead the crews of several ships, being paid off in consequence of the peace, were proving mutinous. Nelson proceeded to London, and for the first time took lodgings in the capital, where for a further three weeks he was fully employed on business connected with the officers and men of his unlamented frigate.

"My time, ever since I arrived in Town, has been taken up in attempting to get the wages due to my good fellows for various Ships they have served in the war. The disgust of Seamen to the Navy is all owing to the infernal plan of turning them over from Ship to Ship, so that men cannot be attached to their officers or the officers care twopence about them."

Lord Hood in London did not forget a young officer of vivid quality whom he had fancied at Sandy Hook. On July 11 he took Nelson to a *levée* at St. James's, and presented him to his sovereign, who had a very kind word for a friend of Prince William, followed by a command for Captain Nelson to come to Windsor to take leave of the Sailor Prince, who was about to embark upon an educative Continental tour.

Fresh from his first attendance at Court, still in the full-dress uniform of his rank, Nelson went to dine with a friend in Lincoln's Inn. Alexander Davison, back from Quebec, was as comfortably lodged in London as he had been on the banks of the St. Lawrence. While the traffic of London at peace, on a late summer's day of 1783, sounded afar, Nelson began to consider with his most interesting friend outside the Service the problem of the future. Davison had political aspirations, and money. Nelson knew that he had closed the war without a fortune; he trusted that he had closed it without a speck on his character. After his very satisfactory reception at Court this morning, he believed that this must be so.

But before he could relax, he had to beg leave to shed his "ironbound" full-dress uniform coat. Davison produced a dressing-gown. They then talked until the sun went down.

Chapter III

1783-1787

(ætat. 24-28)

"SENTIMENTAL JOURNEY"

I

HORATIO NELSON, landing at Calais at 10.30 a.m. on Thursday, October 23, 1783, after an easy passage of three and a half hours from Dover, was amused to discover that Monsieur Grandsire, at whose inn he breakfasted, was the son of Hogarth's landlady. The young sea-officer was, like most young men of his day, familiar with engravings of "Calais Gate", and with Sterne's *Sentimental Journey*. Indeed, in his first long descriptive letter to Locker he compared his experiences with those of Sterne, though he had as yet no incidents at all sentimental to report.

He had not passed through an English summer without contracting one of his heavy colds. Nevertheless, the north of France was his choice for the winter. He had heard too much of the tiresome scenes that took place when one of His Majesty's ships commanded by an officer who knew no language but his own captured a prize. ("Boatswain's mate, pass the word for any man who can speak French to come aft on the quarter-deck.") It was even worse when the papers of a foreign vessel needed examination, for a seaman who had picked up some French or Spanish very likely could not read it. Besides, French was an accomplishment expected in high society.

His first application to their Lordships, for six months' leave of absence to go into France "on my private occasions", mentioned the town of Lisle as his goal. Mr. Stephens, Secretary to the Admiralty, who was receiving many similar letters, failed to reply, and Nelson, after a week's wait, wrote again, having during the interval made his arrangements. When the desired permission came he had nothing left to do except pick up his travelling companion. James Macnamara, messmate of days in Sir Peter Parker's flagship, recommended St. Omer. "Mac", who had the advantage of his friend in that he could make himself understood by French natives, said darkly that if an Englishman settled in a town where there were English, he might find life very difficult, but Nelson had heard that St. Omer was "a dirty, nasty town"—a thing which he could well believe after his first whiff of Calais. After performing a perfunctory tour of that historic city, and dining, they ordered a post-chaise, and prepared to embark for the interior. When the post-chaise arrived, with a flourish, at Monsieur Grandsire's doors, Nelson had another wary smile at French taste. The little postillions, in their large jack-boots, cut most ridiculous figures; the horses which they drove with so much imprecation seemed to a quiet English eye to resemble rats. The officers entered their equipage, and immediately made two discoveries which, taken in conjunction, were serious. Chaises, in France, possessed no springs, and roads were "generally paved, like London streets". The young gentlemen were "pretty well shook together" by the time that they had covered two posts and a half, and by no means inclined to push on to Montreuil-en-Mer, another forty-five miles, at a pace which they calculated not to exceed four miles an hour. "Marquees" had an elegant sound. They decided to spend the night there, and presently drew up at the solitary inn of a small village, situated in dumb, dark country, of salt-laden airs, notably remote and melancholy on an early autumn evening. " 'Inn' they called it—I should have called it a pig-stye. We were shown into a room with two straw beds, and, with great difficulty, they mustered up clean sheets, and gave us two pigeons for supper, upon a dirty cloth and wooden-handled knives. O what a transition from happy England!" But being both five-and-twenty, on holi-day, and determined not to be upset by trifles, they enjoyed a good laugh, and, going to bed, slept very soundly. Next morning, Mar-quise having no charms to detain them, they set out with first day-light for Boulogne, which they found packed with English, but mostly of a type with whom other English would not wish to make closer acquaintance. Nelson thought that the excellence and cheap-ness of the wine with which he was served at breakfast might account for the presence of most of these countrymen.

A week later, safely "fixed" in the place which "Mac" had always favoured, he bought Chambaud's *Grammar of the French Tongue*, on the title-page of which he wrote neatly, "Horatio Nelson began to learn the French language on the first of November, 1783". He never succeeded.

By late December, he was softly humming—

> "But when a lady's in the case,
> All other things, they must give place."

His address, as he had instructed Locker, was *"Monsieur Nelson, chez Madame Lamourie, St. Omer-en-Artois"*, and St. Omer was all and more than "Mac" had promised. It had many old houses, inclining heavily above harbour and canal, but also plenty of well-paved, well-lighted streets of good shops, in which a number of cheerful English were visible, and even two sea-officers, to whom he took the violent instinctive dislike characteristic of travelling English for unintroduced compatriots. Captains Ball and Shephard (for he knew their names, although they had not troubled to call) had adopted the effeminate French addition of *épaulettes* to their uniform, a thing which made him think (quite mistakenly as events proved) that he should dislike them very much if he did get to know them. To find good lodgings with a pleasant French family had been quite easy, and the Mesdemoiselles La Mourie, one of whom made the lodgers' breakfast and the other their tea, were always ready to play a game of cards in the evening, after the officers' dinner had been sent in by the *traiteur*. But until Nelson learnt to address them in their own tongue, his acquaintance with these sirens must be confined to nods and becks and wreathed smiles, for they showed not the slightest intention of ever understanding English. Reinforced in his resolution "I must learn French", he restricted his English visiting list to two names. Mr. Massingberd was brother of an officer whom he had known in the *Lowestoffe*. Mr. Andrews, a clergyman, was blessed with the large number of olive-branches usual for a person of his period and means. After several visits, Nelson was still hazy as to how many children of what sexes there were in the *maison* Andrews. He was clear about three only—a naval son, George, and two grown-up daughters, "about twenty years of age", who played and sang whenever he was invited to dine. These young ladies had "such accomplishments" that Nelson felt sure that had he been a millionaire he would instantly have offered for the elder, who was, besides, a beauty. "I must take care of my heart, I assure you." However, as she could have no fortune, and his income was at present "by far too small to think of marriage", such dreams were vain. He was "very happy in the acquaintance", and there the matter must end. Soon, French, in spite of perseverance and patience (of which he feared he had a small stock), went on but slowly, and as the winter days shortened, and frost set in, his thoughts and steps tended with dusk to turn more and more often towards an English parlour in a French provincial town, where the exile was sure of a warm fire and a welcome. The clergyman parent, the naval brother, the young ladies seated at the instrument all spoke to him of home, and he presently got sad news from home. His sister Anne had died—"at Bath, after a nine days' illness. It was occasioned by coming out of the ballroom immediately after dancing," he told Locker, adding that his sister had been in her twenty-first year. She had, in fact, been twenty-three, but Nelson was always polite where a lady's age was concerned.

On January 14 he addressed a long letter to Uncle Suckling, beginning:

"There arrives in general a time in a man's life (that has friends) that either they place him in life in a situation that makes his application for anything further unnecessary, or give him help in a pecuniary way if they can afford it, and he deserves it. That critical moment in my life has now arrived." [He had discovered that Miss Andrews was not absolutely penniless: she had a small fortune] ... "£1,000 I understand. The whole income I possess does not exceed £130 per annum. Now I must come to the point. Will you, if I should marry, allow me a hundred a year, until my income is increased to that sum either by employment or any other way? A very few years will, I hope, turn something up, if my friends will but exert themselves. If you will not give me the above sum annually, to make me happy for life, will you exert yourself either with Lord North or Mr. Jenkinson, for to get me a guardship, or some appointment in a public office, where the attendance of the principal is not necessary, and of which they must have a number to dispose of?

"If nothing is done for me, I know not what I have to trust to. Life is not worth living without happiness, and I care not where I may linger out a miserable existence.

"I am prepared to hear your refusal, and have fixed my resolution if that should happen; but in every situation I shall be a well wisher to you and to all your family, and pray that they nor you may never know the pangs which at this instant tear my heart.

"God bless you, and assure yourself that I am your most affectionate and dutiful nephew, Horatio Nelson."

Mr. Suckling noted his compliance on the back of this letter, but by the time it reached him, Nelson was already in London. Such a sudden change of plans demands some explanation.

2

The General Election of 1784 has not been much mentioned in biographies of Nelson. He was under orders for the Leeward Islands by the time that polling took place, and already by the end of January hotly announced in a letter to his brother William that he "had done with politics". But there is no doubt that for a few hectic days in the middle of this month he was bitten with the idea of standing for Parliament. Nor was his interest in politics suddenly conceived, or as easily killed as he declared in his first disappoint-ment. Eleven years later he was sufficiently attracted by a tentative approach from some political luminary to suggest that H.M.S. *Agamemnon* should be summoned home, in order that he might present himself as a candidate. But by that time he had learnt much. His account of his public services did not lack colour. His list of sponsors was impressive and strictly *en règle*—as far as family went, the Duke of Portland, via his kinsman Lord Walpole; profession-ally, Lord Hood, Admiral Cornwallis, Lord Hugh Conway. Conversations with Sir Gilbert Elliot had seemed to show him the principal patriotic characters rearranged. In 1795 he was certain that he must stand in "the real Whig interest". In 1784, Mr. Pitt, exactly and rousingly, expressed his political opinions, and Mr. Pitt was said to be throwing his net wide. Nothing came of either project.

When he arrived suddenly in London, he gave correspondents several reasons for his return. He told Locker, "some little matters in my Accounts obliged me to come over". To his brother William he wrote that he needed the advice of good London physicians. He also presented himself in the unexpected guise of man-about-town. "My time has been so much taken up by running at the ring of pleasure. . . . London has so many charms that a man's time is wholly taken up." But in the first week of January, seated in his St. Omer lodgings wrestling with the problem of Miss Andrews, he had realised that Parliament might be dissolved at any moment. "I hope it will, that the people may have an opportunity of sending men that will support their interests." Acting on the idea that "out of sight, out of mind" may work conversely, he had come over to pursue a possibility which cannot have been entirely illusory. He caught a violent cold on arrival and made it worse attending a *levée* at St. James's. He "danced attendance" in other influential circles. He applied for an interview with the First Lord, who asked him whether he wished to be employed, to which he could only answer "yes". Lord Hood, who was himself thinking of standing, in the event of a dissolution, was much more encouraging. He at once invited the young aspirant with a feverish cold to dine at 12, Wimpole Street, and after that first dinner said "that his house was always open to me, and that the oftener I came the happier it would make him". Soon "Brother William" and Locker came to hear more, to receive daily bulletins ("to-night the ministry will try their strength. I shall not conclude my letter till late, as perhaps I may hear how matters are likely to go"), very warm opinions on Mr. Fox and "a turbulent faction that are striving to ruin their Country", and eulogies of Mr. Pitt, together with instructions to William to vote for him at Cambridge. Nelson and his young friends hoped "to unkennel Fox at Westminster", in which they were disappointed. Who these friends were, except that they talked good rank party stuff, and that he met them at the houses of Lord Hood (for whom they were already canvassing, "although not openly") and Captain Kingsmill (who was "looking out for a Seat"), is not disclosed. Captain Kingsmill, born Brice, who had taken the name of his lady when she inherited the estates of her grandfather, found a seat. Unfortunately for Nelson, all his family connections, in this heyday of nepotism, were Walpole—"the merest set of Cyphers—in Public affairs, I mean. . . . As to your having enlisted under the banners of the Walpoles," he told William, who was still hoping for a Walpole living, "you might as well have enlisted under those of my grandmother."

By the last day of January, Nelson's pretensions had received their quietus. "Let who will get in, I shall be left out." He left town as abruptly as he had arrived, and spoke of spending the winter in Norfolk, where "poor little Kate is learning to ride, that she may be no trouble to us". He was waiting for a fair wind for the Lesser Antilles by the time that the results of the Westminster Election convulsed London, and Lord Hood, who had also been the son of a simple country clergyman, was returned at the head of the poll. But the political connections of "the greatest sea-officer I ever knew" had always been valuable. He had entered life under the patronage of the Grenvilles, the Lytteltons and the Pitts. However, if his friends would not get Nelson a seat, they could get him a ship. He was appointed to the *Boreas*, another 28-gun frigate, on March 18. During the interval he had found himself "pulled down most astonishingly". He had considered returning to France, "to many charming women, but no charming woman will return with me". This sounds as if a refusal from Miss Andrews may have been the chief reason for his flight from St. Omer, but it is as likely that he left her full of hope, and gave up dreams of matrimony and a political career together. He took her younger brother George to sea with him in the *Boreas*, so he must have been in friendly communication with the family after his departure.

Whatever the circumstances of his double disappointment, he prepared to sail for the Leeward Isles in an unusually bitter mood. Even William had been surprised at his getting a ship when so many officers were unemployed. "You ask," wrote Horatio crushingly, "by what interest did I get a Ship? I answer, having served with credit was my recommendation to Lord Howe, First Lord at the Admiralty. Anything in reason that I can ask, I am sure of getting from his justice." He was having to take William with him. "Come when you please, I shall be ready to receive you. Bring your canonicals and sermons. Do not bring any Burnham servants." He was, as he expressed it, to be "pretty well filled with *lumber*" on this voyage. "I am asked to carry out Lady Hughes and her family—a very modest request, I think; but I cannot refuse, so I must put up with the inconvenience and expense." Also the ship was "full of young midshipmen, and everybody is asking me to take someone or other". He could not refuse to take Lady Hughes, because she was the wife of the Admiral commanding at the Leeward Islands.

The *Boreas*, said to be a very fine frigate, well officered and manned, was lying in Long Reach, ready to sail, when he went down to take possession of her. His troubles began at once.

"On Monday, April 12th, we sailed at daylight, just after high water. The d——d Pilot—it makes me swear to think of it—ran the Ship aground, where she lay with so little water that the people could walk round her till next high water. That night, and part of the next day, we lay below the Nore with a hard gale of wind and snow; Tuesday I got into the Downs; on Wednesday I got into a quarrel with a Dutch Indiaman who had Englishmen on board, which we settled, after some difficulty. The Dutchman has made a complaint against me; but the Admiralty, fortunately have approved my conduct in the business, a thing they are not very guilty of where there is a likelihood of a scrape."

Lady Hughes and party joined the ship from Portsmouth, and Nelson, crossed in love and done with politics, found that in addition to a large and rustic elder brother, over thirty mothers' darlings, or rejects, and an Admiral's lady who never stopped talking, he was to take charge of a sugary *débutante*. For Lady Hughes had a daughter, and it instantly became sufficiently obvious that the poor "Rosy" was being taken to the Leeward Islands for no other object than to find a husband. The Captain of the *Boreas* came first on Lady Hughes's list, but if he would not offer, almost any other gentleman, even his parson brother, would serve. The methods of Lady Hughes were crude, but she was not blind to the agonising fact that an adored child brought scarcely anything except youth to market. Nelson saw that "the mother will be the handsomer in a few years". His methods also were crude. After his first terrifying vision of the amorphous "Rosy" he hastened to Portsmouth, hired steeds and invited another young lady for an expedition on Portsea Common. Retribution came swiftly and painfully. The "blackguard horse" bolted, and "carried me round all the Works into Portsmouth, by the London gates, through the Town out at the gate that leads to the Common, where there was a waggon in the road". Nelson flung himself from his steed, "unluckily upon hard stones", and "to crown all", the young lady, whose horse had emulated his, was saved by a total stranger "from the destruction she could not have avoided".

Three weeks later Locker received a letter, franked by Kingsmill, now Member for Tregony, who had scribbled on the back, "Nelson's last, I imagine; he sailed to-day. He is a very good young man, and I wish him every enjoyment of life". But as yet the very good young man was not enjoying life at all. As the *Boreas* pursued, in increasingly pleasant weather, that slow course towards sunlit isles of which Lady Hughes nourished such high hopes, the poor lady became increasingly proprietary. She felt proprietary in a frigate which her husband had commanded in '63; she maddened Nelson by calling his ship "*dear Boreas*". On a sheet of paper, headed "Walking the *Boreas* quarter-deck on the 30th May, 1784 at 7 in the evening", he jotted down a list of her passengers and officers: "Lady Hughes, Miss Hughes, Captain Nelson, Lieutenants Wallace and Dent" (he spelt Wallis, who was a stranger, wrongly), "James Jameson, Master, Reverend Mr. Nelson, Masters Mates, Bromwich and Powers. . . ."

Cupid's darts, so anxiously awaited by Lady Hughes, began to fly about, but not in the right direction. Before the voyage was done it was apparent, even to her austere Captain, that both Lieutenants of the *Boreas* and her Scottish Surgeon were paying great attention to the Purser's wife. But for her attendant "specimen of English beauty", he would not have disliked Lady Hughes. He saw that the couple really were "very pleasant good people". They were not sea-sick, and they were delighted with his ship. Lady Hughes, for her part, long after she had given up hopes of such a relationship, continued to feel maternal affection for a young man obviously designed by nature to be a good husband and father; and years later, following a meeting with a brother-in-law of the hero at Bath, she felt impelled to send Mr. Matcham a line on the subject of Captain Nelson's "infinite kindness and goodness of heart displayed in his management of his many young midshipmen. He every day went into the schoolroom, and saw them do their nautical business, and at twelve o'clock he was always the first on deck, with his quadrant." Naturally, not all the thirty "younkers" were bold boys.

"The timid, he never rebuked, but always wished to show them he desired nothing of them that he would not instantly do himself; and I have known him say, 'Well, sir, I am going a race to the mast-head, and beg I may meet you there'. No denial could be given to such a wish; and the poor fellow instantly began his march. Captain Nelson never took the least notice with what alacrity it was done, but when they met in the top, instantly began speaking in the most cheerful manner, and saying how much a person was to be pitied that could fancy there was any danger, or even any thing disagreeable in the attempt. After this excellent example, I have seen the timid youth lead another, and rehearse his captain's words."

The thirty midshipmen included, as well as her own son, a Maurice Suckling, a distant cousin of the Captain, and she little knew that while she beamingly noted the stiff young bachelor's astute and humane treatment of "the young gentlemen who have the happiness of being on his quarter-deck", he was gloomily recording that he could not as yet make much of either Maurice William or the Admiral's son.

During the evening of June 14 "the usual pastimes on Crossing the Line were observed: Old Neptune came on board and received the customary fine", and the Captain seized the opportunity to give a straight talk to his officers and men on the inevitable results of failing to pay due respect to diet and hygiene in the tropics. Twelve days later the *Boreas* anchored in Carlisle Bay, Barbados, and Nelson found himself Senior Captain and Second-in-Command on the station.

3

He was not at first sight favourably impressed by the Leeward Islands, and in his present mood was inclined to be ruthless in comment and act. He reported to the Commander-in-Chief, and found Sir Richard Hughes (whose chosen instrument was the violin) "tolerable, but I do not like him, he bows and scrapes too much for me". Sir Richard, at five-and-fifty, was not a figure for whom it was possible to indulge hero-worship. He had lost the sight of an eye, but not in action. The disability was the result of an accident with a table-fork, when attempting to kill a cockroach. He lived in a boarding-house in Barbados "not much in the style of a British Admiral". He was a baronet; his father and grandfather had both, for many years, been Commissioner at Portsmouth; his lady had been a great-niece of the celebrated Sir Hans Sloane. Nelson, who had taken great pains on the voyage that the Admiral's lady should appear in due state, felt miserably that the Hugheses failed to present themselves with the prestige suitable to their position. The unavoidable sequel to such behaviour was apparent to his critical eye. Between them, the Hugheses, the climate and the piping days of peace were producing dire effects upon an unpopular station. "The Squadron is cursedly out of tune."

The Rev. William Nelson was the first victim of the climate. Three months of the Leeward Islands sufficed for him. Both the Collingwood brothers were on the station, but Cuthbert, the only officer for whom Nelson could feel both affection and regard, was at the moment of his arrival away at Grenada. Another old mess mate, little Charlie Sandys, whom he had known and liked as a merry, laughing lieutenant, had developed a failing not uncommon in exiles. "I am sorry to say that he goes through a regular course of claret every day." Soon poor Sandys, enamoured of a young lady of Antigua, whose beauty struck him speechless, but who had the sense to refuse him consistently, was "between Bacchus and Venus, scarcely ever thoroughly in his senses. . . . I am very sorry for him, for his heart is good, but he is not fit to command a Man-of-War." Dismissing Sandys, with the expectation that the next hurricane months would carry him off, and the remainder of his fellow officers as "geese" and "a sad set", Nelson turned to the one bright spot in his existence. "Was it not for Mrs. Moutray, who is *very very* good to me, I should almost hang myself at this infernal hole." The lady who bore this unmelodious name was the wife of the Commissioner at Antigua. She was much younger than her husband; her family consisted of a single son, aged eleven, destined for the Service. She had leisure, accomplishments and the most distinguished manners ever observed by an impressionable officer who had at present "nobody I can make a confidant of". She did not disturb his lacerated heart by any resemblance to Miss Andrews, who had been a beauty, but, as he realised now, an *ingénue*. The Commissioner and lady offered Nelson hospitality at "Windsor" while the *Boreas* was painting. He at once conceived for Mrs. Moutray one of those perfectly hopeless, desperately respectful passions, as common amongst young exiles as the habit contracted by Sandys. "Her equal I never saw in any country or in any situation." And this sentimental journey had amongst its fascinations for the young romantic the fact that it was doomed from the first. Commissioner Moutray's health was weak. Sooner or later he must go home. "I really am an April day, happy on her account, but truly grieved if I only consider myself." This sentimental journey lasted eight months. She sailed, eventually, in March, and in May he revisited the house on the hill above English Harbour where he had spent his "happiest days in this world", and indulged the pathetic fallacy: "E'en the trees drooped their heads." A certain tamarind, hallowed by some lofty memory, had possessed sufficient sensibility to die. "All was melancholy; the road is covered with thistles; let them grow. I shall never pull one of them up. By this time I hope she is safe in old England. Heaven's choicest blessings go with her."

It may be guessed that after the exit of Mrs. Moutray the stage was set for the entry of Mrs. Horatio Nelson, and that almost any lady of reasonable discretion and attractions might hope to play that part. She had made her first apologetic appearance within a few days of his saying farewell, "with a heavy heart", to her predecessor, and it was hard upon her that she must begin to play with a partner preoccupied by professional trouble, and against a noise of distant but furious dispute, which gave the tropical scene an additionally uneasy, headachey air.

4

About the time that Horatio Nelson decided that "the Admiral and all about him are great ninnies", Sir Richard Hughes began to be certain that in his new Senior Captain he had a trouble-maker. There was a whiff of trouble when the *Boreas* was not properly saluted on beating into Fort Royal Bay, Martinique. On his arrival in English Harbour, Antigua, on February 5, 1785, Nelson received a second and worse shock. The *Latona* was lying there with a broad pendant hoisted. He addressed himself to Commissioner Moutray, who proved to possess a memorandum from Sir Richard, authorising him to act as Commander-in-Chief on the station during the absence of a senior officer. "Until you are in commission I cannot obey any order I receive from you," said Nelson. "I know of no superior officers beside the lords commissioned of the Admiralty, and my seniors on the post list." He wrote to Sir Richard twice, and to the Secretary to the Admiralty. He felt himself on firm ground, as an officer must retire from the active list and be placed on half-pay before he could be appointed Commissioner of a Dockyard. Sir Richard also wrote home, and the result of this skirmish was that their Lordships informed Captain Nelson, "he ought to have submitted his doubts to the Commander-in-Chief on the station, instead of having taken upon himself to controll the exercise of the functions of his Appointment". Their Lordships were clearly supporting a senior officer.

His next difference with his Commander-in-Chief (which, since an answer from home took three months, overlapped his first) was far more serious. It had, indeed, been brewing from the moment of his arrival. Correspondence on the subject had begun with the New Year, and it was to embroil him with every authority in the islands. Sir Richard had been induced to waive the Navigation Laws in respect to vessels of the United States trading in the islands. "His easy temper", said Nelson politely, "had made him the dupe of some artful people." The Admiral's compliance suited nearly every prominent planter, merchant and Customs House official on the station, but not, as Nelson pointed out, "the interests of Great Britain". Sir Richard behaved in character throughout this weary business. When first approached by Nelson and Cuthbert Collingwood, he hedged. He had no instructions from home. Nelson told him that this was "very odd, as every captain of a man-of-war was furnished with the Statutes of the Admiralty, in which was the Navigations Act. . . . He said he had never seen the Book." On being presented with a copy, he "seemed convinced". He had "never seen or noticed" the Act before, but would now issue an order that the Navigation Laws should be enforced. "In December, to my astonishment", Nelson received contrary instructions. Sir Richard, after nearly two months' release from the company of his emphatic Senior Captain, had taken "good advice". After mature consideration, he required his officers not to hinder what was going on. "Let the residents of the various Islands decide the various cases." On finding that Nelson was not prepared to do this, indeed was going to defy such instructions, he sourly washed his hands of him, with a nervous reminder that he would get himself "into a scrape". Nelson stated his views at length, on paper, to Sir Richard, to the Admiralty, again and again, and to Lord Sydney, Secretary of State. ("My name most probably is unknown to your lordship, but my character as a man, I trust will bear the strictest investigation. I stand for myself, no great connexion to support me if inclined to fall.") He also wrote anxiously, for professional advice, to Uncle Suckling, "a person that has been in the Customs House since a boy". In the last resort, when his situation did begin, as Sir Richard had prophesied, to look very ugly, he addressed a humble memorial to the King's Most Excellent Majesty. "I had no alternative to save myself from being ruined."

The news of what he was about soon spread, and he found himself ostracised by the society of the islands. Supported by Cuthbert Collingwood, he visited the Governor, who began by explaining that he was all for suppressing the illegal trade, but his difficulties were many. Americans putting into port would produce wonderful excuses, swear, "even as the sea-phrase is, 'through a nine inch plank' that their vessel leaked, or had sprung a mast. Then the Customs grant a permit to land a part or whole of their cargo to pay expenses, under which permits they land innumerable cargoes." Governor Shirley, relishing the probable results of Captain Nelson's action as little as his Admiral, said at some moment during their interview that "Old Generals were not in the habit of taking advice from young gentlemen", to which Nelson replied, "I have the honour, sir, of being as old as the Prime Minister of England, and think myself as capable of commanding one of His Majesty's Ships as that Minister is of governing the State." (Mr. Pitt was still his idol.) As he expected, he was able to deal with Governor Shirley, but the abuse continued. It was at this point in the struggle that, being upon a cruise to St. Kitts and Nevis, he, and Wilfred Collingwood acting under his orders, turned back every American in sight, and having given four vessels lying in Nevis roads forty-eight hours' warning to hoist their proper colours and depart, seized them. The fat was then in the fire. Sir Richard regretfully gave up the idea of sending another captain to supersede Nelson and court-martialling his disobedient junior. He "stood neuter". "I am sure of casting my gentlemen", said Nelson calmly, and he was right. But a new danger awaited him. When the American masters went on shore they were met by an attorney primed by the furious inhabitants of Nevis, who had clubbed together and raised a sufficient sum for the ships' owners to sue Nelson for assault and imprisonment. Forty thousand pounds was mentioned as the sum claimed for damages. A marine had been on sentry duty at the cabin door while their evidence was taken; he was represented as "a man with a drawn sword", who had put them in terror of their lives. To avoid arrest, Nelson was obliged to stay in the *Boreas* for eight weeks, until the trial came on. Attempts to serve writs on him were frustrated by Lieutenant Wallis. The end of the story came three months later, when orders arrived from England that the costs of Captain Nelson's defence were to be paid by the Treasury. By the same packet came congratulations to Sir Richard Hughes and the officers under his command for their activity and zeal in protecting the commerce of Great Britain.

"Don't let me forget," added Nelson, detailing the saga to Locker, "the President of Nevis offered, in Court, to become my bail for £10,000 if I chose to suffer the arrest. He told them I had only done my duty, and although he suffered more in proportion than any of them, he could not blame me." In the last paragraph of a letter which covers four and a half pages of close print, he tantalisingly mentions, "I think I have found a woman who will make me happy."

5

Mr. John Richardson Herbert, President of the Council of the Island of Nevis, generally referred to by his family as "the President", or "Mr. H.", and by his acquaintance as "the Governor" or "Governor Herbert", was a character ripe for the pen of Sir Walter Scott, Miss Austen, Mr. Thackeray and, in his more despotic moments, even Miss Barrett of Wimpole Street.

Nevis, viewed from the sea, resembled a highly coloured illustration of a treasure-island in a child's picture-book. It was almost circular, and its lower slopes displayed the sharp green of the sugarcane, fringed by groves of coconut. Its conical summit, of a much darker blue than the surrounding waters, was continually capped by the snow-white clouds which had reminded Columbus of the Mountains of Nieves, in Spain. Montpelier, a large white house, guarded by pillars without, and within closely shuttered against West Indian glare, furnished by an owner to whom expense was no object, at a date when fashion expressed itself in terms of much gilding, crystal, floral brocade and polish, was the finest residence in an island measuring only eight miles by six and a quarter, but unequalled in products of the luxury trade.

Nelson, who first visited the President in January 1785, was naturally impressed. "Herbert is very rich and very proud. . . . Although his income is immense, yet his expenses must be great, as his house is open to all strangers and he entertains most hospitably."

The President of Nevis was a widower. He was not at present on good terms with his only child, Martha, who intended to marry Mr. Andrew Hamilton of the island. His household included, in addition to innumerable faithful blacks, a fluctuating number of nieces (who "came out" upon long visits and generally married), and an invalid sister, "Miss Sarah". Nelson brought one of the nieces with him on his second trip to Nevis—Miss Parry Herbert, also niece to the Governor of Barbados, David Parry. ("They trust any young lady with me, being an old-fashioned fellow.") There was also a permanent niece who at the time of his first two visits was absent, staying with friends in St. Kitts. "Dear Fanny", whom the President mentioned portentously as being "as dear to him as a child, perhaps dearer," kept house for a man "who must have his own way in everything"—no easy task. She was a young widow, and a particularly fine boy of five, who occupied the echoing nurseries of Montpelier, was her property. Nelson heard of her, and she also heard of Nelson. For that species of white magic which sometimes informs a female that she has met the future partner of a beloved relative, caused yet another of the nieces to include the following paragraphs in a letter to Mrs. Nisbet.

"We have at last seen the Captain of the *Boreas*, of whom so much has been said.

"He came up, just before dinner, much heated, and was very silent; yet seemed, according to the old adage, to think the more. He declined drinking any wine; but after dinner, when the President, as usual, gave the following toasts, 'the King', 'the Queen and Royal Family', and 'Lord Hood', this strange man regularly filled his glass, and observed that those were always bumper toasts with him; which having drank, he uniformly passed the bottle, and relapsed into his former taciturnity.

"It was impossible, during this visit, for any of us to make out his real character; there was such a reserve and sternness in his behaviour, with occasional sallies, though very transient, of a superior mind. Being placed by him, I endeavoured to rouse his attention by showing him all the civilities in my power; but I drew out little more than 'Yes' and 'No'.

"If you, Fanny, had been there, we think you would have made something of him; for you have been in the habit of attending to these odd sort of people."

Two months passed before Nelson's frigate was again to be seen in Charlestown harbour, and again by a chance he missed Mrs. Nisbet. He arrived too early on the morning of March 11. In the character of chaperon to the lively Miss Parry Herbert, he had hastened his charge up from H.M.S. *Boreas* to the shelter of her uncle's roof. The travellers arrived to find a West India house still asleep. While the new niece from home ran upstairs to announce herself, Nelson waited in a room next to that prepared for breakfast. Children, as well as sea-officers, stir early. He presently found himself regarded by a very bright pair of dark eyes. "Good God!" ejaculated the President to his household, when he appeared late at the breakfast-table, having completed a toilet interrupted by the necessity of descending to greet an early caller, "Good God! If I did not find that great little man of whom everybody is so afraid, playing in the next room, under the dining-table, with Mrs. Nisbet's child."

A few days later the Captain of the *Boreas* came to dine, and the elusive wraith who acted as hostess for her uncle was able to thank him, with that mixture of pride and apology so becoming to a young mother, "for the great partiality he had shown to her little boy". She could not know that she reminded him instantly of Mrs. Moutray, and at a moment when his heart was bleeding for the loss of that paragon. The ladies' points in common were obvious, and where there was a difference, it was distinctly in favour of the younger. Mrs. Nisbet had, like her predecessor, leisure, accomplishments and a single fine son; but no middle-aged husband loomed behind her, making chaste romance impossible. She displayed the same type of elaborate manners which Nelson had so much admired in the Commissioner's drawing-room ("Her manners are Mrs. Moutray's"), but the ceaseless entertainments over which Mrs. Nisbet diffidently presided much exceeded in scope and size those of the lady of Antigua. She was fluent in the French tongue, an exquisite needlewoman, and according to rumour (which lied) her musical talents were beyond the ordinary. The *fichu* gowns of muslin and sash in which she flitted about the groves and drooped in the saloons of Montpelier were inspired by those in which the Queen of France was playing at being a shepherdess or a milkmaid at the Little Trianon. Her features were fine, her eyes dark grey; of her dark curls a lover could not judge, for in 1785 all ladies were in powder by dinner-hour. Most important of all, Mrs. Nisbet's "English complexion" was the pride of the island. Nelson fell in love swiftly, as usual. He saw her first on some day between the 13th and 15th of March, "a few days after" March 11. By June 28 he was confiding to Brother William, "*Entre nous*. Do not be surprised to hear I am a *Benedict*, for if at all, it will be before a month. Do not tell." However, he himself had already said too much. Grave Captain Collingwood had congratulated Mrs. Nisbet on a bloodless conquest. Before he sailed for Barbados in mid-August, Nelson "spoke", and followed up his verbal proposal by a letter.

"My dear Mrs. Nisbit [*sic*],

"To say how anxious I have been, and am, to receive a line from Mr. Herbert, would be far beyond the descriptive powers of my pen. Most fervently do I hope his answer will be of such a tendency as to convey real pleasure, not only to myself, but also to you. For most sincerely do I love you, and I think that my affection is not only founded upon the principles of reason but also upon the basis of mutual attachment. Indeed, My charming Fanny, did I possess a Million, my greatest pride and pleasure would be to share it with you; and as to living in a Cottage with you, I should esteem it superior to living in a palace with any other I have yet met with.

"My age is enough to make me seriously reflect upon what I have offered, and commonsense tells me what a Good choice I have made. The more I weigh you in my mind, the more reason I find to admire both your head and heart. But come, don't say, 'What a vain young Man is this! 'tis a modest way of telling me I have given a proof of my sense by accepting him.' No! To Your heart do I own myself most indebted, yet I trust you approved of me for this obvious reason—'He esteems me, therefore he is the person I ought to expect most happiness from, by a return of affection. . . .'

"My temper you know as well as myself, for by longer acquaintance you will find I possess not the Art of concealing it. My situation and family I have not endeavoured to concial [*sic*]."

"Don't think me rude by this entering into a correspondence with you. Consider that separation from the objects we esteem loses some of its stings by a mutual unreserved correspondence."

The President answered, after an interval, in kindly non-committal vein. "My dear boy," said Nelson ruefully to Collingwood, "I want some prize-money."

"Dear Fanny", as she was to be henceforward, had not written to her "H.N.", but she had never in the course of a rather unsuccessful love-scene given any promise to correspond. He suggested in a postscript to a second attempt, "Do I ask too much, when I venture to hope for a line? Otherwise," he feared, "I may suppose my letters may be looked on as troublesome."

November found him engaged upon the inevitable letter to Uncle Suckling. "I open a business which perhaps you will smile at, in the first instance, and say, 'This Horatio is for ever in love'." He had obtained an interview with Mr. Herbert, an interview at which the President had evidently been majestic. "I have told him I am as poor as Job; but he tells me he likes me, and I am descended from a good family, which his pride likes." The trouble was that Mrs. Nisbet (most surprisingly when one came to think of it) turned out to be without a fortune. For the moment, at any rate, anything which she could bring towards a match must depend entirely upon the generosity of Mr. Herbert, who could not, he declared, "do much in my lifetime. When I die, she shall have twenty thousand pounds; and if my daughter dies before me, she shall possess the major part of my property." Nelson believed that the President might be persuaded to give his niece an annual allowance of two or three hundred a year, but he would much prefer that "whatever he may do at her marriage, may flow spontaneously". Finally, and most agonisingly for an ardent suitor, Mr. Herbert intended retiring in about eighteen months' time, and did not wish to lose his house-keeper before then. But meanwhile he had no objections to Captain Nelson paying his addresses.

Nelson's two letters to his uncle on this subject, both full of mis-statements, show how headlong had been his wooing and how inaccurate the information he had culled about Mrs. Nisbet. To Nelson, an acquaintance of eight months might perhaps fairly be presented as "of pretty long standing", and chivalry, or sheer ignorance, may have led him to subtract five years from her age; but he cannot have heard, either from her or Mr. Herbert, that she had been an orphan since she was two, and that her husband had died eighteen months after their marriage, in Nevis. It is even doubtful whether she can have told him that her husband had "died insane". The facts were quite different. Frances Herbert Woolward, born in the early half of 1758, and baptised at Nevis in May 1761, was a few months older than Nelson. Her father was William Woolward, Senior Judge of Nevis, and her mother, who died during Fanny's infancy, Mary, "Molly", one of the three sisters of President Herbert. Fanny's father survived until she was nearly one-and-twenty, and she married, within four months, the physician who had attended him. The Nisbet family had been settled for two generations in Nevis, at an estate called Mount Pleasant, but Josiah was a second son. President Herbert promised his niece a dowry of £2,000, but this had not yet been paid when the honeymoon couple sailed for England. Their reason for leaving the West Indies was that Dr. Nisbet was suffering from sun-stroke. The oppressed couple performed their long journey "home", and a child, named Josiah, was born, eleven months after the marriage, in England. For a further seventeen months Mrs. Nisbet attended her invalid physician, who then died at a house in the Cathedral Close at Salisbury. For the second time in her life she was left unprovided for, and this time she was in a strange land and with an infant child. She took the only possible course. She appealed to her Uncle Herbert, who provided her with an invitation to Montpelier and a settled home. It is possible that the President, misunderstanding the origin of distressing symptoms which he had observed, told Nelson that Fanny's first husband had died insane. She herself must either have confirmed this impression, or never alluded to a period in which she had suffered severe shock; for Nelson, as an experienced West India captain, was well aware of the difference between being what he called "struck with the sun" and insane. Before leaving the depressing subject of her finances it may be stated that the two or three hundred a year which Nelson had believed that the President would give her on her second marriage, and the legacy of £20,000, eventually took the shape of an annual allowance of £100 and a legacy of £4,000.

Nelson believed at the time of his engagement that Mrs. Nisbet's "little fellow" would in time receive sufficient from his father's and grandfather's estates to make him "totally independent". The President mentioned a legacy of £1,000 and intentions of putting Josiah in the way of making his own living. Josiah's legacy was £500, to be paid when he was twenty-one. He was twelve when Uncle Herbert died, and his stepfather had just been appointed to commission a ship-of-the-line. Uncle Suckling, grimly commenting that the legacy was more than he had expected, offered to advance the first £100, and Nelson, with the words "My objection to the Navy now he is certain of a small fortune, is in some measure done away", took the boy to sea with him.

6

Captain Nelson and Mrs. Nisbet settled down to the eighteen months' engagement dictated by expediency.

He had written home to announce his engagement. William was told:

"The dear object you must like. Her sense, polite manners, and to you I may say, beauty, you will much admire; and although at present we may not be a rich couple, yet I have not the least doubt but that we shall be a happy pair:—the fault must be mine if we are not."

Mr. Suckling learnt:

"Her heart is equal to her head. . . . Her mental accomplishments are superior to most persons of either sex; and we shall come together as two persons most sincerely attached to each other from friendship. . . . My affection for her is fixed upon that solid basis of esteem and regard that I trust can only increase by a longer knowledge of her."

"In due course" a bunch of congratulatory replies arrived. William, led astray, as he might well be, by his brother's original

mention of marriage within the month, concluded Horace a husband by now, and desired his love to Mrs. Nelson. "I am not
married yet", Horatio had to confess. "In England you think these
matters done in a moment"; and to Mr. Suckling, "I have not an
idea of being married till nearly the time of our sailing for England".
Suddenly, he had hopes of return that year. Sir Richard Hughes was
ordered home, but nobody in the squadron had the least idea
whether he was to be replaced, or what was to become of them.
"Lord Howe is so close, nothing is to be got out of him." The
Admiral sailed alone in June, preceded by Lady Hughes, proudly
escorting a married daughter. A bold major of the 67th Regiment
had been the happy man. "O what a taste!" said the Captain of the
Boreas, who never could forgive Rosy, even when she was safely
Mrs. John Browne. This wedding was the first of a series in his
circle. During the next year three announcements from home took
Nelson by surprise. William had married. His bride was announced
as Miss Sarah Yonge, daughter of the Vicar of Great Torrington,
Devon, and sister of Chancellor Yonge of Swaffham. Nobody told
that she was eight years William's senior. Captain Nelson begged
his best respects. "You will treat her kindly and tenderly, I have no
doubt. . . . I believe it is most generally the man's fault if he is not
happy."

His sister Kitty's match was a good one from every point of view.
As well as being a charming and talented man, handsome and energetic, Mr. George Matcham, explorer and author, had inherited
and augmented an East India fortune.

The third wedding in Nelson's family was the most surprising.
Uncle Suckling had answered his nephew's letter of last November
very kindly. He had, as usual, no wish that Horace's heart should
break for lack of a little temporary pecuniary assistance. He would
help, should it be necessary. But something in the letter, a single
sentence, perhaps misunderstood, had struck the recipient as chilly—
had cut him to the quick. The fact was that Mr. Suckling was thinking of getting married again himself, and although he admitted that
the children of his deceased sister had claims, he had children of his
own to consider. Horatio, who knew his uncle thoroughly, told
William that he was "truly glad to hear of this marriage. It will add

to his felicity, for had he not done that, he must have kept a woman, which you will allow would have been very disagreeable."

Mrs. Nisbet's *fiancé* now knew how he stood. The hour had clearly come when he must make a determined effort to discover the intentions of her uncle. He suffered pangs of apprehension after his letter had been sent. He would have preferred to approach the subject in an interview. But that, at present, was impossible. Nor, after twelve months' courtship, mainly on paper, was his "young widow" in the least less coy.

"I will not begin by scolding you, although you really deserve it, for sending me such a letter. Had I not known the warmth of your Heart by this time, I might have judged you had never seen me. However, I have fixed my resolve of not saying more."

Mrs. Nisbet received on May 4 from Barbados her first hint of what it would mean to be a sailor's bride.

"Never, never, do I believe shall I get away from this detestable spot. Had I taken your advice and not seized any Americans, I should now have been with you; but I should have neglected my duty, which I think your regard for me is too great for you to have wished me to have done. Duty is the great business of a Sea-officer. All private considerations must give way to it, however painful it is."

As the hot season of '86 wore on he began to feel less and less well, and correspondingly impatient.

"At first I bore absence tolerably, but now it is almost insupportable, and by and by, I expect it will be quite so. . . . I am alone, in the Commanding Officer's house, while my Ship is fitting, and from sunrise until bedtime, I have not a human creature to speak to; you will feel a little for me, I think. I did not use to be over-fond of sitting alone. The moment old *Boreas* is habitable in my cabin, I shall fly to it, in order to avoid mosquitoes and melancholies."

The mosquitoes also performed their duty, and presently a letter from his lady-love found him stupid with fever, hardly able to read and with only a faint recollection of what he had been about recently. He had to tell her that although his chief complaint was in his chest, he had no pain, and the doctor said there was no fear of a consumption. To Locker he had written quite the reverse, but a lady must be tenderly rallied.

"As you begin to know something about Sailors, have you not often heard that salt water and absence always wash away love? Now, I am such a heretic as not to believe that Faith. For behold, every morning since my arrival, I have had six pails of salt water at daylight poured upon my head, and instead of finding what the Seamen say to be true, I perceive the contrary effect."

Not until the end of September was he able to announce:

"On the 9th of October barring something extraordinary, you will certainly see H.N. again, and I need not say, if it be possible, with a stronger affection than when he left you."

He got his wish for October, but in early November something extraordinary did occur. H.M.S. *Pegasus*, under the command of Prince William Henry, suddenly arrived from Nova Scotia. Sir Richard Bickerton had not yet appeared to succeed Sir Richard Hughes. There was something ironic in the situation, for a society which had cold-shouldered the officer who enforced the Navigation Laws was thrown into a fever of excitement by the prospect of entertaining a Prince of the blood-royal, and every engagement made for the Prince's extended tour of the islands must be passed by his commanding officer and old friend, Captain Nelson.

At the end of seven weeks of hardly any sleep, and much too much full-dress uniform, salutes, strong sun, rich foods and loyal bumpers, the Senior Captain on the Leeward Islands station knew himself no courtier. ("What is it to attend on Princes? Let me attend on you, and I am satisfied. Some are born for attendants on great men. I rather think it is not my particular province.") To add to his trials, after the week's engagements had been somehow accomplished, he had to listen to His Royal Highness's complaints of his officers. Their Lordships had wisely supplied an eager twenty-two-year-old royalty with a scholarly and exact First Lieutenant, aged thirty-four, who had a distinguished West India active-service record. Mr. Schomberg appreciated that he was to "dry-nurse" the Prince, but the Prince by no means appreciated his efforts. Nervous tension was marked by the time that the *Pegasus* arrived at Antigua.

Jogging home over country roads, on the night of January 22, after a good dinner and very fine speeches, Nelson flogged himself to respectful attention while Prince William talked himself into a passion, telling the story of Lieutenants Schomberg and Smollett sending boats ashore without acquainting him. On the following evening, when the Senior Officer the Leeward Islands regained his cabin, he found a formal letter from Lieutenant Schomberg stating that as Prince William Henry had thought fit this morning to accuse him publicly of neglect of duty, he begged for a court-martial. Nelson immediately put Schomberg under arrest, and sent for the Prince; but he was too late. There had been many witnesses of a heated scene in which his Captain had upbraided the First Lieutenant of the *Pegasus* for asking for a court-martial, to which Schomberg had replied that His Royal Highness was grown "so very particular" that no officer could serve under him; that he realised that sooner or later His Royal Highness intended that he should be broke, and that if a court-martial acquitted him, he was going to ask for an exchange out of the *Pegasus*. Nelson's actions pleased nobody. Four days later, having good reason to believe that further officers of the Prince's ship were going to ask for a court-martial, he issued an order directing them not to make such applications on frivolous pretexts at a time when he had not sufficient ships to bring them to trial. He had, in fact, placed Schomberg under arrest because he saw that it was quite impossible for him to continue serving under the Prince. He had a very high opinion of Schomberg. He hoped for the arrival of a Commander-in-Chief, the prevention of a court-martial, and the removal of Schomberg from the *Pegasus*. But no god in the machine arrived, and after many weeks of confinement Schomberg believed himself thoroughly persecuted, while the Prince, who was justly nervous of his august father, and "very uneasy" ("I wish to God it had never happened"), still referred resentfully to his First Lieutenant as "this unhappy and deluded man", and "miserable object".

In the end, Nelson sent the *Pegasus* down to Port Royal, with a private note of explanation to Commodore Gardner ("His Royal Highness, I can have no doubt, gave the orders alluded to, although Mr. Schomberg might have misunderstood them"); and on a station where a court-martial could have been held, it was avoided. Their Lordships, furnished with the whole correspondence, said that Captain Nelson had done wrong in sending the *Pegasus* to Nova

Scotia by way of Jamaica. Schomberg was superseded, and sent back to England, but a few weeks later was appointed First Lieutenant of the *Barfleur*, carrying Lord Hood's flag, whereupon the Prince, who had not yet learnt his lesson thoroughly, sent a regrettable letter to Lord Hood. The last word was said seven months later, when Nelson wrote to the Prince to thank him for having saved a good officer from appearing before a court-martial,

"which must ever hurt him. Resentment, I know your Royal Highness never had ... but, now you are parted, pardon me, my Prince, when I presume to recommend that Schomberg may stand in your Royal Favour as if he had never sailed with you: and that at some future date, you will serve him. ... In full confidence of your belief of my sincerity, I take the liberty of saying that, having seen a few more years than yourself, I may in some respects know more of mankind. Permit me then to urge a thorough knowledge of those you tell your mind to. Mankind are not always what they seem. ... Nothing is wanting to make you the darling of the English Nation, but truth. Sorry, I am to say, much to the contrary has been dispersed."

The "difficult and disagreeable affair" of Lieutenant Schomberg was much more quickly and satisfactorily settled than that of the peculations by His Majesty's Crown Officials in the Leeward Islands, disclosed by Messrs. Wilkinson and Higgins, merchants of St. John, Antigua. They came to English Harbour on April 13, 1787, and delivered to the Senior Officer the Leeward Islands a letter, the duplicate of one enclosed, addressed to His Royal Highness. The Prince, although enjoying "no peace of mind" (since Lieutenant Schomberg had now been under arrest for ninety days), took instant intelligent interest in what he called "the Frauds". As he was just about to leave Antigua, he could only relinquish the matter into the hands of Nelson, who he was sure would do all that was proper and right. Nelson set to work with characteristic energy and enthusiasm. He interviewed Messrs. Wilkinson and Higgins repeatedly, and decided that they were very shrewd, sensible men of business. They had been partners with a Mr. Whitehead, Agent to the Royal Naval Hospital, Antigua. "Having separated, they have possessed themselves of all Whitehead's Books and Papers." Of course they were not disinterested. When His Majesty's Government were convinced, as the result of their disclosures, that vast frauds against the Customs had been committed, they expected a percentage of all sums recovered—15 per cent. "They are certainly men of strong natural parts, and appear wonderfully expert at the percentage."

In the impersonal Italian hand which he had learnt at Norwich Grammar School, when he was the boldest pupil, and his haystack of fair hair had been of a livelier colour, Captain Nelson wrote long letters to Prince William Henry; to Mr. Pitt (for the Prince said Parliament must know of it); to the new Comptroller of the Navy ("Sir, As a Fraud is likely to be discovered in the Naval Department which under your direction", etc.); to Viscount Howe, First Lord; to the Commissioners of the Office for the Sick and Hurt; and to His Grace the Duke of Richmond, Master General of the Ordnance. The results, in every direction, were disappointing.

As far as Nelson was concerned, the curtain rang down after two years and three months with a Delphic utterance from the Duke of Richmond: "With respect to yourself, I can only renew the assurances of my perfect conviction of the zeal for His Majesty's Service which has induced you to stir in this business."

7

The Captains of the *Boreas* and the *Pegasus* talked of more agreeable matters than Lieutenant Schomberg and Messrs. Wilkinson and Higgins as they sailed in fine weather from Barbados to Grenada, back to Antigua, and from Montserrat, by way of Nevis, to St. Kitts and the Virgin Islands. Two youthful figures in blue-and-white uniforms swept with their telescopes the headlands of St. Lucia, Grenada and Martinique and, with especial interest, the small rocky islets called "The Saints" in the channel between Dominica and Guadeloupe. The elder explained how the fleets had manoeuvred on a December day nine years past; on a July day of the following year; in the next April, and particularly on April 12, 1782. Captains Nelson and Prince William were fighting again the actions of Admirals Barrington, Byron, Rodney and Hood in the late war. Unluckily, although he had known these waters both before and after those stirring days, Nelson had not been present at any of the battles he described so well.

They also, since they dined with one another on alternate nights, and were both in their twenties, talked of love—or rather Prince

William did. Like most of the many sons of George III, he adored Romance. Since Nelson had last seen him he had travelled for two years in Germany and Italy, getting into many scrapes. As soon as he discovered that his friend was an intending bridegroom—which was very soon—he made a well-meant but not wholly considerate pronouncement. Nelson must promise him not to get married without his assistance. Indeed, he must undertake the *rôle* of Father of the Bride, and himself give Mrs. Nisbet to his friend. On this occasion, for the first and last time, he would break through his rule of never accepting private invitations. Nelson received the proposal with pleasure and concern. The compliment was great, but the inconvenience equally so. He wrote to tell Fanny that she must prepare to be given away by a Prince, though when he could not say, as his movements depended entirely upon those of His Royal Highness, "and when I shall see you, it is not possible for me to guess: so much for marrying a Sailor". He was also sufficiently ingenuous to tell her that the Prince kept on chaffing him on being such a calm wooer. His Royal Highness was sure that Nelson was already a husband and was keeping it dark. When Nelson told him, "I certainly am not", the Prince, tidying his face to match that of his companion, and really interested, was sure then that Nelson must have a great esteem for Mrs. Nisbet—not "the thing which is vulgarly called love". "No, I won't make use of that word", remembered Nelson, and told Fanny, "He is right, my love is founded on esteem, the only foundation that can make the passion last."

The New Year came, the year in which Mr. Herbert was going home, the year in which it had always been fixed that they should get married, and Nelson seemed as far as ever from choosing his wedding-day. He hoped for a spring date, for the *Boreas* was now so leaky that unless he got her home before the next hurricane season, he foresaw a further twelve months in the Leeward Islands. And he did not at all fancy another hurricane season at anchor in English Harbour, encouraging the ship's company to combine in concerts, dances and cudgelling contests, and shepherding the younger officers through the violent passages always provoked by private theatricals. February saw him at Montserrat, bound for Nevis and St. Kitts, but his plans for seeing much of the hostess of Montpelier were frustrated. The Captain of the *Maidstone*, upon whom he had depended to attend the Prince to the other side of the island, while he enjoyed some privacy with his Fanny, became indisposed. However, he had been able to display both his devotion and the adaptability of the British seaman. The Captain's steward from the *Boreas* had been up to Montpelier to remove an instrument of which its fair owner was making complaint, and as the Captain sat tussling with a difficult letter he was able to announce—"a man is cracking my head with tuning your pianoforte, but there is nothing I wouldn't bear for my dearest Fanny". He had succeeded in pinning down Mr. Herbert to another business interview, but not, he considered, a satisfactory one, for the President now nonchalantly suggested to an ardent suitor—"I might be united to you when I thought it most convenient, or let it alone till we got to England. I objected to the latter for many reasons." One of these needed tactful approach. If the *Boreas* sailed for home with her execrated Captain still a bachelor, "the ill-natured part of these islands would say I have only been playing the fool with you".

On March 6, Fanny received a startling intimation, prefaced by the words, "How uncertain are the movements of us Sailors", and "I am now feeling most awkwardly". H.R.H. was now also rather unwell, so their itinerary was altered. They were returning directly from St. Kitts to Nevis. She had five days' notice in which to prepare herself for her wedding. She would then get a week's honeymoon, in the island in which she had been born and bred, before her bridegroom sailed again, for the Virgins, whence, after a call at Antigua, he would attend H.R.H. to Grenada, which should finish his tour. By mid-May Prince William Henry should be under sail again for Halifax, and the *Boreas* fit for a passage home. "Happy shall I be when that time arrives." His last letter to Fanny before their wedding ended, "Heaven bless you, and I need scarcely say how much I am, your affectionate Horatio Nelson."

So, on Sunday, March 11, 1787, Nelson's last sentimental journey as a bachelor ended. He was twenty-eight. Nevis, like most of the Leeward Islands, possessed its small white church, containing monuments to Service victims of the climate, and less tersely worded memorials to the lives and deaths of members of the colonist families; but fashion, at the moment, prescribed that weddings should take place in private houses, so the Rev. W. Jones, Rector of Figtree church, St. John, was summoned to officiate in the principal reception-room of Montpelier.

The background of the scene has not altered in a century and a half, although the scythe of Time has reaped the rich white house, together with its jocose wedding-guests, fine in muslin, powder, broadcloth and bullion, and their attendant troupe of chocolate faces enlivened by flashing smiles. The stagey backcloth once viewed from drawing-room windows, of panting groves of coconut palms printed against blue skies and seas quivering in the primitive colours peculiar to the tropics in the height of the dry season, stays unchanged.

The guests and clergyman assembled; the bridegroom supported by his blond and large Hanoverian princeling in full-dress uniform and high good humour. The curtseys and deep bows necessitated by the entry of a son of His Majesty were performed. On the bridegroom's side there was present one relative—his midshipman cousin, Maurice Suckling; on the bride's many, including the very fine boy of seven, whom the confident bridegroom was going to treat just like his own children. The Prince offered his arm to Mrs. Nisbet (decked out in Limerick lace of the first quality), who was tremulously sure that to-day would give her the best of husbands and her dear Josiah the best of fathers. H.R.H. on his previous visit to the island, a few weeks earlier, had spent "many happy hours at Montpelier". He found Mrs. Nisbet "pretty, and a sensible woman, and may have a great deal of money, if her uncle, Mr. Herbert, thinks proper: poor Nelson is over head and ears in love. . . . He is now in for it: I wish him well and happy, and that he may not repent the step he has taken." Personally H.R.H.'s predilection at the moment was for striking *débutantes*, but when the knot was tied, with royal tact he congratulated the bridegroom on "having borne off the principal favourite of the island", a sentiment echoed by many of the blue-and-white uniforms present.

After the happy couple had retired, and the guests began to experience the flatness and slight melancholy generally produced by the disappearance of the principal characters of a Comedy, and the drinking of many toasts at an unfamiliar hour in very hot weather, some of Nelson's brother-officers looked gloomy. An admiring midshipman had heard with apprehension that "Captain Nelson has married a complexion", combined with "a remarkable absence of intellectual endowment". Next day, Captain Pringle, a gentleman for whom the bridegroom had a particular regard, was still buttonholing listeners to hear—"The Navy, sir, yesterday lost one of its greatest ornaments, by Nelson's marriage. It is a national loss that such an officer should marry; had it not been for that circumstance, I foresaw Nelson would become the greatest man in the Service."

Another midshipman never forgot his surprise at hearing, a few weeks later, that the Captain of the *Boreas*, whom he remembered dancing a minuet in the Island of Nevis with the widow of a Dr. Nisbet ("a pretty and attractive woman and a general favourite"), had not taken his bride home in his own ship. "Though lately married, he went home in his Frigate and she in a Merchant ship. . . . He was then so ill that it was not expected that he could live to reach England, and he had a puncheon of rum for his body in case he should die during the voyage."

Chapter IV
1787–1793
(ætat. 28–34)

FIVE YEARS ON THE BEACH

I

WHEN the Portsmouth bum-boats bobbed merrily around
the *Boreas* on the evening of July 4, 1787, her Captain had no
other expectation than that she would be paid off in a few weeks.
Nearly two months later he made a flying expedition to London in
order to leave his lady there with her relations. The *Roehampton*, a
luxurious West Indiaman, had had a slow but safe passage. Mrs.
Nelson, "never yet having made the *Boreas* her home" (as the
Captain of the *Boreas* somewhat sadly mentioned), was not likely to
do so now. The exiles' return, so warmly pictured, had taken place
at rather a disturbed moment. There seemed at the date of Nelson's
arrival a strong probability that England was going to war with
France again.

The weather was equally disturbed, and Nelson at once developed
one of his colds. "It is not kind in one's Native air to treat a poor
wanderer as it has done me since my arrival. The rain and cold at
first gave me a sore throat and its accompaniments: the hot weather
has given me a slow fever." He could hardly hold up his head while
the tedious and noisy business of victualling the *Boreas* for three
months was performed, and naturally a ship's company that had
expected release after a three years' cruise was in no cheerful mood.
He had to forward to London descriptions of deserters. He wrote to
ask Lord Howe for a ship-of-the-line in the event of hostilities, but
his orders were to be ready to take the *Boreas* to sea at an instant's
warning, with the squadron at Spithead. He did not himself believe
that France would give ultimate offence for another year, for although England was in a bad state for going to war, yet, "Thank
God, the French are worse". As England was in a bad state, Sep-

tember found the *Boreas* at the Nore, serving as a slop and receiving-ship for pressed men. Even the Rector of Burnham Thorpe realised that now Horace's situation was disagreeable. To Locker, who had been called out of retirement to regulate the impress at Exeter, his pupil wrote, "If the Regulating business is a thing you like, most sincerely do I give you joy of it." He had another trouble with which he did not vex his friends and relations. The Admiralty, on his arrival, had been as ungenial as the weather. Throughout these months of difficult and unpleasant duty he was harassed by correspondence with the various Departments involved in his attempts to enforce the Navigation Laws: and, though this might be no more than chance, every temporary appointment which he had made while Senior Officer on the Leeward Islands station could not, it appeared, for one reason or another, be confirmed. As the autumn wore on, Nelson, who had found himself, at the prospect of "a bustle", "never better", and "fit for any quarter of the Globe", became depressed at "laying seven miles from the land on the Impress service . . . as much separated from my wife as if I were in the East Indies".

The alarm of war, after blowing hot and cold, blew over at last. On November 30 the *Boreas* was paid off, at Sheerness, and the extraordinary and unwieldy collection of impedimenta made by her Captain in a cruise of over three years was hauled to light and dispersed, disclosing some minor tragedies. The dispersal was in itself a business entailing many letters and some private arrangements. Nearly everything had to be sent on by sea to the nearest port to its destination, and for some of his purchases the Captain could not face the enormous duty which the Customs House would demand. Nelson in 1787 wrote quite openly of having to smuggle West India luxury products. He had rum for William and Uncle Suckling, wine, rum and nuts for Kingsmill, wine for Lord Walpole of Wolterton, and a mountain of tropical dessert fruits. Poor Wilfred Collingwood's effects were brought forth, and the shrunk and scanty wardrobe and possessions of a promising young officer, of no private means, who had succumbed to tuberculosis, were put in a boat bound for Newcastle-on-Tyne, accompanied by a feeling note to necessarily harrowed relatives. All the wine chosen for Captain

Erasmus Gower, a person whom Nelson scarcely knew, had run out, a most disobliging circumstance. He had to make good the deficiency from his own store. Nor were all recipients grateful when they had unpacked their orders, or gifts. Locker, whose frankness was an endearing characteristic, when he had received his consignment of 36 pounds of tamarinds, a 60-gallon cask of rum, a dozen *Noyeau*, a dozen *Véritable* and half a hogshead of Madeira, wrote that he thought the wine not good. The apologetic purchaser could only say that he had paid a very good price for it. Mistakes took place at the Customs House. On a winter's day, nearly two years later, when Captain Nelson entertained a few cherished friends, the host's face underwent a sudden change. Instead of the Madeira which he had kept for such an occasion, he was sipping as good Port as ever he had tasted.

Mrs. Nelson and her husband, united at last, and on a holiday of unlimited duration, spent their first Christmas together as guests of Mr. Herbert. The President had sailed from Nevis in May, but not before witnessing the marriage of his only child and heiress to the man of her choice, a romance happily concluded largely owing to the efforts of his niece's unworldly husband.

After his marriage Nelson's view of London was altered. He never again haunted the small, old streets off the throbbing Strand, frequented by impecunious junior officers, and so convenient for visits to the Admiralty, Whitehall and the Navy Office, Seething Lane, the Victualling Office, Tower Hill, the Pay Office and the Sick and Hurt Office, Broad Street, and, last but not least, the coffee-room of Fladong's Hotel, New Oxford Street. The Herbert family revolved around the President's house, 5, Cavendish Square. To be near her kin, even when not actually staying with them, Fanny and her husband lodged in the side-streets of Marylebone—at 10, Great Marlborough Street and 6, Princes Street. He never took to "north of the Park", and when he came to order a house in London, told Davison on no account to choose one "on the other side of Portman Square. I detest Baker Street."

They "rather hurried" to Bath, when the sad little flurry of despatching Josiah to boarding-school was accomplished. Nelson must place his ailing wife at a Spa before he undertook a bachelor expedition. Prince William's ship had arrived at Plymouth from Nova Scotia, and H.R.H. had written inviting his friend to take part in the festivities celebrating his safe return. Nelson went gladly, and found the west-country port *en gala*. Some people who had known and disliked H.R.H. previously, said that he was a most altered young man. The *Pegasus* was allowed by every competent judge to be one of the best-disciplined ships that ever came into Plymouth.

At Bath, too, "sea-folks" were "pretty numerous", but after a fortnight of drinking the waters, a young couple with no money to spare tired of a Spa. With spring, a country clergyman's son was longing to get into the country. A further fortnight of Bath followed a month near Bristol; they then cut themselves entirely loose from the haunts of rank and fashion. They made holiday in South Devon, and by a lucky chance, in early May, met "in this remote corner" just the type of English spring weather dreamt of by West Indians. From "Exmouth Moor", Nelson wrote to Hercules Ross, the patriotic Jamaican who had sent his slaves to man the batteries of Fort Charles, Port Royal, when Admiral D'Estaing was expected. Ross, too, had recently been "united to an amiable woman, the greatest blessing Heaven can bestow". He, however, had retired. "You", wrote Nelson, "have given up the toils and anxieties of business; whilst I must still buffet the waves—in search of what? That thing called Honour, is now alas! thought of no more. . . . My integrity cannot be mended, I hope, but my fortune, God knows, has grown the worse for the Service." He comforted himself that "a uniform course of honour and integrity seldom fails of bringing a man to the goal of Fame at last", but before the month was out had had enough of sunning himself amongst Devon gorse, and was to be seen entering the courtyard of the Admiralty. His object this time was not to ask for a ship, but, in consideration of his services when left in command of the Leeward Islands station, at least the same allowance usually given to a junior officer at Jamaica. His bills for frequent journeys to St. John had all, so far, been settled out of his own pay as Captain of the *Boreas*. He wanted also to see whether it was his fancy that their Lordships were not favourably impressed by his recent exertions. But after doing himself the honour of calling twice upon the First Lord in order to pay his personal respects, and never being happy enough to find his Lordship disengaged, he was obliged to write a letter recounting these and his previous efforts. He also wrote from Cavendish Square to Prince William Henry. Fanny had thought of a way in which she might aid the family exchequer, not in itself uncongenial, though it must mean much residence in London and separation from her husband. Nelson, who knew himself not very good at asking for favours from the great, managed his request as best he could, in the last paragraph of a longish letter.

"There may be a thing, perhaps, within reach of your Royal Highness; therefore, trusting to your goodness, I shall mention it. The Princess Royal must very soon have a Household appointed her. I believe a word from your Royal Highness would obtain a promise of a situation in Her Royal Highness's Establishment not unbecoming the wife of a Captain in the Navy; but I have only ventured to say this much, and leave the issue to your better judgment."

Prince William's answer is not preserved, but Fanny Nelson never shared the fate of Fanny Burney.

Nelson came in sight of his home again with midsummer, and alone. It was not entirely the young couple's fault that they had been so long visiting Burnham Thorpe. When Mrs. Horace had threatened a winter visit, the Rector, who knew what Burnham was like under snow, had commented "Forbid it Fate!" He had written nervously to his daughter Kitty, that he would be very glad to see Horace for a few days. As to Horace's lady, who wrote him the most distinguished letters from Cavendish Square, he imagined that she would form a very valuable part of his family connections, but he could not imagine what she could do at little Burnham. He knew that she had been bred in West Indian luxury. She was a "fine" lady, and would wish to bring her personal maid, what in the eighteenth century was called her "woman". At the thought of Mrs. Horatio Nelson's *suite* scorning his own rustic staff—all strong personalities—the Rector was overcome. Nelson managed the first meeting tactfully. He took his lady upon a tour of his Norfolk relations. They began with the Boltons, a household cheerful, whatever the odds. At present his elder sister was sheltering Edmund, fourth surviving son of the family, who had been a partner with Mr. Bolton, but was now not earning, as he was in a decline. Leaving Fanny at Hilborough, with the William Nelsons, her husband rode over to Burnham Thorpe. In his home thoughts from sea he had most often pictured his birthplace as he found it now—in the weeks of haymaking, the elder-flower and the wild rose.

The Rector's latest additions to his register of family prowess did not make cheerful reading. His youngest son, Suckling, on receiving his legacy under the Comptroller's will, and a liberal benefaction from Uncle William Suckling, had bought the house and stock-in-trade of a grocer and draper at North Elmham. That venture was now at an end, and he seemed willing to take holy orders. The Rector hoped that Suckling might pass "amongst a crowd of undistinguished preachers, and gain some respect in the village of his Residence, from his quiet disposition, his liking for conviviality, and his passion for Greyhounds and Coursing". But taking orders must entail the expense of a private tutor, followed by a university course at Cambridge. And while Suckling had merely lost money, Maurice was in debt. While he shepherded the Captain of the *Pegasus* round the Leeward Islands, the Captain of the *Boreas*, in obedience to letters from home, had not neglected to mention to the Sailor Prince that he had a brother languishing in the Navy Office. He had warned his family, "My interest is but rising". The Rector's account of his eldest brother sent Captain Nelson up to London again, and by the first week in July he had somehow managed to "entirely liberate poor Maurice from the galling chain". On his return to Norfolk he collected his wife for a visit to his younger sister, Kitty. The Matchams had taken a lease of Barton Hall, near Neatishead, where they lived in what the Rector complacently, but unenviously, described as "ease and affluence". Unfortunately, alone of his connections by marriage, Mrs. Horatio Nelson did not fall an instant victim to the charms of "G.M." She thought the admired bridegroom of Kitty Nelson, who had, it is true, the wealthy man's penchant for buying, altering and then selling properties, the most unsettled man she had ever met.

While they stayed at Barton, Nelson read in the *Gazette* that a new Board of Admiralty was appointed. Lord Chatham was become First Lord; Lord Hood one of the two Naval Lords. He wrote at once to assure their Lordships of his readiness to serve whenever they might think proper to call upon his services, followed his letter by a personal call upon Lord Hood, and was able to inform Fanny from London in August that his Lordship had made many enquiries after her, and been most civil. "He assured me that a Ship in peaceable times was not desirable; but that should any Hostilities take place, I need not fear having a good ship."

Nelson on half-pay was receiving eight shillings a day. Fanny and he both received annual allowances of £100 from their uncles. But perpetual holiday is an expensive business, and Nelson was now thirty. On October 8, he wrote to Cornwallis, expressing his desire to serve under him in the East Indies. "Fame says that you are going out with a convoy." Although "set down here in a country life", and "happily married", he was perfectly ready. Five days later he sent a repetition of his desire "to serve under you, and for our Country (although I am as happy in domestic life as a person can be.") The reply was most disappointing. Cornwallis answered that nothing would have given him more pleasure than to have had Nelson in one of his ships. He had thought of him, remembering him as an officer with East Indian experience, but knowing that Nelson had recently achieved a fireside of his own, had not dared to make such a suggestion. For the present, his appointments were made. He could only say that if more ships were sent out, nothing would please him more than to see Nelson in one of them.

The Horatio Nelsons had by this time settled, though not by a fireside of their own. The Rector, on meeting Fanny, and finding that in spite of her *suite* she was unalarming—in fact, rather painfully alive to her situation as a person of limited means—had tenderly invited the young couple to make their home with him and cheer his declining years. They had been planning to winter in France, so that Horace could make one more assault on the language of that country. They gave up their French plan without much struggle.

The old walled garden at Burnham Thorpe showed signs of the havoc wrought by Mr. Matcham's suggestion of "turning" the stream through the grounds, and the season was an interesting one in the gardener's year. "The very energetic Captain" set to work at once to urge his father's outdoor servant, Peter Black, "poor, forlorn, 'tho wise as ever", to lustier effort. Mrs. Nelson began to make acquaintance with a very small home, of low rooms, filled with worn furniture and reflections of greenery, with flagged floors, grateful in warm weather, set down in a landscape two-thirds of which appeared to be occupied by sky. The autumn leaves began to fall, and winds to blow across the steel-grey North Sea. In expectation of promised roses from Barton, Nelson achieved a *parterre*. The boot-and-knife boy, Williamson, helped him to dam the stream, on which he was going to sail a model ship-of-the-line. . . .

All through their first winter at Burnham Thorpe the West Indians shivered and shook. Fanny heaped more and more woollen garments upon her small frame, and finally retired to bed for days together. Even "the most robust Captain" acknowledged "a rheumatick twinge" after his labours in the garden. Presently the wind dropped, the snows came and gardening was no longer possible. When Burnham was winter-bound all was, in the Rector's language, "Hush, at High Noon as at Midnight". Even horse-traffic ceased. Only an occasional hardy village figure plunged past the irregular windows of the small shabby house where the Rector, his naval son and his West India daughter-in-law sat in a brown parlour with a stone floor, under the dim and indifferent portraits of ancestors of higher fortune.

The Rector himself was accustomed to the solitude and climate. Horace was at home, and spent the hours of candlelight with his nautical charts, his model ship-of-the-line, Dampier's *Voyages* (which he thought the most interesting book he had ever read) and his correspondence with their Lordships, etc. Fanny, however, hung heavy upon the Rector's conscience. He wished that some amusement could come her way—"a little society and an instrument, with which she could pass away an hour. She does not openly complain. Her attention to me demands my esteem, and to her Good Husband she is all he can expect." Fanny had her fine needlework, her water-colours and, three times a year, "Master Nisbet for the holidays". When her brother-in-law Edmund arrived home to die, she included him in her kind attentions. But he was listless—past caring for relations new or old; he seemed to prefer the company of his village nurse, Dame Smith. Spring, as usual, came slowly to Norfolk. When the woods began to bud, and the birds to sing, her husband took Mrs. Horatio Nelson, who found Norfolk not so temperate as Nevis, out on bird-nesting expeditions. He knew that the hedge-mongers commonly visited the old yew hedge in the garden. His eye and ear gave him access to a kingdom of simple delights unsuspected by his partner.

He had no private transport, no money to spare and no call to London. He read the local newspapers thoroughly. They told him that in France the Bastille had fallen, and the royal family had been triumphantly escorted from Versailles, by a vociferous mob, to enforced residence in their capital. England was at peace, and her beloved King recovered. Nelson's "interest" could no longer be termed "rising". "Not being a man of fortune", he explained to Locker, who was also unemployed, "is a crime which I cannot get over, and therefore none of the Great care about me. I am now commencing Farmer, though not a very large one, you will conceive, but enough for amusement. Shoot, I cannot, therefore I have not taken out a license; but notwithstanding the neglect I have met with, I am happy, and now I see the propriety of not having built my hopes on such sandy foundations as the friendships of the Great." His princeling had been created Duke of Clarence, but at present the patronage of this royalty was rather a disadvantage than the reverse. The Duke had joined with his brothers in their long, unedifying struggle to establish a Regency, and had delivered himself of some startling speeches.

Half a dozen letters—four concerned with Messrs. Wilkinson and Higgins, two to Locker—confirm Nelson's uninterrupted residence at home in the year 1789, "retired, upwards of 120 miles from London".

2

The west coast of Vancouver Island is generally precipitous, much broken by bays and inlets. One of these harbours, six miles in width, and sending inland three arms, from sixty to a hundred and twenty fathoms deep, was visited by Captain Cook in 1778. He called it by what he took to be its native name—Nootka—and concluded that Spaniards had never been there, but did not formally take possession. In the same year that the *Boreas* was paid off, after an alarm of war with France had died, Spain began to take interest in a fine harbour which Perez claimed to have discovered four years before Captain Cook's visit. In 1789 a little confused and angry shouting took place amongst the woods and waters of Nootka Sound, the echoes of which were to rouse Europe. Two Spanish ships, the *Princesa* and the *San Carlos*, had been sent by the Governor of Mexico to take possession of Spanish property. They found two English merchant vessels, of classical name, in the harbour of Nootka, their crews stolidly and quite openly engaged in trading with the natives of the island. The name and story of Nootka Sound penetrated even to the *Norfolk News*. Suddenly it seemed that England might be going to war with Spain, and presently, as the weeks passed into spring, also with France, as ally of Spain—a serious situation. In early May, after a meeting of the National Assembly in Paris, fourteen French sail-of-the-line were ordered to make ready to go to sea.

Nelson was in London by May 8, but owing to an untoward incident, he might have been in France. After many months completely devoid of noteworthy event, the shades of Burnham had been roughly visited. His brother William, his brother-in-law, Mr. Matcham, had been kind enough after their visits to leave a horse in the Parsonage House stables. With the approach of better weather he decided to buy "a Gallwey, a little pony" at the local fair. On April 26 the Captain arrived home on his purchase, very pleased with the result of his first attempt to deal in horseflesh. Indeed, so great was his satisfaction that not until the pony had been rubbed down and watered and fed did he perceive anything amiss in the atmosphere at home. He had for some time been plagued by letters from solicitors representing clients whose ships he had seized while applying the Navigation Laws in the Leeward Isles. It now transpired that during his absence at the fair, two men, "in appearance resembling Bow-Street officers", had forced their way into his father's house, desired to see his lady, and after making her repeatedly declare that she was the wife of Captain Nelson, presented her with a document, telling her to give it to her husband. The document was the notification of an action to be taken against him by certain American captains, and they laid their damages at £20,000.

He had no great reason for anxiety. The Secretary to the Admiralty had informed him, a month before, in answer to another letter on the subject, that his communication had been referred to the Treasury, with recommendations that he should be defended. But he had much cause for wrath. Fanny had been frightened. The lady of a sea-officer in His Majesty's Service had been insulted. "This affront I did not deserve!" He wrote, on the spot, to the Admiralty, enclosing a copy of the notice "this day served by a person from London". He trusted to their Lordships' protection, hoping they would only think he had performed his duty. But in the heat of the hour of insult he also formed a dramatic resolution. If he did not receive a favourable answer at the earliest possible moment he would retire to France. Maurice should bring Fanny over to join him in eternal exile. A note in his wife's hand tells that "He once spoke of the Russian service". On May 4 he was able to cancel these unhappy plans. Captain Pringle had seen the Right Hon. George Rose, and the Secretary to the Treasury, who had not forgotten a six a.m. interview two and a half years ago, with a strange young man who had exposed peculations in the Leeward Isles, had calmly mentioned that Captain Nelson, "a very good officer", need be under no apprehension. "He will assuredly be supported by the Treasury."

3

At the Admiralty on May 8 he was not able to get an interview with Lord Chatham. That was not surprising, since the situation, as shown in the newspapers, had called up to Whitehall many figures so well known to the porters of the stately Admiralty building that these aloof flunkeys did not trouble to show the poor devils to the waiting-room. In the company of many other officers on half-pay, some of whom looked as if they should get employment and others as if they never would, he wrote a note explaining that he had come up to town immediately on hearing of "the bustle", and was ready to undertake whatever employment their Lordships thought most proper. He went on to Lord Hood's house, and here found his man.

Their interview was brief, and as a result of it Nelson made no further effort to see Hood for over two years. The Admiral who had "found" him could not ask the First Lord for a ship for Captain Nelson. Staggered by this sudden and wholly unexpected removal of favour, Nelson asked outright the reason. Lord Hood, who never lacked courage, made a reply never effaced from Nelson's brain. "The King was impressed with an unfavourable opinion of me." This sentence struck Nelson so near to the heart that he asked no more. He left the house in Wimpole Street in staring silence, determined never again to trouble his Lordship for his interest or influence.

To be unemployed for a couple of years in time of peace had been a growing anxiety, but the prospect of remaining unemployed when "nearly the whole Service had been called forth" was unendurable. He had never lost sight of "the radiant orb" beckoning him on to brave every danger with his King and Country as Patron; but he had not, in his least optimistic moments, considered the possibility of being denied the chance of braving dangers. Nor, now, upon reflection, would he believe that his King and Country did not need him. He decided, in this sickening and lonely hour, that he must, like better men before him, have become the victim of some misunderstanding—"a prejudice at the Admiralty, evidently against me, which I can neither guess at, nor in the least account for". The radiant orb stayed in his heaven. "Neither at sea nor on shore, through the caprice of a Minister, can my attachment to my King be shaken. That", he knew, "will never end but with my life."

He achieved again, in very different spirits, the tiring and expensive journey back to rural spring-tide Norfolk, and told his expectant and affectionate circle that he had done all that was proper, and could but wait the event; many other officers were in the same state of uncertainty. The Rector, in whose character the virtues of humility and resignation were strongly developed, quite honestly considered the existence of an upright and benevolent landowner (too wealthy to be obliged to follow any profession) superior in happiness to that of a sea-officer. He noticed that Horace was restless, but was glad that his son seemed reconciled to any available employment. He could not deceive himself that though Horace's merit was great, "Still, without Interest, I fear it may be over-looked, where a Boldness and some parliamentary weight stands forward". He remembered with uneasiness the day when Maurice "might have catched a gleam of sunshine; it is now clouded". Fanny, who thought the life of a sailor's wife hard, had, in preparation for becoming a grass-widow, settled upon lodgings in the small town of Swaffham—a sad change from Montpelier. Mr. Matcham, ever generous, wished to offer his brother-in-law a pipe of wine when he should have a ship. Outside the family, many acquaintances who had sons to place, or vacant bins in their cellars, enquired the name of Captain Nelson's new ship.

Another General Election took place during this summer. "Noisy nonsense", opined the Rector. But in 1790, "on the beach", out of luck, Nelson knew that he had not the slightest chance of what he called "a land-frigate". Amongst the twelve members elected for Norfolk that year five were new, but not one, according to the Rector, a cause for much elation. Nelson offered himself and lady for a visit to his godparent at Wolterton, a scheme that caused the Rector to entreat Mrs. Matcham to choose for his daughter-in-law, in London, a plain handsome bonnet and a cloak, suitable for dinners, calls, etc. Nelson wrote also to the Duke of Clarence, making no secret of his position. "My not being appointed to a Ship is so very mortifying that I cannot find words to express what I feel on the occasion." By August, getting desperate, he snatched at any excuse to address a person of rank who was of his profession. "The retired situation which I am placed in, affords me seldom any means of information but through newspapers; in which I read with sorrow that your Royal Highness was prevented from being at Windsor on the Prince of Wales's birthday. . . ." The newspapers had also reported, under the heading, "Torbay", August 1. "Wind fair at W.N.W." "This morning Lord Howe's flagship threw out the signal for sailing. Thousands of spectators watched the departure of the Fleet—thirty-one ships-of-the-line, nine frigates, two brigs, two cutters, a fire-ship and a hospital ship. . . ."

On September 26 Nelson tried the First Lord again. "My wish to be employed is so great, that I trespass on your Lordship's time with a letter. I am sensible I have no great interest to recommend me nor have I had conspicuous opportunities of distinguishing myself, but thus far, without arrogating, I can say that no opportunity has been passed by, and that I have ever been a zealous Officer." Mr. Suckling, in the same week, was mentioning his nephew's name to Lord Hawkesbury. The saintly Rector reserved his outward sympathy for "Poor Mrs. Nelson, still kept in the same harry of spirits and uncertainty as she has been for the last six months", and pointed out that war had not yet been declared. If "the present negotiation" terminated in peace, Horace would have been fortunate in not being appointed to a ship. "And if War must be entered upon, he is still in good time." The present negotiation did terminate in peace before October was out. Spain, faced by an English ultimatum, and finding to her chagrin that Louis XVI was not able to declare war without the sanction of the National Assembly, temporised in time. On October 28 the Nootka Convention was signed, by which England gained the right to trade and settle on the north-west coast of the Americas, and Spain relinquished for ever her claims to sovereignty of the coast as a result of discovery.

Cold weather settled down upon the Burnhams again, and the Rector, who found that failing sight and strength made his performance of duties in two churches, neither close to his home, increasingly difficult, took the lease of a cottage in Burnham Ulph village, leaving the government of the Parsonage House to his son and daughter-in-law.

In December Lord and Lady Walpole announced themselves ready to receive guests from Burnham Thorpe, and Captain Nelson and lady set out at last for Wolterton. They stayed for several weeks at a country seat well furnished with lake and woodland, but inhabited by so prosaic a couple that had they not been a peer and peeress, they might not have been much visited. However, they were kin. Nelson, who had recently had good reason to appreciate the necessity for appearing neither hopeless nor obscure, took care to mention his address to the Duke of Clarence, and thereafter the winter stay of his lordship's naval godson and lady became an annual fixture. Annually, also, Nelson made his spring pilgrimage to London to attend a *levée*. "It must one day come to account." And, though he would not trouble Lord Hood again, he never neglected the courtesy when in town of leaving his name at his lordship's doors.

Not a single letter from Nelson's pen in the year 1791 has come to light. From family letters it appears that he took part in the mild provincial gaieties available. At the Lynn Feast and Aylsham Assembly, as season succeeded season, the Horatio Nelsons noticed awkward schoolgirls become extraordinary fine, tall young women, and dowagers, bent on their shilling whist, increasingly garrulous and depleted of front teeth. Violent events taking place in France did not trouble the belles of Aylsham while the fiddles sounded, but even in Norfolk repercussions were noticeable, and Nelson wrote at length on the subject to his Prince, who shared his anxiety lest their country be cast into "the wretched deplorable confusion of France". Nelson's opinions, as expressed to a son of the sovereign, were temperate. He hoped that the justices of Norfolk would find courage to do collectively what not one dared do individually— take away the licences from those of the public-houses that allowed societies calling themselves by such names as "Friends of the People" to hold incendiary meetings. On the other hand, he realised that the poor labourers who flocked eagerly to these meetings were not without reason for desiring a changed world. Part of their wants he supposed unavoidable, but he blamed some landlords for prevailing disaffection, which, however, he did not believe to be as yet very dangerous or widespread. It had been quite easy for the son of a respected country clergyman to penetrate to cottages, asking such homely questions as how much did shoes and cobbler's bills for the family cost per annum? His Majesty himself made such expeditions, and though caricaturists represented cruelly, under the title "Affability", a monarch who gloried in the name of Briton bawling into the ear of a stone-deaf and scared husbandman, Nelson found, as he had expected, that Farmer George was securely seated in the hearts of his people. So that no country gentleman should have it in his power to say that Captain Nelson painted too black a picture, he was careful to enter in his "Account of Earnings and Expenses of a Labourer of Norfolk, with a Wife and three Children, supposing that he is not to be one day kept from labour in the whole year", such extra money as might be won by the woman gleaning,

or the man turnip-hoeing at the appointed seasons. The Duke of
Clarence received from his naval friend a document ending, "Not
quite twopence a day, for each, and to drink, nothing but water; for
beer our poor labourers never taste unless they are tempted, which
is too often the case, to go to the Ale-house." (The Duke never
knew that, upon second thoughts, Nelson had deleted from his
accompanying letter the burning phrase, "Hunger is a sharp thorn,
and they are not only in want of food sufficient, but of clothes and
firing.")

Coursing had been Nelson's favourite relaxation at home, but by
February 1792 he had decided that the pleasure of the sport was
outweighed by the wet jacket and heavy cold that were generally
the sequel. His world was narrowing, do what he would. When old
Dr. Poyntz called at the Parsonage House he left an emphatic
message for William, regarding walnut trees and red filberts.
His host really could not remember the drift of the old gentleman's
long-winded instructions, and feared that his only comment had
been that by the time any trees planted by Brother William this
year were bearing walnuts, William would not be alive. His
thoughts had been elsewhere. He had received letters from
Commodore Cornwallis, by the *Swallow*. . . . No hopes from that
quarter. If Kingsmill had gone to India he had promised to ask for
Nelson. "However, that is over for the present. . . . The Navy is to
be reduced to 15,000 men." The Prime Minister had told the House
of Commons, "There never was a time when, from the situation
of Europe we might more reasonably expect fifteen years of
peace."

In September a family party always sallied forth from the Parsonage House for rough shooting upon a glebe of thirty acres. Most of
the bloodshed was laid at the door of Tom Bolton. William's fire
was remarked to evaporate chiefly in threats. Of Horace, it was
remembered that "he once shot a partridge; but the manner in
which he carried his gun always cocked, as if he were going to
board an enemy, and his custom of firing immediately when any
birds appeared, rendered any attendance on him a service of considerable danger". By September 1792, Horace, who pronounced
"An Enemy floating game is a better mark", had long been

N.—5*

persuaded that he could not shoot. His sixth winter "on the beach" began. On December 15 he wrote to his younger sister that all her family in Norfolk were well. Mr. Matcham had recently built a house on an estate with the charming name of Shepherd's Spring, near Ringwood, in Hampshire, but the couple were at present enjoying London. Nelson told his sister that when she and Mr. Matcham chose to come into Norfolk, Mrs. Nelson would be very happy to receive them at the Parsonage House. He cautiously fancied they would find the spring more pleasant than the winter. "We have had one heavy fall of snow, but it has thawed now."

Eleven days after Nelson watched the thaw from his desk in his Norfolk window, the trial of Louis Capet began in Paris. Once more English newspapers were prophesying war with France—a thing their Prime Minister was most desirous to avoid. But Revolutionaries drunk with power had proceeded to acts intolerable to England. The River Scheldt had been closed to commerce by several treaties. A month before Nelson wrote his Christmas letter to his sister, the Convention suddenly declared the Scheldt open. Three days later the support of France was flamboyantly offered to all nations striving for Freedom. Nelson had written to Lord Chatham in October, asking for a ship, and repeated his request after five weeks had passed without his receiving any answer. Rather to his surprise, his second letter produced a reply, "Sir," wrote the Secretary to the Admiralty, on December 12, "I have received your Letter of the 5th instant, expressing your readiness to serve, and I have read the same to my Lords Commissioners of the Admiralty." No man could have judged from this that the end of his time of waiting had come. But in London the name of Nelson no longer reminded one official only of the sufferings of poor Admiral Hughes; and a whole series of Government officials of endless correspondence with a Post-Captain over vexing discoveries of frauds in their Departments, and a very exalted quarter indeed of a "Memorial" from a young officer who had not done much to prevent Prince William making more of a fool of himself in the West Indies than Nature intended. A capable Post-Captain, well down the list, who had exceeded in zeal, and had been left five years "on the beach", was likely to be employed again in the present crisis.

Whether Nelson was summoned to London in the first week of January 1793 or took the initiative, in a month renowned for its flooded roads and coach-accidents, does not appear, but by January 7 he knew that he was to get a ship and his first of the line. "*Post nubila Phœbus*", he quoted in ecstasy to Fanny. "Your son will explain the motto. After clouds come sunshine. The Admiralty so smile upon me that really I am as much surprised as when they frowned. Lord Chatham yesterday made many apologies for not having given me a Ship before this time, and said, that if I chose to take a Sixty-Four to begin with, I should be removed into a Seventy-Four." By January 26 he was "fixed for the *Agamemnon*, at Chatham", "without exception one of the finest Sixty-Fours in the Service", and unlike the poor *Boreas*, "with the character of sailing most remarkably well". His first, mercifully formal, interviews with Lord Hood passed off as well as possible. Lord Hood, who was hoisting his flag in the *Victory*, hinted that the *Agamemnon* might be ordered to join his fleet at Gibraltar. At the Admiralty their Lordships, most flatteringly, agreed to Captain Nelson's request that no bills asking for men for the *Agamemnon* should be put up in London until the name of her Captain could be announced. His bills were already posted throughout Norfolk, where a Lieutenant and four midshipmen were scouring every port, with instructions to forward the results to Lynn and Yarmouth. Several men from the seven Burnhams had "offered", but even when he had got his stiffening of Norfolk volunteers—worth two of other men, in his opinion—he feared that he would still be upwards of a hundred short of complement. This meant having to rely upon the captures of the press-gangs, having to sail undermanned, or, worst nightmare of a young officer, being unable to sail. He had written to his Service friends in the north to send what they could lay hands upon to Whitby and Newcastle. . . . Locker's broad pendant was flying on board the *Sandwich*, as Commander-in-Chief at the Nore, and the Commodore was discharging Mr. Maurice Suckling and Mr. George Andrews into the *Agamemnon*, and Joseph King, once boatswain of the *Boreas*, out of the *Valiant*, at the request of the Duke of Clarence. Nelson had no scruples in employing "one of the best boatswains I have seen in His Majesty's service", who might, but for his representations, have been out of the Service and in the mad-house. He had been able to secure his old servant, Frank. . . .

During the fortnight before his commission was signed he paid a brief call at home, where the scene was much changed. The doors of the Parsonage House were continually opening, in hard weather, to admit callers arriving in chariots, on horseback or on foot—all on business. The Rev. Dixon Hoste, once squire of Ingoldisthorpe, and now a tenant of Mr. Coke at Godwick House, had a fragile-looking second son, aged twelve, for his distant kinsman's ship. He and the Rev. Mr. Weatherhead had taken the additional precaution of getting their magnificent neighbour of Holkham to recommend the boys to Captain Nelson. The Rev. Mr. Bolton, Susanna's brother-in-law, produced the third Norfolk clergyman's son for the *Agamemnon*. Everyone seemed to have a little "younker" to offer, when what her Captain needed, in view of active service, was a couple of strong-nerved surgeon's mates. Fanny, in her blacks for Uncle Herbert, was fitting out Josiah, and had promised, after the departure of all she held dear, to "take on a new lease of life", aided by the small legacy which had come to her on the death of the President of Nevis. Her husband, "never better in health", and "perfectly indifferent to what quarter of the World we go", was already with her in body only. He told her that "being united to such a good woman, I look back to as the happiest period of my life", and, since that sounded too like an eternal farewell, "Never fear, I shall come laughing back one day."

4

Another anxiety which he had not mentioned abroad had clouded his five years of waiting.

His brother William, married four months before him, was now the father of a Charlotte Mary, aged five, and an Horatio, a year younger. His younger sister, whose marriage had taken place a fortnight after his own, had lost one infant son, but had a fine surviving boy and girl; thirteen more children were to follow. His elder sister, married in 1780, had by 1793 completed her family of seven, opening with twin daughters, now at boarding-school, and had only lost one child. As a bachelor, Nelson had been noticeably

vulnerable to the solemn wiles of infancy, and outside his own family a pronounced child-fancier had been invited to stand sponsor to
several Horatios. He had married, in confident expectation of
children, a lady who had been prompt in presenting an heir to his
predecessor. From no available source does it appear that Frances
Woolward ever became pregnant by her second husband. She
ailed persistently, but rheumatism, relaxed throat, chest colds and
nervous debility are specifically described. Hope had receded
gradually during the five years of Nelson's unemployment. By the
end of that time, when he looked at his small, neurotic, thirty-five-
year-old wife, happy with her shoulder-high midshipman son, he
had realised that she was unlikely to bear again. He alluded openly
to his disappointment once only. In the *Sketch of my Life* produced
in answer to a request from Lord Hood's secretary, John M'Arthur,
after the Battle of the Nile, he mentioned under date 1787, "And in
March this year I married Frances Herbert Nisbet, widow of Dr.
Nisbet of the Island of Nevis, by whom I have no children."

Chapter V

1793–1794
(ætat. 34–35)

SHIP-OF-THE-LINE

I

ON the warm afternooon of Saturday, June 22, 1793, officers of the six sail-of-the-line from Lord Hood's fleet, ordered to water at Cadiz, were entertained before their departure by the naval authorities of that port. Spain, unfavourably impressed by the march of events in France, was showing herself friendly towards England. The visiting captains had been permitted to see what they pleased of the Naval Arsenal of the Isla de Léon, the defensive works of Cortadura, and the dockyards of the wealthiest port of western Europe, one of the first marine cities of the world, headquarters of the Spanish treasure fleets. They had obtained everything that they needed for their ships, except wine, which they could collect at Gibraltar, and the Captain of the *Agamemnon* had succeeded in getting a cask of the famous sherry of Jerez, which, undeterred by past criticism, he was going to send as a gift to the newly appointed Lieutenant-Governor of the Royal Hospital for disabled British sailors at Greenwich—Captain William Locker.

The Captain of the *Agamemnon*, as he feasted with the Spanish Admiral on board the *Concepcion*, of 112 guns, was very well satisfied with all he had seen. There were four first-rates in commission at Cadiz, beautiful ships, not so much undermanned as manned by inexperienced men, without any idea of discipline. "The Dons may make fine ships—they cannot, however, make men. . . . Long may they remain in their present state." The Captain of a Spanish frigate explained that it was no wonder his men were sickly, for they had been sixty days at sea. Now, after sixty days at sea, "our Jacks" would have been getting healthy. The *Agamemnon*, at the moment, was remarkably healthy, and her Captain, delighted at the thought that in a few days' sail they would be up the Mediterranean, was never better. "Indeed, nobody can be ill with my ship's company, they are so fine a set." Since he spoke no Spanish and few of his hosts understood English, he had leisure to reflect as he banqueted in view of a city famed since the days of Ancient Rome for its dinners and dancing-girls, and the sum of his silent reflections was that he, and the five other British Captains present, with a boarding-party of no more than their ships' barges, could certainly have taken this foreign first-rate. Spanish festivities commonly last late; the waters of Cadiz Bay, the turrets of a white-walled city of five gates, giving access to quiet streets displaying much Italian marble, were in colour reminiscent of Spanish gold when the party broke up, but only, it appeared, to proceed to further gaiety. The English officers were to be taken to the something translated as the "Bull-Feast". They presently disembarked at a rocky island among the salt marshes which lined the southern shore of the bay, and after making their way through a noisy concourse of persons, all bending their steps in the same direction, were escorted to a prominent position in an amphitheatre, which they were told would hold 16,000. The audience included many well-dressed women, and the countenances of some of the handsomest bore witness to the fact that Cadiz had, for five hundred years, been under Moorish occupation. The Spanish hosts explained that the better sort of people never missed a Bull-Feast, and that ladies chose their lovers ("husbands", wrote Nelson to Mrs. Nelson) for their dexterity in attacking and killing these animals. As for the lower classes, they would sooner sell their jackets or go without victuals than be absent.

Ten bulls were selected for to-day's entertainment, and amidst violent applause, half a dozen men on foot, attired in spangled yellow and sky-blue tights and scarlet cloaks, marched into the sandy arena, followed by three cavaliers. The first bull was led into the ring: the "Feast" began, and the Captain of the *Agamemnon*, who had quite calmly realised the necessity for providing a ship-of-the-line, likely to see action, with sturdy surgeon's mates, began almost at once to feel sick. A glance at the suddenly stolid faces of his brother-officers told him that they shared his feelings. "We felt for the bulls and horses." The footmen were provided with darts,

paper flags, goads and whips to make a timid beast mad, the horse-
men with spears, capable of penetrating six inches. At first he really
did not think that he would be able to sit the affair out. Had the
horses been killed outright, or even the bulls, it would not have
been intolerable. Some hopelessly gored horses were despatched,
but obviously to get them out of the way, not for humanity's
sake: and as soon as a vanquished bull lay down a fresh one was
prodded forth.

He did sit the "Feast" out, and he believed it was considered a
good one, for five horses were disembowelled and two men very
severely wounded. Had the men also been killed, he supposed that
the entertainment would have been regarded as a complete success.
For his own part, as he watched the excited audience, he believed
that to have seen some of them tossed by an enraged bull would not
much have displeased him.

Afterwards, over a solemn night-cap, the officers of six British
sail-of-the-line from Lord Hood's fleet agreed that they had seen
their last Bull-Feast, and the Captain of the *Agamemnon* wrote to his
lady next morning that how Spanish "Donnas" could sit out, much
less applaud, such an exhibition was astonishing.

2

His experiences since driving away from the doors of the old
Parsonage House on the morning of February 4 had included only
one hour spiced by the expectation of immediate action (under
most disadvantageous circumstances), and that had occurred at
dawn, a week past. "We fell in with a Spanish eighty-gun Ship,
ninety mounted: there being very little wind, and we the only Ship
near her, and fancying her to be French, we fully expected a trim-
ming; for we must have been in action near an hour before any
Ship could have come to our assistance. However, as we sail well,
that is to come." Otherwise, although entirely absorbed professionally, his hasty notes had for the most part communicated "nothing
new here".

He had joined his first ship-of-the-line on February 7 in company
with his First Lieutenant, Mr. Hinton, and Master, John Wilson,
and taking his stand on his quarter-deck and unfolding his papers,

read aloud to his standing officers his commission. The usual business of shaking hands and passing a few words with characters known and unknown had been accomplished in good vein. He had a private word later with the Purser, Mr. Fellowes, one of Locker's recommendations, whom he was very much disposed to like, told Mr. Fellowes this, and also that he would not fail a person called upon to perform many duties necessarily odious, provided that he was very careful. Mr. Fellowes seemed perfectly to understand his instructions. "I daresay we shall do very well together." After his first formal inspection of H.M.S. *Agamemnon*, four days passed before the ship's company completed from the *Sandwich* guardship began to come on board to be passed in review by the Surgeon, Purser and Boatswain. Mr. Fellowes and his clerk plied their pens; Mr. Roxburgh, the inevitable Scots doctor, made his inspection—not very merciless, since men were hard to come by; Joseph King grimly returned to Mr. Fellowes's slop-store such recruits as he deemed unpresentable in their present attire. Uniforms did not exist, but since the old hands knew what was best, keen volunteers were imitative, and the purser's slop-store offered no variety, the men of the *Agamemnon* in 1793 presented a uniform appearance. Their costume was check shirts, white or buff trousers (cut short in the leg and loose at the ankle to show coloured stockings) and scarlet or buff waistcoats. Their blue jackets, cut very short in the waist, had no collars: a handkerchief, knotted round the neck, protected the tunic from the grease of the pigtail, until the hour came when it was needed to protect the ear-drums from the reverberations of gun-fire. Their headgear was a straw hat painted with black enamel, or japanned, sometimes turned up at one side to show a coloured lining. The ship's name was painted on the hat ribbon, or stamped on a small copper plate attached to it.

The wooden-walled cabin, which was to be the Captain's home for three years, was a great improvement on those he had occupied in frigates, but even after Frank had unpacked his master's luggage, was demonstrably designed for service, not show. Its furniture consisted of a carpet and curtains, a table and chairs, a rack for sword, pistols and telescope, and a locker covered by a leathern mattress.

The *Agamemnon* did not go down the river until mid-March.

The sudden expansion of the Navy on a declaration of war, by a country until recently intent upon economy, and without mobilisation plans, had produced the natural results. Lord Hood's fleet was not nearly ready for service. During the first weeks of waiting, Mrs. Nelson, as yet unaccustomed to the unheralded appearances, and equally unforeseen exits, of a sea-officer, was startled by a flying visit from her husband at Hilborough. He mentioned the possibility of another meeting when he got to Spithead, but made no suggestion that she should come to Sheerness, where the "Three Tuns" was acclaimed by British sea-officers, with a sort of perverted pride, as the Worst Inn in the World. In his month there he never slept a night out of his ship. The *Agamemnon's* progress to the Nore from Blackstakes confirmed hopes already high. "We appear to sail very fast; we went, coming out, nearly as fast, without any sail, as the *Robust* did under her top sails." Mr. Nisbet, aged thirteen, was described by an experienced observer as "a little sea-sick". Nelson himself had not yet reached the age when he frankly confessed to miserable, repeated and incurable sea-sickness. A week of smart gales followed, and although on her arrival at Spithead he was told to take the *Agamemnon* to sea for a week, "for two days it blew so strong we could not get up our anchors". A few days later, the *Agamemnon*, still awaiting Lord Hood, sailed as one of a division of five of the line under the command of Admiral Hotham. In a letter headed "12 leagues N.W. of the Island of Guernsey", her husband told Mrs. Nelson that neutrals from French ports said that Nantes, Bordeaux and L'Orient were packed with English vessels, taken prize by French privateers or frigates—a depressing piece of news, if true, and another obvious result of our unreadiness. His next brief line, "Sixteen leagues from Scilly", told of such fog and drizzle that although Hotham's division had joined the main body under Hood a fortnight past, the *Agamemnon* had been quite unable to get a boat hoisted out. Their latest delay had been caused by the necessity of keeping the approaches of the Channel open for a home-bound convoy of East Indiamen, which had passed safely on the evening of June 6.

After this relief events moved quickly. The fleet bore up for the Straits in "the finest weather possible", and in a letter headed "Off

Cape St. Vincent, June 14th", Nelson was able to say that he had at last, a few days past, been able to have himself rowed across to H.M.S. *Victory* to pay his respects to his Commander-in-Chief. Lord Hood had been civil. "I daresay we shall be good friends again."

3

On Sunday, July 7, the Captain of the *Agamemnon* "performed Divine Service to the Ship's Company and presented them with a Psalm Book and a Seaman's Monitor". Next morning the promised Spanish fleet joined Lord Hood off Alicante, but did not, to Nelson's amusement, "after several hours' trial, form anything which could be called a Line of Battle ahead", and soon announced the intention of returning to Cartagena to refit, leaving to England, he noticed, the honour of keeping the enemy in order. "I really never expect to see them again." Eleven days later, Lord Hood's fleet of fourteen of the line stood close in to Toulon, and sent in a flag of truce, to propose an exchange of prisoners. Neutrals, spoken off Cape St. Sebastian, had told of nearly thirty French battleships ready for sea at Toulon. There appeared to be seventeen, and five still fitting in the harbour, amongst them the *Commerce de Marseille*, Rear-Admiral Trogoff's flagship. "Seventeen ports on each deck", wrote Nelson. "The *Victory* looks nothing to her." After several days of heavy gale the flag of truce returned, bringing "no clear answer". Some theorists believed that nothing but hunger would bring the French out, others that when they had equal numbers ready for sea the Toulonese would drive them out. It might be that they would be tempted to attack a diminished enemy. Lord Hood took his fleet up to Nice, "to show ourselves"; but from the Gulf of Lyons, Nelson reported, "There seem to be no French ships at sea; at least we have seen nothing like one". His relations with "the Lord" who did not spare signals to a fleet which failed, in his opinion, to keep as compact order as was desirable, as yet showed no increase in cordiality. The Commander-in-Chief had written to offer the Captain of the *Agamemnon* a 74-gun ship, to which Nelson had replied to the effect that "As the Admiralty chose to put me into a 64, there I stay", and, "I cannot give up my officers". His reasons seemed to have been accepted as sufficient. "So far, well." He had only just, since the *Agamemnon* was kept continually on the move, found time to reply to a truly exasperating letter which had reached him after three months, and dealt with a claim six years old. He pointed out to the Joint Secretary to the Treasury:

> "It has been totally out of my power to take any steps to receive the prize money due to the Ship's company under my command, nor is it possible that every poor seaman can go to Nevis, to receive his money from the Collector of Customs. They look up to their Captain as their friend and protector, and it was my intention, if the money was paid me, to advertize the distribution of it in London, when every Officer and Seaman, or their relatives, would be on the spot. . . . I humbly hope their Lordships will be pleased to order the money to England."

Only confused accounts of what was happening in the interior penetrated to the British fleet watching and waiting on the Mediterranean coast of France in trying weather. The coast road was very bad, very little used. Since they saw no French ships, it was difficult to believe that Provence, a district unable to feed herself, was not feeling the pinch. The English grew "heartily sick" of their daily view of blue sky, bluer sea, rocky islets of a golden or reddish tint, inclining conifers and eternal olive-groves, amongst which glimmered a few lowly, white-washed habitations. The guillotine had been set to work in Marseille, and the master of a ship from that port said that there were only two sorts of persons left in his country —the one drunk and mad, the other dying of hunger. Provence was said to be ready to attempt to form a separate Republic with British assistance. Civil war seemed imminent, in which case, Nelson supposed, war with England would not continue. Unfortunately, he would come home no richer than he had left, if things went on as they were at present. "All we get is honour and salt beef." He fretted increasingly that no action was being taken, either to attack disturbed southern France, or to offer her British protection should she proclaim herself royalist. "We have attempted nothing."

Three days after he penned these words, the fruit of the long blockade dropped quietly from the bough. Commissioners from Marseille arrived on board the *Victory* to treat for peace. They expected to meet their opposite numbers from Toulon, who were ready to declare for Louis XVII and alliance with England, but were detained by riots in the town. Incredible though it seemed, the French fleet was never coming out. The Toulonese, apprehensive of sharing the fate meted out to the inhabitants of Marseille by the Republican General Carteaux, wished to place their ships, citadel and the forts of the adjacent coast provisionally at the disposal of Lord Hood. "The old saying 'That hunger will tame a lion'", wrote Nelson, "was never more strongly exemplified."

The Spanish fleet had made a complacent reappearance as their allies entered "the strongest place in Europe" in triumph, but Nelson was not present to take part in the scene. Lord Hood had chosen the *Agamemnon*, a fast sailer, for a special mission. Her Captain's orders were to proceed, without an instant's delay, carrying despatches for the Vice-Consul at Oneglia (to be forwarded to the British Minister in Turin) and despatches to be delivered personally to the British Envoy and Minister Plenipotentiary to the Court of the Two Sicilies. After watering, he was to rejoin the fleet in Hyères Bay. Nothing could have been less diffuse than Lord Hood's instructions, but at sea, on her passage up to Oneglia, the *Agamemnon* fell in with the *Tartar*, homeward bound with the Commander-in-Chief's despatches, and her Captain, Lord Hugh Conway, sent a hasty line to Nelson. He explained that he had already written to the Envoy at Naples, urging him to ask at the Court of the Two Sicilies for as many Neapolitan troops as possible, to be despatched instantly to assist the Allies to hold Toulon against advancing Republicans. The British and Spanish landing-parties had been barely able to man the essential forts in the Toulon district. "Pray, press Sir W. Hamilton. . . . Will take your commands, if you have any, but in God's name, keep the boat as short a time as possible."

At dawn on September 12, 1793, Nelson completed a long letter, composed in snatches during the last five days: "Begun off the Island of Sardinia, and finished at anchor, off Naples." He had come in sight, with dusk, of the city which mortals are advised to see before they die, and Naples, he was bound to admit, viewed from her bay, at the hour when her windows, from harbour to terraced heights, began to twinkle, did not disappoint. Quickly the operatic scenery took on British national colours, and a lady at Swaffham was told, "We are now in sight of Mount Vesuvius, which shows a fine light to us in Naples Bay, where we are lying-to for the night, and hope to anchor to-morrow." He did not, as he scanned the famous panorama, indulge in any great expectations. "My poor fellows have not had a morsel of fresh meat or vegetables for near nineteen weeks, and in that time I have only had my foot twice on shore, at Cadiz. We are absolutely sick with fatigue. . . . I may have lost an appointment by being sent off; not that I wish to be employed out of my Ship. . . . I have only to hope I shall succeed with the King of Naples." His full-dress uniform was prepared for the morrow's events, which might, or might not, include an audience with royalty. He remembered to tell Fanny that he had captured a vessel worth about £10,000, bound from Smyrna for Marseille. If she was condemned it might mean prize-money—"add something to our comforts". Since the only kindness he could show to his wife was attention to her son, he had ordered Josiah to go ashore with him to-morrow.

Later, in a moment of solitude, before a day which must bring either a chilling repulse or important response, the beauty of the scene touched him to add a breathless postscript: "We are in the Bay all night, becalmed, and nothing could be finer than the view of Mount Vesuvius."

4

The cool classic splendours of the newly decorated royal *suite* in the Palazzo Sessa were indeed a change after nineteen weeks of Mediterranean glare in the Captain's cabin of the *Agamemnon*. Nelson, who had anchored and gone ashore as soon as possible on Thursday morning, had for two days no opportunity to write home describing a mission which had been an unqualified success. The correspondents to whom he addressed himself from the British Embassy on September 14 were his wife and his Uncle Suckling.

Everything had gone right, from the moment of his arrival in Naples, or, to be exact, before he had set foot there, for the entry of a British warship into their bay had been watched with interest by Neapolitans high and low, and the King, who had been a King since he was a boy, and at the age of forty-two retained much of the boy in his habits and manners, had literally come half-way to meet the English Captain. The news of Lord Hood's "most glorious and great" success had been received with enthusiasm and relief by a community already strongly pro-British, or at least anti-Jacobin, and enough could not be done for the officer who brought such tidings. Several accidental circumstances had combined to make Nelson's mission unexpectedly easy. The Queen (whom he did not mention in his letters home) was a sister of the unhappy Marie Antoinette, soon to be carried from the Conciergerie prison to the scaffold. Since she was also a daughter of the late Empress of Austria, and had been accorded by her marriage treaty a voice in the Neapolitan Councils of State, it went without saying that the influence of Maria Carolina was great. Her husband's Prime Minister, who owed his appointment to her machinations, was an Englishman—Sir John Acton—a fortunate chance for a sea-officer who spoke no language but his own. Lastly, the British Envoy and Minister Plenipotentiary enjoyed closer relations with the Court than any of his predecessors. He attended the sport-loving King on what he called Nimrodical expeditions; his wife was more in the Queen's confidence than any Neapolitan lady, a situation partially explained by the fact that Maria Carolina's notions of benevolent despotism entailed the employment of a secret police, drawn from all classes of society. Few persons in her Court dared trust one another.

Twenty years, even thirteen years ago, Sir William Hamilton, cousin of the Duke of Hamilton, cousin of Lord Abercorn, uncle of the Duchess of Atholl and Earl of Warwick, had dreamt of rising in his profession, of exercising his talents at the Courts of Spain and France. The climate of Naples was relaxing; her ladies were not in the first fashion. At sixty-three, his aquiline features, bronzed by the suns of twenty-nine Neapolitan summers and twenty-two ascents of Vesuvius, were of pronouncedly aristocratic cast, but his expression was more interesting than that of the average man of fashion. Though a recent severe illness had shaken him, he was still elegantly spare, muscular and energetic. He and his heir, Charles Greville, were always "Hamilton" and "Charles" to one another, never "uncle" and "nephew". But he had almost given up the idea of serving his country dramatically at a Court where opportunities never offered. The Fellow of the Royal Society, the archæologist, the dilettante had begun to predominate in his character, adding to its attractions. He was beginning to be entirely satisfied with his *palazzo* in the city, from which he could enjoy his morning "roll" in the Mediterranean, and drive daily, during the hot weather, to dine at his seaside casino at Posilipo, renamed "Villa Emma" in compliment to his mistress. For evenings when ice glazed the streets of Naples he had his box at the San Carlo Theatre, or, if "sick of masks and lights", his cabinets of cameos, coins and specimens of volcanic eruptions. (He had once been observed in a picturesque side-street, clad in full Court dress, helping a ragged peasant to carry a basketful of classic vases.) At his "sweet, delightful country house", sixteen miles from Naples, close to their Majesties' rococo palace of Caserta, he spent the months of spring and autumn. He had no family to consider. His first marriage, at the age of twenty-eight, "somewhat against my inclination", to Miss Barlow of Laurenny Hall, Pembrokeshire, had assured him of a fortune which he, who had met great fortunes, mentioned merely as "a little independence". His plain, pious and pathetically adoring wife had died in 1782. Two years past, after consideration, and with the approval of Neapolitan society, he had taken the serious step of marrying a young Englishwoman of obscure birth but far from obscure appearance, who had been his companion at the Embassy for five seasons. She was not only young enough to have been his daughter. Had the only child of his first marriage survived, she would have been several years the senior of the second Lady Hamilton. Miss Hart, who had signed the register at her marriage "Amy Lyon", but was addressed by her husband as "Emma", had been presented by him to his circle as a young countrywoman, come to Italy to study music and the arts. She was very generally known to have been relinquished to him by his impecunious nephew and heir, but the establishment at the Palazzo Sessa had always presented a correct *façade*, so much so that long before the wedding ceremony (performed quietly during a short spell of leave in England) native and even English guests had believed their hostess to be secretly Lady Hamilton. A duenna known as Mrs. Cadogan, Miss Hart's mother, resided under Sir William's roof, acting as housekeeper with self-effacing good manners which suggested that she had long acquaintance with the houses of the great. She also saved her employer much money; for he was apt, in rueful moments, to refer to the British Embassy, Naples, as "The King's Arms"—a hostelry that got good custom from travelling English.

The British Envoy and Minister Plenipotentiary, presented late with a chance of distinction in the diplomatic field, prepared to play his part with gusto. After his first meeting with Lord Hood's messenger, he returned to instruct his lady that Captain Nelson was to be their guest, a decision which surprised her, as no visiting sea-officer had previously been shown such attention. When Lady Hamilton was further instructed that the room redecorated for occupation by the sixth son of her sovereign, Prince Augustus Frederick, was to be put at Captain Nelson's disposal, she realised that more than diplomatic considerations were influencing her husband. Two persons hard at work, from wholly creditable motives, to produce a valuable first impression, had been able to like one another sincerely. Sir William had recognised "no common being". Nelson, who had arrived prepared to act for Lord Hood "with a zeal no one could exceed", had met a character who represented his picture of the ideal *grand seigneur*. A friendship which was to survive unusual circumstances had been formed at sight.

Lady Hamilton also had her task and her reward. Her duty during the busy days that followed the sudden appearance in the Bay of Naples of H.M.S. *Agamemnon* was to entertain the Captain's midshipman stepson, the awkward boy whom, in the language of his day, he always termed "my son-in-law". As Lady Hamilton was devotedly grateful to her husband, and naturally good-humoured, she exerted herself, and her efforts were not unnoticed by a guest who did not mention in his letters home that the beauty of his hostess made greater demands upon the attention than he had been able to bestow. "Lady Hamilton", wrote Nelson to his wife, "has been wonderfully kind and good to Josiah. She is a young woman of amiable manners, and who does honour to the station to which she is raised."

5

Nelson, already "knocked-up" when he arrived in Naples, had little peace during his four days there, though Sir William and General Acton did all possible to smooth his path. There was, from the first, no difficulty about his obtaining an audience with a King who sent for him every day, described the British Navy as the Saviours of Italy, and of his Dominions in particular, and promised to provide for Lord Hood, in his own handwriting, "the handsomest letter that could possibly be". At a dinner at the Palazzo Reale, which occupied a sea-frontage of 800 feet, the visiting English Captain was placed on the King's right hand, although the Ambassador of his nation was present. What was more to the point, Sir John Acton, evidently a person of more ability than his countenance suggested, confidently assured him that six thousand troops of a nation generally averse from disciplined sudden action should be embarked forthwith to support Lord Hood. Sunday (according to the ungodly custom of all foreigners, the gayest day of the week) was fixed for a visit of the King to H.M.S. *Agamemnon*. The difficulties in the way of returning hospitality in a ship which had been at anchor but twenty days in the last five months were great, and Nelson had hoped, in Naples, to rest a ship's company with a sick list of nearly a hundred. Sir William undertook to support the prestige of the British Navy from the cellars and kitchens of the British Embassy.

When Nelson wrote home on Saturday, September 14, he had scarcely had the chance to learn his way about the house in which he had slept for two nights after hot days of kaleidoscopic action. There had been snatched hours, between appointments, in a noble set of rooms on the second floor, filled with diffused southern sun and objects of *vertu*. In Sir William's private apartments his guest had learnt much more of the eminent persons whom he was to encounter than must meet the light of day. The Palazzo Sessa was not an official residence. Sir William had taken the lease of a private mansion from the Sessa family, and spent largely on "improvements". Its situation, half-way up the hillside of the Pizzo-falcone quarter, gave it an unequalled prospect of one of the most famous scenes in the world. Its exterior, like that of most of its kind, was somewhat forbidding. In a country of strong sun, shuttered windows abounded. Within, furnished by one of the first *virtuosi* of Europe, it was an Aladdin's cave. On the ground floor of the central building and wings were accommodated the results of a lifetime as collector of classical antiques, referred to humorously by Sir William as "my lumber". The "English Room" had been constructed to the designs of Robert Adam. There were also worthy reception-rooms in which Lady Hamilton offered the entertainment known as her "Attitudes". This did not sound enjoyable, as it consisted in her posing, generally in dumb-show, with the aid of such adjuncts as a shawl and a tambourine, to represent the primitive emotions, while Sir William directed lighting effects; but, without exception, everyone who had ever witnessed Lady Hamilton's "Attitudes" agreed that they were remarkable. Her husband proudly claimed that she was "better than anything in the antique". Actually, her features, lit by good health and great vitality, although faultless, were far from reminiscent of cold, classical perfection, and destined to find admirers in every generation.

Sunday's festivities began early, with the arrival on board the *Agamemnon* at 10 a.m. of Sir William and Lady Hamilton, the Bishop of Winchester and family, Lord and Lady Plymouth, Lord Grandison and daughter, besides, as her Captain hurriedly noticed, "other Baronets etc." "I gave them breakfast; manned ship etc." According to arrangements, the King was to appear at one o'clock, and Nelson was again to dine on shore with His Majesty. Preparations had been made to hoist the Royal Standard of the Two Sicilies as the King came on board and "entertain him with a cannonading". But after the breakfast, and before one o'clock, Nelson received a note from Sir John Acton which caused him to take the decision of asking his guests to depart at once, as he must get to sea as soon as possible. A French man-of-war, and three sail under her convoy, had anchored near Sardinia. Naples boasted seven sail ready for sea and a Spanish frigate of forty guns, but her Prime Minister's message said nothing of employing them. "Unfit as my Ship was, I had nothing left for the honour of our Country, but to sail, which I did in two hours afterwards. It was necessary to show them what an English Man-of-war would do."

Everything lent from the British Embassy was returned, except a butter-pan, which Nelson apologetically recorded in his letter of thanks twelve days later. This letter was the first of a series to pass between him and Sir William during the five years that elapsed before he met again, under even more encouraging circumstances, a host and hostess whose kindness had left an ineffaceable impression on his mind.

6

The French had got either into Leghorn or some Corsican port. The *Agamemnon* saw nothing of them. Nelson determined to go into Leghorn himself, "absolutely to save my poor fellows". He was too late to save his Surgeon's second mate, whose burial at sea took place with the usual ceremonies, off the north end of Corsica. Nothing could have seemed further than the smiling Neapolitan scene as he waited throughout the night of September 27, in a gale and thick weather, watching an enemy frigate of 40 guns lying at anchor off Leghorn. She had been ready to weigh as he hove in sight, and was obviously waiting for the first dark moment to get out. Luckily she could scarcely hope to escape in such weather, without running aboard the vigilant English 64. As there seemed no hope of persuading her to quit neutral waters while he was in attendance, he gave up the idea of going in to Leghorn, and stood for Toulon. He arrived there on October 5, at the same moment as the second division of Neapolitan ships bringing the troops promised by Acton. Lord Hood, much pleased with an officer who had acted on his own initiative with success, showed his regard by despatching the *Agamemnon* to sea again, after only three days in Toulon. The sealed orders which Nelson opened when he was off the island of Porquerolles told him to place himself under the direction of Commodore Linzee at Cagliari, in Sardinia. Further sealed orders, for Linzee, which he carried, told the Commodore to take his squadron on a mission to Tunis.

Off Corsica on October 11 the *Agamemnon* spoke a ship from Gibraltar, and Nelson got his first letters from home since he had left England. Her present host could not disguise the fact that Mrs. Horatio Nelson, who had not yet "fixed" anywhere, was fretting.

Nelson wrote to his wife in slightly sterner vein than usual. "My dear Fanny, I received a letter from Mr. Suckling yesterday, and was indeed truly sorry to hear you were not perfectly well. Why should you alarm yourself? I am well, your son is well, and we are as comfortable in every respect as the nature of our service will admit." He went on to say that every day at Toulon, at present, afforded "some brilliant Action" on shore. "I have only been a spectator, but had we remained, I should certainly have desired to land."

His first "little brush" with the enemy took place ten days later. At 2 a.m. on the morning of October 22, when running down the island of Sardinia, he came in sight of five sail, which, perceiving themselves observed, altered course. He stood after them, and a couple of hours later got within hail of the hindermost, but was careful not to fire into her, in case she might prove to be a Neapolitan or Sardinian, escorting a convoy. She failed to reply when hailed in French, and made sail, so the *Agamemnon* fired one shot from an 18-pounder ahead of her, and at the same moment opened her lower deck ports. Thereupon the frigate set all her sails. A running fight continued for three hours, the other ships on her weather quarter steering after the *Agamemnon*. With daybreak, the *Melpomene*, of 40 guns, hoisted national colours, and began firing stern-chasers. As she was smaller and faster than the *Agamemnon*, she was able to yaw and deliver broadsides while only the *Agamemnon's* bow guns could bear. Also, since he had been obliged to land many sick men in Toulon, Nelson had only three hundred and fifty men at quarters. By nine o'clock the *Melpomene*, separated from her consorts, had suffered so severely that, had not the wind failed, she must have surrendered or sunk, but the *Agamemnon's* rigging was badly damaged, and three more French frigates, a corvette and a brig were coming down upon her with all sail set. Nelson summoned his officers, to discuss whether he could possibly close with the *Melpomene*, and, without some small refit, and refreshment for his men, prepare to enter upon further action. The unanimous answer was that he certainly could not, so he ordered that "some of the best men be employed refitting the rigging, and the carpenters getting crows and capstern bars to prevent our wounded spars coming down", and, since it might be half an hour before they were engaged by a far superior force, in which case they must expect "warm work", he also ordered that food and wine be served. The enemy, until noon, had the option of bringing the *Agamemnon* to action, but contented themselves with carrying off the *Melpomene*. Eventually, in an almost sinking state, she got into Calvi. The *Agamemnon* was, according to her Captain's report to Lord Hood, "after a very few hours at anchor, in many respects fitter for service than before", an additional tribute to officers and a ship's company who had "conducted themselves entirely to my satisfaction", for her top-mast, main-mast and mizzen-mast had been shot to pieces, and her fore-yard badly wounded. Satisfaction in the *Agamemnon* after her "little brush" was indeed general, and with Christmas a Norfolk rectory received an enthusiastic description of her first engagement of this war. Mr. William Hoste, aged just thirteen, ended his long letter to his father, "Captain Nelson is acknowledged one of the first characters in the Service, and is universally beloved by his men and officers".

7

On one of the last days of November 1793, a small party of European gentlemen, attired in the blue-and-white gold-laced uniforms, black stocks, large cocked hats and long queues affected by British sea-officers at that date, proceeded as swiftly as possible through the tortuous streets of a walled city of North Africa which included, amongst its outstanding features, many camels laden with charcoal, snake-charmers, separate markets for perfumes, carpets, saddlery and jewels, and a notable building of green-tiled domes and walls, enriched with rose-coloured marbles.

Commodore Linzee and his companions, formal in costume and visage, had emerged from another wholly unrewarding interview with the Bey of Tunis. The Commodore's last letter from his brother-in-law, Lord Hood, had opened, "You are to expostulate with His Excellency, the Bey, in the strongest and most impressive manner, on the impolicy of his giving countenance and support to so heterogeneous a government as the present one of France, composed of murderers and assassins, who have recently beheaded their

Queen in a manner that would disgrace the most barbarous savages. . . ." The Captain of the *Agamemnon* had produced this argument, but the reply of the Bey, descendant of a Cretan renegade of ability, had been exasperating. His Excellency, by means of his interpreters, had smoothly agreed that nothing could be more heinous than the murders of the King and Queen of France by their subjects. Yet, if the historians of the great country represented by his naval visitors were to be believed, the subjects of a King of England had once arisen and beheaded their sovereign.

Nelson, after his first glance at the Oriental potentate, had silently fixed His Excellency's price at £50,000. The French convoy from the Levant, lying in Tunis Bay, was worth at least £300,000, so England could have afforded the bribe. That the French had expected Linzee to attack had been obvious: they had, on his arrival, hauled their ships almost aground. When they had found, to their relief, that he was not prepared to do so, that the Bey refused to give them up, and that the English Commodore had patiently sent to Toulon for further orders, their bearing had been unforgettable, even considering that they were revolutionaries of a nation expert in polished malice. Nelson believed that the Bey, presented with a *fait accompli*, would have swallowed a sufficiently richly gilded insult. To attempt to negotiate with such characters only gave them the idea that England was weak. "The English seldom get much by negotiation, except the being laughed at, which we have been; and I don't like it." He knew that the enemy had bought His Excellency, and although Linzee might hesitate to attack enemy ships which had sought the shelter of a neutral port, the fact was that Tunis was little better than a piratical stronghold. In the Commodore's place, he would have seized the French man-of-war and convoy first, and seen the Bey later. However, Linzee had not believed that his instructions authorised him to use force, and from the moment that the Bey and the enemy had realised that, the position had been hopeless.

"The English never yet succeeded in a negotiation against the French," wrote Nelson resignedly, "and we have not set the example at Tunis. Thank God! Lord Hood, whom Linzee sent to, for orders how to act after having negotiated, has ordered me from under his command, and to command a Squadron of Frigates off Corsica, and the Coast of Italy, to protect our trade and that of our new Ally, the Grand Duke of Tuscany, and to prevent any Ship or Vessel, of whatever Nation, from going into the port of Genoa. I consider this command as a very high compliment—there being five older Captains in the Fleet. . . . Lord Hood is certainly the best officer I ever saw. Every order from him is so clear, it is impossible to misunderstand him."

He prepared to see the last of Tunis without regret, except for an opportunity missed. Lord Hood, who had by now heard of the "little brush" of October 22, had sent him a letter quite in his old style. To be given a detached command was "most handsome", and to be empowered to deal with the frigates that escaped him was exhilarating. "The Lord" had written that he looked upon them as "certain, trusting to my zeal and activity". Nelson had learnt their names and strength now, and they had been, as he had suspected, part of the convoy now in Tunis harbour, under the protection of His Excellency the Bey. Two of them were at San Fiorenzo, one at Bastia, and the damaged *Melpomene* at Calvi.

When the *Agamemnon* arrived in Leghorn roads in Christmas week, to water and provision, she found the port in confusion, and received bad news. Lord Hood had been obliged to evacuate Toulon. "For England", wrote Nelson stoutly to Hilborough Rectory, "a most happy event." On the forenoon of December 17, in the dark reception-room of a Toulon merchant's house which had been his headquarters on shore, while the dull thud of distant gunfire sounded, attired in the three weeks' mourning ordered for his fleet on receipt of the news of "the murder of the late good Queen of France", Lord Hood, "the same good collected officer he ever was", had dryly informed a consternated audience of six nationalities that he was about to order his fleet to put to sea, taking with it as many French ships as were ready, and setting fire to the rest. He would himself hold the fort of La Malgue as long as possible. The troops at his disposal had long been insufficient to control the land defences of the port, and gradually enemy artillery had gained command of the roadstead, making his position untenable. A Lieutenant-Colonel, aged twenty-four, with his fortune to make, had been sent from Paris to stir up General Carteaux. Nelson heard the facts, but the name of "Buona Parte" was first written thus by him two and a half years later.

The place had admittedly been held at great cost. Lord Hood would from the first have preferred to remove the French fleet to a place of safety; but the feelings of Allies had demanded consideration. The retiring forces under his orders had now wrecked the arsenal, burnt nine French warships and carried off a dozen frigates and four battleships, including the *Commerce de Marseille* (so large that no dock at Portsmouth could take her). Half the town was said to have been left in ashes. The fact remained that the British fleet now lacked an advanced Mediterranean base, and eighteen French sail-of-the-line had been abandoned, either unharmed or only partially disabled. It had not been possible for Lord Hood to achieve miracles, and he had made chivalrous efforts to save royalist troops and refugees, likely to be shot, guillotined or murdered, by a mob which had arisen in revolutionary fury, as revolutionary troops drew near. Nearly fifteen thousand unhappy Toulonese had been safely embarked.

At Leghorn, Nelson found home letters. His mare had not been sold. The Rector wrote that his having been thrown had been entirely his own fault. He did not believe the poor beast "vitious": he feared, however, that she might be going blind. . . . Mrs. William Nelson had heard of a delicious Mediterranean fish that could be salted; spelt "Tonges", if her brother-in-law deciphered William's handwriting correctly. She would be glad if Horace could bring some home in his ship, since he seemed to think that France, torn by the internal feuds of Jacobin and Girondist, could not much longer continue war against England. The homely request sounded strangely at a moment when the young Captain of a British man-of-war was confronted by a collapsed French female, explained to him as the mother of five, penniless and homeless, whose husband had committed suicide sooner than be left to the mercies of the revolutionaries of his town. "What calamities do Civil Wars produce, and how much does it behove every person to give their aid in keeping peace at Home."

Vessel upon vessel packed with hysterical refugees was labouring into Leghorn, where there was a rumour that, as the port was already short of food, they might be refused admittance: ships bringing wounded troops must be given preference. Nelson never forgot the tales and scenes of horror following the fall of Toulon, which took him by surprise, in Christmas week, 1793. "Fathers are here without families, families without fathers." M. le Comte de Grasse, Captain of the frigate *Topaze*, under his command, was distracted for news of a wife and nursery, and some reports estimated the number of men, women and children left screaming on the quay-sides of the burning town as over 6,000. Many had been drowned by the oversetting of boats, many had taken their own lives in despair, and many been trampled underfoot, swept into the harbour, or torn in pieces by their own countrymen. Lord Hood, who had attempted to rally the flying troops, had been the admiration of everyone, but "the torrent was too strong". The Neapolitans, so swiftly despatched by General Acton in September, had panicked shamelessly. The French and Spanish had been at best inefficient. "Many of our posts were carried without resistance; at others, which the English occupied, every one perished. I cannot write all. My mind is deeply impressed with grief. Each teller makes the scene more horrible." Napoleon Buonaparte also never forgot a scene of which he had been an eyewitness. He enthralled audiences in St. Helena with descriptions of his feelings as he had watched ship upon ship bursting into flames which had matched the blood running into her gutters as the Red Terror took possession of Toulon.

The *Agamemnon* left Leghorn on January 3, to be blown off her Corsican station by some of the hardest gales, accompanied by the heaviest rains, that her Captain had ever trysted with. An enemy frigate took the opportunity to slip down from San Fiorenzo to Calvi, but he believed that his blockade had been so close that the provisions carried by her could only feed the place another fortnight at the outside. He had received further orders from Lord Hood, entrusting him with a negotiation opened by Linzee, but now suddenly of importance. Corsica had been decided upon as a base of operations, and he was "to settle plans for the landing of troops, etc." with the Patriot General Pasquale de Paoli, who had agreed that the island should be ceded to Great Britain on the condition that the British should assist the natives to expel the French. Nelson sent as his "Ambassador to the Chief of the Corsicans" Lieutenant George Andrews, brother of the beauty of St. Omer. The situation needed delicate handling, as Lord Hood was by no means convinced of the good faith of the Patriot General. He had also his own troubles. English troops took San Fiorenzo without difficulty in mid-February. Even the garrison of the renowned Tower of Martello, after two days' bombardment at a distance of a hundred and fifty yards, called for quarter. One of the imprisoned frigates which had escaped the *Agamemnon* was burnt. But General Dundas, supported by Lieutenant-Colonel John Moore, refused, before the arrival of reinforcements from Gibraltar, to proceed to attack Bastia, little more than twelve miles distant across the hills in the north-east of the island. The enemy were adding daily to the strength of their positions there. Lord Hood took the event upon himself, and keeping up a close blockade by sea, ordered Lieutenant-Colonel Vilettes, of the 69th Regiment, and Captain Nelson to land with a force consisting of 1,000 regulars and marines and 300 seamen.

Nelson prepared "to anchor and act with the army" in good health and spirits. "Armies go so slow that seamen think they never mean to go forward; but I daresay they act on a surer principle though we seldom fail. . . . We are few, but of the right sort." He had, during the weeks before San Fiorenzo fell, as well as continuing the blockade, conducted a dashing series of coastal raids—on one occasion "seized a happy moment" to land sixty soldiers and sixty seamen to demolish an essential mill; on another, burnt twelve vessels loaded with wine, and captured four. "At a place called Rocliniar, or Porto Nuovo," he had, with his own hand, struck the national colours hoisted by the natives on the top of "an old castle". At L'Avisena he had taken another fort, Miomo, and driven her garrison up to a position within gun-shot of the walls of Bastia. Naturally, such operations could not be carried out without some losses, but after "a very smart contest" which had ended in a courier boat being carried "in high style", he had a casualty list of no more than six wounded. "My ship's company behaved most amazingly well; they begin to look upon themselves as invincible, almost invulnerable. . . . They really mind shot no more than peas."

The siege of Bastia opened on April 4. Her husband reckoned Mrs. Nelson by now at Bath, where she should find, amongst other friends, Admiral Robinson, "my old Captain with a wooden leg". He told her that Corsica was a wonderfully fine island, her people brave and free. "Paoli has nothing to give them; no honours to bestow." He held out the usual hopes of coming home before long, on the conclusion of the war—not by France's return to a monarchy, but by England's decision to leave her to stew in her own juice, "perhaps the wisest method we could follow". He begged his wife "not to want for anything" at a Spa where prices were always high. "Don't be afraid of money." His own expenses at present were not likely to be great.

8

Always foreseeing that it must be the next place to be attacked, and much hoping to be concerned, he had made himself thoroughly familiar with the appearance of Bastia long before he landed, three miles north of the town, under cover of darkness, during the night of April 3. He had guessed that San Fiorenzo had fallen before he got the news, for the red light from the frigates burning in the harbour there had lit the evening skies beyond the mountains on February 19. Next morning he had taken his second careful look at Bastia, running so close inshore, attended by two of the six frigates under his command, that the enemy had opened fire, from a new half-moon battery below the town, Fort St. Croix, beyond the town, and the forts of the citadel. The bursting of one shell, very close, had shaken the *Agamemnon*, and on their third appearance, merely to reconnoitre, during the afternoon, all three ships had been struck in the hull. But their damage had been easily reparable and they had sustained no casualties, whereas they heard from a Dane, coming out of the mole, that their very accurate replies had destroyed six French guns and killed several gunners.

Nelson felt the siege of Bastia particularly his. "I presumed to propose it." (Uncle Suckling, at Kentish Town, possessed a picture of the town, which did not, however, show the citadel.) He knew that his reports had decided Lord Hood to make the attempt, and therefore his reputation depended upon the result. An Engineer and

an Artillery officer had been sent, at his request, to approve his choice
of sites for a battery on shore and landing-place. Fortunately, both
had been young and enthusiastic. He had now sent Lieutenant
Duncan, R.A., in a fast frigate to Naples, to ask Sir William Hamilton to press the King and Prime Minister for mortars, shells, field-
pieces and stores. He had not been perfectly frank with Lord Hood
in his account of the expected strength of the garrison, fearing that
if he was, his Lordship might incline to the opinion of General
Dundas, shared by that gentleman's successor, General D'Aubant,
that the project in hand was "most visionary and rash". But, to do
him justice, it was not until everything was fixed for the attack that
he received certain information on this point. Personally, he felt
strongly that to let the opportunity slip, merely because it presented
great difficulty, would be "a National disgrace". "What would the
immortal Wolfe have done?" "A thousand men would, to a certainty, take Bastia; with 500 and *Agamemnon*, I would attempt it."
"We are really without firing, wine, beef, pork, flour, and almost
without water: not a rope, canvas, twine or nail in the Ship. . . .
Not a man has slept dry for many months. The Ship is so light, she
cannot hold her side to the wind: yet, if your Lordship thinks or
wishes me to remain off Bastia, I can, by going to Porto Ferrajo,
get water and stores, and twenty-four hours at Leghorn will give
us provisions; and our refitting, which will take some time, can be
put off a little. My wish is to be present at the attack. . . ." He was
relieved that at the end of a fortnight's repetition of such telling
phrases, Lord Hood had told him to do his best with a force of 1,300.

All the defences of Bastia could be clearly viewed from the sea,
as he had told Lord Hood, and the place was, as he had told Mrs.
Nelson, highly picturesque, "the environs delightful, with the most
romantic views I ever beheld". The surrounding country, where
cultivated, displayed the usual Corsican prospect of straggling vine-
yard, cypress, citron and olive grove, pale lower slopes on which
goats and sheep picked up what sustenance they could, villages
perched like sea-fowl on sun-baked cliffs, and, in the background,
heights clothed by forests of sweet chestnut, pine, beech and oak.
Corsica, island of barren rock, rushing streams, bitter honey and
excellent timber for shipbuilding, looked her best in early spring,

when the blossom of apricot and apple was succeeding almond and cherry. Even her uncultivated districts, lying about the lagoons at the mouths of her many rivers, were covered with a vigorous undergrowth of arbutus, myrtle and other aromatic shrubs, called by the natives *maquis*, and so pungent that their presence could be detected even after dark, and from the sea.

By noon on April 4, eight 24-pounders from the lower deck of the *Agamemnon* and eight 13-inch mortars had been landed under cover of gunboats without molestation, and the troops commanded by Colonel Vilettes and Captain Nelson had encamped under a rocky height within 2,500 yards of the citadel. Nelson perceived without dismay that the Corsican patriots holding the adjacent tower of Torga, which they had taken during the night of April 2, knew nothing except how to fire a musket. They watched open-mouthed while Norfolk seamen who had volunteered for a 64 commanded by the son of the Rector of Burnham Thorpe (advertised as a flier, with prospects of good prize-money) made roads, hauled up guns and cut down fragrant Corsican undergrowth and copses to make platforms for guns and cover towards their fort, the weakest point, from which attack might be expected. The future Viceroy of the island was an admiring spectator. The green face of the rocks leading to the fort was, said Sir Gilbert Elliot, steeper than Minto craigs at home. "They fastened great straps round the rocks, and then fastened to the straps the largest and most powerful purchases, or pullies, and tackle, that are used on board a man-of-war. The cannon were placed on a sledge at one end of the tackle, the men walked down hill with the other end of the tackle. The surprise of our friends the Corsicans, and our enemies the French, was equal to the occasion."

When he had mounted a captain's picquet at Torga, with a sentry a hundred yards in front of it, and sent word to the *Scout* sloop to anchor as close as possible to the tower, Nelson resignedly hoped that the mere presence of his Corsican allies might be useful later. In the middle distance of the warmly coloured picture, his sweating seamen had a comforting vision of the *Agamemnon* at anchor, and on the skyline, south of the town, "Lord Hood in the offing".

During the next fortnight he realised that only time could bring success. His first batteries were ready for action by the eighth day after his landing; none too soon, for the camp had been for two days exposed to heavy fire. Lord Hood's flag of truce, sent in before his batteries spoke, had received from the Commissioner in the citadel the reply, "I have hot shot for your ships, and bayonets for your troops"; whereupon Lord Hood had hoisted a red flag at the main-top-gallant mast-head of H.M.S. *Victory*. When Nelson, in reply, hoisted English colours on the rock above his tattered tent, and the order was issued to open fire upon the town, citadel and redoubt of Camponella, every man present gave three cheers. They fired throughout the night and next day, and during the afternoon, Colonel Vilettes, Nelson, Duncan of the Artillery—happily re-turned from Naples with the desired mortars—and two other military officers, attended by a Corsican guide, advanced to examine a ridge about a thousand yards nearer the town. Enemy musketry and grape were pouring towards their camp. The guide was killed, the Brigade-Major was fatally wounded and Nelson received "a sharp cut in the back", first mentioned by him in a letter to his wife four months later, and never again. Next morning he began to superintend the building of two more batteries for mortars and guns from the *Agamemnon*; one close to the Torga tower, the other a little to the rear. They took eight days to complete, but after they had been firing for twenty-four hours, deserters from the town affirmed that the guns of the citadel had been twice put out of action. Nelson's first letters home, dated "Camp, near Bastia", were mainly occupied with descriptions of "my poor seamen dragging guns up such heights as are scarcely credible". Five men from his ship's company had been killed. "They are not the men to keep out of the way."

The Corsican patriots were now directed to make false attacks upon the upper and southern enemy outposts. More British troops were urgently needed, but General D'Aubant, with seven regiments at San Fiorenzo, continued firm in his resolution not to "entangle himself in any co-operation". ("It is enough to make any lover of his Country run distracted.") Nor was co-operation in the camp ideal. Nelson had to write to Lord Hood, asking for a ruling as to whether the seamen landed were under his command or that of

Captain Hunt. The enemy, having got their town batteries into "a tolerable state", reopened very heavy fire, and one of Nelson's best men from the *Agamemnon*, working on repairs during the night, was killed by a shot from the Camponella redoubt. A letter, in neat, slanting Italian hand, was despatched on its long journey to a small home in Swansea.

"From the nature of our profession, we ever hold life by a more precarious tenure than many others, but when we fall, we trust it is to benefit our Country. So fell your Son, by a cannon-ball, under my immediate command, at the Siege of Bastia. I had taken him on shore with me, from his abilities and attention to his duty."

The next battery to be built was on the ridge examined a fortnight earlier, and within 700 yards of the town. Andrews (referred to by General Paoli's staff as "Mr. George") was appointed to fight it with forty-five seamen, but was wounded almost at once. The end, however, was now in sight. In a letter begun on May 1 and ended on the 4th, Nelson was able to tell his wife "as a secret" that Bastia should fall before the month was out. He reminded her that, in the words of Shakespeare, not quite correctly remembered, "a brave man dies but once, a coward all his life long". It was to a correspondent at Leghorn, to whom he had sent for provisions (and who had added to the butter, Dutch cheese and porter ordered, a personal gift of peas and asparagus), that he admitted, "I have had my escapes."

On May 18 a message reached Lord Hood from a brother of the Mayor of Bastia. The garrison, terrified of falling into the hands of victorious Corsicans, and short of food and ammunition, were ready to enter into negotiations for unconditional surrender. The army from San Fiorenzo made the timely appearance expected by Nelson. At 6 p.m. on May 23 the British Grenadiers took formal possession of the town gates, and next morning, with daylight, the combined forces marched into Bastia to the strains of the National Anthem.

Two days later, Nelson sent a brief triumphant note to Sir William Hamilton, enclosing a letter for Lady Hamilton. He promised, "We shall now join heart and hand against Calvi." The embarkation of stores for this purpose was discontinued on news that the French fleet was out of Toulon. Admiral Hotham's blockading squadron had lost touch with it, and lost, as afterwards appeared, an excellent chance of an action much to be desired. He had borne up hastily to join Lord Hood. The enemy retired before superior force, and the *Agamemnon* was sent to Gibraltar, to refit before entering upon a bout of combined operations, which Nelson considered his first in this war, for of the siege of Bastia he commented pointedly, "I may truly say that this has been a Naval Expedition."

9

The siege of Calvi, a place, small but very strongly fortified by art and nature, on the western side of the island, differed in many respects from that of Bastia, chief commercial city of Corsica. The chief point of resemblance was that Nelson's seamen were again employed "dragging cannon up steep mountains, and carrying shot and shell to batteries built, armed and manned under his personal supervision". But the rocks of the Calvi district were far more inhospitable than those of Bastia, and this time there was no question of the Army refusing to co-operate. From the moment that General the Hon. Charles Stuart (a younger son of Lord Bute) came on board the *Agamemnon* to express himself anxious to get on with the attack, if Captain Nelson thought it right to proceed with the shipping (to which the answer was "I certainly do"), affairs moved swiftly.

At 10 p.m. on the night of June 17, H.M.S. *Agamemnon, Dolphin* and *Lutine*, with sixteen sail of transports, victuallers and storeships, anchored after much difficulty about a mile from the shore and three and a half miles west of Calvi, opposite a romantic-looking cove known as Porto Agro, and at 3 a.m. next morning, Nelson, with General Stuart, went ashore, in the hopes of discovering a better place for landing guns and stores. The *Agamemnon* was lying in fifty-three fathoms; sunken rocks, with very deep water between them, extended to within twenty feet of the beach. It was to be feared that with a common sea-breeze such a swell would set in as to prevent boats landing. They examined the enemy's outposts, Fort Monteciusco, close to the south-west of the town, Fort Muzello to the west; and between it and Fort San Francesco, on a rocky peninsula washed at the base by the sea, the Fountain Battery, well tucked away behind a mountain shoulder. The town itself, although not ditched, appeared well fortified. They reluctantly decided that in spite of its distance from their object, and bad landing, Porto Agro must be their base. Nelson repeated that he placed the firmest reliance on the protection of the fleet, under Lord Hood, who would see to it that the French fleet at Golfe Jouan should not molest them, and disembarkation of the troops began. The business of getting field-pieces and military baggage on shore was still in progress when the picture took on dark colours. For the next two days a Corsican thunderstorm of truly melodramatic variety raged over the scene. Most of the ships were obliged to put to sea in such weather as to raise doubts of their reappearance. The anxiety of those landed, however, was nothing to that of Lord Hood, as he powerlessly contemplated from Martello Bay the possible fate of a force which had believed itself "under his wing", deserted on a hostile shore. "I tremble", he wrote to Nelson, "for what may have happened from last night's wind." But that night, amidst thunder, lightning, gale and downpour, Nelson's seamen had begun to make a road for their guns. On the 22nd the weather became "rather more moderate", and although a great deal of surf was running, he got boats off to such ships as were still visible, and much-needed rations and some powder, shot and gun-carriages were landed. The guns began to pass up towards the site chosen for a battery against Monteciusco. On the beach, working-parties of drenched soldiers set to work to fill sand-bags. Next day more reassuring quantities of ammunition and guns were landed, and the *Agamemnon* and transports returned to their anchorage. The "Royal Louis", first battery to be completed, opened fire with dawn on July 4. Two more were in action within three days; still progress was much too slow to satisfy General Stuart, who slept every night in the advanced battery and suffered "more than I can describe" when he was obliged to ask for another night's grace before his working-parties could come up to an intended emplacement where punctual seamen had been waiting with the guns since sunset.

Amongst the first casualties was Captain Serocold of the Royal Navy, "by a grape-shot passing through his head as he cheered the people who were dragging the gun". Nelson made time to scribble a line to his always nervous Fanny, who might see the fact in a newspaper, unaccompanied by the name.

"I am very busy, yet own I am in all my glory. Except with you, I would not be anywhere but where I am, for the world. I am well aware my poor services will not be noticed: I have no interest; but however services may be received, it is not right in an Officer to slacken his zeal for his Country."

He had been dashed that in Lord Hood's despatch announcing the taking of Bastia, he had merely been mentioned as "commanding and directing the seamen, landing guns, mortars and stores". When poor Serocold had heard that Hunt was to be the officer sent home with the Bastia despatch—"a young man who never was on a battery, or even rendered any service during the siege. . . . (If any person says he did, then I submit to the character of a story-teller)" —he, who had himself commanded a battery under Captain Nelson, had hotly announced his intention of "publishing an advertisement". The services of Duncan, the young Artillery Lieutenant whom Nelson had sent with a personal letter of commendation to Sir William Hamilton at Naples, had also been singled out for praise, and Duncan, with a slight flesh wound, promoted to a Company, and an aide-de-camp on General Stuart's staff, was showing an inclination to condescension. "There is nothing like kicking down the ladder a man rises by." However, "Lord Hood and myself were never better friends, nor, *although his Letter does,* did he wish to put me where I never was—in the rear." By the newly appointed Viceroy of Corsica, Sir Gilbert Elliot, Captain Nelson knew that his efforts and position had been recognised; he believed that General Stuart, "a stranger and a landsman", would probably do him the credit "which a friend and brother officer has not given me". Disappointment from that quarter was yet to come.

The enemy, having allowed the British to land and bring guns over the mountains which they had, apparently, considered inaccessible, now opened heavy and concentrated fire upon their works, demolishing two valued 24-pounders from the *Agamemnon* and a 26-pounder. On the morning of July 12 at 7 a.m. Nelson was struck with great violence, in the face and breast, by splinters, stones and sand from the *merlon* of a battery hit by an enemy shell. When the profuse flow of blood from his head-wound had been checked, he found that he had received several superficial lacerations in the face and a deep cut in the right brow, which had penetrated the eyelid and eyeball. The pain was great, but the surgeons who performed the first dressing held out hopes that the eye might recover a measure of sight. "I got", he told Lord Hood, in the last sentence of his daily report forwarded the same evening, "a little hurt this morning: not much, as you may judge from my writing." Lord Hood, in the first sentence of his reply, asked for details and said that he would be sending someone next morning, "to know how you are, and whether you would not have assistance". Nelson's answer was that if a more advanced entrenchment was to be begun the next evening he would be capable of superintending the work. "My eye is better, and I hope not entirely to lose the sight." Three days later he was "much better".

The siege was now proceeding as well, though not as expeditiously, as even he could wish. The guns of the *Commerce de Marseille* had been landed, and the carpenter of the *Agamemnon*, a better man at making a gun-platform than any military gentry, had turned his energies to siege ladders. The news of Lord Howe's glorious victory of the First of June came as a restorative at an hour when an officer who never forgot the Nicaraguan expedition was beginning to receive alarmingly long lists of men down with "the fever". "We have far more to fear from the Climate than the Enemy." His only consolation was that the Army was falling sick in far greater numbers than the Navy, a fact which he attributed to the greater activity of seamen.

Fort Muzello was carried on July 19, two days later than Nelson had expected. Thirty-five pieces of heavy ordnance were playing on the town towards the end of the month, and Calvi, although rejecting an offer to negotiate for terms of peace, asked for a twenty-five days' truce. Her defenders had learnt of the sickness in the English camp, and were playing for time. Lord Hood was reported unwell; General Stuart was visibly very sick. Nelson himself began to experience, in addition to pain from his eye, a familiar cycle of sickening symptoms which threatened to send him down to a hospital ship packed with malaria cases (the *Boreas*), but he hoped that "an active scene" would cure his shivering fits, to which he was so accustomed that they worried him less than those in his company. The weather, also, was becoming intolerable. He discovered that the unremitting glare of what an Englishman termed "the Dog Days" was called by the Corsicans "the Lion Sun". It was certainly something that no man could endure.

Just in time for him, and many others, the enemy hung out a white flag. The garrison marched out on August 10, and amongst the warlike material relinquished by them was the *Melpomene*, "the most beautiful frigate I ever saw". But his spirits were lowered by the realisation that two juniors to whom he was attached by more than Service ties were likely to die. "Little Hoste" returned from the brink of the grave. James Moutray, aged twenty-one, Second Lieutenant of the *Victory*, the only son of his mother, and she a widow, was laid to rest in the church of San Fiorenzo, and Nelson, before he sailed from Calvi (a place he hoped never to see again), composed directions for the inscription on a memorial tablet to be cut by his carpenter.

Back in his cabin in the *Agamemnon*, bound for Leghorn to refit, staring into a familiar small mirror, clapping a hand over alternate eyes, one of which was still painful, he was able at last to come to a decision about the injury sustained by him on July 12. He no longer had a pair of eyes. The pupil of his right eye was now large, irregular in shape and immovable. It nearly covered the blue part—he forgot what the doctors called it. Within four days of being wounded he had been able to distinguish light from darkness, but no object. The efficient, hard-drinking young surgeon who had performed the first dressing on shore had not promised much more. He had since taken two further opinions from more exalted quarters. It was in the sick-bay of the *Victory* that he learnt for certain that he had now only one efficient eye.

While he waited for the *Agamemnon's* guns to be brought on board, he had gone out to consult the medical staff of the Commander-in-Chief's flagship, taking with him Captain Hallowell, a Canadian-born officer, who had been "always on the batteries", even when suffering from the fever. The couple presented a contrast in types, for Hallowell, "though at present much reduced, poor fellow", was of mordant humour, gigantic stature and great physical strength. General Chambers, Surgeon-in-Chief to the Forces in the Mediterranean, had, in a discouraging certificate, dated August 9, stated his opinion that Captain Horatio Nelson's right eye had been so materially injured by stones and splinters struck by shot from the enemy, that he would never recover the perfect use of it. The amiable Dr. Harness, Physician to the Fleet, a person devoted to sick seamen and to citric acid as the antidote to scurvy, merely confirmed the diagnosis of Mr. Michael Jefferson. He wrote of "a wound of the iris of the right eye, which has occasioned an unnatural dilation of the pupil, and a material defect of sight". Nelson had been absent from duty only a few hours, and his name had never appeared in the Calvi casualty list. On October 2 he enclosed the two certificates to Lord Hood, stating the loss of an eye in His Majesty's service. Since August 9 he had indulged in no false hopes. "As to all purposes of use", the eye was gone. "I feel the Want of it but such is the chance of War, it was within a hair's breadth of taking off my head." His intention now, after fears of total darkness of which nobody knew, and a lucky escape, was to keep out of the awful hands of the medical fraternity as far as possible. "Nature does all for me, and Providence protects me." For a sea-officer with twenty-five years' service, to be short of an eye was nothing out of the ordinary. He now confessed to his wife the extent of the "slight scratch" first mentioned to her three weeks after receiving it. He assured her that "the blemish is nothing; not to be perceived, unless told". He also assured her that his hurts had not kept him from his duty. Nothing less than the loss of a limb could have done that.

Chapter VI

1794-1796

(*ætat.* 35-37)

"OLD MEDITERRANEAN MAN"

I

WHEN Lord Hood sailed for Gibraltar, and Portsmouth, without him, on October 12, 1794, Nelson was disappointed, but the duty on which he was ordered offered chances of prizes, and unless a peace should send him home, he was not, at heart, inclined to leave the Mediterranean at present. He knew that after a period of eclipse, his interest was rising again; and he had not yet seen a fleet action. "I trust the time will come when I shall be rewarded, though really I don't flatter myself it is near."

His chief regret was for Mrs. Nelson, from whom letters were arriving to say that the prospect of seeing her dear husband and child so soon made her happy beyond expression. "It has given me health, for before you wrote that you were well, and that Calvi was taken, I had fallen into the same way I was last year."

His Fanny's letters from Kentish Town were read by Nelson in Golfe Jouan, which the fleet had christened "Gourjean", and while he faced a boringly familiar prospect of inclining conifers and rocky islets, in increasingly bad weather, he was mentally transported to a scene typical of Georgian England. Under Mr. Suckling's roof, on September 29, a large party had sat down to dinner, and drunk the health of the absent friend. They had a couple of geese amongst the good fare, as the host was a Norfolk man. In the background stood Price, the black butler, looking blue, poor fellow, since his son had been found drowned in Hampstead ponds. Hickman, another old retainer, had also, on Mrs. Horatio Nelson's arrival, been full of enquiries for the Captain. The blooming and attentive Mrs. Suckling was supported by her father, contemporary of her husband, and other members of her family from Hampstead. The daughter of the house had a wistful look. She had formed an attachment for an Army officer. Her father knew of it, but said the young man must sell out—a hard saying, as he was at present with his regiment on the Continent, where the war was going poorly. If any little thing should come in her husband's way, Mrs. Nelson wished he would bring it home with him as a keepsake for his cousin. "I feel for her." The party had been very merry, and Mr. Suckling had quizzed his nephew's wife, as was his way, saying that he could always tell what was in her good man's letters by her expression. At the close of the feast, his present to her on her husband's thirty-sixth birthday had been truly handsome—"nothing less than £100". The trifle bought by Nelson for his cousin Elizabeth was also handsome—a diamond ring; and, since he would not now be home for Christmas, he sent £200 to his father, to be spent on comforts for the poor of Burnham Thorpe. He said that he thought a large N. could be woven into the blankets.

Christmas saw him at Leghorn again. His itinerary for the present was Gourjean, Leghorn, Porto Ferrajo in Elba and San Fiorenzo in Corsica. His duty was blockade, and his expectation that nothing much was likely to happen till the spring, when, if the French should turn their attention to the invasion of Italy, they would probably succeed. "We don't seem to make much of this War." "Pray let me hear from you often", he had written to his wife in his first moment of dejection at not coming home; "it is my greatest comfort." But Fanny's letters, dated from Bath now, did not bring great comfort. "This winter will be another anxious one. What did I not suffer in my mind, the last! . . . My mind and poor heart are always on the rack!" She told him that his brother Maurice, who seemed at last to be prospering, had grown quite stout, and that Mrs. Matcham was ailing for the usual reason, and that Mr. Matcham, as usual, was dissatisfied with his latest purchase. The manners of her husband's brother William (to whom he was unalterably attached) were growing more and more rough. Uncle Suckling had, since her departure, alarmed his young wife and his daughter by another of his coughing fits, in which he nearly strangled himself. She was deeply interested in the Prince of Wales's forthcoming match with the Princess of Brunswick, and much misinformed on the subject.

"Mrs. Fitzherbert has been long dismissed. . . . The Prince, it is said, is quite happy at the thought of being domesticated." In her husband's family, only his saintly father escaped a Parthian dart. She did not know that he was writing to Mrs. Matcham:

"No letters by Lord Hood from your Bro. His poor wife is continually in a Hurry and fret about him, and I find many others are the same, and worse. In such a state, the blessings of a Marriage union are thus made a torment, and most likely the Health is destroyed, or the temper soured, so as never to be recovered."

Lord Hood had arrived home, and presently news of him reached Nelson from several sources. All seemed to be going well. As the Commander-in-Chief from the Mediterranean had stepped out of his coach in London, the First Lord had been ready with a hand of greeting. From an inn at Devizes, on his road to Bath, Lord Hood assured "my dear Nelson" that he had taken the earliest opportunity of explaining to the First Lord the very illiberal conduct of General Stuart in making no mention of the services rendered by the Captain of the *Agamemnon* in the taking of Calvi. He had put into Lord Chatham's hand, with the understanding that it should be delivered to His Majesty, Nelson's letter enclosing the two medical certificates attesting the loss of an eye. "So you may be perfectly easy upon that subject." Three days later, Fanny took up the story. The Hoods had arrived at 5, Queen Square, and called at 17, New King Street. His Lordship had been as affectionate as if she was a daughter, and held out hopes that within three months her grass-widowhood would come to an end. Lady Hood had privately assured her that if justice was not done to Nelson it would not be his Lordship's fault. A week later she had dined with them, and been "cheerful and well-dressed". Nelson had not received well her pathetic disclosure that sheer worry during the siege of Calvi had undermined her health. ("Why you should be uneasy about me so as to make yourself ill, I know not. . . . The Service must ever supersede all private considerations.") She realised that she must begin to think of Josiah, now nearing his fifteenth birthday, as "my young man", no longer "my child", but found this almost impossible. "My child! I figure him to myself—good and obedient to you, and I hope tells you all his secrets. If he does, you will keep him good." After fierce storms, snow clothed the streets of Bath, a most unusual thing, and a sea-officer's wife could not resist the confession, "I never hear the wind but my dear husband and child are full in my thoughts."

Nelson's reports of his stepson were always favourable. "His understanding is excellent, and his disposition really good. . . . He is a seaman, every inch of him." He had begun to detect signs of what he cautiously termed "a warm disposition"—however, nothing could cool that so thoroughly as being at sea, "where nobody has entirely their own way".

At Leghorn, on Sunday evening, March 8, he was interrupted for the third time while attempting to compose a letter to his wife. He had begun it over a week before, on his return from a very bad cruise, but so far it contained but two paragraphs. For twelve days of January the fleet had been under storm stay-sails. All his letters since the New Year had told of little but gales and lumping seas. "But in *Agamemnon*, we mind them not; she is the finest Ship I ever sailed in, and were she a seventy-four, nothing should induce me to leave her while the War lasts."

He was now fast becoming what he called "an old Mediterranean man", well accustomed to brown shirts and scanty dinners, and he knew the free and neutral port of Leghorn as well as his native Lynn. The Tuscan sea-bathing resort, used by the Mediterranean fleet for refitting and victualling, had not many wholesome attractions for the exile, and when a sterner Admiral succeeded Hotham, he took ruthless measures to check behaviour which had resulted in a lamentable percentage of officers and men being invalided to Ajaccio Hospital. The second-rate hotel and opera charged exorbitant prices. Nelson haunted the house of the Pollards, Levant merchants, and together with Mr. Udney, British Consul, often agents for prizes taken by the fleet. He ordered his portrait in miniature from a local artist, who produced for the admiration of Mrs. Horatio Nelson a curiously pursy-looking sea-captain, with fashionably curly hair. The uniform was conscientiously attempted, but even the men-of-war, dramatically heeling over in the background, did not suggest British reality.

The third interruption to Nelson's letter of March 8 was unexpected, and caused him to close it immediately, with the words,

"I have only to pray to God to bless you." The fleet, "taken rather suddenly", got off at dawn, "pretty tolerably, as to order", and early on the morning of the 10th, Nelson's hope that they had gone to sea for some good purpose seemed likely to be gratified. The fifteen enemy sail-of-the-line reported to Admiral Hotham, by an express from Genoa, to be out of Toulon and steering for Corsica, were sighted at 10 a.m. and Hotham, with fourteen British warships and one Neapolitan, gave the signal for a general chase. Nelson reckoned the English fleet "half-manned", to have but 7,650 men at quarters, while the enemy had 16,900. His chief anxiety was lest the *Agamemnon* might not be able to acquit herself worthily, owing to being short of complement. It was during this day of light and variable winds and mists, typical of the Mediterranean in early spring, that he scrawled, in momentary expectation of his first fleet action, a jerky addition to what might be a farewell letter: "My character and good name are in my own keeping. Life with disgrace is dreadful. A glorious death is to be envied." The action which followed was scrambling and unsatisfactory, but a chance did come for him to distinguish himself.

At midnight on the 10th Hotham hoisted the signal to form in order of battle, but next morning no enemy was visible. Another uncanny day of sighing fickle airs and haze, accompanied by a heavy swell from the S.W., followed. The night was calm. With dawn the enemy were in sight again. Since his ship belonged to Vice-Admiral Goodall's division, it was to this officer, in the *Princess Royal*, that Nelson sent, at 9 a.m., a note expressive of strong emotion.

"My dear Admiral,

"I most heartily congratulate you on our being so near the Enemy's Fleet, and have only to assure you that the *Agamemnon* shall ever most faithfully support you. I wish we had a hundred, or at least should have fifty, good men. Should any of our Frigates get near you, I hope you will order some men for us, even should Admiral Hotham forget us. Believe me as ever, but never more than on the present occasion,

"Your most faithful,

"Horatio Nelson."

A few minutes before 3.15, when Hotham gave the signal "Prepare for Battle", Nelson saw Genoa lighthouse, about five leagues to the N.N.E., and, with that quickening of the visual sense usual at such moments, Genoa, surnamed "the Superb", displayed in all her glory. In the *Agamemnon*, as the *Britannia* broke the red flag, a continual drumming began to sound, and every man hurried to his assigned duty. Wooden bulkheads and canvas screens vanished: tables, chairs, lockers and chests went to the hold: hammocks, piped from below, neatly rolled and corded, were packed in troughs along the tops of the bulwarks. The galley fire was doused, and the fighting decks watered and dressed with sand: the ship's company tied their silks round their heads and cast their footwear, and indeed all wear save their trousers, both in expectation of warm work and because surgeons preferred to operate on wounds uninfected by greasy textiles. The *toilette* of the guns was also completed and the port lids yawned, while along the sanded decks buckets of water, tourniquets and swabs were ranged handy. With the first roll of the drum, nets had been spread from the main-mast aft to the mizzen, and in the hatchway "fearnought" felt fore-screens were hammered into place. Finally, to the orlop, safe under the water-line, repaired a solemn company, including the carpenter with his gang, ready to staunch a mortal wound to under-water timbers, and Mr. Roxburgh, surgeon, with mates rolling their shirt-sleeves to their shoulders. Six minutes was the time allotted for this transformation scene in a ship-of-the-line, but an hour passed on March 13, 1795, before Hotham gave the signal to form order of battle on the larboard tack; and his next signal, half an hour later, was for every ship to carry a light during the night. Nelson's opportunity did not come until the next morning, with fresh breezes and again the order for a general chase.

The enemy, refusing battle, were running as fast as they could, pursued by the English fleet, on a parallel line, the *Agamemnon* and half a dozen other ships well ahead, when suddenly Nelson beheld a French 80-gun ship (afterwards identified as the *Ça Ira*) run foul of another and carry away her own fore and main topmasts. Captain Fremantle, in the leading frigate, coming up fast, with great resolution at once attacked the 80-gun ship, and the first shots of the action were heard; but the little *Inconstant* received heavy punishment and was forced to retire. The *Agamemnon* then stood towards the *Ça Ira*, the *Sans Culotte*, of 120 guns, and the *Jean Bart* (which Nelson, better versed in the names of prominent members of the French Directory than French naval history, wrote down as the *Jean Barras*). It was at this moment that a sacrifice avoided the previous day when clearing the decks for action was performed, and seven live bullocks, purchase of a captain with strong views on the prevention of scurvy, were hove overboard. "We could", considered Nelson regretfully, "have fetched the *Sans Culotte*, by passing the *Ça Ira* to windward, but, on looking round I saw no ship-of-the-line within several miles to support me." He determined to direct his attentions to the *Ça Ira*, presently taken in tow by a frigate, with the *Sans Culotte* and *Jean Bart* standing by to protect her. Moving fairly rapidly through the water, she began firing stern-chasers, with such effect that Nelson, who had intended to touch her stern before he gave the order to fire, decided to reply. "Seeing plainly from the situation of the two Fleets, the impossibility of being supported; and in case any accident happened to our masts, the certainty of being severely cut up, I resolved to fire as soon as I thought we had a certainty of hitting." He continued to manœuvre and hit, unsupported, for upwards of two hours, and during this time had the satisfaction of observing "my poor brave fellows" carrying out his orders with as much calm and precision as if they had been working the *Agamemnon* into Spithead. "Scarcely a shot seemed to miss: the instant all were fired, braced up our after-yards, put the helm a-port and stood after her again . . . never allowing the *Ça Ira* to get a single gun from either side to fire on us." By 1 p.m. the French 80-gun ship was "a perfect wreck", and her commander ordered his towing frigate to pull her round, so that she could bring her broadside to bear. Nelson ran on boldly, and her shots flew over the *Agamemnon*. Such was the state of the engagement when Hotham, instead of hastening reinforcements, hoisted the signal of recall.

Next morning all sail was made to cut off the *Ça Ira*, now towed by a 74, and as the enemy made an attempt to save two ships-of-the-line, a partial action ensued in which the *Agamemnon* was again engaged, and two British ships were disabled. But as soon as the enemy cripples had struck, Hotham, contented with a measure of success, decided against further pursuit.

Having sent the faithful Andrews to board the enemy prizes and hoist English colours, Nelson himself went on board the Admiral's flagship, to urge leaving the prizes, with the two damaged English 74's and some frigates, and continuing the chase in hopes of forcing a general engagement. Hotham, "much cooler than myself", replied, "We must be contented. We have done very well." Nelson, far from contented, when he got on board the *Princess Royal*, carrying with him, by Hotham's orders, the captains of the two enemy prizes, found Goodall of his own mind. This more adventurous officer went so far as to send a hasty line to his Commander-in-Chief, backing Captain Nelson's opinion that, if they could but get close enough, they might have the whole enemy fleet, and "such a day as I believe the Annals of England never produced". "Sure I am," wrote Nelson privately, "had I commanded our Fleet on the 14th, that either the whole French Fleet would have graced my triumph, or I should have been in a confounded scrape." But Hotham, perceiving the possibility of the scrape, refused to make a dangerous attempt, and contemporary comment did not criticise him too severely. He had not, after all, done badly. Corsica was temporarily saved, and two French sail-of-the-line had been captured. Only a few persons of discernment summed up his future from that hour. "I can *entre nous*, perceive", wrote Sir William Hamilton, from his Neapolitan palace, "that my old friend Hotham is not quite awake enough for such a command as that of the King's Fleet in the Mediterranean; although he appears the best creature imaginable." Nelson was obliged to be content with the reflection that he had been lucky enough to command the only line-of-battle ship to get into single action, and with an opponent "absolutely large enough " to have taken the *Agamemnon* in her hold. While the *Ça Ira* and the *Censeur* showed a casualty list of seven hundred and fifty, the *Agamemnon* had, by what seemed like a miracle, since "our sails were ribbons and all our ropes were ends", only thirteen wounded. Also, although Hotham's despatch made no mention of him on the second day of the battle, he soon disovered that in both the British and enemy fleets his services had not been underestimated. As "we are too far from home to be noticed", he told his wife "as a secret" that out here now he was not unknown.

The French poetasters had given Captain Nelson a mistress—"no less a personage than the goddess Bellona".

2

His dissatisfaction with the results of the late engagement was renewed when he heard that the French fleet had, before being encountered, fallen in with and captured the *Berwick*, and afterwards had been joined by six ships from Brest, which should never have been permitted to get into Toulon unopposed.

For above three weeks, while the cautious Hotham kept his whole fleet under his eye at San Fiorenzo or Leghorn, Nelson was "absolutely in the horrors" lest a convoy, momentarily expected from Gibraltar, might share the fate of the *Berwick*. In case the enemy, encouraged by their superior numbers, might make another attempt to take Corsica before the arrival of Lord Hood, he wrote to the Viceroy, offering his services for the command of any seamen landed for the defence of the island. Twelve months had now passed since he had first set eyes upon Sir Gilbert Elliot, a figure who would, by anyone familiar with the type, have been recognised by the gait and set of jaw alone as a Border laird. The Scots Viceroy was one of the most admirable characters yet encountered by Nelson. He was, like most of his race, slightly below middle stature, with a gift of silence and a lightning wit; a man of parts and means, personally disinterested, impossible to fret or daunt. The Vicereine, indulgently described by her partner as "my John Bull wife, who understands a Frenchman no better than Molly housemaid", had arrived safely at Bastia from Roxburghshire in the previous December, with their six children and a young cousin, Miss Eleanor Congleton. From her "fairy-tale palace", overlooking an island-studded bay, Lady Elliot now issued invitations to assemblies and balls at which regimental bands played, and the company were at liberty to wander, in moonlight, through great glass doors on to the terrace of an immense garden, on a cape washed by the sea. She also astonished the natives by being out early for hard walks in mountain scenery which reminded her husband of *As You Like It* and *A Midsummer Night's Dream*, while he astonished her by bringing to her table guests who were precisely her picture of Bluebeard. Even before he had

explained his reason for sending his second son into the Navy, Sir
Gilbert had won Nelson's heart by his insistence upon the attack on
Bastia. ("I like the sea better. The character of the profession is
more manly. They are full of life and action, while on shore it is all
lounge and still life.") The Viceroy was openly in agreement with
Nelson's despair over neglect of the Mediterranean by those at
home. The news of the appointment of Lord Spencer to succeed
Lord Chatham had been a personal blow to an officer still waiting
for recognition of his loss of an eye. ("Now he is out, all hopes
will be done away.") His chagrin vented itself in a long letter
to Locker.

"When I am to see England, God knows! I have, in the present situation
of affairs, determined on staying here till the autumn, or another Action
take place, when all active service will probably be over in these seas. . . .
One hundred and ten days I have been actually engaged at Sea and on shore
against the Enemy; three actions against Ships, two against Bastia, in my
Ship; four Boat Actions and two Villages taken, and twelve Sail of Vessels
burned. I don't know of anyone who has done more, and I have had the
comfort to be ever *applauded* by my Commander-in-Chief, but never *rewarded*; and what is more mortifying, for services in which I have been
slightly wounded, others have been praised, who at the time were actually in
bed, far from the scene of action.

"But we shall, I hope, talk my opinion of men and measures, over the
fire next winter, at Greenwich."

As the spring passed, and no word came of the promised reinforcements, he began to fear that the new Lords were not to be
an improvement on their predecessors—a thing he had scarcely
believed possible. The junction of a single Neapolitan 74, towards
the end of April, was "absolutely matter for exultation" in the
fleet, "not so much neglected as forgotten are we at Home". He
was glad when Hotham, "I believe heartily tired of his temporary
command", at last took his fleet to sea, a proceeding not only more
honourable, but also much safer than "skulking in Port". But
contrary winds held them in Leghorn, while the French Minister
at Genoa triumphantly announced the signature of a peace between
his country and Spain, and Sir William Hamilton wrote ruefully
that if this story was true, we should soon be losing "our Naples
friends", quoting—"As do Spain, so do Naples."

The long-looked-for store-ships and victuallers from Gibraltar made an essential appearance ("Had we lost them, the game was up"), but everyone felt indignation that they had been obliged to run such a risk of capture and that their Admiral was receiving "not the scratch of a pen" from London, where "they should know that half the Ships in this Fleet require to go to England". Presently, unofficial reports of the reinforcements with which Lord Hood was waiting to sail from St. Helens were truly astonishing—only five of the line. "What", demanded Nelson of Uncle Suckling of the Navy Office, "can the new Board of Admiralty be after? We expect the French Fleet to be at sea every hour." On June 15 a disaster which he had long dreaded was announced. Admiral Man joined the fleet with a squadron of seven ships. Lord Hood, while lying at Spithead in the *Victory*, ready to sail, had found it his duty to remonstrate for the last time with their Lordships on the inadequacy of the force on the Mediterranean station, and when Lord Hood felt strongly the result was remarkable, for, in the words of the admiring William Hotham, he had even upon normal occasions "A Something" about him which put inferior officers in much awe. "He was a stranger to any feeling of nervous diffidence." Their Lordships, on encountering this side of Lord Hood, had ordered him to strike his flag and come on shore, which he had accordingly done, never to be employed at sea again. Nelson's dismay was equalled by his indignation. His hopes, like those of Sir Gilbert Elliot, had been "accustomed to rest on the *Victory's* anchor". "Oh, miserable Board of Admiralty. They have forced the first officer in the Service away from his command. His zeal, his activity for the honour and benefit of his King and Country are not abated. Upward of 70, he possesses the mind of 40. . . ." Nelson's belief that his lost leader was a man "equally great in all situations" was justified. Hood, even at this moment, had taken care to send by Admiral Man a letter from Lord Spencer acknowledging the pretensions of Captain Horatio Nelson "to favour and distinction when proper opportunities offer". It was dated before news of the action of July 13–14 had been received at the Admiralty, but also before Hood's difference with their Lordships—a serious consideration, as he had since written to another officer:

"To be candid with you, I can be of no use to anyone, for Lord Spencer is not content with marking me with indifference and inattention, but carries it to all who have any connection with me. You will therefore do well, in any application to his Lordship, not to make mention of my name. I have neither seen or spoken to his Lordship since my flag was struck, and look upon myself as thrown upon the shelf for ever."

Lord Hood's retirement was dignified. In 1795 he expressed his intention of spending "the short remnant of my life" in the happy situation of a private gentleman. Ill-health had been offered as his reason for coming back from the Mediterranean last winter, but on a chill March morning his silver head and hawk-features were observed in the House of Commons at 6 a.m. In the following March he was appointed Governor of Greenwich Hospital, a post which he held for twenty years.

3

While Nelson was "waiting off Minorque, doing nothing . . . out of spirits, though never better in health", he dealt with a matter which he had deferred in hopes of Lord Hood's return. He addressed himself directly to the Secretary at War, asking for the allowance usually made to a land-officer of equal rank ("which I understand is that of Brigadier-General") in respect of his services on shore during the sieges of Bastia and Calvi. A chilly but quick reply informed him: "No pay has ever been issued under the direction, or to the knowledge of this Office, to Officers of the Navy, serving with the Army on shore." He sailed for San Fiorenzo at the end of June, at a tense moment. The French fleet was said to be at sea again, with twenty-two of the line and "innumerable frigates", but a valuable convoy from Gibraltar (this time bringing ammunition and troops) had escaped. "So far, good." On his arrival in Corsica he found that he was to be given a detached command. By what seemed an ironic chance, considering the ill-success of his late application, he was, on account of his experience during the sieges of Bastia and Calvi, being employed to act with forces on shore. His mission had a sound of high romance—"to co-operate with the Austrian General, Baron de Vins, in the Riviera of Genoa". The principal armies engaged against the French Republic now were those of Austria and Sardinia, and France was bringing increasing pressure to bear on technically neutral Genoa.

At San Fiorenzo Nelson found Hotham, happy in the belief that only seventeen enemy sail were at sea, and for no other purpose than to exercise their men. A courtly letter from de Vins at Genoa had assured him that the main fleet was in Toulon, and that allied arms had taken Vado Bay, which should be a useful base for the English fleet. Nelson sailed from San Fiorenzo with five frigates at dusk on July 4, and midway between Nice and Genoa, on the afternoon of the 7th, fell in with the enemy fleet in full strength. They immediately gave chase to his small squadron, and he needed all his seamanship to get back to San Fiorenzo. For seven of the twenty-four hours during which he was pursued, Hotham's fleet had the mortification of watching him in imminent danger of capture. The wind was blowing right into the bay, and most of the British ships were watering and refitting. After great exertions they got to sea— "Twenty-three of the Line, and as fine a Fleet as ever graced the seas", searching for an enemy equal in strength. Five days later they came in sight of their opponents, and Hotham, after spending a long time dressing his line, hoisted the signal for a general chase. He was being given the second chance, rare in the career of a Commander-in-Chief. Many lesser Powers in Europe, and particularly along these shores, were waiting to see whether the English could hold the Mediterranean, or whether the star of France was in the ascendant. The night of July 12 had been wild, and several British ships had split their topmasts. With daylight the wind continued high, and there was considerable swell. The weather favoured the pursuit for a while, but by noon, when the *Agamemnon*, with half-a-dozen other ships of Man's squadron, leading the van, was in touch with the enemy's rear, the French coast near Toulon was also visible, and soon after the *Victory* had opened fire, the breeze swung round to the north, giving the three sternmost enemy vessels the opportunity of bringing their broadsides to bear. The *Victory* and the *Culloden* lost limbs, but the *Alcide*, last ship in the French line, was so badly damaged that she struck and surrendered. Before she could be boarded, she took fire and blew up. While the sun struggled through the clouds, about two hundred of her crew were saved by English boats. Nearly all the prisoners subsequently declared themselves royalists, and Nelson decided that, upon the whole, he found French republicans better specimens.

Although smoke from the gunfire had now produced a perfect calm, the *Cumberland* and *Agamemnon* were again getting into close action when Hotham, eight miles astern, signalled, "The whole Fleet will now retire." In his own words, "Those of our ships which were engaged had approached so near to the shore, that I judged it proper to call them off." Captain Rowley did his best to avoid seeing the unwelcome signal, but the *Victory* repeated it, hoisting the *Cumberland's* distinguishing pendant, and Rowley was obliged to obey. Once more the French fleet had escaped, and even the immediate results of the Battle of Hyères were obviously inferior to that of the disappointing action of the previous March. The eventual results were to include the abandonment of the Mediterranean by the British fleet, the loss of Corsica, and Spain ranged by the side of France. Nelson wrote:

"Thus has ended our second meeting with these gentry. In the forenoon we had every prospect of taking every Ship in the Fleet, and at noon it was almost certain we should have had the six near Ships. . . . To say how we wanted Lord Hood at that time is to say, 'Will you have all the French Fleet, or no Action?' But the subject is unpleasant and I shall have done with it. I am now co-operating with the Austrian Army, under General de Vins, and hope we shall do better there."

4

On July 18, 1795, Nelson arrived in Genoa, and picked up letters and newspapers from home which told him that he had been gazetted Colonel of the Chatham Division of Marines. For some months past the promotions rewarding the Glorious First of June had been expected. He had dreaded that they might give him his flag and send him home. He found that the promotions to Admiral had stopped short seven above him. As he made his way through the streets of Genoa towards the British Minister's house, which stood five miles outside the city, he saw in his mind's eye the grey pile of Holkham presiding over the Norfolk fields close by Burnham Thorpe, and pictured the "very small cottage" now within his means, where he should be as happy as if in Mr. Coke's famous

Hall. He decided to send his dear father a further gift of £200, "since at present I believe that I am the richer man". The recognition of his services, achieved without any interest, raised his spirits. After his evening with Mr. Drake his brow was not so light. He slept on their conversation, and next day sent the Minister a long letter ending, "When your Excellency considers the responsibility of a Captain in the Navy in these matters, I trust you will think it right for me to state my opinion fully." His Excellency had asked him to take a step justly described by him as "vigorous", his favourite adjective at this date. Mr. Drake wished him to stop, not only all enemy vessels, but all neutrals trading with the districts of the Genoa littoral under enemy occupation. Hotham's recent instructions gave him considerable freedom, but a circular order based on advice from London, issued by the Commander-in-Chief to his fleet only a month past, adjured all officers to take extreme care, in their dealings with neutral shipping, not to give just cause of offence to Foreign Powers in amity with His Majesty. He doubted whether Hotham would stand by him if he did give cause for complaint, and as a Captain in the Navy, he was well aware that should neutral owners sue him successfully for detention and damage he would be liable for the payment of sums amounting to so many hundreds of thousands of pounds that the exact probability was not worth his consideration. He therefore asked Mr. Drake to assure him that unless an entire stop was put to all trade, the army with which he was told to co-operate was unlikely to hold its present position. He also asked to be assured that the step proposed was for the benefit of His Majesty's Service. Mr. Drake did so, and with the words, "Political courage in an Officer abroad is as highly necessary as military courage", Nelson agreed without further hesitation to take the responsibility of acting, "not only without the orders of my Commander-in-Chief, but in some measure contrary to them". He issued "proper orders" to "the Squadron under my command", and taking Mr. Drake on board the *Agamemnon*, sailed for Vado Bay. There they found the Honourable John Trevor, now Minister at Turin, awaiting them, and the Baron de Vins, "extremely glad" to see them. Nelson was disappointed with the newly captured base. Had it not been called a bay, he would never have recognised it as one. It appeared to him to be a mere "bend in the land", and his first experience of going ashore from a warship at anchor was not encouraging. He grudgingly allowed that the water was certainly deep, with a good clay bottom, and that a fleet might ride there for a short time during the summer months. With the Allied Army he was better impressed—"3,200 of the finest troops I ever saw"— and the practised charm of an aristocrat of the Imperial Court was not lost upon him. He thought the Baron de Vins an officer who perfectly knew his business, and seemed disposed to act with vigour. "A good man, and I verily believe a good General." Listening to the flowery periods of the old Austrian cavalry General, who informed him that the name and reputation of *M. le Commandant Nelson* were perfectly known in his army, indeed throughout Europe, he could almost fancy himself charging at the head of a troop of horse. When his army entered Nice, as they might do in six weeks, said de Vins, he expected to receive the baton of a Field Marshal, and the English fleet would have Villefranche harbour. Once he was across the Var, Provence would rise. "All War or all Peace" was his motto. It took Nelson nearly two months to discover that talking dramatically was General de Vins's strong point. The General, having appreciated very quickly that the English Commander-in-Chief had sent him a highly exhausting young companion in charge of a few frigates, had privately decided not to move unadvisedly. He meant to continue his careful tactics of spreading small forces everywhere possible, thus never, as his critics claimed, having a main body with which to attack.

Having said all that was necessary for the moment, Nelson sailed again for Genoa, with their Excellencies, promising to return to Vado Bay with all possible expedition. He did not intend even to anchor, but a gale blew him into Leghorn roads, and a week passed before he returned to a business which he soon learnt to describe as "pushing the Austrian General forward". De Vins gradually disclosed his difficulties. He had tried both flattery and abuse on the Piedmontese and Neapolitans under his command. The former were too poor in spirit even to defend their own territory. He had long been patiently awaiting their promised attack, under General Calli, in the Ventimiglia district. He believed that no Neapolitan vessel would stay at sea in winter to save an empire. Still, if Neapolitan gunboats could be obtained, they might serve to check enemy supply vessels streaming out of Genoa after dark, and creeping along the coast in shallow water. He apologised that "the politics of his court so constantly tied his hands". A plan that Nelson should take five or six thousand troops round behind the enemy front and land them between San Remo and Ventimiglia received his polite consideration. The young Englishman himself admitted that it might be a risky undertaking.

Nelson began to suffer from nervous strain. On the bright side of the picture he still ranged the General, "inclined to go forward, if England will but play her part, which I hope she will". Admiral Hotham was "said to be coming to look at us", which sounded promising. With "the Squadron under my command" he was fully satisfied. The squadron, at the moment, consisted of eight little frigates, their names ranging from classic romance to English ports and descriptive attributes—H.M.S. *Speedy*, *Tartar*, *Inconstant*, *Southampton*, *Lowestoffe*, *Meleager*, *Romulus*, *Ariadne*. . . . In three of their captains, Hallowell, Fremantle and Cockburn, he had old friends. The Genoese authorities had begun to be very angry, "but that does not matter. . . . It seems almost a trial between us who shall be first tired—they of complaining, or me of answering them." He disregarded a warning that it would not, perhaps, be wise for him to land there at present. The capture of a Leghorn vessel or two would stop the Leghorn trade. The chief anxiety in London seemed to be lest the Dey of Algiers should be alienated. "But, Sir," he invoked Sir Gilbert Elliot, "is England to give up the almost certainty of finishing this war with honour, to the fear of offence to such beings?"

The dark side of the picture kept him awake at nights, in a ship nearly as crank and in need of a refit as her Captain. After long days of ceaseless vigilance in heavy weather he had formed the disagreeable habit of waking suddenly with a most disquieting sensation, "as if a girth were buckled taut over my breast", and staying awake —remembering that owners of neutral vessels might sue a Captain in the Navy successfully, remembering that Hotham, the best heart in the world, needed a new head, and hated "this co-operation".

His "good" eye began to trouble him. For ten days, in August, he was almost blind and in great pain. The strain of entertaining foreign officers who considered only his rank, not his pay, was having its effect upon his purse as well as his constitution. He had another personal worry, which was an ever-present source of irritation. His servant, Frank Lepée, who had followed him up the dreadful green reaches of the San Juan river on his first expedition, would have to go. Ten months of reprimand and promises of amendment had dragged their weary course. The family circle, with whom the faithful sailor servant was a popular and picturesque figure, would expect an explanation. He achieved this in the least possible words— "Parted with Frank for drunkenness, and when so, mad; never will keep a drunkard another hour." Tom Allen, one of the Burnham Thorpe lads who had volunteered for the *Agamemnon*, was promoted to be what he proudly called "wally-de-sham". He was black-haired, stunted, uncouth, entirely illiterate, and never wrong, but he knew his capacity: Nelson endured him for seven years. ("That beast Allen has left behind, or lost, all my papers. . . . I asked him, in the boat, for my red case, as I did not see it. His answer was, 'Sir, I put it in the stern locker.' I then desired him to take particular care in handling the case up the side, when he knew perfectly well he had not put it in the boat. . . . Huzza! Huzza! P.S., Allen is returned with my case.") Since it did not occur to Nelson to attribute his symptoms to accumulated fatigue and irregular meals snatched amidst the writing of "difficult" letters, he resorted unwillingly to the doctors, who said that he ought to be on shore for a month or two, "without the thoughts of service".

A small successful action on August 26 by "part of my Squadron" —actually six out of his eight frigates—made him feel "better every way". De Vins had sent him word that provisions and ammunition had arrived at Alassio, a place occupied by the enemy. Within an hour of Nelson's appearance he had captured a National corvette, two galleys, one large gunboat and six or seven lesser vessels, one fully laden. Some enemy cavalry fired on his boats from the shore, but without killing or wounding anyone in his boarding parties. casualty was little Hoste, who, in charge of a small boat, cut led with ammunition, but broke his leg falling down her scuttle. Hoste, however, did not spend long picturing "the seat on the starboard side of Papa" at the family dinner-table in Norfolk, perhaps occupied by his next brother. He rather enjoyed his spell in the sick-bay, as Captain Nelson came down so often to see him. He was soon on crutches, loudly singing his favourite "Dearest Peg", and a ship's company, dying with laughter at his efforts, decided that this boy had been born lucky, and began to entertain a partly superstitious affection for him. The capture of the corvette had pleased the men of the *Agamemnon*, for they all recognised *La Résolve* as "the long black polacca ship which came alongside the *Sans Culotte* on the 13th of July, and outsails us all".

The next expedition of "part of my Squadron" was not so successful. On their passage to cut off a ship from Oneglia, Lieutenants Andrews and Spicer, in two small galleys, fell in with three tall Turkish merchantmen, who opened fire. One Turk was carried, but the other two got into Genoa, with six million pounds in hard cash. Nelson had to record—"My gallant Officers and men, after a long contest, were obliged to retreat; and it is with the greatest pain that I have to render so long a list of killed and wounded." As September wore on and he began to despair of getting the Admiral to move, or the General into action, suddenly de Vins appeared to announce that his troops had carried an enemy outpost in the mountains, that they were now within half musket shot of some other point, which, if possible, he meant to attack, and that he was now going to the advanced post. He withdrew, and nothing further happened. His latest difficulty was whispered to be "the non-co-operation of the British Fleet". He complained "heavily" of never seeing the Admiral. Nelson, in whose letters the words "frivolous" and "excuses" had begun to appear, at once went down the coast, as far as Nice, and sounded and examined every port. On his return he offered to land five thousand men, bag and baggage, with their field-pieces, and to ensure their safe convoys. The General, in reply, produced another scheme, which he considered preferable. The only drawback to it was that it entailed "a small degree of assistance from Admiral Hotham". So as not to leave him what he called "a loop-hole", Nelson wrote to Hotham, asking for transports, more frigates and at least one 74. He had hopes of the effects of Mr.

Drake's appointment to reside at the headquarters of the Austrian
Army, but, as he told Uncle Suckling, "My situation with this Army
has convinced me, by ocular demonstration, of the futility of Continental Alliances". De Vins too wrote to Hotham, but only to say
how much he and his staff appreciated the judgment, abilities and
activity of Captain Nelson, and also the discernment of the British
Commander-in-Chief in having made choice of so zealous an officer
to co-operate with them. Mr. Drake duly forwarded this testimony
to Lord Grenville, Secretary of State for Foreign Affairs, and for a
space nothing more was heard of a complaint which had made the
commander of the co-operating British squadron very angry
indeed. In mid-October he went to see his Admiral, who was lying
quiet in Leghorn roads, in the belief that the armies were unlikely
to move until the spring, and that wholesale desertions in the
Toulon fleet were keeping the enemy in port. Six of the line and
eight frigates had got out of Toulon, and were said to be gone
to the West Indies, but Hotham, content so long as month after
month slipped past without any losses, let a fortnight elapse before
he parted with equal numbers to pursue them.

The military action which Nelson had so long desired did take
place that year, although the season was so far advanced, but it was
not engendered by the Allies. The first week of November 1795
was bitterly cold. In the Alpes-Maritimes, after a north wind, the
first snows of the winter had fallen, followed by frost. Austrian
soldiers were said to be dying at their posts in the mountains. In the
French camp, General Kellerman was reported to be going round
every post daily, saying all that he could to encourage his troops.

For some time the Austrians had complained of enemy gunboats
harassing their camp near Loano, fourteen miles west of Vado Bay.
On the night of November 10, while the *Agamemnon* lay at single
anchor in Vado Bay, ready to proceed at the first sound of an enemy
gun, the boats of *La Brune*, a French frigate of 26 guns, crept out of
Genoa, attended by several privateers. An Austrian commissary
travelling to Vado Bay, with £10,000 sterling, pay for De Vin's
troops, was known to be spending the night at an inn in the small
town of Voltri, nine miles east of Genoa. On that wild and bitter
winter's night, a landing-party of about three hundred from *La*

Brune took the neutral post, unopposed and slenderly guarded, robbed the commissary, and seized the corn and flour magazines. Next day, flushed with triumph and rich in booty, their Captain was publicly enlisting men for his army in the streets of Genoa. On the 13th about seven hundred were embarked, to sail under his convoy, to attack a strong post between Voltri and Savona. There a detachment of the French army was to join them and the Genoese peasantry were to be incited to insurrection.

Nelson found himself "in a cleft stick". Mr. Drake, having put his wife and nursery on the road to Milan, was calling with all his might and main for the return of the *Agamemnon* to Genoa. Nelson weighed, and made sail along the shore to the eastward, anchored the same night within Genoa mole, and there did the only thing possible in the circumstances—laid the *Agamemnon* across the harbour's mouth so that no French ship could leave the port. He was aware that while he was in this position he covered the Bochetta Pass (the only possible retreat for de Vins and a force of between eight and ten thousand, should they be worsted in an attack), but he also knew that by leaving Vado he was giving the enemy gunboats their chance to plague the Austrian left flank. He regretted that the *Agamemnon* could not be cut in two.

For several dark late November days he received no certain news. The weather was "so very bad that neither sails, nor ships nor people could remain at sea very long". For ten days, "very anxious and uneasy", he hoped against hope that accounts of a defeat, after a grand enemy attack near Loano, on the 23rd were exaggerated. Hotham had retired to Naples, and Goodall—a greater loss—much hurt at not having been chosen to succeed him, was on the first stages of a journey which was to end in permanent survey of the placidities of Teignmouth. Sir John Jervis, "who I understand is a man of business", had not yet arrived, and Sir Hyde Parker, in temporary command, had by now deprived Nelson of all but one of his frigates. By December 4, he knew the bitter truth.

"The Austrians, by all accounts, did not stand firm. The French, half naked, were determined to conquer or die. General de Vins, from ill-health, as he says, gave up the command in the middle of the Battle, and from that moment not a soldier stayed at his post. . . . It was 'Devil take the hindmost.' . . . The Austrians ran eighteen miles without stopping, the Men without any arms whatsoever, Officers without soldiers, Women without assistance. Thus has ended my campaign."

On the same day he added a postscript to a letter to Brother William, begun a fortnight earlier. "I am on my way to Leghorn to refit. The campaign is finished by the defeat of the Austrians, and the French are in possession of Vado Bay." If he should fall in with the French squadron, which was now ready for sea again at Toulon, and with troops embarked, he thought the situation of the *Agamemnon* would be very precarious. "My Ship and Ship's Company are worn out, but the folks at Home do not feel for us." Actually, folks at home were beginning to hear vaguely of his exertions. An article in the *Gentleman's Magazine* for the following February, dealing with the nomenclature of H.M. ships, mentioned that the men of a certain 64 on the Mediterranean station, disliking classical titles, had renamed the *Bellerophon* the "Bully Ruffian", the *Polyphemus*, "Polly Infamous", and their own *Agamemnon*, "Eggs and Bacon".

No untoward incident such as Nelson feared disturbed his passage to Leghorn, and at that port he learnt news of great interest to him. Sir John Jervis had arrived at San Fiorenzo from Spithead, in the *Lively* frigate, on November 27, "to the great joy of some, and sorrow of others".

5

He had met Sir John Jervis once, years ago, but the chance *rencontre* was not one which the new Commander-in-Chief would be likely to remember. It had taken place in the dimness of the Treasury Passage of the House of Commons. The Member for Yarmouth had recognised an old messmate, from Captain Locker's singular habit of scanning a scene through an eye-glass fitted to the head of his cane. Sir John had stopped, and Captain Locker had begged leave to present his young *élève*, Captain Nelson.

Sir John Jervis, in his sixty-third year, had a reputation not altogether enviable. He was credited with a heart of stone, a most discerning nose for inefficiency, a grim turn of humour, an ungovernable temper and a tongue which did not spare even those of elevated station and birth. Professionally, his prestige stood high:

he had a record of distinguished service in the Seven Years' War, the War of American Independence, and as Commander-in-Chief in the West Indies. But the fleet which the *Agamemnon*, "as fit as a rotten ship can be", joined on January 15, 1796, was not a happy one. On his arrival, the new Chief had begun without loss of time the inculcation of a system of rigid discipline and curtailment of customary privileges, far from agreeable to the majority of his captains, and so much resented that, four years later, the toast, "May the discipline of the Mediterranean never be introduced into the Channel Fleet", was endorsed by a naval wife, "in full coterie", with the rider, "May his next glass of wine choke the Wretch!"

Nelson, after his reception by this character on January 19, 1796, was greeted by a disgruntled brother-officer with the wondering words: "You did just as you pleased in Lord Hood's time, the same in Admiral Hotham's, and now again with Sir John Jervis! It makes no difference to you who is Commander-in-Chief." To this outburst, Nelson, fresh from a surprising first interview with his new Chief, returned "a pretty strong answer", before sailing for his old station off Genoa. He was satisfied that in Sir John Jervis he had, at any rate, met a man who meant to act with vigour. For the Mediterranean fleet there was to be no more peaceful lying at anchor in Fiorenzo Bay, or skulking amongst the Balearic Islands.

He had taken care, as soon as possible, to mention Captain Locker's kind remembrances. But whether or not Sir John Jervis recollected their previous meeting did not matter, for he had at once shown himself friendly, and made the offer of the *St. George*, of 80 guns, or the *Zealous*, a 74. Nelson had respectfully declined either, whereupon Sir John, deserting that subject abruptly, had demanded his knowledge, and even advice, on several matters upon which, in Nelson's opinion, others in the fleet should already have been able to inform the new Admiral. At the end of a very long and interesting sitting, Jervis had regretted that he had at present no means of giving Captain Nelson a squadron equal to his merits, and then asked if he would object to serving under him when promoted. Nelson's reply had been that if the *Agamemnon* was ordered home before his flag arrived, he had many reasons for wishing to go to England. Should his flag arrive (which he could hardly expect) and the war continue, he would be proud to hoist it under the command of Sir John Jervis. He took his leave under the impression that Sir John was writing to the Admiralty that day, to ask that, if the fleet was kept there, his flag might be sent to the Mediterranean. But, cautious after many disappointments, all he would admit in letters home was that, as yet, he appeared to stand well with his new Chief. He did not have to wait long for the appearance of Sir John and the fleet off Toulon, and after his second interview with the Admiral, in a February blizzard, sounded a more confident note.

"Sir John Jervis, from his manner, as I plainly perceive, does not wish me to leave this station. He seems at present to regard me more as an associate than a subordinate Officer; for I am acting without any orders. . . He asked me if I had heard any more of my promotion. I told him 'No'. His answer was, 'You must have a larger Ship, for we cannot spare you, either as Captain or Admiral.'"

The French were making great preparations for opening their spring campaign in Italy. Sardinia was in open rebellion. On March 9, Nelson, who did not know when he had been so ill at sea, stood for Leghorn, to get his damages repaired. The worst north-easterly gale which he had ever experienced in the Mediterranean had stove in the stern of the *Agamemnon*, carried away her starboard quarter-gallery and sprung her main topmast. The coastline of the Riviera di Levante, under deep snow, was intensely cold. Through Paris streets deep in slush, General Buonaparte, aged twenty-six, was arriving late to hurry through a civil marriage ceremony with a graceful widow. His choice, like that of Nelson nine years past, was an elegant, neurotic West India lady, some undiscovered months his senior, who had borne to his predecessor, but by whom he was to have no children. No other points of resemblance existed between the romances.

Two leaders who were to know each other's names well, both at work in hard weather to achieve a remarkable personal touch with sorely tried men under their command, were drawing together. On March 27, Buonaparte, at Nice, issued his first inspiring order to troops whom he found sullen and half-starved:

"Soldiers! you are naked, ill-nourished. The Government owes you much, but can do nothing for you. Your patience, the courage which has carried you amongst these rocks, do you honour, but give you no advantage, no *éclat*. I will lead you into the most fertile plains in the world, where you shall find great towns, rich provinces—within your grasp, Glory, Honour, Riches! Soldiers of Italy! shall you be found wanting in constancy, in courage?"

In the *Agamemnon*, Mr. Midshipman Hoste was meanwhile writing home:

"Our Squadron at present consists of two Sail-of-the-Line and four Frigates, but is to be increased in the summer, when we shall not want for amusement, I make no doubt, as our Commodore does not like to be idle.

"I suppose your curiosity is excited by the word *Commodore* Nelson. It gives me infinite pleasure to be able to relieve it by informing you that our good Captain has had this additional mark of distinction conferred upon him, which, I daresay you will agree with me, his merit richly deserves. His Broad Pendant is now flying; therefore I must beg my dear father to draw an additional cork."

This appointment had been made on the day of Buonaparte's Nice order.

Chapter VII

1796–1797
(ætat. 37–38)

"NELSON'S PATENT BRIDGE
FOR BOARDING FIRST-RATES"

I

THE end of a chapter came on June 11, 1796, when Commodore Nelson shifted his broad pendant from the *Agamemnon* to the *Captain*—a 74. Orders had come from England for a second-rate and the worst ship-of-the-line to go home with a convoy. There could be no doubt that the *Agamemnon* must go, and for a week Nelson seemed likely to go with her. However, Captain J. S. Smith of the *Captain* confessed to a very weak state of health and great anxiety to get home, whereas Commodore Nelson assured Sir John Jervis, on June 3, that in spite of insomnia and chest trouble, to tell the truth, when he was actively employed, he was "not so bad", and on June 5, "Having slept since my last letter, indeed, I cannot bear the thoughts of leaving your command." In the end, he had four hours in which to "change all my matters".

His last days in the *Agamemnon* were, with a single exception, entirely depressing. Throughout May, in strange changeable weather, amongst fogs, brilliant sun, heavy seas and sudden stark calms, his business was to forward to his Admiral news of uninterrupted French successes in Italy. He reported Buonaparte's defeat of the Allies at the battle of Montenotte on April 12, in the gorges of Millesimo, at the village of Dego and at the bridge of Lodi. Sardinia had made peace; Naples was preparing to desert; Spain was getting ready; Genoa had begun to be openly insolent ("Commodore Nelson is very much surprised that, whenever he approaches any Town belonging to the Genoese Government, they fire shot at him"). Milan presented her keys to the conqueror, and on May 15 Buonaparte rode into the capital of Lombardy through the Porta Romana on a little white horse. Nelson mentioned without comment that the first pictures of Italy were being sent to Paris "to decorate the Palace of the Louvre", and that a demand had been made upon Rome for "the famous statue of the Apollo Belvidere". Since his last hopes of assisting the Austrians to retake Vado Bay, or of landing English troops at St. Remo, were now washed out, and he knew that the French were in possession of every supply they needed, he enclosed a note to Jervis, asking that, if he could be in any way more active or useful, his squadron might be recalled, even if this meant that he must strike his distinguishing pendant. Before his Admiral could receive this letter, however, he had the satisfaction of a last small successful action in the *Agamemnon*. Under the guns of Oneglia, on May 30, his squadron captured the siege-train *en route* to Buonaparte at Mantua.

Inevitably he saw the last of the *Agamemnon* with mixed feelings. Her ground tier was giving way. Her appearance, which confirmed his assertion that not an ounce of paint had been sent to him for many months, was, he bitterly said, that of a tub floating on the water. (The last rope sent to him for repairs had been a mere insult, "without exception the worst I ever saw. The twice-laid we make on board is far preferable; indeed I never saw any so bad in my life.") She could have stayed out here, without a thorough refit, for another three months, but not for another winter. Still, as he watched her fade from view on June 18, from Fiorenzo Bay, with his new First Lieutenant, Mr. Edward Berry, by his side, the sum of his reflections was that although the *Diadem* (another 64) was certainly in better plight, yet in point of sailing the *Agamemnon* was much superior.

2

"If I hoist my Flag here," wrote his old pupil to Captain Locker, a few days later, "the *Goliath*, I fancy, will be my Ship!" She was new-coppered, but according to rumour, wretchedly manned and worse disciplined. "However," said he, "the latter I don't mind, if I have but good stuff to work upon." (Brother William received almost a duplicate of this sentence: "I don't mind, if I have but the stuff to work upon.") He had his eye upon a Captain Ralph Willett

Miller as his Flag-Captain, a very solid-looking person, born in New York, thirty-five years past, of a Loyalist family, educated in England, went to sea aged sixteen, three times wounded in action, served under Admirals Barrington, Rodney and Hood; a married man, a father. . . .

The Captain's log of the *Captain*, from the day that Nelson took possession of her in 1796, tells a tale of continual effort, of perpetual motion, under circumstances generally disadvantageous and sometimes heart-breaking. But the latest postscript of a Commander-in-Chief with marked leadership qualities had been "Go on, and prosper". He went on. A blockade of Genoa had to be proclaimed, and very soon of Leghorn, for late in June French troops seized that neutral port so suddenly that only remarkable exertions on the part of Captain Fremantle got away the English shipping and residents. The Pollards were just in time to get on board a French prize, with the best of their furniture and little Hoste, whom Mrs. Pollard had been nursing through malaria. Lady Elliot and her children, returning from a holiday at the Baths of Lucca, embarked with nothing except the clothes in which they had happened to be standing up when Fremantle appeared to hurry them down by-streets to the *Dolphin*.

Another British family, who had fled at top speed from Florence (and arrived at the Consulate to jettison two expensive coaches with scarcely a pang, in their relief to discover that a squadron of the fleet was there), claimed permanent attention from the young officer in charge of the evacuation. The Wynnes were perhaps hardly recognisable as an English family, since Mr. Richard Wynne (of Welsh extraction, son of a passionate Venetian mother and husband of a neurasthenic French lady) had despairingly sold the last of his property in Lincolnshire soon after the birth of his fifth successive daughter, and had since been expending the result in the best society on the Continent. He was an attractive, futile man of two-and-fifty, of the type sent to the guillotine in France, and his *suite* usually included, besides his Catholic wife, grown-up daughter (unhappily married to an Italian) and four schoolgirl daughters, some nineteen dependants, exclusive of dogs and horses. Miss Betsy Wynne, a small and fairy-like creature, chattering French and

Italian, but able to remember England, met in Captain Fremantle of His Britannic Majesty's Navy probably the first straightforward and efficient man of her life. This was fatal to her peace of mind, and before he had left his charges in safety at Bastia, Fremantle too had lost his heart. The situation of the young lovers seemed desperate, for Sir John Jervis had often announced that "an officer who marries is damned for the Service", and had been capable of asking the First Lord to order instantly "to the East or West Indies, to cool" a Captain who had rashly plighted troth with a naval store-keeper's daughter at Gibraltar ("a very bad party for him"). The Commander-in-Chief, however, took an unexpected view of romance when personified by a young lady of good physique, blood and fortune. He dubbed the decorative Wynnes "the Amiables", invited them all on board his flagship, and sheltered them under a benevolent wing for many months. The result was invaluable to biographers of Nelson, for both Miss Betsy and Miss Jenny Wynne kept journals, preserved by their descendants.

From no other source is it possible to appreciate, so exactly, the impression made by Jervis's fleet on an audience to whom Britain's Navy had been previously nothing but a name. Its strong, fine frigates appeared to the bright eyes of these young ladies so remarkably clean. Its ships-of-the-line were "castles" (though the *Victory*, the same size as the *Britannia*, and in the highest order, was possessed of disappointingly smaller and less comfortable "apartments"). On the decks of the *Lively* and the *Inconstant*, "most elegantly dres't up, all the guns being removed", they enjoyed famous suppers after dancing to the strains of crack bands, and the officers attendant always kind, gay and civil, "doing the honors so well", under such difficult circumstances, seemed qualified to win everybody's heart. All were, at first sight, "equally complaissant and good-natured". "They live like brothers together, and give all they have." A tiny, childish candle is held up to the rugged countenances of many of Nelson's daily companions. Foley kept a good table; his ship was "a little town—you get all your desires in it". The penurious Cockburn was sprightly and fashionable, Saumarez the glass of fashion, Bowen could be satirical about a spoilt beauty, Drinkwater was the most agreeable society imaginable; General de Burgh, always writing angry letters, was, by general consent, always wrong. And since the scene was set in real life, on a closer view less happy characters flitted across it—Lieutenants, little, starved-looking and anxious, chattering and forward, married and miserable; Captains, stingy, dark and brutal; military gentlemen drinking remarkably hard. . . . There are brilliant *vignettes* of a convoy at sea—the *Inconstant* coming close enough to the *Achilles* for her Captain to roar out that he was in a great rage at having to run away from the French; "Captain F. going to the Fleet", waving farewell (while the motion of the ship was terrible); "Old Admiral Jervis" bowing and smiling from his stern gallery to young ladies, "a curiosity in his Fleet". Naturally, junior Captains and Lieutenants absorbed most of the attention of diarists in their 'teens. To such, the difference in age between Commodore Nelson, who was thirty-eight, and Admiral Jervis, who was sixty-two, was not discernible. And except that "the noise and crashing of the guns was most tiring", and that when a frigate was cleared for action the ladies dining in the gun-room found the atmosphere induced somnolence, there are few references to the fact that they were guests of a squadron engaged in a death grapple for the possession of the Mediterranean.

3

After the departure of Captain Fremantle's squadron from Leghorn with the refugees, Buonaparte made a dramatic appearance, on a flying visit, took possession of the house of Mr. Udney, Consul, and at dinner with the Grand Duke asked to be shown the road to Rome. Nelson wrote to Sir Gilbert Elliot, in hopes that an attack on Leghorn by troops from Corsica might be engineered, but the Viceroy's reply was that the landing of small parties of Corsicans in the French service in the island was becoming a menace and must be stopped, by the seizure of Elba. Nelson successfully conveyed troops, under the command of his old acquaintance, Major Duncan, from Bastia to Porto Ferrajo and returned to blockade Leghorn and Genoa. Last November, when the date had arrived for the election of a new Doge at Genoa, he had nourished hopes of the election of a firmer character, more kindly disposed towards English interests. But a thing unprecedented had occurred. Signor Giacomo Maria Brignole had been requested, in a period of extreme stress, to continue in office. The French were to make the same request after their abolition of the Genoese constitution in the following May, and keep him for six months in nominal power. Nelson's efforts to persuade an opportunist to remain at least neutral were vain, and on September 18 a letter of the Vicereine of Corsica described the hurried appearance of the Commodore to consult with her husband.

The Vicereine's letters home were stoic. She described Corsica as "still as the sea; we ride every evening till nine o'clock by moonlight, and have no more palpitation, when we meet a man with a gun, than in England a peasant with a stick". But a fortnight later, when, after eight months' silence, despatches from London arrived for the Viceroy, her husband's brow grew very grave, and when Nelson made his second sudden appearance at the palace with great glass folding doors, on the night of September 29, the atmosphere was high tragedy. He came in haste from Leghorn, to protect Corsica from a French landing. Sir John Jervis had appointed him a Commodore, First Class, on August 11, and the sterling Miller was now his Captain. He had, on hearing of the rumoured French expedition, transferred his broad pendant to the *Diadem*, and sent the *Captain* down to Ajaccio, under the command of Berry. On his arrival at Bastia he had received orders from his Admiral, labelled "most secret", which were indeed a thunderbolt. News of the decision of the Cabinet to "withdraw the blessings of the British Constitution from the people of Corsica" and the British fleet from the Mediterranean had reached Sir Gilbert Elliot and Sir John Jervis simultaneously. Only Sir John received part of these summary instructions without strong emotion. He had for some time considered that for England to retain Corsica, when at war with Spain, would not be possible. He now looked forward to an early meeting with the large but rotten Spanish fleet. To Nelson, all the instructions were "sackcloth and ashes". There was a supreme irony in the fact that he, who had been chiefly responsible for the capture of Bastia, should be the officer ordered to conduct its evacuation. In London, the authorities had not yet decided whether his loss of an eye at the siege of Calvi constituted, financially, the loss of a limb. He had not forgotten, and never would forget, the unparalleled exertions of his seamen landed, the loss of Serocold and young Moutray, the Lion Sun and the fever. He had long since outgrown his love at first sight for the rust-red rocks and deep blue waters of a promised isle. Once his orders were digested, he was coolly prepared, if necessary, to "knock down Bastia". But that the fleet should leave the Mediterranean seemed to him a sheer disgrace. "They at home do not know what the Fleet is capable of performing—anything and everything. Of all Fleets I ever saw, I never beheld one, in point of officers and men, equal to Sir John Jervis's, who is a Commander-in-Chief to lead them to glory." He had also, in three years, conceived a strong possessive affection for the Mediterranean—that extraordinary compound of fickle seas, blazing flowers, palm-crowned crags, ancient towers, turning a ruined shoulder to warm sun in midwinter, and bleached towns, famous for two thousand years for their gaiety and the cure of chest complaints. "Indeed, this Country agrees much better with my constitution than England." He foresaw that, shuddering amongst what he called "the cold damps" of home, his fancy would return to villages predominantly of the shade known as "Naples yellow", couched amongst silvery olive-groves, under lavender skies; to happy returns to quay-sides, canopied by stars, where music sounded from every open window; to autumn mists parting at 10 a.m. to display Genoa the Superb; to the glow of Vesuvius, above a ship-of-the-line, becalmed in full moonlight in the Bay of Naples. . . .

He found Sir Gilbert "low and distressed". The Viceroy repeated that he believed Corsica to be at the moment in a state of most perfect loyalty to the King and affection for the British Nation. His astonishment and disappointment at his orders were profound. The embittered and theatrical quarrels between the Corsicans friendly to England, whose thirst for place, and universal vanity, were incredible, had from the first made his life a burden. In the patriot General Paoli, who had now retired to London, disgusted with the favour shown to his compatriot, M. Pozzo di Borgo, his interest had for some time been at a low ebb.

Sir Gilbert believed that the number of French royalists and

Corsicans whom he was bound to remove from the vengeance to come would not exceed six hundred. His own intention was to go directly to Naples, since Nelson agreed with him that no chance must be lost to keep the King, who had already made an armistice, from proceeding to a peace with France. Lady Elliot, Miss Congleton and the children (with the exception of George, now a midshipman) must return to Scotland at once. The prospect for the father of a family was not reassuring. Nelson offered the *Gorgon*, one of his fastest frigates, adding that if His Excellency wanted another ship, he must, and would, spare one. Sir Gilbert said heavily that the *Gorgon* would suffice, and that he would provision her. The childless Commodore could only repeat his confidence in Captain Dixon (who should be told, under all circumstances, to run and not fight), and suggest that Lady Elliot should be begged on no account to quit the "coach"—the apartment near the stern of the frigate usually occupied by the Captain. It was arranged that the *Gorgon* should sail from Gibraltar within the week. The morning of the 21st was settled as the earliest possible date for the embarkation of the Bastia garrison. With the assurance that, as far as his powers and abilities went, he could be relied upon, the Commodore then parted from the stricken but still stately Viceroy, to become very busy.

Their next private consultation took place a fortnight later, and after dark, but in a house from which the mistress and children were already gone, and echoing to the sounds of the removal of luggage. No sooner had the Viceroy given official notice to the Municipality of Bastia that the island was to be evacuated, than they had taken the law into their own hands. They had appointed a Committee of Thirty to carry on the government until the French should arrive, sequestered all British property, forbidden any vessel to quit the mole and sent a delegation to the Corsican Generals in the French service at Leghorn. Nelson arrived, this time, by the garden path. He had not waited for the *Diadem* to anchor. He found the situation fully as serious as he had been led to expect, but the Viceroy in typically resolute mood. During the next twenty-four hours he was fortunately too much engaged to reflect upon "miserable anxiety" for the safety of a gentleman of worth and wisdom. From the Viceroy's house he went, through black darkness and wild weather, to General de Burgh, who told him that there were as many hostile armed Corsican as British troops in the citadel, and that he had not a hope of saving any stores, guns or provisions. The gale, still raging, had driven H.M.S. *Southampton* and every transport from their anchors; a privateer was moored across the mole-head, by orders of the Committee, and Corsican musketeers mounted guard at every post. "Commodore Nelson," reported Sir John Jervis to Lord Spencer, "by the firm tone he held, soon reduced these gentlemen to order."

By midnight on October 15th the streets of Bastia were silent as the grave. Nelson's suggestion to General de Burgh that the gates of the citadel should be closed, to prevent more French partisans entering, had produced peace, not a riot, as had seemed equally likely. The Viceroy was safe on board *La Minerve*, a French prize frigate, philosophically pondering fresh despatches from Whitehall which told him, if it was too late to counter-order the evacuation of Corsica, to retain Elba. "Wonderful", commented Nelson. "Do His Majesty's Ministers know their own minds?" Since it was certainly too late, he set heartily to work to save what time, and a very heavy surf, would permit; an effort which was continued until sunset on the 19th. "Our boats never ceased, night or day." The garrison marched out at midnight, and by 1 a.m. French troops were passing into the back of the town. "From its blowing a gale," stated Nelson in conclusion, "it was dawn of day before the General and myself went into the barge, not one man being left ashore; and we took with us the two field-pieces brought down to cover our retreat." He stood for Elba, with a fine wind, at 6 a.m. (unaware that the Spanish fleet, consisting of thirty-eight sail-of-the-line and ten frigates, was already abreast of Cape Corse), and before dark was able to announce, "Every man and vessel safely moored in Porto Ferrajo, for its size the most complete port in the world." The garrisons from Calvi and Ajaccio came in without an accident, within the week, and his arrangements for the Elliot family were as successful.

4

"I remember", wrote Nelson to Locker, from the *Captain*, at sea, on November 5, 1796, "when we quitted Toulon we endeavoured to reconcile ourselves to Corsica; now we are content with Elba—such things are." Worse were to come. When the fleet arrived at Gibraltar, three weeks later, fears that Admiral Man had, in defiance of orders, taken his squadron home, became a certainty. All ideas of a meeting with the combined French and Spanish fleets in the Mediterranean had to be laid aside by the infuriated Jervis, and Nelson's next orders were to bring away the troops from Elba. To a four-line note addressed to Collingwood, in which he hoped that his friend had heard from home, and prophesied dire consequences to Man, he scribbled the postscript, "If we are at anchor, will you dine here at 3 o'clock?"

Collingwood, who had, five years past, concluded a somewhat slow-paced wooing of a grandniece of his old Captain (now Admiral) Roddam, had been on the Mediterranean station, in command of a 74, for above a year, but the old messmates met so seldom that Nelson had to enquire by letter such facts as "How many children have you?" They kept their friendship in repair by gifts of fresh vegetables and old newspapers, jottings of the latest dates on which they had heard from home, and on their rare occasions of leisured encounter (prefaced by Nelson's "Then we can Talk") they explored every aspect of private and public affairs. Collingwood's confidence in "my friend Nelson, whose spirit is equal to all undertakings, and whose resources are fitted to all occasions", was a steady flame, but the father of Miss Sarah and Miss May Patience Collingwood had been shocked by the breakdown, within the year, of the Prince of Wales's marriage, and could not understand the comment of his less happily situated contemporary, "What have we to do with the Prince's private *amours*? The World says there are faults on both sides: like enough. Thank God, I was not born in high life." Since he had not been born in high life, had heard nothing more of his promotion, and knew that Sir Gilbert Elliot's diplomat brother-in-law had been ordered to Paris to open peace negotiations, one of the questions which two officers high on the post list had to discuss after dinner on a December day of easterly gale off Gibraltar was whether Nelson would do well to seek the interest of newly made but influential friends, all of whom, he believed, would give him a good character to those in high life at home—"a public letter of my conduct, as has come under their knowledge". The fleet was to leave the Mediterranean, therefore he would probably see no more of their Excellencies the British Ministers at Genoa, Naples and Leghorn, and the ex-Viceroy of Corsica. Making such applications was not a very pleasant business, but "God knows," said Nelson ruefully, "ambition has no end." He knew that he stood well with Sir John Jervis, who had done all that he could, and now could but repeat that Lord Spencer had expressed his sincere desire to give Commodore Nelson his flag.

All Nelson's letters were written, and all had produced most kindly response, before the first month had passed of a New Year which was to bring him such an opportunity of distinguishing himself as to render them unnecessary. He wrote also, before he left Gibraltar, to his wife, telling her, "I am going on a most important Mission, which, with God's blessing, I have little doubt of accomplishing. It is not a fighting Mission, therefore be not uneasy." Having hoisted his broad pendant in the *Minerve*, and taken the *Blanche* in company, he then set out, on December 15, on his extremely perilous passage up the Mediterranean to save the Elba garrison.

Five nights later, off Cartagena, amongst fresh gales and cloudy weather, the *Minerve* and *Blanche* encountered two Spanish frigates (one of which carried a poop-light), hailed them, and receiving a defiant answer, commenced action. The *Santa Sabina*, engaged by the *Minerve*, after losing her mizzen mast, her main and fore masts, and having a hundred and sixty-four men killed or wounded, struck her colours. Her Captain, the sole surviving officer, came on board the *Minerve* to surrender himself and give up his sword. His mien was haughty, even for a Spanish grandee. His swarthy visage of high features, which seemed marked by heredity for misfortune, struck some chord of memory. He introduced himself to Commodore Nelson as Don Jacobo Stuart, great-grandson of James II, one-time Lord High Admiral, and King of England, Scotland and Ireland. Nelson recounted:

"When I hailed the Don and told him, 'This is an English Frigate', and demanded his surrender, or I would fire into him, his answer was noble, and such as became the illustrious family from which he is descended—'This is a Spanish Frigate, and you may begin as soon as you please.' I have no idea of a closer and sharper battle. . . . I asked him several times to surrender, during the Action, but his answer was, 'No, sir; not whilst I have the means of fighting left!' "

The *Santa Sabina* was taken in tow, but three hours later another frigate, after hailing her in Spanish, fired a broadside into her. The *Minerve* cast off her prize and engaged the stranger, who, after three-quarters of an hour's warm action, wore and stood away. Daylight displayed her having joined two Spanish line-of-battle ships and a frigate. By 9.30 a.m. the *Minerve*, with all her masts shot through, and furniture much cut, was being chased, and saw, bearing to the east, a fleet which her commander could only suppose to be that of Spain. The *Santa Sabina* and the *Ceres*, both with prize crews on board, were retaken, but after dark the enemy quitted the pursuit. "We very nearly", considered Nelson, on Christmas Eve, "escaped visiting a Spanish prison. Two lieutenants and a number of our men are taken, and we have lost near fifty killed and wounded; but 'tis well it's no more." He finished the day by capturing, off the south end of Sardinia, a French privateer, three days out from Marseille, and dictating letters to His Excellency Don Miguel Gaston, Captain General of the Department of Cartagena, and Admiral Don Juan Marino, couched in old chivalrous style.

"Sir,

"The fortune of war put *La Sabina* into my possession after she had been most gallantly defended; the fickle Dame returned her to you with some of my officers and men in her.

"I have endeavoured to make the captivity of Don Jacobo Stuart, her brave Commander, as light as possible; and I trust to the generosity of your Nation for its being reciprocal for the British officers and men.

"I consent, Sir, that Don Jacobo may be exchanged, and at full liberty to serve his King, when Lieutenants Culverhouse and Hardy are delivered into the garrison of Gibraltar."

On the wet afternoon of Christmas Day he arrived at Porto Ferrajo, to fresh troubles. These, however, were not at once evident. At Porto Ferrajo a Military Ball was toward, and Captains Cockburn and Fremantle had promised to send a barge for the Misses Wynne, who had been mentioning the ball in their prayers, and had made all arrangements to change into their gala at the town house of their friends, the Cantinis. "Commodore Nelson, who was going to take the command of this place", was mentioned in Miss Betsy's carefully kept journal as the leader of the party that "had to trot about in the dirt" of a wet night towards the theatre of the town, where the ball was staged amongst very pretty decorations. It was essentially a provincial affair. Captain Woodhouse got "perfectly drunk". The principal Shylock of the place had managed to secure an invitation, several Italian and Corsican ladies, and some French girls, who, imagining that the Misses Wynne understood no language but their own, commented favourably on the unexpected elegance of the English misses. But as Commodore Nelson and the sea-officers of the station, escorting their countrywomen, entered to be formally received by General de Burgh, Commander of the Garrison, the band struck up "See the Conquering Hero comes!" and this was followed by "Rule Britannia". Before 3 a.m. the Commodore had been brought to realise that an arduous action which he had, in the chagrin of losing his prizes, written down as "an unpleasant tale" would be mentioned in the *Gazette*, "and I may venture to say, it was what I know the English like".

Later on the same winter's morning, he found time to visit Mr. Wynne's country house, and intimate to that vacillating displaced person that "as a friend" he would advise him to take the chance of sailing for Naples, with Captain Fremantle, who was going there on an undisclosed mission. His troubles began with his call on General de Burgh, who was agreeable as ever, but "under a great embarrassment for want of precise orders". "My instructions," explained Nelson, "both written and verbal, are so clear that it is impossible for me to mistake a tittle of them." Sir John Jervis had sent him to take under his command the seventeen ships stationed at Porto Ferrajo, and to remove all troops and stores lately brought from Corsica. The Artillery and First Regiment of Foot were to be landed at Gibraltar; all other troops, British and foreign, were to be carried to Lisbon. The General replied that he had always been of the opinion that the signature of a peace between Naples and France ought to be the signal for his quitting Porto Ferrajo. Now that he was advised that the British fleet would never again come there, he believed that the troops under his command could fulfil no useful object by staying in Elba. But without written authority from London, annulling the orders under which he had been sent to Elba, he could not feel himself justified in taking the responsibility of quitting his post. Restrained letters began to pass daily between the embarrassed General and the impatient Commodore, who declared that whether the troops came or not, he was going to withdraw all naval stores, and as many ships as possible. "The object of our Fleet in future is the defence of Portugal, and keeping in the Mediterranean the Combined Fleets." He was on tenterhooks lest he should miss a fleet action under the flag of Jervis, who had announced that his first meeting with the enemy should be no "half-begotten" battle. Presently, the General was brought to agree that if the ex-Viceroy of Corsica would assure him in writing that the Government wished him to depart, his mind would be easy. Nelson, who had already sent Fremantle to Naples, with orders to stay, if possible, no more than forty-eight hours, while awaiting Sir Gilbert Elliot, or the orders from home which the aggrieved General said that he ought to expect, began to collect his squadron.

Sir Gilbert and staff did not appear until 3 a.m. on January 22. The ex-Viceroy had been upon a valuable tour of the Italian states. But the appearance of this wary Scots politician at Porto Ferrajo by no means simplified the situation. Sir Gilbert, whose own experience of waiting for orders from His Majesty's Ministers was bitter, refused to put his name to any document purporting to interpret their possible pleasure. He disagreed with the Commodore and the General as to the advisability of quitting Elba, and had a slight passage-at-arms with de Burgh, who let slip, with a sneer, the word "politics". The ex-Viceroy of Corsica, fresh from a most cordial reception at Rome and Naples, considered a superior British fleet in the Mediterranean an essential measure for securing Italy, and indeed Europe, from the domination of the French Republic, "politics" which he believed represented the sentiments of all His Majesty's Ministers. After composing a letter which he knew would cause his poor friend the Duke of Portland to raise his spectacles to his forehead, sigh deeply and do nothing for a fortnight, Sir Gilbert gladly went on board the *Minerve*, and prepared for a protracted passage to Gibraltar, since the indefatigable Nelson said that he must, in order to bring his Commander-in-Chief the latest news of the enemy, look in *en route* at Toulon, Mahon and Cartagena.

The Captain's cabin in the *Inconstant* was filled with what Commodore Nelson, invited to view the glowing spoil, could only describe as "pretty things". The efficient Fremantle had managed, during his brief stay at Naples, to secure Miss Betsy Wynne, with £8,000. Two very weak characters had been swiftly overruled by two of great vigour. Mr. and Mrs. Wynne had proved no match for Lady Hamilton, instructed by a British sea-officer. The hasty wedding had been staged at the Embassy, and Lady Hamilton had taken complete charge. The impression made by "the well-known and admired" Ambassadress on a moist bride and bridesmaid had been remarkable. Miss Eugenia Wynne, attending her sister, had noted Lady Hamilton as "four or five and twenty, in the bloom of youth and beauty, full of graces and accomplishments", yet principally admirable for her delicate, warm and sincere attentions "to a husband of past 70".

The Pollards, also refugees from Leghorn, were now struggling to establish themselves at Naples, and Mrs. Pollard had sent Commodore Nelson her kind remembrances, a large box of the Neapolitan native ware which he liked, and an aggrieved message. The Commodore replied at once to say that the box was very handsome, just the thing he wished, that he was far from having forgotten Pollard, and if he had any interest in appointing agents for prizes, would certainly name him amongst them. He hoped that the Pollards might, before long, be happily restored to Leghorn. Since seeing the very handsome things Fremantle had got, he must request Mrs. Pollard to be good enough to lay out ten or twelve pounds on Naples gifts for Mrs. Nelson, anything "such as may please a most elegant woman". What he had particularly admired amongst Mrs. Fremantle's *trousseau* was the Italian silks—"shawls, particularly large handkerchiefs".

Although he viewed with apprehension Fremantle's addition to his cabin of a curly-headed young lady of seventeen in a white gown, who played upon the harpsichord and sang very sweetly, he shouldered some responsibility for the match, and accepted the invitation of the happy couple to dine in the *Inconstant*. Mrs. Fremantle recorded her little party of five sea-officers as "very noisy. Old Nelson very civil, and good-natured, but does not say much".

Nelson during these days had been what he called "active". Having left de Burgh sufficient transports to remove his troops in three days, and a small escort, he prepared to go down to Gibraltar, "sure of a pleasant party, let what will happen". Sir Gilbert Elliot was the best company in the world; his advice was "a treasure", and the ex-Viceroy had brought amongst his staff a successful author, Colonel John Drinkwater, whose *Siege of Gibraltar*, dedicated to His Gracious Majesty, had run into three editions in as many years. The handsome Colonel had a singularly uninformed enthusiasm for life at sea (although his father had at one time been a naval surgeon), painted delightfully in water-colours, and, as *aide-de-camp* to Sir Gilbert, had very properly fallen in love with Sir Gilbert's eligible cousin, Miss Eleanor Congleton. It was something of a blow to Nelson to discover that until after Gibraltar he could not offer Colonel Drinkwater accommodation in the *Minerve*. For Sir Gilbert had also brought with him his late Secretary of State, M. Pozzo di Borgo. Indeed, he had no choice at present but to carry this unfortunate and very sea-sick gentleman everywhere with him, for the name of M. Pozzo di Borgo had not been amongst those mentioned in the general amnesty when French troops landed in Corsica, and on his recent travels in Italy a demand had been made by the French Government for his arrest. His politics at present seemed concentrated in loathing of the Buonaparte family (also of Ajaccio). However, he was a nobleman by birth, and spoke fluent English in a penetrating voice.

Sir Gilbert's Italian tour had been rewarding. At Naples he had been received with more than civility. He had suffered a pang when he bowed over the hand of the Queen of Naples. A family likeness to her sister, the murdered Marie Antoinette, had carried his fancy instantly to the last public dinner attended by him at Versailles, "where the Queen of France, then Dauphiness, was in all the glory and lustre of Burke's morning star". His report on Maria Carolina was favourable. He had spent many pleasant quiet evenings with the royal family, and the Queen, having ordered the Theatre of San Carlo to be lighted up, had herself conducted him around it, taking his arm, "as gracious as any queen could be". The King, toasting the English nation publicly at his dinner-table, and carrying his English guest to view the factory of Belvedere, "where he seemed like a father in the midst of his family", had shown in a better light than after a morning's sport at Carditelli, when he had been sulky at securing nothing more than fifteen wild boars, four foxes, two fawns and a hare. The effusive welcome of the English Ambassadress, delighted to entertain any friend of England and her "Sir Willum", had not been much to the taste of a Border laird. Sir Gilbert admitted that Lady Hamilton's face was beautiful. The pains she had taken to acquire education and accomplishments were remarkable and laudable. After a performance of her "Attitudes" his allegiance had almost been won. But a Scottish gentleman, slightly below middle height and by nature reserved, had recoiled instinctively from a voiceful, glowing, sea-side hostess whose person seemed to him "nothing short of monstrous for its enormity"; and he could not but resent the spectacle of Sir William Hamilton, grandson of a Scottish duke, married in his senescence to a blooming mistress of doubtful antecedents. To his own lady he confided, "With men, her language and conversation are exaggerations of anything I ever heard anywhere; and I was wonderfully struck with these inveterate remains of her origin: though the impression was very much weakened by seeing the other ladies of Naples."

The pleasant party bound for Gibraltar sailed on January 29, the *Minerve* for Toulon, the *Romulus* and *Southampton* in charge of a convoy of transports, in two divisions, and with orders to take different courses, so that one, at any rate, might escape the enemy. The wind was foul for Mahon, so Nelson cut Minorca out of his programme. Finding at Cartagena that the Spanish fleet had left that port, he hurried. At Gibraltar he learnt that the enemy had passed the Rock to the westward, and that Sir John Jervis, determined to intercept them on their passage to Brest, had taken up his station off Cadiz. He paused only to collect his two Lieutenants, Culverhouse and Hardy, with the prize crews taken in the *Santa Sabina*, and weighed in the forenoon of February 11. Two Spanish sail-of-the-line and a frigate, at anchor at the head of the bay, also weighed, and began to chase him. The *Minerve* cleared for action. When Colonel Drinkwater asked the Commodore whether he thought an action possible, the Commodore replied, "Very possible. But", looking up at his broad pendant, "before the Dons get hold of that bit of bunting, I will have a struggle with them, and sooner than give up the frigate, I'll run her ashore."

The Commodore and his party, which now included an author taking notes, presently sat down to dine with true British phlegm, the Spaniards meanwhile overhauling them. Colonel Drinkwater was in the act of congratulating his neighbour, the large and somewhat blockish-looking Lieutenant called Hardy, on his escape from being a prisoner of war, when the warm hum of conversation was arrested by the cold cry of "Man overboard!" The officers of the frigate sped to the quarter-deck. Sir Gilbert and *suite* hurried to the stern windows, and beheld, in February dusk, a white wake whirling into designs more intricate than those of any Oriental magic carpet. At first they could see nothing but most intimidating-looking waters, through which they seemed to be moving very fast, but in an incredibly short time they got an excellent view of the lowering of a jolly boat, in which Colonel Drinkwater recognised, as the officer in charge, his late large dinner-partner. The landsmen watched breathlessly while the current of the Straits, running strongly to the eastward, carried the little boat far astern of the *Minerve* and towards the foremost pursuing Spanish sail-of-the-line. After a breathless interval Lieutenant Hardy made a signal, interpreted to them as, "No sign of the missing man". The boat's crew pulled "might and main" to regain the frigate, but seemed to make hardly any progress. When *Le Terrible*, the foremost Spanish sail-of-the-line, was almost within gunshot of the *Minerve*, "By God!" exclaimed Commodore Nelson, "I'll not lose Hardy! Back that mizzen-topsail." To the landsmen in the *Minerve*, their destruction now seemed only a matter of minutes, but, to their stupefaction, *Le Terrible* proceeded to shorten sail, in order to allow her consort to join her, and in the time given, the *Minerve* dropped down to the jolly boat and took out Hardy and his crew. In the winding of the Straits she soon regained her lost distance and by sunset, steering further to the southward, lost sight of the enemy. The only explanation could be that the Commodore's daring action had been misinterpreted by the Spaniards. They had evidently supposed that the *Minerve* had sighted the British fleet approaching from the west, and was offering action.

Darkness succeeded sunset, and with darkness in the Straits on that February night came fog. The little *Minerve* found herself alone in clammy blue gloom, surrounded by strange sounds, strange sails. Colonel Drinkwater, an author, and in love, sharing the Commodore's cabin with Sir Gilbert Elliot, noticed with mingled admiration and surprise that his employer slept soundly through the Commodore's first wordless incursion. After Nelson's second *affairé* visit he felt himself obliged to arouse Sir Gilbert, and explain that they were apparently either amongst the Spanish fleet or a convoy bound for the West Indies. The Commodore had briefly said that if his second guess was correct, it would be his duty to give the earliest intimation to the British Commander on the West Indies station. Sir Gilbert, faced in the small hours, after an exhausting day, with the prospect of a trip to the Antilles, displayed his usual well-bred imperturbability. With the words, "We are only passengers, and must submit to circumstances", he fell asleep again. When morning broke the passengers learnt that they had passed unscathed through the Spanish fleet.

On the morning of February 13 the *Minerve* joined Sir John Jervis's fleet and Nelson moved back into his own ship, the *Captain*. After all, it seemed, he had arrived in time. During the Eve of St. Valentine's Day the wind shifted to the westward, Spanish signal guns sounded repeatedly, and Sir Gilbert Elliot, a Scottish country gentleman, a politician, forty-seven years of age and the father of six, discovered to Sir John Jervis his great desire to assist at "a general action of the British Fleet". The ex-Viceroy's application to be allowed to come on board H.M.S. *Victory*, as a volunteer, was rejected, but at his earnest request the *Lively* frigate, under orders to carry him home directly, was detained, to carry also the news of the approaching naval engagement.

At dawn on the sunless morning of February 14, 1797, the position of the British and Spanish fleets was twenty-five miles west of the

Portuguese headland of St. Vincent, a hundred and fifty miles north-west of Cadiz, for which port the enemy were running, with a fair wind but in poor order. As far as numbers and size went, the fleets, moving one from the westward, the other from the northward, to a common crossing, were most unevenly matched, a fact which was not confirmed to Sir John Jervis until the dense morning mists clinging to the waters began to part. Amongst the many scraps of conversation recorded of that eventful day, none is more character-istic than that which opened between him and the First Captain of the *Victory* at 10.49 a.m.

"There are eight sail-of-the-line, Sir John."

"Very well, sir."

"There are twenty sail-of-the-line, Sir John. . . . Twenty-five. . . . There are twenty-seven sail-of-the-line, Sir John; near double our own!"

"Enough of that, sir! If there are fifty sail, I will go through them. Eng-land badly needs a victory at present."

Captain Ben Hallowell, whose ship had been wrecked a couple of months previously, was serving on board the *Victory* as a volunteer, and happened to be walking back and forth beside the Admiral on the poop. The huge Canadian-born officer, who had been Nelson's constant companion on the batteries at Calvi, so much forgot himself at this exhilarating moment as to deal his Commander-in-Chief a thump on the back, exclaiming, "That's right, Sir John, that's right! And, by God! we shall give them a damned good licking."

The fleet under Jervis's command numbered fifteen sail-of-the-line, of which the *Victory* and *Britannia*, of 100 guns, the *Barfleur* and *Prince George*, of 98, and the *Blenheim* and *Namur*, of 90, were three-deckers. He had eight 74's—H.M.S. *Culloden*, *Colossus*, *Captain*, *Excellent*, *Egmont*, *Goliath*, *Irresistible* and *Orion*. The *Diadem*, a 64, four frigates, a sloop and a cutter completed the array with which he proposed to engage the Spanish Grand Fleet of twenty-seven of the line, ten frigates and a brig. Half a dozen of the Spanish three-deckers carried 112 guns, and the four-decker *Santissima Trinidad*, flagship of Don José de Córdoba, mounted 136. With the exception of one 80, the *San Nicolas*, the other Spaniards were all 74's. But these fine ships, graphically described by the Signal Lieutenant of the *Barfleur* as "Thumpers, looming like Beachy Head in a fog", had been forced to sea in haste, and were all undermanned. A large proportion of their ships' companies were pressed landsmen, and their officers were inexperienced. When they discovered the proximity of the British, they were taken by surprise. They were proceeding leisurely, in a long, straggling line, some side by side in pairs, others in groups of odd numbers, and a gap of some seven miles stretched between their leading division of six and the remaining one-and-twenty. Jervis, before they had time to recover, took the risk he had announced of going through their line. Ten of his ships had been under his command for a couple of years, the other five had recently joined him from the Channel Fleet. "Confident in the skill, valour and discipline of the Officers and Men I had the happiness to command, and judging that the honour of His Majesty's arms, and the circumstances of the War in these seas required a considerable degree of enterprise", at 11.42 a.m. he ordered six of his ships to put on a press of sail and get through the enemy gap. "We flew to them", wrote Collingwood to his wife, "as a hawk to his prey." Troubridge led the van, in the *Culloden*, Collingwood brought up the rear in the *Excellent*.

As they drew near the enemy, nine Spanish ships had passed to the eastward. The gap in their loose formation was wide, but it seemed that, as the two lines were steering, a collision between the tenth Spaniard and the *Culloden* was inevitable. Her First Lieutenant drew the attention of his Captain to this, and received the reply, "Can't help it, Griffiths. Let the weakest fend off." A distant cannonade broke out between the leading ships on either side, but the *Culloden* reserved her fire for the ship which threatened her with collision.

The Spanish backbone was broken, and Jervis's next signal was to tack in succession, his intention being to engage the bulk of the enemy fleet to windward, before the discomfited nine ships to leeward could assist them. By the nine now cut off but a feeble attempt at molestation was made, and only one, running down the British line, and passing to the stern of the *Excellent*, regained the eighteen.

The battle was half won as the British ships proceeded, one by one, to turn towards the north, but the possibility remained that

THE BATTLE OF CAPE ST. VINCENT

February 14, 1797

Reproduced from *Sea Kings of Britain*, by Sir Geoffrey Callender.
By kind permission of Messrs. Longmans, Green and Co., Ltd.

the larger Spanish detachment, by bearing up to pass astern of them, might rejoin the small division, and perhaps escape to Cadiz. It was at this point that a 74, third from the rear of the British line, altered course to the west and threw herself in defiance across the bows of the Spaniards. An independent squadron was needed in this position, to prevent the battle degenerating into the "half-begotten" engagement despised by Jervis; and Nelson, with the *Captain*, had resolved to represent it, offering himself to the attack of at least seven enemy sail-of-the-line. He wore out of his station, and came into close action with the *Santissima Trinidad*, largest fighting ship in the world. In quitting the line he was aware that he was not only acting without orders, he was deliberately disobeying them. A friend came to his assistance.

"I was immediately joined, and most nobly supported, by the *Culloden*, Captain Troubridge. . . . For near an hour, I believe (but do not pretend to be correct as to time), did the *Culloden* and *Captain* support this apparently, but not really, unequal contest; when the *Blenheim*, passing between us and the enemy, gave us a respite, and sickened the Dons."

Two Spanish ships dropped astern, and "being fired into, in a masterly style" by Collingwood, the *San Isidro*, of 74 guns, struck. Nelson believed that the larger *Salvador del Mundo* had also struck, after being attacked by Collingwood, at a distance which that north-country officer reckoned as not longer than a certain well-remembered garden on the banks of the Wansbeck.

"But Captain Collingwood, disdaining the parade of taking possession of beaten enemies, most gallantly pushed up, with every sail set, to save his old friend and messmate, who was to appearance in a critical state."

Jervis, having seen and recognised the brilliance of Nelson's action, had ordered the *Excellent*, last ship in the line, to support him instantly, and the *Blenheim* was soon followed by the *Prince George* and *Orion*. The larger enemy division resumed its former course, but by now the engagement had become close and general. "The *Blenheim*, being ahead, and the *Culloden* crippled and astern, the *Excellent* ranged up within ten feet of the *San Nicolas*, giving a most tremendous fire." At this moment the Spanish 80 luffed incontinently, and the great three-decker *San Josef*, which almost simultaneously received the fire of the *Prince George*, fell foul of her. Nelson's second opportunity of the day had come. His ship had by this time been so much mauled as to be incapable of further service, in the line or in chase. She had lost her fore topmast; her wheel had been shot away. "Not a sail, shroud or rope was left!" He ordered her helm to be put down, and called for a boarding-party. "Captain Miller so judiciously ordered her course" that the *Captain* was laid aboard the starboard quarter of the *San Nicolas*; her sprit-sail yard passed over the Spaniard's poop, and hooked in her mizzen shrouds. The first man to board the enemy 80 was Berry, "late my First Lieutenant", a passenger in the *Captain*, as he had recently been promoted Commander. Miller, anxious to lead, had been directed to remain in charge of the crippled *Captain*, while Nelson undertook this duty. Many "old Agamemnons" were equally eager. "The Soldiers of the 69th Regiment, with an alacrity which will ever do them credit", headed by Lieutenant Charles Pierson, were amongst the foremost. Nelson, with his boarding-party, which included three midshipmen, passed from the fore-chains of his own ship into the enemy's quarter gallery, where the butt of a marine's musket smashed an upper window for their entry. The doors of the cabin in which they found themselves were. locked, and some startled Spanish officers discharged their pistols through the sky-lights, but the doors were quickly forced by the marines, who then opened fire, and amongst the enemy officers to fall, mortally wounded, retreating to the larboard side of the quarter-deck, was the Commodore, Don Tomaso Geraldino.

On the quarter-deck Nelson found Berry in possession of the poop, engaged in hauling down the Spanish ensign. The lower-deck guns of the ship were still replying to the *Prince George*, which was firing into her starboard bow, but as Nelson passed towards the forecastle several officers delivered their swords. This ceremony was interrupted by a spatter of pistol and musket fire from the Admiral's stern gallery of the *San Josef*, and seven men of the boarding-party were instantaneously killed. This much larger ship, inextricably entangled aloft with the *San Nicolas* (now on fire), seemed determined to expel the handful of invaders from her. Nelson, without hesitation, decided to carry a Spanish first-rate from the decks of a Spanish 80. He ordered his marines to return the fusillade, stationed sentinels at the hatchways to keep the enemy below decks, called to Miller to push more men into the *San Nicolas*, and to the cry of "Westminster Abbey, or Glorious Victory!" charged on. Berry was at hand to help him into the main-chains, and another headlong scramble from ship to ship was painfully achieved. But the appearance of resistance from the *San Josef* was deceptive. As the depleted boarding-party came in view, a Spanish officer, looking over the quarter-deck rail, hailed to say that she surrendered. This news, "most welcome" to Nelson, was treated with caution until he found himself on the quarter-deck of the first-rate, where her Flag-Captain, on bended knee, presented his sword and explained that his Admiral, Don Francisco Xavier Winthuysen, was dying of his wounds below. On being assured that the *San Josef* had struck, Nelson gave her Captain his hand, and then asked him to summon his officers and ship's company to hear an announcement of the surrender. This was done, and

"on the quarter-deck of a Spanish first-rate, extravagant as the story may seem, did I receive the swords of the vanquished Spaniards, which, as I received, I gave to William Fearney, one of my bargemen, who put them, with the greatest *sang-froid*, under his arm. I was surrounded by Captain Berry, Lieutenant Pierson (69th Regiment), John Sykes, John Thomson, Francis Cook, all old Agamemnons, and several other brave men, seamen and soldiers. Thus fell these ships."

6

As the announcement, in the Spanish tongue, of the surrender of the *San Josef* died upon the foggy air, Nelson found his hand seized by one of his boarding-party. The man was muttering that "he might not soon have such another place to do it in, and was heartily glad to see me". Spirits were running high amongst a ship's company who realised their achievement as something new in the annals of naval warfare. Nelson's own view of the exploit was temperate. He had had "good fortune" such as did not fall to every man. He afterwards told Locker that he did not pretend that the ships might not have been taken had he not boarded them, but it was far from impossible that they might have forged into the enemy fleet, been taken in tow and reached Cadiz. This disappointing result did occur in the case of two other disabled ships, the *Santissima Trinidad* and the *Soberano*.

He experienced the sensation of being "in a dream" a few moments later, when the *Victory* passed the interlocked group of the *Captain*, *San Nicolas* and *San Josef*, and her men, lining her bulwarks, saluted him with three cheers, an example afterwards followed by every ship in the fleet that day, when they distinguished Commodore Nelson's broad pendant.

The *Captain* was, for the present, useless, but Nelson believed that there might be further work for him to do. The *Minerve* was sending a boat for him. He returned to the *Captain*, and in her cabin addressed himself to his second-in-command—"Miller, I am under the greatest obligations to you." The phrase was modern, but accompanied by a mediæval gesture. Captain Miller found himself the possessor of a sword and a ring—the sword, very fine, lately the property of Don Tomaso Geraldino, the ring of no commercial value, a pale semi-precious stone set round with brilliants, drawn from the finger of a British sea-officer of better blood than fortune.

Nelson ordered Captain Cockburn to put him on board the nearest uninjured ship-of-the-line, which proved to be the *Irresistible*; but, as he regretfully discovered, "the day was too far advanced" for him to venture upon the project of taking possession of the Spanish Admiral's flagship. In February, in poor weather, light fails soon. Jervis was gathering his fleet to protect his prizes and cripples. He had decided to rest content with the possession of four enemy sail-of-the-line (two of them first-rates), more especially as he had only twelve ships left capable of fighting, while the enemy seemed likely to be reinforced by nine which had scarcely been into action. His casualty list was light, and the Spanish fleet had been demonstrably beaten. Córdoba, with his surviving Rear-Admiral and six of his Captains, was to be court-martialled and dismissed the service. By five o'clock all firing had ceased. Gradually the fleets separated, the British standing for Lagos, the Spaniards for Cadiz. Nelson's description of his reception by his Commander-in-Chief was marked by the same temperateness which distinguished all his accounts of personal adventure that day. "At dusk, I went on board the *Victory*, when the Admiral received me on the quarter-deck, and having embraced me, said he could not sufficiently thank me, and used every expression to make me happy." Many months later, in private conversation with his brother-in-law Bolton, he drew a more highly coloured picture of this darkling and dramatic scene. Jervis received him with open arms. Nelson's appearance was remarkable. Most of his hat had been shot away, his shirt and coat were in tatters, and his countenance was freaked with the smoke of gunpowder. (But for that matter, the Admiral himself had been standing too near a marine killed by a shell.) "On my return on board the *Irresistible*," ends Nelson's narrative, "my bruises were looked at, and found but trifling, and a few days made me as well as ever." This was another understatement. His name appeared in the casualty list as "bruised but not obliged to quit the deck". He had, in fact, received a super-ficial wound from a shell-splinter; he had not slept on the nights of the 11th and 13th, and he had been engaging in some violent ac-tivity. The surgeons, perceiving symptoms which might signify internal injury, were uncommunicative, and some rumour of their anxieties spread through the fleet that night. For a week Nelson's "contusion of no consequence" caused him acute pain, and though he reported himself "not near as much hurt as the Doctors fancied", he felt so unwell that he achieved only the briefest of lines to assure his wife—"I am well, Josiah is well." Something a little less per-functory, to Collingwood, was a duty which must be achieved without delay.

"My dearest Friend," he wrote, discarding for the only time in a long correspondence his customary, "Dear Coll.",

" 'A friend in need is a friend indeed,' was never more truly verified than by your most noble and gallant conduct yesterday in sparing the *Captain* from further loss; and I beg, both as a public Officer and a friend, you will accept my most sincere thanks. I have not failed, by letter to the Admiral, to represent the eminent services of the *Excellent*. Tell me how you are; what are your disasters? I cannot tell you much of the *Captain's*, except by Note of Captain Miller's at two this morning, about sixty killed and wounded, masts bad, etc. etc. We shall meet at Lagos; but I could not come near you without assuring you how sensible I am of your assistance in nearly a critical situation. Believe me, as ever, your most affectionate

"Horatio Nelson."

Collingwood, an officer renowned for his icy reserve and unbending demeanour, answered within the hour, offering "My dear good Friend" his congratulations on distinguished services. "You formed the plan of attack—we were only accessories to the Don's ruin. . . . It added very much to the satisfaction which I felt in thumping the Spaniards that I released you a little."

7

On the morning after the greatest naval battle since the Saints, Colonel Drinkwater was delighted to hear the voice of Commodore Nelson enquiring for Sir Gilbert Elliot. He was further delighted when the hero of the hour, finding that Sir Gilbert had gone with the Captain of the *Lively* to the *Victory*, said, "I hoped to have caught him before he saw the Admiral; but come below with me."

"Seated alone with the Commodore", the eager author began by offering, "in the most expressive terms", congratulations on his safety, and on the very distinguished part taken by his ship in yesterday's action, of which many particulars had by this time reached the *Lively*. He added (redundantly, since every officer in the fleet who could spare a moment on a morning which was busy was engaged scribbling a letter home) that, of course, the *Lively* would be bearing the glorious news to England. Nelson, who had received his congratulations with great modesty but evident pleasure, then, "in the most good-natured manner", acceded to a pressing request to give as many details as possible of the proceedings of the *Captain* yesterday, and as he continued, after a brief professional statement, to let drop priceless musings, the author drew towards himself a sheet of paper and a pencil. Presently, the saga, begun with the words, "I'll tell you how it happened", ceased, and the Colonel bound for London began to calculate comfortably the Honours List which must follow such an affair. "The Admiral will, of course, be made a peer, and his seconds in command noticed accordingly. As for you, Commodore, they will make you a baronet." He was arrested by a hand on his arm. "No!"

Nelson returned to the *Irresistible*, to send a line to Sir Gilbert, but it stated little more than the condition of his ship, and his satisfaction that his Admiral thought his reputation "had not been diminished by the events of yesterday". Sir Gilbert's answer, prompt, was in his best style:

"To have been foremost on such a day, could fall to your share alone. Nothing in the world was ever more noble than the transaction of the *Captain,* from beginning to end, and the glorious group of your Ship and her two Prizes, fast in your gripe, was never surpassed, and I daresay never will. I am grieved to hear you are wounded, however slightly you talk of it. . . . I was in hopes you were unhurt, by seeing you on board the *Minerve,* and hearing the cheers you were saluted with. . . . May you speedily recover, and enjoy your honours, and the gratitude and admiration of your Country for many years."

Encouraged by this "affectionate and flattering" letter from the man possessed of "interest", who was accompanying the Admiral's despatches to London, Nelson wrote next day, "If you can be instrumental in keeping back what I expect will happen, it will be an additional obligation." After the victories of Lords Rodney and Howe, in 1782 and '94, baronetage had been bestowed on their junior flag-officers. Nelson mentioned that he was far from disposed to hold such a distinction light, but strongly felt that to accept, without having the means to support, an hereditary title, was a situation that should, if possible, be avoided. As things were, he was having difficulty to "make ends meet", and on taking flag rank must forfeit his pay as a Colonel of Marines. He tentatively added, "There are other Honours, which die with the possessor, and I should be proud to accept, if my efforts are thought worthy of the favour of my King."

The news brought by the *Lively* frigate reached London on March 3, and a *Gazette Extraordinary* was published the same night. Although his fleet had included two Vice-Admirals, a Rear-Admiral and a Commodore, Sir John Jervis's despatch mentioned by name only Calder, his First Captain. His accompanying private letter to Lord Spencer, explaining that "the correct conduct of every Officer and man made it impossible to distinguish one more than the other", went on to name Vice-Admiral Waldegrave, Captains Troubridge, Collingwood, Berry and Hallowell, and Commodore Nelson, "who was in the rear, on the starboard tack, took the lead on the larboard, and contributed very much to the fortune of the day". Nelson had certainly expected that the despatch would tell his family details of his actions which he had not had time to describe in his letter carried by the *Lively*, and when the despatch was seen it aroused criticism in the fleet. It was murmured that an original draft, giving due prominence to Nelson's outstanding services, had been suppressed on a reminder by Calder that the Commodore had, by his unauthorised departure from the prescribed order of attack, created a dangerous precedent. Nelson himself credited an anecdote that when Calder had reported—"Sir, the *Captain* and *Culloden* are separated from the fleet and unsupported, shall we recall them?" Sir John's reply had been, "I will not have them recalled. I put my faith in those ships." He also believed that Sir John was, like himself, not quite satisfied with the engagement, although he could not say so publicly. "We ought", he was still fretting, two months later, "to have had the *Santissima Trinidad* and the *Soberano*, seventy-four. They belonged to us by conquest, and only wanted some good fellow to get alongside them and they were ours. But it is well, and for that reason only, we do not like to say much."

England, which had been badly needing a victory, had no doubt that "it was well". Every gift in the hands of Government was showered on the victors. The thanks of both Houses of Parliament were voted by acclamation; His Majesty sent a personal message to the fleet, and gold medals to the Admirals, Commodore and every Captain of a ship-of-the-line. Sir John Jervis was, as Drinkwater had prophesied, made an Earl (it was said that the King himself had chosen the title—"of St. Vincent"). Admirals Thompson and Parker became baronets, and Waldegrave, already possessed of a courtesy title, was presently rewarded with an Irish peerage; Captain Calder was knighted, and the Order of the Bath was conferred upon Commodore Nelson. Sir Gilbert had not failed him.

Congratulatory letters began to reach Nelson on April 1, but they had all been written a week before the news of the Battle of Cape St. Vincent had reached home. On a promotion of flags, dated February 2, he had become, in the ordinary course of seniority, a Rear-Admiral of the Blue.

At Bath, on February 22, Captain Fane, of the Royal Navy,

literally ran from the coffee-house where he had been scanning the newspapers, to carry the good tidings to a modest couple established in Bennet St., and "I never", wrote Mrs. Horatio Nelson, "saw anything elevate our father equal to this." Little more than a fortnight after the ageing Rector had accomplished a patriarchal screed, opening "My dear Rear-Admiral", came the news of St. Vincent, and he found himself obliged to seek the shelter of his lodging in haste, to shed a private tear, and, in his easy chair, in front of the fire, spend "a useless hour" reflecting gratefully on "the various Events of a long life". On his daily potter to the Market perfect strangers were stopping him to say "Hansom" things of Admiral Nelson's courage and judgment. The post was bringing more letters than Mrs. Horatio could answer in a month. Lord Walpole had written that London was ringing with the name of his relative: at Bath it was being mentioned at the theatre and in the grey streets by the common ballad-singer. The cities of London, Bath, Bristol and Norwich had voted the Admiral their Freedom, and to the capital city of the county of his birth he was sending the sword of the Spanish Admiral Winthuysen. A little before it must be mentioned abroad, he warned his family of his "mark of the Royal Favour, which I was once given to understand I had no likelihood of enjoying", and Maurice was, at his request, communicating with York Herald as to coat-of-arms, crest, motto, etc., for Sir Horatio Nelson, K.B.—

"the supporters, on one side a Sailor, properly habited, holding in his hand the Broad Pendant, on a staff, and trampling on a Spanish flag; on the other side, the British Lion . . . *Crest*—on a wreath of the colours, the stern of a Spanish Man-of-War, proper, inscribed, 'San Josef'. *Motto*—what my brother William suggested, turned into English, 'Faith and Works'."

He added to a holograph copy of his "Few Remarks relative to myself in the *Captain*, in which my pendant was flying on the most glorious Valentine's Day, 1797" a note, "There is a saying in the Fleet too flattering for me to omit telling—viz., 'Nelson's Patent Bridge for boarding First-Rates', alluding to my passing over an Enemy's 80-gun Ship".

More letters than could be answered in a month penetrated to Nelson too, but much more slowly. The first set, congratulating him on his promotion, reached him off Cape St. Mary's; the second, on his performances in the Glorious Action of Valentine's Day, came in the same ship as orders from Jervis to sail for Corsica; the third, on his decoration, found him blockading Cadiz.

His wife wrote:

"My dearest Husband,

"Yesterday I received your letter of February 16th. Thank God you are well, and Josiah. My anxiety was far beyond my powers of expression. M. Nelson and Captain Locker behaved humanely, and attentive to me. They wrote immediately, Captain Locker assuring me that you were perfectly well, Maurice begging me not to believe idle reports, the 'Gazette' saying you were slightly wounded. Altogether, my dearest husband, my sufferings were great . . . . I shall not be myself till I hear from you again. What can I attempt to say to you about Boarding? You have been most wonderfully protected; you have done desperate actions enough. Now may I—indeed I do—beg that you never Board again! *LEAVE* IT for *CAP-TAINS*."

Her next letter repeated her last injunction:

"I sincerely hope, my dear husband, that all these wonderful and desperate actions—such as boarding ships—you will leave to others. With the protection of a Supreme Being, you have acquired a character or name which, all hands agree, cannot be greater; therefore, rest satisfied."

Chapter VIII

1797
(ætat. 38)

IN-SHORE SQUADRON, CADIZ BAY:
SANTA CRUZ, TENERIFFE

I

ON the fresh spring night of April 11, 1797, two old friends of East India days, seated in a patched-up cabin of His Britannic Majesty's Ship *Captain*, at anchor off Cadiz, held deep and private counsel. Their prey, as might be guessed from the maps and charts spread before them, and lit by swaying lanterns, lay in the Atlantic Ocean, in a Spanish-owned archipelago, some sixty miles west of the north-west African coast. Nelson's scheme for a daring combined operation, to which he brought characteristic enthusiasm, might, he claimed, not only immortalise the undertakers and ruin Spain, but actually put an end to the war.

He had gone to sea in the *Irresistible* on March 5, at the first possible moment after the last gasp of a formidable gale, taking with him *La Minerve*, the *Zealous* and the *Culloden*; his instructions had been to look out for the Viceroy of Mexico. This dignitary, also with three of the line, two of them first-rates, was believed to be on his passage to Cadiz, from Havana and Vera Cruz, laden with the gold of the Americas; so a meeting with him might have brought gaudy reward, and was regarded as a most covetable chance. Spain depended so much on the safe arrival of these specie ships (reported to be carrying between six and seven million sterling) that some people were sure her fleet would be obliged to come out, to meet and protect them. Nelson, who had, as he expected, cruised in vain between Cape St. Vincent and the African coast covering the approaches to Cadiz, had no belief in the readiness of the enemy to see further action at present. On his arrival this morning he had found himself, though junior flag-officer, appointed to the command of the in-shore squadron, an honourable post, and in emergency practically independent; but not what he had wanted. Troubridge, who had been on their recent cruise, and had come to dine in the *Captain* after picking up the gossip of the fleet, had mentioned that two frigates were being sent to look for the missing treasure-ships at Santa Cruz of Teneriffe, and that the Chief had said he would be interested to hear Nelson's opinion on the possibility of an attack on that place. Nelson forthwith disclosed "my plan", which had long occupied his thoughts and during his late weeks at sea had been carefully considered.

His letter to Lord St. Vincent urging the attack on Santa Cruz had many points in common with past letters to Lord Hood pleading to be allowed to take Bastia. Given the means he asked, he was equally confident of success. He opened by dealing with the operation by sea. Santa Cruz of Teneriffe, or de Santiago, a sea-port, the capital of Teneriffe and of the Canary Islands, occupied a small plain, bounded by rugged rocks and seamed by water-courses, generally dry. Water was brought to the town in wooden troughs, so the stoppage of this supply should induce a quick surrender. The anchorage was good, and a mole facilitated landing. The shore, although not easy of access, rose steeply from deep water, enabling transports to run in and land an army in twenty-four hours. "I will undertake, with a very small squadron, to do the Naval part." The bay was open to all winds between E. by N. and S.W., and a swell was generally setting in. From April to October the N. or N.E. wind blew upon the island, roughly from 10 a.m. to 6 p.m. In summer this wind produced a dense stratum of sea-cloud, and as a rule, when making Teneriffe from the northward during these months, land was seldom recognisable till within twenty miles of it. The approach by sea to the anchoring place was under very high land, and three valleys —Teneriffe and the adjacent Gomera being twin peaks of a volcanic mass. Spanish ships generally moored with two cables to the sea and four from the stern to the shore. "Therefore, although we might get to be masters of them, should the wind not come off the shore, it does not appear certain we should succeed so completely as we might wish." A surprise attack by night was indicated, and "as to any opposition, except by natural impediments, I should not think it would avail".

Having given a fair picture of every possible difficulty besetting the attempt by sea, he proceeded to unfold "my plan", which entailed military support. By a happy chance, 3,700 trained men, with every necessary munition and store, were already embarked, and since Teneriffe, in its history of three hundred years of Spanish occupation, had never been besieged, the hills that commanded the town had no fortifications. The only drawback was that the detachments at sea were the old Corsican garrison, and he was doubtful whether General de Burgh (who had flatly refused to leave Porto Ferrajo for Gibraltar without London orders) would consent, however rich the prize and propitious the moment, to a suggestion of Lord St. Vincent that men ordered for service in Portugal should be deflected to take part in a combined action on an island of the Canary group. Should General de Burgh refuse to act, he could only suggest that General O'Hara, Governor at Gibraltar, should be approached. This valiant old gentleman, a native of County Sligo, known in the fleet as "Old Cock of the Rock", was constitutionally far from averse from a sporting chance and sudden violent action.

2

On March 7 the First Lord had written, "Admiral Nelson will, I find, prefer a two-decked ship to a larger one, and Admiral Parker may therefore have the choice of the *Victory* or the *Barfleur*." It was from St. Vincent's new flagship, the *Ville de Paris*, on May 27 that Nelson sent a note to Miller, telling him to anchor the *Captain* near the *Theseus*, and transfer his personal effects. Such officers as wished to go with him into the *Theseus*, and such men as came from the *Agamemnon*, and volunteered, might make their preparations. Miller and he could discuss details later. In fact they had much to settle. His new ship had also arrived from Portsmouth. She was not the dreaded *Gibraltar*, but she came with the curse of a bad reputation. St. Vincent called her "an abomination". However, the Commander-in-Chief was flatteringly confident that her condition, the result of a weak Captain and a bullying First Lieutenant, would soon be put to rights by Admiral Nelson and Captain Miller. Amongst the three congratulatory letters from his princely naval friend awaiting Nelson, the one of latest date contained typically violent opinions of the recent trouble at Spithead. "Pardon my gloom", concluded the bachelor Prince (after drawing a lurid picture of "the Fleet at Spithead, during a War, for a whole week, in a complete state of Mutiny", and Ireland, in open rebellion, awaiting French invasion). "I have a very large stake in this Country, and a family of young children to protect." (The first detachment of young Fitz-Clarences to be brought to him by Mrs. Jordan, the famous comedy actress, was openly established at Bushey Park.) Nelson's view of the respectfully expressed demands of the Spithead malcontents was that shared by most well-informed persons. "I am entirely with the Seamen in their first complaint. We are a neglected set." At home, patriotic persons had learnt with horror that the navy's rations were maggoty and underweight, that their medicines were embezzled by their ships' surgeons, and that their leave, wages and pensions were lamentably in arrears and insufficient. Parliament had been quick to vote the necessary sums for increased pay, the Admiralty had made concessions, the sovereign had been prevailed upon to extend a general pardon. For the far more dangerous and largely politically inspired mutineers of the Nore, news of whose misdeeds was yet to reach St. Vincent's fleet, Nelson had presently no sympathy whatsoever. They were scoundrels, and he would be glad to command a ship against them. His immediate object was to discover whether he had got scoundrels or "the stuff to work upon" with the *Theseus*. She had certainly been sent to St. Vincent from the Channel fleet because she had been prominent among the disaffected ships. In a letter to Alexander Davison, headed "*Theseus*, changed from the *Captain* this day ", he made no other mention of his new ship, though he expressed at length his indignation that their Lordships, instead of adequately reinforcing St. Vincent, who was now faced with the possibility of encountering forty-five enemy sail-of-the-line with a force of twenty-two, had seen fit to spare a squadron to cruise, actually on his station. The squadron had, apparently, been sent to catch "the dollars" from Havana, which every veteran under St. Vincent's command considered his perquisite.

On the same night, the report of Captain Miller, after that reliable officer's first inspection of the *Theseus*, was illuminating. The ship, carrying papers which showed that she had been provisioned in March for foreign service, was on May 27 absolutely destitute of stores of all kinds. The boatswain had nothing in his charge; the carpenter could not produce a single nail. As things were at present, should even a rattlin be shot away in action, she had no means of replacement. As she had, as yet, seen no service, nothing could have been used except for routine cleaning. His Flag-Captain withdrew, and Nelson presented his compliments to his Commander-in-Chief, thanked him for his confidential letter delivered by hand ("You may depend on me"), and warned him that the Captain of the Fleet would shortly be receiving a very heavy demand for stores for the *Theseus*. When some of these arrived, it was obvious to every "old Agamemnon" that Admiral Nelson was preparing for action of an interesting nature. They were being set to teach their new companions to make ladders, such as they had constructed before the sieges in Corsica. During the next few weeks, specimen escalade ladders, some over thirty feet long, kept on passing between the Commander-in-Chief's flagship and the *Blenheim* (whose carpenter was late of the *Captain*) and the *Theseus*. Admiral Nelson came to look at them often, and said that they would not take more than ten men at a time—"the actors in our *Comedy* must not be too anxious to *mount*".

Admiral Nelson, it appeared, knew even when the fresh greens, which were always bought largely for his people, failed to arrive in sufficient quantities, and himself interviewed the Spanish market boatmen engaged to deliver them. He had, moreover, gone to the *Swiftsure*, where two poor fellows, suspected of shamming mad in order to get their discharge, were lying in irons, after an attempt to destroy themselves. The result had been that he had written to the Commander-in-Chief asking that Dr. Weir, Physician to the Fleet, should pay a visit to these cases. He had offered to give fifty pounds out of his own pocket to send the younger and less afflicted fellow to a proper place for his recovery, and had recommended both men for discharge. . . .

Within a fortnight of his move into the *Theseus*, a soiled paper, of difficult script, found "dropped on the quarter-deck" during the middle watch, was brought to his hands.

"Success attend Admiral Nelson! God bless Captain Miller! We thank them for the Officers they have placed over us. We are happy and comfortable, and will shed every drop of blood in our veins, and the name of the *Theseus* shall be immortalized as high as the *Captain's*."

It was signed in large block capitals, "SHIP'S COMPANY".

3

The Spanish fleet did not come out on the First of June. On May 30, Rear-Admiral Nelson sent word to His Excellency Admiral Don Josef de Mazaredo that, as June 4 was the birthday of his Royal Master, Lord St. Vincent intended firing a *feu de joie* at 8 p.m., and desired him to mention this, "that the Ladies of Cadiz may not be alarmed". The answer of His Excellency was that "the Ladies of Cadiz, accustomed to the noisy salutes of the vessels of war", would sit to hear what the British Admiral meant to regale them with, and that the Spanish nation, as a whole, could not but interest itself in so august an occasion. Calling upon his Maker to preserve Rear-Admiral Nelson for many years, and kissing his hands, Don Josef (very courteous for a Biscayner) signed himself, "attentive servant". Nelson also was attentive. St. Vincent, out of a strength of twenty sail-of-the-line, eventually spared him ten. The ships-of-the-line had to keep their distance to avoid the shoals, but the small craft of the in-shore squadron kept a ceaseless guard on the harbour mouth, and with darkness every night they reported alongside the *Theseus*, their crews armed with pikes, cutlasses, broad-axes and chopping-knives. Every boat was provided with handspikes, sledge-hammers and ropes to tow off captured vessels, and when they had received their orders, Nelson visited them at their stations. Even on his quarter-deck he was "barely out of shot of a Spanish Rear-Admiral", and close enough to admire the languorous ladies of Cadiz, pacing the walls and Mall of their town, and the merchants peering out anxiously every morning to see whether the Havana convoy had fallen into the hands of the blockading British overnight.

On June 15 the combination of unusual signals, the unmooring of thirteen Spanish ships-of-the-line, and information that their men had been in the market buying much food, raised Nelson's hope of a meeting sufficiently for him to order all ships of his squadron to clear for action. After nearly three weeks of existing in the miserable discomfort unavoidable when the bulkheads were down, he was feeling "very indifferent", and "almost tired of looking at these fellows". A Spanish report said that Mr. Pitt was out of office. From England, first descriptions of the outbreak at the Nore were worrying. Austria had succumbed to Buonaparte and signed the Peace of Leoben, and a French army of invasion was waiting to sail from the mouth of the Texel under cover of a Dutch squadron. By July 3, the *Thunderer* bomb-ketch and *Urchin* gunboat having arrived from Gibraltar, St. Vincent (who had been receiving almost daily letters from Nelson, on the subject of ladders, ammunition, artillery and a devil-cart necessary for the Santa Cruz Expedition) agreed to a bombardment of Cadiz, in the hopes of either bringing out the Spanish fleet or raising a revolution in the town. Nelson wrote what should make a beautiful last letter to his lady—who had begged him to leave dangerous actions to subordinates—opening: "Rest assured of my most perfect love, affection and esteem for your person and character, which the more I see of the world, the more I must admire", and to St. Vincent two very cheerful notes, the first of which ended, "I intend, if alive, and not too tired, to see you to-morrow". His second note asked that all the launches of the fleet, with their cannonades and ammunition, and all the barges and pinnaces, well provided with pikes, might be with him by 8.30 at latest. He hoped to begin "to make it a warm night at Cadiz" at 10 p.m. The town batteries and the fleet were, he knew, expecting him—"Gun boats advanced etc. So much the better. If they venture from the walls, I shall give Johnny his full scope of fighting. It will serve to talk of, better than mischief." The enemy were expecting him on their "soft side". He stationed the *Thunderer*, with a detachment of artillery on board, within 2,500 yards of "the strong face of Cadiz", near the Tower of San Sebastian, covered by the *Urchin*, launches and barges of the fleet. The ketch began to do her duty, and several shells fell into the town, to be followed by smoke and flames, streaming towards the midsummer night sky. The town was soon well alight in three places. The *Thunderer* was not, of course, left long undisturbed. Seventy pieces of cannon on the line-wall came into action; she was disabled, and a vigorous attempt was made by enemy mortar-gun boats and armed launches to carry her. "Rear-Admiral Nelson", in the words of St. Vincent, "always present in the most arduous enterprises", after signalling her to retire to the protection of three frigates kept under sail for such an emergency, himself sped to her rescue. In the *mêlée* which followed, the craft attending him boarded and carried two Spanish gunboats, but the launch of St. Vincent's flagship, the *Ville de Paris*, was sunk by a raking shot, and his own barge was singled out for attention by the Commander of the Spanish flotilla, Don Miguel Tyrason.

The attack on Cadiz on the night of July 3 was a small affair, but it claimed a full paragraph in the succinct *Sketch of my Life* later supplied by the Victor of the Nile to a biographer. As yet he had never in his life been more nearly despatched in hand-to-hand fighting. "This was a service, hand to hand, with swords." His barge, with its common crew of ten men, a coxswain, Fremantle and himself, was attacked by that of the Spanish commander, rowed by twenty-six men, and carrying four officers. Fremantle was slightly wounded, and John Sykes, coxswain, who had stood by his Captain's side on the quarter-deck of the *San Josef* on Valentine's Day, twice saved his life by interposing his person. On the second occasion, Sykes fell, with severe head injuries. But the enemy, in overwhelming force, were not only beaten off. By the time that the Spanish armed launch of much superior size had been captured, every survivor had been wounded, and her Commander had been taken prisoner.

In the small hours, Nelson, with a hundred and seventeen prisoners on board the *Theseus*, thirty of whom were not to survive, was able to dictate a decidedly satisfactory report to St. Vincent, who next day had the pleasure of learning that "the active intelligent mind of Captain Fremantle" had got his launch up, and was supervising repairs on board H.M.S. *Culloden*. Another bombardment was planned for the 5th, this time on "the soft side", on the outside of the lighthouse, where Mr. Jackson, Master of the *Ville de Paris*, knew of a good berth for the *Thunderer*, now reinforced by the appropriately named mortar-boats, *Terror* and *Stromboli*. Nelson was "merely a spectator" of the attempt on the night of July 5. From the first the shore batteries had got the exact range of his bomb-ketch and mortars, and as their gunboats kept close under the sea-wall, no opportunity offered for Bowen of the *Terpsichore* to "make a dash at them". When some forty-odd shells had been successfully landed in the town and harbour, and the *Thunderer* had been shot in the hull and both masts, Nelson signalled Bowen to tow her off.

St. Vincent had his own good reasons for ordering these nightly distractions. On the 7th and 8th four mutineers of the *St. George* were being tried by court-martial on board his flagship. Their trial did not terminate until after sunset on the Saturday, so he decreed that the sentence should be carried out at dawn on the following morning. Nelson, who was ordered to be present, with the boats of the in-shore squadron, approved the speedy carrying out of the sentence, though on a Sunday, but "Vice-Admiral Thompson having presumed to censure the execution on the Sabbath in a public letter, I have", reported St. Vincent, "insisted on his being removed from the Fleet immediately." One of the mutineers, when interviewed by the chaplain, had disclosed that his scheme had been in contemplation for six months, and that he had confederates in the *Britannia*, *Diadem*, *Captain* and *Egmont*. The condemned men had asked to be allowed five days in which to prepare for death, "in which they would have hatched 500 Treasons. Had it been Christmas Day, instead of Sunday," said Nelson, "I would have executed them." He believed that if the same spirit of determination had been shown by the authorities at home, the disturbances in the Channel and North Sea fleets need never have got out of hand. But he still thought that old Lord Howe's sending back the Spithead men's first petition had been quite wrong.

On the hot and uneasy night of the 8th, after the court-martial had risen, his plan of a third operation on Cadiz having been frustrated by a gale which made it impossible to get the *Thunderer* up to the chosen point of attack, he summoned and addressed his ship's company, under, perhaps, the most difficult circumstances of his career. "We, in the advance, are night and day, prepared for battle. Our friends in England need not fear the event." An unusual silence pervaded the men of the *Theseus*, lately "an abomination". They dismissed very quietly. They were ordered to assist at to-morrow's scene, so Nelson hoped that he had spoken with good effect. Next morning the sentence was duly carried out, and the action of twenty-seven enemy mortar and gunboats, which advanced to cannonade his ten sail-of-the-line, on observing the barges and pinnaces of his squadron proceeding to the execution, was decidedly helpful to *morale*.

In the postponed third attack on the town, made on the night of the 10th, since the *Theseus* "had the honour of every gun from the southern part of Cadiz, and of every gun and mortar boat", she suffered a few casualties, but Nelson, who had much rather see fifty men shot by the enemy than one mutineer dangling from his yard-arm, welcomed the shot flying about her as likely to do her good. He had now forced the enemy from their outer into their inner harbour, so his squadron should, in future, have notice of the emergence of the Spanish fleet; and next morning, to his great interest, he saw a red flag hoisted on board seven enemy ships, including that of an Admiral. He seized the chance of sending a flag of truce into the town, with some ninety of the prisoners taken on the 3rd, and the officer in charge reported, on return, that when he had asked if the Spanish fleet was "*à la Nore*", he had received an unbelievably languid reply, "Yes, that the men were demanding their wages". The merchants of Cadiz, however, were offering a small fortune to any volunteer who would board the dreaded *Thunderer*.

Quite suddenly, only a few hours after he had written to St. Vincent asking for more mortars from the Rock, came the orders for which Nelson had long been hoping. After receiving them he wrote to his wife, telling her that as he now had a prospect of being absent from the fleet for a short time, she must not be anxious if she heard nothing awhile. On the morning of July 14, at 8 a.m., he weighed, and stood towards the main body of the fleet. Noon was the hour appointed by the Commander-in-Chief for a tense, though not long, interview, and next morning at 6 a.m., having received orders to take under his command H.M.S. *Theseus*, *Culloden*, *Zealous*, *Leander*, *Terpsichore*, *Seahorse* and *Emerald*, the *Fox* cutter and *Çacafuego* mortar-boat, Nelson made sail to the westward.

4

The circumstances under which the Expedition sailed for Teneriffe on July 15 were by no means those visualised by Nelson and Troubridge on the hopeful night of April 11.

St. Vincent had not been successful in persuading either de Burgh or O'Hara to part with troops "to attempt the surprise of Santa Cruz in the Grand Canary". O'Hara, indeed, describing himself as out of spirits, had counter-attacked, asking for an addition to the naval force at Gibraltar. These refusals were serious considerations, as Nelson, when presenting his original plan, had stipulated for either the Corsica garrison of three thousand seven hundred, or one thousand six hundred men from the Rock. Nor, as St. Vincent admitted, was the capture of Teneriffe quite the grand object it had been when Nelson suggested the enterprise. Captains Cockburn and Hallowell (sent thither to cruise, with a roving commission, so long as their provisions lasted) had ascertained that the Viceroy was not sheltering in Teneriffe.

The news from Lisbon was that, hearing of the result of the engagement of Valentine's Day, and hoping for a peace, the Mexican treasure fleet had decided not to run the enormous hazard of attempting a homeward passage until the war was over. It had not sailed. On the other hand, by the first week in May, St. Vincent knew for certain that two register ships belonging to the Philippine Company, bound from Manila for Cadiz (one of them the famous *El Principe d'Asturias*), were at Santa Cruz, and had not as yet unloaded their rich cargoes. And O'Hara, although he would not part with troops and expressed wrath at the request to do so, was willing to supply the train of artillery, ammunition and devil-cart demanded by Nelson. As this news gradually dropped in, St. Vincent kept Nelson advised, by letter and by the impenetrably discreet Jackson, and finally asked him to pronounce on the possibilities of a wholly naval operation—"Turn this in your mind." Personally, St. Vincent had always hoped to live to see the day when there was not a foot-soldier left in Great Britain, or the colonies, except the King's Guards and the Artillery. "A very considerable corps of Marines" in their place was one of his dreams for a peace establishment.

Nelson, without the least hesitation, answered that given two hundred extra marines for his landing-party, "with 'General Troubridge' ashore and myself afloat, I am confident of success". Thereupon, St. Vincent agreed that the moment his fleet was reinforced by the four sail-of-the-line for which he had asked repeatedly and strongly, he would be ready "to dash you off".

On June 7 St. Vincent wrote, "We must have something from England soon, together with your ribbon, and the patents for the Admirals", but a month later he had not been reinforced and he was trying mutineers. He was now convinced that the Spanish fleet was not coming out, at least during the season while he could keep his present station, and while Spain had between thirty and forty sail-of-the-line in port at Cadiz and a division at Cartagena he could not hope to return to the Mediterranean. In these black weeks he persuaded himself that hopes of a success at Teneriffe under a lucky commander were "well-grounded". His temper at this period was at its most formidable, and not only mutineers felt it. "I dread not the seamen. It is the indiscreet, licentious conversation of the officers which produce all our ills, and the presumptuous discussion of the orders they receive." The *Captain*, under her new Captain, was not what she had been. Acting on a belief that her wardroom was enjoying the dainties of the fresh fare obtainable, the Chief issued a General Fleet Order that ships' companies were to be first served. "When at sea, we do not make snug for the night, as in the Westward Squadron." Colonel Flight, commanding officer of marines, being summoned to the quarter-deck of the *Ville de Paris* at 2.30 a.m., arrived armed at all points, imagining that the enemy were out. "I have sent for you, Colonel, that you might smell, for the first time in your life, the delicious odours brought off by the landwind from the shores of Andalusia. Take a good sniff, and then you may go and turn in again." On another morning, a too well-liking Lieutenant came on board to answer a signal. "Calder," observed the Commander-in-Chief, "all the Lieutenants are running to belly. They have been too long at anchor. Block up the entering port except for Admirals and Captains, and make them climb over the hammocks."

But to Nelson he could not have shown more spacious favour.

He allowed him to choose the ships and officers to accompany him, although the old friends chosen by Nelson were the cream of the late Mediterranean Fleet—Troubridge, Fremantle, Miller, Waller, Bowen, the young Sam Hood. . . . The senior captain of marines was also Nelson's choice. The worthy Oldfield had been wounded in his company on the night of July 5. The Lieutenant of Artillery, Baynes, also direct from Gibraltar, belonged to the Rock, dynastically and professionally. Lord St. Vincent, who had long known both his parents, had commended this officer, of a good Service family, to Nelson before the young man had distinguished himself shelling Cadiz from the *Thunderer*. Thompson, the only Captain not present, had special knowledge of the Canaries, was cruising down there now, and would join the squadron at sea, as would Bowen, who had taken the *Terpsichore* to Lisbon for supplies.

An hour before the Expedition sailed on the early morning of the 15th the Captains of the squadron came on board the *Theseus*. They were given their orders, and, in case of separation, the *rendezvous*. The scene was not peaceful, for the boats of the fleet were delivering scaling-ladders, ammunition and marines to be transferred to the *Leander* ; but Lord St. Vincent's instructions were as usual unmistakable. Admiral Nelson was to proceed with the utmost expedition to the Island of Teneriffe, to take possession, by a sudden vigorous assault, of the port of Santa Cruz. If successful, he was authorised to seize *El Principe d'Asturias* with her whole cargo, and all treasure in the port belonging to the Crown of Spain. Should the inhabitants object, he might levy a heavy contribution upon them and endeavour to take, burn, sink or otherwise destroy all enemy vessels of every description on the coast of Africa, even those engaged in the fishery. Lord St. Vincent's order closed: "And having performed your mission, you are to make the best of your way back to join me." Nelson had assured him: "Ten hours shall either make me a conqueror or defeat me", and, "We shall get hold of something, if there is anything moving on the face of the waters." Still, in his note of farewell, the Commander-in-Chief displayed more good wishes than high expectations: "God bless you and prosper you. I am sure you will deserve success. To mortals is not given the power of commanding it."

At 9 a.m. on July 15, H.M.S. *Alcmene*, nearing the end of her passage from Portsmouth to Cadiz, in charge of a convoy, beheld a cheering and business-like sight. The British squadron which she spoke in the mouth of the Straits consisted of three 74's, a couple of frigates (one of 60 guns) and a cutter with a gunboat in tow. The early morning had been very cloudy, but the wind was now moderate from the S.S.W., and before the squadron passed from view the smaller frigate had parted. Waller, in the *Emerald*, had been sent ahead to look out for Bowen. The *Terpsichore* joined next evening, and Captain D'Arcy Preston of the *Blanche* carried to his relative, Lord St. Vincent, the news that at 6 p.m. on Sunday he had seen Admiral Nelson's squadron standing on for Teneriffe with light airs and clear weather.

Nothing further was heard of the Santa Cruz Expedition for exactly a month, when the swift *Emerald* arrived alone, with a despatch and two letters written in an almost indecipherable strange hand, the contents of which caused the Commander-in-Chief extreme anguish.

5

The Expedition had sailed on a Saturday morning. On the Monday the Captains of the squadron came on board the *Theseus* again to bend their brows over a large-scale plan of Santa Cruz Bay, drawn by a Lieutenant of Engineers, in which the valley to the north-east of the town, known to the inhabitants as "Lion's Mouth", was labelled "E", and the heights and battery behind it, and commanding the port, were "F" and "G". It was agreed that the boats carrying the landing-parties should proceed in six divisions, kept together by towing, that they should disembark their men simultaneously, and that the moment the attempt was discovered, the *Çacafuego* should open fire on the town and keep on doing her duty until she saw a flag of truce hoisted—"from either the Enemy or from us". Frigates were to anchor as soon as possible after either the alarm had been given or the forces were on shore, and as near as they could to "F" and "G", which would be immediately stormed. The Admiral recommended that every possible seaman disembarked should be provided with a marine's greatcoat or jacket; certainly canvas crossbelts. He had not the slightest doubt of the boldness and efficiency of his "Jacks", but they were few. "Red-coats have their use in dazzling the eyes of the Enemy" and of genuine marines he had but two hundred and fifty. The knowledgeable Thompson, whom he had summoned from Cadiz and intended to employ as second-in-command to Troubridge, had not yet joined. He empowered all Captains who wished to do so to land at Santa Cruz and command their men, together with as many men above the number detailed from each ship as wished to volunteer, only providing that sufficient were left to manage the ship and man her boats. The 74's would be kept below the horizon until the surprise night attack had been launched, and then make their appearance, ready to bring their broadsides to bear against the line-wall battery and mole-head. All Captains were instructed to set their men to work to make iron ramrods, since wooden ones were apt to break when used in haste, and Troubridge, Fremantle and Hood were, in addition, provided with a sketch, showing sections of gun platforms. Next morning the *Theseus*, too, echoed to sounds of carpentry. She was making a sledge to drag eighteen-pounders. Other ominous sounds startled the summer seas as the squadron drew nearer to the "fortunate isles" of Plutarch and Ptolemy. After a general signal for midshipmen, small-arms men exercised themselves firing at a target. At 8 a.m. on Friday the 21st, the Captains came on board for their final conference. A blue cone, of barbaric contours, uncannily girdled by drifting cloud, and seemingly based on air, was looming momentarily larger. Indeed, since with sunset yesterday the visibility had suddenly become uncommonly good, the Peak of Teneriffe had been clearly discernible, against fading skies, at thirty miles distance.

The last conference was held. Captains Hood, Fremantle, Miller, Waller and Bowen "very handsomely" offered their services on shore. The ninety men detailed had been augmented by about a hundred volunteers. "General" Troubridge, "Commander of the Forces ordered to land", was entrusted with his Admiral's formal summons to the Governor or Commanding Officer of the port, which he was recommended to present, as he thought best, either before or after proceeding against the town and mole-head battery.

His orders, which gave him great scope to use initiative, advised that his first step should be the capture of the mountain fort "G", and ended, "Having the firmest confidence in the ability, bravery and zeal of yourself, and all placed under your command, I have only to heartily wish you success." The squadron wore to the eastward and hoisted out the boats which were to transfer the landing-parties to the frigates *Terpsichore*, *Emerald* and *Seahorse*. All oars for the boats designed for the night operation had been muffled with pieces of kersey or canvas. Scaling-ladders, each provided with a lanyard four fathoms long, many sledge-hammers, wedges, broad-axes, ramrods and "every implement I thought necessary for the success of the enterprise" were also transferred. Nelson, with his line-of-battle ships, then retired to the eastward, to wear and tack throughout the hours of darkness in increasing anxiety, as no unusual and hoped-for sounds disturbed the night. At 3.30 next morning, he bore up for the island, and through the clouds of daybreak could see three British frigates and a mortar-boat off Santa Cruz, and the ships' boats pulling off-shore. Evidently the dash in the dark had not taken place. At 6 a.m. a trio of solemn figures presented themselves to report a setback. Troubridge, Bowen and Oldfield wished "to consult what was best to be done". Their lamentable tale was that, although the frigates had been within three miles of "Lion's Mouth" by midnight, by the unlucky conjunction of a strong gale of wind in the offing and a strong current against them in-shore, they had not been able to get within a mile of beach "E" before light came. The surprise attack had been frustrated by the elements, and the enemy were now well aware of their presence, and in high commotion. Still, Troubridge believed that if he could capture the mountain overshadowing "Lion's Mouth", he might storm the fort, halfway up it, from the rear, and turn its guns upon the town.

Nelson assented, and by nine o'clock the frigates had anchored and begun, in broad daylight, to put the landing-party on shore. But Fortune again refused to "favour the gallant attempt", and his effort to "create a diversion" with his line-of-battle ships, by battering fort "G", was rendered impracticable by a flat calm and contrary currents. With darkness came gales and cloudy weather. The 74's struck their top-gallant masts and wore. The sole success of the expedition took place with dawn, when the *Zealous* captured a merchant vessel from another of the Canaries, bound for Teneriffe, with stock. At 7 a.m. Troubridge appeared, dead-beat, to announce that he had failed to get possession of "F" or "G", but had gathered his landing-party and re-embarked it on board the frigates. Nelson signalled the frigates to weigh and join him. The landing-party was carried back to its various ships, and all boats were hoisted in. As the wind still permitted of no closer approach to the shore, the squadron continued under sail for two days.

By Monday morning, July 24, "foiled in my original plan", Nelson was ready with another, so hazardous that all serious-minded persons, on hearing of it, made their preparations. "Convinced there is nothing which Englishmen are not equal to, and confident in the bravery of those who would be employed", he had decided, during those two days of blowing weather, upon a direct attack on the town, in the centre of the bay, at the earliest possible moment; and this time he would lead it himself. The weather that day remained persistently unfriendly, with strong gales but good visibility, but by 5.30 p.m. he had anchored the squadron about two miles north of the town, and anyone who had not taken a closer look was able to satisfy his curiosity as to the attractions of Santa Cruz of Teneriffe on a wet summer's evening. It was a small old town, in the Spanish style, with an exiled air. It possessed one prominent square church tower. Its white houses, flat-roofed and faced, crouched, half in eternal shadow, below weirdly shaped and seamed volcanic heights. Most of the greenery in the picture was provided by cacti.

Nelson's display of every indication that he was about to bombard the heights had the desired effect. As dusk closed in, he was able to observe detachments of troops hurrying from the town to the mountain fort, which he meant to leave undisturbed. The only unexpected incident of the afternoon was a welcome one. The *Terpsichore's* signal for a strange sail heralded H.M.S. *Leander*. Her two hundred marines were added to the landing-force, and Captain Thompson, chosen for his knowledge of the island, was immediately ready to volunteer his services on shore. At 6 p.m. the boats of the squadron received the same directions as on the preceding

Friday. Complete darkness could not be relied upon, even on a poor day, until shortly before midnight. As light faded, Lieutenant Nisbet, Officer of the Watch, summoned to his stepfather's cabin, found the Admiral busy, this July night, sorting and burning Lady Nelson's letters. The dress of Josiah announced that he was prepared to embark with the landing-party, and a dramatic dialogue followed his war-like entry.

"Should we both fall, Josiah, what would become of your poor mother? The care of the *Theseus* falls to you. Stay, therefore, and take charge of her."

"Sir, the Ship must take care of herself. I will go with you to-night if never again."

That Josiah's memory did not exaggerate the tone abroad that night may be judged from the letter written by his stepfather, after his exit, to the Commander-in-Chief.

> "*Theseus, off Santa Cruz,*
> "*July 24th.* 8 p.m.

"My dear Sir,

"I shall not enter on the subject while we are not in possession of Santa Cruz; your partiality will give me credit that all has hitherto been done which was possible, but without effect. This night, I, humble as I am, command the whole, destined to land under the batteries of the Town, and to-morrow my head will probably be crowned with either laurel or cypress. I have only to recommend Josiah Nisbet to you and my Country. With every affectionate wish for your health, and every blessing in the world, believe me your most faithful

> "Horatio Nelson."

"The Duke of Clarence, should I fall, in the service of my King and Country, will, I am confident, take a lively interest for my Son-in-Law, on his name being mentioned."

Before setting out for what he himself afterwards described as "a forlorn hope . . . I never expected to return", Nelson proceeded to sup with Mrs. Fremantle, in the *Seahorse*.

Besides the logs of the various ships concerned, four first-hand accounts of the events of that dark and fatal night are available. Nelson's "Journal", despatch and detailed report to St. Vincent, with which he enclosed a letter to himself from Troubridge, record in official language the events of a disastrous night operation against hopeless odds in foul weather. Josiah Nisbet and an anonymous "officer who was present" add some valuable details, but their story was not collected for at least seven years. Two young persons left behind to await the return of the party wrote their impressions on the spot. Betsy Fremantle kept her diary. William Hoste sent a letter home.

6

When Captain Fremantle, at Gibraltar, received orders to change into the *Seahorse* and join the fleet off Cadiz, he was not much pleased. His expectation had been to carry his foreign-bred bride home in the *Inconstant*, and settle her amongst his affectionate family while he pursued a brilliant career. But Captain Oakes of the *Seahorse* was in a deplorable state of health, the *Inconstant* was due for a thorough refit, and his Betsy was enchanted at the prospect of more of his company. When he got to Cadiz, and heard of the project in hand, his wife noticed "much better spirits". He told her that there were good hopes of peace, which, after two experiences of sitting up for him while he was "out all night with Admiral Nelson to bombard the town", she was glad to hear. His outings with Nelson sounded very noisy, and from one of them he returned, having received "a blow". On the day before the Expedition sailed for Santa Cruz, the bride felt "not well, but I don't know what makes me feel so". Her husband had by now given her an explanation of the duty on which they were bound. "We are going", she calmly instructed her diary, "to take the island of Teneriffe." The island, to be sure, did not seem quite so easy to take as she had been led to expect, and after two days in a small bay at a short distance from the town, but out of gunshot, she was delighted at the order to weigh and join the Admiral and 74's. "Had they been with us, the place would have long been taken."

By the night of July 24, when the Admiral, attended by Captains Bowen, Miller and Hood, came to sup with her in the *Seahorse*, Mrs. Fremantle was "pretty well". The only drawback to her happiness as a hostess, that dark, rough night, was the noise made by the men of the *Theseus* as they went on board the boats bound for the mole of Santa Cruz. During the last three days she had found these three hundred and fifty guests "the most tiresome, noisy, mutinous people in the world", and noted that they seemed to annoy Fremantle. But it appeared that their temporary presence was a necessary evil. "They are all", she explained to her diary, "to land in the Town." Satisfied by the brief explanations of her supper-party that "the taking of the place seemed an easy and almost a sure thing", she received their polite farewells with *aplomb*, and went to bed, "apprehending no danger to Fremantle".

He had fitted up a lower cabin for her, and for the past four nights had seen to it that she had a woman within call—the sail-maker's wife. When she heard "much firing" during the night, the ailing bride had no doubt that the English were by now masters of Tene-riffe. "Great was our mistake. This proved to be a shocking unfor-tunate night."

7

Of what followed after the last of Mrs. Fremantle's guests had gone over the side of the *Seahorse* into darkness, Troubridge's experiences may be given first. At 10.30 the marines and seamen from the various ships, numbering between six and seven hundred, began to go on board the heaving boats alongside the three frigates. A further hundred and eighty men were embarked in the *Fox* cutter, and eighty in the Spanish merchant vessel taken at dawn. Fremantle and Bowen went with the Admiral, to lead the central division in the attack. The Captains of the remaining five divisions had all received orders to land on the mole and make for the principal square of the town as fast as possible. There, they were to form, in preparation for whatever services might be necessary. By 11 the last boat had put off. The night was pitch black, and there was a heavy sea running—circumstances which prevented the enemy from discovering the approach of the invaders, but also prevented them from finding their way. Troubridge's division was almost the unluckiest. After more than an hour and a half's steady pulling against stinging rain and raving wind, he heard the roar of the surf breaking on rocks. He realised then that he must, as he had feared, have missed the mole. Almost immediately he knew that someone must have been more successful, for a crackle of musketry sounded

from end to end of the town, the sky lit, cannon opened fire close
overhead and all the bells of Santa Cruz began to peal. The expectation of the veterans of St. Valentine's Day that Spanish soldiers
would show no more fight than Spanish seamen was quite mistaken. Decadent Spain, like Rome, kept her best legions in her
outposts. There were tough men (though mostly irregulars), under
a competent commander, awaiting the arrival of the English; and
although large detachments had been sent to the fort on the moun-
tain-side, forty guns had been trained on the mole-head all day, and
every house overlooking it had musketeers posted in the windows.
Troubridge found himself under the battery to the south of the
citadel. He pushed on shore, and landed safely on a narrow beach,
at the same time as another boatload, whose commander he presently
recognised as Waller. But only two or three boats out of their two
divisions followed them. The surf was so high, many put back in
despair; many more, cast violently against the inhospitable rocks of
Santa Cruz Bay, filled and sank instantly. He collected what men
he could, and, together with Waller, fought his way over the line-
wall and battery, taking some prisoners, and managed to reach the
central square. At this *rendezvous* he waited, while the scene
gradually but unmistakably took on every aspect of the night
operation which has gone very wrong.

8

William Hoste, midshipman of the *Theseus*, endured a most
wretched vigil after he had seen the ship's boat depart for H.M.S.
Seahorse and the mole of Santa Cruz without him. Lieutenant
Weatherhead, his best friend, and Lieutenant Nisbet, to whom he
was not so devoted, had both gone. Hoste, although he had entered
the Service at the same date as both these officers, and was only
three months junior to Nisbet, was still a midshipman. A serious
attack of typhoid after the siege of Calvi, a broken leg, from which
he still sometimes felt twinges, and a long experience of malaria at
Leghorn last year, had deprived him of many months of service
afloat. He was, at the moment, recovering from a deep cut in the
right palm, which he had got in one of the hand-to-hand boat
attacks in Cadiz harbour. Four years and four months had passed

since Captain Nelson had commissioned the *Agamemnon*, and a noticeably small boy of twelve, with the blunt, short features, direct, blue gaze and flaxen hair of his Flemish ancestors, had said a wondering farewell to Godwick House, Norfolk. He thought that if he was to be set down at Tittleshall, he could still find his way to his father's house; but from no further village. (He could not, in his home thoughts from sea, remember the roads.)

The *Theseus*, cleared for action, was not a "floating heaven". At 1 a.m. on the morning of July 25, Hoste's pricked ears were rewarded by "one of the heaviest cannonades I ever was witness to". It came from the town and was doubtless directed upon the boats which had pulled away into stormy darkness after supper. The attempt had been discovered, and the landing must now be in progress; the next few hours would be critical.

But less than an hour had passed when he suddenly heard, above the confused clamour of a dirty night, the unexpected sound of Admiral Nelson hailing the *Theseus*. There was a very brief pause after the suggestion had been repulsed of a chair from the main yard-arm to hoist in the Admiral, wounded. The boat, it seemed, must immediately go back to the mole, where men of the *Fox* were struggling in the surf. Then William Hoste, peering into the noisy blackness, straining his eyes and ears, experiencing feelings so strong that he knew not how to describe them, perceived "him, whom I may say has been a second father to me, his right arm dangling by his side, while with the other he helped himself to jump up the ship's side". He next heard a familiar voice snapping at a consternated audience, "with a spirit which astonished all", "Tell the surgeon to get his instruments ready, for I know that I must lose my arm, and the sooner it is off the better."

9

As the central division of boats, led by Nelson, got within half gunshot of the mole of Santa Cruz, rockets climbed the skies, and blue lights threw a sudden ugly glare on the scene. Above the jangle of alarm bells, he shouted to the boats to cast off from one another, give a huzza, give way for their lives and remember their orders. Grape and canister began to tear the water just outside of them.

Only the parties led by Thompson, Fremantle and Bowen succeeded in landing at various points on the mole, which they quickly carried, although it was defended by between four and five hundred men. They spiked its six twenty-four-pounders, but proceeded no farther. By the time that this had been achieved "we were nearly all killed or wounded". Nelson received his wound, a grapeshot shattering the right elbow, as he was in the act of drawing the dress-sword, regarded by him as a talisman. The gift of Captain Maurice Suckling, originally the property of Captain Galfridus Walpole, dropped from his right hand, but he snatched it up with his left. One account declares that he was, at the moment, stepping out of the boat, and that the same fire wounded seven other men in their right arms. Another describes him as having landed, being hit while pressing forward on the mole and falling, to lie for several moments in the dark confusion, until Josiah Nisbet, missing him, returned in search, and finding him senseless, carried him on his back to their boat.

He was laid in the bottom of a boat, and his stepson, noting that the sight of his blood seemed to increase the patient's faintness, took off his own hat and laid it on the Admiral's breast. A bargeman named Lovel had pulled off his shirt to form a sling, and helped to adjust a tourniquet. Nisbet, in this, his great hour, collected five other men, and after an alarming delay, got the boat, which had grounded from the falling of the tide, afloat again. He took an oar and shouted to the steersman to go as close as possible under the guns of the mole battery, which were firing. The young, raised voice attracted Nelson's attention, and the Admiral asked to be lifted, "that he might look a little about him". The night was so dark that there was little to be seen except a stormy sea lit by gun-fire, but his change of position was made at the moment that the Fox cutter went down, taking with her her commander and ninety-seven men. She had been hit in her under-water timbers, and sank rapidly. The water became alive with struggling figures, and Nelson insisted that his boat should go out of its way to pick up as many survivors as possible. After half an hour, the boat, pulling for the Theseus, got within hail of a frigate, but on hearing that she was the Seahorse, Nelson refused to approach her. He was strongly advised that further exposure in an open boat, over-full of drenched men, might mean the loss of his life—"Then I will die; for I would rather suffer death than alarm Mrs. Fremantle by her seeing me in this state, when I can give her no tidings whatever of her husband." The boat, accordingly, made on towards the ships-of-the-line, and although boarding on such a night was difficult, even for a sound man, the Admiral, twisting a rope round his left arm, went up the side of his flagship unaided. "Let me alone! I have got my legs left, and one arm."

The amputation to which he had resigned himself from the moment he was hit was performed as soon as possible, and it appears that the tale, often doubted, that Nelson's arm was taken off by a Frenchman is founded on fact. M. Ronicet, Assistant-Surgeon of the *Theseus*, was a French royalist refugee, collected by Lord Hood at Toulon, in August 1793. Like the Principal Medical Officer of the *Theseus*, he had followed Nelson, who had the highest opinion of him, from the *Agamemnon* into the *Captain*. From the surgeon's point of view there was much for which to be thankful. There were not many other wounded urgently needing attention, the ship was at anchor and her guns were not in action. Nevertheless, the circumstances were far from favourable. The lantern light was dim and shifting; the ship was rolling; and the patient was exhausted and chilled. However, his unselfish resolution not to alarm Mrs. Fremantle seemed to have brought its reward, for after his ordeal he congratulated himself on "a good surgeon", whereas Fleming, of the *Seahorse*, who attended Fremantle, got praise from no quarter. Within half an hour his Flag-Captain was by Sir Horatio's side, receiving necessary orders, "as if nothing had happened", and a large outer audience presently heard that the Admiral had undergone his operation "with the same firmness and courage which have always marked his character". When asked whether he wished his limb to be embalmed and sent home for burial, he had said, "Throw it into the hammock with the brave fellow that was killed beside me." "He was in a fair way of recovery." He certainly did not get a fair chance.

Throughout the night the town batteries continued to fire, and at 4 a.m. a number of boats which had been tossing in the bay for five hours, unable to reach the mole, came alongside and began to discharge their landing-parties. With first daylight came sudden and shattering noise. In the market-square of Santa Cruz, Troubridge and Waller were marching in quest of Hood. The enemy were responding by a bombardment of the English shipping in the bay. In the *Theseus*, watched by Tom Allen, who had been present at the amputation, the patient stirred. Captain Miller was again summoned, and the Admiral, who had ordered the squadron to weigh, heard the measured clank of the capstan as the cable came in, the rumble of the guns being run out, and familiar patterings and bellowings as the port-lids opened. The *Theseus*, standing off and on the town, returned enemy fire regularly for the next two hours, during which time a boat which had managed to escape from the town arrived, bringing the dark tidings that every man of the landing-parties who had contrived to reach the *rendezvous* had been obliged to surrender. Persons who had begun to pride themselves on having silenced the enemy batteries fell silent.

Comparative peace continued until 9 a.m., when a flag of truce came off the mole, with Waller and a Spanish officer carrying the Governor's very handsome terms. Before noon Lieutenant Weatherhead was conveyed on board the *Theseus* in a cradle. William Hoste, again experiencing feelings so strong that he could not describe them, told himself that "this was not a time to give way", and bustled round, getting everything in his power ready for the reception of his friend. With his first glance at John's changed face, some instinct told him that this was Death, and the surgeons, after examining the mute boy, held out no hopes of his long survival, a diagnosis confirmed by his collapse and quiet passing four days later. "I had almost forgotten", added Hoste to his long letter home, "to say that on the death of Weatherhead, Admiral Nelson gave me a commission to act as Lieutenant in his vacancy; happy would it have made me, had it been in any other."

Nelson's arm had been taken off "very high, near the shoulder", at an early hour on the 25th, and once the deed was done he eagerly reclaimed command of what he called "my carcase". His Medical Officers, very ready with frequent wet dressings, found their examinations resented, and as far as possible avoided. Tom Allen, full of importance and invention, guarded his sick master, who would not be sick, with the devotion of a dog, the jealousy of a woman. In preparation for blowing nights on their return passage to the fleet, Tom had rigged up a cord, attached to his shirt collar, by which means Sir Horatio, needing anything, need only give a twitch to summon his *valet-de-chambre*. By the 26th the patient was dictating a letter to the humane and courteous Commandant of the Canaries, begging His Excellency's acceptance of his sincere thanks and (in a postscript) a cask of English beer and a cheese. His Excellency replied, sending his best wishes for the Admiral's recovery, and a couple of flasks of finest Canary wine, whereupon the Admiral gallantly offered to carry to Cadiz His Excellency's despatches for the Court of Spain—"thus making himself the herald of his own defeat". Next day he dictated a despatch to St. Vincent, and to the enclosed list of two hundred and fifty-odd officers, seamen and marines, killed, wounded, drowned and missing, appended his second effort at a left-handed signature. (Little Mrs. Fremantle had already received a line of enquiry for her husband, and assurances that he himself was "coming on very well".)

At last the weary preparations for leaving the Fortunate Isles were complete. The men of the landing-parties had all been returned to their proper ships; the squadron, provisioned from the town, by courtesy of the Governor, was at liberty to depart in peace, and Nelson might settle to the business of recovery. Only the wind stayed unfriendly and refused to carry the vanquished out of sight of a shore now detested by more than Mrs. Fremantle. The body of Captain Bowen was brought on board his ship and committed to the deep. As his squadron lay becalmed, Nelson attempted his first letter. The days of his conventional, fine sloping hand, long since degenerated into an over-driven scribble, were gone for ever. His new writing, unmistakable, foursquare, at present spider-thin and tending to wilt backwards, slowly and painfully came into sight. With the humiliating effort and the sudden heat and peace, came the inevitable reaction. He realised that of late he had received "flattery enough to make me vain, and success enough to make me confident". His memory recurred with futile insistence to the loss of Bowen and "a great many gallant officers and men". He believed the grey-headed Lieutenant of the *Fox* to have left, in indigence at Hastings, "an only daughter, the darling of his heart". The Admiral's attendants were obviously nervous, and perhaps with reason. His first letter rambled, in style as well as script.

"My dear Sir,

"I am become a burthen to my friends, and useless to my Country; but by my letter wrote the 24th, you will perceive my anxiety for the promotion of my son-in-law, Josiah Nisbet. When I leave your command, I become dead to the World; I go hence, and am no more seen. If from poor Bowen's loss, you think it proper to oblige me, I rest confident you will do it; the Boy is under obligations to me, but he repaid me by bringing me from the Mole of Santa Cruz. I hope you will be able to give me a frigate, to convey the remains of my carcase to England. God bless you, my dear sir, and believe me, your most obliged and faithful,

"Horatio Nelson."

"You will excuse my scrawl, considering it is my first attempt."

10

On the afternoon of Wednesday, August 16, he came in sight once more of Lord St. Vincent's flag, and his spirits rose. The Commander-in-Chief's note of greeting combined in the happiest manner the grandiose and jocose: "Mortals cannot command success." He was sure that Nelson and his companions had deserved both success and fame. The *Seahorse* should waft him and Fremantle to England the moment she was provisioned, and they need not fear missing anything interesting here, as his Lordship had just betted £100 on the preliminaries of a peace being already signed, and a definitive treaty before mid-September. He sent his love to Mrs. Fremantle, and hoped to salute her, and bow to Nelson's stump, to-morrow morning.

But "a left-handed Admiral" who had asked nothing more than that he might get to some "very humble Cottage" as soon as possible, in order to make room for a better man, was now desirous to display himself as most suitable for further employment afloat. When the *Theseus* anchored at 3 p.m., Tom Allen had already got his master into his coat, and to the surprise of Captain George and Sir Charles Grey, a figure, drawn in countenance but eager in speech, appeared at Lord St. Vincent's dinner-table. He stayed an hour, and that night his host reported to the First Lord that Rear-Admiral Nelson had joined with his squadron, and in such health that nothing could prevent his coming on board the *Ville de Paris.* "He dined with me, and I have very good ground of hope he will be restored to the service of his King and Country." Privately, he had promised Nelson to ask for him again as soon as possible.

One letter very irritating to the invalid was awaiting him. Rear-Admiral Parker had heard from friends at home that "then Commodore Nelson", in a statement of the action of Valentine's Day, had not given him that credit which properly belonged to him. To this letter, which was of great length, he received the curtest of replies, and not until after Nelson had sailed for England. For four days Dr. Weir, Physician to the Fleet, was allowed full access to his stump; then, in record time, the *Seahorse* was ready, and Admiral Nelson came on board in great spirits. Mrs. Fremantle, who now saw him for the first time since his loss, found "it looks shocking to be without one arm". Sir Horatio had brought with him four years' luggage, a surgeon, an extraordinary body-servant, and a number of sick and wounded from the *Theseus,* and Mrs. Fremantle liked the look of Mr. Eshelby sufficiently to confide her own symptoms before the day was out, whereupon the Principal Medical Officer of a ship-of-the-line valiantly supplied suitable pills and confirmed hopes which made her know that she was very happy, though feeling very ill.

What the Admiral described as "a fine fair wind", and his hostess as "a nice breeze", carried the frigate to the westward of Cape St. Vincent, and presently it seemed that the Admiral, although very hearty, was not free from pain. Next morning the *Seahorse* was rising at her fences, and Fremantle, whose flesh wound seemed to be getting larger and wetter instead of drier and smaller, was easily persuaded, after a bad night, not to attempt to get up. His ministering angel was utterly miserable; even the Admiral confessed that the motion of the ship hurt his arm. As for the sick and wounded of the *Theseus,* they suffered most noisily and with incredible persistence.

But being driven far to the westward, at great speed, was preferable to their next experience, a foul wind, which made the Admiral fume and become worthy to be acidly classed, together with Mrs. Fremantle's adored husband, as "a very bad patient". The succeeding complete calm was not reflected in the *Seahorse*. Fremantle, big-eyed, hot and restless, announced his resistance almost exhausted, and voiced in the same breath apprehensions of a lingering illness. His little wife drooped to see him so low. The Admiral wryly reported himself "very indifferent". His unspoken belief was that Fremantle would have to face amputation before the month was out.

In the fullness of time a fair wind was the only comfort of a party of wrecks. It brought them, by the penultimate day of August, in sight of Home, and Mrs. Fremantle, aged eighteen, who had not seen Home for nine years, thought "the light of Scilly, plain in the evening" had a lovely look. Next afternoon, when they should have been seeing land, came a foul wind again, and the Admiral mutteringly wished himself back with the old Mediterranean Fleet, off Cadiz. In the mist of a gloomy first of September, the pretty Isle of Wight did not display herself nearly clear enough for patriotic Mrs. Fremantle's taste. The *Seahorse* came to anchor at Spithead before dinner, and immediately after that meal, although the sea was much too rough for a lady to consider leaving the ship, a one-armed Admiral descended to his barge, and was pulled, in whirling rain, amongst swooping gulls, towards fishy smells, and wet house-faces, and the "George", Portsmouth.

Chapter IX

1797

(*ætat.* 38–39)

DOCTOR'S ORDERS

I

SUNDAY, September 3, 1797, was a lovely day, sunny and pleasant, and light lingered long, but shutters were closed against night air, candles were lit and a very quiet family in the dead season for Bath were thinking of bed, when suddenly a wife's ear detected the sound of a familiar voice, accustomed to shouting commands. The house of the late Mrs. Searle, which the Rector had rented furnished for three years, stood just round the corner of the street, and Admiral Nelson was directing his coachman where to stop. A moment later he was in the room, "come laughing back", as he had always prophesied.

He had now attained the appearance made familiar by the most famous series of his portraits, for which the original sketches were made during the next few months. Time and the enemy were yet to strike a blow at him. One more visible scar was to be added to his brow. He grew in the eight seasons remaining to him more meagre and haggard. At the last, shrunk inside a weighty uniform and orders, almost as fragile as an autumn leaf, he appeared to the uninitiated, on formal occasions, a truly alarming compound of direct manners and elaborate dress. But essentially the unexpected figure which electrified the Bath parlour that night was already that which would be recognised by members of every succeeding generation as Nelson. His hair, originally light auburn, had been since the fatal Nicaraguan Expedition so white as to require in his opinion no powder. Fashionable women wrote indulgently of his shock head, and, never a man of fashion, it seems that after he was largely dependent upon a *valet* to get him into a complicated costume, his dress and person suggested additionally the mild dissociation early remarked by Prince William Henry. The fixed dim right eye, the empty right sleeve, were painful novelties to his family, but that his old infective high spirits were untouched was at once equally obvious; and these spirits were so distracting a characteristic that witnesses called upon for a description of a great man often confirmed on a note of surprise that he was not above middle height, very slight, far from handsome, unaffectedly simple in address, and of no great dignity, "indeed, in appearance nothing remarkable either way". In vain they catalogued a face of irregular worn features, a complexion whipped and spoilt by sea-winds, a grave nose, a vulnerable mouth, an eye still boyish. The outstanding impression of those who encountered Nelson while the radiant orb shone upon the burning glass was of a man so active in person, so animated in countenance and so apposite and vehement in conversation that little else was recollected.

Only one member of the party surprised that night seemed to the home-comer quite unchanged. He had been much forewarned to expect alteration in his parent. To his delight, his good father looked to him exactly as he had done on a snowy morning of January 1793. Over four years of perpetual ailment and fret had inevitably taken their toll of the looks of a lady nearing forty, but his wife had always dressed well, and possessed fine features. He gladly pronounced on his return "my domestic happiness perfect". His elder sister, as befitted a matron of daughters nearly marriageable, was now chiefly remarkable for a formidable cap, nose and chin, and the young lady by her side was, of course, quite unrecognisable as "the little Kate" remembered as a round-eyed child, sitting about disconsolate at Burnham Thorpe, wondering how her mama could have sent her to so dull a place. To this future Captain's lady the arrival of her distinguished naval uncle spelt romance. Her cousin and confidante, Mary Anne Bolton, had already received an offer from an "old Agamemnon". Lieutenant Pierson, the bearer of letters to East Anglia after the battle of February 14, had not been idle when invited to spend some weeks of convalescence at Hollesley Rectory. News of Mary Anne's brother, also an "old Agamemnon", was eagerly awaited. But it soon transpired that the traveller's arm, which still required attention, had not been dressed since dawn.

Late though the hour, Mr. Nicholls, medical adviser to Lady Nelson, had to be fetched, and presently a lady so nervous that she dared not open a letter which might contain bad news found herself called upon to attend the dressing of an amputation case. Moreover, her husband expected her to acquire the skill to perform this business, when necessary, unaided. Since he was cheerfully firm, and she was devoted, resolution was summoned, and the first great effort made. After an interval, a paler Admiral and lady reappeared, and the Bath physician, accustomed to plucking the golden goose and prescribing for nothing more shocking than the results of English fare and weather after East or West Indian service, had no objection to offer to his patient's desire for a London opinion. Next morning Lady Nelson wrote to Mr. Maurice Nelson, asking him to engage London lodgings. Next morning also, and for several days, newspapers published full accounts of the total failure of the expedition against Teneriffe.

The journals scanned by the returned Admiral at Bath were typical of their date. In the advertisement columns, since Britain's Fleet was still fast expanding, sea-officers were tempted by offers of succulent ship's stores—Beef-rounds, Portable soups, Morello cherries, Anchovies, Truffles, white Walnuts, and particularly Mr. Skill's delicious genuine six-pounder Stilton cheeses. In the gossip columns, Margate was reported very vulgar, Ramsgate very gay, Tunbridge very full, Brighton extremely modish and Southampton deserted. Lord Spencer was on holiday at Althorp, and the Prime Minister, at his country house, was combining exercise and amusement by swinging a hatchet. All papers gave pride of place to the failure at Teneriffe, and no journalist had been able to resist dwelling gloomily upon the loss of the *Fox*. Otherwise, comments differed according to the political complexion of the organ. The *Courier* noted, with erudite and ghastly gaiety, that "the Fortunate Isle of the Ancients is evidently not one of Billy Pitt's". Several much mistaken persons represented ageing Lord St. Vincent as meekly submitting to bloodthirsty orders from Home; others resented the brevity of the Commander-in-Chief's despatches, and there was bickering about contradictory numbers in the casualty lists. On one point only the Press were agreed. No blame attached to Rear-Admiral Nelson, "just landed after his gallant though unsuccessful attempt, in good spirits and health except the loss of his arm". It was recalled that the Puerto Rico Expedition had been a failure, although it, too, had been entrusted to a commander of approved merit. Bad information as to the degree of enemy force to be encountered and as to recently strengthened defences was averred in his defence. A Bath journal was possessive: "Arrived at Bath—Lady Ann Mahon, Sir John Snow, Sir William Addington, Admiral Sir Horatio Nelson. . . . The Rear-Admiral, who was received at Portsmouth on the 1st with a universal greeting, reached Bath on Sunday evening in good health and spirits, to the great joy of his Lady and Venerable Father, and gratification of every admirer of British Valour." "The brave Admiral certainly owes his country no service; he has signalized himself in as exemplary a manner as any hero that graces the Naval Annals of this country, and with the loss of a right arm—

> 'Having purchased in his youth renown,
> To make him lov'd and valued when he's old,'

it might have been supposed that he would set quietly down 'with all his budding honours thick about him'. But it is said that he eagerly longs to repair to that station on which his name has been the pride of the British Fleet and the terror of the enemy." One writer paid him the supreme compliment of alluding to him without title or Christian name: "Protected by such as NELSON we may defy the malignant threats of our Enemies, and look with contempt upon the wild project of an Invasion, confiding in the superintendence of Providence to afford us safeguard, and in our Wooden Walls."

On the Wednesday following his entry, pens were active in Mrs. Searle's house. Lady Nelson wrote to Mr. Suckling explaining that they could not as yet come to Kentish Town, since the Admiral's wound required a daily dressing by a surgeon. "My husband's spirits are good although he suffers a good deal of pain—the arm is taken off very high, near the shoulder. Opium procures him rest, and last night he was pretty quiet." Her husband was simultaneously writing to William, "As to my personal health, it never was better, and my arm is in the fairest way of healing", but "the truly affectionate William" was already on his road to Bath. Letters from distinguished quarters continued to surprise the quiet household. Lord Hood sent what Lady Nelson called "such a letter!" The First Lord wrote most handsomely, hoping to see Rear-Admiral Nelson in Town as soon as possible. The Duke of Clarence longed to be one of the first to shake his old friend by the left hand, and considerately begged that Lady Nelson might report. In slow and laboured characters the old friend himself replied:

"Sir,
  "I trust your Royal Highness will attribute my not having sent a letter since my arrival to its true cause—viz., the not being now a ready writer. I feel confident of your sorrow for my accident; but I assure your Royal Highness, that not a scrap of that ardour with which I have hitherto served our King has been shot away."

At last all the letters were written, the London surgeon and lodgings were engaged, and Sir Horatio Nelson and lady, the Reverend William Nelson, the Admiral's sailor servant and her ladyship's woman took the road for the capital. The months of July and August had been remarkably tempestuous, and September was proving very wet, but warm, and with pleasant sunshine between the thunder-showers. There were gossamer floats in the hedgerows of the clean-washed landscape through which the travellers passed, and although Provence roses were still to be seen in cottage gardens, the large golden leaves of the horse-chestnut were sailing to the ground through still airs, evenings were vaporous, the swallows were congregating and the song of the robin had been heard. They broke their journey at Newbury, and on the evening of Wednesday, September 13, in sunshine after heavy rain, drew up safely at the doors of 141, Bond Street. The lodging-house kept by Mr. Jones stood on the west side of the fashionable street, a little south of Grosvenor Street, and near enough to St. George's, Hanover Square, for a wakeful man to hear the hours tolled from that modern classic building throughout the long night, after the last coach had rolled home, the last laugh had died away outside, the last pair of heels had ceased to trouble the pavements, and there was no other sound in the world remarkable, except the too-fast heartbeats bred by rising fever.

N.—9*

2

Nelson, who persisted in regarding his condition as the result of an accident, not an illness, and who realised that he had been arrested at a critical moment in his career, was disappointed after he had displayed his arm to his first London surgeon. Mr. William Cruikshank, late partner of Dr. William Hunter, brought his young son-in-law, Mr. Thomas, a person who had been chief dresser to the great but brusque Hunter at St. George's Hospital. After five days of their treatment, a most impatient patient found himself not the least better than when he had left the hands of good Dr. Weir at Cadiz. The London experts confirmed his gloomy opinion that only time would bring him about again. Meanwhile, since he would not be an invalid, and must perform the duty known as "keeping in touch", he repaired nearly every morning to the Admiralty.

Here he learnt, amongst other things, the very welcome news that he was to get a pension of £1,000 a year. Custom decreed that he must first make a formal statement of his services to his Sovereign. The document, when accomplished, was impressive. He could claim to have assisted at four fleet actions, three with frigates, six engagements against batteries, ten cutting-out expeditions and the capture of three towns; in which service, humbly submitted for His Majesty's consideration, he had lost his right eye and arm. But the business was by no means finished when he had drawn up his memorial and forwarded it with a covering letter to Lord Spencer. A fortnight passed before the Surgeons Company notified him that the hour of 6 p.m. on the first or third Thursday of every month had been appointed for such examinations as that of the injury to his eye. To an officer who possessed no carriage, and was enduring daily dressings after an amputation, an invitation to present himself in the City, after dark, in the height of the London fog season, for the examination of an injury sustained three years past, did not seem reasonable. He took a firm line; addressed himself to the Commissioners of the Navy, offering to appear at Surgeons Hall any day between the hours of ten and four, carried his point, and presented himself in jocund mood, accompanied by his brother-in-law

Bolton. ("Oh! this is only for an eye: in a few days I shall come for an arm: and in a little time longer, God knows, most probably for a leg.")

There were other advantages in daily attendances at Headquarters. The word that Nelson was in town, lodging in Bond Street, in the surgeons' hands, passed like lightning from the outer chambers of Whitehall to the clubs, and particularly to the coffee-room of an hotel at the Strand end of Oxford Street. Callers began to knock at the doors of Mr. Jones's house. Mr. Richard Bulkeley, one of the survivors of the San Juan Expedition, appeared one evening after candles were lit, bringing two boys, to whom Sir Horatio showed his sword. The Lieutenant-Governor of the Royal Hospital, looking older and less rubicund, but benevolent as ever, came up from Greenwich. He had been quite unable to wait to see a favourite pupil until the *levée* at the end of next week. He had also a confession to make and a plot to weave. After Valentine's Day, a small print-seller of George Street, Woolwich, had come to the Hospital, begging leave to engrave any likeness of Admiral Nelson which might be in the possession of his old Captain. Locker had unhung from his gallery of future heroes the portrait of a Lieutenant by J. F. Rigaud, R.A., and on August 14 (an unhappy date in Nelson's story, when he was toiling back to the fleet from Teneriffe) Mr. Shipster had given to the world a small oval portrait in stipple, entitled "Horatio Nelson, Esq., now Sir Horatio Nelson, K.B., Rear-Admiral of the Blue Squadron". The engraver had been obliged to guess as to the changes wrought by twenty years' service, and had not guessed very happily. Lady Nelson, also approached by a print-seller (who intended to dedicate the result to H.R.H. the Duke of Clarence), had been as guilty, but either more discerning or fortunate. The miniature by an anonymous artist of Leghorn, sent to her two years past, had been entrusted by her to Mr. Robert Laurie, of Messrs. Laurie and Whittle, trading at the Golden Buck, Fleet Street, and Mr. Laurie, a mezzotinto engraver of considerable merit, working upon a portrait much inferior to that given to Shipster, was still engaged altering a Captain's uniform to that of an Admiral, adding the Star of the Bath, and removing Sir Horatio's right arm. Locker now considered that it was the duty of his friend to sit again as soon as possible for something authoritative, and he had an artist in mind. Lemuel Abbott, who abode in Caroline Street, Bloomsbury, in domestic disquiet and such penury that he could employ no assistants, was of a persevering disposition, and could present the speaking likeness of a sea-officer. He was willing to come to Greenwich when the Admiral was visiting the Lieutenant-Governor.

About noon on the fine but sunless morning of September 25 Admiral Nelson, bearing with him the two gentlemen he was to present—his large, robustious elder brother and slight, diffident Captain Berry—performed the short journey downhill from Bond Street to the St. James's Palace, where the first *levée* of the autumn season was to be held. When an officer had newly lost an arm—no unusual occurrence—the procedure as regards uniform was conventional. The upper sleeve of the close-fitting coat was slit or gashed to allow a servant to insert his hand and ease the painful stump into the tight garment: three neat bows of black or navy blue ribbon fastened the opening. All portraits of Nelson showing three ribbon bows on his right upper coat sleeve belong to the four months before the stump healed.

The *levée* was typical of its date. The Turkish, Sardinian, Portuguese and Neapolitan Ambassadors were present. The diplomats, headed by a deaf peer with a high nose and waving white locks, were ranged to receive the first share of royal notice. Six blue and eight scarlet coats were marshalled into line below them. Old Lord Howe had many enquiries to make after Lord St. Vincent. The officers of the navy included one other survivor of the Teneriffe expedition—Waller. The King, who had come up from Kew for the day, with two daughters to look after him on the journey, walked into the long gallery of the old blackened red-brick palace at 12.30, attended by the Duke of York. Lord Malmesbury, fresh from his unsuccessful attempt at peace-making with France, presented two soft, handsome youngsters of his staff, drawn from the Grand Whiggery of Devonshire House—Lord Morpeth and Lord Granville Leveson-Gower. Admiral Nelson's turn came next, but did not find him unready. The obstinate, pink-faced old gentleman with a bright light blue eye, for whom he nourished the warmest and most reverential feelings, was suddenly exclaiming before him. "You have lost your right arm!" observed the King. "But not my right hand, as I have the honour of presenting Captain Berry." Few outside their immediate circle heard the *riposte*, but Berry repeated it to the girl he hoped to marry.

Afterwards came the ceremony of investing Admiral Nelson with the Order of the Bath. It was just a happy chance that someone who so much appreciated the romantic fact should have been invested by the sovereign personally. Orders had been sent to Cadiz six months past for Lord St. Vincent to perform the ceremony, but by the time they had arrived Nelson had already sailed for Teneriffe. Strictly speaking, he had not been Sir Horatio until to-day, and St. Vincent and others of the fleet had been exact, but even the Secretary to the Admiralty and the Duke of Clarence had so addressed him.

Times had much changed since the *levée* after which an ardent Post-Captain had repaired to Alexander Davison's Lincoln's Inn chambers to discuss every subject under the sun. Davison, like the officer whom he called "H.N.", had prospered during the past five years. At the opening of the war with France he had been concerned with the commissariat of the Duke of York's ill-fated Flanders expedition, and now that large bodies of troops were being retained at home in expectation of invasion, he was acting as a Government contractor on a large scale. His factories, furnishing barrack supplies, from tents and boots to coal and candles, covered an area of Millbank. He had bought a Northumbrian property called Swarland Park, where he was making improvements. At a house in aristocratic St. James's Square he was forming a collection of historical oil-paintings by British artists. Nelson, vaguely disturbed by the large talk of a man now deep in Cabinet, princely and City secrets, offered in vain a word of caution.

On October 5 a congenial party set out for the Royal Hospital, Greenwich. Sir Gilbert Elliot, invited to dine with the Governor, had gladly accepted the offer of a seat in the carriage bespoken by the Nelsons, bent upon a stay with the Lieutenant-Governor. The ex-Viceroy, who had just heard that he was to be raised to the peerage, as Baron Minto, and had decided upon a Moor's head as his crest, was chiefly exercised by the thought of having to face the criticism of his Eton son. However, he had written to tell his tutor to apologise to young Gilbert, and Mr. Reed reported that the heir had resignedly pronounced, "Well, if it is to be so, it must be so." Sir Gilbert, who had not seen Nelson since his loss of an arm, thought that he looked, nevertheless, "better and fresher than I ever remember him". Nelson confessed that his arm was by no means well, and that he was still suffering a good deal of violent pain—taking opium every night. His surgeons were talking of a further operation, which, they warned him, would not be easy, as the stump was already very short, but to which he would gladly consent if there was any hope of success, as he was very impatient to get to sea again. Sir Gilbert himself was feeling far from well, and resented the gout which had first begun to afflict him during the nerve-racking last days of his Viceroyalty. He, too, was anxious to be employed abroad again for his country's good as soon as possible, and his lady, "less of a coward than myself", wrote rousingly from Scotland, urging high deeds upon him. He was to kiss hands on Wednesday or Thursday next, and poor Pozzo di Borgo still haunted him.

The carriageful of cheerfully talking invalids jolted into the echoing grey precincts of the Royal Hospital, seen at its best on an autumn day of cloudless skies, when every massive building which had succeeded the ancient palace of Placentia rose clear-cut against a background of wooded heights and flashing, tumbled waters, well covered by slow and swift-moving merchandise, although England had now been at war again for nearly five years. The houses of Lord Hood and Captain Locker stood opposite one another, the Governor's facing the noble Grand Court on the west, and the Lieutenant-Governor's on the east—therefore, as far as outlook and prospects of summer sun went, infinitely preferable. The Nelsons passed through a commodious entrance-hall to a drawing-room in which Mrs. Locker and family awaited them, and afterwards through a panelled room to the dining-room. The panelled room, which was of notable charm and comfort—exactly the room pictured by an officer thinking of home on blowing nights—was generally used by the Lieutenant-Governor as his sanctum, and old Miss Elizabeth Locker loved in long-after years to describe to an author nephew how she had, as a child, helped Nelson on and off with his undress uniform coat, before and after every sitting given by him to Lemuel Abbott in her father's apartment at Greenwich Hospital.

3

A few days later, when winter was beginning to settle down upon eighteenth-century London, deep sunk in brown fog and mire, an elegant caller presented himself at 141, Bond Street, where, although prices were high, guests could only be offered what Lady Nelson deprecatingly styled "a family dinner". Colonel Drinkwater soon mentioned a rumour current in Whitehall this morning that an engagement between our North Sea Fleet and that of the Dutch was hourly expected. The result surprised him. "Drinkwater!" exclaimed Nelson, starting from his seat, in his peculiar energetic manner, "I would give this other arm to be with Duncan at this moment." In the shadows, her constant rôle, Lady Nelson endeavoured in vain to restrain her husband.

At dawn on October 13, a gloomy morning of black clouds, later discharging heavy rain, Lieutenant Brodie of the *Rose* cutter arrived at the Admiralty with a despatch, and before dusk the guns of the Tower and Park had fired salutes in honour of what to-morrow's newspapers would describe as "Admiral Duncan's total destruction of the Dutch Fleet at Camperdown". Illuminations were ordered in official quarters, and late though the hour and poor the visibility, most private houses in the fashionable streets put out some evidence of enthusiasm. A crowd of cup-shotten patriots thundered at the doors of 141, Bond Street, where every window was dark. Their repeated knockings and shoutings dragged back from the borders of drug-induced sleep an invalid who had retired to bed early after a bad day. Oddly enough, nobody in this house most interested in a naval action had heard either the guns or the news. Everyone leapt to the conclusion that the visitors brought an alarm of fire. Presently the rough voices faded apologetically and heavy boots retreated. On being informed at Mr. Jones's house that Admiral Nelson, badly wounded at Teneriffe, lodged there, their leader had withdrawn the intruders with the words, "You will hear no more from us to-night."

The mere thought of a decisive action at which he could not assist had been maddening to Nelson, now beset by four surgeons, a physician and an apothecary. The late Principal Medical Officer of the *Agamemnon* had come to his old Captain's aid, and at the request of Mr. Bulkeley, Dr. Benjamin Moseley, late of Jamaica (now Physician to the Royal Hospital, Chelsea), had been called in. Still the ligature applied on board H.M.S. *Theseus* on a July night held fast to the artery and nerve. The stump was now hot and swollen, requiring poultices. The advisability of cutting down upon the nerve-bulb had been discussed *ad nauseam*. Mr. Cruikshank was nervous of a further operation. Finally, the opinion of Mr. Thomas Keate, Surgeon-General to the Army and Surgeon to the Prince of Wales, had been sought. Mr. Keate, although little likely to agree with any crony of Dr. Hunter (especially one given to intemperance), pronounced himself averse from violent methods. He advised that the cure should be left to Time and Nature. A patient who knew that he was playing a game in which Time mattered had to resign himself to keeping up his spirits and proceeding with what activities were possible. He achieved an astonishing amount.

On November 3, when his preparations for leaving London for Norfolk were well in train, two young visitors were ushered in to him. A lady, little more than a child herself, but within a few weeks of opening her nursery, possessively shepherded a naval Captain with an arm in a sling and the heavy pallid look of one deprived of accustomed hard exercise. Mrs. Fremantle had asked for Lady Nelson (a person she had never met), but on hearing that her ladyship was not at home, the callers had leapt at an offer of "the good Admiral". The Fremantles (who had no notion that they were pathetic) had been in London five days, and had been shopping, and to the Shakespeare Gallery, and to see the King go to open Parliament, "very grand, and amusing enough", and Fremantle had felt the benefit of being out of Portsmouth, but was still far from well. He had borne the jolting of a journey to the capital pretty well, but the inquisitors of the Surgeons Hall, at their favourite 6 p.m., had so pulled him about that he had subsequently been obliged to desert a family party at the play at Drury Lane.

However, he had seen Lord Spencer, who had been very civil, and the surgeons had pronounced his wound equal to the loss of a limb, and he had been instructed to memorialise His Majesty with regard to a pension.

At last Susanna's brother-in-law, Sam Bolton of Akenham Hall, near Ipswich, seemed to have heard of a house of the right size in the right position. Roundwood was not flimsy or glaringly new. It had been built to last, in 1700. "All looks like a gentleman's house." It was not the romantic cottage of Nelson's early dreams, but neither was it one of the unmanageable, decaying mansions thrust upon his notice, as so cheap, by the large-minded William. Before Nelson had seen the house, the Rector had guessed that he meant to buy it if at all possible, and this expectation was fulfilled. The moment was suitable for the setting up of a new home, for the Rector was thinking of retirement.

On the night of November 28, at 11 p.m., back in Bond Street, Nelson wrote to Berry, who had announced his engagement to a cousin, Miss Louisa Forster, elder daughter of Dr. Forster of Norwich. The Admiral's first paragraph expressed congratulations on the prospect of becoming "one of *us*", and hopes of meeting Mrs. Berry. The second was important. Although his arm was still obstinate, his daily visits to the Admiralty had not been fruitless. He had heard to-day that he was to have the *Foudroyant*, of 80 guns, due to be launched in January and commissioned in February. Lord Spencer had also told him that he must be in Town on December 19, which had now been fixed for the King's going to St. Paul's in procession to offer thanks for the naval victories of the war. To this pageant, likely to be very fine, Captains Berry and Noble should attend him. He wrote cheerfully, for he had just emerged from one of those functions his soul dreaded. In spite of his early political aspirations, and ample practice in addressing a ship's company, the thought of having to make a ceremonial speech of thanks to a complimentary civilian audience, to "be stared at", still poisoned his life for hours beforehand. He had to study his few sentences carefully, and depart for the ordeal at last on the dogged note—"Anything better than ingratitude". At the Guildhall this afternoon, Mr. Chamberlain John Wilkes, presenting the Freedom of the City of London, in a gold box of the value of one hundred guineas, had addressed him with penetration.

"Many of our Naval Commanders have merited highly of their country by their exertions, but in your case there is a rare heroic modesty which cannot be sufficiently admired. You have given the warmest applause to your Brother Officers and the Seamen under your command but your own merit you have not mentioned, even in the slightest manner. . . ."

Five nights after he penned his late line to Berry, Nelson went to bed as usual. Outside the streets were quiet, for on the 29th snow had fallen from 9 a.m. without intermission, and throughout the next three days there had been snow-showers, and although to-day no snow had fallen, the skies were heavy again, and it was Sunday night. He went to bed as usual, but did not stir till daylight—an extraordinary thing, something which had not happened since last July. He had slept the night through, like a child, and woke almost free from pain. He had returned to a sane world, nothing resembling the distorted scene through which he had been forcing his way, almost a soul dragging about a corpse, from the moment that he had felt himself hit in the right elbow, on the mole at Santa Cruz.

The reason might easily be guessed, and when the surgeon (hastily summoned) undid the bandages, the ligature came away at the slightest touch. The knotted thread attended by evil odours fell into the dressing like a spent snake, to trouble no more. Within a few days his stump was fast healing.

He attended another *levée*, and heard that the *Foudroyant* would not be ready for him in time, now that he was well. On the night of December 8 he wrote two short notes. The first was to his future Flag-Captain.

"To Captain Berry, R.N., Dr. Forster's, Norwich.

"SECRET, except to Dr. Forster and Miss.

"My dear Sir,

"If you mean to marry, I would recommend your doing it speedily, or the to be Mrs. Berry will have very little of your company; for I am well, and you may expect to be called for every hour. We shall probably be at sea before the *Foudroyant* is launched. Our Ship is at Chatham, a Seventy-four, and she will be choicely manned. This may not happen, but it stands so to-day,

"Ever yours most faithfully,
"Horatio Nelson."

But since he was also the son of the Rector of Burnham Thorpe, he did not, in his moment of relief, forget another duty. He sent across a note to the clergyman of the nearest parish church, St. George's, Hanover Square: "An Officer desires to return thanks to Almighty God for his perfect recovery from a severe Wound, and also for many mercies bestowed upon him. December 8th, 1797 (for next Sunday)."

Chapter X

1798

(*ætat.* 39)

THE NILE

I

ON April 24, 1798, two handsome peers, seated in Whitehall, where the lilacs were budding in the First Lord's garden, held under the cloak of a casual morning call an interesting conversation. *The Times* that morning had published a circumstantial account of the French armament collecting in Mediterranean ports. Lord Minto, whose sources of information were reliable, had heard that the Government was at last thinking seriously of the Mediterranean..He supposed that Sir Horatio Nelson would be the fittest man in the world for such a command, and, glancing round the apartment in which he found himself, added, "He is as well acquainted with the Mediterranean as your lordship is with this room we are sitting in."

Lord Spencer listened patiently to an agreeable man who might get himself another important post abroad. He did not much relish being told that anyone appreciated better than himself the possibilities of junior Admirals, but any flag-officer who could serve under Lord St. Vincent for a considerable period without the noise of an explosion penetrating to Whitehall merited attention, and he had taken the trouble to study Nelson during his months of sick-leave, a thing rendered easy by the Admiral's zealous attendance in his waiting-rooms and drawing-room. Lady Spencer, the simplicity of whose grandeur sometimes startled her gentle sister-in-law, the Duchess of Devonshire, had thought Nelson an extraordinary-looking creature before he spoke, and after he had opened his mouth, more extraordinary still. The Lady of the Admiralty, who was determined that her husband's tenure of office should be marked by brilliancy and high moral tone, was undecided whether Nelson was an idiot or a genius. On his first arrival in her drawing-room he had appeared so shockingly ill she would rather not look at him. He had certainly performed a feat in getting a hostess of pronounced hauteur to break through her well-known rule of never noticing a sea-officer's wife. All officers of the rank of Captain and above received an invitation to dine at the First Lord's before they sailed to take up a new command. Nelson had said that he had not asked permission to introduce his lady, but that if Lady Spencer could notice her, after his departure, it would make him the happiest man alive. He was convinced that Lady Spencer must like Lady Nelson, who was beautiful, accomplished and, above all, an angel whose care had saved his life. He had been invited to bring the angel to dine that very day, and he had upset Lady Spencer's table arrangements by handing his own wife in to dinner and asking to be allowed to sit next to her. He had said that he saw so little of her that he would not voluntarily lose an instant of her company.

Lord Minto's panegyric ended, and Lord Spencer thought that he might venture to assure his companion that if the Government should take such a decision with regard to the Mediterranean, the name of Nelson would certainly be the first to suggest itself to him. Actually, Lord St. Vincent must nominate the officer. But he knew well how high was the opinion held of Nelson in that quarter. He would express to Lord St. Vincent his own and the Government's view. Making a great gesture of throwing off the official mask, he mentioned a squadron of eight of the line as the first reinforcement likely to be sent to Cadiz. Lord St. Vincent might be able to spare Admiral Nelson another four, and competent frigates. There was no chance of any other officer being chosen. He thanked his caller for confirming an opinion he had already held, and said that he would always be glad to hear the valuable suggestions of the ex-Viceroy of Corsica.

Lord Minto returned to his Roehampton villa to send a long letter to Nelson, confessing "the step I have taken on my own responsibility", and Lord Spencer wrote five days later to Lord St. Vincent, pointing out that, if he determined to send a detachment into the Mediterranean, the activity, disposition and experience of Sir H. Nelson seemed to qualify him in a peculiar manner for this service. His letter marked "Private and Confidential" waited at the Admiralty until May 2 to accompany a long official document headed "Secret Instructions", and arrived in Cadiz Bay on May 24, a date which found Nelson already on his way to Toulon, and overtaken by disaster. In the following winter, when people had long ceased to complain of so junior an Admiral being chosen, His Majesty's sailor son asked Berry to tell Nelson that, as a matter of fact, the person who had chosen him and "formed the whole plan", resulting in the victory of the Nile, was his august parent.

Nelson's progress since he had seen the *Vanguard* out of dock on December 18 had been entirely successful, though not so speedy as he had hoped. In France, during the early months of the year, while General Buonaparte (abruptly summoned from Italy) was inspecting the invasion ports of the north coast, Nelson, at Bath, was receiving the usual flood of letters from persons who had relatives or friends to place. By early February the *Vanguard* had gone down the river to the Nore. Berry was bringing her round to Spithead, and if the present wind held, Nelson reckoned that the next thing he would hear would be orders to hoist his flag. He hoped to stay at Portsmouth not above forty-eight hours. The Admiral, "as usuall in Great Good Spirits, panting to be in Actuall Service", said farewell to his father and moved up to Bond Street again, this time to No. 96. A fortnight later he had heard nothing from Lord Spencer. A large convoy, which he was to escort, was slowly assembling. On March 14 he made his final appearance at a *levée*, and after that had nothing further for which to wait, except a line from the Admiralty. Lady Nelson would set off for Bath, taking with her little Kate Bolton (to whom she meant to be very kind), at the same moment that he took the Portsmouth road. William, come up from Norfolk to see the last of a hero, was given an affectionate letter for very old Miss Mary Nelson, the Rector's sister, and two pounds of tea, a gift easily come by at the moment, for stores of every description were beginning to shower upon the Admiral's lodgings. Already he knew of three passengers whom he would have to entertain at his table, and an Admiral must at least present the appearance of having everything handsome about him. To be remarkably shabby or frugal was bad for discipline. A crate labelled

"China" was sent off by coach. The tailor, haberdasher and linen-draper delivered new gear, marked and numbered in cross-stitch. Lady Nelson, her maid and niece packed; still the collection of parcels seemed to increase, and Mrs. Cuthbert Collingwood might yet be sending treasures to be carried to her husband at Lisbon. The last days in London were trying, not the least of the difficulties being that the Admiral's sailor servant had taken the measure of the Admiral's lady. Lady Nelson's spirits were low as the hour of parting approached. Her orders were to settle as soon as possible at Round-wood. "I am clear it is right you should be in your own cottage."

At 8 p.m. on the night of March 29, Sir Horatio broke his flag, blue at the mizzen, on board the *Vanguard* at Spithead, and entered into his new kingdom. The scene for the next forty-eight hours was just as busy as that he had quitted in London, but much less distressing. "Berry is married, but still goes with me." He found very little wrong in his flagship. He greeted Captain Peyton, made the acquaintance of the two land-officers whom he was to carry to Lisbon, and began to employ a new character, his Secretary. The First Lieutenant, Galwey, another stranger, displayed every mark of the good officer risen without the help of friends. Michael Jefferson was Principal Medical Officer. Cork reports mentioned that the chops of the two channels were crowded with home-bound ships waiting the first spurt of a southerly wind to enter their destined ports. The *Vanguard* was off with the lark on April 1, but, the wind coming to the westward at noon, was forced to return to St. Helen's. All passengers went ashore, but Sir Horatio remained "fixed". In the Admiral's state-room, amongst mahogany which would soon be reflecting Mediterranean sun, Tom Allen unpacked doggedly. Lady Nelson had kindly slipped in her own little blue pillow, but in the bustle of departure had gone off with the Admiral's old watch, and, apparently, the keys of his dressing-stand. On the other hand, just the weights of her ladyship's scales were here. Tom had obeyed her ladyship's orders to lock the bedroom door before he opened any of his master's luggage at the inn on the road down (the trunks being full of small parcels); all the same, many things were missing. Letters began to fly between the

Admiral, detained for ten days by the wind blowing as foul as it could ("So much for Admiralty delays"), and her ladyship, watching the vane on Queen Square Chapel, Bath, to see whether the *Vanguard* had sailed. He could not find the old pieces of Portuguese gold given him by his father, or his black stock and buckle. (It was true that the buckle had only cost him 1s. 6d., but it was a friend of eighteen years' standing.) In an evil hour, while it blew so strong as to prevent all intercourse with the shore, he went through his linen, and found it very different from his dearest Fanny's list. The brightest spot was sixteen cambric handkerchief's instead of thirteen. The magnitude of the most serious deficiencies (eleven pairs of new silk stockings and ten huckaback towels) led him to hope that they had never been sent. Lady Nelson replied that Bath was over-full of country families who had run there supposing it a safe place in case of the Invasion. She was trying to exert her spirits. "I wish very much it had been in my power to send your things more comfortably." She believed that his buckle and keys must come to hand. "I will leave this mortifying subject." She sent her love to her "child", and invoked God to protect and bless her husband. "I rejoice to see you so exact. Times will make us all very careful." His last words were, "Nothing in the world can exceed the pleasure I shall have in returning to you", and "I hope, when you travel, you will not trust yourself in a stage."

2

"I am very happy", wrote the First Lord to Lord St. Vincent, on March 30, 1798, "to send you Sir Horatio Nelson again, not only because I believe I cannot send you a more zealous, active and approved officer, but because I have reason to believe that his being under your command will be agreeable to your wishes." "I do assure your lordship", replied Lord St. Vincent, on May 1, "that the arrival of Admiral Nelson has given me new life. You could not have gratified me more than in sending him. His presence in the Mediterranean is so very essential that I mean to put the *Orion* and *Alexander* under his command, with the addition of three or four frigates, and to send him away (the moment the *Vanguard* has delivered her water to the in-shore squadron) to endeavour to ascertain the real object of the preparations making by the French."

Lord St. Vincent had continued to suffer since he had last seen Nelson. "What", he demanded, "do they mean by invariably sending me the mutinous ships? Do they think I will be hangman to the Fleet?" Captains were forbidden to entertain one another at dinner, and all officers to go ashore at Lisbon or Gibraltar, "on what is called pleasure", except in correct uniform. (The coloured clothes and round hats which the Commander-in-Chief had observed might, he feared, cause these supercilious and licentious-spoken young gentlemen to be mistaken for shopkeepers.) Lights out by 8 p.m. was the rule for ships' companies, and since the utmost frugality in fuel consumption was necessary, no fires were to be lit except between 11 a.m. and 3 p.m. Breakfast could be cooked on stoves. While the Captain of a ship newly arrived from home reported to the Admiral, one of his bargemen, perceiving the bronzed countenance of a veteran peeping out of a lower-deck port of the *Ville de Paris*, ventured to ask, "What have you fellows been doing while we have been fighting for your beef and pork?" "Take my advice", was the awful reply, "and say nothing at all about all that out here. For, by G—d if old Jarvie hears ye, ye'll be dingle-dangle at the yard-arm by eight o'clock to-morrow morning."

Raging neuralgia, mutineers and "the vain conceit and flippancy of manner of inexperienced officers" were not the worst things mourned by St. Vincent during the months of Nelson's absence. "The nerves of Mr. de Pinto are totally unstrung!" Portugal, England's only remaining ally, gave her at present nothing but the use of the Tagus, and Portugal, like nearly every timorous neutral, appeared blind to the expediency of uniting openly and effectively with Great Britain, while time remained. All watched fascinated to see whom the revolutionary crocodile would devour next. Austria (never ceasing to lament that her Italian campaign had been ruined by the withdrawal of the British fleet from the Mediterranean) had signed the definitive Treaty of Campo Formio in October, relinquishing Belgium, and receiving in exchange the city and part of the former territories of despoiled Venetia. Holland, Switzerland and the Italian Republics were all occupied by French troops, and exercising government under French control. The death of the Anglophil Catherine of Russia had been immediately followed by the breakdown of Lord Malmesbury's peace mission, for France had little fear of obstruction from her successor. It was under these circumstances that Pitt "began to think of the Mediterranean", where it was obvious that France was planning some new operation on a grand scale, but with commendable secrecy. Ireland, the West Indies, Naples, Sicily, Portugal were all considered as the possible destination of the fleet fitting out at Toulon, and the troops and transports collecting in large numbers at every southern French port, in Genoa, Civita Vecchia and Corsica. At all costs the junction of this force with the Brest squadron, or the Spanish fleet still held in Cadiz, must be prevented. A new coalition was now Pitt's dream —an auxiliary Russian squadron in the North Sea, France vexed by a renewal of war on the Continent by restive Austria and perhaps her satellite Naples; but before it could be realised, these Powers must be reassured that Britannia ruled the waves. While Nelson dined with Lord St. Vincent on April 30, Lord Spencer's letter urging "the appearance of a British squadron in the Mediterranean is a condition on which the fate of Europe may at this moment be stated to depend" was not yet despatched from Whitehall.

Nelson found his host very friendly, very violent, obviously unwell, and, although he was close about this, hinting at retirement. ("The person to succeed me should possess both temper and good nerves, or he will be in continual hot water, and terrified at this anchorage.") Not only professional matters were discussed. The Commander-in-Chief had done his best for the large lowering lad of eighteen, who sent Nelson stilted notes beginning, "My dear Father". The Captain of the *Dolphin*, according to Lord St. Vincent, had acquitted himself marvellously well as an officer on three recent occasions, and was improving in manner and conversation. ("Pretty quick promotion", resignedly commented William Hoste.)

On Sunday evening, May 20, as the rays of a spectacular spring sunset gilded the green paint of his cabin, Nelson, pacing up and down it, knew himself "exhilarated beyond description". Yesterday it had blown strong from the N.W. This evening the wind had dropped away, and the *Vanguard*, with top-gallants set, was not moving as fast as his wishes. Still, the picture framed by slanting stern-gallery windows was handsome, for she was attended by H.M.S. *Alexander* and *Orion*, 74's, four frigates and a sloop. The Gibraltar garrison had been very civil and very merry. English beef and buttons, chained to the Rock, announcing themselves forgotten in London, generally were in spirits. But the scarlet coats had shown an inclination to *fête* sea-officers who had better be watering their ships, and having no taste at present for social gaieties, the Admiral had been glad to slip out of Rosia Bay with dusk, his eastward course marked by no unfriendly eye. Despite his loss of a right arm, he was up the Mediterranean again, with secret orders "to look after the French", and the men of the corvette *La Pierre*, captured by one of his frigates four days past, and separately examined, all agreed that General Buonaparte had arrived at Toulon on the 6th, where fifteen of the line and numerous transports were ready to go to sea, and twelve of forty thousand men were already embarked. Cavalry had been pouring into the city as the polacca left the harbour. Nelson reckoned that he should now be in the exact position for intercepting enemy supply ships bound for Marseille and Toulon. He had sent the usual line to his wife, telling her that she must not be surprised if she did not hear from him again for a little. He would not be going on any fighting expedition. Nor need she now fear the invasion of England by Buonaparte this summer. (Although the Conqueror had now abandoned the Italianate version of his name, to Nelson he was ever "Buonaparte" and never, except in derision, "Napoleon".) He had addressed the letter to "our Cottage", where he hoped that she would soon be fixed in comfort. The evil months of his protracted convalescence, permeated by the sickly fragrance of dressings and opium, were safe wiped from his record, and almost from his memory, as the *Vanguard*, with her squadron about her, stood in towards Cape Sicie, with a moderate breeze. He knew that his squadron, "small but very choice", expected much of him, and he returned the compliment.

The sun sank, and the weather began to appear not so promising, but as the ship had been prepared for a gale, his mind was easy. By midnight the *Vanguard*, under a main storm-stay-sail, was at close grips with trouble. At 2 a.m. her main-topmast went over the side, with the top-sail full of men, followed within half an hour by the mizzen-topmast. The fore-mast soon gave an alarming crack, and at a quarter past three went by the board, with a resounding crash, falling in two pieces across the forecastle. The shrieking of the wind began to be punctuated by an ominous thumping sound. The wreck of the fore-topmast and fore-mast, together with the best bower anchor, were beating against the ship's bottom. The smooth face of young Captain Berry, who could not help fearing that such a series of disasters might not have overtaken a more experienced officer, grew long. The *Vanguard*, without masts and rolling unspeakably, was shipping so much water that it became necessary for him to order the scuttling of the lower deck. The wind did not drop until Tuesday afternoon, when the *Alexander* took the *Vanguard* in tow and made a daring attempt to bring her into Oristano Bay, Sardinia. Captain Ball, although signalled by the Admiral to shift for himself and leave the flagship to her fate, continued wonderful exertions. The worst moment for Berry was shortly before dawn on Wednesday, when a heavy western swell was driving them towards invisible rocks on which he could clearly hear the surf breaking. Daylight found the *Alexander*, with the flagship still in tow, about five miles off an island south of Sardinia. The imperturbable Saumarez appeared with the *Orion* to announce and guide them into the bay of St. Pietro. At about 6 a.m. a breeze at last filled the sails of the *Alexander*, and before noon the *Vanguard*, a perfect wreck, having weathered the rocks to the southward of the little isle, anchored in six fathoms and fine smooth water. The Admiral, as soon as possible, went on board the *Alexander* to express unreserved gratitude, and enter upon a new and life-long friendship. There was irony in the chance that had made him so much obliged to Ball, for although they were almost contemporaries, their paths had never crossed, except at St. Omer, fourteen years past, when Nelson had decided that if he should ever come to know this wellfavoured son of a considerable Gloucestershire landowner, he should very much dislike him.

On the last day of May, Nelson addressed a four-line letter to St. Vincent:

"My dear Lord,

"My pride was too great for man, but I trust my friends will think I bore my chastisement like a man. It has pleased God to assist me with His favour, and here I am again, off Toulon."

His pride was not entirely dead, for he had written to his wife that if the ship had been in England, months would have passed before she came out of dock. "Here my operations will not be delayed. The *Vanguard* will in two days get to sea again, as an English man-of-war." Captain Ball had again come to the rescue of young Captain Berry (who was nervous that the Admiral might shift his flag to a more effective ship), and a character of dour visage, with near thirty years' experience in the Royal Service, had been lent to advise a newly commissioned ship's company as to the repair of very extensive damage. For three days and four nights the disappointingly unfriendly shores of St. Pietro echoed to sounds of sawing and hammering, while persons on their mettle, under the direction of Mr. James Morrison, shipwright of the *Alexander*, rigged jury masts; then Berry was able to announce that the *Vanguard* was not only equipped, but actually at sea, and "not bound (I would have you observe) to Gibraltar or any English port, to be refitted, but again cruising after the enemy on their own coast!"

On the day after she left St. Pietro the *Vanguard* spoke a merchantman from Marseille, and learned that Buonaparte was at large. He had sailed from Toulon, on the day before the storm in which the *Vanguard* had been dismasted, and he had taken with him thirteen ships-of-the-line and four hundred transports. Nelson made all possible speed to his appointed secret *rendezvous*, where he hoped to find the frigates never seen since the gale. He reached it on June 9, but it was deserted. It was with dawn next morning that a despatch brig joined the 74's, and the solid figure of Captain Hardy came on board the *Vanguard*. His news was startling, and almost wholly welcome. The frigates were safe, but at Gibraltar, whence they had betaken themselves, never doubting that a ship so severely damaged as the *Vanguard* must return to a dockyard. Urgent instructions from the Admiralty, dated May 2, had reached Cadiz Bay, and the Commander-in-Chief, promised reinforcements, and given the choice of either taking his whole fleet or sending a considerable squadron up the Mediterranean, had appointed Admiral Nelson to this detached command. Next day, at ten minutes past one, a strange fleet was sighted near Cape Corse, which proved to be ten of the line under Captain Troubridge, sent off by St. Vincent as soon as the reinforcement from Portsmouth, under Sir Roger Curtis, had been visible from the masthead of the *Ville de Paris*. Indeed, since every ship designed for Nelson had been ready to put to sea at a moment's notice, Troubridge had actually been out of sight, on his course to Gibraltar, before Sir Roger cast anchor at the British station off Cadiz. "Choice" and "active" were favourite epithets in Service diction at this date, and St. Vincent's private letter, accompanying Nelson's commission, promised him "some choice fellows of the in-shore squadron". He had, in fact, deprived himself of his best officers and ships, and at a moment when the Spanish fleet, in obedience to French pressure, was making a feint of coming out. Troubridge also brought additional secret instructions. Nelson was advised to exact every supply he might need from the Grand Duke of Tuscany, the King of the Two Sicilies, the Porte, Malta, and the *ci-devant* Venetian state. The Dey of Algiers was well-disposed, the Bey of Tunis perfectly good-humoured and neutral, and the Bashaw of Tripoli probably friendly. He was empowered, in his efforts "to take, sink, burn or destroy the Armament preparing by the Enemy at Toulon", to pursue the French to any part of the Mediterranean, the Adriatic, the Greek archipelago or even the Black Sea. "It is hardly necessary", ended the Commander-in-Chief, "to instruct you to open a correspondence with His Majesty's Ministers at every Court in Italy, at Vienna and Constantinople, and the different Consuls on the Coasts of the seas you are to operate in."

Three major difficulties confronted Nelson when he received these flattering but large orders. He was becalmed, he knew that Buonaparte had already sailed, "with a long start" (but he knew not in what direction), and he lacked the essential equipment for discovery—"Frigates, the Eyes of the Fleet". Captain Thomas Thompson, "an active young man", who had regretted orders to remain at Gibraltar a month ago, made a welcome appearance within twenty-four hours, with the 50-gun *Leander*, but he had to be left behind to redirect Ball and Saumarez, who had been detached to look out for Troubridge. Nelson's only recent information was that the troops gathered at Genoa had not yet sailed, so he hoped that Buonaparte might have given them a *rendezvous* in Telamon Bay. He told Hardy to look in there, set off himself round the north of Corsica for the Italian coast, and (since he must have frigates, and the King of the Two Sicilies, hourly expecting invasion, certainly possessed them) he wrote to the British Ambassador at Naples in very clear terms. Fortunately this official was Sir William Hamilton, with whom he had been in friendly correspondence at intervals ever since his visit to the Palazzo Sessa five years past. His letter of June 12, however, was entirely formal, and suitable to be shown to Sir John Acton, Chief Minister at the Court of Naples. His Excellency was asked exactly what co-operation was intended by the Court, whether all the ports of Naples and Sicily were open to His Britannic Majesty's fleet, and whether their authorities had received orders to give him supplies. If it was *convenient*, Nelson much wished for the loan of some fast-sailing vessels. "I want information of the French Fleet; for I hope they have passed Naples. I want good pilots, say six or eight, for the Coast of Sicily, the Adriatic, or for whatever place the Enemy's Fleet may be at, for I mean to follow them if they go to the Black Sea."

On the night of Friday, June 9, at Wimbledon, the Right Honourable Henry Dundas, Secretary of War, slept ill, and during the next two days twice addressed himself to the First Lord. "My dear Lord, Did the instructions to Lord St. Vincent mention that *Egypt* might be in the contemplation of Buonaparte's expedition? It may be whimsical, but I cannot help having a fancy of my own on that subject." "My dear Lord, *India* has occupied my thoughts all night. ..." Such fancies were no novelty to the First Lord, or, for that matter, to Mr. Dundas, who had received a mysterious warning in April that French officers were being sent to Egypt *en route* for Hindustan. A British sea-officer with a romantic record, prisoner-of-war in France, had managed to send Lord Grenville, as long ago as last January, a message that the Directory had designs on Egypt and British trade in the Levant. On Captain Sidney Smith's escape, last month, the First Lord had given him breakfast and taken him to a *levée*. Lord St. Vincent seemed the person to deal with an officer of initiative, inclined to be rather talkative. Captain Sidney Smith's latest tall tale had been that Buonaparte's *troupe* included mathematicians, historians and geologists, ordered to report upon the antiquities and develop the resources of captured Egypt and India.

Five days after Lord Spencer had received Mr. Dundas's second note, Nelson wrote to him, from off the Ponza Islands:

> "The last account I had of the French Fleet was from a Tunisian cruiser, who saw them on the 4th, off Trapani, in Sicily, steering to the eastward. If they pass Sicily, I shall believe they are going on their scheme of possessing Alexandria,—a plan concerted with Tippoo Sahib, by no means so difficult as might at first be imagined."

Hardy had rejoined, reporting "nothing in Telamon Bay", and since the Admiral had not, as he had hoped, been welcomed by a cruiser from Naples, he had decided to send Troubridge in the *Mutine* to talk to Sir William Hamilton and General Acton, get the news and repeat his distress for frigates. ("Troubridge will say everything I could put in a ream of paper.")

On June 17, while he lay with his squadron, outside neutral waters, in Naples Bay, awaiting the return of his envoy, he received four letters from the Palazzo Sessa. The Ambassadress, as well as her husband, had written. Lady Hamilton's first note, well though hastily performed in a thin, slanting hand, expressed on behalf of herself and the Queen of Naples best wishes for his success and happy return.

> "God bless you, my dear Sir, I will not say how glad I shall be to see you. Indeed, I cannot describe to you my feelings on your being so near us. Ever, Ever dear Sir, your affte and gratefull Emma Hamilton."

Her second effort, an almost indecipherable scrawl on a scrap of the same paper, contained an enclosure.

> "Dear Sir, I send you a letter I have this moment received from the Queen. *Kiss it*, and send it back by Bowen, as I am bound not to give any of her letters, Ever yours Emma."

The words "kiss it" were underlined, and Nelson replied, in equal haste, before sailing forthwith for the Straits of Messina.

"My dear Lady Hamilton, I have kissed the Queen's letter. Pray say I hope for the honor of kissing her hand when no fears will intervene, assure her Majesty that no person has her felicity more at heart than myself and that the sufferings of her family will be a Tower of Strength on the day of Battle; fear not the event, God is with us. God bless you and Sir William, pray say I cannot stay to answer his letter, Ever yours faithfully, Horatio Nelson."

The news with which Troubridge had returned within two hours was not entirely satisfactory. Sir William Hamilton had carried him and Hardy directly to General Acton, who had been the person to beg the Admiralty to send a fleet into the Mediterranean for the protection of the Kingdom of the Two Sicilies. It had been correct etiquette that the shifty, effeminate and anti-British Marquis de Gallo, Secretary of State, should be present at their interview, and the scene must have been a remarkable one, for both the sea-officers were, in appearance and manner, British oaks, and Troubridge, according to Sir William, "spoke straight to the point"; but the much-desired frigates were not forthcoming. An extremely delicate negotiation with Austria was in progress, and if the Emperor should learn that his brother-in-law had lent vessels of war to an English squadron, bent on the destruction of Buonaparte's fleet, he certainly could not be expected to continue to consider proposals to support Naples, should she suffer an unprovoked attack by France. The lethargic King, whose fears of invasion had been temporarily allayed by the French fleet passing Naples on the 8th to attack Malta, was "perfectly at peace with France", and by the terms of the late treaty with the Directory not more than four belligerent ships at a time might enter his ports. However, General Acton, "a true man of business", had furnished Troubridge with an informal order, "in the King's name" (what the anxious Sir William Hamilton described as "a sort of credential"), empowering all Port Governors of the Two Sicilies to give Admiral Nelson every necessary assistance and supply, "under the rose".

Nelson, (who, on Troubridge's return, had not even waited to read Gallo's prevaricating replies to his previous letter to Sir William) achieved during his swift passage to the Straits a cheerful note headed "private", in which he begged Sir William, if he thought proper, to tell their Sicilian Majesties and General Acton that they might rest assured he would not withdraw his fleet from the Mediterranean, except upon positive orders from his Commander-in-Chief or (underlined) the *impossibility of procuring supplies*. He repeated that his distress for frigates was extreme.

"I cannot help myself and nobody will help me. But thank God, I am not apt to feel difficulties. Pray, present my best respects to Lady Hamilton. Tell her I hope to be presented to her crowned with laurel or cypress."

In a long official communication, dated two days later, "off the Pharos of Messina", he reminded the Ambassador that although, on his arrival in the Bay of Naples, he had found plenty of goodwill towards England and hatred of France, he had also found no assistance, and no hostility to France. The French Minister had been permitted to send off vessels to Buonaparte's fleet, reporting the arrival, strength and destination of the English squadron, but no corresponding information had been available for Captain Troubridge. When His Britannic Majesty's Ministers heard that *no co-operation* had been offered at Naples, who could say whether they would decide to keep the squadron, so pressingly demanded, in these seas? He drew to a close with a telling warning. "I have said, and repeat it, *Malta is the direct road to Sicily*."

On the 22nd of June, off Cape Passaro, the *Mutine* fell in with a Ragusan brig from Malta, and Hardy learnt the unpleasant news that the French, having taken the island on the 15th, and left a garrison there, had sailed again next day, as it was supposed for Sicily. But as the wind had blown strong from the westward since that date, and the Sicilian Government was not calling for aid, Nelson was convinced that Alexandria was their goal. He immediately signalled four of his Captains to come on board the *Vanguard*. The handsome Saumarez, Troubridge, Ball and Darby (a lively Irish officer whose nationality was proclaimed by both his countenance and voice) made up the first of many councils held in the Admiral's flagship during those hot, weary weeks of vain search. His own guess was that the enemy might at the moment be safe in Corfu, and his officers agreed; but without frigates they could only guess. He sent Hardy ahead with a despatch for the British Consul at Alexandria ("Pray do not detain the *Mutine*, for I am in a fever at not finding the French"), and prepared to follow with all possible speed—six days' passage. Saumarez, as the squadron crowded all sail for the chief port of Egypt, thanked Providence that the sole responsibility for the decision did not rest with him. It would have been too much for his irritable nerves.

In Alexandria, on June 28, the roads were empty. That is to say, the old port displayed one Turkish ship-of-the-line and four frigates; and what was called "the Franks' port" held about fifty sail of merchant vessels of various nationalities. The ship-of-the-line (alarmed by the tidings brought by an English brig, and a Leghorn report) was landing her guns, and the town was filling with troops.

An officer of the British Navy, of large stature, with a sweet Devon accent, had a sorry but clear tale to tell. Hardy had been obliged to bring back the Admiral's urgent letter to Mr. George Baldwin, British Consul, and the accompanying reviews and magazines, "pleasant though old". Mr. Baldwin, according to the Vice-Consul (who was neither English nor intelligent), had left this place twelve weeks past. The disappointment was bitter, but the squadron did not waste time in vain regret. Ball, on being shown the long explanatory despatch composed by the Admiral next day, at sea, said that he thought it quite a masterpiece of clarity and accuracy, but strongly advised that it should not be sent. "I should recommend a friend never to make a defence before he is accused of error." Nelson, who had good reason to fear that he was already being criticised, forwarded it on its long journey. He knew that he had been appointed in preference to senior Admirals. From Cadiz, on June 16, Sir John Orde had sent to the First Lord a letter, opening, "Sir Horatio Nelson, a junior officer, and just arrived from England, is detached from the Fleet in which we serve. . . . I cannot conceal from your lordship how much I feel hurt." He had not, either, concealed it from Lord St. Vincent, who, after a stormy interview, had ordered him home and presently announced "the removal of a certain baronet from this squadron has produced a wonderful effect".

On July 12, off Candia, Nelson wrote again to his Commander-in-Chief, but he had now been without news of the enemy for a month, and the strain was beginning to tell. "After receiving

Captain Hardy's report, I stretched the Fleet over to the Coast of Asia." In the interval since his last despatch he had been up the Aleppo coast and into the Turkish gulf of Antalya. Many years later he bade Troubridge, "Don't fret . . . I wish I never had." The return to Syracuse, he said, had broken his heart. July 18 was the date mentioned by him as finding him at his lowest ebb.

By July 20 he was back in Syracuse again, with ships some of which had not been watered since May 6, and all of which, although provisioned for another nine or ten weeks, lacked the anti-scorbutics which were part of his creed. His intention, if he heard nothing further within six days, was to try the Morea, Constantinople, and, failing them, Cyprus. "The devil's children", he wrote to Sir William Hamilton, "have the devil's luck." Addressing himself to His Excellency two days later, he found himself unfortunately obliged to send hot complaint of having been refused entry by the port authorities of Syracuse. "I understood that private orders at least would have been given." His postscript explained that it was only "as a public man" that he had to complain. Every personal courtesy had been shown to him. Both these letters were endorsed, "Sent on shore, to the charge of the Governor of Syracuse."

To Lord St. Vincent, he reported on the 20th that he was watering, and "getting such refreshments as the place affords", and hoped to get to sea in a few days, and on the 22nd, "Our treatment in the Sicilian Ports is shameful. If they had the force, this Governor says, they are bound by their orders to prevent our entry. Acton promised to send orders. *None has been sent*. What (do you) think of this ?" Lady Hamilton, who had written to him warmly, got an equally indignant note on the 22nd. Next day he suddenly announced to her husband, "The Fleet is unmoored, and the moment the wind comes off the land, shall go out of this delightful harbour, where our present wants have been most amply supplied, and where every attention has been paid to us." Then, before concluding with professions of respect to the Ambassadress (never omitted from his private letters), he added something irreconcilable with his first paragraph, and inexplicable, unless it was intended to exculpate those who had aided him "under the rose"—"But I have been tormented by no private orders being given to the Governor for our admission."

The squadron, having got to sea two days earlier than Nelson had expected when he first wrote to Cadiz, made the Gulf of Coron, in the Morea, within the week, and Troubridge, sent to ask for news from the Turkish governor, returned in a few hours with an enemy wine-brig in tow, and news that Buonaparte's fleet had been seen steering to the S.E. from Candia about four weeks earlier. Another vessel confirmed this to the *Alexander* within the day. It now began to be clear to Nelson that after all he had been correct in going to look for the enemy in Alexandria, but that, far from having missed them by delay, he had arrived too soon. This was what had happened.

As he had no frigates to bring him information, he had twice missed the French by a matter of hours. The first occasion had been during the night of June 22, soon after leaving Sicily, in thick weather, when, having believed that Buonaparte had left Malta six days before, he had unwittingly crossed his route, and passed so close to his slow-moving Armada that British signal guns had been heard and caused Admiral de Brueys to steer in alarm for the security of Crete. On June 29 watchers from the Pharos of Alexandria had scarcely seen the sails of Nelson's squadron disappear rapidly over the north-eastern horizon than the immense French flotilla had begun to come in view from the N.W. Within three weeks of landing, Buonaparte had taken Alexandria, won the Battle of the Pyramids and entered "Grand Cairo" in triumph. Lower Egypt, with all its possibilities, was his.

Nelson's second passage to Alexandria occupied only four days. It had always been his hope to fall in with the enemy at sea, and the squadron had sailed in order of battle, in three compact divisions, two of which were to engage the French warships, while the third paid deadly attentions to the reported four hundred transports. Of the efficiency of that famous young Corsican, "the Conqueror of Italy", as a General, he could not pretend to judge, but as a sea-officer of more than twenty-five years' experience he grimly longed "to try Buonaparte on a wind; for he commands the Fleet as well as the Army". Throughout the cruise, gun and musketry practice had been kept up, and whenever possible he had summoned his Captains on board his flagship for conference. Consequently, the disposal and conduct of each ship, when attacking the enemy under every likely combination of circumstances, had been so often discussed and calculated as to render signals almost unnecessary. Nevertheless, some fresh ones, which might be needed, had been inserted in his signal-book. When he approached Alexandria for the second time his theories and intentions were well known to his officers, and they appreciated that he had the highest opinion of, and reliance in, every Captain under his command. There was not a weak link in that chain. The squadron's health was good, and its *morale* as it reached the end of its long quest was high. In the *Vanguard* the Officers of the Watch who breakfasted with the Captain at 8.30 when they came off duty remarked that the Admiral had asked the time of night rather often. Not even Troubridge knew until afterwards that, as day after day had slipped past without bringing the hoped-for encounter for which he was momentarily ready, Nelson had reached such a state of nervous tension that the slightest unfamiliar sound sent his heart pounding as it had done during his experiences of high fever. This bad habit, he said, persisted whenever he was startled, either by pleasure or pain, in after years. He believed that those weeks had, in the colloquial phrase, "taken years off his life". "More people perhaps die of broken hearts than we are aware of."

With dusk on the last day of July, he made the signal for his fleet to close, and early next morning the *Alexander* and *Swiftsure* were detached to look into Alexandria. The fleet came in sight of the Pharos and Pompey's Tower with a top-gallant wind, in clear weather, soon after noon on August 1. As before, neither harbour displayed French sails. The signal to turn eastwards down the coast was given, and in every ship-of-the-line the main meal of the day, usually served at 1.30, began. Looking back, Captain Saumarez did not recollect ever feeling more hopeless than when he sat to eat that day.

"Judge what a change took place when, as the cloth was being removed, the Officer of the Watch came running in saying, 'Sir, a signal is just now made that the Enemy is in Aboukir Bay and moored in a line of battle.'"

As he reached his quarter-deck cheers were sounding. The masthead look-out of the *Goliath* had been the first man to sight sixteen enemy warships at anchor in a strange bay on the larboard bow, about fifteen miles east of Alexandria. Lord Minto's second son, Mr. Midshipman Elliot, had run direct to Captain Foley, without having hailed the quarter-deck; but before the *Goliath* could signal "Enemy in sight", her jealous but devoted consort, the *Zealous*, had anticipated her.

In the *Vanguard*, Captain Berry noticed "the utmost joy which seemed to animate every breast" reflected in the countenance of the Admiral, "perhaps more heightened". Having signalled his squadron "Prepare for Battle", Nelson then ordered his dinner to be served, and on rising from that meal, remarked to his officers, "Before this time to-morrow, I shall have gained a Peerage or Westminster Abbey."

3

Admiral de Brueys had been ordered, after Buonaparte's victorious disappearance inland, either to take the French fleet into Alexandria, to sail for French-occupied Corfu or to assume a strong position on the coast and prepare to repel attack. The old harbour of Alexandria was difficult of entry for large ships, he still had army stores on board and he was insufficiently provisioned for the passage to Corfu. After the event, when he found the army which he eventually deserted cut off in Egypt, Buonaparte declared that he had repeatedly ordered de Brueys into Alexandria.

When first accounts of a Fleet action penetrated to the Admiralty, *via* a Paris newspaper, on September 21, the name "Béguieres" puzzled experts until it was recollected that Béquier was the old French form of the Arab "Al-Bekir", distinguishing a district including a bay of shoals, stretching for many miles between a promontory, village and island, and the Rosetta mouth of the Nile. The shores of the southwards-curving bay were sandy, with waters deepening so slowly that anchorage for ships-of-the-line could not be found within three miles of the coast, and the promontory at its western extremity was linked by rocks to the small island, which it sheltered from north-westerly winds. Aboukir Island, protected on its seaward side by further rocks and shoals, had, when Nelson came in sight of it, been newly fortified, and the French fleet, anchored in a single line, with a slight bend in the middle, stretching from N.W. to S.E., was actually composed of thirteen ships-of-the-line and four frigates. But the ships-of-the-line included one of 120 guns—the inspiringly named *L'Orient*, de Brueys's flagship—three 80's, *Le Franklin*, *Le Tonnant* and *Le Guillaume Tell*, and nine 74's. Nelson's fleet, lacking at the moment the *Alexander* and *Swiftsure*, detached on scouting duty, and the *Culloden*, nine miles astern with her wine-brig in tow, consisted of his flagship, the *Vanguard*, H.M.S. *Goliath* (Foley), *Zealous* (Sam Hood), *Orion* (Saumarez), *Audacious* (Davidge Gould), *Theseus* (Miller), *Minotaur* (Louis), *Defence* (Peyton), *Bellerophon* (Darby) and *Majestic* (Westcott), all 74's, the *Leander*, of 50 guns (Thompson), and the *Mutine* brig (Hardy).

De Brueys, anchored on the edge of shoal water, with the fortified island to the windward end of his line, had reckoned correctly on the English being unprovided with charts of the reefs protecting his position. Ben Hallowell had given Nelson, a few days previously, a rough sketch of the bay, taken out of a French prize. Sam Hood possessed an English map which he soon discarded as useless; Foley, always well-found, had a good chart in a modern French atlas—"Bellin's Collection". De Brueys, expecting attack from seaward, had taken the precaution of placing his strongest vessels, including his own flagship, in the centre of his line. His next heaviest ships occupied the only other position which he considered vulnerable, his rear. His van, of which the leading ship should have been so close to the island as to make it impossible for the enemy to pass between it and the shore, contained his oldest and least effective craft. There was also room for ships to pass through his line.

When a French 74 signalled, in rapid succession, around two o'clock, "Strange sail in sight", "Enemy in sight", and "Enemy moving on the bay", the French Commander-in-Chief proceeded to call a council of war. He was so short of provisions that his frigates had not been on the look-out, and the boats of many of his ships-of-the-line, with many men, were on shore, filling water-casks and digging wells, a business at which they had to be protected by guards against Bedouins. Only one of his flag-officers, Blanquet-Duchayla, advised that he should order his fleet to weigh and stand out to meet Nelson, and for three precious hours hopes were entertained that as the brief twilight must be fading by the time that the sails approaching out of the west could enter the bay, the

English would not attempt a night action in uncharted waters. During the hours of darkness, de Brueys considered, he might form his line in closer order, nearer the shore, or even contrive an escape. But the English ships continued to bear up for the bay, now with a whole sail breeze, and were presently observed to be coming to the wind in succession, so at 5.30, *faute de mieux*, he signalled that he intended to engage them, at anchor, and his ships were hurriedly cleared for action on the seaward side. The hot and weary working-parties had been recalled, but many men failed to return in time, and although "good seamen" were taken from the frigates to strengthen the crews of the 74's, eventually revolutionary France fought two-thirds short of complement.

De Brueys's preparations showed a complete misconception of his opponent. Nelson had repeatedly promised, "I will bring the French Fleet to Action the moment I can lay hand upon them", and as all the possibilities of a night attack upon a stationary enemy had been discussed by him with his Captains, he had nothing for which to wait. Indeed, as he realised at once, dangerous though the attack must be under existing circumstances, delay could only advantage his adversary. In the words of Berry, he viewed de Brueys's dispositions, from the first moment, "with the eye of a seaman prepared for attack". He gave the signals to prepare for battle, to get ready to anchor by the stern, and communicating his intention to attack the enemy's van and centre, as they lay at anchor, "according to the plan before developed". At about 5.30 his fleet began to form line of battle "as most convenient". "No further signal was necessary." Every Captain appreciated what Nelson had eagerly and instantly noted—"that where there was room for a French 74 at single anchor to swing, there was room for a British 74 to anchor", and he was alive to the probability that the French would have lumbered up their guns on the in-shore side. It had always been his intention, if he found the enemy at anchor, to throw his whole weight on a part of their line and crush it, before assistance could come—"first to secure the victory, and then to make the most of it, according to future circumstances." As de Brueys had disposed his line, this blow would fall on the oldest and weakest enemy vessels. The risks taken by Nelson were great, for he was

entering a strange bay with nightfall, without charts or pilots; and
the possibility of his own ships firing into one another when attacking enemy ships lying between them could not be disregarded. That
the batteries on the island were as ineffective as they proved, he
could not guess; all that he could do was to keep as far out of their
range as reefs would allow.

The ten British 74's hauled sharp to the wind to weather the foul
ground to seaward of the island, sounding as they came into the
shallows—fifteen fathoms, thirteen, eleven, ten. . . . As they came
abreast of the end of the shoal at the entrance, Nelson hailed Hood
to ask him if he thought they were far enough to the eastward to
clear it. Hood replied composedly that he was in eleven fathoms,
and that he had no chart, but that, "If you will allow me the
Honour of leading you into Battle, I will keep the lead going."
Nelson said, "You have my leave, and I wish you success", and took
off his hat. The lofty-statured Hood, attempting to return the
courtesy in a fresh breeze, lost his hat, and his First Lieutenant caught
the words, "Never mind, Webley! There it goes for luck. Put the
helm up and make sail." The *Goliath* was on their larboard bow,
striving for place. The efforts of the French brig *Alerte* to lure them
on to the outer shoals and within range of the island batteries were
coldly disregarded, though she manœuvred almost within gunshot.
(Afterwards, Contre-Admiral Blanquet-Duchayla, prisoner-of-war,
remarked to his host, Ball, that the English Admiral had *sans doute*
pilots of experience. "He did not pay any attention to the brig's
track, but allowed her to go away; he hauled well round all the
dangers!") At 6.28, the enemy having hoisted their colours and
opened fire, the *Goliath* fulfilled her Captain's hopes of leading the
fleet inside the French van. Foley crossed the bows of *Le Guerrier*,
raking her with a broadside, but his sheet anchor hung, whereupon
Hood took up the station he had intended. Foley brought up on the
inner quarter of *Le Conquérant*, next in the line, and the *Orion*,
Theseus and *Audacious* followed them round. As the fiery sun of
August 1, 1798, sank below the horizon, the five leading English
ships, all inside and at closest possible quarters, were bringing an
overwhelming fire to bear upon the enemy van, the more distressing to its recipients because their larboard guns were not only loose,

but piled up with baggage and mess furniture, a certain source of deadly splinters. The *Vanguard*, the sixth ship to come into action, was the first to anchor outside the French line, abreast and within pistol-shot of *Le Spartiate*, already engaged at longer range by the *Theseus*. But until the *Minotaur* had drawn the fire of *L'Aquilon*, fourth in the French line, the *Vanguard* was hard pressed.

By 7 o'clock, total darkness having fallen, and the scene being lit by nothing but gunfire (as five French 74's, undermanned and able to fight only one broadside at a time, were being swiftly beaten into helplessness by eight British), Nelson signalled all ships to hoist distinguishing lights. Only one enemy Captain at the very rear of the French line, waiting horrified for inevitable destruction, spread his topsails in an appeal which brought no response.

The eighth and ninth of Nelson's ships, arriving to a smoke-hung and darkling scene, sustained the heaviest casualties. The *Bellerophon*, missing *Le Franklin*, first of the French 80's (at the moment most gallantly attacked by the *Leander* frigate), brought up abreast of *L'Orient*, and received the undivided attention of a vessel of double her own force. The *Bellerophon's* masts were entirely shot away, and she wore out of the line to the lee side of the bay. The *Majestic* ran her jib-boom into the main-rigging of *L'Heureux*, and while she hung in this position, suffered heavy loss. Her Captain, Westcott, was fatally wounded in the throat by a musket ball; but her First Lieutenant, getting her free, and anchoring on the bows of the next enemy astern, instantly began an unsupported action with *Le Mercure* (and having fought his ship resolutely throughout the Battle of the Nile, Mr. Cuthbert was next morning promoted to the vacant command).

The battle had reached this stage, round about 8 o'clock, when Nelson, standing on his quarter-deck with Berry by his side (according to tradition looking at Hallowell's sketch of the bay), was struck on the head by a piece of flying langridge—the scrap shot much used by the French for the destruction of British sails. The fragment cut his brow to the bone, above his old wound, and a flap of flesh, falling down over his "bright" eye, accompanied by profuse hæmorrhage, blinded him. He fell, and Berry, catching him in his arms, heard the words, "I am killed. Remember me to my wife."

4

This was the end he had long foreseen, and it was indeed as good as he could ever have hoped, for he had fallen when a victory, to be greeted as "the most signal that has graced the British Navy since the days of the Spanish Armada", was already assured. He proceeded to carry everything in the high style dear to him and Shakespeare. Towards the cockpit, inefficiently lit by lanterns curtseying to the roll and thud of gun-carriages, and amid unintelligible sounds, prefaced by shouts and followed by explosions, seventy-odd wounded were trooping with bent heads, or being carried. He would not allow the Principal Surgeon to be told that the Admiral was amongst them. To the relief and surprise of those about him, Jefferson, after probing the wound, pronounced the visible damage superficial. Since all wounds, and especially head-wounds, were dangerous, he cautiously diagnosed "no immediate danger". But the son of the Rector of Burnham Thorpe, struck on the head and in total darkness at last, could not believe that this was not the end. He sent for Mr. Comyn, Chaplain, and messages were delivered for Lady Nelson and for Louis of the *Minotaur*, who had so boldly and efficiently relieved the Admiral's flagship from the dual fire of *L'Aquilon* and *Le Spartiate*—"Your support prevented me from being obliged to haul out of the line." While he lay awaiting his dressing, cheering sounded above, and Berry entered, to acquaint him with what that young man described, with considerable meiosis, as "pleasing intelligence". *Le Spartiate*, long dismasted, had ceased to fire at 8.30. Berry had sent Galwey to board her with a party of marines. The First Lieutenant had returned with the French Commander's sword, which his Flag-Captain delivered to the Admiral, together with the assurance that *L'Aquilon* and *Le Souverain Peuple* had struck, and although *L'Orient*, *Le Tonnant* and *L'Heureux* were not yet taken possession of, "they were considered as completely in our power. . . . It appeared that Victory had already declared itself in our favour."

The surgeon had stitched and bandaged his brow, and urgently entreated him to remain quiet. Nelson withdrew, in order to clear the cockpit. A quiet place, at such a moment, and in a ship so shaken as the *Vanguard*, could with difficulty be found. He was settled in the bread-room, in the hold, a place of great capacity, far removed from the din of battle, where a man might walk upright; and it was to these surroundings that the Admiral's Secretary was summoned to take down a despatch to the First Lord. But the sight of the Admiral, blinded by bandages, identifiable only by his stump and his St. Vincent medal, ghastly pale, cold as ice and highly impatient, was altogether too much for the newcomer, who had himself been hit. He afterwards explained his incapacity as the result of emotion on seeing his employer blinded and suffering much pain. He was dismissed from the bread-room, and, within a fortnight, from Nelson's life. ("My Secretary I have recommended to be Purser of the *Franklin*. He has not activity for me.") Mr. Comyn made another appearance, offering his services, but Nelson himself had taken up the pen and, pushing up his bandage, begun to trace the words, "My Lord, Almighty God has blessed His Majesty's Arms in the late Battle." This was the correct style for a victorious Admiral. He well knew that after the Battle of the Saints, Rodney had begun—"It has pleased God, out of His divine providence, to give His Majesty's arms a most complete victory."

He was interrupted by another entrance of Berry, this time to report that *L'Orient* appeared to be on fire, in her cabin. Disobedient as usual to doctor's orders, Nelson demanded to be assisted on deck, and emerged into the soft but smoke-hung Egyptian night at about the moment that *Le Conquérant*, *Le Guerrier* and an unrecognisable 74 struck to H.M.S. *Audacious*, *Zealous* and *Minotaur*. Firing was still brisk. Gradually a ruddy light began to swell upon the battle scene, until it was so bright that the Admiral, focusing his imperfect and painful gaze on every quarter in turn, could distinguish the colours flown by the respective ships, and judge of the situation with some certainty.

L'Orient had been repainting, and the flames had spread to oil-jars and paint-buckets lying on her poop. He at once told Berry to do what he could to save as many as possible of the crew of the enemy flagship, which he judged "completely beat", and the indefatigable Galwey, with the only boat of the *Vanguard* in condition, set off towards a warm spot.

In the dramatic shadows, to the north-west of Aboukir Island, a British 74 lay at a dejected angle. This pitiful spectacle represented Troubridge, who, having received permission by signal to cast off his prize, and hastening to the engagement through the perilous defile with a failing wind, had struck the tail of the shoal. All his own endeavours, combined with those of the smaller craft commanded by Thompson and Hardy, had failed to get the *Culloden* off, and the only assistance that could be afforded during the Battle of the Nile by the Captain described by Lord St. Vincent as "the ablest adviser and best executive officer in His Majesty's Service" was serving as a beacon to the vessels coming up astern. Ball and Hallowell, arriving late on the scene, gave the *Culloden* and the island batteries as wide a berth as possible, and sweeping down to anchor on either side of the ships of the enemy centre, already heavily engaged, had presented the terrifying aspect of an untouched British reserve. Hallowell with judgment withheld his fire while a disabled and unlighted 74 drifted past him—the *Bellerophon*, with Darby and one-third of her crew casualties.

As the poop of *L'Orient* was alight, the new arrivals concentrated their fire on that spot, rendering all attempts to check the conflagration quite impossible. Men continued to serve her lower-deck guns until they were driven from them, but flames began to race up tarred rigging, along her newly painted sides and down towards her magazine. As her destruction became imminent, many gesticulating figures, silhouetted against the glow, leapt into the sea, and ships to the windward of her veered, or slipped their cables. Only Ball, having drenched the *Alexander*, held his station until he was sure of the doom of *L'Orient*. She blew up at 10.5, with a detonation which startled French troops at Rosetta, ten miles distant, and was believed by workers below decks in the *Goliath* to signify an explosion in the after-part of their own vessel. Adjutant-General Moutard, although wounded, swam to the nearest ship—the *Audacious*—and several stunned men were tugged in to safety through the lower ports of British 74's, but Commodore Casabianca and his intelligent ten-year-old son, who had been clinging to the wreck of the main-mast in the water, never reappeared, and it was reckoned that Galwey's boat, and those from other ships

⚓L, ⚓A, ⚓S show the anchoring-places of Leander, Alexander, & Swiftsure

TIMOLEON
GENEREUX
GUILLAUME TELL
MERCURE
HEUREUX
PEUPLE SOUVERAIN
Majestic
TONNANT
ORIENT
Bellerophon
S⚓
FRANKLIN
Orion
L⚓
Defence
AQUILON
Minotaur
Theseus
SERIEUSE
Leander
Goliath
Vanguard
SPARTIATE
Audacious
Swiftsure
CONQUERANT
Zealous
Alexander
GUERRIER

N

Culloden
Wind

THE BATTLE OF THE NILE
August 1, 1798
Reproduced from *Sea Kings of Britain,* by Sir Geoffrey Callender.
By kind permission of Messrs. Longmans, Green and Co., Ltd.

which had followed his example, rescued not more than seventy of the four hundred-odd men noticed in the water before the explosion.

L'Orient took with her to the depths of Aboukir Bay the body of Admiral de Brueys, dead of his wounds on his quarter-deck, £600,000 in ingots of gold and diamonds wrested from the Swiss Republic and Roman State to finance Buonaparte's Eastern expedition, and, what was irreplaceable, the storied treasures of the Most Venerable Order of the Hospital of St. John of Jerusalem. Malta of the Knights, under her first and last German Grand Prior, and well prepared by propaganda, had made the feeblest show of resistance when the French fleet had appeared in Valetta harbour, and for the past three months their treasure, with the exception of three relics, had been in the hold of the French Admiral's flagship.

For a few minutes after the explosion (calculated by various eye-witnesses as between three and ten) complete darkness reigned: then firing broke out again. Meanwhile, masts, yards, red-hot ammunition, charred fragments of rope, timber, metal and corpses rained from the eastern skies into the troubled waters and on board the surrounding ships. At the Battle of the Nile, Republican France, crippled by every inevitable result of National Revolution, fought with ardour, though largely uninstructed. ("Fire, fire, steadily", urged Admiral Duchayla in the dismasted *Franklin*. "The last shot may give us victory.") As the moon rose on the scene of triumph and wreckage, struggling through a pall of black smoke, Nelson was persuaded to go below. He did not rest, and continued to issue orders, but although until 3 a.m. firing continued spasmodically, and broke out again at dawn with renewed vigour, the "follow through" of the Battle of the Nile was not sufficiently effective to satisfy him. The fact was that the experience of Miller was characteristic throughout the fleet:

"My people were also so extremely jaded, that as soon as they had hove our sheet anchor up, they dropped under the capstan-bars and were asleep, in a moment, in every sort of posture, having been working then at their fullest exertion, or fighting, for near 12 hours."

With the light of day came the garnering of the fruits of victory. Out of thirteen enemy sail-of-the-line, nine had been taken and two burnt. Of the four frigates, one was burnt and one sunk. Rear-Admiral Villeneuve, in his flagship *Le Guillaume Tell*, accompanied by *Le Généreux* and the frigates *Diane* and *Justice*, weighed before noon and stood out to sea, to fight another day. Hood made an attempt to chase, despite the state of the *Zealous*, but no other vessel was in a condition to accompany her: he was recalled. The British casualties were estimated by Nelson at about 200 killed and 700 wounded; the French loss as 5,225 taken, drowned, burnt and missing, 3,105 sent on shore by cartel, and 200 kept to serve the fleet. During the first day succeeding his victory (which he rightly styled a Conquest), though jarred and sick, he knew little rest. His desk was littered by letters written over-night by his Captains, of which Davidge Gould's was a fair example:

"Sir,

"I have the satisfaction to tell you the French ship *Le Conquérant*, has struck to the *Audacious*, and I have her in possession. The slaughter on board her is *dreadful*; her Captain is dying. Our fore and mainmast are wounded, but I hope not very bad. They tell me the foremast is the worst. I give you joy. This is a glorious victory."

Nelson signed Hardy's commission for the *Vanguard* (as Berry was to go home in the *Leander* with despatches), and lest Berry might meet with an accident, he decided to send his Signal-Lieutenant, Capel, together with Hoste, to Naples in the *Mutine*, with duplicates. He wrote to the French Commandants of Aboukir and Alexandria to arrange for the reception, under cartel, of their wounded into hospital, and he issued a memorandum of congratulation and thanks to all captains, officers, seamen and marines of the squadron. In the evening he entertained French officers. A large proportion of the company, of both nations, were suffering from head-wounds. The prisoners, although some obviously came of monarchist stock, were frankly atheist, and expressed their surprise and admiration at the discipline which had enforced attendance at the religious services of thanksgiving held throughout the victorious fleet in the heat of the day, this afternoon. The scenes on board the battered men-of-war had been picturesque—the ship's companies ranged around their black-gowned chaplains, on the quarter-deck, under an awning formed of the ship's ensigns, through which the sunlight of 2 p.m. had cast a rich glow. As darkness fell, Arabs and Mamelukes lining the shores of the bay kindled bonfires. The guests took these to mean that some military success had been achieved over Buonaparte, and took their departure heavily. Afterwards, Miller, visiting Nelson in his cot, found him "weak but in good spirits".

5

The days following the Battle of the Nile, when the stricken victor lay in Béquier Roads, totally unable to communicate with the outer world, were amongst the strangest in his story. His Captains, headed by the mortified Troubridge, urged their men to super-human efforts, under Egyptian sun, amidst unparalleled débris. The burial at sea of poor Westcott took place, and many enemy corpses were interred below the sands of Aboukir Island, now to be renamed Nelson's Island. Throughout the hours of daylight the sounds of carpentry never ceased, and ships' boats plied incessantly amongst the hulks aground on the shoals.

After their toil and labour, the gentlemen were not idle. On the night of August 2, in Saumarez's ship, Nelson's Captains inaugurated "The Egyptian Club", and a solemn document, signed by all present, invited Sir Horatio to accept the gift of a sword and have his portrait taken for the Society. Berry, scribbling replies on behalf of his Admiral, assured Miller, "He is now more easy than he was this morning, the *rage* being over." But for many days yet Nelson could not be easy. Until the *Leander* was ready, on the 6th, his despatches had to wait for transport. The casualty list as usual omitted his own name. ("Were I to die this moment", he added in a note to Lord Spencer, " 'Want of frigates' would be found stamped on my heart.") He enclosed a packet of intercepted enemy letters, including one from Buonaparte himself. "He writes such a scrawl, no one not used to it can read; but luckily we have got a man who had wrote in his Office to decipher it." These letters, and a later packet (travelling to Buonaparte from France, and recovered from the waves by dauntless tars, when the crew of a French gun-boat tried to sink them), were published in London before the year was out, and the second volume was provided with a frontispiece displaying Admiral Nelson's left-handed signature.

After studying the captured enemy correspondence, large issues troubled Nelson's brain. Buonaparte, blockaded in Egypt and Syria, could only attack Constantinople overland, and the Victor of the Nile was sending an express to advise the British Minister at the Porte that if the Grand Signior would but trot an army into Syria, the career of the Conqueror of Italy and Egypt was finished. But unless Indian waters were watched, Tippoo Sahib might still get French reinforcements by the Red Sea. It appeared that Foley's Fourth Lieutenant (a cousin of Drake of Genoa) was ready to travel by Alexandria, Aleppo and Basra to warn the Governor of Bombay. "A very clever young man" came on board the *Vanguard* and was provided with letters commending him to the British Consuls, Vice-Consuls and merchants on his route, and authorising him to draw upon the East India Company for his expenses. If the Company objected, Sir Horatio took their repayment upon himself. "As an Englishman I shall be proud that it has been in my power to be the means of putting our Settlements on their guard."

At last, by August 15, Capel and Hoste had left with the duplicate despatches for Naples, and Admiral Blanquet-Duchayla's sword for the Lord Mayor of London—"Relying on your zeal and judgement, I have only to wish you a good voyage by sea and by land." The fleet had unanimously appointed Mr. Alexander Davison sole agent for the prizes captured at the Battle of the Nile, and Saumarez had sailed for Gibraltar with six of the prizes and seven of the line. Sam Hood had received orders to blockade the coast while his Admiral departed down the Mediterranean with his three worst-damaged 74's. Reports from the friendly natives of the interior suggested that such of Buonaparte's garrisons as had not been murdered by them were being decimated by water-borne fever. At last, too, despatches and frigates from Cadiz had traced Nelson to the mouth of the Nile. The Commander-in-Chief, who had heard nothing since the squadron had quitted Syracuse for the second time, but who had never ceased to send messages of good cheer, and deprive himself of frigates which had been missing the squadron consistently, now forwarded urgent secret orders for it to return to the westward and co-operate in an expedition against Minorca. Lord St. Vincent also sent Admiral Nelson's stepson to receive a scolding for bad behaviour, and letters which showed that the Victor of the Nile was in disgrace at home for missing the enemy—"such is the chance to which officers' characters are subject".

Suddenly in touch with Europe again, kept from sleep by a perpetual cough, Nelson replied at once in his own hand, "My head is so upset that really I know not what to do; but by to-morrow will arrange matters in my mind, and do my best." Next day he ordered three enemy ships which could not be refitted within a month to be burnt. He could only hope that the prize-money for them would be granted.

Then, thick-coming fancies crowding upon him, he succumbed. Now that there was, for the moment, no more to be done, "That fever of anxiety which I have endured from the middle of June" fastened down upon him. Jefferson, in charge of an illustrious but impossible patient with a long case-history, running a high temperature, began to answer enquiries sourly.

6

Nelson's despatches, sent by Naples, announcing the Victory of the Nile, took two months and a day to reach England, and were beaten by five days by a circumstantial message from Hamburg. A French brig which had made a dash for the open sea just before L'Orient blew up had reached Rhodes with a tale of disaster, and the Governor had informed His Britannic Majesty's Minister at the Porte, who had expeditiously notified his opposite number in Vienna. Fortunately for those whose reputation was deeply engaged by the choice of so junior an officer as opponent to Buonaparte, the headlines of English papers were much occupied for many months of 1798 by rebellion in Ireland. Still, they had much to endure. By August 1 the public, agitated by persistent dark hints of an action in which seven British warships had been lost, was getting restive, and one editor voiced their feelings in a querulous article, headed, "Where is Buonaparte? Where is Admiral Nelson?" Pitt, supplied with French prints, some of which claimed a success of Buonaparte over Nelson, concluded that "something has happened", and while waiting patiently for authentic accounts, resolutely supposed that even French authorities would not long be able to disguise entirely what that "something" had been. Admiral Goodall, when asked "What is your favourite Hero about? The French Fleet has passed under his nose!" stoutly promised, "something capital".

But by mid-September, tired of what the First Lord called "the extravagant accounts propagated nearly all over Europe of Sir Horatio Nelson having won a decisive victory", Mr. Dundas was "in charity" presuming that when Sir Horatio reappeared to tell his own story he would be able to give a good reason for having missed Buonaparte. It was known at the Admiralty by now that Nelson had left Syracuse for the second time, and Lord Grenville was insistent that he must be ordered to protect the Kingdom of the Two Sicilies, and not attach himself to Buonaparte's fleet. The First Lord replied coolly that he hoped Sir Horatio Nelson would have "a pretty good story to tell, at least. His missing the French fleet both going and returning is certainly very unfortunate but we must not be too ready to censure him for leaving Alexandria when he was there, till we know the exact state of the intelligence which he received there." Only his staff realised, when the good news—far surpassing the most extravagant rumour—did arrive, what had been Lord Spencer's anxiety. On being told that the victory had been achieved without the loss of a single British ship he turned and, without speaking a word, fell flat in the passage outside his office. At Naples, both the Queen and the British Ambassadress had fainted, but Lady Hamilton had been well enough, before the day was out, to drive about the streets, with young Capel and Hoste, wearing round her forehead a bandeau inscribed "Nelson and Victory".

Berry and Thompson did not arrive in London until the last week of November, having passed through very trying experiences. After a six-hour action off Candia, with Le Généreux (the French 74 to escape with Villeneuve from Aboukir Bay), the 50-gun Leander had been captured. The Republicans treated Nelson's Captains with discourtesy. They not only relieved Captain Berry of his full-dress uniform, they actually removed some of the instruments with which the ship's surgeon was at the moment operating upon Thompson. Both officers were severely wounded, and Thompson was observed on the night of his arrival "walking halt up White-hall". However, Berry had the satisfaction of being able to assure Lord Spencer at dinner that the Battle of the Nile had been won before *L'Orient* blew up, an important point on which he found the First Lord, together with the whole nation, at fault. He was knighted on December 12 and Thompson in the following February.

The rewards conferred upon Nelson were many, but of most of them he did not hear for many weeks, and congratulatory letters from home did not reach him till mid-January. The first gifts to be announced came from the Sultan of Turkey, and were of Oriental profusion and magnificence. The Grand Signior sent a sable pelisse, a purse of 2,000 sequins to be distributed among the wounded, a canteen, a dress sword, a gold-hilted scimitar, an ivory- and silver-mounted musket, and a diamond ornament called a "Chelengk", taken from one of the Imperial turbans. (Hearing that Nelson was wearing this Eastern jewel in his hat, Lemuel Abbott, called upon to supply more and more portraits, attempted the Chelengk unseen, and got it very wrong.) Many royalties sent diamond-studded boxes. That from the criminal lunatic Czar of Russia contained his own likeness in miniature. One of particular beauty, in the shape of a rose, came, it was whispered, from the Dowager Sultana, mother of the Grand Signior. From the East India Company came a grant of £10,000. The City of London, recipient of the sword of Admiral Blanquet-Duchayla, replied with swords for Nelson and his Captains, who all received gold medals from His Majesty; and before the year was out, Messrs. Potter, Haberdashers of Charing Cross, were ready with the medal ribbon. Mr. Alexander Davison, sole prize agent, also provided medals, at a personal cost estimated at £2,000. Davison's medals, in gold for captains, silver and copper-bronzed for seamen and marines, were handsome. The obverse presented Hope, with an olive branch in her right hand, supporting on a rugged rock a medallion with the profile of Nelson. The reverse showed the opposing fleets lit by the sinking rays of the radiant orb, encircled by the opening words of the Admiral's despatch—"Almighty God has blessed His Majesty's Arms". Only the peerage, bestowed in November, together with a pension of

£2,000 for three lives, was not considered by Nelson's friends adequate. Lord Hood had told Lady Nelson, on the best authority—that of Mr. Pitt—that she was likely to find herself Viscountess Alexandria. Jervis had received an earldom after St. Vincent, and Duncan a viscounty after Camperdown. Neither of these victories had been so complete or in any degree comparable in importance with that of the Nile. The reason offered for the award of nothing more than a barony was that as Nelson had not been a Commander-in-Chief, but merely detached in charge of a squadron, the Admiralty could find no precedent for offering a higher rank.

The news of the Battle of the Nile roused an enthusiasm at home the echoes of which have never died. The good tidings, so long and anxiously awaited, spread very quickly. In a west-country cathedral city, within forty-eight hours, the landlord of a leading tavern, having attired himself as a British Tar, stood on his threshold welcoming guests, beneath a balcony on which the local volunteers played "Heart of Oak" and "A Royal Standard flew above the disgraced Tricolour". In the adjacent seminary, young gentlemen, given a holiday, were cutting out silhouettes to be carried in a torchlight procession. Their labours represented "the Hero of Italy in the mouth of a Crocodile, and the French Admiral delivering up his sword to our single-handed Conqueror". By a happy chance, the essential features of this naval success of the first order were easily to be understood and to the last detail dramatic. The public eye fastened with eager comprehension on the picture of the Republican fleet anchored in a crescent formation, under Eastern skies of turquoise and rose, while British 74's, eagerly watched by turbaned and dusky natives from the roof-tops and shores of a palm-crowned bay of shoals, advanced unhesitatingly out of the west, after a long chase, to match a couple of ships to every vessel of an ill-disposed van. The young Admiral's despatch, in which he gave all credit to his subordinates ("My band of friends was irresistible"), his failure to enter his own name in the casualty list, his gift of the French Commander's sword "as a remembrance that Britannia still rules the waves", were recognised by a seafaring nation as breathing the heroic spirit of an antique day. They touched a note which had not been struck with like vigour since the Renaissance. By the close

of the year, a shower of souvenirs, ranging from the purely orna-
mental to the functional, and within reach of every purse, had been
produced to meet a huge popular demand, and the likeness of the
Victor of the Nile, on canvas, paper, porcelain, pottery, glass,
muslin and metal, was as familiar in cottage and castle as that of His
Majesty. "Nelson with his one lame arm and gallant fighting spirit"
had won a place in British hearts from which he was never to be
deposed.

Chapter XI

1798
(ætat. 39–40)

NAPLES

I

"MY HEAD", wrote Nelson to St. Vincent, off Candia, on the first day of September, "is splitting—splitting—splitting ..." He made three efforts at the word.

He had seen the last of Aboukir Bay at 8 p.m. on Sunday, August 19, and decided then that if "my half-head" was not particularly needed in the Mediterranean now, he would apply for leave to go home, for the complete rest so much urged by the doctors. At Naples he would say nothing, except that he was going to Cadiz in a fortnight's time. The mere thought of having to tussle, in his present state of health, with the Marquis de Gallo sickened him. He hoped that his command might devolve upon poor Troubridge. ("The copy is a d—d deal better than the Original.") His plan had been to put Troubridge into the *Vanguard*, "with the *Culloden's* masts, yards, etc.", but the *Culloden*, it soon became evident, must be hove down before she could be trusted out of port. With oakum and canvas fothering her damaged bottom, she sailed dreadfully. Nevertheless, she was to reach the dockyard of Castellammare, in the Bay of Naples, before the Admiral's flagship. His progress towards the Court of the Two Sicilies, with light and contrary winds ("I detest this voyage"), was necessarily slow, but correspondingly curative. By September 7 he felt so much better that he decided not to "give up" for a little while, and advised Sir William Hamilton that he intended to spend not more than four or five days in the most populous city of Italy. Syracuse should in future be his port, and his sphere of operations from Malta to Syria. "These times are not for idleness." He felt also, with returning health, more cheerful about his stepson, in whom he hoped that

Lord St. Vincent had been a little mistaken. Josiah was young for his age, but "very active". The stuff to work upon was there, the anxious proxy parent assured himself. "He may have lain too long at Lisbon." The lad, "certainly ungracious in the extreme", brightened at the news that a request for "a good frigate" for him had already been forwarded to the First Lord.

Within the week, off Stromboli, more frigates joined the small division, and, as always, the home mails for His Majesty's ships brought months-old news, important, trivial, glad and tragic. Troubridge, already wrestling with a dark hour, learnt that he was no longer a husband. Lady Nelson, at Roundwood House, was now sitting opposite her Admiral's portrait. "The likeness is great; I am well satisfied with Abbott."

Next evening the *Mutine* joined, back from Naples, bringing the first letters of congratulation. Sir John Acton presented at length to the Saviour of Europe the felicitations of his royal employers. Sir William Hamilton, who had but once sheltered the victor under his roof, for four nights, five years past, but who had (especially recently) been in continual helpful correspondence with him, hailed, on behalf of "myself and Emma", "our bosom friend". "History", announced a much-moved Fellow of the Royal Society, "does not record an Action that does more honour to the Heroes that gained the Victory, than the late one of the first of August. You have now completely made yourself, my dear Nelson, *immortal*." Lady Hamilton also had written, enclosing two letters from "my adorable queen", but her description of the Queen's emotion on hearing the news of the Nile was such as to make a convalescent hope that he might not be called upon to witness the renewal of such a scene. His apartment, wrote the Ambassadress, was preparing, and his hostess was dressed from head to foot, "*alla* Nelson. Ask Hoste. Even my shawl is Blue with gold anchors all over." She sent some "Sonets", but a separate ship would have been required to carry all being produced by the Neapolitans, mad with joy. Lady Hamilton, who would sooner have been an English powder-monkey in Nelson's victory than an Emperor out of it, was walking on air with pride, "feiling I was born in the same land. . . . Write, or come soon." He had already written, trusting that the fact that she would find him much mutilated would not cause him to be less welcome.

As before, his moment of elation was closely followed by minor tragedy. At 7 a.m. on the morning of the 15th, in a sudden squall, the *Vanguard* lost her foremast, the head of her main-topmast and her jib-boom. Four seamen were carried away with the main-mast, and several survivors of the Nile were severely wounded. The Admiral's flagship performed most of the remainder of her slow progress towards Castellammare dockyard in tow of a frigate. Nelson's cough and fever returned. He doubted whether he should see St. Vincent's face again.

The triumphal entry into the Bay of Naples of what he sadly called "the wreck of the *Vanguard*" was the subject of description by many pens. All eyewitnesses agree that from dawn, when the British men-of-war were observed, in picturesque silhouette against the rugged rocks of Tiberius, off Capri, the day promised to be remarkably fine and warm even for southern Italy in the month when the fig and grape are dropping. The *Vanguard*, towed by the *Thalia*, and followed by H.M.S. *Minotaur* and *Audacious*, was visible many hours before she anchored; in any case, the festival-loving Neapolitans had been provided with something in the nature of a dress-rehearsal of welcome to the battered victors of the Nile, when Ball and Troubridge had brought the *Alexander* and *Culloden* into port four evenings previously. By 10 a.m. on Saturday, September 22, the waters of the famous bay, smooth as a mirror, reflected the many-coloured sails of more than five hundred pleasure-boats, overfilled with musically inclined parties. Professional bands, including one from the principal Opera House, well knew the British National Anthem, and had learnt for the occasion "Rule, Britannia" and "See the Conquering Hero". The quays were crowded by enthusiastic *lazzaroni*, a speciality of Naples—beggars, named after Lazarus, but masterful, highly organised and regarded by their monarch with paternal indulgence. In the city, where tier upon tier of houses, parchment-coloured, terracotta, yellow and coral, were backed by hazy heights clothed with cypress, many native as well as English residents had hung flags and bunting from balconies already loaded with dependent carnations and roses.

The British Ambassador's barge, accompanied by a boatload of musicians in his employ, was the first to come alongside the *Vanguard*, and was greeted by a salute of thirteen guns. Nelson himself, a few days later, from the grateful shades of the Palazzo Sessa, sent his wife an account of what followed.

"Alongside came my honoured friends: the scene in the boat was terribly affecting; up flew her ladyship, and exclaiming, 'Oh God, is it possible?' she fell into my arm more dead than alive. Tears, however, soon set matters to rights. . . . I hope some day to have the pleasure of introducing you to Lady Hamilton, she is one of the *very best* women in this world. How few could have made the turn she has. She is an honour to her sex, and a proof that a reputation may be regained. I own, it requires a great soul. . . . Her kindness, with Sir William's, to me, is more than I can express: I am in their house, and I may now tell you, it required all the kindness of my friends to set me up. Lady Hamilton intends writing to you. May God Almighty bless you, and give us, in due time, a happy meeting."

A further salute, this time of twenty-one guns, sounded from the *Vanguard* an hour later. The King of the Two Sicilies, in a much-gilded state galley with spangled awnings, was paying the British Admiral the extraordinary compliment of coming out nearly three leagues to meet him. Ferdinand IV, perspiring in powder, black velvet and gold lace, was five years grosser than when Nelson had last obtained an interview with him. The large and loosely hung Spanish-Bourbon king was still remarkable for the nose which led his boon-companions of the fish-market to call him "Il Rè Nasone", but his swarthy features appeared at their best illuminated by relief, and the royal oration of welcome certainly came from the heart. He warmly clasped Nelson by the hand, hailing him as "Deliverer and Preserver", and expressed, with the boyish vigour which he never outgrew, his wish that he could have assisted at the battle of Aboukir Bay under Nelson's orders. The Austrian-born Queen was unavoidably absent, detained by a bout of ague, aggravated by the sudden death of her youngest child, the Princess Elizabetta, but she was represented by the Hereditary Princess, born the Archduchess Clementina, seventeen years of age, doubly first-cousin of her mate, and eight months pregnant. The King, who prided himself upon being a seaman, stayed three hours on board the *Vanguard*, gently moving towards his capital, quite unconcerned that his dismal daughter-in-law had swooned at an early stage in their inspection of the ship. As the illustrious company sat to an elegant breakfast, a further important guest made a brief professional appearance. Commodore Caracciolo, Bailli of the Order of Malta, a man of aristocratic family, forty-six years of age, who had learnt his seamanship under Rodney, was in charge of the nautical education of the King's nine-year-old son, Leopold. Caracciolo was known by at least one of the feasters present to have expressed, within the last few days, long-smouldering resentment of Nelson's conduct in the engagement on March 14, 1795. The spectator to record with interest his "seemingly genuine" congratulations to the conquering hero was an authoress. Miss Ellis Cornelia Knight, who had accompanied the Hamiltons in their barge, was a figure venerated by the English colony at Naples. She was the only child of the second marriage of the late Sir Joseph Knight, Rear-Admiral of the White, and for the past twenty seasons, in company with her accomplished but impecunious and invalid mother, had moved incessantly in the best Continental society. Their last move had been from threatened Rome.

The flutter of the wings of many liberated birds, towards skies of intensified colour, had been arranged to coincide with the moment of Nelson's setting foot in Naples. A multitude of vociferous fishermen, holding aloft curiously shaped wicker baskets, let loose their captives as he stepped on shore, amongst sun, dust and scattered petals. The Admiral, the British Ambassador and Ambassadress, and the authoress gained an open waiting carriage with difficulty, and clattered away over lava pavements, uphill, towards the Palazzo Sessa, easily recognisable by the particularly vivid hangings of not quite British scarlet, white and blue festooning its façade, on which, when darkness fell, the words "Nelson of the Nile" and "Victory" were to spring to life from three thousand lamps.

During the drive Nelson mentioned that except for a few hours on board his Commander-in-Chief in Cadiz Bay on April 30, this was the first occasion for six months that he had been out of his ship.

2

On the evening of Nelson's arrival, while his name blazed from its balconies, the doors of the British Embassy were closed except to a few favoured compatriots. Ball and Troubridge were amongst the blue coats seated by candlelight beneath the likenesses by modern artists of one of the most beautiful women of any age. Sir William, before possessing himself for life of the glowing original, now happily presiding at his table, had never lost an opportunity of securing a copy. The three three-quarter-length portraits of Emma, now Lady Hamilton, by Romney, decorating the walls of the Palazzo Sessa, showed her as herself (a model, in her teens), in a pink silk gown and a black hat; as a Bacchante, in classic weeds, with auburn tresses flying, casting a bewitching glance over her shoulder; and in white draperies, with palms closed and eyes raised to Heaven—Saint Cecilia. The son of the Rector of Burnham Thorpe most admired his hostess as a Santa, and when Lady Knight, an acquaintance of Lady Nelson, supposed that the day of his victory was accounted by him as the happiest in his life, he replied repressively: "No; the happiest was that on which I married Lady Nelson."

Everyone present was in need of rest, after an exhausting day of triumph in strong sun, following weeks of anxiety. Sir William confessed himself much run down; Lady Hamilton was still suffering from bruises sustained in her swoon on hearing the news of the Nile. The atmosphere on that first night, deceptively, promised opportunities for relaxation.

The room prepared for the Admiral was on the upper floor, where a boudoir, unique in her experience, had long been a source of admiration to the much-travelled Miss Knight. The semicircular window commanded a prospect of the bay, which was reflected in mirrors covering the entire opposite wall. When the full moon seemed to arise out of the ruddy crater of Vesuvius, illuminating a little flotilla of native craft engaged in the tunny fishery by torchlight, the effect was romantic. Nor did dawn, broad daylight or dusk bring disenchantment. From the upper floor of the Palazzo Sessa the eye could discern, beyond masts and sails, clouds resting upon the mountains behind Sorrento, Vesuvius dominating the fertile Campania, gardens, mainly filled in the unsatisfying Italian style with topiary and statues (curving along the shore towards the grottos of Posilipo), and a medley of flat-faced and flat-roofed dwellings of all sizes, five and six storeys high, separated by thoroughfares, noisy, steep and tortuous. Nelson soon found that for him to venture into these streets, either on foot or in a carriage, produced a mob, and that his expectations of a rest at Naples were utterly illusory. "Between business and what is called pleasure, I am not my own master for five minutes."

Within, the large and echoing Italian house still presented to the stranger a bewildering assortment of staircases, grand and subsidiary, narrow, tall folding doors, minor galleries, spacious and sombre, with unmeant-looking views of closely surrounding masonry, and an army of servitors, mostly native. The ground floor was given up to reception-rooms, but since the Ambassador was a man of taste, these were not furnished in the perfunctory manner usual in official residences. At the moment, several redoubtable galleries, with walls and floors of carefully selected alabaster and marble, stood empty, as, in preparation for flight, he had recently transferred the gems of his Etruscan collection to packing-cases. But this circumstance was providential, for his wife had invited eighteen hundred guests to celebrate Admiral Nelson's fortieth birthday, on the 29th. Sounds of hammering penetrated to the upper floor, where His Britannic Majesty's representative and his lady untiringly entertained the hero of the Nile *en famille*. A rostral column, engraved with the words "Veni, Vidi, Vici", and the names of the Captains of the Battle of the Nile, was to be unveiled by Lady Hamilton at a dramatic moment during next Saturday's revelries. It was, of necessity, solidly incorporated in an apartment destined to be shaken by the feet of so many rejoicing Neapolitans, and she declared that it should never come down while she and Sir William occupied this house.

Sir William, whose ideas of hospitality had been learnt in the great country houses of the mid-eighteenth century, had been truly fortunate at an age when many single gentlemen, fond of comfort, are reduced to marrying their housekeeper. Travelling English, calling at the Embassy, were sometimes startled by being asked their business by an elderly person in apron and keys, and more surprised when they heard that *La Signora Madre* was their Ambassador's mother-in-law. But, as that astute gentleman had foreseen, most Neapolitans accepted without further question what they deemed a stock figure of light opera. Nelson, on coming to know her, joined heartily in a devoted daughter's admiration of Mrs. Cadogan, a strong spirit.

His new Secretary, Mr. John Tyson, late purser of the *Alexander* (who believed that his hostess was, like himself, Lancashire born), adapted himself to improved circumstances with speed, but Nelson, despite the kindness of an accomplished host and hostess, fretted throughout his first week at the Palazzo Sessa, and closer acquaintance with the outstanding characters of the Court of the Two Sicilies by no means bred regard. Even an old Mediterranean man was taken aback by much that the British Embassy, long inured to Neapolitan morals, took for granted, and Admiral Nelson, attired night after night in full-dress uniform by a perfectly complacent sailor servant, read, unhappily, word from Captains Hardy and Troubridge that the squadron was in distress for slops and bedding. (Lady Hamilton, distressed by his small appetite, was, at this moment, offering him the services of the Embassy *chef* for his flagship.) The only idea of the leaders of the circle in which he found himself at present seemed to be competition as to who could offer him the most spectacular entertainment. After an hour with the Marquis de Gallo, the English Admiral's ire was roused. The polished and not brainless Marquis, elaborately studying his snuff-box, decorations and ring, managed very successfully to convey the impression that "he has been bred in a Court, and I in a rough element". General Mack, sent from Vienna to take command of the Neapolitan army, was hourly expected, but so was a new French Minister. Nelson hoped that M. La Combe St. Michel might make so tactless a speech on presenting his credentials that he would be given his *congé* forthwith, but this wish was not fulfilled, and General Mack, who required five carriages for his personal effects, still lingered on the mountain roads.

The problem of Malta was pressing. A deputation had offered the island to His Sicilian Majesty, and his colours had been hoisted on every fort with the exception of those of Valetta. But at Naples the authorities could not be brought to declare more than that they had no official communication from Malta since September 5. They hoped that Nelson would be able to take the place for them. He sent off a frigate to the island, and meanwhile made an expedition to Castellammare to see the *Vanguard's* foremast stepped. As he had feared, not all the exertions of Hardy or scoldings of the bereaved and maddened Troubridge had availed to get the refitting of his damaged ships as far forward as he had intended. He reminded himself that he had always known Naples was a bad place for such a business. "Beside the rest, we are killed by kindness." The phrase had originated with Lady Hamilton. A tendency to quote her, verbatim, had become noticeable in his hurried letters, though he himself was not without his *bon mots* during these days of Court life. As the party from the British Embassy passed in the Admiral's barge, between the enemy ships taken in the late action, Sir William, referring to absurd French claims, said, "Look at those, and ask how they can call it a drawn battle!" Nelson's reply, treasured by the ubiquitous Miss Knight, was, "They are quite right, only they drew the *blanks* and we the *prizes*."

It was impossible, he wrote to his wife, not to be touched by the childlike eagerness with which Lady Hamilton gradually revealed all her surprises for his birthday. Sir William had not stinted, and Neapolitan fingers were clever at fashioning glittering trifles of tinsel and satin for carnival favours. Every button and ribbon to be distributed amongst Saturday's guests bore Nelson's name, and the new dinner-service, ordered from the royal porcelain factory at Portici, had "H.N." and "Glorious First of August" on every piece. An additional verse to the National Anthem had been composed for the occasion by Miss Knight, and more songs and sonnets than he would ever open were being delivered. Lady Hamilton was making translations, and her collection of newspapers for despatch to Lady Nelson was growing formidable. It was almost a relief when the auspicious day dawned with broken weather, though this inevitably meant a heavy swell in the bay, further retarding the process of refitting, and a packed assembly within the walls of the Palazzo Sessa.

Next morning the Admiral penned a memorable note to Lord St. Vincent.

"I trust, my Lord, in a week we shall all be at sea. I am very unwell, and the miserable conduct of this Court is not likely to cool my irritable temper. It is a country of fiddlers and poets, whores and scoundrels. I am Etc.

"Horatio Nelson."

One of his reasons for irritation was understandable. Captain Nisbet had chosen Lady Hamilton's *fête* as the scene for a display of juvenile inebriety. Captain Troubridge and other officers had removed the young man swiftly, but not before a considerable section of the enervated Neapolitan society had gathered with amusement that the stepson of the Victor of the Nile was complaining that the British Ambassadress was receiving attentions due to his mother.

Their guest made two expeditions with the Hamiltons during the early days of October. At the royal factory of Portici, a service ordered by the Queen to be decorated with his portrait and scenes from the various engagements in which he had taken part was in hand. Fine porcelain always attracted him, but he prudently and tactfully confined his purchases to a set of busts of the royal family. When he came to pay, he was told that anything chosen by Admiral Nelson was to be delivered free. "It was handsome of the King." The Queen was at last ready to receive him, privately. His first comment after he had recorded, "I have been with the Queen, she is truly a daughter of Maria Theresa", was, "This Country, by its system of procrastination, will ruin itself: the Queen sees it, and thinks as we do."

The royal stateswoman whose dignity and distress had so much impressed Nelson had never been accounted a beauty, and a grand air, a fine hand, a long throat and the unmistakable Habsburg lip completed the catalogue of the attractions of Maria Carolina in 1798. She was forty-five, and had borne eighteen children, of whom eight survived. Her complexion was waxen, her eyelids were puffy and her figure was at once gaunt and massive. Like her sister Marie Antoinette, she had been over-early married, to a boor whom she despised. The story of the sisters had much in common, as the glassy eye and frozen look of Maria Carolina proclaimed to all beholders. Her dread and hate of republicans was hysterical, and she honestly believed that her own day of reckoning was drawing near. She had always been the subject of much scurrilous gossip, which might not have approached a princess in whose character levity was unsuspected, but the *façade* displayed to Nelson on that October night was convincing and bound to enlist his wholehearted support. It was as the enemy of the French Anti-Christ, the daughter of Maria Theresa and the mother of many children that Maria Carolina appealed to a British officer whose unusual appearance proclaimed that he was not likely to be absent in the day of battle. Of course, also, like all injured foreign royalties, she hoped for money from Great Britain.

General Mack reached the palace of Caserta, sixteen miles north of the capital, on October 9, and Nelson and the Hamiltons were bidden to meet him there two days later. Nelson, who had bitter experience of Austrian Generals, and had already formed his opinion of this one (but prayed he might be mistaken), prepared to impress his personality with care. He felt that it was important that he should gain the entire confidence of the military leader to whom their Sicilian Majesties were about to entrust their army. The setting also was impressive. The party from the British Embassy arrived beneath a main portico one hundred and thirty-four feet high and divided into three vestibules by sixty-four columns, and ascended a state staircase to a first floor of gilded reception-rooms, decorated with frescoes and tapestries in which most figures were of much more than life size. The royal residence seemed primarily designed to make all inhabitants appear insignificant, but the atmosphere of the small party that presently sat to dine was from the first moment hopeful, in spite of the fact that the General sent to command Neapolitan troops understood no Italian, and the Admiral spoke no language but his own. French was employed, and the Hamiltons translated for Nelson. Their hosts introduced the British Admiral and the Austrian General to each other with every expression of esteem and regard, the Queen adding impulsively to Mack—"General, be to us by land, what my hero, Nelson, has been by sea!" The Emperor had desired the King of Naples "to begin", and promised support. Nelson returned from the entertainment to record, "I have endeavoured to impress the General with a favourable impression of me, and I think I have succeeded. He is active, and has an intelligent eye, and will do well, I have no doubt." Field-Marshal Baron Karl Mack von Leiberich was a much more promising person than he had expected. He was, unlike the Austrian General previously encountered, neither fine-drawn nor of noble birth. A visible scar testified to his services against the Turk. He was a blunt, dry-spoken Bavarian. The fact that the imported military leader was prepared to march in ten days had surprised and relieved Nelson, and Mack had privately agreed that the moment the war began, their confidence should be placed in the Queen and Sir John Acton.

Having set affairs in Naples in what he believed to be good train, and entertained the King and Prince Leopold to breakfast on board his flagship, Nelson sailed for Malta. Knowing that the French were well supplied, he was not so sanguine as the Neapolitans, as to the fall of Valetta, and he was right. Malta, although closely blockaded under his supervision, held out for two years. He was thankful to get his squadron, with the exception of the *Culloden* (still waiting for the pintles of her rudder), out of Naples Bay, though he himself was now bound by promise to their Majesties to return there. He had given up, with reluctance, his plan of going to Egypt to complete the destruction of Buonaparte's shipping. Turkish and Russian squadrons should soon be on that coast to relieve Hood, but his unwillingness to return to Naples was not only because he was uneasy at entrusting any blockade to Allies. In a letter dated October 4, now speeding towards Cadiz Bay, he had confided to Lord St. Vincent:

"I am writing opposite Lady Hamilton, therefore you will not be surprised at the glorious jumble of this letter. Were your Lordship in my place, I much doubt if you could write so well; our hearts and our hands must be all in a flutter. Naples is a dangerous place, and we must keep clear of it."

When this letter arrived at Admiral's House, Rosia Bay, the Commander-in-Chief wrote at once to the British Embassy, Naples. To Nelson he struck the professional note, mentioning his relief that the ladies of Naples had not detained him from duties that only he could perform. "You're great in the Cabinet as on the Ocean, and your whole conduct fills me with admiration and confidence." To Lady Hamilton he suggested:

"Ten thousand thanks are due to your Ladyship for restoring the health of our invaluable friend, on whose life the fate of the remaining governments in Europe whose system has not been deranged by those devils, depends. Pray, do not let your fascinating Neapolitan dames approach too near him; for he is made of flesh and blood and cannot resist their temptations."

3

A Portuguese squadron had joined Ball off Malta, and on Nelson's arrival, after a very slow passage, the Marquis de Niza expressed every flowery courtesy. But it instantly appeared that these allies were going to be rather a burden than a help. "It is ridiculous to hear them talk of their rank, and of the impossibility of serving under any of my brave and good Captains." Nelson thanked the Marquis for his zeal in proceeding to the blockade of Malta, ordered him to take his ships instantly to Naples (where they were needed), and repeated that none but Portuguese ships were under His Excellency's orders. He sent a formal summons to the French General and Admiral in command at Valetta, landed British stores, and ordered Ball down to the little island of Gozo, which was also flying French colours. The French in possession of Gozo, threatened with bombardment if they failed to surrender, did so with alacrity, and leaving Ball with five sail-of-the-line to continue the blockade, Nelson sailed again for Naples, after dark on the 30th of October. Letters from Lady Hamilton had told him that he was urgently needed. Since his departure, in spite of all her efforts, the Government were dropping back into their former condition of fascinated helplessness. General Mack had not even performed his avowed intention of visiting the troops on the frontiers. He said that he was working night and day, and that when he left Naples it would be for good. "I tell her Majesty, *for God's sake, for the Country's sake, and for your own sake, send him off.*" The picture painted by Lady Hamilton to the Queen had included "her friends sacrificed, her husband, children and herself led to the Block; and eternal dishonour to her memory, after for once having been active". The result had been satisfactory. A council had been summoned, and the King had agreed to join his army in a few days and not to return. "The Regency is to be in the name of the Prince Royal, but the Queen will direct all." The happiest passage in Lady Hamilton's very long letter described the Grand Signior's gifts to the Victor of the Nile, now on their way in a frigate from Constantinople.

She drew to a close with talk of children. Little Prince Leopold had been detected yesterday attempting to run away to sea to join Nelson, and had cried himself sick on being recaptured. The Court was at Caserta, awaiting the *accouchement* of the very pusillanimous Hereditary Princess, and after being summoned to sit in gala attire during a false alarm which had lasted twenty-four hours, the English Ambassadress had retired with a headache, humming the old English catch, "Oh dear, what can the matter be?" She sent her love to her "dear little fatherless Faddy", the fourteen-year-old son of a Captain of marines killed on board Nelson's flagship in Aboukir Bay. "I will be his mother as much as I can." She ended, "Love Sir William and myself, for we love you dearly. He is the best husband, friend, I wish I could say father also; but I should have been too happy if I had the blessing of having children, so must be content."

4

Nelson's journey of sixteen miles towards the Hamiltons' country house at dusk on November 5 came at the close of a wearisome day. Miss Cornelia Knight, through her telescope, had watched from her hotel window from the moment that Admiral Nelson in the *Vanguard*, together with the *Minotaur* ("Captain Louis from Malta"), had appeared over the horizon; "and they were all day coming in". When the Admiral reached the vicinity of the palace, the scene was one of unpromising confusion, and the air was rent by the pealing of bells and discharge of guns. The Hereditary Princess had at last been brought to bed, though not of an heir. Court officials who had been tied to the spot for weeks were departing in glad haste, and the King had announced his determination to join his army at the camp of San Germano. Lady Hamilton, who had found it impossible to be happy away from Naples while "our ships" were there, was in good spirits, but after a visit to the palace, Nelson recounted in the heavy manner which had previously succeeded an interview with Maria Carolina, "I am, I fear, drawn into a promise that Naples Bay shall never be left without an English Man-of-War. I never intended leaving the Coast of Naples without one; but if I had, who could withstand the request of such a Queen?" He had presented to His Majesty the French colours captured at Gozo, and told Ferdinand that he had sixteen thousand new subjects. Leghorn, where the attitude of their Majesties' son-in-law, the Grand Duke, was causing anxiety, was his next objective. He returned to the *Vanguard*, not the Palazzo Sessa, but when summoned, within the week, to consult with Mack and Acton at the camp spelt by him, "St. Germaines", he travelled with the Hamiltons. The weather was fine, and the military spectacle stirring. Thirty thousand of what Mack called "La plus belle Armée d'Europe" were drawn out for Nelson to see. He politely pronounced that as far as an officer of the navy could judge, the rank and file appeared healthy and good-looking. Privately, he noted that the force was, "with some few exceptions, wretchedly officered", and he was much struck when the monosyllabic Mack, attempting "the courtier-like" to their Majesties, regretted that so fine an army should not have the prospect of encountering an enemy more worthy of its prowess.

After dark, after the long day of the review, a council in the field was staged. It was ultimately agreed that a force of four thousand infantry and six hundred cavalry should be landed in the enemy's rear, at Leghorn. With the Emperor's advance, the French should be caught between three fires. Nelson volunteered to be responsible for transporting the infantry.

At 6 a.m. next morning the Admiral went to take leave of their Majesties, and found a sad change. Despatches received overnight from Vienna had not brought any solid assurance of support from what Lady Hamilton called "their poor fool of a son-in-law". M. Thugut, the highly neurotic Austrian Minister to Naples, was evasive, and much wished that the French could be presented as the aggressors. Nelson, feeling far from well, ventured to tell their Majesties, without aid of an interpreter, that one of two things was bound to happen, and His Majesty had his choice—"Either to advance (trusting to God for His blessing on a just Cause), to die with '*l'épée à la main*', or remain quiet and be kicked out of your Kingdoms". Ferdinand, startled, replied that he would go on, and trust his Maker, but Nelson was asked to delay his departure and hold further conference with Baron Mack on what their Majesties described (but he refused to recognise) as "a new face on affairs". Two days later the question of financial support from Great Britain was again mooted, and on the 18th Lady Hamilton received a letter from the Queen "full of the idea" that English money was essential to their effort. The British Ambassadress was desired to show this letter to Admiral Nelson and ask him to say what he saw. Nelson's reply was blunt. He had long ago told the Queen that he did not think Mr. Pitt would go to Parliament to ask John Bull to throw good money after bad. When his country once saw that Naples was taking up arms on her own behalf, he had no doubt that an ally in distress would be supported. As to what he saw, he could say that briefly. He saw the finest territory in the world, full of resources, unable to supply her public wants, and all persons of influence who could get at public money or stores helping themselves.

At last, on November 22, he sailed for Leghorn, and two days later Mack's army crossed the frontiers into the Papal States. Nelson's part in the enterprise proceeded, if not without difficulty, to complete success. "It blowing a strong gale on that night and the next day, none but British ships kept me company." He anchored in Leghorn Roads on the afternoon of the 28th, and, in concert with General Naselli, sent in a summons. By 8 p.m. the Governor of the city had come on board the *Vanguard* to surrender unconditionally. The Neapolitan troops were then landed, despite a heavy swell, together with their cannon and baggage, and having won a bloodless victory, proceeded to take possession of the town and fortress with loud rejoicing.

Two letters from Lady Hamilton met Nelson on his return journey to Naples. The first, beginning, "My dearest Lord,—How unhappy we are at the bad weather. How are you tossed about? Why did you not come back?" told him that the army had marched. Lady Hamilton, who had not slept for two nights, thinking of his sufferings, had not yet seen the Queen, who had arrived in the capital, nor could her ladyship hope to do so for another two or three days, as she was kept indoors by a feverish chill. She adjured the Admiral not to go ashore at Leghorn, where the stiletto of many a republican would be ready for him. Her second letter told a story that sounded too good to be true. On the approach of the Neapolitan army, General Championnet had retreated. The King had written to the Queen from Frascati, and was about to enter Rome in triumph.

The Naples to which Nelson came back on December 5 was an uneasy place, full of rumours. On the last day of November the British Embassy had heard that after a battle resulting in heavy casualties, Mack had been taken prisoner. There had been no such bloody encounter, but many men who had marched with the Baron were secretly home again, having shed their uniforms. "La plus belle Armée d'Europe" had already suffered, though not from the foe. Its officers, as Nelson had foreseen, "did not like fighting". Some were suspected, by those under their command, of "liking the French". Its ranks had been stiffened, at the last moment, by old soldiers, condemned by military tribunals, and robust convicts from civilian gaols. At the first opportunity such leaders had shown recruits how to plunder a countryside and their own convoys, and they had cause for complaint, for already, on their road to Rome, they had been left three days without rations. Even the King and his staff had been thirty-six hours without food or a change of clothing. On the day following his return Nelson informed St. Vincent that the French had thirteen thousand troops at a strong post called Castellana, and that although the force with which Mack had gone against them numbered twenty thousand, "the event in my opinion is doubtful". If Mack was defeated, he had no doubt that Naples would be lost within a fortnight. "For if the Emperor will not march, this Country has not the power of resisting." He prophesied that unless Mack succeeded quickly in dislodging the French from Castellana, he must fall back to the frontier, for "the French have driven back, to say no worse, the right wing of the King's Army, and taken all their baggage and artillery". He had gathered this unfortunate state of affairs during a painful audience with "the great Queen", who admitted that her husband's troops were behaving in a manner which broke her heart, that Mack was in despair, and that she put no faith in the remainder of her subjects, whom she termed "rabbits". For three days after this, nobody from the British Embassy was summoned to the royal palace, but from letters from the Queen to Lady Hamilton, "painting the anguish of her soul", and from other sources, Nelson was able to form a picture of the "bad behaviour" of her husband's troops deplored by Her Majesty. This he pronounced with unusual sarcasm, upon the whole, not so bad as he had expected. "The Neapolitan officers have not lost much honour, for God knows they had but little to lose, but they lost all they had."

Early on the 14th Naples enjoyed its most startling rumour yet. Amongst the soldiers in civilian disguise who had slipped back home was His Majesty. A large mob gathered in the square below the palace, and his *lazzaroni* roared until the figure of Ferdinand appeared on the balcony.

5

The day of the King's ignominious reappearance was a busy one in the Bay of Naples. "Arrived also", noted the journal of the *Vanguard*, "the Marquis de Niza, in the *Principe Real*, and the *Alcmene* from Egypt, bringing despatches from Captain Hood of H.M.S. *Zealous*, and the Turkish Ambassador and his suite, bringing presents from the Grand Signior."

The smiling and unsuspicious old Kelim Effendi, attended by his long procession of staff, in charge of a Mr. Pisani, employé of Mr. Spencer Smith, Minister at the Porte, had been duly decanted at the Palazzo Sessa, where a group of armed *lazzaroni* stood on guard night and day, under orders from their chief, Egidio Pallio, to attend the British Ambassador wherever he went. Arms were now carried by many such persons, who met deserters at the gates of the city and relieved them of their equipment, and the King, who on his arrival home had declared that he would await the French surrounded by his loyal subjects, was beginning to share his wife's opinion that "*les scènes de Varennes avec toutes leurs suites*" were about to be repeated in his own capital. On December 18, a despatch from Mack, in full retreat, besought His Majesty to move before the French took possession of Naples.

On the previous day Nelson had written to Spencer Smith, "I do not know that the whole Royal Family, with 3,000 Neapolitan *émigrés*, will not be under the protection of the King's flag this night." He had shifted the *Vanguard* to a new berth, out of range of the Neapolitan forts, an act that had brought residents—not all British—panting to the Palazzo Sessa, as much taken aback as if the Rock at Gibraltar had moved. The King's consent was not obtained until the 19th, when he suddenly became pressing to be gone, but from the 15th onwards the Queen had been delivering, under cover of darkness, to the British Embassy, the belongings of ten members of her family, "it may be for life". Lady Hamilton sat up nightly, to receive an astonishing jumble, ranging from "the diamonds of the family, both male and female", and three dozen casks of doubtful security containing gold ducats, to small coffers of linen which would be needed by the children on the voyage, tapestries, pictures, furniture, sculpture and plate.

Nelson reckoned the value of the royal property personally collected by Lady Hamilton, received by her at the Embassy, and delivered to his seamen and marines, labelled "Stores for Nelson", at £2,500,000. Sir William and he avoided the palace during these days of tension, but although Lady Hamilton visited the Queen as usual, Maria Carolina also wrote to her daily.

Nelson had originally fixed the flight for the night of the 20th, but until the 19th the problem of how to get the royal family from the palace to the landing-stage called Vittoria, on the little quay known as the Mola Figlio, had not been solved. The solution in an Italian palace was, of course, a subterranean passage.

The morning of the 21st dawned exceedingly foul, and Acton, who sent to Nelson and Hamilton during the day at least eight contradictory notes, suggested a further postponement on various pretexts, one of which was that the Admiral might find it impossible, owing to the swell, to transfer the sacred persons of their Majesties and household from the landing-stage to his expectant men-of-war. Nelson's reply was to postpone the first embarkation by an hour and a half. A note of the 20th, with underlined corrections in his own hand, preserved by Hope of the *Alcmene*, shows how detailed had been his preparations.

"*Most secret.*

"Three barges, and the small cutter of the *Alcmene*, armed with cutlasses only, to be at the Victoria at half-past seven o'clock precisely. Only one barge to be at the wharf, the others to lay on their oars at the outside of the rocks—the small barge of the *Vanguard* to be at the wharf. The above boats to be on board the *Alcmene* before seven o'clock, under the direction of Captain Hope. *Grapnells to be in the boats.*

"All other boats of the *Vanguard* and *Alcmene* to be armed with cutlasses, and the launches with carronades to assemble on board the *Vanguard*, under the direction of Captain Hardy, and to put off from her at half-past eight o'clock *precisely, to row half way towards the Mola Figlio. These boats to have 4 or 6 soldiers in them. In case assistance is wanted by me, false fires will be burnt.*

"Nelson."

"*The Alcmene to be ready to slip in the night, if necessary.*"

A note entirely in his own hand, delivered at Lady Knight's hotel, just as the invalid and her daughter were preparing to go to bed on the night of the 21st, secured immediate obedience.

"My dear Madam,

"Commodore Stone will take care of you. Do not be alarmed, there is in truth no cause for it.

"Ever your faithful servant,
"Nelson."

Amongst Nelson's larger instructions had been a summons to Troubridge from Leghorn ("For God's sake, make haste!"), and to Foley from Malta, and a warning to Ball not to send any Neapolitan ships with the *Goliath*. The Queen's fear that there were traitors in her husband's Marine had been confirmed. The ships' companies and several officers of the *Parthenope* and *Sannita* had abandoned their ships and come ashore. Caracciolo's application to be allowed to carry his royal master and mistress in a ship of their own navy had been refused, and Miss Knight, meeting the gentleman at a dinner-party a few evenings before the flight, had remarked that, "I never saw any man look so utterly miserable. He scarcely uttered a word, ate nothing, and did not even unfold his napkin." Amongst the ill presages which afflicted the Queen on the fatal morning was the news that Count Vanni, an officer once employed by her, had shot himself. "The White Terror of Naples", who had been responsible for the arrest and imprisonment of hundreds, could not face the prospect of republicans occupying Naples.

Nelson, in better health than recently, "my mind never better and my heart in the right trim", drove with the Hamiltons and Mrs.

Cadogan after dinner at the Embassy to attend a farewell reception offered by Kelim Effendi. At the Palazzo Sessa servants proceeded to lay a supper-table. Their Excellencies' carriage, ordered to fetch them home in two hours' time, was already outside the scene of the entertainment when all members of the Hamilton party withdrew on foot. Lady Hamilton noted that she had fifteen minutes in which to reach what she called "my post". Faithful to her dramatic promise to follow her royal companion to the scaffold if necessary, she hurried to the palace to support a royal lady who had repeatedly and unpromisingly announced, "My head is quite gone."

Nelson landed at the corner of the Arsenal at 8.30 and entered the palace by the long subterranean tunnel communicating with the Vittoria landing-stage, on which Count Thurn, an Austrian Commodore in the Neapolitan service, was posted with instructions which included two passwords—"All goes right and well", and "All is wrong, you may go back". The descent of the royal family, escorted by Nelson, began punctually, and soon the first party of hooded and muffled passengers urged towards a heaving barge had entered upon half an hour's experience of Naples Bay with a heavy ground swell. The Knights, who went with the main party of British refugees, were less fortunate.

"The night was cold, for we were in the month of December, and it was between twelve and one before we were in the boat. There were several persons already in it, and an English child fell in the water, but was taken out unhurt. We had a long way to go, for the ships had cast anchor at a great distance from the city, to be beyond the range of the forts in the event of treachery or surprise. When we came alongside the Admiral's ship, the Captain, Sir Thomas Hardy stepped into the boat, and told my mother that the ship was so full there was no room for us. In vain we entreated to be taken on board. The thing was impossible."

The Knights passed on perforce to the *Rainha de Portugal*, commanded, they were assured,

"by an Englishman, who had formerly been a Master in our Navy, but was now a Commodore.... The young midshipman who conducted us was constantly jumping about in the boat to keep himself from falling asleep, for during the last 48 hours he had been unceasingly engaged in getting the baggage and numerous attendants of the Royal Family on board."

In the chief cabin of the Portuguese man-of-war the Knights found many ladies of various nationalities, of whom only one, a Russian of high rank and great wealth, had secured a bed. They now heard, for the first time, that their destination was Palermo.

In the *Vanguard* conditions were not much better. Captain Hardy had set sailmakers to make cots for the royal family three days past, and the wardroom and offices under the poop had been hastily repainted, but his notice to get his ship ready for sea had been short, and during the week he had been obliged to send men on shore to fetch the royal valuables. "The first embarcation" of about thirty persons came on board between 9.30 and 10. The gentlemen passengers were directed to the wardroom; the Admiral's quarters had been prepared for the ladies and children. When the "second embarcation", consisting of more than an equal number of royal attendants, several Neapolitan nobles and their *suites*, and many British merchants, arrived, about two hours later, the *Vanguard* (rolling at single anchor) began to appear uncomfortably crowded. It became known that their Majesties' linen and bedding was not to be found. That of the Hamiltons was successfully traced to the transport *Samuel and Jane*. Throughout the hours of darkness, boats bringing refugees swarmed around the flagship. The British were referred to the three transports of their nation and the ships of the Portuguese squadron. For the frantic royalist-French and Corsican *émigrés*, the British Ambassador had chartered two Greek polaccas, and arranged that they should be provisioned by English victuallers.

After a broken night, the dishevelled passengers arose to witness a storm so violent that for several hours no communication could take place between the ships. The King's Confessor fell out of his crib, and fractured a forearm. Nelson, hoping for the arrival of Troubridge to relieve his overcrowding difficulties, had worse problems with which to contend. A letter from Captain Sir Sidney Smith, containing enclosures from their Lordships, must be left to burn a hole in his pocket until he had leisure to attend to it. Not even the promise of double pay had availed to persuade Neapolitan ships' companies to return to their 74's. Such officers as remained explained that their men were naturally too anxious about the fates of their homes, which they would be leaving unprotected. It was

Nelson's duty not to leave any men-of-war to fall into enemy hands, but their Majesties, who remembered what their 74's had cost, could not be reconciled to the prospect of their destruction. The Admiral did what he could—directed the Marquis de Niza to get all out of the mole, and equip as many as possible with jury masts for a passage to Messina. The remainder, if the French captured Naples, or the Neapolitan Jacobins revolted, must, he insisted, be burnt. He decided to leave the *Alcmene* behind under de Niza's command, and their Majesties left Count Thurn.

Next day, the weather being more moderate, several deputations from the town approached the *Vanguard*, desiring audience of the King. Ferdinand, however, had made up his mind for Palermo. Towards dusk came a visitor whom Nelson scarcely recognised. Baron Mack—"worn to a shadow"—had to announce that all that was left of his army was already at Capua, with the enemy on its heels, and that Tuscany had been invaded. He could only, before making a tragic exit, beg the King to sail as soon as possible. "My heart", said Nelson, "bled for him." A month later Nelson had to admit that Mack seemed lost. The Baron had taken refuge from the remnant of the Neapolitan army in the French camp.

At 7 p.m. on December 23 the *Vanguard* weighed and made sail, in company with the Neapolitan corvette *Sannita* and the *Archimedes*, 74, the three British transports and about twenty merchant vessels. "Next day", in Nelson's opinion, "it blew harder than I have ever experienced since I have been at sea." The wind with which he had sailed had been easterly, but he had hardly cleared Capri when it chopped round to the westward, in heavy squalls, with rain. The *Vanguard*, with a disagreeable coast under her lee, began to labour prodigiously. Although all rest was out of the question, comparative quiet began to reign amongst the passengers. The horse-laugh of the King was no longer heard. Mrs. Cadogan, who attended sufferers in the wardroom, was acclaimed by him as an angel. All the Neapolitan servitors, who should have been performing the duties undertaken by the *Signora Madre*, were invisible, or on their knees engaged in last prayers. At about 1.30, at a moment when Nelson had just left the quarter-deck to look at the ship's position on the chart, a furious blast from the W.S.W. gave the *Vanguard* a heave, and blew her topsails to pieces, together with the driver and fore-topmast staysail. Count Esterhazy flung to the waves, in appeasement, an expensive snuff-box embellished with the likeness of his Italian mistress. In the ladies' quarters, the Duchess of Castel-cicala cut her head on Admiral Nelson's sideboard, and little Prince Alberto fell into convulsions. Tom Allen, assuming knowledgeable airs, had told the groaning ladies that they would be all right "while the sticks stand". Hearing barefooted seamen hurrying with axes to cut away the wreck, they judged that the worst had happened and that they had escaped being torn to pieces on shore only to be lost at sea. Lady Hamilton, and one of the Queen's stewards, Saverio Rodino, "a faithful and sure man", were the only passengers to keep their heads. The Ambassadress, in the words of the admiring Admiral, from the moment that she had come on board a British man-of-war, had put him and the whole royal family under an eternal obligation. When her own bedding and linen had been brought to light, she had instantly given up all to the party of women and children in his cabin (which included a swaddled princess, aged seven weeks), "and become *their slave*, for except for one man, no person belonging to Royalty assisted the Royal Family, nor did her Ladyship enter a bed the whole time they were on board". "Good Sir William", he added, "also made every sacrifice for the comfort of the august Family." Another officer told a tale which showed the aged antiquary in a more characteristic attitude.

"During the height of the gale, when Lady Hamilton could think of nothing more wherewith to console the desponding Queen, she looked around for Sir William, who was not to be found. At length it was discovered that he had withdrawn to his sleeping-cabin, and was sitting there with a loaded pistol in each hand. In answer to her Ladyship's exclamation of surprise, he calmly told her that he was resolved not to die with the 'guggle-guggle-guggle' of the salt-water in his throat; and therefore he was prepared, as soon as he felt the ship sinking, to shoot himself!"

Next morning, although the wind moderated and drew round to the S.E., "there was still much for such passengers to endure". The British officers made a brief appearance to express good wishes for the season and regrets that they could not offer more worthy fare for Christmas Day. Prince Alberto, apparently entirely recovered, ate a hearty breakfast. Soon afterwards the child began to display symptoms of agony, and by 7 p.m. was dead in the arms of Lady Hamilton. He had reached the attractive age of six, and was, she said, her favourite amongst the royal children.

The *Vanguard* anchored within Palermo Mole at 2 a.m. next morning, and Nelson escorted the stricken Queen and Princesses on shore, *incognita*, before day dawned, returning at 9 a.m. to assist at the entry of the King into his second capital. "Manned ship, and cheered him until on shore; could not salute him by reason of being in the Mole."

His Sicilian Majesty's Royal Standard flying at the main top-gallant masthead of a British warship had been visible for many hours, and the authorities of the town, including Mr. Tough, British Consul, had arrived to pay their respects. Ferdinand was received by his subjects with the loudest acclamations and apparent joy.

Chapter XII
1798–1800
(ætat. 40–41)
"INACTIVE AT A FOREIGN COURT"

I

THE refugees' first impression of Palermo, in December rain, was wholly chilling, but on the day after he had taken the royal family on board the *Vanguard*, Nelson had received some instructions which had made him warm whenever he had time to think of them. Their Lordships had at last discovered a suitable way in which they might employ Sir Sidney Smith, whose address and pretensions were considerable. Good relations with Turkey were now of additional importance, he knew Constantinople well, and his own younger brother—who must be accustomed to him—was Minister there. He had been appointed to a vaguely defined combined naval and diplomatic post, and sent to St. Vincent with orders to forward him to the Levant. Sir Sidney's own view of his position was quite clear—in a splendidly engrossed and sealed passport, which presently found its way to Nelson's desk, he styled himself "*Chevalier Grand Croix de l'Ordre Royal et Militaire de l'Épée de Suède, Ministre Plénipotentiaire da sa Majésté Britannique près la Porte Ottomane, et Chef de son Escade dans les Mers du Levant*". ("We are not", was Nelson's comment, "forced to understand French.") Sir Sidney had written to inform Sir William Hamilton that he was going to conduct operations in Egypt, and had been allowed by their Lordships to choose Captain Miller as his second-in-command Sir William, at present, was in no fettle for strife. He was confined to bed by a familiar variety of bilious fever, brought on by anxiety, cold and fatigue, and he objected strongly to the house in which their grateful Majesties had established him after two nights as their guest in the gloomy Colli Palace. Sir William had been far too unwell to attend the effective, though hastily planned, Reception given by their Majesties, this dark Sunday afternoon, to the nobility and gentry of their second capital (a function which had entailed an apologetic note from the Queen to Lady Hamilton, begging that the big cases, which she had rashly said might be thrown into the hold of our brave liberator's flagship, might be sent up to the Colli at once, as they contained all the Court dress of the family).

The Ambassadress, who had been up to the palace several times to weep with the Queen, was, after a succession of sleepless nights —twelve, she claimed—and the loss of three elegantly furnished houses and six or seven carriages, naturally, in her husband's opinion, able to weep easily. She said that to do so was now the only comfort of two women of sensibility, and disliked being told that she was not yet a philosopher. Their guest also was not yet a philosopher. A left-handed scribe, who covered a sheet slowly and had waited a week, sat down in the long-untenanted Villa Bastioni that night to tell Lord St. Vincent that, since much abler officers had arrived in a district which he had believed to be under his control, he hoped that unless his health (at present much affected by uneasiness of mind) should shortly improve, he might be allowed to resign his command to one of the brave officers who had so gloriously fought at the Battle of the Nile. Next morning he addressed his Commander-in-Chief privately.

"*I do feel, for I am a man,* that it is impossible for me to serve in these Seas, with the Squadron under a junior officer:—could I have thought it!—and from Earl Spencer! Never, never was I so astonished as your letter made me. As soon as I can get hold of Troubridge, I shall send him to Egypt, to destroy the Ships in Alexandria. If it can be done, Troubridge will do it. The Swedish Knight writes Sir William Hamilton, that he shall go to Egypt, and take Captain Hood and his Squadron under his command. The Knight forgets the respect due to his superior Officer: he has no orders from you to take my ships away from my command, but it is all of a piece. Is it to be borne? Pray grant me permission to retire, and I hope the *Vanguard* will be allowed to convey me and my friends, Sir William and Lady Hamilton, to England."

Having ordered Sir Sidney to Alexandria, and assured him that all instructions coming from their Lordships and the Commander-in-Chief should be most strictly complied with, he could do no more than await results, which meant months of waiting.

The results of Nelson's letters began to be apparent in mid-February, when Lord St. Vincent wrote, "Employ Sir Sidney Smith in any manner you think proper." A long despatch from Lord Spencer, received at the end of April, mentioned "very great misunderstanding", and Sir Sidney was obliged to relinquish his self-appointed rank of Commodore flying a broad pendant. His very gallant and successful services in Egypt fully confirmed their Lordships' hopes of him, but as far as his relations with Nelson went, his desire to re-establish the control of the Porte in Egypt (even though it meant giving passports to French troops deserted by Buonaparte and fast dying of malnutrition) was fatal to good understanding. "The Great Plenip:" continued, while Nelson remained in the Mediterranean, to be a thorn in the flesh.

Not only the inhabitants of the Villa Bastioni were miserable as the early weeks of 1799 dragged slowly past, bringing execrable weather and unrelievedly bad news from Naples. The Queen, shuddering with cold and ague amongst the flaking gilt and dusty plumes of the only habitable part of the Colli Palace, quickly perceived her new home to be the appointed background for royal assassination. She pointed out that if she had to make another escape from republicans, the only road to the quay was over two miles in length, and one of the main thoroughfares of the town. To add to her anguish, she found her influence with her husband and his counsellors much diminished.

The densely populated side-streets of Palermo presented many eating-houses, but only lodgings for bag-men. There was but one hotel in the town—in Sicily, said cynics—at which a French proprietress was accustomed to receive (and charge accordingly) an occasional English milor' who had read in a library overlooking green parkland of the mosaics of Monreale. The hotel swallowed up about a score of the 2,000 unexpected exiles whose pallid but supercilious *valets* and *femmes de chambre* had not yet learnt that mention of Naples was loathed by Sicilians. The remainder gradually established themselves, in colonies, in vacant *palazzi,* with reception-rooms of great size, where ceilings were beautifully painted with cupids and clouds, but marble-topped tables and mirrors were cracked, and furniture was scanty and untrustworthy. To the more

nervous of the refugees, the very independence of the Sicilian character suggested republican leanings, and their feeling of insecurity
increased as they heard of Jacobinism spreading to the very toe of
Italy, and Trees of Liberty planted in Calabrian towns. When the
newly appointed British Consul-General to Naples arrived from
England, after a three months' passage, he found, "We should have
been on 'le pavé', but for the Ambassador's exertions, for a lodging
is not to be had." The appointment of young Mr. Charles Lock
(obtained through the influence of Lord Robert Fitzgerald and Lord
Craven) was not a happy one. Mrs. Lock was first cousin to Charles
James Fox, and stepsister of "the notorious Irish rebel", Lord
Edward Fitzgerald, husband of "La Belle Pamela", illegitimate
child of Philippe Egalité, Duc d'Orléans, who had voted for the
execution of Louis XVI. Nothing in the subsequent conduct of the
Locks persuaded their Majesties of the Two Sicilies from the
opinion that the couple were Jacobins. The Locks conceived violent
animosity against "Lady Hamilton, who governs the Queen and
Lord Nelson", and attributed all her troubles to her "female vanity
which could not bear that any English woman should be admired
by her countrymen except herself".

After a short pause, consequent upon the royal flight having
outstripped news, dire tales of what had followed in Naples arrived,
at irregular intervals at the Colli Palace, where, as Nelson deplored,
although sometimes three councils were held in a day, nothing
resulted, except that the Sicilians, naturally concerned for the
defence of their country, were estranged by the King's preference
for Neapolitan advisers. General Pignatelli, who had been left as
Regent in Naples, soon proved quite unequal to a task which he did
not relish. He proceeded to treat with the French for a two months'
armistice, in the terms of which his Sovereign's name nowhere
appeared, whereupon the *lazzaroni* revolted and elected Prince
Moliterno and the Duke of Roccaromana in his place. Of these, both
presently joined the republicans, but the Duke eventually returned
to royalism. Ghastly atrocities had already been committed in a city
divided against itself, and terrorised by mobs led by the section of
the community devoted to the dynasty. The *lazzaroni* had freed all
prisoners in the gaols of the town, and massacred in cold blood all

available characters suspected of Jacobinism. On the arrival of the French they put up a fierce though disorganised resistance, but by February 4 Nelson knew that what he called "the tricoloured flag" was flying from every fort in Naples, and that a provisional government, under French protection, known as the Parthenopæan Republic, had been established. A great number of persons lately holding Court appointments, some of whom were convinced republicans, or considered themselves deserted by the King, had accepted office in hopes of salvation from anarchy.

Nelson, who dubbed the new régime "the Vesuvian", wrote to Brother William, "My situation here is not to be envied, and I hope very soon to be released from it"; but in their hour of darkness he considered himself "tied so fast by their Sicilian Majesties that I cannot move".

He shifted his flag to the *Bellerophon*, while she underwent repairs after her passage, and ordered Cockburn to take the *Vanguard* and *Minerve* to Malta to see if they could be of any use to Ball, who was calling desperately for corn. He told Ball that he hoped soon to be able to return her Purser to the *Alexander* for a few days, but at the moment was quite unable to spare Tyson. "My public correspondence," he explained to William, "besides the business of sixteen Sail-of-the-Line, and all our commerce, is with Petersburg, Constantinople, the Consuls at Smyrna, Egypt, the Turkish and Russian Admirals, Trieste, Vienna, Minorca, Earl St. Vincent and Lord Spencer. This over, what time can I have for private correspondence?" Nevertheless, all old friends who had sent congratulations received answers in his own hand, all on a note of deep dejection. Admiral Goodall was told, "Palermo is detestable, and we are all unwell and full of sorrow"; Lady Parker, "You who remember me always laughing and gay, would hardly believe the change"; Davison, "I am ready to quit this world of trouble, and envy none but those of the estate of 6 feet by two." To Louis, waiting off Leghorn to rescue the royal families of Tuscany and Sardinia, he wrote, "Darby will tell you what is *not* passing here, for none can tell what we *are* doing." His note to Lady Nelson was the saddest of all: "I wish I could say more to give you any satisfaction about Josiah, but I am sorry to say, with real grief, that he has nothing good about him. He must, sooner or later, be broke, but I am sure neither you nor I can help it." But on February 2, the wheels at the Admiralty having duly revolved, he was able to tell Josiah's mother that Captain Nisbet had been appointed to the *Thalia*.

The defence of Messina, the key of Sicily, was absorbing him on the early February date when persons scanning the *Gazette* in London coffee-houses read that, on a promotion of Admirals, Lord Nelson had risen from Rear-Admiral of the Blue to Rear-Admiral of the Red.

2

The climate of Sicily, although both the Hamiltons and Nelson abused it, was famous for its equability, and towards Easter-tide of 1799, when the *tramontana* ceased to blow, Palermo began to show herself in her true colours. Under dazzling skies, suddenly warm and wide, country girls, accompanying gaily painted carts loaded with spring flowers, pressed upon passers-by stiff bouquets of violets and freesias. Pastry-cooks' windows were filled with sugar lambs; every morning small new shops opened. They displayed embroideries, executed in cottages of the landscape, models of ships and Sicilian vehicles (eagerly demanded by Neapolitan children), tastefully arranged furnishing fabrics, native pottery and sailors' hymns (which last afterwards enjoyed great popularity in London). It appeared to Miss Knight that the Sicilians, an active and intelligent people, had only needed encouragement for their industries. "It was wonderful to see the improvement and resources which started up in Palermo after the arrival of so many strangers." All that met the eye of the English authoress was admirable, but by the following winter, when Palermo had assimilated over 3,000 Neapolitan and Tuscan exiles accustomed to luxury, the jackals of the entertainment trade, having smelt money, had provided much that had hitherto been uncalled for in "La Città Felice". In the crowded rooms of a *palazzo* on La Nova, leased by a committee of titled exiles for concerts and balls, in imitation of the *Accademia de' Nobili* of Naples, company was less closely scrutinised than it would have been at Almacks in St. James's, play was high, hours were late and liquor flowed.

The background of Nelson's life underwent a change. The Hamiltons had moved to what Miss Knight mildly described as "a larger villa near the Mole", where Lady Hamilton was again able to entertain on a resplendent scale. "I find", wrote Captain Ball, in February, "that you fascinate all the Navy as much at Palermo as you did at Naples." "Patroness of the Navy" was his name for her. Three travelling Scotsmen, Captain Pryse Lockhart Gordon (who was bear-leading delicate Lord Montgomery) and young Lord William Gordon (who wrote verse), were also frequently invited to view the spectacle described by their hostess as "Tria Juncta in Uno" (in witty reference to the motto of the Order worn by both Sir William and Lord Nelson). Tom Allen, bearing a note, a bouquet or a bottle of Tokay, now rolled up many marble steps towards a palace of pretensions. The property had been, in fact, so much beyond the Ambassador's means that until Nelson had arranged to take up residence there and bear a share of the expenses, Sir William had been doubtful of the wisdom of the move. Even when two other English families—the Gibbses and the Nobles—had arrived as paying guests, there was room to spare in a house which struck the happy mean between town house and country; for the Palazzo Palagonia had the advantage over the Neapolitan palace of standing apart from all other buildings, in its own spacious gardens.

Letters from Brother William and Alexander Davison, and a packet from Lady Nelson, dated December and February, reached Nelson early in April. A paragraph in a newspaper had been his first intimation that during the dark week of the flight from Naples a character very important in his early life had passed away quietly at Kentish Town. William's letter told him that Uncle Suckling had left him co-executor with an unknown Mr. Hume, and a legacy of £100. "I love his memory," replied Nelson, "and am not sorry that he has forgot me, except as his executor, in which I will be faithful. I loved my dear uncle for his own worth." Three months later, when he heard of the death of his younger brother, his expressions of regret were less warm. To the tender-hearted Maurice and uninhibited William he was sincerely attached, but Suckling had never been anything but a source of anxiety. Davison wrote, somewhat enigmatically:

"I cannot help again repeating my sincere regret at your continuation in the Mediterranean; at the same time, I would be grieved that you should quit a station, if it in the smallest degree affected your own feelings. You certainly are, and must be, the best and only judge. Yet you must allow your best friends to express their sensations . . . Your valuable better-half writes to you. She is in good health, but very uneasy and anxious, which is not to be wondered at. She sets off with the good old man to-morrow—for Bath. . . . Lady Nelson this moment calls, and is with my wife. She bids me say, that unless you return home in a few months, she will join the Standard at Naples. Excuse a woman's tender feelings—they are too acute to be expressed."

Nelson already knew that his wife was no longer living under what he liked to think of as "my own roof". His father had explained as long ago as September that "Lady Nelson is apprehensive this place might be too cold for the winter and moreover the House wants paint etc." Mrs. Matcham had been desired to find a small furnished house in a good situation in which her parent and sister-in-law might pass another Bath season. A most dutiful son had hastened to assure the Rector that if Roundwood and the Ipswich neighbourhood were not as pleasant as could be wished, he trusted that the generosity of his country would soon allow him to choose a more comfortable resting-place for his family. The note of his reply to his lady, dated April 10, could not be called encouraging.

"You must not think it possible for me to write even to you as much as I used to do. In truth, I have such quantities of writing public letters, that my private correspondence has been, and must continue to be, greatly neglected. You would, by February, have seen how unpleasant it would have been had you followed any advice which carried you from England to a wandering sailor. I could, if you had come, *only* have struck my flag, and carried you back again, for it would have been impossible to set up an establishment at either Naples or Palermo. Nothing but the situation of affairs in this country has kept me from England; and if I have the pleasure of seeing their Sicilian Majesties safe on their throne again, it is probable that I shall yet be home in the summer. Good Sir William, Lady Hamilton, and myself, are the mainsprings of the machine which manages what is going on in this country. We are all bound to England when we can quit our posts with propriety."

The outlook, like the weather, had begun to improve, suddenly and progressively, exactly a month before this letter was written. The arrival of General Sir Charles Stuart to occupy the garrison of Messina with two English regiments from Minorca had been hailed by Nelson as "an electric shock, both to good and bad subjects of his Sicilian Majesty". A fortnight later came news of the capture of Corfu by the Russian and Turkish squadrons under Vice-Admiral Ouschakoff and Abdul Cadir Bey. That the Emperor should move had always been regarded by Nelson as essential to the re-establishment of the Neapolitan monarchy, and Austria, having waited to be attacked, had by mid-April inflicted some startling reverses on the enemy. Tales from Naples were all of strained relations between the authorities of the Parthenopæan Republic and their masters, and since the Roman State and Southern Italy were in revolt, the French were beginning to realise that the troops holding down their Neapolitan conquest were in a precarious position. The most unexpected item of good news (which continued to pour in as inexorably as that of disaster had arrived last autumn) concerned a counter-revolution engineered from Palermo. Cardinal Fabrizio Ruffo, a politician of princely though impoverished family, had left the Court on a January night when *morale* at the Colli Palace had been low. He had landed in his native Calabria with only eight companions. Within a few weeks his "Christian Army of the Holy Faith" consisting mainly of peasants and brigands, but numbering 17,000, were carrying the Sicilian royal standard, and considerable terror, towards Naples, through a country in which he had great influence. Ruffo, described by Nelson as "a swelled-up priest", had never taken orders. His Cardinal's hat had been bestowed upon him on his retirement from the posts of Papal Treasurer-General and Minister of War. His followers, termed by himself "all ferocious men", were reinforced by some Turks and Russians who had crossed the Adriatic. His most spectacular lieutenant was a bandit called Michele Pezza, generally known as "Fra Diavolo", and by Nelson as "The Great Devil". Nelson's interest, during the spring months of good hope in 1799, centred in the progress of the one force in which he could repose entire confidence—the squadron under Troubridge, sent by him to the Bay of Naples, with orders to blockade it and get into communication with the royalists of that capital. Since their Sicilian majesties considered the presence of Admiral Nelson (even without his flagship) as necessary to their feelings of security, and the Bashaw of Tripoli was intriguing with

Buonaparte, he transferred his flag to the *Culloden* while the *Vanguard* went to show herself at Tunis, and for two days after Troubridge's departure and before the return of the *Vanguard*, to the transport *Samuel and Jane*.

Troubridge, who sailed on the last day of March, was able by April 3 to announce that all the islands in the immediate neighbourhood of Naples had re-hoisted the Royal Standard. A week later Salerno had fallen to Hood and the royal colours were flying at Castellammare. "Your Lordship", wrote Troubridge, "never beheld such loyalty", but he was embarrassed that amongst their expressions of loyalty the faithful had hastened to deliver on board his men-of-war all natives of their island who had held prominent office under French control, seven or eight of whom, he was told, merited death. He wrote to ask that their Majesties would send Neapolitan troops and an honest Judge to conduct trials. Nelson, after a hurried visit to the Queen and Acton, replied that a Neapolitan ship-of-the-line should instantly bring what was desired. "Send me word some proper heads are taken off; this alone will comfort me." The Admiral's reason for present discomfort was that although he preached incessantly to the now rejoicing and relaxed Court that speedy rewards and quick punishments were the only foundation of good government, "unfortunately, neither the one nor the other have been practised here".

Their Majesties were now agreed upon only one point—that they would not return to Naples until it was "entirely cleansed", and that they must be supported by British men-of-war and troops. The arrival of Vincenzo Speciale, forwarded to Troubridge with assurances from the Queen and Acton that he had a reputation for severity, only increased the troubles of a British officer in charge of prisoners whose countrymen were howling for their blood, and a heated scene took place on board H.M.S. *Culloden* on May 7. "Mr. Judge", pronounced by Troubridge, "the poorest creature I ever saw", and "frightened out of his senses", had come at intervals during the past fortnight to hint that he needed support. At least seventy families were involved in the cases under his consideration: also he could not execute disloyal priests without their having been degraded by a Bishop. He wished a British ship could be spared to take the priests to Palermo. Troubridge, by now, had delivered all the provisions in his power to the islanders, put his name down for a relief fund for seven ducats (more than he could afford) and pledged his name that supplies promised by the Queen were hourly expected. The conduct of the trials which had dragged on for the past fortnight appeared to him curious. "Frequently the culprit is not present." When "Mr. Judge," unwillingly impressed by an inflexible audience, proceeded to ask for the services of a British hangman, the temper of an increasingly grim officer (avowedly "completely stupid" after the examination since 4 a.m. of "vagabonds, none of whom ever give a direct answer") broke in a thunderstorm. "This treachery fairly does me up." The storm broke, not upon the head of "Mr. Judge", but upon that of the equally feeble Neapolitan General who refused to land the troops sent from Palermo. Realising that the odium for anything that aroused criticism would be thrown upon Nelson's squadron, Troubridge spoke his mind. "I desired the General and all his cowardly gang to get out of a British man-of-war. We want people to fight; he does not come under that description. I told him plainly that his King will never do well until he has hanged half his officers."

Among the officers who had turned his coat was now, beyond doubt, Caracciolo. The Commodore had left Palermo for his own estates on February 4, his reason being that the Parthenopæan Republic were preparing to seize the property of all absentee landlords. Ferdinand's farewell to him had been pointed. "Beware of intermeddling with French politics. Avoid the snares of Republicans. I know I shall recover the Kingdom of Naples." For as long as possible both Nelson and Troubridge had discredited reports that an officer who had learnt his seamanship under Rodney had deserted his royal master. There was reason to believe that such of the nobility as had been unlucky enough to find themselves in Naples under French control had been obliged by the occupying enemy to undertake humiliating duties in the militia. But by mid-May the fact that Caracciolo had taken the offensive against his King was indisputable. On the evacuation by the French of every part of Naples except the castle on St. Elmo, the authorities of the Parthenopæan Republic had begged him to take charge of their crippled navy, and on May 17, in an attack upon the Island of Procida, he had fired upon the vessel which had once been his own flagship.

Nelson was in hopes of embarking their reluctant Majesties for Naples within a fortnight, when suddenly all such plans had to be laid aside. A brig arrived at Palermo with news that a French fleet of nineteen sail-of-the-line had escaped from Brest under cover of a fog, and had been seen off Oporto steering for the Mediterranean. The Spanish fleet, with which it was expected to make a junction, was reckoned at twenty-five sail-of-the-line. Having summoned Troubridge and Duckworth, Nelson put to sea on the night of May 19. The decision had been difficult. "If I go, I risk, and more than risk, Sicily, and what is now safe on the Continent." But to stay, when there was the prospect of action, would have broken his heart. A note to Lady Hamilton was achieved before he sailed.

"To tell you how dreary and uncomfortable the *Vanguard* appears, is only telling you what it is to go from the pleasantest society to a solitary cell, or from the dearest friends to no friends. I am now perfectly *the great man*—not a creature near me. From my heart I wish myself the little man again! You, and good Sir William, have spoiled me for any place but with you."

3

On the afternoon of June 25 Cardinal Ruffo came on board Admiral Nelson's flagship in Naples Bay and was saluted with thirteen guns. Dusk had fallen before the prelate took his departure, and Nelson opened a fiery letter to Duckworth with the words, "As you will believe, the Cardinal and myself have begun our career by a complete difference of opinion." His experiences during the past month had been varied, but all ultimately unsatisfying. He had put to sea four times. June 4, the anniversary of the birth of His Britannic Majesty, had fallen between the two first occasions, and since the desired financial support from England now seemed likely to be forthcoming, and the weather was magnificent, the day had been one of unbroken festivity. "A Grand Dinner" at the Palazzo Palagonia had been followed by a Court Ball offered by their grateful Majesties. "Two or three very fine India shawls—the price is no object", purchased at the request of Nelson by the British

Minister at Constantinople, had arrived in time for presentation to
Lady Hamilton, who employed such adjuncts in her "Attitudes".
But Nelson's letter of thanks to Spencer Smith, written the morning after the *fêtes*, displayed that grand dinners and balls were not at
the moment congenial. In short, nervous sentences, he described
what was keeping him "on the alert". The French fleet, which had
sailed on April 26 and had been joined by five Spanish warships, had
passed through the Gut by May 5. Lord St. Vincent had left Gibraltar on the 8th with twenty sail-of-the-line, and letters from his
lordship were dated the 15th, off Minorca. "This is the whole I
know." He did not mention that a report that St. Vincent had
applied to go home on account of bad health had caused consterna-
tion in his squadron and evoked a passionate appeal:

> "For the sake of our Country, do not quit us at this serious moment. I
> wish not to detract from the merit of whoever may be your successor, but
> it must take a length of time, which I hope the War will not give, to be in
> any manner a St. Vincent. We look up to you, as we have always found
> you, as to our Father, under whose fostering care we have been led to
> Fame. If, my dear Lord, I have any weight in your friendship, let me entreat
> you to rouse the sleeping lion."

A fine new second-rate arrived at Palermo on the day after this
letter was despatched, and on June 8 Nelson shifted his flag from
the *Vanguard*, and took with him into H.M.S. *Foudroyant* "Captain
Hardy, five lieutenants, Mr. Comyn, Chaplain, and many mates
and midshipmen." "Hardy was bred in the old school. I never have
been better satisfied with the real good discipline of a ship than the
Vanguard's." An odd trophy of the Nile which also accompanied the
Admiral lay for several days on the grating of the quarter-deck of
his new flagship, arousing much interest amongst such of his officers
as were new to his command. They heard with surprise that Lord
Nelson was accustomed to dine with a coffin behind his Windsor
chair. Captain Ben Hallowell had recently sent his lordship this
unusual gift, made by the carpenter of the *Swiftsure* from part of the
main-mast of *L'Orient*. Coming out of his cabin one June morning
to discover his officers staring at this blunt reminder that all flesh is
grass, Nelson remarked, "You may look at it, gentlemen, as long as
you please; but depend upon it, none of you shall have it."

His second return to Palermo, on June 15, had been occasioned by a despatch from Lord Keith, who had now succeeded Lord St. Vincent, telling him that the Combined Fleets were believed to be bound either for Naples or Sicily. He had just quitted Palermo, taking with him "my little squadron", 1,700 troops and the eldest son of the royal house, entrusted to him by the Queen in a typical letter. Considering "that the best defence for their Sicilian Majesties' dominions is to place myself alongside the French", he disembarked the Prince and troops, and cruised off Maritimo for four days, but without seeing anything of the Franco-Spanish armada. On the 21st, having been joined by Ball with the *Alexander* and *Goliath* from Malta, he sailed again for Naples, calling at Palermo for two and a half hours *en route*. He did not anchor, but he made an expedition to the Colli Palace, and he took with him as passengers the British Ambassador (much shaken by the tragic intelligence that H.M.S. *Colossus*, carrying the treasures of his classical collection, had been lost off the Scillies) and "my dear Lady Hamilton, my faithful interpreter on all occasions", to whom he had written almost daily during his absence. On the passage he learnt that Ruffo, panic-stricken by the news of the Combined Fleets being at sea, and sickened by the behaviour of his own army in Naples, had concluded a three weeks' Armistice with the enemy. When Nelson arrived in Naples Bay, on the afternoon of the 24th, he found flags of truce flying on the sea-forts of Uovo and Nuovo (held by the Neapolitan Jacobins), from the castle of St. Elmo (held by the French) and upon the frigate *Seahorse*, whose commander, Captain Foote, had been left, on Troubridge's recall, in charge of a small flotilla. Foote's orders had been to co-operate with the Cardinal, and with the Russian and Turkish detachments in the blockade, and (as he explained, when he came on board the *Foudroyant* at 4 p.m.) he had supposed the Cardinal "the confidential agent of his Sicilian Majesty", and the French fleet more likely to appear than Nelson's. But the document, "already signed by the Cardinal and the Chief of the Russians", to which he had put his name, with much misgiving, yesterday morning was, so far as the Neapolitan Jacobins were concerned, no Armistice, but a definite capitulation. Foote had thought its terms "very favourable to the Republicans", as indeed they were, for the Cardinal had offered to his countrymen, in arms against their sovereign, that on their evacuation of the sea-forts they should be permitted to march out with the honours of war and all their property. Such as wished to retire by land might do so, while those who had no desire to remain in their native city should be evacuated by sea to Toulon. The French commander in St. Elmo, General Méjean, had ratified the capitulation before Nelson's squadron came in sight, but made no terms for his own force beyond the three weeks' Armistice. He still hoped for the arrival of the Franco-Spanish fleet to solve his difficulties. Finally, the Neapolitan nobleman who had taken charge of the negotiations with Méjean—the Cavalière Micheroux, accredited to the Turkish and Russian forces—was regarded by the Cardinal as a supernumer-ary character, and was upon the worst of terms with him.

Nelson did not waste much time upon an officer left in charge of a detached squadron who said that he had been unprovided with "instructions or any document to assist or guide me". He told the harassed Foote that he had blundered—"had been imposed upon by that worthless fellow, Cardinal Ruffo, who was endeavouring to form a party hostile to the interests of his Sovereign"—gave him credit for having acted in an unpleasant and arduous situation with all possible zeal, and dismissed him with orders to draw up a detailed narrative of his dealings with Ruffo.

The *Foudroyant* anchored in thirty-five fathoms at 8 p.m., and during the hours of darkness, while the squadron stood on and off Naples Bay with light winds, the Hamiltons gave audience to a melodramatic old acquaintance. Egidio Pallio, chief of the *lazzaroni*, had come out to offer the services of 90,000 loyal subjects of His Majesty, who were, however, without the arms necessary for a sanguinary attack upon the Jacobins. Next morning Pallio was promised arms, but adjured, for the present, to restrict his efforts to keeping peace in Naples until the arrival of the King. Nelson, who had annulled what he had believed to be an Armistice, by signal, before anchoring, now moored his fleet of eighteen sail in a close line of battle before the city, and summoned the twenty-two gun and mortar vessels lying at the islands, to flank his ships-of-the-line. "If the French Fleet should favour us with a visit, I can easily take

my position in the centre." He sent to Ruffo, by Ball and Troubridge, his "opinion of the infamous terms entered into with the
rebels" and two documents to be forwarded to the castles flying the
white flag. He demanded unconditional surrender from the French.
To "the rebellious subjects of His Sicilian Majesty, in the castles of
Nuovo and Uovo", he simply announced that he would not
permit them to be embarked or quit those places. "They must
surrender themselves to His Majesty's Royal mercy." His "Observations on the Armistice" were endorsed in his own hand: "Read,
and explained, and rejected by the Cardinal". Ruffo refused to forward either document, and replied to Troubridge's direct question,
that if the British Admiral chose to break the Armistice, and reopen
hostilities, he must do so without assistance. The Cardinal was
"tired of his situation". During the afternoon he appeared in person
to repeat his theories that his Jacobin countrymen who had taken
office under the French had done so *faute de mieux*, and that the best
hope for the peaceful re-establishment of the monarchy was a policy
of forgiveness for all, except perhaps a very few, who should not be
judged quickly. Nelson's unvarying and furious reply was that both
the Treaty and Armistice were at an end by the arrival of his fleet,
and that neither the Cardinal nor he had the authority to agree to a
capitulation so entirely contrary to the expressed instructions of
their Sicilian Majesties. Sir William Hamilton acted as interpreter
during the early stages of an interview which soon degenerated into
an altercation, and when he retired, worn out, Lady Hamilton took
his place. How difficult was their task may be judged from the fact
that when the Admiral spoke of "the rebels" and the Cardinal of
"the patriots", they were referring to the same body of men.

The ship was loading beef, lemons and fuel, and her launches were
watering, at the pace of forty butt per launch. A great number of
officers, arrived to pay their respects, also came alongside, but not even
the Cavalière Micheroux gained admission to "the Great Cabin".

Presently, since they seemed unable to agree upon first principles,
Nelson broke off the discussion, convinced that "an Admiral is no
match in talking with a Cardinal". He would write. His written
opinion could be condensed into a single sentence. "Rear-Admiral
Nelson, who arrived in the Bay of Naples, on the 24th of June, with

the British Fleet, found a Treaty entered into with the Rebels which, he is of opinion, ought not to be carried into execution, without the approbation of his Sicilian Majesty, Earl St. Vincent, Lord Keith." Ruffo withdrew, saving his dignity by the announcement that he must consult his Russian and Turkish allies, and would let them know at the castles of St. Elmo, Nuovo and Uovo that he could not answer for Lord Nelson's allowing of the Armistice to continue. The night of terror prophesied by him followed in Naples, although not exactly according to his expectations, since most of the disorder was caused by natives attempting to fly from the capital, convinced that, between them, the French from St. Elmo and the British from the sea were about to reduce their homes to a heap of stones. Such of them as were unlucky enough to be mistaken for, or recognised by, the *Sanfedisti* or *lazzaroni* as Jacobins, were either murdered on the spot or carried prisoners to ships in the bay which took them to Justice, as practised at Procida.

Next morning, very early, the two documents which Ruffo had said that Nelson might send in "if he pleased" were despatched to the sea-forts and St. Elmo, and Sir William Hamilton sent the Cardinal a hasty assurance that Lord Nelson would do nothing, pending instructions from Palermo, to break the Armistice—a statement which Nelson (who had not altered his opinion that only the King could agree to a capitulation not yet carried into effect) later confirmed in his own hand. Ruffo, for his part, was now asking for the marines, refused by him yesterday, to be landed for the defence of the city against Jacobins, and French troops reported to be marching on Caserta. In the expectation that hostilities were about to recommence, he had ordered his own irregulars and the Russians, covering the forts, to retire, an action which aggravated the tumult in the town. After receiving Nelson's note he put them back again. He had also privately offered the Jacobins of the sea-forts the option of seeking sanctuary in Naples. They, however, having mostly no desire to fall into the hands of the *Calabresi* or *lazzaroni*, and realising that they could not sail for Toulon in defiance of Nelson's fleet, proceeded to surrender before the day was out. They were not accorded the honours of war mentioned in the terms of the capitulation, and the vessels to which they hurried were not allowed to sail. Thirteen hundred seamen and marines at once invested the forts, and next morning Troubridge, having been joined by five hundred Russians and some *soi-disant* "loyalists" (half of whom Nelson believed to be rebels, and knew to be cowards), advanced to the siege of St. Elmo. From Castello dell Uovo ninety-five persons had chosen to embark in the transports, and thirty-four to retire, under cover of night, to their homes in the town. The Cardinal attended a service of thanksgiving in the Church of the Carmine, and wrote polite letters of gratitude and congratulation to Nelson, and to Sir William and Lady Hamilton, to which the Ambassador replied cordially.

On the morning of the 28th letters from the Colli Palace arrived. Acton wrote that no conditions except unconditional surrender were to be made with the Neapolitan Jacobins. The transports were forthwith brought in under the guns of the fleet, some of their most notorious passengers were brought on board the British men-of-war, and Nelson issued a proclamation to those who had returned to their homes, to the effect that they must surrender to the King's mercy within twenty-four hours, or be considered as still in active rebellion. These actions caused an immediate termination of his brief harmonious relations with the Cardinal, who stepped back to his old position of refusing to assist in the siege of St. Elmo, and in addition published an order that nobody in the city was to be arrested except by his command. For a few hours, as Nelson wrote to Acton, it was "a toss-up" whether or not he arrested Ruffo, but eventually he decided to send Foote with the *Seahorse* and a cutter to Palermo to beg the King, the Queen (thrice underlined) and Acton himself to embark for Naples, while he endeavoured to "keep things tolerable", until their appearance. He had come to Naples prepared if necessary "to take off the Cardinal's head", and he did not now inform that inveterate intriguer either of his invitation to the King or the fact that he had been given authority, if he thought fit, to arrest him and forward him to Palermo to explain himself.

4

The weather on the morning of June 29 was noted in the Journal of the *Foudroyant* as moderate and cloudy. Captain Hardy was on deck, watching the arrival of the Portuguese *Rainha* and the *Balloon* brig from Messina, when his attention was distracted by a sudden clamour amongst the Neapolitans on board his ship. Several minutes passed before he understood that the reason for their unwholesome excitement was that "the traitor Caracciolo was taken". The appearance of the Commodore, "pale, with a long beard, half dead, and with downcast eyes", being urged on board the flagship in handcuffs, by a party of Ruffo's irregulars (who had brought him out from Naples in a small boat), shocked Sir William Hamilton. Hardy immediately ordered that the prisoner's arms should be unbound, and that while the officers commanding the Neapolitan ships in the bay were signalled, the Commodore should be confined from the violence of his countrymen in a cabin guarded by a lieutenant and two marines. He sent refreshments, of which the prisoner refused to partake.

Caracciolo had not been amongst the Jacobins to surrender two nights previously. He had fled from one of the sea-forts as long ago as June 17, and made his way in a peasant disguise to a country villa in the neighbourhood, upon the estate of his uncle, the Duke of Calvirrano. A warning that he had been betrayed, and that a price was set on his head, had caused him to leave the villa for a hut. Some of Ruffo's men, under a leader called Scipione La Marra, had dragged him forth into Neapolitan sunshine from the depths of a well. His capture had taken place on the 25th, and Nelson, who had received the news within twenty-four hours, had sent a message to Ruffo on the 27th that if his Eminence thought proper to deliver the Commodore, together with the other rebels, on board his flagship, he would "dispose of them". Determined to choose a glaring case for an example of the "quick punishment" he had always urged upon their Majesties of the Two Sicilies as the only foundation of good government, his plans were made before the prisoner was delivered. By 10 a.m. a court-martial, convened at his order, and composed of the five senior officers of the squadron in the Neapolitan service under the presidency of Count Thurn, was in progress in the wardroom of the *Foudroyant*. The proceedings, which lasted two hours, were conducted in Italian, and Nelson was not present. Caracciolo's actions were a matter of common knowledge to all his judges, and undeniable. He had accepted the command of the republican fleet and acted with considerable vigour. By his attack with gunboats upon the British and Royal Neapolitan ships approaching Castellammare he had, in Nelson's words, "spirited up" the republicans in the naval arsenal. Off Procida, firing impartially upon British and Neapolitan ships, he had damaged *La Minèrva*, once his flagship. The charges made against him were rebellion against his lawful sovereign and firing at his colours. His request to be tried by British officers was refused, and Count Thurn, after calling upon the court to identify him, informed him of the charges and asked if he had any defence to offer. Caracciolo, although obviously suffering from deadly fatigue, roused himself to reply at length. He pleaded "not guilty", saying that he had been given the choice of being shot or accepting the command of the republican fleet. Cross-examined by Thurn, he repeated that he had, on every occasion when he was called upon to attack His Majesty's ships, done so under compulsion. He admitted to having been with the division of gunboats which went out to prevent the entry of His Majesty's troops at Castellammare, but said that he had mistaken Ruffo's hordes for "insurgents". He confessed to having issued "written orders tending to oppose His Majesty's forces". Asked why he had not attempted to fly to Procida, he answered that he had feared to be ill-received there. Shortly after noon the court was cleared, and Thurn called upon the five officers to declare their verdict. Four, including himself, voted for death, two against. He reported to Nelson, who ordered that the sentence should be carried out at five o'clock on the same evening. A suggestion by Thurn, supported by Sir William Hamilton, that the condemned man should be allowed twenty-four hours in which to prepare his soul, was disregarded by an officer who had observed the results of Lord St. Vincent's methods with mutineers.

Mr. George Parsons, Signal Midshipman of the *Foudroyant* (who forty-five years later published *Nelsonian Reminiscences, Leaves from Memory's Log*), remembered Caracciolo as a "short thick-set man of apparent strength, but haggard with misery and want, his clothes in wretched condition, but his countenance denoting stern resolution to endure that misery like a man". Caracciolo spoke a sentence to Parsons in good English when summoned to the court, and according to the young officer, his defence included a dramatic period unrecorded by Thurn. When accused of treason, he retorted that his King had deserted him and all loyal subjects. Though the accused was, in fact, forty-seven years of age, Parsons remembered him as "a wretched old man and grey-haired, who, however, walked with a firm step when conducted to the British Admiral's barge for removal to the scene of his execution".

At 5 p.m., accordingly, Commodore Caracciolo was drawn by his own men to the foreyard-arm of His Sicilian Majesty's frigate *La Minèrva*, which he had once commanded, drums rolled, a gun was fired, and English seamen, clustering like bees on the rigging of eighteen ships-of-the-line, on a heavy evening, watched him launched into eternity. At sunset, in obedience to Nelson's orders, the body was cut down and thrown into Naples Bay.

Next day Ruffo came on board the *Foudroyant* to dine, having withdrawn his hostility towards the attack on St. Elmo. "Certainly", wrote Sir William Hamilton, "this quick justice has had a great effect." The King's letter to the Cardinal and order to Nelson for the Cardinal's arrest remained throughout the meal locked in the Admiral's writing-box, in a sunlit cabin decorated by the gaily dyed French and Parthenopæan flags, collected on the evacuation of the forts. Nelson's first comment on hearing of Caracciolo's defection had been, "This man was fool enough to quit his master when he thought his cause was desperate." Maria Carolina, who had always believed Caracciolo's actions the premeditated result of professional chagrin, wrote, "All his rage was at not having us embark with him, to have us at his disposal and at the disposal of his felon and traitor friends." After his death she alluded to "the sad but merited end of the unhappy and crazy Caracciolo".

Sir William Hamilton was in great uneasiness until July 10, when the Royal Standard fluttered from the masthead of the *Foudroyant*, signifying that His Sicilian Majesty had arrived to take up his headquarters there; but his anxieties were quite unnecessary.

Lord Spencer, on October 7, wrote to Nelson, "In answer to your letter of the 23rd of July. . . . I can only repeat what I believe I have before said on the subject—namely, that the intentions and motives by which all your measures have been governed, have been as pure and good, as their success has been complete."

Not until the following May did Nelson hear any criticism from England of his proceedings in the Bay of Naples in midsummer 1799.

5

On February 3, 1800, a day upon which Nelson was writing a letter beginning, "My dear Lady Hamilton, Having a Commander-in-Chief I cannot come on shore till I have made *my manners* to him", trouble for the Admiral was blowing up in the House of Commons. On the Motion for the Address, thanking His Majesty for refusing to negotiate with the French republicans, Mr. Fox had risen to suggest:

"I wish the atrocities, of which we hear so much, and which I abhor as much as any man, were indeed unexampled. I fear they do not belong exclusively to the French. When the Right Honourable Gentleman speaks of the extraordinary successes of the last campaign he does not mention the horrors, by which some of these successes were accompanied. Naples, for instance . . ."

Mr. Fox believed that a party of Neapolitan republicans, sheltering in the fortress of Castello dell Uovo, had made terms with a British officer which, although absolutely guaranteed, had resulted in their being delivered, not, as they had expected, with all their property, into safety at Toulon, but to dungeons and strangulation. His source of information was probably his cousin-by-marriage Charles Lock, who had written home privately, from Naples, on the previous 13th of July:

"You will hear with grief of the infraction of the articles convented with the Neapolitan Jacobins and of the stab our English honour has received in being employed to decoy these people, who relied on our faith, into the most deplorable situation. . . . But *the sentiment of abhorrence expressed by the whole fleet* will I hope exonerate the nation from an imputation so disgraceful, and charge it where it should lie, upon the shoulders of *one or two*."

Nelson, on hearing of Fox's speech on May 9, 1800, wrote at once to Davison, forwarding amongst other papers his "Observations on the infamous Armistice entered into by the Cardinal".

He begged his friend to show them to the Right Hon. George Rose, and if necessary, give them to the Press. But he was too late to efface the impression, founded upon fact, that Neapolitan royalist vengeance had been ferocious, and when Captain Foote arrived home on leave in the same year, that worthy but not brilliant officer was dismayed to discover that Nelson's part in the transactions in the Bay of Naples last summer had become the subject of violent controversy, and, amongst some level-headed persons, sincere regret. He was dissuaded by Service friends from asking for a public inquiry, but the wound festered, and seven years later, two years after Nelson's death, he published a "Vindication" of his own conduct (which had never been attacked by any authoritative person) and a notably confused criticism of that of Nelson, which he had not, until now, made any attempt to question. Meanwhile, he had been provided with additional material. In 1801, Miss Helen Maria Williams, an English authoress in her fortieth year, who during residence in France had adopted the principles and ideas of the Revolutionaries with a whole heart, published a work in two volumes, called *Sketches of the State of Manners and Opinions in the French Republic, towards the end of the Eighteenth Century*. It included a lively but unconscientious report of the Neapolitan revolution and counter-revolution. She accused Nelson of having tricked and trapped the garrisons of Uovo and Nuovo, including Caracciolo, and she passed very severe comment on the assistance of Lady Hamilton at the scene. A copy of what Nelson wearily called "that Mrs. Williams' book", with marginal corrections in his own hand, is to be seen in the British Museum.

The next writer to inflame the brooding Foote was Lady Hamilton's *protégé* Harrison, who published for the first time, in 1806, Nelson's letter of July 13, 1799, to Lord Spencer, in which the Admiral described the capitulation arranged by Ruffo as "Infamous". That Foote had not heard the word used upon the occasion is improbable, as it appears in every letter written by Nelson at the time, but he resented Harrison's strictures on his part in the transaction exceedingly, and took up an unaccustomed pen to defend himself and the document to which he had put his name in Naples Bay. Harrison, delighted at the consequent demand for a further large edition of his book, refused to delete the passages objectionable to Foote, who thereupon commenced pamphleteer. He censured Nelson for the execution of Caracciolo, and for having acted, with regard to the capitulation, without consulting Lord St. Vincent and Lord Keith. Following the lead of Miss Williams, he accused him of having been influenced by guilty passion for Lady Hamilton. The fact that Nelson soon detached him on immediate service "to some distance from Naples" now appeared to him suspicious. The Rev. John Clarke, engaged on an unhappy chapter in his biography of the Admiral (due for publication in 1809), involved himself in an ultimately acrimonious correspondence with the pamphleteer. Dr. Clarke, after conversations with Admiral Foley and Sir Thomas Hardy, had been forced to revise his unfavourable opinions of Nelson's behaviour, but believed that Lady Hamilton had "indecently and unjustly accelerated" the trial and execution of Caracciolo, and that "this wicked siren" had attended the carrying out of the sentence. Three years later, Robert Southey, Poet Laureate, added to his chapter on the events of midsummer 1799 the inaccuracies of Miss Williams and Captain Foote, and some of his own invention. His conclusion was "A deplorable transaction! A stain upon the memory of Nelson, and the honour of England!"

It was left to Captain Edward Pelham Brenton, in 1823, to insert in his *Naval History* a fiction that Lady Hamilton had made an expedition with Nelson in his barge, expressly to gloat over the pendent corpse, a spectacle which had haunted her midnight hours to the day of her death, evoking "horrid screams". "A lady who lived many years with Lady Hamilton and who scarcely ever quitted her room during the last few weeks of her life" bravely ventured into print to say that Lady Hamilton had not been in the habit of having nightmares and never mentioned the name of Caracciolo. Commodore Sir Francis Augustus Collier, whose widowed mother had delivered him to Nelson's care at a tender age, loudly denounced "an arrant falsehood", and what Brenton described as "a person signing his name John Mitford, R.N." sent a polished letter of denial to the *Morning Post*. "I called on this man, but could never find him", said Brenton. "I discovered he lodged over a coal-shed in some obscure street near Leicester Square, and that he was not an officer in the Navy." Had Captain Brenton persevered, he would have discovered further that Mr. Mitford, who since his discharge from the Royal Service as insane, in 1814, had been in and out of the mad-house, and whose sole possessions now were a candle, a pen, a strip of bedding, a bottle of ink and a bottle of gin, had indeed been a midshipman in a ship-of-the-line at Santa Cruz, and an eye-witness of the death of Caracciolo.

But Lord Holland, in his *Memoirs of the Whig Party*, had spoken of Lady Hamilton's "baneful ascendancy" over Nelson's mind as the chief cause of indefensible conduct at Naples, and Lord Brougham and Mr. Alison, the historian, had credited Miss Williams and the Laureate. In 1830, Major Pryse Lockhart Gordon, who had been present in the bay, in Hood's ship, published memoirs of remarkable inaccuracy. Until Commander Jeaffreson Miles took up the defence in 1843, lacking essential documents and with un-skilled impetuosity, no author attempted the task of catching up a contemporary rumour that Nelson, languishing under the spell of Lady Hamilton, confidante of a bloodthirsty and dissolute queen, had acted towards a guiltless Neapolitan with ill-faith, precipitance and cruelty.

6

Cardinal Ruffo's pronouncement that the English were hateful, even to the well-disposed amongst the Neapolitans, "because they burned our Fleet", had not been forgotten by the royal exiles. Ferdinand IV returned to Naples, with a convoy of troopships and escorted by H.M.S. *Seahorse*, but in a Neapolitan frigate. He had been loath to leave Palermo, where he was comfortably settled in a new country house, from which good sport was available. As his wife told her daughter, the Empress, "*Naples est pour lui comme les Hottentots*". Throughout the four weeks of blazing midsummer Mediterranean weather spent by him in Naples Bay, while Nelson completed the reconquest of his kingdom, he never once went on shore. He conducted all his business of state on board the English Admiral's flagship, and held *levées* on her quarter-deck. Some months later, wishing to describe a scene of irritating confusion, Troubridge said that it reminded him of the "buzz" above the gangway ladder of the *Foudroyant* when at Naples. A number of the nobility and officials who hastened to welcome their increasingly hilarious King brought their ladies, and in the Great Cabin which had witnessed a heated interview between Ruffo and Nelson, Lady Hamilton, acting for the absent Queen, received messages protesting devotion from many congratulatory persons, some of whom she remembered as having been openly pro-French before the flight of the royal family. She also received a flood of heartrending letters begging for her intercession on behalf of political prisoners languishing either in the polaccas or the gaols of the town ("compared to which", said Troubridge, "death is a trifle"). It was difficult, even for British officers present, to realise that the chief source of influence available to the Ambassadress was the Queen, whose advice was anathema to the King. Domenico Cirillo, a scholarly and benevolent man, Court Physician, and formerly medical attendant at the Palazzo Sessa, was a personal friend, and it appears that in his case, at least, Lady Hamilton did break through her rule never to ask favours from Admiral Nelson, who described the correspondence received by her as "excuses from rebels, Jacobins and fools", and was determined not to interfere after the arrival of a King upon whom he had always urged speedy punishment of the guilty and reward of the loyal as the only foundation of good government. The result of efforts on behalf of the humanitarian Cirillo, who frankly confessed in his letter to very mild co-operation with the enemy, under compulsion, was mortifying. The Doctor, according to Nelson, "might have been saved, but that he chose to play the fool, and lie; denying that he ever made any speeches against the government, and that he only took care of the poor in the hospitals". Cirillo was hanged on October 29, a date which supports the story of Clarke and M'Arthur that Maria Carolina went on her knees to beg this life from her husband, who had by then rejoined her at Palermo. The Queen's letters to Lady Hamilton during the weeks while her unpopular Majesty was what she called "banished" from her husband's triumphal reappearance all repeated her resolution not to appear to question Neapolitan sentences on her former ill-companions. An English gentleman, writing from Posilipo to Lady Hamilton, apologised for troubling "again" "your Ladyship, who

is the general patroness of the distressed in these perilous times";
yet, before the year was out, Neapolitan Jacobin refugees, and even
royalist representatives in Pisa, Vienna, Paris and London, were
spreading the tale that the sanguinary vengeance still in progress in
their capital was inspired by the Queen and her English friends. The
task of throwing the odium on the British was, as Troubridge had
foreseen, thoroughly accomplished, and a century later English
visitors, touring Neapolitan public and private collections, viewed
with dismay the portraits of noblemen of liberal sentiments and
baby-faced ladies of birth, all attended by gruesome anecdotes of
execution while eighteen British sail-of-the-line, under Nelson's
command, lay at anchor in Naples Bay. That the Bourbon dynasty
overthrown in the nineteenth century was entirely corrupt and
decadent was by this date obvious: but that Nelson, when called
upon to support it, believed himself to be saving Naples from a
Terror analogous to that which in Paris had outraged humanity,
was by no means understood.

Public executions in the Piazza del Mercate were a permanent
feature of entertainment in Naples from July 1799 until the following May. Nightly during the King's stay, boats plied to and fro
amongst the polaccas, collecting victims required for interrogation
by the Junta sitting in the Castel di Carmini. As at Procida, some of
the accused were condemned without being present at their trials;
others, having given evidence against fellow delinquents, were, as
surprisingly to British spectators, released. By mid-August, when
the polaccas sailed for Toulon, only one-third of their original
passengers survived. The execution, on the 20th, of a particularly
brilliant group, noted by Troubridge as "princes, dukes, commoners
and ladies", led that officer to hope that the judges would "soon
finish, on a great scale, and then pass an act of oblivion", but the
gallows were not taken down for another nine months. Ferdinand
IV had been badly frightened. For three days after his arrival the
bombardment of St. Elmo formed a noisy background to the
scenes of festivity on board the *Foudroyant*, and in the following week
he had a bad moment. A fisherman at dawn had brought a story
that Caracciolo, "who had risen from the bottom of the sea", was
coming as fast as he could to Naples. The wind being favourable,

Nelson obliged the curious King by standing out to sea. A body, moving upright in the water, was presently noticed to be directing its course towards the flagship. Sir William Hamilton saved the situation by saying in courtier-like vein to a mentally unstable royalty that Caracciolo had been unable to rest until he had implored his monarch's pardon, and the horrible corpse was towed by Nelson's orders to Santa Lucia, where it received Christian burial in the fishermen's church of Santa Maria La Catena.

The anniversary of the Nile brought the news that Capua and Gaeta, the last Jacobin strongholds in the kingdom, had fallen to Troubridge's seamen and marines, and the rejoicings in the Bay of Naples were sufficiently superb to evoke a description from Nelson to his lady.

"The King dined with me; and, when His Majesty drank my health, a Royal salute of 21 guns was fired from all his Sicilian Majesty's Ships of War, and from all the Castles. In the evening there was a general illumination. Amongst other representations, a large Vessel was fitted out like a Roman galley; on its oars were fixed lamps, and in the centre was erected a rostral column with my name; at the stern were elevated two angels supporting my picture. In short, my dear Fanny, the beauty of the whole is beyond my powers of description. More than 2,000 variegated lamps were suspended round the Vessel. An orchestra was fitted up, and filled with the very best musicians and singers. The piece of music was in a great measure to celebrate my praise, describing their previous distress. *But Nelson came, the invincible Nelson, and they were preserved and again made happy.* This must not make you think me vain; no, far, very far from it. I relate it more from gratitude than vanity. I return to Palermo with the King. May God bless you all. Pray say, what is true, that I really steal time to write this letter, and my hand is ready to drop."

On the day that St. Elmo had hoisted Royal Neapolitan colours he had received a second despatch from Lord Keith, who had been out of touch with the French fleet for three weeks. The Commander-in-Chief, who believed Minorca to be threatened, ordered Nelson to send him, at once, as many ships as could be spared from Naples. Nelson, believing Minorca to be in no danger, had decided that "at this moment I will not part with a single ship". "It is better to save the Kingdom of Naples, and risk Minorca, than to risk the Kingdom of Naples to save Minorca." "I am fully aware", he wrote to Lord Spencer, "of the act I have committed, but, sensible of my loyal intentions, I am prepared for any fate which may await my disobedience. . . . Do not think, my dear Lord, that my opinion is formed from the arrangements of any one. *No*, be it good, or be it bad, it is all my own." When Keith wrote again, peremptorily demanding "the whole or the greater part of the force under your Lordship's orders", Nelson sent Duckworth with three sail-of-the-line and a corvette. None of his letters of explanation reached his Commander-in-Chief until Keith had left the Mediterranean and the French fleet was again back in Brest, a fact which probably prevented strong action being taken by the Admiralty. In due time he received a measured rebuke from Whitehall, but also temporary succession to the command left vacant by Keith. That he had been right as to enemy intentions, and Keith wrong, was a fact, but that he had disobeyed orders was not forgotten, and bore fruit. It was true that in attaching himself so unreservedly to the Royal Neapolitan interest he was acting under previous instructions, but more than a suspicion was by now current that he was held in such close and prolonged attendance on the Court by private considerations.

7

Nelson sailed for Palermo on August 5, leaving Troubridge in command in Naples Bay with orders to hoist a broad pendant, so that his authority over the expected Turkish and Russian squadrons could not be questioned. His opinion of the allies was not high. "The Russian Admiral has a polished outside but the bear is close to the skin. . . . He is jealous of our influence. . . . As for the Turks, we can do anything with them. They are good people, but perfectly useless."

Ferdinand IV did not scruple to make the return voyage in the *Foudroyant*, and on their arrival, in the heat of noon, his Queen and children came on board to dine, after which, to the sound of a salute of twenty-one guns, answered by every fort of the capital, the royal family went on shore. Two days later, Lady Hamilton, at the Queen's request, broke to Nelson the news that the King intended to bestow upon him the Sicilian duchy of Brontë, accompanied by feudal domains reported to produce an annual income of about £3,000. From the Palazzo Palagonia, in weather of a moist warmth denounced by him as intolerable, Nelson wrote to offer his father an immediate gift of £500 a year. It was all he dared promise until he had seen a year's returns from the duchy, for he had refused payment for their Majesties' expenses while on board his flagships, and did not yet know whether the Admiralty would refund him. The grateful King, whose gifts included a diamond-hilted sword, had written to England for permission for him to bear the Sicilian title, and empowered him to settle the succession to it as he chose. It should pass, in Nelson's opinion, to his father, brothers and their children, and after them, sisters and their children. (Five lives at the moment stood between the dignity and the eventual heiress, the twelve-year-old Charlotte, daughter of his brother William.) Actually, the duchy, represented as belonging to the Crown, was Church property, sequestered a century past, and in a state of decay. It did not include the small mediæval mountain town from which it took its name. Its predominant architectural feature, the fortress of Maniace, was a picturesque ruin. A farmhouse called "La Fragila" was the only habitable dwelling of any size on the estate, and since they lacked roads to send their produce to market, the tenants made no active efforts to improve their condition.

Nelson, who was determined that the Brontese should know a model landlord and English methods, appointed Graeffer, the landscape gardener, *protégé* of Sir William Hamilton, as his agent. His first letters after his adoption of the title were signed "Brontë Nelson"; later he chose the form "Brontë, Nelson of the Nile" and finally, "Nelson and Brontë". According to Sicilian legend, the original Brontë, one of the Cyclops, had forged the trident of Neptune and thunderbolts of Jove, so the name was judged particularly suitable to the Admiral of the *Foudroyant*, who had reseated the Bourbon monarch on his throne; and in the fullness of time Lady Hamilton and Nelson's sisters proudly alluded to a person mild in the family circle as "Great Jove" and "My Lord Thunder".

Sir William Hamilton, now professionally complacent, accustomed to the Neapolitan midsummer habit of turning night into day, and much restored by his cruise, was the most cheerful inhabitant of his house during the month of unbridled festivity which succeeded the King's return. The bereaved Miss Knight, who had been entrusted to him with her mother's dying breath, was now a permanent guest at his table. His wife and even his mother-in-law were prostrated by the heat. The Admiral was suffering from eye-strain. On the 16th of August, writing to Duckworth to inform him that he was sending Hardy in the *Foudroyant* to Malta, Nelson mentioned apprehensively, "We are dying of heat, and the feast of St. Rosalia begins this day. How shall we get through it? Our dear Lady has been very unwell, and if this *fête* to-night does not kill her, I daresay she will write you." Maria Carolina, while deserted, had been busy. The *festa* of the patron saint of Palermo, for which she had urged the return of the victors of Naples, was generally disposed of in five days, but the Queen's characteristic efforts did not culminate until September 3, when all officers of His Britannic Majesty's fleet were invited to a midnight *fête-champêtre* in honour of her British friends. The occasion left an indelible impression on the memory of Midshipman Parsons, whose account casts a sudden beam of light into the cockpit of an eighteenth-century ship-of-the-line while young gentlemen are getting into ballroom order. The midshipmen of the *Foudroyant* dressed to shouts of "Two dirty shirts nearly new for one clean one", and "Who will lend a pair of uniform breeches?" A clumsy, apple-cheeked English boy who had ruined a shipmate's "number one" coat at his last turn-out promised a new one made by Stultz "when we both reach old England", if his friend, who was on duty to-night, would but part with a pair of breeches not yet worn out by pipe-clay. As they were unaccustomed to hiring transport, their joint resources when they assembled on the Prado amounted to fivepence. They commandeered a nobleman's carriage for their four-mile journey uphill, and fifteen of them packed into or upon the box of the roomy vehicle. The "fairy scene" at which they alighted surpassed Vauxhall on a gala night, and after witnessing a display of fireworks, representing the blowing-up of *L'Orient*, they flocked with a crowd, which included grave Turkish officers and the fairest of Italy's nut-brown daughters, towards a Temple of Fame. This edifice was surmounted by a goddess blowing a trumpet, and occupied by waxworks of Admiral Nelson, the British Ambassador and "Lady Hamilton, Britannia's pride". After the playing of a patriotic air, the nine-year-old Prince Leopold, who was represented by his fond mother as the originator of the *fête*, placed a laurel wreath on the head of the very life-like effigy of the Victor of the Nile, and running to thank "the guardian angel of his papa for recovering his realm", was received into the kneeling Nelson's one arm. Tears coursed down the weather-beaten cheeks of the Admiral as the trumpets blew to a point of war, and bands struck up "See the conquering hero". Midshipman Parsons, searching for a handkerchief, remembered too late that he had been obliged to place the leg of an old white silk stocking in the pocket designed to display the missing article. The entertainment ended sadly as far as he was concerned, for towards its close some of his ebullient contemporaries charged the King's Foot-Guards with dress dirks, whereupon one insulted guardsman fired "and shot a fine boy through the thigh, who did well. For this notable and ill-timed feat Lord Nelson stopped our leave for six months."

A clash of temperaments more serious in its result summoned the ailing Commander-in-Chief from the Palazzo Palagonia on the following Sunday night. A quarrel had broken out in the over-hot and over-full town between some Palermitans and Turks. A considerable number of Cadir Bey's seamen had been killed, and their fellows, forbidden to take worthy vengeance, had proceeded to mutiny. Nelson went on board the Turkish Admiral's flagship, "and subdued the disturbance".

Plans for the forthcoming winter already occupied his busy mind, although Lady Elgin, bride of the peer appointed to succeed Spencer Smith, was "literally gasping" on board H.M.S. *Phæton*, at anchor before Palermo, and only kept from swooning by bathing her brow with vinegar while "the thermometer in the shade" stood at ninety. In what was called the cool of the evening, a little hot air puffed seawards from cobbled streets crowded with seamen of many nationalities, but at 8 p.m. eighty-two degrees were still registered. The Portuguese squadron had been recalled to Lisbon. Admiral Ouschakoff had explained that no Russian ship could be expected to keep the sea during the cold and blowing months. For that matter, as far as Nelson could observe, they had shown no desire to do so in the summer. He began to consider which of his own ships must go home for a thorough refit, and which could be dealt with at Gibraltar or Minorca; for if he was to be continued in his present command, he was determined not to keep a single useless ship devouring stores in the Mediterranean next season. He was disconcerted by the undeniable fact that the King preferred to stay, and spend, in Palermo, a state of affairs which roused justifiable discontent amongst Neapolitans. "Indeed, sick and tired of this want of energy", he mentioned emphatically that if he found it impossible to be of use to His Majesty he must retire from his present "inactive service". In the end of September, Troubridge, still unaided by English troops, but supported by a Russian division forwarded by Marshal Suvárov, reported the capitulation of Rome and Città Vecchia. Nelson, amused by the fulfilment of a prophecy, made to him in Naples by an Irish priest, "that I should take Rome with my ships", pointed out that the last objection to the return of the royal family to their Neapolitan capital had been removed. Still the King would not move. "I am almost mad with the manner of going on here."

"The unpleasant paragraphs in the newspapers" regarding their Commander-in-Chief, deplored by Commodore Troubridge in letters to Governor Ball, were not in very wide circulation in England as yet, but Gibraltar was so full of gossip on the subject that the Elgins had arrived determined to accept as little hospitality as possible at the Palazzo Palagonia. "They say", wrote young Lady Elgin to her mother in Scotland, "that there never was a man turned so *vain glorious* (that's the phrase) in the world as Lord N. He is now completely managed by Lady Hamilton." Her husband found that "they" had not spoken strict truth as far as Lord Nelson was concerned. On business, particularly in private, the young diplomat was penetrated by the "infinite fire", decision and refusal to be daunted by difficulties displayed by a prematurely aged man, who appeared to have a film growing over both eyes. But in private, too, the Admiral told him solemnly that he had now lived a year in the same house as Lady Hamilton, and that her beauty was nothing in comparison to the goodness of her heart. Sir William, in Lord Elgin's opinion, ought to go home, and he wrote to England to say so. Lady Elgin found that Lady Hamilton was pleasant, sang remarkably well, and at dinner, quite in an undress, looked very handsome. "My Father would say, 'There is a fine Woman for you, good flesh and blood.' She is indeed a Whapper!" The famous Emma, however, appeared to her fellow Ambassadress lacking in reserve, and Lady Elgin felt really humiliated as she watched Nelson's obvious devotion. "Lord Nelson, whenever she moved, was always by her side. . . ." "He seems quite dying, and yet as if he had no other thought than her." When the *Foudroyant* sailed for Minorca, and probably Gibraltar, Lord Elgin had so much fallen a victim to the Admiral's personality as to give the toast "Lord Nelson" at Sir William Hamilton's table, whereupon, to Lady Elgin's amusement, "my-Lady actually *greeted*".

Nelson had warned Ball and Sidney Smith that he was going to Minorca to get together ten sail-of-the-line in order to meet a squadron of fourteen enemy warships, including one three-decker, reported off Finisterre. He was satisfied that they were not bound for the Mediterranean, and that the British outward-bound convoy was their prey. This consisted of seven hundred sail, escorted by a few frigates, English authorities having been assured—quite correctly—that the French were blockaded in Brest. On the evening of October 12, having called at Port Mahon, the squadron of the temporary Commander-in-Chief on the Mediterranean station, under sail for Gibraltar, fell in with the *Bulldog* sloop of war, and Sir Edward Berry, recovered of his wounds of the Nile, and fresh from England, brought news from Admiral Duckworth that the supposed French were Spaniards who had already put into Ferrol. The squadron returned to Port Mahon, but in a four-hour interview with Sir James Erskine, Nelson did not succeed as he had done with Lord Elgin. The military commander could not at present consider sparing 2,000 men to assist in the reduction of Malta, where the conciliatory Ball, appointed Governor, was on the best of terms with the afflicted natives, but still without the troops necessary to drive "the accursed French" out of Valetta. Amongst other business despatched by Nelson at Port Mahon, on the same day as a court-martial, was a literary effort, "which I am sensible wants the pruning knife". Mr. John M'Arthur, who had been Secretary to Lord Hood, and Purser of the *Victory*, had explained that the first volume of his *Naval Chronicle*, for which a "Sketch of my Life" by

Lord Nelson was essential, was already in print. Nelson's "Sketch of my Life", which he realised would be read in English homes, closed on a trumpet note. "Perseverance in any profession will most probably meet its reward. Without having any inheritance, or having been fortunate in prize-money, I have received all the Honours of my Profession, been created a Peer of Great Britain, and I may say to the reader, 'Go thou and do likewise.' " The moment was a sad one for him to address himself to the rising generation. His sister Susanna, whose family opened with daughters, had at last been able to fulfil her dream of sending a son into the navy. The Admiral had just heard that George Bolton, aged twelve, had died on his passage from Gibraltar to Minorca.

When the *Foudroyant* returned to Palermo on October 22, Berry was again her Captain, "my friend Hardy" having gone into the *Princess Charlotte*, "to make a Man-of-War of her".

8

The English Press, as the last months of the old century wore out, was principally concerned with the ignominious end of Tippoo Sahib at Seringapatam, something in the nature of a *coup d'état* in Paris, and what Nelson knew as "the Secret Expedition". The Fourth Lieutenant of the *Goliath* had safely performed his long journey to the Governor of Bombay, and Lord Mornington and his military brother, Colonel Wellesley, had acted promptly in India on hearing of the victory of Aboukir Bay. On the day after Nelson, delighted by Sidney Smith's successes, had written to Troubridge, "*Adieu, Mr. Buonaparte!*" that character had deserted his army in Egypt. Buonaparte had landed six weeks later at one of those small French Mediterranean ports so well known to officers of Hood's and Jervis's fleets, and had been received with enthusiasm by a handful of surprised and obscure inhabitants. In his own phrase, "the pear was ripe", but "the Secret Expedition", which had just been launched, appeared to all English readers of newspapers much more important. After a year of preparation, since invasion of their own shores had been frustrated by the Battle of the Nile, English troops had invaded the Continent. Holland had been their choice for a landing-place, and, so far as Nelson knew, affairs were proceeding according to plan; but the Mediterranean fleet, while affairs in Mediterranean waters were "pretty nearly at a standstill", seemed to him quite forgotten, and in his darker moments he suspected that this neglect was intentional. He had attempted to justify his failure to obey Lord Keith.

"Much as I approve of strict obedience to orders—even to a Court-Martial to inquire whether the object justified the measure—yet to say that an Officer is never, for any object, to alter his orders, is what I cannot comprehend. The circumstances of this War so often vary, that an Officer has, almost every moment, to consider—What would my superiors direct did they know what is passing under my nose? The great object of this War is—'Down, down with the French.' To accomplish this, every nerve and by both services, ought to be strained."

Two days before Christmas, writing to his Flag-Captain, he mentioned that he had heard nothing from home since October 22, "and then only a miserable letter from the Admiralty", indeed "a severe set-down". His offence now, of which he felt himself quite guiltless, was, ironically enough, failure to keep their Lordships informed. He had replied that, as an acting Commander-in-Chief, without the usual appointments or salary, he had been "thrown into a more extensive correspondence than ever, perhaps, fell to the lot of any Admiral, and into a political situation, I own, out of my sphere". His situation for some months now had been, as he mourned to Lord Spencer, "most uncomfortable. Plain commonsense points out that the King should return to Naples, but nothing can move him. . . . Unfortunately, the King and Her Majesty do not, at this moment, draw exactly the same way. Do not, my dear Lord, let the Admiralty write harshly to me—my generous soul cannot bear it, being conscious it is entirely unmerited." He was "almost in desperation about Malta", and in anxiety lest the long-suffering Maltese, when they learnt that England was deferring to the Czar's desire to restore the Order of St. John with his Imperial Majesty as Grand Master, should give up the long struggle. He was working night and day to get them troops from Messina and corn from Girgenti. He was ready to sell the Czar's diamonds, and had pledged Brontë. "Nothing in this Country is well done." Acton continued to promise, but not to act. The Bashaw of Tripoli, who was now far

from averse from concluding a peace with His Sicilian Majesty
(which should ease the passage of supplies for Malta), wished first
to know what sum he would be paid for it; as if he made peace with
King Ferdinand he must find some other monarch to fight, or lay
up his cruisers. "Very good reasons for being at war", wrote Nelson
on the back of the English Consul's explanatory letter. "Well said,
Bashaw!" Lord Elgin was calling for a strong squadron in the
Levant, and the Austrians for one to blockade Genoa. The murder
of an English seaman in Palermo by two Genoese who could be
identified had been reported. For the last twelve months British
ships had been losing valuable men in tavern and quay-side affrays
with Genoese. A firm letter to the Marquis Spinola was sent on its
way.

Mr. Charles Lock, "mortified beyond what I ever was in my
life", had been persuaded by Sir William Hamilton to send Lord
Nelson a letter of abject apology for spreading "malicious and
scandalous" rumours that the Victualling Board were grateful to
him for exposing Captains' and Pursers' frauds, and saving the
Government forty per cent. on the provision of stores for Lord
Nelson's fleet.

"I declare that circumstances compelled me against my will and against
my sense to appear in the light of a Public accuser. As it was far from my
intention to assail your Lordship's integrity by any expression which may
have fallen from me, and as every purpose of Justification is already
answered which a further inquiry could produce, I trust your Lordship will
deem it unnecessary to press the matter further."

But Mr. Lock still felt sore, for he had been thanked by the
Victualling Board for his zeal—though unofficially. His interest at
home was good, and his father had written to him that Mr. Marsh,
a Commissioner of the Board, felt very much obliged to him for
"interference"; and Miss Lock reported that Sir William Belling-
ham, Chairman, at a family dinner-party, had repeated the sentiment. Suggestions by Mrs. Lock, however, that "Lord Craven and
Lord Bathurst should be informed of it all", had been disregarded
by her prudent father and father-in-law; and unfortunately, in one
of many heated letters to the Admiral, Mr. Lock had accused Lord
Nelson of forwarding false statements of his conduct to the Board.

("I wish I had said 'erroneous' instead of 'false', as the expression is offensive.") The Board, disingenuously, replied to a complaint from the Admiral that they had never had correspondence with Mr. Lock; but the Admiral's letters also had been heated, and one had contained a sentence bound to arouse criticism at home—"Nelson is so far from doing a scandalous or mean action as the Heavens are above the Earth."

Palermo, this Christmas-tide of hard gales, was very gay, gayer than ever, and Troubridge, whose letters of warning were becoming a familiar feature of Nelson's correspondence, had produced a maddening theory that the Queen, an inveterate employer of secret agents, was privately acting against the British she favoured so openly. The Commodore believed that his letters to his Commander-in-Chief were seen by Her Majesty before they reached their destination. Last September he had believed "some person about Sir William Hamilton's house sends accounts here, as I have frequently heard things which I knew your Lordship meant to keep secret". Now a story that Nelson was gambling was driving him frantic. The facts were that Nelson, who began his day at 5.30 a.m. and had told the Secretary to the Admiralty, "till after 8 o'clock at night, I never relax from business", had fallen into the habit, during the winter months, of attending the Hamiltons to the concert, ball and card rooms on La Nova. Supper-parties at the Palazzo Palagonia were also enlivened by high play at Faro. Nelson never played, but Lady Hamilton had begun to do so, and the mere appearance of the British Commander-in-Chief dropping asleep at the table, by the side of a gambling lady, had been delightful to the Jacobin Press and Neapolitans who loathed the Queen and her English friends. A story that Sir William had challenged the Admiral had not survived, as they were always seen together on the best of terms, but one that the Admiral and Ambassadress, in disguise, haunted quay-side taverns *incognito* was popular. "You may not know", wrote Troubridge heavily to Lady Hamilton, "that you have many enemies. I therefore risk your displeasure by telling you." To his relief, she took his admonition in good part, saw his point and gave up playing. The mischief, however, was done, and Sir William Hamilton's successor was told, and reported to London, that Lord Nelson had ruined his health and fortune playing Faro, and other games, at Palermo, in the company of Lady Hamilton.

The new century opened with a week of pacific skies and sunshine, at the end of which Nelson learnt that his acting command had come to an end. Lord Keith, from Vigo, announced that the Admiralty had directed him to proceed into the Mediterranean. He was going to look into Genoa, and ordered Nelson to join him. Keith received, without any assumed pleasure, a chagrined and personally unsympathetic officer whom he intended to treat with great tact. He fixed a critical eye upon the *Foudroyant* and brilliant young Sir Edward Berry, one of Nelson's "swans". Lord Keith had brought his lady with him, and this personage, though like Lady Elgin a Scottish heiress, and of far more formal manners, availed herself of an invitation to the Palazzo Palagonia while the *Queen Charlotte* was in port. The moment was not a happy one. During his absence a thunderbolt had fallen upon the house in which Nelson abode with the Hamiltons. Sir William had been abruptly informed that the Honourable Arthur Paget, in a fast frigate, was on his way to relieve him of his duties. It was true that in 1798 Sir William had mentioned to Lord Grenville that he would like to come to England to look after his Pembrokeshire estates, and that if leave could not be granted the Foreign Minister might dispose of his post; but he had heard nothing further on the subject, either publicly or privately. Now, their Sicilian Majesties' representative at St. James's had blandly written to Sir John Acton that Sir William's retirement was at his own wish. A philosopher, Sir William valiantly supposed that he was the victim of "a cabinet job" (some provision for a young son of Lord Uxbridge being necessary at the moment), but his lady was horrified at the prospect of retirement, and the Queen, according to her own account, was "half dead with grief". All rallied. Sir William announced that after thirty-six years' service he had been "either kicked up or down out of my post". Time would show which. "I have now not a doubt but we shall have the extreme satisfaction of returning home with our dearest friend, Lord Nelson." But when Nelson sailed for Malta, with Lord Keith, on February 12, after what that dour character described as "the *long* eight days I was at Palermo", all felt that the end of a chapter was drawing near. The capture of Valetta and the two enemy warships which had escaped from the Nile was all that remained to bring Nelson's professional career in the Mediterranean to a triumphant finish.

Amongst the unpleasant news received by Nelson, after a long, ominous silence, was that Marshal Suvárov had retired to Prague, ready to act either with or against the Austrians, as events proved; for a French envoy was treating for peace at Vienna. That the combined English and Russian invasion of Holland had not been a success was becoming apparent. The Czar was passing into disgust for both his allies. Consequently, Admiral Ouschakoff had accomplished his long-threatened withdrawal from his station off Malta. Ball, looking back upon the events of the following week, said that Nelson was indeed a lucky Admiral. For sixteen months the blockade had been carried on without any serious enemy interference. No sooner did Nelson arrive than a frigate brought word that a French ship of the line, in charge of a convoy bringing 4,000 troops and grain from Toulon for the relief of Valetta, had been seen west of Sicily. Keith, with his division, approached the island in unusually good weather for the season, but Nelson's journal on the anniversary of the Nile was achieved in low spirits.

"At 9 o'clock went on board the *Queen Charlotte*. Lord Keith just got up. Went into the breakfast-room. (N.B. Everything very dirty, and the table-cloth not changed since we sailed.) Got no information of Lord Keith's intentions about me. Came on board very unwell. Had all the officers and midshipmen of the ship, who were in the battle of this day, to dine with me. Blew fresh all night." [Next morning they were close off St. Paul's.] "Asked the Admiral, by signal, if I should lead into port. Answer, 'No.'"

He realised, what he had foreseen, that Keith had no intention of admitting him to the confidence or giving him the free hand to which the leadership of St. Vincent had accustomed him. On learning from the *Lion* of the approach of the enemy, Keith signalled to Nelson to chase to windward, with four of the line, and for three days and nights, carrying all sail possible, in very dirty weather, Nelson gloomily entered, "Nothing in sight". The Sicilian troops embarked on board the *Foudroyant* suffered, and he grimly noted, "Nothing is off Valetta to prevent the entry of any vessel.

The Commander-in-Chief knows best." To Lady Hamilton he misquoted Shakespeare, "If it be a sin to covet glory, I am the most offending soul alive", adding dismally, "But *here I am*, in a heavy sea and thick fog". Next morning, through the mist, he heard the note of cannon, and steered towards it. The scene is henceforward illuminated by the irrepressible Midshipman Parsons, whose description, recollected for an early-Victorian audience, opens at the moment that the masthead look-out is hailing the quarter-deck.

" 'The stranger is evidently a man-of-war—she is a line-of-battle ship, my lord, and going large on the starboard tack.'

" 'Ah! an enemy, Mr. Staines. I pray God it may be *Le Généreux*. The signal for a general chase, Sir Ed'ard' (the Nelsonian pronunciation of Edward). 'Make the *Foudroyant* fly! . . . This will not do, Sir Ed'ard, it is certainly *Le Généreux*, and to my flagship she can alone surrender. Sir Ed'ard, we must and shall beat the *Northumberland*.'

" 'I will do the utmost, my lord. (Get the engine to work on the sails—hand butts of water to the stays—pipe the hammocks down, and each man place shot in them—slack the stays, knock up the wedges, and give the masts play. Start off the water, Mr. James, and pump the ship.)'

"The *Foudroyant* is drawing ahead, and at last takes the lead in the chase. 'The Admiral is working his fin' (the stump of his right arm). 'Do not cross his hawse I advise you.'

"A strange sail ahead of the chase" is the next report, and Parsons, ordered to the masthead, after being damned by the Admiral for starting to climb without his telescope, shouts:

" 'A sloop of war, or frigate, my lord.'

" 'Demand her number.'

" 'The *Success*, my lord.'

" 'Captain Peard; signal to cut off the flying enemy—great odds, though, thirty-two small guns to eighty large ones.'

"The *Success* has hove-to athwart hawse of the *Généreux*; and is firing her larboard broadside. The Frenchman has hoisted his tricolour, with a Rear-Admiral's flag.

" 'Bravo—*Success*! *At her again!*'

" 'She has wore round, my lord, and firing her starboard broadside. It has winged her, my lord—her flying kites are flying away altogether.'

"The enemy is close on the *Success*, who must receive her tremendous broadside. The *Généreux* opens her fire on her little enemy, and every person stands aghast, afraid of the consequences. The smoke clears away, and there is the *Success*, crippled, it is true, but bull-dog like, bearing up after the enemy. . . .

" 'Then signal for the *Success* to discontinue the action and come under my stern,' said Lord Nelson, 'she has done well for her size. Try a shot from the lower deck at her, Sir Ed'ard.'

" 'It goes over her.'

" 'Beat to quarters, and fire coolly and deliberately at her masts and yards.'

"*Le Généreux* at this moment opened her fire on us, and, as a shot passed through the mizzen stay-sail, Lord Nelson, patting one of the youngsters on the head, asked him jocularly how he relished the music; and observing something like alarm depicted on his countenance, consoled him with the information that Charles XII ran away from the first shot he heard, though afterwards he was called 'The Great', and deservedly from his bravery. 'I therefore', said Nelson, 'hope much from you in future.'

"Here the *Northumberland* opened her fire, and down came the tricoloured ensign, amidst the thunders of our united cannon."

Nelson gave the signal to cease fire, and Berry boarded the prize, soon to return with the sword of Rear-Admiral Pérée, who was dying of wounds. But the victor's reception by his Commander-in-Chief next day was very unlike that usually given by St. Vincent to a favourite and successful officer. Not a muscle of Lord Keith's face moved as he listened to Nelson's report, and when Nelson added that he had made a vow that if he took *Le Généreux*, he would strike his flag, crushing silence followed. Nelson believed that he had again disobeyed Keith, in leaving him without a signal ("The way he went, the *Généreux* never could have been taken"), but Keith, writing to the Admiralty, gave him credit for skill and address in comprehending signals in very bad weather, and prepared to leave him in charge of the blockade of Malta, offering him the choice of Syracuse, Augusta or Messina as a more convenient *rendezvous* than Palermo. "I could no more stay fourteen days longer here than fourteen years", explained Nelson, in a private letter, accompanying his request for a fortnight's sick leave, "to go to my friends at Palermo". To Lord Minto, he burst out, "Greenwich Hospital seems a fit retreat for me, after being *evidently* thought unfit to command in the Mediterranean." For a few days, hopes that the *Guillaume Tell* and other enemy ships were likely to come out of the harbour detained him; then, in spite of anguished protests from Troubridge, he sailed. The *Speedy* brig, from England, brought him a note of warning from another good friend shortly before he weighed. Old Admiral Goodall, seated in a mansion of Mayfair on a short November day, had brought to a duty letter all his wonted address.

"My Good Lord,

"I hope, as the sailor says, 'this will find you well, as I am at this present.' I have wrote at different times three letters to you in favour of my protégé, Captain Broughton of the *Stromboli* Bomb, and flattered myself that I should have heard you had had an opportunity of giving him Post. Keep him in your mind's eye, and let it be so.

"They say here you are Rinaldo in the arms of Armida, and that it requires the firmness of an Ubaldo, and his brother Knight, to draw you from the Enchantress. To be sure 'tis a very pleasant attraction, to which I am very sensible myself. But my maxim has always been—*Cupidus voluptatum, cupidior gloriae.* Be it as it will, health and happiness attend you."

Nelson replied at length to a man who had himself known what it was to be passed over for the command in the Mediterranean, but did not mention the Hamiltons except as his present hosts, and in that capacity "nonpareils". The weather was most unfavourable for an invalid suffering from symptoms which he believed signified fatal heart trouble, and he was again without a secretary. ("I wish", said Ball, " he could be prevailed upon to write less, because I am very apprehensive he impairs his health by leaning so much.")

On his arrival in Palermo, Nelson sent Berry back with the *Foudroyant*, to take part in the blockade of Valetta, and again hoisted his own flag on board a transport, in view of the windows of the Palazzo Palagonia. The latest festivity to take place in that hospitable house had been depressingly characteristic of Neapolitan Court circles, and confirmed his growing mistrust and dislike of their Majesties' chief Minister. Sir John Acton, aged sixty-four, had been married, by dispensation, to his niece, who still lacked three months to her fourteenth birthday.

The *Foudroyant* arrived back on her station just in time to capture the *Guillaume Tell*, and from the moment that he got the news Nelson's plans for going home began to take active shape.

"My task is done, my health is lost, and the orders of the great Earl of St. Vincent are completely fulfilled. I hope the *Foudroyant* will be able to come here, to carry us first to Malta, and from thence, taking the Queen of Naples to Leghorn, proceed with us, at least to Gibraltar, if not to England."

9

The censorious young gentleman called by the Queen "the fatal Paget" had arrived some weeks past. On April 22 Sir William Hamilton presented his letters of recall, and next day a party from the Palazzo Palagonia sailed with Nelson in the *Foudroyant* for Malta. Miss Knight had at first declined the Admiral's invitation, but on being assured that it was his intention to visit Syracuse, could not resist the temptation. Since there were two authors on board, vivid glimpses of this cruise are available. Miss Knight noted in the Admiral's Great Cabin an immense tricoloured plume, carved in wood, a relic from the figure-head of the *Guillaume Tell*, four muskets taken from the *San Josef*, the flagstaff of *L'Orient*, and many new publications, sent from England by Lady Nelson. The officers of the ship were in turn invited to dine, and the Admiral kept a good table, although nothing about his appointments was ostentatious. Owing to contrary winds, their passage to Syracuse was slow, and Lady Hamilton's birthday, April 26, was celebrated on board with toasts and songs, one of which, composed by Miss Knight for the occasion, was set to the old tune "Heart of Oak". It was coyly dedicated "To a lady who is leaving Sicily with great reluctance", and opened:

> "Come, cheer up, fair Delia, forget all thy grief,
>   For thy ship-mates are brave, and a Hero's their chief."

After two days' sightseeing in ancient Syracuse, the party again set sail, and late in the evening of May 3 joined the blockading squadron off Malta.

On the night of their arrival off Valetta a breeze unexpectedly came in from the sea, with the result that the *Foudroyant* dragged her anchor, and, being given cable, brought up within gunshot of the shore-batteries. Sir Edward Berry, roused from slumber by the Officer of the Watch, said, "Very well, Mr. Bolton, we will shift our berth at daylight", but with dawn the enemy began target-practice upon the flagship. "Lord Nelson was in a towering passion, and Lady Hamilton's refusal to quit the quarter-deck, did not tend to tranquilize him." Their welcome by all the English authorities at Malta was hearty. General Graham and Commodore Troubridge invited the whole party to dine on several occasions during their stay of seventeen days. Governor Ball addressed Lady Hamilton as "my dear sister". An application of the Admiral to the Czar (as Grand Master of the Order of St. John) to notice the bravery of Captain Ball, and the exertions of the lady of the British Minister at the Court of the Two Sicilies to procure supplies for the Maltese, had resulted in the arrival of decorations for both. Ball had been named *Commandeur Grand Croix*, and Lady Hamilton *Dame Petite Croix*.

Everyone concerned wished that Nelson would wait to witness the fall of Valetta, which they represented as imminent, but on May 20, having been at anchor in the little bay of Marsa Sorocco since the 11th, the *Foudroyant* got under weigh. Ball's last letter to Lady Hamilton, who had failed to attend a farewell dinner, wished her prosperous gales and every blessing in this life. He attributed Nelson's heart-attacks to fatigue and anxiety. "I therefore rejoice at your being on board." Their return passage was not attended by the desired favourable winds, and during it a report that Lady Hamilton was suffering from fever caused stillness to be observed in all parts of what Parsons called "this Noah's Ark". To give Lady Hamilton rest by night, the Admiral ordered the ship to be run off before the wind, with her yards braced. To his great joy, and indeed to the pleasure of all on board, this remedy appeared efficacious. She was pronounced convalescent when they made the port of Palermo, late on the last night of May.

Full strength was necessary to face the week of official leave-taking which lay before the party. On June 5 Sir William responded with a farewell banquet (also celebrating the birthday of his sovereign). At the last moment the Queen, in a flutter caused by the news that Buonaparte was crossing the Alps to recover Italy, postponed her departure for three days. Her alleged object in going to Vienna was to exert diplomatic pressure upon the Court of her daughter and son-in-law, but it was common knowledge that the King was thankful to be relieved of her company. She was taking with her her three unmarried daughters, her younger son and a *suite* calculated at about fifty. Nelson, who had sent for the *Alex-*

ander, prophesied, "The ship will be overflowing". The Queen came on board the *Foudroyant* eventually, early on the morning of the 10th, thanked the Admiral again and again as he bent to kiss her hand, and turning to his officers, with inimitable grace, ordered their presentation to her daughters, the future Queens of Spain, France and Sardinia. The passage of the royal family to Leghorn was swift, and Parsons was in a seventh heaven, as the most ravishing of the princesses was a good sailor, and when her mother and sisters were presently prostrated, much enjoyed herself on the quarter-deck, being taught by the younger officers to use the speaking-trumpet. They came in sight of their destination on June 14, and as Tuscan guns fired a royal salute, the Queen murmured, in tones of rapture, "Leghorn! Leghorn!" "No doubt", decided Miss Knight, "as being on the way to her native land." A boat was sent ashore, with great difficulty, and the Queen began to present her parting gifts. It was therefore something of an anticlimax that, owing to the weather, she was detained on board a further two days, but at the end of that time she landed, to be received by the Governor and conducted to a service in the cathedral. The doors of her ducal son-in-law's palace closed upon her, much to Nelson's relief; the Hamiltons drove on to the official residence of Mr. Wyndham, British Consul. But the Admiral's troubles, far from being at an end, were only beginning. Boarding on such a night was not easy, and when he regained his cabin, it was "truly a hog-stye". Many of his belongings were afloat. The results of the *Foudroyant's* sharp action with the *Guillaume Tell* were apparent after rough weather, and a cold which had kept him in bed for four days of the past week was still heavy upon him. Although he knew that he would see her next day, he wrote to Lady Hamilton before he slept.

The Queen, on parting from him, had admitted that she was not perfectly satisfied with the news. Lord Keith's capture of Genoa on the 5th was well confirmed, but Leghorn reports of a major encounter between the Austrian and French armies differed. At midnight on June 18 a despatch from Keith told Nelson that the Austrian Commander had signed a convention abandoning Northern Italy, as far as the Mincio, to the French, to whom were to be given up all fortresses, including Genoa. On the day that the Austrian-born

Queen had come in sight of Leghorn, her countrymen had been
totally defeated by Buonaparte at Marengo. Keith ordered Nelson
to sail at once for Spezia, to take possession of the garrison of that
place; next day a further despatch directed that, in view of the
changed situation, should the Queen wish to return to Palermo, no
British ship-of-the-line must be employed. An earlier order, which
had missed Nelson, had forbidden him to take ships off the blockade
of Malta to transport royalty. Nelson sent off the *Alexander* and one
frigate, but remained himself, with the *Foudroyant*, ready, if necessary, to evacuate "my sacred charge". Keith's next communication,
labelled "most confidential", explained that he had just seen "a man
who has come from Buonaparte. Let the Queen go to Vienna as
fast as she can." Buonaparte had said publicly, "There is one Power
still in Italy to be reduced before I can give it peace", and Keith
believed that if the French fleet got a day's start of his own, Sicily
would be captured. Nelson, who had no belief that the Brest fleet
would come into the Mediterranean, commented, "But if they do,
Lord have mercy upon them!" With regard to the Queen, he said,
"Until I have got rid of my charge, nothing shall separate me from
her. I should feel myself a beast, could I have a thought for anything
but her comfort."

On the 24th Keith arrived in person, to land fugitives from
Genoa, and, as he informed the First Lord, "to be bored by Lord
Nelson for permission to take the Queen to Palermo, and princes
and princesses to all parts of the globe". The Queen, now highly
hysterical, asked with tears for the *Foudroyant* to carry her back to
her husband. According to the British Consul, whose relations with
Sir William Hamilton had never been harmonious, Keith had added
to his refusal that "Lady Hamilton had had command of the Fleet
long enough". He had already ordered the *Foudroyant* to Minorca
for repairs, and informed Nelson, who had shifted his flag to the
Alexander, that if he was determined to accompany the Queen to
Vienna from any Adriatic port, he must send the *Alexander* to
Mahon. The Commander-in-Chief had further formally offered
Lord Nelson and Sir William Hamilton and party, should they
wish to return to England by sea, accommodation as passengers in
the *Seahorse* frigate, or a troopship from Malta.

On June 26 Nelson sent to his lady "a line, not to say that I am contented or happy, for neither the one nor the other is near true—but enough of that!" He told her that he wore the Order of the Crescent above that of the Bath, and that he was going to give up two years' rent from his Sicilian estate for its improvement. "It is my intention to fulfill a Prophecy that one day it should be called Brontë, the Happy."

On the evening of July 9 the Queen and her children suddenly came on board the *Alexander*. News that the French were within twenty-four miles of the town had roused excitement, and the sister of the murdered Queen of France believed that the mob gathered below the palace windows meant to hold her and her family as hostages. Actually, the populace (who had illicitly armed themselves from the arsenal, and were strongly anti-French) were calling for Lord Nelson to be their leader against Buonaparte. Next day the idea of sailing round the peninsula to Trieste was abandoned, and the Queen returned to the palace. Lady Hamilton (translating for the Admiral) had successfully adjured the mob from the balconies to return their stolen weapons of war and depart in good order. Nelson struck his flag on the 13th, and it was announced that the whole party were about to travel overland, by way of Florence to Ancona, and there embark in small Austrian vessels for Trieste. Miss Knight heard of her future with dismay amounting to wrath, and in her farewell letter to Sir Edward Berry glanced severely at her hostess. She was astonished that the Queen, a sensible woman, should consent to such a journey. Poor Sir William Hamilton said he should die by the way, and looked likely to do so. Lord Nelson, although well, and keeping up his spirits amazingly, was clearly going upon an expedition of which he disapproved. Everyone, in short, was to be inconvenienced, because Lady Hamilton had suddenly discovered that "she cannot bear the thought of going by sea. . . . She hates the sea, and wishes to visit the different Courts of Germany." But, as Miss Knight broodingly realised, "The die is cast, and go we must."

The Queen left on the 15th, and they followed two days later. A letter delivered to Nelson before the *Foudroyant* sailed was cheering.

"My Lord,

"It is with extreme grief that we find you are about to leave us. We have been along with you (though not in the same Ship) in every Engagement your Lordship has been in, both by Sea and Land; and most humbly beg of your Lordship to permit us to go to England as your Boat's crew, in any Ship or Vessel, or in any way that may seem most pleasing to your Lordship.

"My Lord, pardon the rude style of Seamen who are but little acquainted with writing, and believe us to be, my Lord,

"Your most humble and obedient servants
"Barge's Crew of the *Foudroyant*."

Two communications from Lord Spencer which had reached him during his Leghorn stay were less calculated to bring him comfort. The First Lord expressed his regret that the state of Lord Nelson's health had obliged him to quit his station off Malta. Should the enemy come suddenly into the Mediterranean, Lord Spencer would be concerned to hear that Lord Nelson had learnt of this either on shore or in a transport at Palermo. It was by no means Lord Spencer's wish or intention to recall Lord Nelson, but he believed that all friends would join with him in deciding that Lord Nelson would be best advised to come home at once, rather than remain inactive at a foreign Court while active service was proceeding in other parts of the station.

Chapter XIII

1800–1801

(*ætat.* 41–42)

STORMY HOMECOMING

I

ACCORDING to Miss Knight, the officers and ship's company of the *Alexander* saw the last of the Admiral with additional regret at the thought of the dangers to which he was going to expose himself. His first day's journey must take him within a couple of miles of advanced enemy posts. Another disadvantage of the overland *route* was already obvious. Almost at once Miss Knight began to deplore "the helplessness" of her travelling companions, and as days passed the impression deepened. In Vienna, to her relief, a factotum called Oliver (long known to Sir William in Naples, and an accomplished linguist) was engaged. The authoress had promised Sir Edward Berry that if she did not die on the way, or find herself in a French prison, she would keep him informed of the Admiral's progress, and from Ancona and Trieste she was better than her word.

Owing more to good fortune than prudence, in her opinion, the party, pressing on through the heat of the day and darkness of the night, reached Florence in twenty-six hours. On the next stage of their journey, near Castel San Giovanni, the leading coach overturned. Nelson reported no injury, but both the Hamiltons were bruised, and a wheel of the equipage was broken. It was repaired, but fell to pieces again at Arezzo. The Queen and her *suite* had now gained two days on the road, and the French were said to be again on the move. "It was therefore decided", explained Miss Knight with simple dignity, "that they should proceed, and Mrs. Cadogan and I remain with the broken carriage, as it was of less consequence we should be left behind, or taken, than they." Lord Nelson was, apparently, lost to every consideration except the well-being of Lady Hamilton. Two Englishwomen, left with a broken coach, spent three days awaiting its reappearance, and when that glad moment came it was coupled with the tidings that the French were now about to cross their road, and Neapolitan deserters were streaming down it. The couple travelled day and night, and rejoined the important members of their party in a state of exhaustion. On their arrival at Ancona it was decided that the Queen, Nelson and the Hamiltons should embark in the flagship of Count Voinovitsch, the officer in command of a Russian squadron, about to sail. Nelson would clearly have preferred to go with the unimportant members of the party, in a frigate commanded by an old English sea-dog, Captain Messer. (Whatever was done to turn off the conversation, the *Foudroyant* was the Admiral's constant topic, and Miss Knight heard him talking with Messer, who had once served with Lord Howe, of the manœuvres he intended if he accepted another command.) When the travellers met again, after an uneventful passage, those who had sailed with royalty had a sad tale to tell. Count Voinovitsch had never made an appearance, pleading illness, and his First Lieutenant, a Neapolitan, had displayed himself as the most ignorant and undisciplined of beings. ("Think what Lord Nelson must have felt!") Nelson's only comment was that a gale of wind would have sunk the ship. They had now reached safety, so far as enemy action was concerned, but unaccustomed hours and diet had taken their toll, and the physicians of Trieste had to be summoned to attend the Queen and thirty-four of her *suite*, Miss Knight and Sir William, all of them "very unwell". Providentially, the British Vice-Consul, a Mr. Anderson, was bound for Vienna and ready to escort the party when convalescent.

In Vienna the British Ambassador awaited their appearance with feelings of almost unalloyed vexation. Lord Minto's speech in the Lords upon the occasion of a vote of thanks to the Victor of the Nile had been a little masterpiece, and he had particularly stressed the lofty moral character of his gallant friend. A Mr. Rushout, a son of Lord Northwick, who had taken part in the royal flight from Naples, had brought incredible gossip from Palermo, confirmed by Mr. Wyndham, fresh from Florence, and judging by Nelson's letter to him, the British Ambassador feared the worst.

"He does not seem at all conscious of the sort of discredit he has fallen into, or the cause of it, for he writes still, not wisely, about Lady Hamilton and all that. . . . He tells me of his having got the Cross of Malta for *her*, and Sir William sends home to Lord Grenville the Emperor of Russia's letter to Lady Hamilton on the occasion. All this is against them all, but they do not seem conscious."

From Palermo, Mr. Charles Lock had written home: "*She* is now gone, thank my stars!"

Nelson found the British Ambassador established in a palace on the slopes of St. Veit, "from Vienna, about Roehampton distance from London". He walked into one of the "extremely spacious" reception-rooms of the Mintos' hired home, and straight back into their hearts. One of his first utterances to his hostess was that he owed everything to her husband. But for the interest taken in him by Lord Minto he would never have been rewarded for his services after his first successful action, or been placed in a situation to obtain his second. "He is just the same with us as ever", exclaimed Lady Minto in delight. "I don't think him altered in the least." "I wish", she said to him presently, "that you had the command of the Emperor's army." "I'll tell you what", replied Nelson, with the schoolboy directness which later fascinated and horrified political luminaries. "If I had, I would use only one word—*advance*."

The British Ambassador prepared to present Lord Nelson and Sir William Hamilton at the Imperial Court, while Lady Minto presented Lady Hamilton, and Nelson appeared, "a gig, from ribands, orders and stars". The Crescent sent to him by the Grand Signior was dazzling, but Lady Minto was disappointed in the famous Chelengk, which she thought ugly in design, and "only rose diamonds". Having found that he had not altered his "honest simple manners", she was disappointed also as to "Lady Hamilton and all that". "He is devoted to *Emma*, thinks her quite an *angel*, and talks of her as such to her face and behind her back, and she leads him about like a keeper with a bear. She must sit by him at dinner to cut his meat, and he carries her pocket-handkerchief." But gradually, with amused relief, the British Embassy realised that Nelson's visit to Vienna, at a moment when England was not popular, was a great personal triumph. When he arrived at the playhouse, the audience rose to applaud a hero—a thing unusual in the Imperial city. It was told that on his road villagers had brought their children to touch him, and when he had hoisted a little boy in his single arm, the mother, bursting into tears, had cried out that now her son should have a lucky life. In fashionable society throughout Europe dress was undergoing a violent change. No hoops were now worn in Vienna, even at Court. The classic style, of which Lady Hamilton was a leading exponent, reigned supreme. Dressmakers, reduced to decorating muslins with gold and silver, hung out a portrait of the Victor of the Nile to attract custom, and milliners produced "the Nelson cap", in cocquelicot velvet.

The English visitors, so kindly received, lingered in a city notoriously romantic in the golden weeks of early autumn, and invitations to country palaces flowed in upon them. The Empress showed them her nursery at Schönbrunn, and Nelson, enjoying "the noise of five fine healthy children for an hour", made his bow to an Archduchess aged eight, the future second wife of Buonaparte. Prince Esterhazy, an old Naples acquaintance, was his host for four days. The Prince, scion of a house as musical as it was magnificent, had arranged for four concerts during Lady Hamilton's stay, and summoned from retirement in the Mariahilf suburb a modest, sensible person, nearing his seventieth year, who had been Ober-kapellmeister to two successive heads of the Esterhazy family. Mr. Franz Josef Haydn, who had met the Hamiltons on one of his London tours, brought with him a copy of his solo cantata for voice and pianoforte, "Ariadne in Naxos", and when Lady Hamilton sang, to his accompaniment, the "Nelson Aria", composed at her request, to words by Miss Knight, the authoress found the effect grand.

On September 19, accepting a last invitation to St. Veit, Nelson repeated a suggestion that "the neglected Queen of Naples" would be gratified by even an informal call from the British Ambassador. Luckily, Lord Minto (reflecting that in some ways a great hero could be a great baby) was relieved from the necessity of excusing himself. Maria Carolina, after the departure of her best friends, was going to take a Baden cure. Her farewell letter to Lady Hamilton, prophesying that she foresaw clouds lowering upon her fortunes, sent "a thousand compliments to the Chevalier, and to the hero, and to you—everything". She still hoped to see her "dear, dear Emma" again at Naples; in any case, her attachment and gratitude to "my friend and sister" would terminate but with her existence. "To you, I shall never change."

2

The Rector of Burnham Thorpe had accepted his son's often-deferred homecoming with his usual humility. "He soars in spheres unknown to private Stations." Personally, the Rector would have preferred to stay the year round in East Anglia, alternating between Burnham Thorpe, where a curate was now installed in the Parson-age, and Roundwood, although nothing of the proposed improve-ments had been carried out there. His hopes had run high, last year, when his daughter-in-law had announced Yarmouth Baths instead of Brighton as her choice for the cure, but June 1799 had seen Lady Nelson in London again, where the Walpole family, now very attentive, had lent the lady of the Victor of the Nile their chairmen, etc., to carry her to their Majesties' drawing-room, at which her husband had told her to make an appearance.

For the winter of 1799, since the hero still tarried, what the Rector described as "a house engaged until the Sun returns to us" was taken at 54, St. James's Street, a modish address. Although they were paying seven guineas a week, their accommodation did not sound very inviting. The Rector slept in the back drawing-room, and Lady Nelson promised "a light closet, on a floor, quite large enough for you and my Josiah should you think it right for him to come home". Her letters never ceased to express hopes for her husband's safety, but she explained that, living so quietly and writ-ing so often, she found little to say. A proposal by William that she should drop a gentle hint to Mr. Windham on the subject of recog-nition for the Nelson family had thrown her into a flutter of right-eous indignation. "Some women can say and do anything; I cannot, and feel happy it is my disposition, by which I never get myself into any scrapes."

Stories of her attentions to his father were always, his lady knew, welcome to Lord Nelson. Indeed, only in talking of the Rector and her son did she ever display emotion. ("Rest assured, my dear, no one thing that can be done for our good father shall be omitted.") In early March 1800 she had a fine tale to tell. Sir William Beechey was the fortunate man chosen by the Rector to paint his portrait. She had ventured to the artist's studio at her father-in-law's command, with instructions to look at the pictures, ask prices, and then, if the great man would come to an invalid. Sir William's answer had been, "No". He really never went to any person outside the Royal Family. "But, may I ask, madam, who is the gentleman?" "Yes, sir, my Lord Nelson's father." "My God! I would go to York to do it! Yes, madam, directly." For a week, while sittings for what promised to be an excellent likeness proceeded, she did not know whether the result was to be a gift to the Rector's son or daughter-in-law, but presently it became clear that the surprise—a profound secret—was for the Victor's return. In the last letter from his wife received by Nelson before he left Leghorn, delighted at the news that Lord Keith had sailed (since she believed that this meant that her husband would come home), she stated, *apropos* of nothing, "I can with safety put my hand on my heart and say it has been my study to please and make you happy." The Rector also sent praises of her to a quarter where, if disturbing rumours were to be believed, they were very necessary. "I well remember, that on my receiving a wound, you promised to heal it, by giving to me another daughter. Indeed, you have, Lady Nelson's kindness as a friend, a nurse, a daughter, I want words to express." But he set off for Roundwood this spring, to assure himself that the shrubs were all trimmed up to receive my Lord, alone, but for servants.

Loving enquiries from his lady for a son who did not write much had caused the Admiral many pangs during a painful period in his career. His directions when sending Josiah down to Constantinople in charge of the Turkish Ambassador had gone into detail on the subject of discipline, and a few weeks later, on learning that his application to Lord St. Vincent on behalf of his stepson had been successful, and that Captain Nisbet was "on his own bottom now", his anxiety had become acute. "I *wish* he may deserve it; the thought half kills me." His fears were soon realised. Apologies to an indignant St. Vincent were called for within four months. Josiah, finding the state of a Captain lonely, had fallen into the habit of messing in the gunroom. A reprimand in the handwriting of his stepfather's secretary recalled him to his senses, and in his abject and somewhat disarming letter promising to reform all his conduct, he declared that he well knew his dear father was the only person in this world that had his true interest at heart. After another four months, when sending H.M.S. *Thalia* to Admiral Duckworth with regrets that he could say "nothing in her praise, inside or out", Nelson hoped, "Perhaps you may be able to make something of Captain Nisbet; he has, by his conduct, almost broke my heart." Silence fell for nine months. Then in June 1800, at a moment when Nelson could stand very little more criticism, came a shattering letter. Knowing the near connection of Captain Nisbet to his lordship, Admiral Duckworth had to divulge with the gravest concern that H.M.S. *Thalia* had joined his squadron at Gibraltar in a low state of discipline. He proceeded to enumerate such facts as the Principal Medical Officer (above three months under arrest) asking for a court-martial on his Captain, and the First Lieutenant ready with a string of complaints, designed for Lord Nelson's eye, some of which, to say the least, would be sufficient to destroy the reputation of Captain Nisbet. Needless to add, while the Captain and his officers were visibly at daggers drawn, minor characters had taken liberties, rightly resented by a young gentleman of a warm disposition. Duckworth believed that possibly his lordship's having given the First Lieutenant authorisation to advise an inexperienced Captain might in some degree be responsible for the present dilemma. He had taken action which he was confident would result in the whole affair being buried in oblivion, and after some labour—having represented to all parties that they were at fault—had arranged a compromise, by which the surgeon was released and requests for a public investigation had been dropped. There could not, however, be two opinions as to the necessity for the parties being divided, and, if he might suggest, the state of H.M.S. *Thalia* justifying her being paid off, his prescription for Captain Nisbet was "a few months with Lady Nelson".

3

Lord Nelson and party arrived in Prague after dark on September 27, and the Hôtel Rothes Haus was splendidly illuminated in their honour, but, as Miss Knight afterwards noted, the host did not forget to charge for the lights on their bill.

A passage to Dresden by water had been advised by the Mintos, and for two days the English tourists proceeded at a gentle pace, in a canopied boat, down an alternately shining and sombre river, presented with a succession of views of forest-clad crags and mouldering mediæval castles, in the high romantic style dear to the artists called upon to decorate the panelling of contemporary palaces. After dark, the Admiral played cribbage with the ex-Ambassador.

The party arrived in the small but picturesque Saxon capital in holiday spirits, and took up residence at the Hôtel de Pologne, whence they joyfully apprised the British Minister of their arrival. It is possible that they had not been forewarned that Lord Minto's far more handsome and brilliant younger brother was already a disappointed man. Amongst his talents was that of finding himself generally superior to his company. In Dresden, languidly described by him as "a good sofa to repose upon", they savoured a foretaste of the reception to be accorded to them in some circles in London.

A young Irish widow, herself an authoress, musician and beauty, had been playing chess with Mr. Elliot when he received the dire news of Lord Nelson's approach, and Mrs. Melesina St. George had been called to the rescue. She let Lady Hamilton borrow several of her gowns, but accepted gushing praise of them with reserve, as she thought the lady's own taste in dress frightful. ("Her waist is absolutely between her shoulders.") She listened without sympathy to indiscreet after-dinner doubts whether Queen Charlotte would condescend to receive the ex-Ambassadress, and after accompanying Lady Hamilton upon the piano, elegantly explained that she had never before "seen or heard of, the sailor's way " of ending all songs with "a bumper, and the last drop on the nail". (To the Elliots she confided alarm at the quantity of champagne enjoyed by all the visitors.) She came, at Lady Hamilton's request, to see Lord Nelson attired for his audience with the Elector, "a perfect constellation of stars and orders". But none of the party grew upon her: she found Sir William's affectation of youthful agility ridiculous, Miss Knight a person who never opened her mouth except to flatter her friends, Lady Hamilton more "stamped with the manners of her first situation than one would suppose, after having represented Majesty, and lived in good company, for fifteen years", Lord Nelson "a willing captive", and Mrs. Cadogan "what one might expect".

The Court artist, Johann Heinrich Schmidt, was summoned to the Hôtel de Pologne, and obtained sketches for pastels of Lady Hamilton wearing her decoration and Lord Nelson in full-dress uniform. Two breakfasts, after which Lady Hamilton performed her "Attitudes", amidst applause, were endured by Mr. Elliot; then, having heard from a King's Messenger that a frigate awaited his guests at Hamburg, he "ventured to announce the fact". On his return from seeing what he called "Antony and Moll-Cleopatra" embark upon the Elbe, he plaintively begged his wife and Mrs. St. George, "Now don't let us laugh to-night. Let us all speak in whispers, and be very, very quiet."

In North Germany the riverside inns were poor. The party found small rooms with sanded floors, no carpets or upholstered furniture, and but scanty fare. On their arrival in Hamburg, after a journey of eleven days, they were disappointed to discover that Mr. Elliot's information had been incorrect. Nelson wrote to England to ask for a frigate, and they settled down to waiting, and more feasting. Their welcome was warm. The English merchants of the town arranged a Grand Gala, consisting of dinner, concert, supper and ball. Baron de Breteuil gave a breakfast, at which all the other guests were titled *émigrés* with the manners of the *vieille cour*. Towards its close a short, shabby gentleman, with a military air, stumped in, as if by accident. General Dumouriez had, in fact, been very curious to meet Admiral Nelson. The Victor of Jemappes was living in retirement, having refused to enter the service of the First Consul, and was supporting himself by his pen. Nelson, who had not forgotten what he called "the pinch", managed at a further meeting to secure the acceptance, by a brave officer, of a gift of £100. An elderly German poet called Klopstock, engaged in writing sublime odes, not to be understanded of the people, also welcomed the English party, and while they were in his parlour, an unexplained reverend person, attired in canonicals, entered to them, with a book in his hand. Although upwards of seventy, this country pastor had journeyed forty miles to obtain the signature of a Christian hero on the fly-leaf of the Bible belonging to his village church.

The travellers had set out from Leghorn, in July, in intolerable heat. At Hamburg, in late October, candles flickered in hotel rooms at midday, the air was distractingly raw, and beneath banks of fog the sea was in motion, and noisy. Miss Knight, who had for some time been "uneasy on many accounts", went shopping with the Admiral, and assisted with pleasure in the choice of splendid lace to decorate a Court gown for Lady Nelson.

On the last day of October, their patience being at an end, the party sailed from Cuxhaven in the *King George* mail-packet, and after a very stormy passage landed at Yarmouth at noon on Thursday, November 6. The weather was thoroughly English, but so was their welcome. "The frugality of our Administration" in failing to send a frigate to fetch the Victor of the Nile had been resented in Norfolk. Bells began to peal, stout volunteers were ready to drag his carriage up from the quay-side to "The Wrestler's Arms", and the band of the Infantry quartered in the town struck up a national air as Lord Nelson appeared on the balcony of an inn overlooking a harbour in which every vessel had colours flying. While rain fell steadily, Lady Hamilton stood by his side, attired in a muslin gown designed for a Sicilian *fête*, with a border of oak-leaves and laurel enclosing the words "Nelson" and "Brontë". The Mayor and Corporation, "with promptitude which did them credit", shrugged into the irregalia and came to present the Freedom of the town and escort the Admiral to a religious service of thanksgiving. Before he had set out on his journey across a continent suddenly disturbed again by Buonaparte, an officer who had gone to sea at a tender age, and left part of his heart with the *Foudroyant*, had faced facts. When blue dusk filled the bottle-end windows of a cosy sea-port hostelry, outside which muskets crackled and bonfires spluttered, two letters in his hand were already in the post. He had written to the Secretary to the Admiralty announcing his health perfectly restored and his desire to serve immediately. "I trust that my necessary journey, by land, from the Mediterranean, will not be considered as a wish to be a moment out of active service."

His second letter was addressed to "Lady Nelson, Roundwood, Ipswich, Suffolk.

"My dear Fanny,   Nov. 6th, 1800.

We are at this moment arriv'd and the post only allows me to say that we shall set off tomorrow noon, and be with you on Saturday, to dinner. I have only had time to open one of your letters, my visits are so numerous. May God bless you and my Dear Father, and believe me ever, your affectionate
                                        "Brontë Nelson of the Nile.
"Sir [sic] and Lady Hamilton beg their best regards and will accept your offer of a bed. Mrs. Cadogan and Miss Knight with all the servants, will proceed to Colchester.
"I beg my Dear Father to be assured of my Duty and every tender feeling of a son."

4

Next morning, an unheralded corps of cavalry drew up outside the inn in which the Admiral had spent the night, and escorted him, not only to the town's end, but to the boundary of the county. Ipswich was equally ready with improvised compliments, and in Colchester the streets had been lined ever since the news of his arrival in Yarmouth had become known; but when the carriage containing Lord Nelson and his friends made a short détour in the neighbourhood of Ipswich, on a late autumn afternoon of heavy clouds enlivened by occasional lightning, no one in the party had any expectation of enjoying more than a private welcome that night. His attempt to show hospitality to the Hamiltons at his small country house, however, was a failure. At Roundwood silence reigned, and it presently became known that Lord Nelson's father, who had been living there alone, had left early on Friday morning to join her ladyship in Town. Letters for Lady Nelson were being forwarded to 64, Upper Seymour Street, Portman Square. It was true that, in his letter from Vienna, the Admiral had told his lady not to attempt to come to Portsmouth, but to be ready to greet him in the house which Davison was taking for them; but this address could not mean that she had obeyed those instructions, as he had particularly told Davison to avoid the Portman Square district. The carriage bringing Nelson home turned away down the short drive from a house in which he had never spent a night and was never to see again, and the journey to London was resumed by easy stages.

He met his wife and father, eventually, in the hall of Nerot's Hotel, 17, King Street, St. James's, at 3 o'clock on the afternoon of Sunday, November 9, to the accompaniment of a thunderstorm.

The worst storm since 1703 had been threatening ever since he had landed, and the tempest broke over London when he was two hours short of the capital. Several members of suburban congregations, returning from Sunday morning service, were killed by falling masonry, and outside Kensington Palace trees were torn up by their roots. After a few days came country tales of drowned infants and cattle, and even a casualty list from Paris.

"The Arrival of Lord Nelson and Sir William Hamilton" was a heading likely to sell many copies of a journal, and one had printed in full, on Saturday morning, "Miss Knight's clever song" the "Ode to Lady Hamilton on her Birthday", boldly substituting "Emma" for the discreet "Delia" of the original. A reporter from the *Courier* was on the spot when "Sir William Hamilton's German travelling carriage" ended its long journey at last, in a dark, narrow street, amongst huzzas from drenched admirers. He noted that Lord Nelson (looking extremely well) was wearing full uniform, two medals and two stars, and that although both the Admiral and the ex-Ambassador were thin in person, "Lady Hamilton looked charmingly, and is a very fine woman". A black female, attendant upon Lady Hamilton, followed the party into the hotel, and ten minutes later the Duke of Queensberry, to enquire for Sir William Hamilton, was announced. The Honourable Charles Greville, nephew to Sir William, had called earlier, on the same errand. The Nelsons and Hamiltons dined together at 5 o'clock, and at 7.30 the vigil of a damp but dogged gentleman of the Press was over for the day. Lord Nelson had left the hotel for the Admiralty, to report to the First Lord, followed after a short interval, in a separate carriage, by Lady Nelson, bound, it was hazarded, for a friendly hour with Lady Spencer.

In Albemarle Street, meanwhile, unnoticed by any reporter, the burly and concerned figure of Sir Thomas Troubridge was approaching a "family" hotel, in which Miss Cornelia Knight had just dined with Mrs. Cadogan. The Commodore, who was on his way to take up his appointment as Captain of the Channel Fleet, under the command of Lord St. Vincent, had come to suggest to a spinster lady that she had better dissociate herself from the Hamilton party immediately.

On the same evening Lord St. Vincent was writing to the Secretary of the Admiralty, from a west-country house:

"It is evident from Lord Nelson's letter to you on his landing, that he is doubtful of the propriety of his conduct. I have no doubt he is pledged to getting Lady H. received at St. James's, and everywhere, and that he will get into much *brouillerie* about it. Troubridge says Lord Spencer talks of putting him in a two-decked ship. If he does, he cannot give him a separate command, for he cannot bear confinement to any object; he is a partisan; his ship always in the most dreadful disorder, and never can become an officer fit to be placed where I am. . . ."

All through the night of Nelson's arrival at a close, fashionable hotel of St. James's distant thunder growled and winds sighed. It appears that the Admiral had an awful homecoming in every sense. Two brief notes from his saintly father, announcing to other members of the family the safe arrival of the hero, breathe joy tempered by bewilderment. Lady Nelson had, with her own eyes, begun to appreciate what she called "the wonderful change, past belief". Her husband's own pen had informed her of his boundless admiration for another man's wife. Gradually, after his triumphal return to Naples from the Nile, he had become a perfunctory correspondent. A letter in which he had been mad enough to tell her of the marvellous "improvement" wrought in her rough and mannerless son by Lady Hamilton had been angrily annotated by a doting mother. He had arrived after long delay, involving professional reprimand, in the company of an enchantress of doubtful antecedents, and beyond doubt displaying every symptom of a man in the condition generally known as "madly in love". A delicate lady, who would have been at home in the pages of a novel by Miss Austen, found herself called upon to play a part in a tragedy in the style of Shakespeare's "dark period". For as long as possible Lord St. Vincent had tried to pass off lightly a sad state of affairs. Unhappily attempting the character of the man of the world, he had admitted that "the Almighty had been in a glorious mood when he had formed Emma", and alluded to the couple as "a pair of sentimental fools". Devoted officers of the Mediterranean squadron had been amazed by, and naturally had not much relished, the spectacle of their Chief with his Famous Woman in tow, behaving with all the ingenuous-ness of a lad in his first affair, changing colour like a maiden when she sang of his victories, and confiding to all and sundry praises of her enormous kindness, angelic nature and brilliant understanding. Some of those who loved him best protested to the last that a devotion so openly expressed was innocent, and were persuaded that "the attraction between her and our hero was something of a kindred enthusiasm in the cause of their Country", but by the time of his arrival in London the cynics had no doubt that the struggle between love and duty was over, and they were right, though they much under-estimated its violence and duration. It had lasted from September 1798 until February 1800. "Ah! my dear friend," he wrote a year later, "I did well remember the 12th February, and also the two months afterwards. I never shall forget them and never be sorry for the consequences."

The time had now come when all persons important to him had to make up their minds that the situation was serious, and they were beholding, not a preternaturally drawn-out Mediterranean *amour-ette*, but a passion which would be remembered with the name of Nelson. Hugh Elliot, at Dresden, had not been wide of the mark when he slightingly referred to "Antony and Moll-Cleopatra", but at the time hardly any spectator of events realised this. There is no satisfactory contemporary authority for the often-repeated state-ment that "Lady Nelson's reception of her husband was extremely cold and mortifying", but that their remaining few weeks together were miserable is borne out by his outburst to Davison in the following March, "sooner than live the unhappy life I did when last I came to England, I would stay abroad for ever". Lady Ham-ilton, for her part, was soon confiding in Mrs. William Nelson (with whom she formed one of her "friendships at first sight" scorned by Mrs. St. George) that on meeting the terrified glare of

Nelson's wife "their [*sic*] was an antipathy not to be described".

The Hamiltons had been invited by the millionaire William Beckford (whose wife, Lady Margaret Gordon, had been a cousin of Sir William) to consider his house, 22, Grosvenor Square, their own. Having discovered that Beckford really meant this, Sir William, who was now more than £2,000 in debt to Nelson, gratefully moved from Nerot's. The house taken by Davison for Nelson was 17, Dover Street, and Davison had interpreted his friend's instructions liberally, for he had taken the house for a year, and though it was not small, he had staffed it so amply that the astonished Rector commented, "The Suite of nobility is long." He found his son "active and well, but always on the wing. I myself can only see him for a moment. He has asked for employment."

Although they were no longer under the same roof, the Nelsons and Hamiltons met daily, and since the situation, agonising to Lady Nelson, was *piquante*, reporters chronicled every appearance of the family party. In any case, the arrival of Nelson had been a godsend to the Press of a capital disturbed by bread riots, and his movements from the moment that he landed can be traced from many sources. November 9th was a Sunday, therefore the festivities of Lord Mayor's Day were transferred to the 10th. On the Monday morning following the Great Storm Sir William sought out Lord Grenville at the Foreign Office, and Nelson, after reporting at the Admiralty, repaired to the Navy Office in the Strand, in which neighbourhood he was recognised and mobbed. Davison's carriage rescued him for a private expedition. They went together to a large dog shop in Holborn, and it appears that a dog of strong personality captured the imagination of an officer who had never before been commanded to make such a purchase, for "poor Nile", although provided with a silver collar announcing that he was "Nileus", the property of the Right Hon. Lord Nelson, strayed, or was stolen, within six weeks. Advising Lady Hamilton as to a further companion, Nelson suggested that a less active dog might be more amenable to London life. He could not describe his unlucky choice as "a domestic animal". He went on to watch the procession of peers to the House of Lords from the Duke of Clarence's apartments, and later that winter's day was guest of honour at the Lord

Mayor's Banquet. His carriage was dragged by the populace from Ludgate Hill to the Guildhall doors, where seamen had been admitted to a prominent position by an affected mob. "The illustrious Tar, landing from his carriage", shook several "old Agamemnons" warmly by the hand, and displayed unerring memory for names and services. A pompous scene followed, at which gold plate and show fruit were lit by the soft glow of many candles, while London fog settled outside. Nelson's reply to the oration of the City Chamberlain was brief, but having been conducted to his station under a triumphal arch, he "hoisted the sword of the value of two hundred guineas" voted to him by the City, and promised that he hoped soon to use it, to reduce to due limits Britain's implacable and inveterate enemy.

John Bull was vociferous, but the Press had provocatively announced that morning that Lady Hamilton, who was a Woman of the Bedchamber to the Queen of Naples and had been decorated by the Czar, was to be presented at the next drawing-room, while, in fact, the only member of the royal family to express any desire to behold her was the Prince of Wales. Their Majesties, who had been adamant on Sir William's marriage, had issued no such command, and Sir William, to Nelson's dismay, was resignedly prepared to make his bow alone, at a Court which would never countenance his wife—"and such a wife!" Accordingly, on the morning following the Lord Mayor's Banquet, Sir William Hamilton, on his return from the Court of Naples, and Baron Nelson of the Nile and Burnham Thorpe, upon striking his flag in the Mediterranean, attended a *levée*. At St. James's Palace the scene was unchanged, but the King, after a curtly expressed hope that his health was improved, turned from the Victor of the Nile without waiting for his answer, and engaged in nearly half an hour's earnest conversation with a military officer. "It could not be", wrote Collingwood furiously from Cawsand Bay, "about *his* successes."

Nelson, after this experience, arrived to dine at Admiralty House looking like thunder. Lady Spencer's duty dinner-parties had never been renowned for their conviviality, and in November 1800, guests at her board were being rousingly presented with the choice of a potato or rice in lieu of the staff of life. On the last occasion that she had entertained the Nelsons, the Lady of the Admiralty had been ruffled by a homely request that a husband might sit next to his wife. After this evening she announced, "Such a contrast I never beheld!" At table, according to her spirited description, Lady Nelson, "perhaps inadvisedly, but with good intention", pushed across to her lord a wine-glass filled with walnuts, which she had attentively peeled for a one-armed man. He thrust it aside so awkwardly that it hit a dish. Lady Spencer remained mistress of herself, though china fell, but Lady Nelson burst into tears, and afterwards, in a stately and frigid drawing-room, while the gentlemen in the adjoining dining-room settled to their wine and talk, "she told me how she was situated". Lady Nelson's reserve broke seldom, but the wife of an officer applying for employment could not have chosen a more disastrous scene or *confidante*, for the tongue of Lady Spencer, a high-priestess of the conventions, was dreaded even by her *débutante* nieces. It may have been upon the Nelsons' homecoming together, after this dreadful entertainment, that an incident gloatingly described by Harrison took place, and the Admiral "in a state of absolute despair and distraction" set out on foot, alone, to spend the remainder of the night wandering the streets of London. "He rambled as far as the city; perambulated Fleet Market, Blackfriars Bridge, etc., and, exhausted with fatigue, as well as overpowered by mental suffering, reached the house of Sir William Hamilton in Grosvenor Square about four in the morning." Harrison claims that the ex-Ambassador suggested to his unexpected guest "to seek that happiness in his professional pursuits which it seemed unlikely he would ever find at home." Meanwhile, as far as the world could see, the Admiral was enjoying the pleasures of leave.

Davison gave a banquet in honour of his celebrated friend at his mansion in St. James's Square, where every delicacy of the season was served up, and the other guests were the Prince of Wales, five Cabinet Ministers (headed by Mr. Pitt), the First Lord and a couple of Admirals. The East India Company feasted Lord Nelson at the London Tavern. It was known that he was sitting to Mrs. Damer, the aristocratic sculptress, for a bust to be placed in the Guildhall. On December 8 he sat to an artist called De Koster for a little sketch, of which engravings were soon on sale at Brydon's, the printseller most affected by him.

On the 20th he took his seat in the House of Peers, and after a dinner and concert given on the following night by the Hamiltons in Grosvenor Square, at which minor royalty were present, Lady Nelson was reported slightly indisposed; but she was at her post again four days later, to witness Kemble as Rolla in "Pizarro" at Drury Lane. An announcement that Lord Nelson had taken seats had filled the house to suffocation, and when his party entered the stage box at 6.10, it was eagerly scanned. It comprised his father and wife, the Hamiltons and the Neapolitan Princess Castelcicala. Lady Nelson was dressed in purple satin, with white sleeves and a turban with two upstanding ostrich plumes. Lady Hamilton's classic draperies were all white. Lord Nelson clapped Rolla heartily during the first act, and Mr. Kemble, playing up to a great house, over-reached himself. ("The pantaloons were cut through and the knee bled profusely.") During the second act, at the conclusion of the scene in which Rolla and Elvira plan the death of Alonzo, a scream from the stage box threw the house into confusion. Lady Nelson had shrieked and fainted. Her father-in-law and Lady Hamilton took her home, but her husband saw the piece out. She made her last publicly recorded appearance in his company a few days later, when they drove down together with the Hamiltons (who were bound upon a week-end visit) to dine with Lord Abercorn at his Stanmore villa. Nelson set out with his friends for a mock-Gothic Yuletide at Beckford's Wiltshire country seat, but without his lady. The invitation to a national hero from an admirer who pronounced himself "dead to the world in general", but still "a genuine Briton", had reached him via Lady Hamilton, and had not included his wife.

At Salisbury, on a very foggy day, he received the freedom of that city, enclosed in a box of Heart of Oak, and amongst the crowd outside the Council House recognised old shipmates, one of whom had actually assisted at his amputation. The people of a cathedral city, even before learning that the Mayor had been presented with a very liberal benefaction for the poor of their town, decided that "Lord Nelson unites a feeling and generous heart, a quick discernment of occasion, and popularity of manners." Mounted volunteers, with a band of thirty playing "Rule, Britannia", led his carriage at a processional pace through the park of Fonthill to its grand entry, where Beckford stood posed under a tower 278 feet high, in a marble hall, surrounded by local gentry and Londoners of distinction, including Mr. Wyatt the architect, and Mr. West, President of the Royal Academy. For three days of poor weather a large house-party enjoyed the splendours of a modern palace, built at a cost of a quarter of a million derived from West India property, and the brilliant conversation of a spoilt man.

On the 26th, amidst the first snow of the season, the party broke up, the Hamiltons to return to Grosvenor Square until their new purchase, No. 23, Piccadilly, was ready to receive them, and Nelson to 17, Dover Street. The London in which his wife and father had spent Christmas without him had been, by all accounts, unrelievedly gloomy. Miss Knight, who had been accustomed upon the Continent to hear the English capital acclaimed as the most flourishing and potent in Europe, had been horrified by the shortness and darkness of London days, and by fashionables who spoke of "the impossibility of going on", and their desire for peace at almost any price. She had withdrawn from all connection with the Nelson and Hamilton circle, and for a month past had steadily refused invitations to Grosvenor Square. Princess Castelcicala, realising that her English acquaintances were *mal vus* at the Court of their native land, was following suit. In Naples and Palermo it had been indulgently accepted that both the British Ambassador and his lady were "bewitched by the gallant Admiral", but in London not only the Press was busy with the names of Nelson and Hamilton. James Gillray, the caricaturist, whose sketches, exhibited in Mrs. Humphrey's print shop in St. James's Street, always gathered a crowd, and who had produced a very complimentary cartoon of the Hero of the Nile two years past, was again at work, and in his most brutal vein. His first comment upon a *ménage* which was attracting criticism, published on February 6, 1801, and labelled "Dido in Despair", depicted a lady of mountainous figure lamenting with outstretched arms and large tears the departure of a fleet, visible through the open window of a bedroom littered with classic busts and unpaid bills, in which a night-capped septuagenarian still slumbered. Below this sketch ran the doggerel verse :

> "Ah; where, and oh! where is my gallant sailor gone?
> He's gone to fight the French for George upon the throne.
> He's gone to fight the French, t'lose t'other arm and eye,
> And left me with old Antiquity, to lay me down and cry."

A companion picture, published six days later, and called "Cognoscenti contemplating the Beauties of the Antique", represented Sir William, senile and slippered, peering through his spectacles in a gallery where the exhibits included likenesses of himself as Claudius and of his lady as the Serpent of the old Nile, pledging her Antony in a bumper.

At 5 a.m. on the first Saturday of the New Year Nelson arose in the lowest of spirits to struggle into uniform by artificial light before embarking for the parish church of Addington, Kent. "I will assuredly attend the remains in my own carriage." He left his house wishing the funeral could have been his own. A note was sent to Grosvenor Square, saying that he hoped to call that night, and the redundant staff of Dover Street were notified that his lordship would not be home to supper. The death of his old sea-daddy had not been unexpected. Judging by Lady Nelson's accounts, Captain Locker had been failing for some time. Indeed, it had been almost a relief to her when the old gentleman had ceased to call, to desire her to say everything that was affectionate and kind on his behalf to Admiral Nelson, always coupled with the explanation that although he still had his legs, he could not use his hand to write nowadays.

5

Nelson, whose promotion to Vice-Admiral of the Blue had been gazetted on New Year's Day, 1801, had known since mid-November that he was to be employed again, and "mine will not, I hope," he wrote bitterly to Berry, "be an *inactive* service". The word repeated in Lord Spencer's letters of reproof received by him at Leghorn had not been forgotten. Ball, notifying him of the fall of Valetta, told him that the Mediterranean Fleet much hoped for his appointment in succession to Lord Keith, who was said to have quarrelled with their Lordships and asked to be recalled; but Nelson knew that second-in-command of the Channel Fleet was his probable fate. Hardy was to be his Captain, and St. Vincent, from Torbay, told him that the *San Josef* had long been in his eye as the most appropriate ship for the officer who had boarded her on Valentine's Day. There was at the moment an additional awkwardness in the prospect of serving under his old Chief, for their respective agents were still engaged in a long-drawn-out tussle on the subject of prize-money. The solicitors employed by Davison on his friend's behalf were Messrs. Booth and Haslewood of Craven Street, and on a morning shortly before Nelson left London, one of the partners of that firm was invited to the breakfast-table of a man whose days were overcrowded with appointments. Mr. William Haslewood was the witness of a painful scene in which Lady Nelson, upon her husband mentioning something said or done by Lady Hamilton, suddenly rose from her seat and burst forth, "I am sick of hearing of dear Lady Hamilton, and am resolved that you shall give up either her or me!" Her manner was very vehement, but his attorney noted with approval:

"Lord Nelson, with perfect calmness, said, 'Take care, Fanny, what you say. I love you sincerely, but I cannot forget my obligations to Lady Hamilton, or speak of her otherwise than with affection and admiration.' Without one soothing word or gesture, but muttering something about her mind being made up, Lady Nelson left the room, and shortly after drove from the house. They never lived together afterwards. I believe that Lord Nelson took a formal leave of her ladyship before joining the Fleet, under Sir Hyde Parker ; but that, to the day of her husband's death, she never made any apology for her abrupt and ungentle conduct above related, or any overture towards a reconciliation."

The details of an anecdote recollected forty-five years later are inaccurate, but that a husband and wife who were not to meet again parted on January 13, after an unhappy scene, is certain. It is equally certain that neither as yet guessed that they had said their last farewell. Roundwood, in which Nelson had never spent a night, had been disposed of, to a Mr. Robert Fuller, before the Old Year was out. The Rector wrote to his daughter Kitty, on January 9, that "as things are now circumstanced", he expected to leave for Bath soon after his son's departure, but made no mention of his daughter-in-law's intentions. Nelson's last words to his wife were, according to her testimony, "I call God to witness, there is nothing in you, or your conduct, I wish otherwise." His four lines, written the same night, ran:

"Southampton,
"January 13th, 1801.

"My dear Fanny,

"We are arrived and heartily tired; and with kindest regards to my father and all the family, believe me, your affectionate

"Nelson."

He left her in the Dover Street house, which had been taken for a year, and before leaving London he had instructed his agents to pay £400 into her account. Whether a copy of the following undated and unsigned letter was ever despatched by Lady Nelson is not to be discovered:

"My dearest Husband,

"Your generosity and tenderness were never more strongly shewn than your writing to Mr. Marsh yesterday morning for the payment of your very handsome quarterly allowance, which far exceeded my expectations. Knowing your income, and had you left it to me, I cou'd not in conscience have said so much. Accept my warmest, my most affectionate and grateful thanks. I could say more, but my heart is too full. Be assured every wish, every desire of mine is to please the man whose affection constitutes my happiness. God bless my dear husband. . . ."

Nelson found his Commander-in-Chief so cheerful that he guessed him to be "riding post for something good", and he had hardly entered when the arrival of a letter from Sir Hyde Parker gave their conversation a confidential and highly interesting turn. They parted next morning without a word having been said on the subject of prize-money, so Nelson was not compelled to bring into action "a broadside, as strong (and backed with justice) as any he can send". His carriage rattled over the cobbles of Plymouth dock-yard with dusk on January 17, and when his flag was hoisted, blue at the fore, in the *San Josef*, it was cheered by the whole fleet. Hardy reported that as far as he was concerned, the ship was ready for sea, but the dockyard had not nearly done with her. The Admiral's cabin was not finished, not even painted yet. Hardy's, however, had been vacated, and contained two splendid easy-chairs of green morocco and mahogany, designed by Messrs. Foxhall and Fryer, who worked for Beckford at Fonthill. The chairs had side pockets into which a one-armed man might slip documents; a pad on the right arm had been provided, and the bill was £20. Lady Hamilton was thanked for her thoughtful choice, but Lady Nelson's efforts had been more than usually ineffective, and "a letter of truths about my outfit" was despatched to that withdrawn figure. Hardy, the ideal Flag-Captain, never in the way and never out of it, proceeded silently to take an unframed portrait of Lady Hamilton to the carpenter's shop, and the people of the dockyard, who had not believed that Admiral Nelson would want to go to sea until the winter was more worn away, suddenly became all bustle. His statement that he wished to get the *San Josef* alongside the Commander-in-Chief's flagship in Torbay within seven days (coupled with a mention that she would be the finest ship in the world) had produced a wonderful effect.

From newspapers which published the fact on January 24 her husband learnt that Lady Nelson had left London for Brighton, and also that Mr. Davison was taking the lease of a fine London mansion for Lord and Lady Nelson. His comment as he sat watching deep snow on Plymouth roofs was, "Let her go to Briton [*sic*] or where she pleases. I care not", and that if she was to take Shelburne House, "I am not, thank God, forced to live in it".

He had heard, four days past, that Lady Hamilton was alleging "a very serious cold", and since he believed that he would be in Torbay before the 26th, he had told her to address all further letters to Brixham. Almost frantic himself, he urged her, against his own belief, "Keep up your spirits, all will end well. . . ." Letters redirected from Brixham began to arrive, but when he sailed for Torbay at last, in the teeth of a south-westerly gale, on January 31, he had received nothing dated later than the 27th.

6

The *San Josef* anchored in Torbay early on the morning of February 1, and Nelson went at once to report to St. Vincent at Torre Abbey. From the first moment all the news that wild Sunday morning was good. An order was awaiting him to transfer his flag to the *St. George*, a three-decker, of lighter draught than the *San*

Josef, and therefore considered more suitable for Baltic service. The First Lord had settled that he was "to go forth as the Champion of England in the North". The expedition foreshadowed by Sir Hyde Parker had been decided upon, with Nelson as second-in-command, but he was not to lose "my *San Josef*". She was to be held for his return, which he believed would be within a few weeks, after which he hoped to be given the chance of another knock at his chosen foe, republican France. He had to acknowledge that their Lordships had behaved handsomely in this instance, and that his prospects "could not be better".

He got the letter from London for which he had been waiting, on his return to the ship. It was blowing fresh, and he had been two hours pulling from Lord St. Vincent's house. When he had mastered the contents of a mysteriously worded message, he burnt it, with the exception of two lines which he cut out, and meant to keep for ever. The child begotten in the *Foudroyant* last April was safely and secretly born, and Lady Hamilton was well. He was the father of a daughter. He found himself laughing and crying at once as he tried to offer a prayer of thanks for "this gleam of future comfort". Since he must not show any of his feelings, he thought at first he would go mad. The post was just leaving, so he was obliged to sit down to write immediately, amidst disturbance. Captain Darby, entering the cabin, noticing a newly framed likeness of the famous Emma, and an engrossed figure, waggishly desired his compliments to her ladyship and sent wishes they could see her down here, instead of merely her portrait.

As letters sent by the post were liable to fall into unintended hands, a fictitious couple had been invented. Thompson, or Thomson (for they carelessly spelt his name both ways), was supposed to be a young father in Nelson's ship, on whose behalf he wrote daily to Lady Hamilton (at present kindly looking after "Mrs. Thomson" and their new-born child). An uncle stood in the way of the lovers' marriage. In his letters of the next few days Nelson offered marriage "as soon as possible", as often and contritely as any village lad, and indeed his fancy painted, in one such declaration, a country scene in humble life. "If you was single, and I found you under a hedge, I would instantly marry you." Now that his child was in the world, his mortification that it must be unacknowledged was so enormous that he could not bring himself to mention the fact, and he hastened to do all in his power to repair the damage. "Aye, would to God our fates had been different!" Soon he had brought himself to believe that a union so unlike his marriage, and so promptly fruitful, must have been intended by Heaven and would be blessed by more children, born in wedlock. He harped upon the innocence and probable loveliness of the daughter of "the most beautiful woman of the age". Her baptism occupied his thoughts much, and St. George's, Hanover Square, was his first choice for the ceremony. As the son of a clerical family he was well aware that a private christening, if necessary, could precede a public one, but that the place of birth and names of parents would be demanded in either case. He could only suggest "born at Portsmouth, or at sea", and that he and Lady Hamilton should take the child to church and stand sponsors, before he sailed, stating to the clergyman that both the Thomsons were at the moment "out of the kingdom". From the day that he learnt of her existence, he never failed to send his love and a blessing to "our little girl." As he had not dared to count upon the infant's survival, no names had been chosen. He now hoped for an "Emma", but Lady Hamilton had decided upon "Horatia". A lock of Horatia's hair was put by him into the case containing that of his shadowy mother, and as far as he could judge, the bright colour resembled what he remembered of his own in childhood. His "good eye" was giving him such trouble that he had been driven to consult the Physician to the Fleet, who prescribed an operation as soon as possible, meanwhile, no writing, and green shades. ("Will you, my dear friend, make me one or two?") He took far-sighted measures to provide for mother and child in case of his sudden death. Since a married woman could possess no property, he must ensure that in the event of both Sir William and Lady Hamilton predeceasing his child, her little fortune (which he hoped to make great) should not fall to Sir William's heirs, headed by Greville, described by him as "that other chap" who had used his love "ill enough". In his wilder moments of impatience, he proposed that when he returned from the Baltic, they should fly together to Brontë, and there settle, with Horatia, the world forgetting. But in time of war he was tied to his profession, and Sir William was visibly failing. For the present all he could offer was that they should marry on the death of "Mrs. Thomson's uncle", or on a declaration of peace. Still another "impediment" which he said that God alone could remove remained, for such plans, never very hopefully suggested, presupposed his own freedom, and divorce never entered his calculations. The word never appears in his letters.

His admiration for the woman whom he had considered perfection even before she had become hallowed in his eyes as the mother of his child swelled into lyrical language. His thoughts turned to his favourite playwright, and a paraphrase of Romeo's speech in Capulet's garden—"Good-night, and good-night. I could say it till to-morrow!" On one of the four occasions when he was able to deliver a letter by the hand of a private messenger he gave full vent to his passion. Davison, who had taken the trouble to travel upwards of two hundred miles from his Northumbrian estate in early February, came to Torbay to discuss his friend's impending law-suit with St. Vincent. He had called on Lady Hamilton on his way through London, brought a letter from her, and carried one back with an enclosure. Troubridge and Captain Edward Parker also took charge of packets, of the contents of which they were entirely ignorant. Oliver, the factotum picked up in Vienna, went down to Spithead in March, and carried back a letter which settled for posterity the question of Nelson's relations with Lady Hamilton and the parentage of Horatia.

In one of the Davison letters, Nelson, regretting that duty forbade him to be the bearer, paid characteristic tribute to his "non-pareil". The figure of Elizabeth Tudor, "our Elizabeth, a victorious and high-spirited woman", had early captivated his fancy.

"I know you are so true and loyal an Englishwoman, that you would hate those who would not stand forth in defence of our King, Laws, Religion, and all which is dear to us. It is your sex that makes us go forth, and seem to tell us, 'None but the brave deserve the fair,' and if we fall, we still live in the hearts of those females who are dear to us. It is your sex that rewards us, it is your sex who cherish our memories. And you, my dear honoured friend, are, believe me, the *first*, the best, of your sex. I have been the world around, and in every corner of it, and never yet saw your equal, or even one which could be put in comparison with you."

In the letter carried by Oliver, opening, "Now, my own dear wife, for such you are in my eyes, and in the face of heaven, I can give full scope to my feelings", he proceeded, "I love, I never did love any one else. I never had a dear pledge of love till you gave me one. You, my beloved Emma, and my country, are the two dearest objects of my fond heart—*a heart susceptible and true*. My longing for you, both person and conversation, you may readily imagine. It setts me on fire. . . ." He ended incoherently—"My love, my darling angel, my heaven-given wife, the dearest only true wife of her [*sic*] own till death. . . ." His postscript adjured her —"Kiss and bless *our* dear Horatia—think of that!"

7

He had no notion, when he thanked God that his *non-pareil* had never borne a child to anyone else, that a younger Emma, the result of a very early indiscretion, was already nineteen. Greville's cynical suggestion for the future of a snub-nosed, low-statured young woman who spoke with a bad accent and showed no signs of any but rural origin and upbringing had been—"a little money might be an inducement for a clergyman to marry her, and then I could help him on; but if she does not make an impression on a good sort of man, I am sure I cannot find one for her". Nelson, when he heard, in the autumn of 1801, that Sir William objected to his lady entertaining her connections, the Connors, at 23, Piccadilly, at once offered the hospitality of his own country house, and added, "I hope, Emma, you take care of your relative; when you can get her well-married and settled, we will try and give her something." Five Miss Connors, including the Sarah to whom his words probably refer, came, but there is no evidence that he was ever told that "Emma Connor" was half-sister to his own child. Sir William had not known of her existence until Greville, infuriated by the news of his uncle's marriage, had forwarded the pathetic bills for her keep.

The weather in which Nelson's Torbay letters were written suited their matter. "My dear amiable friend, could you have seen the boat leave the ship, I am sure your heart would have sunk within you." Sometimes for two and three days together it was impossible to send a boat ashore, either to send or receive the post.

The sea came over the *San Josef's* forecastle, and in the Admiral's after-cabin the motion was so great that he could not sit. But "a miserable fellow, shut up in wood", thanking Providence, "who keeps a look out for Poor Jack", that his ship had new cables, still swore himself, "in fair or foul weather, at sea or on shore, for ever yours".

Too often during the gales of this new year neither the writing nor receipt of his love-letters brought anything but misery. A usual accompaniment of illicit passion was driving him to the borders of insanity, both just before and for many weeks after the birth of his child. Jealousy, of the strength observed by Shakespeare before he drew the characters of Leontes and Othello, put him on the rack and brought him almost to a condition of trance. Since the woman whom he could not claim as wife professed herself equally untrusting, the situation was degrading, and both images suffered distortion. His fears, which were reasonable, though unreasonably expressed, centred around the figure of the Prince of Wales, who had idly told a circle, which had hastened to repeat it, "how Lady Hamilton had hit his fancy". After a few efforts to dine in Sir William Hamilton's house *en famille*, discouraged by Sir William's lady at her lover's command, a royal personage unaccustomed to rebuffs troubled no more. Lady Hamilton's fears included all women, and imposed refusal of all invitations at which any might be encountered, and, to satisfy her, her lover disparaged any whom he might chance to meet.

The diction of Nelson's love-letters of these weeks is unmistakably that of the early nineteenth century, but the cadence, especially of those which he believed would be instantly burnt after being delivered by hand, is that of the passionate lover of all time. He scribbled them late every night, after the day's interruptions had ceased, and he set down everything that came into his head.

8

At 7 a.m. on the morning of Tuesday, February 24, 1801, a carriage which had travelled through the night drew up at 23, Piccadilly, one of the smaller houses overlooking the Green Park. Nelson's three days' leave in London passed unnoticed by the Press.

Throughout his stay the Park was crowded by the equipages of loyal subjects, all bent in one direction. The King, who had caught cold in chapel on the 15th, was now unconscious. A Regency seemed inevitable, the accession of George IV, at any moment, a dreadful possibility. That the monarch had suffered a return of his "old disorder", brought on by the worry and excitement of a change of Government, caused more grief than surprise, but the rock upon which Pitt had foundered was unexpected. The man who had long been pressing the more vigorous prosecution of a war of which his country was tired had been unable to satisfy his sovereign on the subject of Catholic Emancipation. Personal encounter with the statesman who had been Nelson's idol in the days when he had nourished political aspirations had not developed into friendship, and two characters so diverse were never to approach intimacy; nevertheless, he had been heartily sorry to hear that Mr. Pitt was "out", because "I think him the greatest Minister this country ever had and the honestest man". The change also interested him professionally, for under the leadership of the late Speaker, Mr. Addington, Lord St. Vincent had succeeded Lord Spencer, and Troubridge had become a Lord of the Admiralty. The appointment of two such resolute officers at a moment when Great Britain's command of the sea was her only cause for congratulation had been popular, but a very general opinion of the new Government had been neatly expressed by the member for Calne. "They have got up the 'Beggar's Opera' without Macheath." London, in February 1801, was not a cheerful city. An expedition under Sir Ralph Abercromby should have arrived in Egypt by now, but nothing was known of its progress. The news from the Continent was all deplorable. Paris was celebrating, with a Grand Fête organised by the brother of the First Consul, the treaty between France and Austria signed at Lunéville on the 9th. From Vienna, Lord Minto, who had looked upon Pitt as "the Atlas of our reeling Globe", had sadly written to Lord Grenville asking for his letters of recall. The Neapolitan Government had bound itself to close its ports to British ships and admit French garrisons. Leghorn, Arezzo, Ancona, every restless, sun-baked city in which Nelson had received so noisy a welcome on the first stages of his journey home, was back under Buonaparte's heel, and Portugal, threatened by Spain, was wavering. The First Consul, whom even Nelson still failed to recognise as the sole inspiring figure of a perfectly new alignment of French ambition and enmity, had most successfully courted Paul of Russia. Denmark, Prussia and Sweden had agreed, at the suggestion of the Czar, to revive the "Armed Neutrality of the North"; no new thing, but at the moment particularly agreeable to France. The result might break the blockade of Brest, and must close the Baltic to British trade.

Nelson arrived in London "almost beside himself with expectation". He had little doubt that the result of this leave would be a brother or sister for Horatia. But Lady Hamilton announced herself in health only "so-so", though in spirits, to-day, excellent. A month ago he had written to her as strongly as he dared, advising her to keep her bed for a week at least after her "very severe cold", and to make no attempt to go out of the house for a fortnight. Her dangerous business having been despatched with complete success, a very resilient character, obsessed with the idea of keeping her secret, had over-taxed a remarkable constitution and was now paying the penalty. Three days had seen her not only out of child-bed, but in full dress.

But face to face with "Mrs. Thomson" at last, "poor Thomson" forgot "all his anger, anxiety and sorrows!" His arrival had been unexpected: their time together was short. As he had found his Dover Street house shut up, he had taken rooms at Lothian's Hotel, Albemarle Street. Essential matters were discussed at break-neck speed, between interruptions. He feared that, as a second-in-command, Lord Nelson might be given no scope. "Everybody except you, tears him to pieces." Lady Hamilton stalwartly assured him that he would find "much to do". Her opinion of the Czar was lower than his. . . . Eight weeks should, he hoped, conclude the Baltic campaign (therefore, "Cheer up! fair Emma!"), and then, "Peace in a cottage, with a plain joint of meat, doing good to the poor, and setting an example of virtue, even to king and princes", was his breathlessly expressed theme, in a newly decorated Piccadilly drawing-room. Arrangements in case there should be any discovery of "poor dear Mrs. Thomson's business" during his absence had to be made, and an officer who was about to proceed on active service promised recklessly to be at hand, at need. If her "uncle" persisted in bringing bad characters to his house, she must quit it. A less dramatic plan for inviting Mrs. William Nelson up to London again, to bear her constant company, was originated. "What signifies a few hundred pounds to make your dear mind a little at ease?" When intrusive royalty found that Lady Hamilton was always from home, dining with the Nelsons, Sir William would soon discover that His Royal Highness did not come for the pleasure of his company. But "Reverend Sir", who could be a bore, and his little woman, whose tongue never lay still, must have beef-steak in their own lodgings two or three times a week, for it must never be said that Sir William Hamilton supported the Nelson family.

At the Admiralty Lord Nelson did not neglect to press for a frigate for Captain Nisbet. At Davison's house all his business was confidential. Lady Hamilton had sold her diamonds in order to furnish 23, Piccadilly (which included a Nelson Room), and Sir William was selling some of his best vases and pictures. To her lover's dismay and wrath, he had learnt that amongst the pictures to be put up to public auction was Romney's "Lady Hamilton as St. Cecilia". This cold-blooded and decidedly ignominious procedure revived all his terrors that a husband who could act so would be prepared to sell the original, when a Prince Regent was the bidder. ("Can this be the great Sir William Hamilton?") He entrusted Davison to secure the picture privately and keep it for his return, packed up, without mentioning the transaction or showing it "to any soul breathing".

At some hour during the next two days, the last of the principal objects of Nelson's flying visit to London was accomplished. Lady Hamilton, who had been enabled to pay well, had also chosen well. Mrs. Gibson, of 9, Little Titchfield Street, Marylebone, was beyond doubt a good woman, and a good reason for a widow in reduced circumstances having accepted the sole care of a new-born child of gentle birth whose parents were unknown to her was present in the shape of an attendant figure—a little daughter of her own, "Mary", slightly deformed. A widow who had been a mother herself had remarked that the infant brought to her on a winter's night by "Hond: Lady Hamilton", unattended, in a hackney coach, was not more than eight days old, but whatever questions troubled the brain of a very quiet woman on that winter's morning, as she watched an open-handed, quick-spoken naval gentleman, with one eye and one arm, take more than civil interest in a brother-officer's child, she asked no questions. His unspeakable thoughts were, "A finer child never was produced by any two persons. It was in truth a love-begotten child."

On the third morning of his leave he received orders to embark 600 troops under Lieut-Colonel the Hon. William Stewart and proceed to join Sir Hyde Parker, who had already left London for Yarmouth. He cancelled his room at Lothian's, told Allen to pack and prepared to drive through the night to Spithead. The farewell of a lady renowned for her classical attitudes was interpreted by him as that of the Roman matron, "Return with your shield, or upon it", and his own was, "No fear of death, except of parting from you."

Chapter XIV

1801
(ætat. 42)

COPENHAGEN

I

BY an extraordinary coincidence, the crowned heads of three of the four northern countries banded together in a Confederation directed against Great Britain were insane, and the fourth, Frederick William III of Prussia, was a character so amiably indecisive as to be personally negligible. Prussia had no fleet, but the remaining three allies represented a force double the strength of that which sailed from Yarmouth on March 12, 1801, under the command of an Admiral "a little nervous about dark nights, and fields of ice". In Sweden the great house of Vasa was almost bred out. In Denmark the Crown Prince had long acted as Regent for an imbecile sire. Nelson viewed Paul I as the first enemy to be disposed of, and thought that his lesson should be severe. The trunk being cut down, he foresaw no difficulty in lopping off the branches. His hope, therefore, was to proceed directly to attack the Russian squadron ice-bound at Revel, and the fact that Lord St. Vincent had recommended to him a Captain Thesiger, late of the Russian service, who was sailing with the expedition as a volunteer, seemed to him to augur well. A lightning blow at Russia would have been his advice. But he found himself, as days passed, ostentatiously excluded from conference.

Sir Hyde Parker was a respectable officer, aged sixty-two, who had gone afloat at twelve. He had grown rich during four years in command at Jamaica and had recently married a bride of eighteen, who reminded Lord St. Vincent of batter pudding. It may have been that he had observed expressions of pity mingled with the congratulations of friends when they learnt that he had been provided with a thunderbolt as second-in-command. The arrival of the squadron from Portsmouth had certainly surprised him. The *St. George* had gone to sea in such haste that she had carried her caulkers and painters to St. Helen's. ("If the wind proves fair, they shall be sent up the harbour; if unfair, no time will have been lost.") The appearance of Nelson at Portsmouth had produced more than the usual activity, for on dismounting from his carriage, his lordship had sent for the officer in charge of the military and announced that he meant to sail with the first tide. Colonel Stewart, an ardent young man, had received the intended impression, and the detachments of the 49th and 95th regiments waiting on Southsea Common to be embarked for special service in the North Sea had all been on board their long-attendant transports within two hours.

At Yarmouth, nine days later, Lord Nelson received many thanks from the First Lord for "using the spur", and Sir Hyde Parker an express ordering him to take his fleet to sea. Lady Parker's ball had to be cancelled. Sir Hyde, who on Nelson's courtesy call, accompanied by Hardy, had told him nothing, remained thereafter invisible. At first Nelson merely regretted that this would mean having to go on board his Commander-in-Chief at sea. (His stepson, after observing the humiliating efforts of a one-armed man to go up the side of a ship in blowing weather, had hoped that some day he would slip and break his neck—and the observation had been mischievously repeated, cutting Nelson to the heart.) The newspapers and Yarmouth fisherwomen had said that he was going to the Baltic. The rumour in the fleet was that they were to wait outside Cronenburg while Mr. Drummond, British Minister in Copenhagen, negotiated. ("I disapprove most exceedingly.... Weak in the extreme.... A fleet of British men-of-war are the best negotiators in Europe.") Dommet, the Captain of the Fleet, had apologetically revealed that Sir Hyde had struck his pen through every recommendation made by his second-in-command. Colonel Stewart, already a confirmed admirer, was disgustedly noting "studied neglect" of a hero. (His hundred sharp-shooters were "ready to fire out Paul's right eye".)

The season was the worst in the year for an expedition to the Baltic. The tedious passage of Nelson's squadron from Spithead to Yarmouth had been achieved, in his own words, "blindfold".

Fog, as thick as mud, had been all that was visible from gunport or stern-window, and he had always left the quarter-deck hoary or wet through. As the fleet of eighteen of the line, eleven frigates, and sloops, brigs, cutters, fire-ships and bombs, amounting in all to fifty-three sail, battled its way northwards, the temperature fell, and gentlemen from England, where daffodils had begun to peer, entered upon a second winter. Ice glistened on the rigging, and snowstorms alternated regularly with sleet. On March 15 the violence of the gale caused Lord Nelson in the *St. George* and Captain Fremantle in the *Ganges* to lay aside half-finished letters. The Admiral regretted that in the Great Cabin of his hastily refitted flagship enough draught came through to turn a mill; Fremantle complained that the hacking coughs of his ship's company ceased not day nor night. It was a relief when, early on the 18th, through flying snowflakes, a long, low sandy arm of land became intermittently visible. This was the Skaw, northernmost point of Jutland, last seen by Nelson twenty years past. The fleet, which had been in some measure scattered, collected, and next day turned southwards down the Cattegat. Nelson observed a frigate sent away by the Commander-in-Chief, and guessed that it carried a diplomat bound for Copenhagen. ("I hate your pen and ink men.") On the following morning, so that no attention should be wanting on his part, he paid a further call upon Sir Hyde, and at the end of an hour's conversation had "ground out something". The rumour that negotiation was to be tried first was evidently true, but he could not achieve anything approaching the confidential note which he considered essential as between a Commander-in-Chief and his second. Next evening the fleet anchored eighteen miles from the boasted defences of Cronenburg and Elsinore, and there waited three days, although the wind was now fair for Copenhagen. At last, on the 23rd, Sir Hyde called a council, and Nelson attended in revived spirits. The *St. George* had been cleared for action a week past. Hardy assured him that the ship's company "would do", and "I take the *Ghost's* word". Amongst his efforts to "brush up" strangers had been the importation of a band, borrowed from the Channel Fleet. Before leaving his cabin he scribbled a line to Lady Hamilton. During the passage he had added a codicil to his will, in which he had left her the Sultan's sable pelisse and the Chelengk. "Now we are sure of fighting", he wrote, "I am sent for. When it was a joke I was kept in the background; tomorrow will, I hope, be a proud day for England."

But on board the *London* the atmosphere nothing resembled what he had pictured. Lieutenant Layman, who steered his gig, noted with awe that "all the heads were very gloomy". The mission of Mr. Nicholas Vansittart, in conjunction with Mr. Drummond, had been a failure. The Danes were not only far too frightened of Russia to accede to Great Britain's request for their withdrawal from the Confederation: they were actively hostile. Moreover, the diplomats had returned with dreadful accounts of newly strengthened defences at Elsinore and Copenhagen. When Nelson arrived, a long-faced council had come to the conclusion that to stay in the Cattegat until the united naval force of the Danes, Russians and Swedes came forth to offer battle was the only prudent course.

Colonel Stewart had noticed that when Lord Nelson was highly dissatisfied, he generally gave vent to less than he felt. Nelson now began by questioning the hushed gentlemen from Copenhagen in close detail, not only as to the strength, but as to the position of the enemy. Having gathered that the Danes had placed their strongest ships at the head of their line, he proceeded to consider the possibilities of coming up to take their rear by surprise. This would mean an entry into the Baltic by the Great Belt, which would entail loss of time, a most important factor. However, attack as soon as possible was his advice—"Let it be by the Sound, by the Belt, or any how, only lose not an hour", and his enthusiasm was so infectious, his eloquence so potent, that by the time the council was dismissed an approach to Copenhagen by the Great Belt had been decided upon. He had warmly advised the necessity of disregarding Government instructions in view of an unexpected situation, and in giving farewell to the diplomats who were sailing for England he heartily wished them so slow a passage that the question might have been settled by a victory before they reached London. On his return to his own ship, he addressed himself to his Commander-in-Chief, and next day forwarded probably the ablest letter he ever dictated.

"My dear Sir Hyde,

"The conversation we had yesterday has naturally, from its importance, been the subject of my thoughts; and the more I have reflected, the more I am confirmed in opinion, that not a moment should be lost in attacking the Enemy. They will every day and hour be stronger; we shall never be so good a match for them as at this moment.

"The only consideration in my mind is how to get at them with the least risk to our Ships. By Mr. Vansittart's account, the Danes have taken every means in their power to prevent our getting to attack Copenhagen by the Passage of the Sound. Cronenburg has been strengthened, the Crown Islands fortified, on the outermost of which there are twenty guns pointing mostly downwards, and only eight hundred yards from very formidable batteries placed under the Citadel, supported by five Sail-of-the-Line, seven Floating batteries of fifty guns each, besides Small-craft, Gun-boats &c. &c. And that the Revel Squadron of twelve or fourteen Sail-of-the-Line are soon expected as also five Sail of Swedes.

"It would appear by what you have told me of your instructions, that Government took for granted you would find no difficulty in getting off Copenhagen, and in the event of a failure of negotiation, you might instantly attack; and that there would be scarcely a doubt but the Danish fleet would be destroyed, and the Capital made so hot that Denmark would listen to reason and its true interest. By Mr. Vansittart's account, their state of preparation exceeds what he conceives our Government thought possible, and that the Danish Government is hostile to us in the greatest possible degree.

"Therefore here you are, with almost the safety, certainly with the honour of England more entrusted to you than ever yet fell to any British Officer. On your decision depends, whether our country shall be degraded in the eyes of Europe, or whether she shall rear her head higher than ever: again do I repeat, never did our Country depend so much on the success of any Fleet as on this. How best to honour our Country and abate the pride of her Enemies, by defeating their schemes, must be the subject of your deepest consideration as Commander-in-Chief; and if what I have to offer can be the least useful in forming your decision, you are most heartily welcome.

"I shall begin with supposing you are determined to enter by the Passage of the Sound, as there are those who think, if you leave that Passage open, that the Danish Fleet may sail from Copenhagen, and join the Dutch or French. I own I have no fears on that subject; for it is not likely that whilst their Capital is menaced with an attack, 9,000 of her best men should be sent out of the Kingdom. I suppose that some damage may arise amongst our masts and yards; yet, perhaps there will not be one of them but could be made serviceable again. You are now about Cronenburg: if the wind be fair, and you determine to attack the Ships and Crown Islands, you must expect the natural issue of such a battle—Ships crippled, and perhaps one or two lost; for the wind which carries you in, will most probably not bring out a crippled Ship. This mode I call taking the bull by the horns. It, however, will not prevent the Revel Ships, or Swedes, from joining the Danes; and to prevent this from taking effect, is in my humble opinion, a measure absolutely necessary—and still to attack Copenhagen.

"Two modes are in my view; one to pass Cronenburg, taking the risk of damage, and to pass up the deepest and straightest Channel above the Middle Grounds; and coming down the Garbar or King's Channel, to attack their Floating batteries &c. &c. as we find it convenient. It must have the effect of preventing a junction between the Russians, Swedes and Danes, and may give us an opportunity of bombarding Copenhagen. I am also pretty certain that a passage could be found to the northward of Southholm for all our Ships; perhaps it might be necessary to warp a short distance in the very narrow part.

"Should this mode of attack be ineligible, the passage of the Belt, I have no doubt, would be accomplished in four or five days, and then the attack by Draco could be carried into effect, and the junction of the Russians prevented, with every probability of success against the Danish Floating batteries. What effect a bombardment might have, I am not called upon to give an opinion; but think the way should be cleared for the trial.

"Supposing us through the Belt, with the wind first westerly, would it not be possible to either go with the Fleet, or detach ten Ships of three and two decks, with one Bomb and two Fire-ships, to Revel, to destroy the Russian Squadron at that place? I do not see the great risk of such a detachment, and with the remainder to attempt the business at Copenhagen. The measure may be thought bold, but I am of opinion the boldest measures are the safest; and our Country demands a most vigorous exertion of her force, directed with judgment. In supporting you, my dear Sir Hyde, through the arduous and important task you have undertaken, no exertion of head or heart shall be wanting from your most obedient and faithful servant,

"Nelson and Brontë."

Communications in 1801 were slow. As this letter was being carried from the *St. George* to the *London*, off Elsinore, on the night of March 24, a party of Russian officials, mostly in, or dismissed from, the Imperial service, were advancing through the streets of St. Petersburg upon the Mikhailovsky Palace. The night was calm but moonless. All the gentlemen had dined over-well. By the time that a British fleet bent upon the Battle of Copenhagen, as a preliminary to the defeat of the Northern Confederation, had weighed and turned for the Great Belt, Paul I had been strangled, and his large and visionary son, whose tendencies were anti-French, was giving audience to his father's murderers, headed by Counts Pannin and Pahlen. But since communications were slow, Nelson did not learn of "the death of Paul" for three weeks.

2

On March 25 it blew too hard for men-of-war to lift their anchors. Next morning, after a few hours' progress in the direction of the Great Belt, the fleet was brought to, and orders were issued for a return towards the Sound. Sir Hyde's Flag-Captain, Otway, was sent to apprise his second-in-command of the reasons. Nelson's unofficial reply was," I don't care a d—n which passage we go, so that we fight them." But Sir Hyde now found it necessary to send a message to Governor Stricker, of Elsinore, enquiring his intentions if a British fleet were to pass the Sound, and two officers from Copenhagen (the younger an aide-de-camp of the Regent) came on board the *London* in defiant mood. While writing a note in Sir Hyde's Great Cabin, the younger soldier called out, "Admiral, if your guns are no better than your pens, you may as well return to England." He was very curious to hear who commanded the various ships, and the name of Lord Nelson startled him. ("What, is he here? I would give a hundred guineas to see him! Then, I suppose it is no joke, if he is come!") Governor Stricker's reply, of course, was that he could not suffer a fleet whose intentions were not known to pass Cronenburg, and this was interpreted by Sir Hyde as a declaration of war. For a further three days, then, head winds and calms detained the fleet six miles from Cronenburg. Meanwhile, Nelson's general scheme for an attack on Copenhagen having been provisionally adopted, he made a complete change of personal plans. He must leave the *St. George* for a lighter ship. His choice was H.M.S. *Elephant*, a 74, commanded by the omniscient Foley, who had led the victors of the Nile inside the French line in Aboukir Bay. On the 30th, the wind coming fair, the fleet again weighed, and drew towards "the fancied tremendous fortress of Cronenburg". This landmark was a four-square mediæval pile, crowned by turrets of unfamiliar design, likely to remind English observers that they were now approaching Scandinavia and Russia. The passage through the narrows was achieved in perfect order and with surprising ease, for, finding that the Swedes did not open fire from Helsingborg, the stately flotilla kept close to the Swedish coast, and clear of the Danish guns, which blazed away ineffectively. The *Elephant* did not even trouble to reply.

During that afternoon Nelson at last came in sight of Copenhagen. Eighteen days had passed since he had sailed from Yarmouth. If he had been in command, he would have been attacking the Danish capital in eight. The fleet anchored some five miles below the city, and Sir Hyde, Nelson and a party of senior officers at once embarked in the *Skylark* lugger, to reconnoitre the harbour and channels. It was soon apparent that their delay had been most obliging to the enemy, and that the accounts of Messrs. Drummond and Vansittart had erred, if anything, on the side of understatement. The Trekroner (Three Crowns) battery had been admirably strengthened, and all buoys of the North and King's Channels had been removed or misplaced.

In the *Elephant*, the Scottish Principal Medical Officer, up late, was disturbed at grim preparations by the sound of a gig coming alongside. He recognised, amongst the cloaked figures who had been out amongst floating ice-blocks during the hours of darkness, the officer whom he had already accepted as "the first man in the world". Presently "light showed me a path which had been trackless". Under the personal supervision of Nelson, British masters and pilots had begun to place the buoys necessary to guide his squadron to the attack.

Nelson's opinion of the Danish line of defence was: "It looks formidable to those who are children at War, but to my judgment, with ten sail-of-the-line I think I can annihilate them; at all events, I hope to be allowed to try." On the afternoon of the 31st another council was called, at the end of which he knew that he was to be allowed to try; but he had to fight for permission, for Sir Hyde was, not without reason, alarmed at the prospect.

Copenhagen was always protected by the Trekroner fort, mounting seventy-odd guns, commanding the point at which the entrance to the harbour branched off from the Inner or King's Channel. Any ships approaching from the north would come under its fire; shattered vessels would have no hope of retreat, and no obstacle would prevent the promised Swedes and Russians arriving to assist their allies. Also in the present emergency, the Danes, working day and night, had moored eighteen dismasted warships, mounting 634 guns, in a line a mile and a half long, stretching from the Trekroner along the King's Channel. Two more hulks, and a squadron of two ships-of-the-line and a frigate, guarded the mouth of the harbour. A shoal known as the Middle Ground lay between the Outer and Inner Channel. Nelson's proposal was to pass with a northerly wind up the Outer Channel and then wait for a southerly wind to take him with ten of the line and all the small craft available down the Inner Channel, to fall upon the rear, the weakest part of the long line stretching south-east from the Trekroner. This plan offered the undoubted advantage that damaged ships could retire after action to join the fleet, which would be lying between the enemy and reinforcements. When he had sketched his plan and offered his services, in the most energetic manner, he had to listen to discussion and criticism, for although most of his audience were agreed upon "the necessity for striking a blow", even some of his greatest admirers thought him sanguine. (Admiral Graves feared that they would be "playing a losing game, attacking stone walls". Captain Fremantle secretly held that they were already a week too late.) Nelson, who had slept only in snatches for the past six days, paced the cabin impatiently. He dismissed fears of a Swedish squadron of superior force with the sharp observation, "The more numerous the better", and when the Russians were reported as likely to be even more formidable, repeated, "So much the better— I wish they were twice as many. The easier the victory—depend upon it." "Close with a Frenchman, but out-manœuvre a Russian" was his dictum. He had been out with the leading artillery officers that morning, in a frigate, to take the closest possible view of the Trekroner defences—and incidentally, in approaching the leading ship of the line, had come under its fire.

Sir Hyde, once his decision was taken, acted handsomely. He offered two more ships-of-the-line than Nelson had asked (although his own position, should the Russians or Swedes appear upon the scene during the action, would then be very unpleasant); he thenceforward left all arrangements to Nelson's direction. That night the buoying of the Outer Deep was completed, and next morning (April 1) Nelson made a final examination, in the *Amazon* frigate. The activity and skill of her Captain, Edward Riou (a man whose scholarly countenance was shaded by what contemporaries described as "a pleasing gloom"), had impressed him, and when he gave the signal to weigh, at an hour after noon (which was received with cheers in every ship), the *Amazon* led the division down the Outer Channel to moor at the southern end of the Middle Ground. The wind was light but favourable. As the *Elephant* dropped her anchor, the Admiral called out loudly, "I will fight them the moment I have a fair wind!" His thirty-four ships, crowded close together, were lying within range of the mortars of Amag Island, as a few shots discharged around 8 p.m. demonstrated, but the Danes, preoccupied with their defences, failed to avail themselves of the opportunity.

That evening, at a late hour for the date, Nelson sat down to dine in Foley's well-appointed ship, with a large but choice party of comrades in arms. The signal to prepare for battle had been given. Darkness had hidden the sullen line of enemy hulks and substantial fortress guarding a northern capital of fantastic towers and steeples. Candle and lantern light illuminated the faces and figures of Nelson's second-in-command, Admiral Graves, an old and valued acquaintance; Colonel Stewart, whom he had met for the first time at Portsmouth; Riou, whom he had met for the first time yesterday; Hardy, Fremantle and many others whose names would be for ever remembered together with his own. He was in the highest spirits, and drank to a leading wind and to the success of the following day.

Soon after 9 o'clock the Captains departed to their respective ships, with the exception of Riou, who retired to the after-cabin with Foley and Nelson, to arrange the Order of Battle and detailed instructions for every vessel. About 11 p.m. Hardy appeared. He had been out taking soundings in the channel, and with a long pole had personally explored the depths round the rearmost of the enemy ships. At 1 a.m. a procession of secretaries was settled in the Great Cabin, ready with quills poised to transcribe orders. Nelson, since the embarrassingly attentive Tom Allen insisted, had gone to his cot, or rather had caused it to be placed on the deck in a position from which he could still dictate. His urgency for the clerks to hurry increased during the small hours, when reports of the wind coming fair were brought in to him. He was up and dressed before six, when the scribes finished their complicated labours, and an hour later he made the signal for Captains. After the Captains had all been provided with their instructions, the pilots came on board. These men, mostly mates of vessels accustomed to trade from Scottish and northern English ports to the Baltic, were unanimous in displaying "a very unpleasant degree of hesitation". All declared that to take ships of deep draught up the channel indicated would be a desperate business. "At eight o'clock in the morning of the 2nd of April", noted Nelson, "not one pilot would take charge of a ship. I experienced . . . the misery of having the honour of our Country intrusted to pilots who had no other thought than to keep the ships clear of danger, and their own silly heads clear of shot." One was found, at length. Mr. Alexander Briarly, Master of the *Bellona*, volunteered to lead the column. He was a veteran of the Nile, where he had been master in Davidge Gould's ship, the *Audacious*. At 9.30, the signal to weigh in succession having been thrown out, "the *Edgar* proceeded, in a noble manner, for the channel". The morning was cloudy but fine. "Not a word was spoken through the ship save by the pilot and helmsman, and their commands, being chanted very much in the same manner as the responses in a cathedral service, added to the solemnity."

3

The Battle of Copenhagen opened disastrously. The *Edgar*, passing along the front of the enemy line, took the shot of the rearmost Danes without reply, anchored abreast the third ship, in seven-fathom water, and opened fire, according to programme; but the *Agamemnon*, who should have followed her, failed to do so. She could not weather the shoals at the entrance to the channel and never came into action. Signal was then made for another 64, the *Polyphemus*, who should have been last of the line, to take up the station assigned to the *Agamemnon*. She promptly obeyed, and was very roughly handled. The *Isis* followed, and took the berth always intended for her, and the *Glatton* and *Ardent* were equally successful.

The *Bellona* then grounded, on the east side of the Middle Ground, within range, but at too great a distance for fully effective fire upon the southernmost hulks which covered the front of the city from bombardment. (Later in the day the bursting of her lower-deck guns caused heavy casualties in this ship.) The *Russell*, last but one in the order of sailing, lost sight of her leader, the *Defiance*, owing to the smoke of battle, and mistakenly following the *Bellona*, shared her fate. From the outset, Nelson's division was reduced from twelve to nine of the line, and the gunnery of the Danes was superior to his expectations. His agitation on perceiving the *Agamemnon* signalling inability to proceed, and two 74's failing to obey his orders to engage more closely, was extreme, but the signal to advance was kept flying. He starboarded the *Elephant's* helm, passed to larboard between the grounded ships and the enemy line, gaining comparatively deep water, and made for the position left vacant by the failure of the *Bellona*. As the *Ganges* passed, he hailed Fremantle to place her as close as possible ahead of his flagship. (By one of the many unhappy chances of this forenoon, the only men in the *Ganges* to be hit before she anchored were the Master, who was killed outright, and the pilot, who lost an arm. Fremantle himself carried his ship in.) The *Monarch* imitated the example of the *Ganges*, and dropped into the berth originally intended for the *Elephant*. By seventeen minutes past eleven the battle had become general, each ship, as she arrived opposite to her number in the Danish line, anchoring by the stern and presenting her broadside to the enemy. Graves, in the *Defiance*, was the last to take up his position, ahead of the *Monarch*, who had already lost her Captain. From that moment, in Nelson's words, "Here was no manœuvring. It was downright fighting." Riou led his squadron of small craft to attack the Trekroner batteries. He knew that it had been intended, if opportunity served, during the smoke of battle, to land the military (from the flat-boats towed by every ship-of-the-line) to storm these two heavily fortified artificial islands. Nelson had left him a free hand, and owing to the accidents to the *Agamemnon, Russell* and *Bellona* the Trekroner was going unmarked. It had also been intended that Sir Hyde, with the remainder of the fleet, including the heavy ships, should make a menacing appearance from the

Wind of April 2nd.

AGAMEMNON

RUSSELL
BELLONA
EDGAR
DANEBROG
ELEPHANT
TREKRONER

MIDDLE GROUND

OUTER DEEP

Nelson's advance

Wind of April 1st.

AMAG ISLAND

COPENHAGEN

HARBOUR

CITADEL

⚓ P   Parker's anchorage.

⚓ N   Nelson's anchorage on the night of April 1st.

The shallows to the left of the map are the Saltholm flats.

THE BATTLE OF COPENHAGEN
April 2, 1801

Reproduced from *Sea Kings of Britain*, by Sir Geoffrey Callender.
By kind permission of Messrs. Longmans, Green and Co., Ltd.

north; but the Commander-in-Chief was still more than four miles distant, beating up against Nelson's fair wind. He had heard the enemy batteries open at 10.40. Two hours later the fate of the day still hung in the balance, and according to Danish accounts, their fire was undiminished. As their crews fell, fresh men were sent from the shore to the Trekroner batteries, and to the hulks, and in some cases rehoisted colours which had been shot away, with the result that ships which appeared to have struck reopened fire, much to the wrath of English boarding-parties.

About 1 o'clock, Sir Hyde, who could see little of what was happening, but realised that Nelson had met with mishaps, and that the Danish resistance was stronger than had been expected, began to feel himself called upon to discontinue the action. He was strongly dissuaded by his Flag-Captain, who obtained permission to go on board the *Elephant* to discover what had happened, but before Otway reached Nelson, Sir Hyde had acted.

Nelson, at 1.30, was, as he had been throughout the action, walking the starboard side of his quarter-deck. The *Elephant* was hotly engaging the Danish flagship *Dannebrog* and two floating batteries ahead of her. As a shot passed through the main-mast of the *Elephant*, sending a few splinters flying about them, he remarked with a smile to Colonel Stewart that this was "warm work". He stopped at the gangway for an instant, and his look and next sentence were imprinted on Stewart's memory for ever. "But, mark you, I would not be elsewhere for thousands." When Sir Hyde's signal was reported to him he continued his walk. The Signal Lieutenant, meeting him at the next turn, asked whether he should repeat it to the squadron. Nelson ordered him to acknowledge its receipt but to keep "Number 16", the signal for close action, still flying. "Mind you keep it so." Stewart noticed that his companion now walked with increased speed, working the stump of his right arm, and after a few more turns, Nelson asked, "in a quick manner", "Do you know what's shown on board of the Commander-in-Chief? Number 39." Stewart had to admit that he did not understand what that number might signify. "Why, to leave off action!" explained Nelson, adding, "Leave off action! Now damn me if I do."

He gave a shrug, and addressing himself to Foley, said, "You know, Foley, I have only one eye. I have a right to be blind sometimes." He raised his spy-glass to his right eye, and announced, "I really do not see the signal."

4

About 2 p.m. the Danish ships astern of the *Elephant* had been silenced. When Fremantle came on board at 2.30 he found Nelson exercising what the Press called his quick discernment of occasion and popular manners. Floating gunboats and batteries were drifting helplessly from the enemy line. The Great Cabin was filled with strange uniforms, and the English Admiral was heartily telling melancholy Danes how he wished they had been Russians, and how he longed to see the Russians down. He thrust a note into Fremantle's hands, saying that he had sent for him to get his opinion whether it would be practicable to advance, with such ships of the division as were least damaged, upon the uninjured northern end of the enemy line of defence.

Fremantle read:

"To the Brothers of Englishmen, The Danes.

"Lord Nelson has directions to spare Denmark, when no longer resisting; but if the firing is continued on the part of Denmark, Lord Nelson will be obliged to set on fire all the Floating-batteries he has taken, without having the power of saving the brave Danes who have defended them.

"Dated on board His Britannic Majesty's ship *Elephant*, Copenhagen Roads, April 2nd, 1801.

"Nelson and Brontë, Vice-Admiral,
under the command of Admiral Sir Hyde Parker."

Fremantle was strongly averse from the further attack suggested. He pointed out that the Admiral had several ships aground, and most of those engaged were so crippled that it would be advisable to attempt to remove them from a very difficult channel while the wind was yet fair. Foley agreed, and Captain Thesiger, fluent in Danish as well as Russian, was immediately sent off in a flag of truce with the original of the note they had just read. It was waiting, signed and sealed, and was in the Admiral's own hand. He had scribbled it on the casing of the rudder-head, with Foley's purser, Thomas Wallis, at his elbow, taking a copy as he wrote, and he had surprised his audience by sending to the cockpit for a candle and wax, as he wished to make a seal. The first man sent did not return, and it was reported that a cannon-ball had taken off his head. The Admiral's comment was, "Send another messenger for the wax." It was pointed out to him that there were wafers on his table, by which a folded sheet could be well secured, but he repeated, "Send for the sealing-wax." It was brought, and he inspected with satisfaction a perfect impression of his own coat-of-arms. Afterwards he explained to Stewart that a wafer would still have been damp when the note was delivered, telling a tale of stress and haste to end the action; the wax would be hard and cold.

Nelson's note was delivered by Captain Thesiger to the Prince Regent himself, whom he found near the sally port, "animating his countrymen in a spirited manner". The two leading ships of Sir Hyde Parker's division had now arrived on the scene, causing the remainder of the Danes ahead of the *Elephant* to strike. Commodore Fischer had shifted his broad pendant from the *Dannebrog* to the *Holstein*, the second ship from the north end of his line, and finally to the Trekroner. The *Dannebrog* was drifting in flames before the wind, spreading confusion in her path. Only the four ships within the harbour were still intact, and, together with the Trekroner and the battery on Amag Island, still firing. Half of their shot was unavoidably striking a group of their own ships which had surrendered, and the British replies were causing more havoc in these unmanageable and unresisting hulks. Adjutant-General Lindholm was directed by the Prince to go to Admiral Nelson without delay, "to ask the particular object of sending his flag of truce". On his way, he ordered the Trekroner to cease fire, whereupon the *Elephant* made the same signal to her division.

An action which had endured for five hours closed about 4 p.m. Nelson's reply to the Crown Prince was again in his own handwriting, but this time the document did show signs of having been composed in haste.

"Lord Nelson's object in sending on shore a flag of truce is humanity, therefore, consents that hostilities shall cease till Lord Nelson can take his prisoners out of the Prizes; and he consents to land all the wounded Danes, and to burn or remove his prizes. Lord Nelson, with humble duty to His

Royal Highness, begs leave to say that he will ever esteem it the greatest Victory he ever has gain'd if this flag of truce may be the happy forerunner of a lasting and happy Union between my most Gracious Sovereign and His Majesty the King of Denmark."

Wallis afterwards corrected the grammar in his copy, but the Admiral's own holograph was that delivered by Thesiger. The Adjutant-General was referred to Sir Hyde Parker, and no sooner was he gone than the signal was made for the *Glatton*, *Elephant*, *Ganges*, *Defiance* and *Monarch* to weigh in succession. The *Monarch* immediately hit on a shoal, but was pushed over it by the *Ganges* taking her amidships. Within a mile of the now silent Trekroner both the *Defiance* and *Elephant* ran aground, and in spite of all efforts made by their fatigued crews, remained fixed for the night. Nelson ordered his gig, and prepared to follow the Adjutant-General to the *London*, four miles distant. As he embarked to encounter his Commander-in-Chief, he exclaimed in Stewart's hearing, "Well, I have fought contrary to orders, and perhaps I shall be hanged. Never mind; let them!" The *Dannebrog*, having also grounded, had just blown up, with heavy loss of life. Graves, unable to make out the response of the *Elephant* to the Commander-in-Chief's signal of recall, had repeated it, and the gallant Riou, hauling off his battered light craft to safety, with the words, "What will Nelson think of us?" had been cut in two by a raking shot from the Trekroner. The Captain of the *Bellona*, Thompson, one of the heroes of the Nile, had lost his left leg.

The calculation of casualties, the scene of devastation through which he passed in the light of a northern sunset, seemed to his companions to have lowered Lord Nelson's spirits as he drew towards the *London*. "First to secure the victory, and then to make the most of it" had been his programme in Aboukir Bay. Physical exhaustion may have been taking its toll, but he was, in fact, considering how best to secure by negotiation what he had won to-day by force. The future of the whole Baltic campaign hung upon his taking the right decisions, and his opinion of his diplomatic talents was not high. ("A negotiator is certainly out of my line.") When the Adjutant-General took his leave at 8 o'clock that night a twenty-four hours' truce was all that had been agreed upon, but it had been suggested by Sir Hyde that his second-in-command should go on shore to converse with His Royal Highness.

Nelson slept in the *St. George*. Before he slept, he wrote to Lady Hamilton, to tell her that all the flower of the Danish marine was in his possession. "Of eighteen sail, large and small, some are taken, some sunk, some burnt, in the good old way." He enclosed a verse entitled "Lord Nelson to his Guardian Angel", endorsed, "*St. George*, April 2nd, 1801, at 9 o'clock at night very tired after a hard fought Battle."

5

Next morning, while daylight was still growing, officers of the *Elephant* were pleasantly surprised to find a gig—the Admiral's favourite conveyance in these waters—alongside. He, too, was pleased and highly congratulatory to find his flagship no longer aground, but at anchor, in Copenhagen Roads, in $6\frac{1}{2}$ fathoms. He took one of his characteristic snatched meals, and set off at once to interview a Danish Commodore. Nelson's call concerned the irregular conduct of a Danish 74, the *Syaelland*. She had been driven by the waves under the protection of the Trekroner batteries, and was refusing to acknowledge herself a captured ship. He had ordered a brig and four long-boats to approach her. The celebrated English Admiral's affable explanation not only gained his point: he left the *Elephanten* as much admired by her officers as he was by those of the *Elephant*. (His personal arrival had indeed taken them by surprise, for when they had opened by saying that the 74 would surrender to no one but Lord Nelson, their early-morning caller, casting off an old green boat-cloak, to disclose a coat decorated with three stars and an empty sleeve, had briskly identified himself, "I am Lord Nelson. See, here's my fin.") In the *Syaelland*, however, as active British tars lashed a cable to her bowsprit, preparatory to their gun-boat taking her in tow, feeling ran high, and Captain Stein Bille, in a burst of patriotic despair, hurried to ask the commander of the Trekroner why he had not opened fire and sunk their fine 74, sooner than allow her to be thus tamely carried off.

On his return to the *Elephant* Nelson made the necessary change in his costume before proceeding to the Amalienborg Palace to dine with a nephew of His Britannic Majesty. Hardy was the only officer ordered to accompany him on an expedition deemed by many who watched them set out to be dangerous. It was known that the carnage in the enemy vessels had been terrible, and Nelson's arrival would coincide with that of the Danish wounded. The morning of Good Friday, 1801, was overcast and hazy. In Copenhagen Roads English men-of-war were refitting with as much precision as if they were at Spithead. Their prizes had, with two exceptions, been secured over-night, but many boats were still plying to and fro, distributing prisoners at the rate of a hundred per ship-of-the-line. The word had gone forth from on high that these prisoners were patriotic fellows, mostly artisans and agricultural labourers, with a stiffening of Norwegian seamen. Young gentlemen from the University, serving as volunteers in the batteries, had, it was whispered, put in the charge before the shot. The Danes, a peace-loving, God-fearing people, were England's natural friends. They had never heard a shot fired in anger until their leaders had been seduced, for his own ends, by the Tyrant of Russia. British pursers who had been insisting on the necessity of a return to Yarmouth or Leith, as they watched so many plump prisoners come on board, were relieved to learn that the prizes had been found excellently well provisioned.

Colonel Stewart afterwards heard that Nelson's passage through crowded streets to the palace had evidently been expected to be a touch-and-go business. The strong military guard on the *route* had been ordered as much from fears of an incident as from compliment. In the event, "the populace showed an admixture of admiration, curiosity and displeasure". Nelson saw and heard only what he had intended, and next morning, over breakfast, told Fremantle that they had been welcomed with cheers, to the annoyance, he fancied, of H.R.H. and Count Bernstorff. "I hate the fellow." (This dislike was not based on personal contact, for Count Bernstorff had been delivered into his clutches for a moment only. In that moment the Foreign Minister had heard that he had acted very ill in involving two countries that ought never to quarrel, in their present situation: a Court official immediately announced that His Royal Highness was ready to receive Lord Nelson, and on Nelson's reappearance, the Count was called to go in to the Prince.)

At the banquet which preceded his audience the chief guest worked hard, the cynosure of many eyes, for the townsfolk were permitted, not only to throng the hall and staircase of the palace, but to watch the lordly ones eat. "The people", recorded Nelson, who trusted his touch with them, "received me as they have always done." As a one-armed English Admiral won his way through the many courses of a Danish state dinner, he told his host that he had been in 105 engagements, but that yesterday's had been the greatest. The French, in action, generally behaved well, but could not for one hour have stood what the Danes yesterday had endured for four.

At the interview which followed the Regent was supported by Lindholm; Nelson stood alone. The Prince opened by graciously thanking Admiral Nelson for his humane attentions to the Danish wounded, but Nelson, going straight to the point, said that every man in England, from His Majesty down to the lowest person, would be painfully affected to hear that Denmark, leagued with her furious enemy, had fired upon the British flag. His Majesty's nephew interrupted to say that Admiral Parker had declared war on Denmark, whereupon Nelson, with equal sharpness, requested royalty to send for the papers to read the direct contrary, and in the silence which resulted, asked if he was permitted to speak his mind freely. When his freedom of speech had included the suggestion that if Denmark was to pursue the policy outlined by the Prince, the Baltic would soon be known as the Russian Sea, his host, shying perceptibly, countered with imitative frankness, "For what is the British Fleet come into the Baltic?" Nelson's answer (intended to be unmistakable) was, "To crush a most formidable and unprovoked coalition against Great Britain." The Prince spoke much and unhappily of "misunderstandings", said that his uncle had been deceived, and presently was rash enough to acknowledge that it was not in the interest of a peace-loving commercial country to see England crushed, to which his guest dryly acquiesced. He repeated, again and again, that he had offered his services as mediator between his uncle and the Czar, but Nelson held that a mediator must be at peace with both countries. The Admiral's plain offer was, "Either join your fleet to ours, or disarm." He asked, first, for a free entry of the British fleet into Copenhagen (and the Prince interrupted eagerly to say, "That you shall have with pleasure"). The demand that Denmark should suspend her treaty with Russia, while Sir Hyde Parker, for his part, suspended his plain and positive orders for an attack upon the Danish capital, caused a royal personage who had seemed "to quake on many points" obvious misery.

Nothing that occurred during the next five days was calculated to cheer Nelson. He went with Fremantle to call upon Sir Thomas Thompson. In the *Bellona*, four wounded midshipmen had heard that their Captain was not dangerously ill, after the amputation of his leg. Thompson (whose private view was, "I am in great pain. . . . I am now totally disabled and my career is run through, only at the age of 35") pronounced himself as well as could be expected, and Fremantle found his spirits very good, but was staggered at the prospect of getting an officer "of very full habit" from the *Bellona* to the *Isis* for a passage home, on a day when it was blowing so hard that communication with the shore was difficult. Mosse, of the *Monarch*, had left a widow and six children; Riou, an invalid mother. Nelson's "heart ran out at his eyes", as he began a letter to St. Vincent, recommending to the protecting hand of the First Lord the wives and families of those men who had lost their lives for their King and Country under his orders. The catalogue brought too freshly to his recollection his hand-grasp and good wishes to every Captain on the morning of April 2. The Armistice was being renewed at twenty-four-hour intervals, and Count Bernstorff sent vague and unsatisfactory notes to Sir Hyde. While the Commander-in-Chief stayed inactive, his second-in-command was so busy by day he had not time to turn round, and at night could not sleep. "All here hang on my shoulders." Fremantle, in letters home, was meanwhile describing him as "the life and soul of the squadron". After Nelson had, with great labour, in bad weather, got out his prizes (some of them, in his opinion, in good condition and easily reparable), he was obliged to organise their immediate destruction. Sir Hyde, who was in no great need of prize-money, and was nervous of the approach of the Russian and Swedish fleets, had decreed that all except one 74 (which he had commissioned as a hospital ship, and was sending home) must be burnt.

At last, on the morning of April 9, the terms of a sixteen-weeks' Armistice were ready for presentation, and Nelson prepared to land again. He was not entirely satisfied with the terms, and not sanguine as to their acceptance, for he was convinced that fear of Russia, not desire for further slaughter, was keeping the Danes from receding, even temporarily, from the Armed Treaty of Neutrality. He wrote to St. Vincent that he only wished to finish Paul and then retire, and to Addington that if the Armistice was not approved, he hoped he might be superseded and allowed to seek the shade of a chestnut tree on his estate of Brontë. Captain Lindholm, Adjutant-General of the Fleet, and Major-General Count Ernst Walterstorff, Royal Chamberlain, had been appointed by the Regent to act on the part of Denmark. Lord Nelson and Colonel the Honourable William Stewart, Member of Parliament for Wigtownshire, were named by Sir Hyde Parker, who was lending his own Foreign Secretary, the Rev. Alexander John Scott, to act as interpreter. Nelson also took Foley, young Edward Parker and Fremantle with him, and they went in Fremantle's barge. Cold rain was lashing a capital which required sunshine to display its charms, and since the sea was very rough, uniforms suffered, in spite of "dreadnought" boat-cloaks. Lindholm had come to meet his fellow Commissioners, and the warmth of the dignified greeting between him and the famous Englishman produced a good effect upon a mourning people who had now buried their dead and were hoping for peace. Stewart gathered that their aspect was much less lowering than it had been upon the previous occasion.

The Commissioners met in a ground-floor chamber of the Amalienborg Palace, and after several hours' conference nearly parted upon Article VII, the clause fixing the duration of the Armistice. Nelson, who had represented his Commander-in-Chief and himself as "English Admirals come to treat with open heart and hand", frankly admitted that he needed sixteen weeks in which to deal with Russia. When an angry Dane muttered in French that they had better renew hostilities, he picked up the phrase and repeated "Renew hostilities! Tell him" (turning to Dr. Scott) "that we are ready at a moment; ready to bombard this very night." The Commissioner, who had believed that because an English Admiral did not speak in any tongue save his own, he understood nothing else, apologised in confusion, and business recommenced with increased amiability: but by 2 o'clock, when the conference broke up to attend a *levée*, Articles VI and VII were still in dispute. As he climbed a grand staircase, on the arm of one of his compatriots, stiff, hungry and tired of being what he described as "shut up in a room in a palace half-wet-through", Nelson murmured, "Though I have only one eye, I see all this will burn very well." A banquet for which fifty covers had been laid awaited him upstairs. He buckled to his task again, and blonde ladies of the Court, looking in at the doorway during the feast, to see a celebrated figure seated on their Prince's right hand, observed with relief that much cordiality prevailed. Nelson, while his well-chosen *suite* made a strong impression on peace-loving, patriotic Danes, was closeted with the Prince for a long final tussle, and after much hesitation, the Prince agreed to an Armistice for fourteen weeks, instead of the sixteen mentioned in the treaty. He did not enter into further thorny dispute on the subject of neutral ships-of-the-line being stopped and their convoys searched for contraband of war by belligerents. His fatigued suggestion was that some means might be contrived by which such mortifications might be prevented. A smiling British Admiral replied, "I think there might very easily", and later went into the problem in close detail with the efficient Lindholm, promising to forward the result of their discussion to Mr. Addington. He did not take his leave without a last cheerful shot: "Now, Sir, this is settled, suppose we write 'Peace' instead of 'Armistice'?" But a Prince who had already gone too far could only muster a smile in return, and say that such a happy state of affairs must be brought about slowly, so as to cause no new wars. Darkness was falling by the time that the Commissioners proceeded, through cheering crowds, to the *London*, for the signature of the Armistice.

Nelson reached his flagship fagged out, to find letters from home awaiting him. While he devoured them, gentlemen at the Amalienborg Palace were also heaving sighs of relief. A message had arrived from St. Petersburg that the Czar had been found dead in his bed, on the morning of March 25. This was the form in which the news of the assassination of Paul I first reached the courts of Europe.

6

"I do not believe", wrote Nelson to Lady Hamilton, on April 13, "we shall fire another shot in the Baltic."

Acting on this belief, he had written to St. Vincent, asking for leave to come home, and begged Lindholm to get him passports to travel overland, by Lübeck, to Hamburg, where, if no better chance offered, he intended to take the Yarmouth packet. Colonel Stewart had sailed, with the terms of the Armistice, and instructions to call at 23, Piccadilly, to introduce himself and collect "Lady Hamilton as St. Cecilia". This portrait (which, having been privately secured, had never left Sir William Hamilton's house) had cost the purchaser £300. "If it had cost me 300 drops of blood, I would have given it with pleasure." Still, he marvelled at Sir William's *sang-froid*. Captain Bligh ("one of my seconds on the 2nd"), bearing a letter in which he was commended as a steady seaman and a good and brave man, was being entrusted with a gift of Copenhagen porcelain to be delivered at the same address. "It will bring to your recollection that here your attached friend Nelson fought and conquered."

In London, at Brooks's Club, Mr. Coke of Holkham was laying Sir T. Miller fifty guineas "that Nelson is neither taken prisoner or capitulated". In Copenhagen the rumour ran that the new Czar was willing to give up all English vessels, goods and subjects detained in Russia. Sir Hyde hesitated no longer to enter the Baltic along the Grounds, between the islands of Amag and Saltholm. All his heavy ships had been ordered to remove their guns; nevertheless on their passage most touched, and several grounded, underlining how perilous had been their situation on the 2nd. Fremantle, who had brought his 74 to draw only twenty-two feet two inches, led the fleet the whole way, though very nervous to be running in four fathoms and a half, and frequently less, for more than four miles. The squadron was safely at anchor in Kioge Bay by nightfall on April 12, with the exception of the *St. George*, the *Agamemnon* and a few frigates.

While he was lying, detained by foul winds, some twenty-four miles from his Commander-in-Chief, a message from Sir Hyde told Nelson that a British look-out frigate had seen the Swedish fleet at sea. The hour was 6 p.m., the temperature was, even in the opinion of tough Mr. Alexander Briarly, "pretty sharp". This admiring Scottish expert, who had stayed in the *St. George* to see her over the shallows, was the witness and chronicler of a characteristic minor incident. The moment that Nelson received the news he ordered a boat to be manned and jumped into her (without even waiting for a boat-cloak), calling for Briarly to attend him. His fear lest the fleet should have sailed before he got on board a ship was his only topic during six hours of hard pulling, mostly in darkness, against wind and current. Briarly, offering a great-coat, received the answer, "No, I am not cold; my anxiety for my Country will keep me warm." He heard Nelson's voice repeating, "Do you not think the Fleet has sailed?" and ever replied, "I should suppose not, my Lord." But even he was shaken by the Admiral's next decision. "If they are, we shall follow them to Carlskrona, in the boat, by God!" Fortunately they were not called upon to cover a distance of some fifty leagues in a six-oared boat, without a morsel to eat or drink. They reached the fleet about midnight, and went alongside the *Elephant*, where her commander gave a warm response to an enquiry, "in true Norfolk drawl", whether Captain Foley could be so good as to be plagued again by Admiral Nelson. The fleet proceeded in the leisurely manner typical of Sir Hyde Parker's command towards "the Swedish Portsmouth", and Nelson vented his irritation in letters of complaint to Lindholm of an official report of the action of the 2nd, composed by Commodore Fischer, who had commanded the Danish line on that occasion. On the 19th, back in the *St. George* again, he came off Carlskrona, to be presented with a beautiful picture of eight Swedish sail-of-the-line and two frigates, "very snug", shut up in their fine harbour, where they were protected not only by their batteries, but also by a profusion of the bronzed and glistening rocks typical of the Scandinavian coastline. Nelson sadly commented, "Thus all our hope of getting alongside them is at an end; they will not trust themselves out again this summer", and Sir Hyde, having received a letter from the Russian Minister at Copenhagen saying that the Czar had ordered his fleet to abstain from all hostilities, returned to an anchorage in Kioge Bay, near the Danish capital, there to await further instructions from England.

Warmer and longer days succeeded one another. Fremantle, who landed and spent a late April day on "a little bit of an island called Ertholmar", thought himself almost at the end of the world. Innumerable tanned children, with linty locks, scrambled fearlessly by the side of the splendid Captain of an English man-of-war as he solemnly promenaded with an amiably slow-witted Governor around a kingdom consisting of seven rocky islets, covering not more than a square mile, and containing nothing but a lighthouse, barracks and fishermen's huts. Two days later he received one of those reminders for which Admiral Nelson's most devoted officers did not much care.

"My dear Fremantle,

"If you don't come here on Sunday to celebrate the Birthday of Santa Emma, Damn me if I ever forgive you. So much from your affectionate Friend, as you behave on this occasion,

"Nelson and Brontë."

"*St. George,* April 24th, 1801."

Two dozen guests, including Sir Hyde and "his parson secretary", assembled on the 26th to drink Lady Hamilton's health in a bumper of champagne. She was possibly in Wales by now, on a tour of Sir William's Pembrokeshire estates. Her last letter showed that she had been vexed by persistent newspaper reports of the purchase of a house for Lord and Lady Nelson. Her lover had assured "Mrs. Thomson", "he has never wrote his aunt since he sailed, and all the parade about a house is nonsense. He has written to his father, but not a word or message to her. He does not, nor cannot, care about her; he believes she has a most unfeeling heart." Before he issued his invitations to Lady Hamilton's birthday feast, he had sent a note of instructions to Davison.

St. George, April 23rd, 1801.

"My dear Davison,

"You will, at a proper time, and before my arrival in England, signify to Lady N. that I expect, and for which I have made such a very liberal allowance for her, to be left to myself, and without any inquiries from her; for sooner than live the unhappy life I did when I last came to England, I would stay abroad for ever. My mind is as fixed as fate; therefore you will send my determination in any way you judge proper."

Before he sailed, he had written again to old William Marsh, senior partner to Messrs. Marsh and Creed (now Marsh, Page and Creed), who had been his agents for seventeen years, asking him to pay £400 quarterly to Lady Nelson. He intended the sum as a permanent arrangement, a separation allowance, but had not stated this explicitly, and the "parade about a house" was not quite all nonsense. His brother Maurice's account of him on his last leave (obliged to lodge in a London hotel) had alarmed his family. His sister Susanna had bravely addressed herself, from Norfolk, on March 8, for the good of the family, to a person whom she had never liked.

"Will you excuse what I am going to say? I wish you had continued in Town a little longer, as I *have heard* my Brother regretted he had not a house he could call his own when he return'd. Do, whenever you hear he is likely to return, have a house to receive him. If you should absent yourself entirely from him, there never can be a reconciliation. . . . I hope in God I shall have the pleasure of seeing you together as happy as ever. He certainly, as far as I hear, is not a happy man."

The Rector had written, four days later, even more tactfully. He said he had heard nothing of his daughter-in-law for a long time. He asked if he could have done anything which might have offended her, and if there was any acceptable way in which he could exert himself on her behalf. But both these efforts arrived too late. The birth of Horatia, of which he had learnt since his last unhappy interview with his wife, had decided Nelson to seek no reconciliation. What he intended to be his last letter to her had been achieved as he lay in thick fog, in the Downs.

"Josiah is to have another ship, and to go abroad, if the *Thalia* cannot soon be got ready. I have done *all* for him, and he may again, as he has often done before, wish me to break my neck, and be abetted in it by his friends, who are likewise my enemies; but I have done my duty as an honourable, generous man, and I neither want or wish any body to care what becomes of me, whether I return or am left in the Baltic.

"Living, I have done all in my power for you, and if dead, you will find I have done the same; therefore my only wish is to be left to myself; and wishing you every happiness, believe that I am,

"your affectionate Nelson and Brontë."

His wife superscribed the sheet, "This is my Lord Nelson's letter of dismissal, which so astonished me that I immediately sent it to

Mr. Maurice Nelson who was sincerely attached to me, for his advice. He desired me not to take the least notice of it, as his brother seemed to have forgot himself."

By the night of May 4 Nelson was ready to leave the Baltic. His heavy luggage had gone on board the *Blanche*, a frigate which was only awaiting the arrival of the next despatch vessel from England to sail with return letters. He had been feeling so fagged that he had given up the idea of a journey to Hamburg by land; but his spirits improved as he gave his Flag-Captain orders for the forwarding of his private correspondence, and watched Hardy and young Parker sealing up his valuables.

The vessel, expected for a week past, joined the fleet late that night, and Colonel Stewart came on board the *London* at 1 a.m. Sir Hyde Parker, who had been well satisfied with his Command, found himself abruptly ordered home. Nelson, who was already in spirit in England, was appointed, with much compliment, to succeed him. The blow to both was painful, and Nelson (who had been resigned to the possibility of his Chief becoming "Lord Copenhagen"), in his first moments of bitterness, believed that Sir Hyde had "worked his leave" and deserted him "to die a natural death" on a station where there would be no more fighting and (since he was forbidden to take prizes in the Baltic) no prospect for a penurious Admiral but "prison for debt". An interview with Sir Hyde soon convinced him that he had wronged that unhappy man, and by 4.30 p.m., his baggage having been removed from the homebound frigate, and that of Sir Hyde having taken its place, the *Blanche* sailed, carrying to eternal retirement an officer verging on old age, undisguisedly "low".

Nelson's first signal as Commander-in-Chief was to hoist in all launches and prepare to weigh. He had sent St. Vincent an urgent note asking that another Admiral might be sent out, and begged the influential Davison to do all that he could to get him relieved of a most unwelcome Command. His letter to Lady Hamilton (which he was convinced would be seen by ten people before her) told her, "We must cheer up for the moment, at the present we are in the hands of others", and that meanwhile, since activity must be his watchword as Commander-in-Chief, "I am on my way to Russia".

7

All the news in letters carried by Stewart had been ill, and the amiable Colonel had not even been able to bring with him the likeness of Lady Hamilton by George Romney. He feared that poor Saint Cecilia would think him a very uncivil sort of gentleman, but the fact was that his last day in London had been a nightmare of tedious immurements in the War Office, the Admiralty and Downing Street, culminating in orders which brooked of no delay, and offered no excuse for a farewell visit to Piccadilly. He had therefore left without her ladyship's promised letters to his friend, and the last received by Nelson had explained that Lady Hamilton was distressed for "Mrs. Thompson's child". She had dismissed an unsatisfactory wet-nurse. The class, Nelson knew, was essentially untrustworthy, and too often disease, occasioning the loss of her own child, was the proxy's reason for availability. The hireling summoned by the lady of fashion always tended to be lazy and greedy. He pictured Horatia, hastily weaned, losing weight and colour, ailing and wailing. Painful tears coursed down the cheeks of a remorseful father ("Dear innocent! she can have injured no one") as the Baltic fleet, bound for Russia under his command, approached Bornholm Island, in blowing weather. He had at last been granted the Victory near Home which always filled the eye and ear of John Bull (and which he had, years past, from a sick-bed, envied Duncan), and handsome things had been said of him in both Houses; but the Prime Minister's letter told him that the Armistice achieved by him after so much labour had only been approved "considering all the circumstances", and Davison, whose intelligence was good, reported in disgust that a Viscountcy was likely to be his sole reward. "*That* you ought to have had long ago, and any additional distinctions short of an Earldom, in my humble opinion, would be degrading." Davison, who received "several epistles daily" from 23, Piccadilly, had naturally, but maddeningly as events had turned out, supposed that Colonel Stewart would be carrying all the latest from that quarter. He was at the moment confined to his house, after a carriage accident, and had therefore been unable to visit Mr. Maurice Nelson, who was dangerously ill with what he described as an inflammation of the brain. He had sent his own physician to take charge of the case, and Sir John Hayes, who attended the Prince of Wales, was hopeful.

On the evening of May 12, in cold, clear light, which reminded him of a January day in England, Nelson came in sight of Pakerot Lighthouse in the Gulf of Finland. He had left the main body of his fleet, under George Murray, off Bornholm Island, to watch the Swedes and cover his communications, and had taken with him, on a visit to be represented as complimentary to Russians now supposed to be friendly, a chosen squadron of ten of his best-sailing 74's, two frigates, a brig and a schooner. But at Revel, next day, to his disappointment, he found that the twelve Russian sail-of-the-line had got out ten days past and gone up to Cronstadt. A polite note to the Governor of the Esthonian capital, requesting pilots, brought French-speaking Russian officers on board the *St. George*, and Lord Nelson was obliged to accept an invitation to land and visit the Governor of a picturesque city of great antiquity, which, in his present mood and health, charmed him not at all. The crowd to which he had become accustomed followed him attentively during his three hours on shore, and all the Russians seemed to have taken it into their heads that he resembled a national hero. Everywhere he heard murmurs of "Suvárov!", "Le jeune Suvárov!" The Military Governor assured him that his letter to Count Pahlen, Foreign Minister, announcing his arrival, had been forwarded by express to St. Petersburg, but M. Balaschoff could not, without further authority, allow him to bring armed vessels within range of cannon-shot, so he had a seven-mile pull from his flagship to the town. He was amused at the surprise evidently felt by both his own squadron and the Russians at finding a British fleet in Revel, but he could not help reflecting with irritation that if, in February, he had been given the Command which he now held, and come straight here, he could not only have destroyed half the Russian fleet: many lives lost at Copenhagen might have been spared. On the following day he returned hospitality, and made his cough much worse escorting innumerable gentlemen of high-sounding title round his ship. Stewart noticed that the Cossack officers showed most intelligent interest in a British man-of-war, and that the disgraceful circumstances attending the death of the late Czar were by no means concealed.

Count Pahlen's reply arrived about 3 p.m. on May 16, as the Commander-in-Chief was about to dine. He studied it with evident displeasure, but did not speak. During the meal he left the table, and in less than a quarter of an hour summoned his secretary. The signal to weigh was immediately thrown out, and although contracts had been made for provisions not yet delivered, the squadron stood out to sea, leaving the *Skylark*, a three-masted, 14-gun schooner, to collect and settle. At this time of year, in this latitude, darkness lasted but a couple of hours, and with dawn the squadron proceeded down the Baltic. Count Pahlen's letter had not been civil. He had announced, on behalf of his Imperial master, astonishment that the whole fleet of a nation expressing friendly intentions should have come into the Gulf of Finland. The only guarantee of loyalty which he could accept was its instant withdrawal.

On the 20th, at night, the squadron fell in with the *Latona* frigate, having on board Lord St. Helens, newly appointed Ambassador to St. Petersburg. A very mild nobleman of attractive address discoursed for three hours in the Great Cabin of the *St. George*, but dashed an Admiral who liked quick results, by saying that he hoped, in a month, to be able to send him some decisive intelligence as to the attitude of Russia. Nelson (who had written to the British *chargé d'affaires* at the Russian capital asking him to call a meeting of British merchants to decide how he and his fleet could be useful to them) considered that two hours should have been sufficient. He was saddened, as he made on with a fair wind, by a letter of condolence from the Comptroller of the Navy, delivered to him by St. Helens. At last his brother Maurice had been promoted, but a rather unlucky man had not lived to enjoy the fruits of thirty-three years' conscientious toil. Maurice, who had obediently departed from a Norfolk parsonage at the age of fifteen to drive a quill in Seething Lane, had died a bachelor, but had left dependants. The Commander-in-Chief in the Baltic remembered with a pang that an elder brother's slender purse had always been open to a struggling Lieutenant, and forgot that he had more than once settled Maurice's debts. He wrote urgently, by three channels, to Davison, asking him to do all that was kind for a lady whom he would always regard as his brother's honoured wife. ("Be liberal.") He begged Lady Hamilton to call upon and comfort "poor blind Mrs. Nelson" (who was legally Mrs. Ford).

8

At dawn on May 23 the squadron from Revel joined the main fleet off Bornholm, and Rear-Admiral Totty, newly arrived from home with a reinforcement, was directed to relieve Captain Murray on that station. Detachments were ordered to Kioge Bay to water, and to Dantzig to buy bullocks, hay, biscuit and particularly wine (the Commander-in-Chief owning himself a strong advocate for serving wine to ships' companies instead of spirits). All his business having been completed by dusk, he proceeded with eight of the line and a frigate to provision at Rostock. On the first night after his arrival there he was amused and satisfied by the sequel to his Russian expedition. Count Pahlen was now singing to a very different tune. He most warmly invited Lord Nelson to visit his Imperial master at St. Petersburg, was horrified by their previous misunderstanding, and added that, as a first step towards solid peace, the Czar had instantly taken off the embargo from English shipping in all parts of his domain. As the Russian lugger left the fleet with a gracious reply to a gracious letter, she fired a salute, and Colonel Stewart heard Nelson say to Wallis, "Did you hear that little fellow salute? Well, now, there is peace with Russia, depend upon it. Our jaunt to Revel was not so bad after all." It had, however, cost him dear.

Since April 27, when he had done what he called "the civil thing" at Revel, he had not been out of his cabin. The keen air of the North had cut him, he said, to the heart. He had written to Troubridge that he hoped his successor might be as strong as a horse. He seemed to have lost the art of sleep, and was coughing up what he believed to be the last of his lungs. He could not find out from his medical attendants whether they shared his fears, but they told him that the prevalent sickness in his flagship was undoubtedly "the influenza".

Hearing that "the prince or duke of these parts" had left for the coast, he hurried on his preparations, and was ready to sail for Kioge Bay with a fair wind, when a letter from the Duke of Mecklenburg-Strelitz told him that His Serene Highness, who had come to Rostock to see him, desired he would appoint the time for his coming on board. A very homely country gentleman, sixty-one years of age, bringing with him "no less than a hundred men, women and children", presented himself next afternoon. Queen Charlotte's brother, who offered ten thousand apologies for bringing such a large family, was obviously made happy by two salutes of twenty-one guns and the gift of a "Davison" Nile medal. In the Admiral's quarters he paused to admire three likenesses of a beautiful woman, and waited in vain for the proud explanation, "Lady Nelson".

May slipped into June. By June 11 Nelson reckoned that it was thirty-seven days since he had received a post. With warmer weather, coughs and colds vanished, and a Commander-in-Chief who possessed what the First Lord described as "the magic art of infusing the same spirit into others", was happy to report "a finer fleet never graced the Ocean". For his own part, he found that either the warm milk forced upon him at 4 a.m. every morning with Captain Foley's compliments, or Captain Murray's lozenges, had produced a miraculous cure. His return to health had certainly been accelerated by the kindness of everyone. "I should be a wretch not to cheer up." Even Totty, an entire stranger, had written to say that he hoped to God it was not true that Lord Nelson was going to England, or, if true, that "your Lordship will take us all with you".

On the night of June 12, Nelson could not sleep for joyful expectation. A cutter, reported in sight during the afternoon, had joined at 11 p.m. His old friend Charles Pole, now a very portly Adonis, was coming to relieve him. His Viscountcy had been gazetted, and he was directed to invest Graves with the Order of the Bath. Two days later, Hardy having "trimmed out the quarter-deck of the *St. George* in his usual elegant manner", the ceremony was performed, with all possible dignity under the circumstances. The green morocco armchair from the Admiral's Great Cabin (chosen for him by Lady Hamilton) represented the Throne. It was draped in the Union Jack, and set under a canopy made of the

Royal Standard. A guard of marines and men of the 49th Regiment
was ranged on either side of the quarter-deck, and all Captains of the
squadron attended in full-dress uniform. The red ribbon, Star and
Commission were carried on a blue satin cushion (also provided by
Lady Hamilton), and Nelson, acting the King "as well as I could",
dubbed Sir Thomas knight with the gold crocodile-hilted sword
presented to him by the Captains of the Nile. A salute was fired as he
put the red ribbon over the shoulder of the new Companion. Above
the scene of closely packed, rigid figures and primitive colours
blazed a cloudless sky, and all around it a glassy sea. Silently, the
Commander-in-Chief was wishing that he had a rope fast to Admiral Pole, who would never get on in such weather.

The *Æolus* frigate pathetically lacked a wind for a further five
days. His release from a station where there was little hope of any
further action came on June 19, when he quitted the Baltic for
England, sailing in the *Kite* brig, so as not to deprive the fleet of a
larger vessel.

Chapter XV

1801–1803

(*ætat.* 42–44)

"SQUADRON ON A PARTICULAR SERVICE"

AND

"EXPERIMENTAL PEACE"

I

SINCE his arrival at Yarmouth on July 1, 1801, the name of Nelson had been daily in the papers. Every reporter had drawn the picture of him passing slowly from bed to bed of the Naval Hospital and presenting every nurse with a guinea, before departing for London in a garlanded post-chaise and six with postillions attired as British tars. The toast in the Baltic Fleet on the day of his departure was said to have been, "May he, who is no longer our Commander, be our Example." The first choice for a few days' country quiet of a man who had no home in England had been a picturesque inn well known to sea-officers. "A very pretty place, and we are all very happy." Burford Bridge, set in a green shade under the yew-covered shoulder of Box Hill, was also a haunt of artists and poets. But a Portsmouth road posting-house at all seasons was a scene of activity. At Shepperton, host Tom White could provide patrons with ideal recreation. Sir William Hamilton was an expert angler; the Admiral had, in boyhood, and during his years of unemployment, often whipped a Norfolk stream. Their engrossed silhouettes were daily attended by others, much junior. The party to assemble on the banks of the Thames had both the look and sound of a family party. The Rev. William Nelson had brought his small, talkative lady and well-behaved daughter. Merry little Captain Edward Parker, who needed a holiday but could ill afford one, had been invited to act as aide-de-camp. He made arrangements for the Admiral to visit the Staines Quarter Sessions dinner, at which, after the usual three cheers, three times three were voted for the British Navy. A day which the Admiral remembered as very happy had been spent at poor Maurice's house at Laleham. Parker ordered the transport, settled the bills, dealt with the tipping and presented the receipts to his lordship.

An almost unclouded reunion was brought to a close on the 20th by a summons which caused a man invalided home from the Baltic to hurry up to Whitehall and Downing Street. On the day of his arrival at Yarmouth a statement that preparations on the coast of France were in great forwardness had been prominent in the Press. Buonaparte, relieved by the Peace of Lunéville of war on the Continent, had been for four months at leisure to reconsider his favourite scheme for invasion of England. Nelson realised when he accepted the command of a large squadron of light craft, for the defence of the coast between Orfordness and Beachy Head, that a reassuring name had been needed by those making an emergency appointment necessitated by popular apprehension. He believed that both St. Vincent and Troubridge were at work to keep him from the company of Lady Hamilton. But a bare three weeks' experience had convinced him that he could not happily make holiday in time of war. Besides, if the war continued, he wanted the Mediterranean Command. He had seen Horatia, and told Lady Hamilton to look out for a country house for him. At 4 a.m. on July 27 he left Lothian's Hotel for Sheerness, having met his father for a brief interview at the hotel on the preceding day.

A letter received by Nelson during his Shepperton stay had run:

"My Dear Husband,
"I cannot be silent in the general joy throughout the Kingdom. I must express My thankfulness and happiness it hath pleased God to spare your life. All greet you with every testimony of gratitude and praise. This Victory is said to surpass Aboukir. What my feelings are, your own good heart will tell you. Let me beg, nay intreat you to believe no Wife ever felt greater affection for a Husband than I do, and to the best of my knowledge I have invariably done everything you desire. If I have omitted anything I am sorry for it.
"On receiving a letter from Our Father, written in a melancholy and distressing manner, I offered to go to him, if I could in the least contribute to ease his mind. By return of post he desired to see me immediately, but I

was to stop a few days in Town to see for a House. I will do everything in my power to alleviate the many infirmities which bow him down. What more can I do to convince you that I am truly,

"Your Affectionate Wife,
"Frances H. Nelson."

The direct question, the tacit suggestion of a meeting, had been alike disregarded by a husband who had closed his ears to the voice of duty, but a too candid lover had duly reported the call from the past, and since (finally very angry) protestations on his part had failed to convince the mother of Horatia that she was not being played false, a heavy cloud, culminating in a storm, had preceded his daybreak departure "on a particular service".

2

As he dined at Sheerness, after a quick and easy journey, he privately considered that England's defenders, as here exemplified, would make a good caricature. Vice-Admiral Graeme, Commander-in-Chief at the Nore, who lived in one of the hulks, was, like himself, short of a right arm. The officer in charge of the military proved to have a wooden leg. An easterly gale rattled the windows as they feasted, and he thought, "If the Dutch mean to put to sea, this is their time." His flag was flying in the *Unité* frigate, and he had gone on board at once, "in order to show we must all be at our posts as speedily as possible".

During his week at Lothian's Hotel he had carefully studied the mass of material available in the Admiralty and elsewhere on the subject of Buonaparte's avowed design of invasion. At Downing Street Mr. Addington, detained in Town by the growing alarm, had been frank. In Hyde Park the Prince of Wales was reviewing volunteers. The capital was, as usual in late July, almost empty of fashionable folk, but John Bull was alarmed. The facts seemed to be that there were some 36 gun-sloops, over 200 gunboats and a large number of smaller vessels collected along the northern French coast, from Flushing to Cherbourg; and in the Pas de Calais and Flushing districts a considerable number of troops, possibly 40,000. The picture which filled the eye of the gentry on holiday, and the dusty crowds cheering in Hyde Park, was of a calm night or hazy day, during which the French flotilla might slip across and land their invasion army on British soil while Britain slept. The reports of secret agents (mostly French *émigrés*, who had to live) were probably exaggerated, but the Grand Army mentioned by them exceeded in number any British regular army ready to offer opposition, and there had recently, beyond doubt, been much building of flat-boats in enemy ports. The Press had succeeded in killing the holiday season for most sea-bathing resorts of Kent, Sussex and Essex, and refugees from south-eastern towns were pouring inland, whilst heated volunteers on the coast erected beacons. After considering the evidence, Nelson had drawn up and submitted a Memorandum on the defence of the mouth of the Thames and the coasts of Kent, Sussex and Suffolk. His plan was based on the supposition that a descent on London might be made from Flanders and Flushing, in conjunction with an appearance of the Dutch Fleet. An officer of the naval service accustomed to using his own judgment was convinced that in order to gain the advantages created by a diversion, Buonaparte would divide his force and land troops at two places simultaneously.

He was all day at his desk on the 28th, issuing orders to the little ships of his new command, some of which bore names very appropriate to their present duties—H.M.S. *Defender, Conflict, Attack, Cracker, Boxer, Bruiser, Firm, Haughty, Gallant, Ardent*. . . . Seven o'clock next morning saw him in his chair again. By noon, to the awed admiration of Parker, he pronounced himself ready to leave for Faversham and Deal, by post-chaise, having dealt with thirty of the ships at Sheerness, "made everyone pleased, filled them with emulation, and set them all on the *qui vive*". A line in the heroic vein from Lady Hamilton, received just as he set out, had chimed with his mood, and "naturally called forth all those finer feelings, of the sort none but those who regard each other as you and I do, can conceive". At Faversham, where his business was "to examine the organisation and readiness to serve of the Sea Fencibles", his arrival gathered staring and cheering crowds. The Reservists looked "with wild but most affectionate amazement at him who was once more going to step forward in defence of his country". A local gentleman, passing rich ("got it by the Fair

Trade", was the Admiral's private comment), explained that the men, "always afraid of some trick", lacked, he was sure, nothing but a word from Lord Nelson, on behalf of the Admiralty, to reassure them that when the invasion was frustrated they would be allowed to return to their own homes. Until Lord Nelson's appointment had been published, nobody had rightly realised that "the thing" was serious. Lord Nelson, who had not himself realised that his new duties might include having to get up and harangue like a recruiting sergeant, supposed that if necessary, since he was "come forth", he could undertake something very disagreeable as well as any other. His immediate instructions to an eager audience on a windy day were easily to be understood. "Whatever plans may be adopted, the moment the Enemy touch our Coast, be it where it may, they are to be attacked by every man afloat and on shore; this must be perfectly understood. *Never fear the event.*"

The anniversary of the Nile saw Nelson at sea, in the *Medusa* frigate, trying to get off Boulogne. A report that the enemy were coming out had caused him to put to sea in a bustle at 10 p.m. on the preceding night, attended by some bomb-ketches. He saw already that the report had been incorrect.

Three days later, as first light revealed a mouse-coloured old *Haute-Ville*, clustering on the slopes of a wooded hill, and a *Basse-Ville*, where soldiers were already busy erecting new guns and mortar batteries, he prepared to make Boulogne an unpleasant spot, though without doing unnecessary damage to the civilian population. The brilliant sun of a late summer's day broke through, and the people of Dover, hearing gun-fire, collected in crowds on the cliffs to hear "Nelson speaking to the French", and since the visibility was very good, to see what they could. By noon his bombs had sunk three flat-bottomed boats and a brig, and disabled six more. As he visited the ketches, the enemy were "most attentive", both to his barge and the various vessels visited by him. By 6 o'clock, when another French vessel went on shore, he was writing to the Secretary to the Admiralty that to-day's business was of no great moment, except to show the enemy that they could not with impunity come outside their ports. He assured St. Vincent, the Duke of Clarence, Davison and the Hamiltons that wherever invasion was coming from, he could now venture to predict that it was not Boulogne.

A mountain of paper-work was awaiting him at Margate. The announcement of his appointment had brought the inevitable flood of letters from friends, acquaintances and strangers. More than a hundred of the letters required replies, and the Admiral, "half-sea-sick", prophesied, "I believe my head will be turned with writing."

When Mr. Spence, maritime surveyor of this part of the coast, came on board the *Medusa* during the morning of August 10, he found a famous stranger of fascinating manners "in a fix". Admiral Nelson, who had been out in a cutter since 6 a.m., explained, "We have got the *Medusa* into this hole, but cannot get her out again, through the proper channel, while this wind remains, and although I have two or three pilots on board, neither they nor the Harwich pilots will take charge of her. I must get to the Nore to-night in her." The *Medusa* had been lying at anchor in the rolling ground off Harwich for two days, imprisoned by an easterly wind. In her passage between the Ridge and Andrew's Shoal, she had touched once or twice, and pilots who were nervous of trying to bring her into Harwich and Hollesley Bay absolutely refused to consider taking her over the flats extending seawards from the Naze. Mr. Spence, adjured to devise some means to get her into the Swin (a distance of some eleven miles), immediately agreed to take the risk at high water, and to the satisfaction of an Admiral who thought he ought to know all that there was to be known of the navigation, and believed he had been a tolerable pilot for the Thames-mouth in his teens, his flagship achieved a hazardous passage which created a record for ships of her size, and was thereafter known as the *Medusa* Channel.

While he waited for the Admiralty to pronounce upon a large project for an expedition with 5,000 troops against Flushing, he went "over the water" again. His preparations for a boat attack on the vessels moored outside Boulogne were elaborate, and he believed that it should be possible to destroy or carry off the whole flotilla. On August 16 he reported to St. Vincent, "I am sorry to tell you that I have not succeeded in bringing out or destroying the

Enemy's Flotilla moored in the mouth of the harbour of Boulogne. The most astonishing bravery was evinced by many of our officers and men." His casualty list was 44 killed and 128 wounded. "No person", he was careful to state, "can be blamed for sending them to the attack but myself. . . . All behaved well, and it was their misfortune to be sent on a service which the precautions of the enemy rendered impossible."

He anchored in the Downs the same night, and himself chose lodgings in Deal for Parker and his Flag-Lieutenant. Frederick Langford went ahead steadily, but from the first the case of Edward Parker was serious. Seated between their beds, Nelson wrote to St. Vincent. "Nothing to be done on the great Scale" was his description of his present duties, and he repeated his request that a junior officer of less damaged frame might be appointed. "The services on this coast are not necessary for the personal exertions of a Vice-Admiral." His belief that Buonaparte's invasion was a mere empty menace was perfectly correct, as were his suspicions that peace was in the air.

Another consideration which was causing him anxiety was that he had only £3,000 in hand, and at any moment Lady Hamilton might find a house for him. "The Baltic expedition cost me full £2,000. Since I left London it has cost me (for Nelson cannot be like others) near £1,000 in six weeks. If I am continued here, ruin to my finances must be the consequence, for everybody knows that Lord Nelson *is amazingly rich*."

The arrival of Francis Oliver, on August 19, with letters from Lady Hamilton, mentioning a house at Merton in Surrey, and the news that Sir William, on his return from Milford Haven, was likely to bring his lady and Mrs. Nelson to the coast for sea-bathing, threw Nelson into a fever of expectation. He hurried to engage bedrooms at an inn, and reception-rooms, with a gallery overlooking the beach, at the "Three Kings", Deal. A bathing-machine was secured for the ladies. On the day that his guests were due to arrive, duty called. Captain Owen of the *Nemesis* had reported from off Flushing that he believed a successful attempt might be made against an enemy flotilla there. A squadron from Margate joined the Admiral off North Foreland, and he stood for Flushing with a force numbering thirty sail, and including bomb-ketches and fire-ships. He took with him several Artillery officers and half a dozen pilots, and, when he was at sea, summoned for conference one of the odd characters with whom he had become more closely acquainted in the pursuance of his present duties. The opinion on the ground of old Yawkins, an ex-smuggler, "a knowing one", now Master of the *King George* cutter, weighed more with him than that of Captain Owen, whose zeal, he suspected, had caused him to overlook such trifles as tides and sandbanks; and two days later, after an expedition up the Welling Channel in the *King George*, he was satisfied that he had come on a wild-goose chase.

On his return to the Downs, he entered upon a fortnight of mingled toil and holiday. He escorted his guests over his flagship, to the Naval Hospital, and daily to the lodgings of Langford and Parker. Lady Hamilton promised to leave behind her chaise, to take out the convalescents, and sent to Piccadilly for a sofa for the Flag-Lieutenant. Sunlit excursions to Ramsgate, to Dover Castle and Walmer (where Mr. Pitt was not yet in residence), were success-fully undertaken. Not all officers of the squadron, however, were happy at the situation. "Lord Nelson", wrote acting Lieutenant William Cathcart to his father, "is, I believe, still at Deal, and if he is wise, he will stay there during the equinoxes. . . . He talks of sailing directly Sir William goes to town. I hope and trust he will not, as his so acting will give rise to a good deal of newspaper chit-chat, which to me will be very unpleasant."

The condition of Parker was already lowering Nelson's spirits when the day drew near for the party to break up. The Hamiltons put off their departure for four days, and an operation was pro-nounced successful, but the little Captain, who had told Lady Hamilton, "To call me a *Nelsonite* is more to me than making me a Duke: I would lose a dozen limbs to serve him", was now so altered that when the Admiral had to quit his bedside, "he got hold of my hand, said he could not bear me to leave him, and cried like a child. . . . I came on board, but no Emma. No, no, my heart will break. I am in silent distraction. . . . My dearest wife, how can I bear our separation? Good God, what a change! I am so low that I cannot hold up my head." He despairingly noticed that he could not even enjoy the sight of a hundred West Indiamen coming through the Downs. He determined to go to look at his Dungeness squadron, but bad news, and lack of a wind, brought him back from Folkestone. Several deceptive rallies led him to hope that Parker might yet "take possession of his room at the Farm". Dr. Baird kept him advised of every change in the patient, and the Admiral fondly repeated, to many correspondents, details of the gradual dissolution of an obscure junior officer. "He was my child, for I found him in distress." On the morning of September 29 Parker died, and since he had youth and hope on his side, died hard. Nelson, who attended the funeral next day as chief mourner, was observed to shed tears as a body which represented to him hopes unfulfilled in his stepson was lowered into the cold earth.

He went under Dungeness in deep dejection, and planned another attempt on the Boulogne flotilla, this time with a fire-brig commanded by the indefatigable Owen, to be attended by H.M.S. *Eugénie* and *Jamaica* and the *King George* cutter. Yawkins had volunteered as pilot. While the Admiral was thus engaged, a Public Letter from Nepean instructed him that as the French Minister might have occasion to send despatches to his Government, their Lordships had directed that no vessels or boats of any description should at present proceed to France. This could mean only one thing, and on October 4 Nelson learnt that preliminaries of a peace treaty had been signed. The days while the peace awaited ratification were remarkable for their beauty. Nelson noted, with growing calm, "a beach remarkably smooth,—not a curl on the shore". A neat note from his schoolgirl niece called forth from a weary man the grateful comment, "Hers is a nice innocent letter." He had expected to be granted leave on the morning of the 6th, and Allen had actually packed, when, instead of the looked-for order of release, came a letter from the Prime Minister expressing the opinion that it was of the utmost importance that Admiral Nelson should keep his flag flying till the definitive treaty had been signed. Troubridge, on behalf of St. Vincent, mentioned a fortnight as the probable interval between the ratification and cessation of hostilities, after which everything that could be attempted to meet his lordship's wishes (short of striking his flag) should be done. "I must submit, for I do not wish to quarrel with the *very great folks* at the Admiralty, at the last moment", explained Nelson to Davison, whose offer to lend any sum necessary for the purchase of a house had aroused a reply in the style of a Walter Scott hero. ("Can your offer be real? Can Davison be uncorrupted by the depravity of the world? I almost doubt what I read; I will answer, my dear friend, you are the only person living who would make such an offer.")

On the day that he had told St. Vincent, "Whenever I am released I shall always be ready to come forth again", descriptions of the welcome given by London to a French General bringing the ratification threw him right out of temper. Like many other officers in His Majesty's service, he was doubtful of the durability of a peace which seemed very convenient to Buonaparte. After a spectacular gale, the autumn rains set in, followed by fogs, and he contracted one of those devastating colds in the head which he believed might last the season, if he was kept "thumping in the Downs". Mr. Pitt, calling on the afternoon of October 13, found him in a frigate's cold cabin, half sea-sick and racked with toothache, convinced, "I should have got well long ago in a warm room, with a good fire and sincere friends." The statesman agreed that it did seem very hard that he should be kept here still, "now all is over", and an invitation to dine at Walmer was issued, but Nelson, although he privately believed that "Billy Pitt" might yet be of use to him, would not face being dragged through a night surf to dine with the angel Gabriel. Troubridge, "one of my Lords and Masters", had advised him not to think of leaving his station, to take health-inducing walks ashore and wear flannel next the skin. "Does he care for me? *No;* but never mind." He made formal application to be allowed to strike his flag, pointing out that the service for which he had been called forth was now at an end, and the state of his health required repose. His request was crossed by a notification that he might have ten days' leave from the 22nd. "What a set of beasts!"

3

Merton Place, Surrey, which, even after he had set eyes upon it, he persisted in calling "the Farm", had been his since September 18, when, after a brisk negotiation (in the later stages of which Lady

Hamilton feared that Mr. Haslewood had not been very civil to Mr. Greaves), it had been secured, furnished, for £9,000. Possession had been promised for October 10, and Lady Hamilton had conducted all the business with the lawyers unaided. (Davison was in Scotland, and Sir William, who had not taken his famous lady with him when he visited his Milford property or his relatives at Warwick Castle, had, after their Deal jaunt, departed again alone, this time to Newmarket.) Nelson, who could not at the moment command more than £3,000, had borrowed from Davison and his late secretary, Tyson, and had so far paid £7,000 in two instalments. "As to asking Sir William, I could not do it. I would sooner beg." He was of opinion that everything in the house should be his, "even to a Cook and a Book", and that Sir William and Lady Hamilton should contribute nothing. "You shall have the whole arrangement. . . . To you I may say that my soul is too big for my purse, but I do earnestly request that all may be mine in the house, even to a pair of sheets, towels, etc. . . . You are to be, recollect, Lady Paramount of all the territories and waters of Merton, and we are all to be your guests, and to obey all lawful commands." He wrote to his solicitor, urging him to get Mr. Greaves out, and Lady Hamilton in, by the 6th, so that Sir William should be presented with a *fait accompli*. ("I wish I could have got up for four or five days. I would have roused the lawyers about.") Mr. Greaves held to his date, but an old diplomat, having once stated that he would be paying half the household expenses while he and his wife stayed in the country house of their best friend, reported on October 16, in his most imperturbable manner:

"We have now inhabited your Lordship's premises some days, and I can now speak with some certainty. I have lived with our dear Emma several years. I know her merit, have a great opinion of the head and heart that God Almighty has been pleased to give her; but a seaman alone could have given a fine woman full power to chuse and fit up a residence for him without seeing it himself. You are in luck. . . . The proximity to the capital and the perfect retirement of this place, are for your Lordship, two points beyond estimation; but the house is so comfortable, the furniture clean and good, and I never saw so many conveniences united in so small a compass. You have nothing but to come and enjoy immediately; you have a good mile of pleasant dry walk around your own farm. It would make you laugh to see

Emma and her mother fitting up pig-sties and hen-coops, and already the
Canal is enlivened with ducks, and the cock is strutting with his hens about
the walks. Your Lordship's plan as to stocking the Canal with fish is exactly
mine. I will answer for it, that in a few months, you may command a good
dish of fish at a moment's warning."

His farm had filled Nelson's thoughts and letters as he pitched
and rolled at anchor in the Downs. He pictured his flocks folded in
peace in view of his windows. "Take care that they are kept on the
premises all night, for that is the time they do good to the land."
He had no fears that his stock would decrease, "for I never expect
that you will suffer any to be killed". Indeed, he foresaw Emma
"getting all the old dogs in the place about her", and also two-
legged and lame dogs—"for every beggar will find out your kind
heart".

It was with dawn of Friday, October 23, 1801, that his chaise-
and-four charged underneath a village-made triumphal arch, past
an unpretentious lodge and gates, and up a drive of no great length
(thickly planted towards the high-road) to the principal entrance of
a red-brick house of two storeys, about a century old, facing east
and overlooking grounds intersected by a small branch of the river
Wandle, spanned by a light Italian bridge. Lady Hamilton had
regretted in her latest letters that the leaves were falling in Surrey,
and feared, as she looked at her hasty purchase in the cold light of
autumn, that her confiding friend might not like Merton. His first
sight of it was at the hour when vitality is at its lowest, and before
fires were lit on a sharp morning, but a weary traveller never
doubted that he had found Paradise.

"To be sure," he had written from the Downs, "we shall employ
the tradespeople of our village, in preference to any others, in what
we want for common use, and give them every encouragement to
be kind and attentive to us." On the night of his arrival, a rustic
community, glad that so celebrated and reputedly generous a man
should have taken up residence in their midst, marked the occasion by
illuminations. Merton was, as he had hoped, a village, no more, and
the names of the tradesmen supplying Merton Place were incredibly
bucolic. Greenfield was the butcher, Woodman the chandler,
Peartree the stable-keeper. Messrs. Wyld and Gadd were his cheese-

monger and baker, Mrs. Cummins took in washing, and his next-door neighbour was Mr. Halfhide. The problem of neighbours had troubled him as he lay in the Downs. Lady Hamilton set the highest value on her "regained reputation", which had been assailed by no tongues during the ten years that she had spent at the Neapolitan Court since Sir William had raised her to what she proudly called "honors, rank, and what is more, innocence and happiness". There could be no doubt that her reputation had suffered since the appearance of the Victor of the Nile as her outspoken admirer. Her regard for the conventions was so strict that he had hesitated to suggest that he should come to Piccadilly, and run down to see Merton in her company, while Sir William was away. ("You would not, perhaps, think it right for me to come.") She had never lost a chance of assuring embarrassed acquaintances that Lord Nelson's regard for her was "the purest flame". Nevertheless, in fashionable London there had been galling scenes when he had attempted to thrust her, in the character of "my particular friend", upon eminent company, and he blamed himself for them. His decision for the future at Merton was, "No person can take amiss our not visiting. The answer from me will always be very civil thanks, but that I wish to live retired." Almost at once, however, it appeared that at Merton Lady Hamilton was not to be reduced, as in Piccadilly, to the society of gentlemen who came without their ladies, leading ladies of the stage and opera, and a very few ladies of the *vrai monde* who remembered Neapolitan hospitality with gratitude, realised that the situation was now quite different, but had always been a law unto themselves. The largest landowners of the district were the Goldsmids, of a family devoted to music and acts of charity. When Abraham Goldsmid gave a *fête* at Morden Hall, descriptions occupied a full column in London newspapers. An elder, but lesser, brother, Benjamin, resided in competitive state at Roehampton. At Wandle Bank House, Mr. Perry, editor and proprietor of the *Morning Chronicle*, was always ready to extend to anglers an invitation to fish in waters which nearly surrounded his mansion and were decorated by many species of water-fowl, including swans. Amongst smaller householders, the Newtons and the Halfhides (who had a field to sell to Lord Nelson) were profuse in friendly attentions. Dr. Parrett, the medical practitioner, introduced himself promptly, and the Vicar of the parish church, Mr. Lancaster, whose appointment dated from the previous April. Almost immediately Lady Hamilton was able to announce with *aplomb* to Mrs. William Nelson, "We *could* have plenty of visiting in the neighbourhood, but we none of us like it."

The punctual appearance of the Merton Place party at Matins in the church of St. Mary the Virgin on the first Sunday after the great man's arrival had aroused feelings of interest and reassurance. "Have we a nice church at Merton?" the son of a country clergyman, now a landed proprietor, had eagerly enquired. "We will set an example of goodness to the under-parishioners." Throughout the service a charming little schoolgirl, with a smooth black head, found the places for her celebrated uncle, and gravely handed his prayer-book to a man who had lost his right eye and arm in the service of his country. Only two descriptions of Nelson in civilian dress survive. There is unreliable mention of him strolling the Hamiltons' London house in a crumpled hat, with a striped brown overcoat thrown round his shoulders. (This garment may have been a boat-cloak, since these were generally supplied in brown plaid camlet lined with green baize.) A nephew remembered him, very neat, in a simple suit of black, doing the honours of his Merton table. In uniform, his "old checked *surtout*" and "cocked hat put on square, and much lower than the others" were famous.

On Monday mornings, since Merton was, as the owner of Merton Place explained, "exactly one hour's drive from Hyde Park or the Bridge", the landowners of the district, almost without exception, took the London road early. The chariots of the Goldsmid brothers hastened to Finsbury Square, in order that their occupants might direct the hidden channel of gold flowing towards London from their native Amsterdam and further capitals; Mr. Perry posted to Fleet Street; Sir Robert Burnett's carriage took the accustomed route to the Vauxhall Distilleries; Sir William Hamilton's emblazoned equipage carried the owner to the British Museum and Mr. Christie's auction rooms, Miss Charlotte Nelson to her desk, and his lady to 23, Piccadilly. The Admiral had appointments with the First Lord and Lord Hood, and had told Messrs.

Webb to send a representative to collect his peer's robe, which must be altered to that of a viscount before Thursday. Lady Hamilton also had made an appointment for him. A letter directed on Saturday to a quiet house off Oxford Street had desired:

"Dear Mrs. Gibson,

"Will you come to Piccadilly with Miss Thomson on Monday at 10 o'clock, not later? I hope my dear god-child is well.

"Ever yrs, E. Hamilton."

Nelson returned out of the fog to the roaring fires and welcoming candlelight of his country house from his first London expedition, alarmingly exhausted, to describe himself, "Not yet well. The cold of the Downs gave me a severe shake", and Lady Hamilton reported to his sister-in-law in some agitation, "I am sorry to tell you I do not think our Dear Lord well. He has frequent sickness, and (is) Low, and he throws himself on the sofa, *tired, and says 'I am worn out'*. But yet he is better, and I hope we shall get him up. He has been *very very* happy since he arrived, and Charlotte *has* been very attentive to him. Indeed, we *all* make it our constant business to make him *happy*."

Lord St. Vincent was no longer to be found in Mortimer Street. The First Lord had moved into Admiralty House, and Nelson, whose memories of that august mansion had not generally been happy, had found this morning's interview depressing. The Earl, gruffly pronouncing himself "very unwell, a most severe cough", had received an indispensable officer, whose actions in private life were causing him deep displeasure, much as might have been feared. Nelson's letters to various Service applicants, dated from his country study during the following week, stated wearily, "Your letter shall be given to Lord St. Vincent, with a note from me on the back of it. I have very little interest." "I wish I could have congratulated you on your good son's being made Post, but I can assure you I have not the smallest interest." "I have not a scrap of interest, but believe me, I am ever your most obliged and affectionate friend." He had thought that the thriving ten-months-old child displayed to him at Piccadilly had a look of the mother about the brow. He had a heavy list of public appearances before him, and after his introduction in the Lords must produce a maiden speech for the following day. His task was suitable—seconding a vote of thanks "to Rear-Admiral Sir James Saumarez, K.B., for his gallant and distinguished conduct in the Action with the Combined Fleet of the Enemy, off Algeciras", but after all was over he thought he had acquitted himself only fairly well. To sit for Ipswich, in the Commons, had been his desire when he was younger. He had toiled for Rachel, and they had given him Leah. John Bull, personified by a butcher of Cheapside, seized him by the hand, in an uproarious City crowd scene, lit by rosy winter sunshine, this Lord Mayor's Day. "How are ye, my hearty? Glad to see ye back!" shouted the butcher, as a carriage long since relieved of its horses rocked the Admiral towards the Guildhall. His weeks were assuming a regular pattern. From Monday to Friday he drove down to Merton every night, after fagging London days. He commonly took a turn in his grounds before setting out, and held confabulation with Thomas Cribb, his head gardener, who had known and loved his property long before him, and was to do so long after. On November 12, the owner of Merton Place told Captain Sutton:

"Yesterday was a busy day—between gardening, attending the House, and eating, drinking, and hurraing . . 150 dined at the London Tavern, and I, being the Cock of the Company, was obliged to drink more than I liked; but we got home to supper; and a good breakfast at eight this morning has put all to rights again."

A few days later the best authority in his world found him "in better health, and happier in himself than in good truth I have in any past time observed him to be". The first adult guest to stay under his roof was his father, and to have won the Rector to Merton was a triumph, for there had been times during the past twelve months when the happy relationship of a lifetime appeared threatened. Lady Nelson had taken a London house, in Somerset Street, Portman Square, and it had been customary for her father-in-law to spend his winters with her. Some tale that she was acting with harshness to Captain Nisbet (who still lacked employment, and some months after the separation had still been calling at 23, Piccadilly) had, apparently, been credited by Nelson, for on September 26 he wrote, "I had yesterday a letter from my father; he seems to think that he may do something which I shall not like. I suppose he means going to Somerset Street. Shall I, to an old man, enter upon the detestable subject; it may shorten his days. But I think I shall tell him that I cannot go to Somerset Street to see him. . . . If I once begin, you know, it will *all out*, about her, and her ill-treatment to her son." More than a week later, when he had not yet composed a reply, he reported a second communication from Burnham, "which has hurt me". The Rector, already disturbed, had been incensed by an anonymous letter accusing him of unkindness to his famous son. "This is unexpected indeed." He had written with some frigidity to ask if he might be personally informed as to his son's plans for future residence, now that peace was happily returned to Britain. A country clergyman, who had never lacked moral courage, and had inevitably, in the course of forty-five years of pastoral duty, observed the misery of the broken home, stated firmly, "If Lady Nelson is in a hired house, and by herself, gratitude requires I should sometimes be with her, if it is likely to be of any comfort to her." (To his daughter Kitty, he was deploring, "No prospect of better times for her, nay I think worse.") For five days Nelson toiled at drafts of an explanation—"that I shall live at Merton, with Sir William and Lady Hamilton—that a warm room for him and a cheerful society will always be there happy to receive him—that nothing in *my conduct* could ever cause a separation of a moment between me and him. . . ." "Tell me, my dear Friend," he appealed to Lady Hamilton, "do you approve? If he remains at Burnham he will die, and I am sure he will not stay at Somerset Street." At length he achieved something ("I could not say less") which he endorsed, "When read, send it to London to be put in the post", but the result was only moderately encouraging, for the Rector's acknowledgment of "many kind invitations" from his son and Lady Hamilton, "which it is my intention to accept", went on to explain that for the present he had engaged to be elsewhere. November 9 found him at Somerset Street, where, he announced, he meant to stay a fortnight, but within ten days the carriage and manservant which a victorious son had provided for an invalid after the Battle of the Nile made a quiet arrival at Merton Place.

Three grandchildren—his eldest daughter's twins, and William's

Charlotte—were his fellow-guests, and his letter of thanks, after a visit of ten days, showed that an ex-Ambassadress had excelled herself in well-considered arrangements for his comfort, and an ex-Ambassador in delicate eulogy of a national hero. The Rector retired to spend the winter with the Matchams at Bath, sadly convinced that his son never meant to live with his wife again, but relieved that "the Breach" in his family need extend no farther. His children were instructed that the love and affection of their famous brother for all of them and theirs "depend upon it is very sincere and unshaken", whereupon the Matchams, last of the family to take the decision, offered themselves for a visit, and entered upon terms of warm and lasting friendship with Lady Hamilton at the cost of relinquishing the acquaintance of Lady Nelson. That the William Nelsons and the Boltons were influenced by anxiety to provide for their young is arguable, but no such consideration can explain the conduct of the Matchams, and George Matcham left amongst his papers a character sketch of "Lord Victory", which contains illuminating passages. In the opinion of his brother-in-law, Nelson's marriage had been a failure from the first, and long before Lady Hamilton came upon the scene, "his heart sickened and revolted" by perpetual complaint and reproach, Nelson had made up his mind not to attempt further home-life in England. After long separation, two very unsuited persons might perhaps have managed to spend the sunset of life together peaceably and comfortably (as was desirable), but, on the other hand, if Lady Hamilton had not filled the gap, some other artful female would certainly have hastened to do so. "Generous in heart, feeling, and full of sympathy, he would readily have been engaged in friendship, and as readily have been attached in love. . . . He early felt the want of that domestic comfort."

With mid-December 1801 the Rector sent thanks to Merton Place for a box of gifts—an elegant set of porcelain for the Matchams and for himself a plaid, chosen by Lady Hamilton, shyly acknowledged as "very handsome". "From an old man you will accept the old-fashioned language at the approaching happy season, which is, 'I wish you a merry Christmas and a happy New Year.' " The weather had turned bitterly cold, and after the House rose

Nelson did not visit London, except for a couple of hours on business, for a full month. He watched a heavy fall of snow from his Merton window on November 27, and by Christmas week skating parties. Lady Hamilton took drastic measures to ensure that he was happy.

(Postmark, 12 o'clock, December 14th, 1801 Nt.)
"My dear Mrs. Gibson,
    "If you will take a post-chaise to-morrow, Tuesday, and set off at half-past ten o'clock, and bring my god-daughter and your little girl with you, I shall be glad to see you. Tell them to drive you to Merton, and the best way you can come is over Clapham Common. Hire the chaise for the day. You can go back at three o'clock. *Do not fail.*
                                "Ever yours sincerely,
                                        " E. Hamilton."

The owner's first Christmas at Merton, before a number of acquaintances with no real claim upon his hospitality had found their way to a comfortable house, was quiet enough. Only Brother William and family were guests under his roof. Count Walterstorff came down for a day, and promised a further call, frustrated by a fashionable cold known in Paris as "La Grippe". Mr. Greville, similarly indisposed, sent his uncle a gift of moor game, and regrets. Lady Hamilton received a long letter from her beloved Queen, who magnanimously sent a thousand compliments to the Hero of the Nile, despite his recent speech in the Lords on the subject of Malta. The peace made by England with France, and the failure of her friends to condole with her on the untimely death of her sainted daughter-in-law, had also caused Her Majesty pained surprise. She thought, with the spring, of rejoining her husband (a situation described by her as "going to die at my post"), and was glad to hear a rumour that "the Chevalier" had bought an estate near London. Sir William, in fact, since Government was still insufficiently grateful, was at present primarily concerned with getting through one more winter tolerably, in an abominable climate. He thought that the air and early hours of Merton seemed to agree with him, and believed that if he could hire a post-chaise by the month to carry him to such London diversions as he still affected, he might subside into retirement, solvent. But to be paying half-expenses in another man's country house while a Mayfair house of his own, fully staffed, yawned untenanted, vexed him, nor was he favourably impressed by his wife's latest "Attitude" as Lady Paramount. In Italy he had never failed to remind a very headstrong young woman, for her own good, of her shortcomings. He feared that entirely uncritical encouragement of a lavish *châtelaine* by the heroic owner of Merton Place would benefit nobody, and confided in his nephew and heir on January 24:

"Nothing at present disturbs me but my debt, and the nonsense I am obliged to submit to here to avoid coming to an explosion which would be attended with many disagreeable effects, and would totally disturb and destroy the comfort of the best man and best friend I have in the world. However, I am determined that my quiet shall not be disturbed, let the nonsensicall world go on as it will."

He had also, in reserve, a plan, not quite his own, for regaining prestige and, incidentally, comparative affluence. Last Christmas, at Fonthill, his kinsman by marriage had sounded him on a scheme which he thought might succeed. A peerage for Sir William, in recognition of his diplomatic services, with reversion to Beckford, was the prize to be demanded. In return, Beckford offered to Sir William an annuity of £2,000, to Lady Hamilton (upon widowhood) an annuity of £500, and to "H.M. Minister, two sure seats in the Commons" (and two more which might, under favourable circumstances, be secured). He suggested that the first approach to the fount of honours should be made by Sir William, via the head of his family, the Duke of Hamilton. He had good reason to believe that the Duke's heir was likely to make Miss Beckford Marchioness of Douglas.

But, upon reflection, an old diplomatist, hibernating, upon the whole very comfortably, in the London villa of a hero, during the first winter of what His Britannic Majesty himself called the Experimental Peace, decided to let this matter wait awhile.

4

The correspondence with which the owner of Merton Place laboriously dealt, in a country library, was not much less than that which had oppressed him while in command in the Mediterranean and Baltic. Indeed, with the prospect of peace, and the sweeping economies in the service proposed by Lord St. Vincent, a certain feature of it rather increased.

"To Lieutenant Baker, R.N., Dover-Street.
"Sir,
"Every officer who has lost a limb has certainly a right to a pension, and by application to the Admiralty you would certainly have one granted. I have, I can assure you, no power whatever to meet your wishes by getting you to the West Indies."

The Chairman of Lloyd's was approached on behalf of Captain Johnson, promoted after the Battle of Copenhagen. ("In nine days from the loss of his arm, he did his duty again as First Lieutenant of the Ship. Such spirit in the Service is never to be overcome.") His lordship's old secretary, Tyson, wrote from Malta in misery, afflicted like Job after two months' slow fever. Tyson's efforts to send agricultural implements and seeds to the duchy of Brontë had been attended by a variety of mischances, and the only payments from the estate as yet forwarded to him by Graeffer amounted to less than £800. The Admiral cast up his accounts, and wrote in haste to Messrs. Marsh, Page and Creed, telling them to have £2,000 ready to pay to Mr. Tyson on his arrival in London, even if this meant that they must sell Lord Nelson's India Stock. Amongst the thirty-five younkers to sail for Copenhagen in his flagship, three had been *protégés* of Lady Hamilton. Young Banti and the engagingly nicknamed "little potatoe Harris" must take their chance, but for her ladyship's cousin he wrote thrice to Sutton, asking him to keep Charles afloat if possible, and if not in his own ship, with any good frigate captain who would give the lad his chance, preferably of foreign service. A stricken-looking guest, on a long visit, drowsed opposite the Admiral as he ended his letter to Sutton, "What a gale!" Poor Langford's leg was still throwing out fragments of bone, and the shadow of amputation now hung over him. Distinguished foreigners were still addressing themselves in compliment to the Victor of the Nile and Copenhagen. The Baron d'Eiker and Ekoffen wrote from Bamberg to announce that the West of Europe had not waited for the conclusion of peace between England and France to testify its veneration for Viscount Nelson. The Chapter of the Order of St. Joachim had universally, and by acclamation, decreed that the dignity of a Knight Grand Commander be offered to him. The East also had not been neglectful. His old acquaintance, Admiral Cadir Bey, wrote from Alexandria, and Lord Elgin from the Porte, to congratulate him on the Sultan's bestowal of a further honour in recognition of the victory of April 2. When writing to the Prime Minister to ask for the permission of his own sovereign to wear these alien decorations, Nelson reverted sadly to an omission which had been the subject of many of his letters this winter. He had long been concerned that as yet nothing except his own Viscountcy and Graves's K.B. had been awarded after Copenhagen. In July he had understood from St. Vincent that medals would be issued, and had accordingly reassured his Captains. When the City had voted its thanks to the two services for operations brought to a successful close in Egypt, his anxiety that protracted silence as to Copenhagen was intentional had become acute. He had written to Downing Street and Whitehall, enclosing copies of a letter of complaint to the Lord Mayor, and after waiting three days for any answer, posted the original. St. Vincent dryly but promptly thanked him for letting him see a document which he had seen fit to forward, and in two longer letters, while regretting that worry was making Lord Nelson ill, stated that no recommendation for any issue of medals celebrating the Action at Copenhagen was going to be made. Addington, after a week's delay, asked him to call. What was said at the ensuing interview did not reach the public ear. It was surmised that His Majesty's Ministers did not wish to give offence to the part of Sir Hyde Parker's fleet not engaged in the action: the feelings of Denmark must be considered. The visible result was that Nelson dropped his enquiries about medals or promotions, and asked the Lord Mayor to consider his letter withdrawn. But in the following June he requested that a motion of thanks to him for his subsequent efforts in command of coast defence against invasion should not be tabled, and in September 1802 he refused to dine with the Corporation at the Guildhall, and in November with the Lord Mayor. "Never, till the City of London thinks justly of the merits of my brave companions of the 2nd of April, can I, their commander, receive any attention from the City of London." On a change of administration, in May 1804, he wrote from the Mediterranean, asking a new First Lord for a reconsideration of the decision of his predecessor. A quarter of a century after Nelson's death his surviving Captains were still petitioning in vain that the most difficult of his victories might be recognised as he would have desired.

Inevitably, amongst the correspondents of a public character were numbered the lunatic, the charlatan and the abusive letter-writer. When a person signing himself Thomas Tugbear begged His Honour to bring back with him the Emperor Paul of Russia (as Mr. Tugbear needed an outlandish wild beast to carry about with him as a show, in order to support a wife and six children), the Admiral, just setting off to the Baltic, replied in his own hand that he would do his best. After the unsuccessful attack on Boulogne, a Mr. Hill, who gave Lord Nelson the choice of forwarding a Bank note for £100 by return of post or seeing an exposure of his conduct in the Press, received an answer at once so suave and terrifying that he never stirred again. There is only one recorded instance of an appeal addressed to the most generous and punctilious of correspondents being crudely returned to the author without any word of solace. A sheet in a familiar handwriting reached Merton in Christmas week, 1801.

"16, Somerset St.

"My dear Husband,

"It is some time since I have written to you; the silence you have imposed is more than My affection will allow me and in this instance I hope you will forgive me in not obeying you. One thing I omitted in My letter of July, which I now have to offer for your accommodation, a comfortable warm House. Do, my Dear Husband, let us live together. I can never be happy till such an event takes place. I assure you again I have but one wish in the the world, To please you. Let everything be buried in oblivion; it will pass away like a dream. I can only now intreat you to believe I am, most sincerely and affectionately,

"Your wife,
"Frances H. Nelson."

On this redirected letter appear the words "Opened by mistake by Lord Nelson, but not read", signed "A. Davison".

Lord Minto arrived to stay at Merton Place, in time for dinner on Saturday, March 20, 1802, determined to disapprove of all he found. He stayed until the Monday morning, and on his return to London, wrote to his lady in Scotland:

"The whole establishment and way of life is such as to make me angry, as well as melancholy; but I cannot alter it, and I do not think myself obliged or at liberty to quarrel with him for his weakness, though nothing shall ever induce me to give the smallest countenance to Lady Hamilton. She looks ultimately to the chance of marriage, as Sir W. will not be long in her way, and she probably indulges a hope that she may survive Lady Nelson; in the meanwhile she and Sir William and the whole set of them are living with him at his expense. She is in high looks, but more immense than ever. She goes on cramming Nelson with trowelfuls of flattery, which he goes on taking as quietly as a child does pap. The love she makes to him is not only ridiculous, but disgusting: not only the rooms, but the whole house, stair-case and all, are covered with nothing but pictures of her and him, of all sizes and sorts, and representations of his naval actions, coats of arms, pieces of plate in his honour, the flagstaff of L'Orient, etc.—an excess of vanity which counteracts its own purpose. If it was Lady H's house there might be a pretence for it; to make his own a mere looking-glass to view himself all day is bad taste. Braham, the celebrated Jew singer, performed with Lady H. She is horrid, but he entertained me in spite of her. Lord Nelson explained to me a little the sort of blame which had been imputed to Sir Hyde Parker for Copenhagen."

Three days later the Peace of Amiens was signed. England had surrendered all her colonial conquests of the late war, except Trinidad and Ceylon. Malta was to be restored to the Knights of St. John, Minorca to Spain, the Cape to the Dutch, and Martinique and Guadeloupe to France. France's part in a most advantageous bargain was to evacuate Egypt and Naples, recognise the integrity of the Turkish Empire and Portugal, and indemnify the House of Orange. Buonaparte, elected Consul for life by a grateful country, henceforward signed only his Christian name, or initial, on all documents.

Nelson was sitting for more portraits. In May Sir William Beechey was paid £36 13s. for a half-length, exhibited at last year's Academy. Joseph Farington, R.A., after a visit to the studio of Hoppner on March 29, noted that this year "Hoppner had intended not to exhibit, but has been persuaded by Lord Carlisle to send a Kit-cat portrait of a girl leaning, which he painted with a view to Rembrandt's works. He will also send a portrait of Lord Nelson, full-length."

5

A letter to the landlord of "The Star" Inn, Oxford, from George Matcham, Esq., of Bath, bespeaking rooms and dinner for himself and eight guests at 5 p.m. on Wednesday, July 21, 1802, had not aroused in that quarter any suspicions that the hostelry of a university city was to harbour a national hero. Eventually, "The Angel" in the High Street, on the south side of the sacred bend, almost opposite Queen's College, was the appointed *rendezvous* of a party consisting of a large clergyman attended by a young Etonian, three gentlemen, all of unusual appearance, though very different stature, a smaller schoolboy, and three ladies, two of whom were in deep mourning. The Matchams, with their first-born, aged twelve, had come from Bath. The William Nelsons, who were going to accompany Sir William and Lady Hamilton and Lord Nelson on a three weeks' tour, had come with them direct from Merton.

The Rector of Burnham Thorpe had died rather suddenly on April 26, and his famous son, although warned that the end was near, had not been present at either the death-bed or funeral of a parent who had never failed to hold up the highest ideals to him. The only person to perform the miracle of keeping upon terms with both Lord and Lady Nelson was now gone, for although his daughter-in-law refused to visit him, the Rector had never ceased to write to her, and a letter in his enormous childish handwriting, opening simply, "My dear" (his usual form of address to the ladies of his family), had been dated April 18. George Matcham, writing on the 24th, had merely asked for instructions from Lord Nelson, who had replied two days later, "Had my father expressed a wish to see me, unwell as I am, I should have flown to Bath, but I believe it would be too late; however, should it be otherwise, and he wishes to see me, no consideration shall detain me for a moment." On April 26, Lady Hamilton's birthday, Merton Place was the scene of a christening, and Cribb, the gardener, always remembered the procession of three carriages to the village church, for the baptism, by the names of Fatima Emma Charlotte Nelson Hamilton, of her ladyship's black maid, a great favourite with her, "taken out of a slave-ship", and entered in the parish register as "from Egypt, a negress, about 20 years of age, under the protection of the Right Hon. Lady Hamilton". The Admiral, on hearing the expected sad news next day, had cancelled an engagement to appear at the Academy Banquet, and decided not to attempt a pilgrimage to Norfolk. Lady Hamilton wrote to his brother, describing his condition as probably necessitating a surgical operation. William, who had been advised from Merton, not Bath, and too late, had taken huff, and in his character as sole executor of a very small estate had "not half liked" the sharpness of Mr. Davison, representing Lord Nelson. However, he had excelled himself in arrangements for the interment, and everything (paid for by the Admiral) had been as the deceased would have chosen—the funeral order given to the local under-taker, and an old body-servant and Bath apothecary handsomely remembered. "I don't think", said William, whose bulletins arrived daily, "any proper people were left out. We have sunk ye grave in the chancel, alongside our mother's—plenty of room." Dr. Nelson (who had reminded Lady Hamilton that this was his correct style, since the degree of D.D. had been conferred upon him in January by his own University) arrived in Oxford in what his relations described as "a diamond humour—that is in the very best". The Dean of Exeter had at last expired, but should his brother's applica-tion to Mr. Addington fail, he had just read in a newspaper that Stalls were vacant at Durham and York. A Peace Election was dis-turbing the country, and on his recent visit to his old college for the purpose of voting for Mr. Pitt, he had been gratified by "a bow from Billy" in the Senate House. "So I made up to him and said a word or two."

Other characters in the Admiral's immediate circle were thinking of preferment. Beckford, on hearing that the Duke of Hamilton had honoured Merton to partake of a family dinner and make the acquaintance of Lord Nelson, had jogged his kinsman's elbow, and Sir William, before leaving Merton, had accomplished his difficult letter to the Marquis of Douglas. He urbanely presented "an old plan of Beckford's" as one "which Lord Nelson and Lady H. have taken up warmly". In fact, Nelson's comment on Beckford's scheme, privately delivered to Lady Hamilton, was not flattering. He thought it "dirty" and "a rub-off"

Until April 10, when Admiral Nelson had received permission to strike his flag and come on shore, he had been nominally on leave, and still in command of his "squadron on a particular service". Repeated applications for his discharge had been met by steady refusals until peace was signed, an event which had been celebrated throughout the country with somewhat unbridled revelry. To inspect Buonaparte's Paris, unless detained at the hustings, was the popular programme for an English gentleman this season. For an Admiral who loathed everything French, and took no great interest in the Election, a tour of various towns of his native land which had offered him their Freedom, combined with a visit to Sir William's estates, in the company of his dearest friends and a contingent of his family, seemed a preferable way of obtaining a change of air and scene while Merton underwent some improvements. He had paid £23 for Halfhide's strip, and was now in treaty with an elderly Mr. Axe of Birchin Lane for a field which alone separated Merton Place from the abbey wall. Mr. Axe was agreeable, but a tenant to whom the field was let was not, so he could only suggest that his Lordship should buy the whole farm, consisting of 150 acres, for £8,000. The Matchams were going to share in the investment, so while Oxford bells tolled outside on a wet summer's day, business as well as pleasure was under discussion. Upstairs, two competent Italian *valets*, who had travelled in the second coach from Merton, were preparing the Stars and Orders for to-morrow's ceremonies. The red ribbon worn by both distinguished gentlemen was that of the English Order of the Bath; that of the Neapolitan "St. Ferdinand and Merit" was blue with a narrow red border; a moss green accompanied the laurelled cross *patée* of St. Joachim, and a fondant pink belonged to the golden Crescent, bearing the sign manual of Selim III. Tom Allen, discharged from His Majesty's Service, master of £95 and a bride to whom Lady Hamilton had been attentive during his absence in the Baltic, had retired to raise a family in his native Norfolk. To Francatello and Gaetano their task was reminiscent of Embassy days, and indeed for all the principal members of the party the next three weeks bade fair to resemble their homeward journey of two years past.

On Thursday, July 22, the City of Oxford bestowed the Freedom, in a golden box, upon Lord Nelson, and the Senior Burgess, a fair, stout, untidy gentleman, with a very polished manner, had a kindly paw for young George Matcham, introduced as a future lawyer. Sir William Scott, friend of Samuel Johnson, and a very good friend of the Bodleian, put into his pocket a copy of Lord Nelson's *Plan for Manning the Navy*, with professions of much interest. Friday, a day of boisterous weather, was dedicated to the University. In full Congregation the Honorary Degree of Doctor of Civil Law was conferred upon Lord Nelson and Sir William Hamilton, presented by Dr. Blackstone, Vinerian Professor of Civil Law. Dr. Collinson, Lady Margaret Professor of Divinity, presented the Rev. Dr. Nelson of Christ's College, Cambridge, Doctor of Divinity of the University of Cambridge, on his admission to the same degree in the University of Oxford. Having left behind him a present to be distributed amongst the prisoners in the city gaol, Nelson left Oxford after dinner. The party spent the night at a Woodstock inn, and next morning prepared to view the splendours bestowed by a grateful sovereign upon a military hero.

But at Blenheim a disconcerting incident occurred. Neither Lord Nelson nor Sir William Hamilton was acquainted with the owner, a nobleman whose habitual hauteur was translated by friends as partially the result of shyness. The ducal family, although in residence, made no welcoming appearance. After a lengthy pause (necessitated by the carrying out of an order issued to the kitchens of a palace), refreshments in the park for Lord Nelson and friends were announced. Last season newspapers had published daily, with uncharitable comment, the highly ingenuous love-letters of the heir of the house (the father of a young family) to the unhappily married lady of the Member for Bridport. Nothing could have been less desired at Blenheim than a party containing any more famous names linked by scandal. It does not appear that any of the rebuffed sightseers realised anything but personal affront. Sir William expressed pained surprise, Lady Hamilton wrath. The collation so coldly proffered was as coldly declined by Nelson, carriages were called for, and, as his careful accounts of the expenses of his Tour record, horses from Troymill to Burford, their next stage, cost £3 14s.

At Gloucester the footfalls of what the Press called "Lord Nelson's tourists" sounded in cloister and aisle, and here, after an affectionate farewell, the Matchams turned off for Bath, taking with them the bad weather. High summer heat settled upon the increasingly sylvan landscape through which the diminished party headed for the very tip of South Wales, where belief in fairies, witches and ghosts was general, and fisherwomen wore scarlet cloaks and steeple hats. But the glades of the Forest of Dean spoke to a sea-officer primarily of wooden walls: he enquired much as to the cultivation and preservation of oak-timber from the landowners in whose company he sat during the following month in public hall and private house, and the results were noted, in his own hand, for a report to the Prime Minister. Greville was waiting for them at Milford, and in a district in which Sir William's name also was potent his heir had drawn up a list of engagements which included laying the foundation stone of a new church, attendance at a Fair, Rowing Match and Cattle Show (which it was hoped might become an annual event on the anniversary of the Nile), and a Banquet. The Lord Lieutenant was coming, Lord Kensington, Captain Thomas Foley and Lord Cawdor (whose 750 rustic volunteers, together with a couple of naval lieutenants, had captured an invading force of 1,400 French on a freezing February night five years past). The company was well chosen, and the setting was cheerful—a perfectly modern marine hotel, with a dazzling view. It was remarked that Lord Nelson looked particularly happy on the night of August 1, and his praise of their splendid harbour pleased both the purely patriotic and those who had commercial interest in its development. He compared Milford favourably with Trincomalee, in the East Indies, and Sir William closed the festivity by presenting to the room in which they were gathered a remarkable oil-painting of his renowned friend performed by Guzzardi of Palermo, at a date when the hero was suffering from the wound on the brow sustained at the Nile.

Seaside days, beneficial to all, slipped away easily, though perhaps not quietly, since some expedition into a landscape of mild airs and sub-tropical vegetation was undertaken every day.

The travellers swept through Pembroke (destined to secure the dockyard and arsenal hoped for by Greville and Sir William for Milford) and at Swansea "a choice body of exultant tars" drew the Admiral to receive the Freedom of the town, where his speech of thanks containing a word on National Service addressed to the rising generation was printed for distribution by an enterprising Portreeve. The carriages were greased that night, in preparation for the long homeward journey through the Midlands, and the day of their second arrival at Monmouth was ideally spent, for the ruins of Chepstow Castle were admired before dinner at Piercefield Park, and those of Tintern Abbey by sunset. Next morning, early, the Admiral drove in a carriage and four up to the Kymin Pavilion to inspect the only Naval Temple in England and partake of another Public Breakfast, during which a band played and cannon were discharged; and since the day was very fine, he walked back to the town through the Beaulieu Grove to dine with the Mayor and Corporation. Venison had been sent by the Duke of Beaufort to the "Beaufort Arms". "Lady Hamilton charmed the company with several songs sung to the tunes of 'Rule Britannia' and 'God save the King' ", and again the speech of thanks made by a happy man was felicitous:

"It was my good fortune to have under my command, some of the most experienced Officers in the English Navy, whose professional skill was seconded by the undaunted courage of British Sailors; and whatever merit might attach itself to me, I must declare that I had only to show them the Enemy and Victory crowned the Standard. . . . In my own person I have received an overflowing measure of the Nation's gratitude—far more than I either merited or expected; because the same success would have crowned the efforts of any other British Admiral, who had under his command such distinguished Officers and such gallant Crews. And here let me impress it on the mind of every Officer in the Service, that to whatever quarter of the Globe he may be destined, whether to the East or West Indies, to Africa, or America—the eyes of his Country are upon him. . . ."

Nelson's arrival at Birmingham was prudently timed for two hours before he was expected. The piece presented at the playhouse that night was *The Merry Wives*, and "Blissett, the Bath actor, supporting the character of the Fat Knight extremely well", "set the house in a roar by turning to the stage box as he rolled forth the line, 'Before the best Lord in the land, I swear it!' " Citizens carrying torches escorted the guests back to Styles's Hotel, and the tour of the factories of "the first toy-shop in Europe" undertaken next morning was conscientious. The tourists struck Watling Street at Towcester, and, moving fast thereafter, reached Merton on Sunday, September 5, having been absent six instead of the intended three weeks. "We have had", wrote Lady Hamilton to Davison, "a most charming Tour, which will Burst *some* of *Them*." Mrs. Matcham was more elegantly informed: "Oh, how our Hero has been received! I wish you could come to hear all our Story—most enteresting."

Nelson's 1802 Tour is important in his story for several reasons. He had made holiday before, unnoticed, in the days of his obscurity. He had been enthusiastically received in English towns before, and was to be again, but always on his way to or from a campaign. Accustomed to long hours of nervous strain and far worse discomforts, he returned from his Tour in glowing health and confirmed in his belief that John Bull and he understood one another. Upon the many who caught sight of him, arriving in a dusty carriage, bowing from a balcony, escorted through institution, aisle and factory, or rising to reply to a toast, his image was fixed, the embodiment of the vigilance and resolution of the Service he represented. His speech was unvarying in essentials. By the grace of God it had been his good fortune to command in many engagements officers and seamen of unmatched courage, skill and discipline. Should this nation ever be called upon again to repel attack, he had no fear of the result.

"You have but to say to your fleets and armies—'Go ye forth, and fight our battles, whilst we, true to ourselves, protect and support your wives and little ones at home. . . .' " I have not the slightest doubt, from the result of my observations during this tour, that the native, the inbred spirit of Britons, whilst it continues as firmly united as at present, is fully adequate."

He brought back from his Tour another conviction upon which he did not publicly enlarge. Within a few weeks of his return he had ascertained that if hostilities should recommence he was to command the Mediterranean Fleet.

6

Sir William Hamilton, after a very exhausting experience, found himself soon called upon to take the road again, and to a place devoid of resource for the elderly antiquary—a fashionable seaside resort in the height of the season. A most unsatisfactory letter from the Marquis of Douglas had reached him. His kinsman politely but flatly refused to touch Beckford's peerage scheme. Shortly after their arrival at Ramsgate his wife addressed a remarkable note to him. (Her temper, too, had been frayed, and by an accident which she could not announce. She had lost the address of the Margate lodgings to which Mrs. Gibson had been ordered by Nelson to take Horatia for a seaside holiday.)

"As I see it is a pain to you to remain here, let me beg of you to fix your time of going. Weather I dye in Piccadilly or any other spot in England, 'tis the same to me; but I remember the time when you wished for tranquility, but now all visiting and bustle is your liking. However, I will do what you please, being ever your affectionate and obedient E.H."

The ex-Ambassador's comment written on the back of the sheet was characteristic.

"I neither love bustle nor great company, but I like some employment and diversion. I have but a very short time to live, and every moment is precious to me. I am in no hurry and am exceedingly glad to give every satisfaction to our best friend, our dear Lord Nelson. The question, then, is what we can best do that all may be perfectly satisfied. Sea-bathing is usefull to your health; I see it is, and wish you to continue it a little longer; but I must confess that I regret, whilst the season is favourable, that I cannot enjoy my favourite amusement of quiet fishing. I care not a pin for the great world, and am attached to no one so much as to you."

That storm blew over, but before the month was out he found himself obliged to address her again in dissatisfaction much more seriously:

"I have passed the last 40 years of my life in the hurry and bustle that must necessarily be attendant on a publick character. I am arrived at the age when some repose is really necessary, and I promised myself a quiet home, and altho' I was sensible, and said so when I married, that I shou'd be super-annuated when my wife wou'd be in her full beauty and vigour of youth. That time is arrived, and we must make the best of it for the comfort of both parties. Unfortunately our tastes as to the manner of living are very different. I by no means wish to live in solitary retreat, but to have seldom less than 12 or 14 at table, and those varying continually, is coming back to what was so irksome to me in Italy during the latter years of my residence in that country. I have no connections out of my own family. I have no complaint to make, but I feel that the whole attention of my wife is given to Ld. N. and his interest at Merton. I well know the purity of Lord N.'s friendship for Emma and me, and I know how very uncomfortable it would make his Lp. Our best friend, if a separation shou'd take place, and am therefore determined to do all in my power to prevent such an extremity, which wou'd be *essentially detrimental* to all parties, but wou'd be more sensibly felt by our dear friend than by us. Provided that our expences in housekeeping do not encrease beyond measure (of which I must own I see some danger), I am willing to go on upon our present footing; but as I cannot expect to live many years, every moment to me is precious, and I hope I may be allow'd sometimes to be my own master, and pass my time according to my own inclination, either by going my fishing parties on the Thames or by going to London to attend the Museum, R. Society, the Tuesday Club and Auctions of pictures. I mean to have a light post chariot or post chaise by the month, that I may make use of it in London, and run backward and forwards to Merton or to Shepperton, etc. This is my plan, and we might go on very well, but I am fully determined not to have any more of the very silly altercations that happen but too often between us and embitter the present moments exceedingly. If really one cannot live comfortably together, a *wise* and well *concerted separation* is preferable; but I think, considering the probability of my not troubling any party long in this world, the best for us all wou'd be to bear those ills we have rather than flie to those we know not of. I have fairly stated what I have on my mind. There is no time for nonsense or trifling. I know and admire your talents, and many excellent qualities, but I am not blind to your defects and confess having many myself; therefore let us bear and forbear for God's sake."

The result was that no separation took place, and during October he accomplished many excursions on the Thames, from one of which he brought back, in revived spirits, more than sixty pounds of fish. With the opening of the autumn season, Nelson accompanied him to meetings of the Literary Society. On Christmas Day a young party sat down to Merton turkey, and fifty wood bavins formed the Yule fire. Lady Hamilton told Mrs. Matcham, who was hopeful again, "here we are as happy as Kings, and much more. We have 3 Boltons, 2 Nelsons, and only need two or three Little Matchams to be quite *en famille*." She gave a Children's Ball for the country-house party early in the New Year, and, his nieces and

nephews having been allowed by an indulgent hostess to dance till
3 a.m., Nelson found next noon that so far he was the only soul
about in his house. He went up to 23, Piccadilly, with the Hamiltons in mid-January, and a tottering courtier, who had not lost hope,
presented himself at Her Majesty's Birthday Drawing-Room. Lady
Mansfield had promised Lady Hamilton to get poor Sir William
near the King. Nelson's winter, so far as professional life went, was
quietly spent. "I really am so little in the world", he explained to
Davison, "that I know little, if anything, beyond [what] newspaper
reports say, respecting our affairs on the Continent." The First
Lord was out of Town for a long spell, ill, but he saw both St.
Vincent and Troubridge occasionally. Neither ever offered to visit
Merton. He submitted to the Admiralty careful memoranda on
three subjects—Manning, Desertion and Prize-Money—and having,
in his own opinion, entirely failed to carry his points, was too dis-
heartened to forward a fourth document dealing with the flotilla
for Coast Defence. He had two ports of call during this winter at
which his repeated appearances passed unsuspected by the world. He
often sent in his name at an unfashionable hotel in which a Naval
Chaplain was lying collapsed after a disastrous trip to the Jamaicas.
He had long had his eye upon the Rev. A. J. Scott, an expert in
languages, as a desirable member of an Admiral's staff. Before proceeding to his next inconspicuous destination, he sometimes paused
at a toy-shop, and on one occasion gave sixpence for a watch which
would tick audibly. ("She was always fond of my watch.") Mrs.
Gibson, whose charge was unafraid of her illustrious god-father,
would tactfully withdraw, having brought in Horatia, and the
couple would play together for hours, upon the carpet.

A call from a nightmarish past reached the Admiral in the first
week of February. He had, like the rest of the newspaper-reading
world, been aware since November that one of the Despard
brothers, well known to him on the San Juan expedition, had been
under arrest on a dreadful charge. The career of Lieut. Edward
Marcus Despard, of the 50th Regiment, since Captain Nelson of the
Hinchingbrooke and he had served together, nearly a quarter of a
century past, had been unhappy. Colonel Despard, recalled to England from Yucatan in 1790 to answer a number of charges for

cruelty and illegal action brought against him as Governor by the settlers, had been kept hanging about the Secretary of State's office for a couple of seasons before being informed that, although his post had been abolished, he would not be forgotten. Six years later a violently spoken unemployed man had been arrested and imprisoned for a few weeks. In 1800, during a third period of detention, he had begun to plot against the Government. According to the evidence given at his trial by his spies, his scheme had been to seduce the Guards, seize the Tower and Bank of England, stop the English outgoing mails and assassinate the King on his way to open Parliament. Nelson, to his discomfiture, found himself subpœnaed to give evidence for the defence, at the New Sessions House, Horsemonger Lane, on February 7. He could not refuse, and duly testified that in the year 1780, "on the Spanish main, we were together in the enemies' trenches and slept in the same tent. Colonel Despard was then a loyal man and a brave officer." The Attorney-General, prosecuting, paid a tribute to a national hero, "a man on whom to pronounce an eulogy were to waste words", and Nelson's testimony produced a recommendation to mercy from the jury. But the evidence was too strong, and at 3 a.m. on the 9th Colonel Despard was condemned to death for High Treason, a sentence which included hideous details. Every circumstance of the remaining days was horrible, for between his sentence and execution the condemned man sent a high-flown letter to Nelson, saying that he would ask no further inscription on his tomb than the character provided by his old comrade-in-arms. He enclosed, almost without mention, a petition which Nelson forwarded in equal silence to Addington, and the Prime Minister and family, studying it together after supper, were moved to tears. Despard was dragged to the block on a hurdle, together with half a dozen of his poor associates, on February 21. He had refused the Sacrament, and he made a long speech on the scaffold, before being first hanged, then decapitated. The remainder of the sentence was remitted. Nelson, visiting Lord Minto in Spring Gardens on the following day, divulged that Mrs. Despard, who had insisted on being present at the final scene, was "violently in love with her husband". He had solicited a pension for her from the Government, but believed that Despard's shocking conduct in denying the Chaplain admittance must render it ineffectual.

Throughout the Session, Admiral Nelson spoke in the Lords on professional subjects with growing ease and eloquence. On March 8 a message from the King to Parliament stated that, in view of the activity in French ports, His Majesty had judged it expedient to make suitable preparations for the security of his realm. That night, at 23, Piccadilly, while London traffic slurred through melting snow, the Admiral sat late at his desk. Some months had passed since, on the eve of a campaign, he had mentioned to Lady Hamilton that he was going to dine quietly with an elderly officer "forced to go to sea, owing to the extravagance of his children". With child-like faith he had applauded his ideal woman when she had told him that she was settling a few small debts before the move to Merton. "You are right, Emma. Poor trades-people cannot afford to lay out their money." The sheet achieved by him on the night of March 8 ran as follows:

LORD NELSON'S INCOME AND PROPERTY

My Exchequer Pension for the Nile	£2,000	0 0
Navy Pension for loss of one arm and one eye	923	0 0
Half-pay as Vice-Admiral	465	0 0
Interest of £1000	30	0 0
	£3,418	0 0

OUTGOINGS OF LORD NELSON

To Lady Nelson	£1,800	0 0
Interest of money owing	500	0 0
Pension to my Brother's Widow	200	0 0
To assist in educating my Nephews	150	0 0
Expenditure	£2,650	0 0
Income	£3,418	0 0

The result, as the most elementary mathematician could see, was "For Lord Nelson £768 0s. 0d. per annum", and in a single week of this year (to be sure an exceptionally heavy one, that following the return from his Tour) bills at Merton and Piccadilly had amounted to £117 8s. 2½d. The Tour itself had cost £480 odd. Next afternoon, while the Debate on the King's Speech was in progress in the Lords, he left his seat to scribble a reminder to the Prime Minister, "Whenever it is necessary, I am *your* Admiral."

More than a week later "nothing positive concerning Peace or War" was generally known. The reason for the King's message had been kept a close secret. The Militia had been called out, but it was guessed that as the strong measures taken in London had not produced an instant rupture with Paris, negotiation was still proceeding. Nelson returned to Merton, reasonably sure that in any case he would soon find himself afloat again. He was known to be in favour of a continuation of the peace, if possible, and therefore unlikely to act provocatively, and his mere appearance in the Mediterranean might cause Buonaparte to hesitate. His flagship was named, much to his satisfaction. "For I know the weight of the *Victory* in the Mediterranean." Towards the end of the month an event threatened which affected him personally, but did not alter his plans. Sir William Hamilton suffered a sudden collapse, entailing a period of unconsciousness. He recovered, to summon gentlemen of Lincoln's Inn to Merton Place and add a codicil to his Will, but he had recognised unmistakable symptoms, and he desired to be moved up to London, to await the inevitable hour with all possible dignity under his own roof. His physicians, headed by Moseley of Jamaica, pronounced his case hopeless. He felt no pain, and welcomed members of his family to his bedside, but he lay, after his safe arrival, "going off", said Nelson, "as an inch of candle".

As the lengthening spring days dragged by, in a hushed town house, cut off from London activities, Nelson declared, "I shall almost hate April. Look at the last three years!" The month which would bring the anniversaries of the deaths of his brother Maurice and his father opened, and he pictured the outside world hanging on news from 23, Piccadilly. "All London is interested in such a character." Actually, although obituaries were graceful, the departure of a retired Ambassador, a notable collector of classical antiquities, was quickly forgotten. Sir William, wandering in mind at last, ceased to breathe on the morning of April 6, without a sigh or a struggle, in the arms of his wife, and with Nelson holding his hand. Both attendants were exhausted from nights and days of watching and previous false alarms; both uttered the language of genuine grief. "The World", wrote Nelson, "never lost a more upright and accomplished gentleman. . . . I lose a friend who has spoken well of me for thirty-seven years." Lady Hamilton tragically noted, "April 6th. Unhappy day for the forlorn Emma. Ten minutes past ten, dear, blessed Sir William left me." The proprieties were strictly observed. Mrs. William Nelson had already arrived from Norfolk, but despite his sister-in-law's presence, Nelson at once took lodgings at 19, Piccadilly, over a saddler's shop, and never again dated a letter from 23. Lady Hamilton directed Mrs. Gibson to keep Horatia indoors until after the funeral, "as we are very close and sincere mourners", and applied to Greville to know what provision had been made for her, whether he would pay her debts, and how long she might remain in her late husband's house. A hatchment, displaying the sable ship of Arran and the bleeding heart of Douglas supported by silver antelopes, ducally gorged, was delivered and erected over the front door of 23, Piccadilly, and Sir William's coffin set off on its long journey to his Pembrokeshire estates and burial by the side of his first lady.

Early in May his Will was read, in the presence of his assembled noble kin, in a house of mourning noticeably gaunt. As all the furniture was hers, Lady Hamilton had already installed it in a smaller house in Clarges Street, close by. The actual Will contained no surprises. Greville was, as had always been understood, his uncle's heir; the provision for Lady Hamilton was, as Nelson had always anticipated, insufficient to keep her in the style to which she had been accustomed as Sir William's lady. She received an immediate gift of £300, and an annuity of £800, of which £100 a year was to be paid, while Mrs. Cadogan survived, to her mother. However, Lord Melville had responded promisingly to applications from Greville, Nelson, and the widow herself, for some continuation of the ex-Ambassador's pension, and Merton should be hers (with £100 a month from the owner, for housekeeping). The codicil, added after Sir William's seizure, displayed anxiety that his nephew should complete his engagement "to pay Emma's debts" (calculated as no more than £450), but suggested as the source "the arrears due to me from the Treasury as the King's Minister at Naples", an old grievance, unlikely to yield profit. There was affectionate particularisation of a violin admired by the Marquis of Douglas, and long designed for that valuable connection. Only the legacy to Nelson was worded in a style which must arouse comment:

"The copy of Madame le Brun's picture of Emma, in enamel, by Bone, I give to my dearest friend, Lord Nelson, Duke of Brontë; a very small token of the great regard I have for his Lordship, the most virtuous, loyal, and truly brave character I ever met with, God bless him, and shame fall on those who do not say 'Amen'."

Nelson meanwhile had been warned to prepare for departure, and had summoned to 19, Piccadilly the tradesmen to be favoured with orders to supply the Commander-in-Chief of a Mediterranean Fleet. He had been down to Merton to settle matters there. He had seen his new Secretary, Mr. John Scott, lately Purser of the *Royal Sovereign*. On May 13 Mrs. Gibson, provided with written instructions to give the clergyman and clerk double fees and bring back a record of the baptism, carried her charge to Marylebone Parish Church, to be christened by the names of Horatia Nelson Thompson.

A ceremony of Installation of Knights Elect of the Order of the Bath had been fixed to take place in Westminster Abbey on May 19, and Nelson had invited his old secretary, Tyson, and his nephews Horace and Tom, to be his esquires. The preparations had been great, and the family disappointment at the prospect of a cancellation was commensurate. But on Lord Nelson's requesting that a young connection in His Majesty's Service might act as his proxy, he was informed that not only might Captain William Bolton, R.N., represent him; his proxy would receive the honour of knighthood on the preceding day. The compliment gave pleasure, for the young man (one of the boys to go to sea with him in his first ship-of-the-line) was engaged to be married to a first cousin, the little Kitty Bolton who had been present in a Bath lodging on a Sunday evening when her famous uncle had returned to his family from Santa Cruz. Lady Hamilton had furthered the match ("the girl may thank you (if it is worth thanking) for her husband"), and the wedding, at which the

Admiral would not now be present, was to take place at Clarges Street on the night of the 18th. He left London at about 4 a.m. on that morning.

He breakfasted at Liphook, and arrived at Portsmouth, almost smothered with dust, at exactly 1 p.m., to be greeted by Captains Hardy and Sutton, the former in very high spirits. The harbour was dark with merchantmen awaiting convoy. The *Victory* was lying so far out that he could scarcely distinguish her, and the *Amphion*, the frigate in which Hardy was going to accompany him to the Mediterranean, was entirely beyond his powers of vision. During his past months of better health he had been haunted by fancies that the sight of his "good" eye was failing, and there had been discussion with Moseley of an operation. His own opinion had been that if it was necessary, the sooner it was done the better, but Moseley (given *carte blanche*, with a cheerful reminder that his patient could not very well spare another eye) had hesitated.

Portsmouth two days after a declaration of war was much as might have been expected. The thunder of 13 guns about 3.30 p.m. signified that Admiral Lord Nelson, who had hoisted his flag on board H.M.S. *Victory*, was saluting the Commander-in-Chief. The High Street and Parade were blocked by carriages and post-chaises, but the heaviest wheeled traffic converged upon the landing-point, where a continual service of tradesmen's carts, delivering livestock, groceries, liquors and crockery for newly commissioned ships-of-the-line, were in competition with hallooing porters trundling officers' luggage over the cobbles on barrows. With dusk the pandemonium increased. Heated and vociferous midshipmen scudded along the row of drinking- and dancing-houses for which the back of the Point was infamous, and forcibly recovered from the arms of their gaily dressed but tipsy Dulcineas the crews which must be waiting to pull the Captain to his ship. Sailors, clustering on the tops of hired coaches, waved their tarpaulin hats and cheered as their vehicles collided, and shouted witticisms to one another and their admirers.

Lord Nelson's heavy luggage began to make its appearance after dinner, and his new secretary ran about in a promising manner. His lordship's sofa and a treasured large chair were not in any list.

His wine was still in the Customs House; the parcels containing his table linen had not been so labelled, and his cot had been sent to the *Amphion*, in the belief that the *Victory* could not be ready. She seemed, indeed, to her new master, "in a pretty state of confusion", and he was inclined to be vexed with the amiable Sutton, who, when the wind was fair, reported that the ship would be ready in every respect for sea by Friday morning. "A good man, but not so active as Hardy" was told to try to make it Thursday night, and the Admiral retired genially, after a quiet meal, to write to their Lordships ("must keep them in good humour") and to assure Lady Hamilton that, so far as personal belongings went, he had never gone to sea so well provided. To his relief, the Commander-in-Chief had been engaged to dine out. ("They say there is much drinking.") Next morning, after an interview with Lord Gardner, he comforted himself with the old adage, "We shall get no rest, till we get to sea", but the fact that the *Victory* would have to sail half manned was, besides alarming, maddening to an expert whose suggestions for manning H.M. ships had been shelved at Whitehall. Dinner with Lord Gardner on Thursday could not be avoided, but his lordship had most civilly invited Mr. Davison (who was not going to leave the *Victory* until she was under sail) and Lord Minto, also just arrived from London, with his brother, Mr. Hugh Elliot, who had been ordered, at twenty-four hours' notice, to take up the post once held by Sir William Hamilton.

On Friday, May 20, 1803, Portsmouth reporters ended a chapter in Nelson's story. "Such was the anxiety of Lord Nelson to embark, that yesterday, to one that spoke of his sailing, he said, 'I cannot, before to-morrow, and that's an age!' This morning, about 10 o'clock, his Lordship went off, in a heavy shower of rain, and sailed with a Northerly wind." Letters began to trickle back to Clarges Street. The first came from the "George", Portsmouth, "By Messenger": "The boat is on shore, and five minutes sets me afloat. I can only pray that the great God of heaven may bless and preserve you, and that we may meet again, in peace and true happiness. I have no fears." He wrote again before noon, from a Great Cabin which had been the background for the figures of Keppel, Kempenfelt, Howe, Hood and St. Vincent, and in which the smell of fresh paint was no worse than he had anticipated. "You will believe that, although I am glad to leave that horrid place, Portsmouth, yet the being afloat makes me now feel that we do not tread the same element."

Five days later, his voice sounded distant indeed: "Here we are, in the middle of the Bay of Biscay—nothing to be seen, but the sky and water. . . ."

MEDITERRANEAN COMMAND

I

THE ROCK was surprised on the night of Friday, June 3, 1803, when Lord Nelson, appointed to the Mediterranean Command, appeared flying his flag in a 32-gun frigate. At Gibraltar nobody had even known that England was at war again.

His orders were to make the best of his way to Malta, and having conferred with Governor Ball and taken Sir Richard Bickerton's squadron under his command, proceed with all possible despatch off Toulon. His last instructions, brought on board the *Victory* at Spithead at 1 a.m. on the morning before he sailed, had been on no account to miss making the offer of that first-rate to the Commander-in-Chief of the Channel Fleet. He did not himself believe that Cornwallis could want the *Victory*, and after going to the Black Rocks off Brest, and hearing from a frigate that his old friend had a *rendezvous* at sea, he was assured that fears of the enemy putting out from that port were at present groundless. He searched for Cornwallis for twenty-four hours (losing a wind which would have carried him to Portugal) before deciding to act in strict obedience to his orders, but against his judgment. The saddened Sutton was told that if he did not fall in with Admiral Cornwallis within a week he must return to Plymouth for further orders; a change made very difficult by a strong wind and heavy sea was effected shortly before dark on May 23, and at 10 p.m. that night Nelson lost sight of the *Victory*, "to my great mortification". His letter to Cornwallis had begged that, if the Channel Fleet did not need the *Victory* "to add to the show off Brest", she should be ordered to join him without a moment's loss of time, and he had left behind in her his steward and all his stock, with the exception of a few trunks of linen.

He had expected that in the *Amphion* he and his staff must be truly uncomfortable, and a foul wind, blowing fresh, and a nasty sea, were soon their lot. Not a vessel was to be seen on the face of the waters as they laboured off Cape Finisterre. The Admiral's Interpreter saw a whale, and noted it in his diary. The Admiral caught a head cold, and began to imagine that the worst might happen, owing to his delay in getting to his station. In feverish moments he feared that Buonaparte might even seize Sicily. But he told himself, "Patience is a virtue at sea", and gradually came to realise that his *suite*, in spite of sleeping seven and eight in a cabin, were not unhappy; that, in fact, a particularly invigorating atmosphere pervaded a small frigate in the highest possible order, doing her utmost. ("Hardy takes good care of us and the *Amphion* is very comfortable.")

A pastel of a fashionably dressed woman, wearing a foreign decoration (an excellent likeness, and one of the handsomest Mr. John Scott had ever seen), was toasted in the third and last bumper every evening. The secretary's engagement had come at a very welcome moment from the financial point of view, but from the domestic, tragic. Lady Hamilton had promised to send him news of Mrs. Scott's confinement. He had been provided with the remedy for the Admiral's spasms, and took care to report regularly. Below the picture of Lord Nelson's Guardian Angel hung a crayon sketch of his adopted child—a stout two-year-old, with cropped fair hair and rosy cheeks, dressed in a mob cap, ankle-length muslin gown and morocco shoes, standing in a garden, with its finger in its mouth. Their owner felt revived every time he looked at his hostages to fortune, and prayed for a short war—"just long enough to make me independent in pecuniary matters".

After passing Lisbon, the *Amphion* was blessed with a gentle fair wind, which so much freshened during hours of darkness, off Cape St. Vincent, that she entered the Straits at 2 p.m. on June 2, having made a run of more than a hundred leagues since eight o'clock on the previous morning. She captured a French brig shortly before coming to anchor in Rosia Bay, and learnt that Buonaparte's brother, Jerome, had passed a few days before, in the *Jemappes*, from Martinique. "If we had proceeded direct in the

Victory, we should have had her to a certainty." A single night and forenoon were spent in Gibraltar. Mr. Elliot sent a messenger to Hookham Frere, his opposite number at Madrid, to ask how England's declaration of war had been received in that capital. The British Consul at Cadiz thought that Spain must join Buonaparte, but his theories were not supported by any signs of activity in the Cadiz Naval Arsenal. Lord Nelson landed at 5 a.m., paid his respects to the Lieutenant-Governor, Sir Thomas Trigge; gave instructions to Mr. Pownall, Naval Storekeeper, and the officers of the dockyard; saw the surgeon of the Naval Hospital; detailed the frigates to guard the entry to the Straits and keep up communications with the Barbary coast; and made arrangements with the agent of a Quaker gentleman, Mr. Edward Gayner, merchant of Rosas, who was to prove useful. He took his leave of all before dinner, and the *Amphion* weighed at 4 p.m. In Tetuan Bay she cleared for action, and next day, Trinity Sunday, captured a French and a Dutch brig. A week later, in full view of the mountains of Mauretania, Mr. Elliot, supplied with letters both official and personal to every influential character at the court of the Two Sicilies, was transferred to H.M.S. *Maidstone* for a direct passage to Naples. He took with him also the body-servant of his predecessor. Gaetano Spedilo, who had been *valet* for thirty years to Sir William Hamilton, promised to return to Lord Nelson when he had seen his wife and children, but his present master doubted whether he would ever see the efficient Neapolitan again.

The remainder of the *Amphion's* progress to Malta was distressingly tedious. The Admiral (as he watched coral-fishing fleets fade into summer haze, and a familiar, eternally brown, burnt-up coastline, presenting the silhouettes of mosques) dictated letters announcing his appointment and arrival to the various authorities of the Mediterranean coasts. The temperature had been rising ever since they left the Rock, and on July 1, as he ascended between cheering crowds towards the white courtyards of the Governor's Palace at Valetta, attended by the Governor, to visit General Vilette and the lady of General Bickerton, and to drink tea with Lady Ball, he found himself cured of his cold but gasping for fresh air. His brief call was, upon the whole, unsatisfactory. Malta, like Gibraltar, had heard nothing of the war. Sir Richard Bickerton's squadron had sailed to cruise between Sicily and Naples on the same day that Lord Nelson had left Portsmouth. Governor Ball was very pleased to see him, but the man seemed to have become sadly desiccated. Drawing around him the solemn mantle of *le Corps Diplomatique*, Sir Alexander hinted that there were negotiations which could not be divulged to an Admiral.

Nelson's thirty-six-hour call to the island convinced him that "this out of the way place" would never suit him as a base for operating against an enemy in Toulon. "The Fleet can never go there if I can find any other corner to put them in. It takes, upon an average, seven weeks to get an answer to a letter." His present experience was a three weeks' passage. In the Straits of Messina what he described as "the lower class of boat-people" swarmed on board, bringing fruit and flowers. Their expressions of loyalty to their King and delight at seeing the English were strong. When asked if there were any Jacobins in their city, they replied with appropriate gesture, "Yes—the gentry who wear their hats so—on one side of the head!" "Bond Street loungers", commented the Admiral, receiving their protestations of affection with extreme caution. On June 25 he came in sight of "*Dear* Naples, if it is what it was. God send me good news!" The shape of Vesuvius, the circle of palaces and villas ranged around that radiant, sickle-shaped bay, aroused so many memories that he could scarcely restrain himself from flying on shore; but he had resolved not to add to their Majesties' difficulties by presenting himself at their court as yet. French troops had begun to take possession of Pescaro, Brindisi, Otranto, Taranto. The constant presence of a British ship-of-the-line in their Bay, always ready to take on board the complete royal family, would be at the moment a more tactful attention. The frigate which had carried Mr. Elliot to his new appointment reappeared, and brought reports that the news of Lord Nelson's approach had inspired all Naples with confidence.

Nearly everyone to whom he had written had answered by the *Maidstone*. He was a little disturbed that the Queen's reply did not mention her particular friend, of whose impoverished widowhood he had sent a clear account. He comforted himself with the reflection "hers is a political letter", and vowed, "If she can forget Emma, I hope God will forget her!" (Emma's belief was, he knew, "She never will, or can.") Mr. Elliot had not as yet been summoned to the King, who was said to be very dejected, living mostly at the Belvedere. Rumour declared that His Majesty would like nothing so much as to resign the throne of Naples, at least, to his son, and retire to Sicily—a situation often prophesied by Sir William Hamilton. To his master's surprise, Gaetano had returned, having apparently seen enough of conditions at home to realise himself lucky in his employment.

The owner of Brontë had heard, while upon his Welsh tour, that Graeffer, his residential agent, had died at his post. He had applied to his banker friends, Gibbs and Noble, for tidings of his estate, but Gaetano had found that both gentlemen were gone on business to Malta, so, as he did not wish to trouble Sir John Acton unnecessarily, an absentee landlord could only wait for their return, and hope that Sicily was not attacked meanwhile.

Other frigates had by now joined, bringing him official letters containing the first of the peck of minor troubles which must be the fate of a Commander-in-Chief. The ex-Ambassador to the Porte was a prisoner. On the morning of May 2, a fortnight before England had declared war on France, Buonaparte had struck his first lightning blow. He had summoned the Governor of Paris to his study at 1 a.m. and delivered to him an order to seize the persons of all Englishmen, from the ages of sixteen to sixty, at present in France. Amongst the visitors to Paris that week had been Lord Elgin, on his way from Constantinople to London. Mr. Drummond, from Naples, had been sent to succeed him, but the Earl's prestige in the Levant had been high, and his present ignominious situation must arouse undesirable reflections in the Oriental mind.

As he toiled slowly past Monte Cristo, Bastia and Cape Corse, Nelson concluded a report to the Prime Minister, marshalled under place-headings in block capitals. At *Gibraltar* he had left Sir Thomas Trigge, not unjustifiably worried that Dillon's Regiment, composed entirely of foreigners, was part of his garrison in war-time. With regard to *Algiers*, he forwarded the Consul's statement with a warning that if the Dey was given way to in the least degree, at a moment when he considered England embarrassed, his insolence would increase. At *Malta* Lord Nelson had found the populace vociferous in their desire never to be separated from England, but having admitted that he regarded the island as a most important outwork to India, and its possession valuable in connection with all Levantine and South Italian dealings, he repeated that nothing but dire necessity would force him to take the fleet there under present circumstances. *Sicily* called for a long paragraph. He thought its condition as bad as possible. It possessed no troops worthy the name. The decadent nobility were rightly unpopular, the middle classes were ready for almost any change of rule, and the peasantry were starving. *Sardinia* had declared herself neutral, and was allowing no foreign troops to land. He could only hope that she might be able to defend herself against a French invasion. It was difficult to know whether to look upon unfortunate *Tuscany* as friend or enemy. Perhaps H.M. Ministers would consider the possibility of blockading Leghorn while the French were in occupation. *Genoa* was undoubtedly as much French as Toulon, and its blockade ought to be declared instantly. "If not, it will be what it has always been, the granary of the South of France, and the north part of Italy." He came last to the *Morea*. He had no doubts that the French agents at work there were preparing it either for the arrival of an army of their own or a Greek revolt against the Porte. In either case it would be used as a base for another attempt on *Egypt*, the mention of which brought to his mind that Mohamed Bey Elphi desired a passage to England in order to solicit Britain's aid against Turkish oppression. "Government will know how to steer between the Turks and Mamelukes." His long letter ended with a calculation of the number of French troops now in Italy—13,000 in the Kingdom of Naples, 8,000 in Leghorn and more arriving every day. Buonaparte was drawing them even from Switzerland.

The *Amphion* was off Monaco on July 5, "looking out sharp for the *Victory*". Three days later, at 2.43 a.m., she saw a strange fleet. At 4.30 she made a private signal, which on its repetition ten minutes later was answered. She bore up, to salute Sir Richard Bickerton, with 11 guns, and at 7 o'clock Nelson took under his command H.M.S. *Gibraltar* (of 80 guns), the *Triumph*, *Belleisle*, *Superb*,

Renown, *Donegal* and *Kent* (all 74's), the *Agincourt* and *Monmouth* (64's), the *Medusa* frigate, and the sloops *Termagant* and *Weazle*.

A Chief of renowned ability, who had come amongst "perfect strangers", announced himself without a finger's ache since he had left England, and firmly of the opinion that the Mediterranean was about to become an active scene. His intention was to send his ships into port in turn, to prepare for a winter's cruise. "We are not very superior, if anything, in point of numbers. . . We must keep a good look-out, both here and off Brest, and if I have the means, I shall try and fight one party or the other before they form a junction." Officers were reminded that they must always have lead, or plenty of shot, attached to their despatches. . . .

The response, from the first, was promising. Sir Richard Bickerton hastened to ask Lord Nelson to mention to the First Lord that he was very desirous of remaining in the Mediterranean. Captain Keats, a character recommended by the Duke of Clarence, affirmed that he was recovering from an illness, but looked so shocking that he was at once ordered to Naples, with leave to remain there for a fortnight. He was back within nine days, knowing his lordship so short of ships at his *rendezvous* off Toulon. Frigates had been despatched to San Fiorenzo, Genoa and Leghorn, to get the number of troops there, and to look out for an enemy squadron reported to be coming either from the West Indies or Brest to join the Toulon fleet. Sloops were gone to the Bay of Rosas and Barcelona to enquire as to watering facilities, and the purchase (under the rose) of bullocks, fresh greens, oranges, lemons and onions. The *Agincourt* had sprung a leak, and must accompany Sir Richard's flagship, the *Kent*, to Valetta. The *Victory* was "in this country". She was at Malta, having taken a French frigate and two or three ships from San Domingo, worth £8,000, but within the limits of Admiral Cornwallis's station—"my usual prize luck!"

The first "scrape of a pen" to reach anyone in the squadron which had sailed from Portsmouth on May 20 also arrived from Naples in the *Phœbe*, on July 29. Lady Hamilton, who had been writing without cease, had chanced a line, fit for any eye, to the care of Messrs. Gibbs, Falconet and Noble, of Naples and Palermo. She was going to visit Lord Nelson's family in Norfolk, before a trip to Southend for sea-bathing, and she sketched plans for winter retirement with Lord Nelson's adopted daughter, at Merton, where she intended improvements. She enclosed a packet of business letters from Davison, and one item of news mentioned by his friend in his accompanying private note gave Nelson such a shock that for several days his thoughts recurred to it persistently. He had already been caused "very serious uneasiness" by paragraphs in English papers headed "Ilchester Election", reporting the first of the evidence being given before a select committee of the House of Commons. Davison, "a good deal alarmed about the bribery", had withdrawn his candidature, and was confident that he could surmount a situation engineered by his personal enemies, but Nelson longed to hear that his friend was quit of a business in which he smelt danger. "Not a day has passed without that I have thought of you." Every day, too, he noted his longing for the *Victory*. She came in sight, at last, on the morning of July 30, while he was at his desk, and that evening her log recorded: "5.30. Joined this Ship, Captain T. M. Hardy, and superseded Captain Sutton. Hoisted Lord Viscount Nelson's Flag."

2

Lord Nelson had two officers in the *Victory* named Scott, obviously an inconvenient circumstance. He solved the problem by calling his Chaplain, the Rev. Alexander John Scott, "Doctor", an anticipatory promotion, as the degree of D.D. was not conferred upon Mr. Scott by Cambridge University until after Trafalgar. This uncomplaining character, who had first attracted his attention as the Chaplain of a 74 in Lord Hood's fleet at Toulon, and afterwards as "Sir Hyde's parson-secretary", was an Original. Languages were his prey, and to his noble employer, who never attained proficiency in a single one, there was fascination in presenting a person of cadaverous countenance and luminous orbs with a captured French despatch, letter, pamphlet, or foreign newspaper, out of which they would together tear the heart in a few minutes. As Admiral's Interpreter, Dr. Scott received £100 per annum in addition to his pay as Chaplain of the *Victory*, but he was often useful in an unsuspected capacity. No Tuscan, Neapolitan, Algerine,

Sardinian or Spaniard, beholding an invalid archæologist admiring their ancient monuments, guessed him to be collecting information and provisions; and in fashionable circles Lord Nelson's Chaplain on sick-leave was more than once able to arrange amicably a concession which could not be granted on paper. His *Recollections of Life in the "Victory"* did his employer as much posthumous service, for Dr. Scott's was the voice to assure early Victorian England that Lord Nelson had been "a thorough clergyman's son. I should think he never went to bed or got up without saying his prayers." Every morning, unless other duties interposed, the pair met, after breakfast, to sit in two leather armchairs supplied with ample pockets, stuffed with matter awaiting translation, and the translator was repeatedly startled by his companion's skill in investigation, and ability to sift the few grains of intelligence lost in a bundle of apparent rubbish. Dr. Scott's considered opinion was "that man possessed the wisdom of the serpent with the innocence of the dove".

Mr. John Scott, official Secretary, bore equally enthusiastic testimony within a few weeks of taking up his duties. "I have heard much of Lord Nelson's abilities as an officer and statesman, but the account of the latter is infinitely short. In my travels through the Service, I have met with no character in any degree equal to his Lordship; his penetration is quick, judgment clear, wisdom great, and his decisions correct and decided: nor does he in company appear to bear any weight on his mind, so cheerful and pleasant, that it is a happiness to be about his hand."

In the *Victory* Nelson had three commodious rooms at his disposal, under the poop, immediately under those of Hardy. They consisted of state room, "great cabin", or reception-room, dining cabin and sleeping cabin, and, taken with his gallery and steward's room, accounted for rather more than a quarter of the whole upper deck. The state room, in which his labours with his secretaries were conducted, was fifteen feet long, and had a row of nine sash windows in the stern, where its width tapered to twenty-five feet. It had two doors communicating with the thirty-five-foot-wide dining-room, in which he had a staircase constructed so that he could reach the quarter-deck without loss of time. Two further doors from the dining-room led to a lobby, subdivided for kitchen and pantry, and his sleeping cabin, measuring twelve feet by twenty. The decks of all were covered with canvas, painted with a pattern of black and white squares, and the furniture, although solid and handsome, was strictly functional. He had, like Buonaparte and other men of action, formed the invaluable habit of being able to sleep in short snatches, from which he would arise filled with new vigour. Sometimes, according to Dr. Scott, he used the two black leather armchairs in his state room, lashed together, as a couch, but the *suite* included an ottoman and a folding bedstead. A dining-table, circular pedestal tables, other chairs, a sideboard, tall-boy and washstand, all of mahogany and typical mid-Georgian design, used during these years, have been preserved, and a replica of his cot is still to be seen in his sleeping cabin.

A Physician to the Fleet and a Surgeon of the *Victory*, neither of whom took up his appointment until the following season (a time when conditions were unchanged), also recorded impressions of daily life in the *Victory*. Dr. Gillespie was called at 6 a.m. by a servant who brought a light and informed him of the hour, wind, weather and course of the ship. He presented himself for breakfast at the Admiral's table at about quarter to seven, together with Murray, Hardy, the two Scotts and one or two other officers, and their fare was tea, hot rolls, toast and cold tongue or other cold meat. Afterwards, in fine, or at least moderate, weather, they repaired upon deck to enjoy a majestic sunrise above a watery perspective, hardly ever obscured by cloud. The *Victory*, "a floating city", mounting 110 guns, and designed to carry water and provisions for four months and a ship's company of nine hundred, went through the Mediterranean with the greatest steadiness, followed, in regular train, by other "lofty and tremendous bulwarks of Britain". During the last three-quarters of an hour of his morning's professional duty the physician worked to the accompaniment of a band, and the Admiral's 3 o'clock dinner was announced by a drum beating to the tune of "The Roast Beef of Old England". Three courses were usually served, followed by a choice dessert, and accompanied by three or four wines, including champagne and claret. "If a person does not find himself perfectly at his ease, it must be his own fault, such is the urbanity and hospitality which reign here, notwithstanding the four orders of Knighthood worn by Lord Nelson, and the well-earned laurels which he has acquired." After coffee and liqueurs the company walked the deck again, while a band played for nearly an hour. Tea was served before seven, and this was the hour after which the Admiral, if not otherwise occupied, sent for "my family, to sit and talk", and generally "unbent himself", although he was "at all times as free from stiffness and pomp as regard to a proper dignity will permit, and is very communicative". At eight a rummer of punch, with cake or biscuit, was the prelude to wishing the Admiral a good night. Mr. Beatty noticed that Lord Nelson partook sparingly of the good things at his table, liked vegetables and eschewed salt. A liver or wing of a fowl, and a small plate of macaroni, sometimes taken with a glass of champagne, often formed his main meal, and after dinner he never exceeded four glasses of wine, and seldom drank three, all of which were diluted by Bristol water. He was generally on deck six or seven hours in the day, and generally, in the opinion of the medical man, insufficiently protected from the weather.

3

On August 17, Lord Nelson's fears that the Admiralty had forgotten him were assuaged by the arrival of H.M.S. *Canopus* from Plymouth, under the command of Rear-Admiral George Campbell. She was welcome, though small craft were his pressing need, and she brought the great batch of letters for the Mediterranean Fleet which had been collecting in London up to July 3. His own large portion contained one piece of confidential intelligence not uncommonly received in a squadron three months after leaving home. Either the recipient or the subsequent thief of his ecstatic reply, addressed to "Mrs. Thomson", obliterated passages with the intention of making it incomprehensible.

"My dearest Beloved,

"To say that I think of you by day, night, and all day and all night, but too faintly express my feelings of love and affection towards you ********** unbounded affection. Our dear excellent good ******* is the only one who knows anything of the matter; and she has promised me, when you ****** again, to take every possible care of you as proof of her never-failing regard for your own dear Nelson.

"Believe me that I am incapable of wronging you in thought, word or deed. No; not all the wealth of Peru could buy me for one moment; it is all yours, and reserved wholly for you and *** certainly ********* from the moment of our happy, dear, enchanting, blessed meeting. The thoughts of such happiness, my dearest, only beloved, makes the blood fly to my head. The call of our country is a duty which you would deservedly in the cool moments of reflection reprobate, was I to abandon; and I should feel so disgraced by seeing you ashamed of me; no longer saying—'This is the man who has saved his country! This is he who is the first to go forth to fight our battles, and the last to return!'

"And then all these honours reflect on you. 'Ah!' they will think, 'What a man! what sacrifices has he not made to secure our homes and property: even the society and happy union with the finest and most accomplished woman in the world.'

"As you love, how must you feel. My heart is with you, cherish it. I shall, my best beloved, return—if it pleases God—a victor; and it shall be my study to transmit an unsullied name. There is no desire of wealth, no ambition that could keep me from all my soul holds dear. No! it is to save my country, my wife in the eye of God, and ********************* will tell you that it is all right; and then, only think of our happy meeting.

"Ever, for ever, I am yours, only yours, even beyond this world.

                                          "Nelson and Brontë."

"For ever, for ever, your own Nelson. August 26th."

But the arrival of Admiralty instructions after so long a hiatus had coincided with symptoms which led him to believe that the enemy were on the verge of putting to sea. Nine days passed before he gave vent to this passionate response, and since he had no safe means of despatching something so unguarded, he kept it, perforce, until an opportunity offered, which was not for three months. His only perfectly secure method of ensuring that a letter reached Lady Hamilton unopened, during a period of two years, was to see it go into the breast-pocket of somebody who would deliver it into her hand, and this generally meant the Captain of a ship of his squadron going home for repairs. He was not often able to employ a despatch brig—the swiftest means of communication—and their Lordships, sending matter to which they needed an answer, together with everything else which had collected at headquarters, always expected him to return the vessel instantly. He began to write letters almost in journal form, adding a paragraph as a fancy or an anniversary suggested. Lady Hamilton often replied c/o

Messrs. Gibbs, Falconet, and when Falconet, the French refugee partner, became so terrified of Buonaparte that he dared not oblige Lord Nelson by the purchase of a little macaroni, an unexpected character stepped into the breach. A Quaker merchant of Rosas Bay was already getting intelligence from inside Spain, which he transmitted to Nelson's officers when they called to water and provision. On a wild December night of 1803 a small Spanish merchantman joined the fleet off Toulon, and a solemn figure came on board the *Victory*. Friend Gayner, who had never before set foot in a man-of-war at sea, had taken a romantic fancy to see Lord Nelson. "I was, of course, very attentive to him and he is gone back quite delighted with our regularity." The guest was duly carried next morning by the Chief to attend Sunday morning service with a ship's company, "very healthy and very unanimous". Henceforward he sent private letters for Lord Nelson, enclosed in his own correspondence, to a business connection at Bristol.

4

An old Mediterranean man had noted that the strength of the north-west gales did not seem to have deteriorated since he was last in this country. "The happiness of keeping a station is always to have a foul wind, and never to hear the delightful sound, *Steady*." The *Victory* was so easy at sea that he hoped she might never sustain any material damage, but the *Canopus* had lost her fore-yard within a few days of joining. However, his mind was made up: "Never to go into Port till after the Battle, if they make me wait a year, provided the Admiralty change the ships who cannot keep the Sea in winter", nor, as the season advanced, and he heard from St. Vincent, "We can send you neither ships nor men", did he alter his resolution. "I bear up for every gale, I must not, in our present state quarrel with the north-westers. By always going away large, we generally lose much of their force, and the heavy sea. By the great care and attention of every captain, we have suffered much less than we could have expected. . . . We either run to the southward, or furl all sails and make the ships go as easy as possible." He believed that the three danger points in his command were the Straits of Gibraltar, the heel of Italy, and Toulon. This view entailed keeping a division on the watch over the mouth of the Adriatic and the Straits of Messina (through which narrowing trade-routes merchant vessels were continually requiring convoy); and whatever the Admiralty might say, he was determined always to keep at least a frigate in the Bay of Naples, ready to remove the royal family. His desire "to send many of our ships who want what I cannot give them, to England, towing a line-of-battle-ship" was appreciated in his fleet, and the anti-scorbutics in which he put great faith, and which he had acquired for his ships, at sea, with much difficulty, had also done their work. As early as August 24 he was able to state, "This day, only six men are confined to their beds in the whole Squadron", and by early October his description had a familiar ring. "We are healthy beyond example, and in great good humour with ourselves, and so sharp set that I would not be a French Admiral in the way of some of our ships for something. I believe we are in the right fighting trim, let them come as soon as they please." He ended less happily, "Would to God the ships were half as good, but they are what we call crazy. I know well enough that if I was to go into Malta, I should save the ships during this bad season, but if I am to watch the French, I must be at sea, and if at sea, must have bad weather."

A position thirty to forty miles west of the harbour mouth had been his summer *rendezvous*. He admitted that it was unusual. He had chosen it to prevent the junction of the Spanish Fleet, and to be able, if necessary, to take shelter within a few hours, either under the Hyères Islands or Cape San Sebastian. He was indignant when congratulated from home on the success of his blockade of Toulon. His intention had always been to let the enemy fleet come out, and annihilate it. "Nothing ever kept the French Fleet in Toulon or Brest, whenever they had a mind to come to sea. I have no Frigates to watch them, and must take my chance." If he missed them, "which God forbid", he was provisioned for a voyage to Madras, and ready to follow them to the Antipodes. "Our weather-beaten ships, I have no doubt, will make their sides like a plum pudding."

Nevertheless, autumn mornings, "as thick as buttermilk, and blowing a levanter", found him "confoundedly out of humour". Desertion from ships in Spanish ports was not yet stamped out, and he had found all his ships short of men. To St. Vincent he confided on October 5, "I am—don't laugh—dreadfully sea-sick this day." Another old friend was told, "Our gales are incessant and you know I am never well when it blows hard." Ten days later he was "absolutely in a fever of the mind", for the latest rumours were that 10,000 troops embarked in Toulon and Marseille were bound for Ireland, for Sardinia, for Messina, the Morea or Egypt. "I have as many destinations sent me as there are Countries." The *Canopus*, ordered to water off the north-east end of Sardinia nearly three weeks past, had not yet returned ("I am uneasy about her"), and the attitude of Spain to his ships was so uncivil that he expected to hear at any moment of her having entered the war. He had written to Mr. Frere, asking to be personally advised from Madrid, as, if he was to wait for the official intimation from England, he would have to wait two or three months. To crown all, on a morning following a storm which had blown him off his station, "a lame story" had been brought to him, from a Spanish source, of a strange fleet of twelve sail seen off Minorca, steering to the westward. "If I should miss these fellows, my heart will break. I am actually, only now recovering from the shock of missing them in 1798, when they were going to Egypt."

It was on such occasions that a surgeon of the *Victory* noticed with professional disapproval that "his lordship's wonderful activity of mind prevented him from taking ordinary repose", and even kept him on deck throughout the night, attired in a thin overcoat, his favourite leather and flannel waistcoats, and light footwear. (He always preferred shoes, which he could kick off in his cabin, where, sooner than summon a servant to undertake a duty very difficult for a one-armed man, he would pace the carpet in his stocking-feet until they were dry.)

The worst of his anxieties of October 15 were banished during the hours of darkness by a signal from the *Seahorse*. She had been sent in to reconnoitre Toulon in company with the *Renown* five days earlier, but his expectation had been that his frigates would neither be able to see the enemy nor find him if they did. "Relieved for the first time in my life by being informed the French were still in Port", he retired to consider a scheme for running with his whole squadron to water at an open roadstead on a neutral coast recommended by one of his officers. Towards the end of the month, when the moon would be full, a couple of frigates could be left to watch an enemy very unlikely to move. His own private journal of his first voyage to the Maddalena Islands conjures up a fearsome picture. The distance was only two hundred miles, but four days after leaving their Toulon *rendezvous*, daylight found a fleet with many split sails no more than five leagues directly to leeward of Rosso, an islet which it had left the night before, and with a very strong current against it. "The Fleet being absolutely in distress for water, I determined to persevere. . . . We worked the *Victory* every foot of the way, from Asinara to this anchorage, the wind blowing from Longo Sardo, under double-reefed topsails." On the evening of the eighth day the whole squadron tacked under Sardinia, and stood into "a beautiful little bay, or rather harbour", hitherto unnamed, and next morning the Governor of Maddalena, coming on board H.M.S. *Victory*, was saluted with nine guns, and Captain Ryves was sent a highly congratulatory note on a most correct chart of "Agincourt" Sound. This officer had been in command of the *Agincourt* in March of the preceding year, when he had been sent with a small detachment to prevent the French seizing these islands. The French had made no such attempt, but a man of resource had filled in his time in carrying out a survey of "one of the finest harbours I have ever seen", which possessed, moreover, the decisive advantage of two entrances.

Nelson, having found the "hole to put the Fleet in" for which he had been searching ever since he had dismissed Malta from his considerations, repaired there six times before the following May, and since the Physician to the Fleet had represented that the country into which the wooding and watering parties must be sent bred fever, he ordered a dose of Peruvian bark to be administered twice a day to every man on this duty.

5

He told himself that in the Mediterranean the weather was not so raw as what they would have experienced in the Channel at this season, but it was undeniable that the monotony of their existence could not have been surpassed. "Our days pass so much alike that having described one, you have them all. We now (October 18) breakfast by candlelight; and all retire at 8 o'clock to bed. . . . We cruise, cruise, and one day so much like another that they are hardly distinguishable." In October he noted wanly that days could be remembered "by the difference of a gale of wind, or not", but for a month from mid-January this distinction was absent. Despite the horrible link between the inscribed page and sea-sickness, he entered always twice, and sometimes as many as six times a day, in his own hand, in two small books, the state of the barometer, weather and wind. (His best barometer in variable weather, however, was always, he said, his stump.) How to combat monotony—what he described as "not allowing the sameness of the prospect to satiate the mind" —was his over-riding problem. He attacked it by changing the cruising ground continually, "sometimes by looking at Toulon, Ville Franche, Barcelona, and Rosas; then running round Minorca, Majorca, Sardinia and Corsica; and two or three times anchoring for a few days, and sending a Ship to the last place for *onions*, which I find the best thing that can be given to Seamen; having always good mutton for the sick, cattle when we can get them, and plenty of fresh water. In the winter it is the best plan to give half the allowance of grog, instead of all wine. These things are for the Commander-in-Chief to look to; but shut very nearly out of Spain, and only getting refreshments by stealth from other places, my Command has been an arduous one." "You will agree with me", he added, to his old medical friend Moseley, "that it is easier for an Officer to keep men healthy, than for a Physician to cure them." Acting on this belief, he sent to Malta for sweet oranges (which he knew could be packed in paper at the proper season), and deputed his second-in-command to discover on the spot why all the bread from this quarter should arrive infested with weevils. He wrote to Gibraltar to order more cheese, cocoa and sugar and less rice. To his chagrin, ships' companies in general did not much like rice, or, when in health, the macaroni so sonorously recommended by Dr. Snipe as "a light wholesome and nourishing food". A Captain who had forwarded vouchers for five bullocks and six bags of hay was asked to explain so large a purchase of fodder for beasts immediately slain. The mystery of a transport which had arrived at Malta an eighth short of her normal stowage was solved by the discovery that the Master had not known that baskets of coal should be heaped. A complete specimen of a seaman's cot was sent to Naples, with enquiries as to the time and cost of supplying duplicates in bulk. Lord Nelson recommended that the Guernsey jackets, of a new pattern, should be made three inches wider and up to ten inches longer so that they should not work out of the trousers of seamen on the yards; and he sent back to England, with a message that "the Contractor who furnished such stuff ought to be hanged", frocks and trousers of "coarse wrapper stuff". "Best Russia duck" was his demand for the seamen of H.M. Navy. The Naval Hospital to be established in a palace at Valetta occupied his thoughts much. It must have a garden in which convalescent seamen and marines could take the air and enjoy gentle exercise.

As to the state of affairs at home, and elsewhere in Europe, during these weary months, he had to guess from newspapers obtained through Spain and never less than ten days old. In April 1804 he complained, "I have only had two dispatches sent me since leaving England."

When Sir William Bolton joined, in the *Childers*, on October 6, 1803, he brought an answer to the Commander-in-Chief's first long letter to the Prime Minister on Mediterranean politics, two bundles of respectively forty-eight and fifty-four printed Admiralty orders for distribution to officers of the squadron, instructions to proceed to the blockade of Genoa and Spezia, and a few private letters for the Admiral, of which only one packet was not dated "Admiralty". The bearing of the Admiral's official Secretary became very uneasy. Fortunately it soon appeared that Lady Hamilton had mentioned Mrs. Scott's being brought to bed. The *Childers*, a 14-gun sloop, the result of Lord Nelson's repeated requests on behalf of his nephew, had been ordered to join him in such haste that no mail for the fleet had been carried. Her Captain had looked out until the last possible moment for some promised packages from Mr. Davison. The Rev. Mr. Este (who had particularly desired to provide a gallant son with a letter to the Commander-in-Chief) had almost wept, when led panting to Sir

Thomas Troubridge's room, to be very kindly told that he was come too late.

Not all the matter brought out with such speed was agreeable to its recipient. The Prime Minister, not having time to read Lord Nelson's political letter, had passed it on to Lord Hobart, Secretary of State at War and for the Colonies. Lady Hamilton was shocked at her expenses, especially as Davison seemed to think that she was going to pay for the improvements at Merton out of the £100 a month allotted to her for housekeeping. She wished to come out to the Mediterranean. The Commander-in-Chief had heard something of this plan already, from Davison, and reasoned with her gently. "How would you feel to be at that nasty place Malta, with nothing but soldiers and diplomatic nonsense, and to hear that the Fleet is gone out of the Straits?" It was true that Lady Bickerton had been unwise enough to maroon herself at Valetta. Knowing what attachment was, Lord Nelson took every opportunity of ordering Admiral Bickerton to Malta. But for a Commander-in-Chief watching Toulon, Malta was about as useful a base as Spithead. "I assure you that Merton has a greater chance of seeing me." The same applied to Sicily and Naples, with the additional disadvantage that if he did ever see them it would be during an action, and only for a few days; besides, sad to say, "nobody cares for us there". A wilder suggestion was quickly quashed. "Imagine what a cruize off Toulon is! Even in summer time we have a hard gale every week, and two days heavy swell. It would kill you, and myself to see you. Much less possible to have Charlotte, Horatia, etc. on board ship! And I who have given orders to carry no women to sea in the *Victory* to be the first to break them!"

With regard to her financial anxieties he was equally gentle but much less firm. "I am not surprised, my dearest Emma, at the enormous expense of the watering place, but, if it has done my own Emma service, it is well laid out." Indeed, he did not find it easy to admonish a lady who, upon receiving from his own eldest sister a family saga of school-fees, doctor's bills and wish for more remunerative employment for the master of the house, had instantly forwarded £100. "Your purse, my dear Emma, will always be empty" was all that he could say, except that he wished Mr. Addington would give her £500 a year pension, and if the Queen of Naples had so far done nothing he should begin to write her down as a time-serving woman. On second thoughts, he did not wish his Emma to be beholden even to Addington. "Whilst I have sixpence, you shall have fivepence of it. . . . We can live on bread and cheese. . . ." He instructed Davison a little curtly that there must be no question of Lady Hamilton being called upon to pay for alterations at Merton, and that everything ordered by her must be undertaken.

Two more features of the "dear delightful letters" for which he waited with so much joyful expectation were not calculated to set his mind at ease. As before, during his absence on foreign duty, his idol could not resist telling him of the attentions paid to her by other gentlemen, and glancing at his wife. But he no longer responded on either count, and as far as her "titled offers" went, was jocular. "I hope one of these days you will be my own Duchess of Brontë, and then a fig for them all!" While she had been the wife of a man who might compel her to receive dissolute royalty he had been anxious, but now she could choose her own company, and his belief in her constancy was absolute. A lady of experience took the hint, and neither of these topics recurred. But she did not settle at Merton, or have Horatia there, except for short visits, and she kept on her London house.

Horatia's name had begun to appear increasingly often in her father's letters. He had studied nursery growth sufficiently to know that she must now be running and talking all day. "How I long to hear her prattle!" He was not happy until she had been "inoculated with the cow-pox", and was most unhappy when the result was a very bad arm. "I dreamt last night, I heard her call 'Papa', and point to her arm, just as you describe."

The thought that the child might be left unprovided for, dependent "upon smiles and frowns", haunted him. He had already sent a note to his solicitor, headed, "Private for yourself—and most secret" and opening, "I send you home a Codicil to my Will, which you will not communicate to any person breathing." Amongst its clauses was a high-handed scheme to ensure that his daughter got an amiable husband, and bore his name. If his dear nephew should prove worthy, in Lady Hamilton's estimation, of such a treasure, it was his wish that the boy Horatio should marry "my adopted daughter". He heard with pleasure that Horatia showed spirit. "Aye! she is like her mother; will have her own way, or kick up the devil of a dust." He wrote twice to ask that a strong netting should be placed round the "Nile" at Merton, "that the little thing may not tumble in". On pitch black nights, when the wind was blowing half a gale and the rain was coming down in torrents, he "whose whole soul is at Merton" could see the red-brick English country house almost as clearly as if the nine windows of the aft-most wall of his state room had looked forth on orna-mental waters of Surrey, instead of "the stormy gulph of Lyons".

"The entrance by the corner I would certainly have done; a common white gate will do for the present, and one of the cottages, which is in the barn, can be put up as a temporary lodge. The road can be made to a tem-porary bridge, for that part of the 'Nile' one day shall be filled up. Down-ing's canvas awning will do for a passage. For the winter, the carriage can be put in the barn. The new building the chamber over the dining-room, you must consider. The stair window, we settled, was not to be stopped up. The underground passage will, I hope, be made, but I shall, please God, soon see it all."

It had always been his intention with the first prize-money he got ("I *long* to be out of debt") to pay Mr. Greaves, whose last instal-ment was due on October 1. Next on his list came Davison.

He was well pleased with the Steward provided by Davison, and indeed often told the astute Chevalier that he wondered he had not set up an hotel years past. But even "living as frugal as my situation will permit", he was saving practically nothing, and he now knew why he had received no rent from Brontë for three years. The obliging Gibbs had made a pilgrimage to the estate on the wrong side of Etna. The last thirty miles had to be accomplished on horse-back. The spreading building under the volcanic mountain which had startled the eyes of the equestrian Englishman had explained all. The deceased Graeffer, letting his æsthetic sense overrule his reason, had been fitting up a perfect palace there, far more worthy to receive the Duke of Brontë than the best existing farmhouse on the estate, which was what he had been told to put in order for occa-sional residence. Graeffer's widow was demanding a pension of at least £200 per annum for herself and her orphan child. By 1805, with care (said Gibbs), a rental of £2,000 should be forthcoming. The hour was not propitious, but as he had already orders to *let*, might he enquire, would his lordship (supposing His Sicilian Majesty himself suggested the idea) find the *sale* of his property anything against his inclination? "Quite the contrary" wrote his lordship in the margin. As affairs were marching, he thought the French were likely to see Brontë before its Duke. He had, in any case, quite given up ideas of settling there. His instructions to Gibbs included a melancholy paragraph:

"I paid more attention to another Sovereign than my own; therefore the King of Naples' gift of Brontë to me, if it is not now settled to my advantage, and to be permanent, has cost me a fortune, and a great deal of favour which I might have enjoyed, and jealousy which I might have avoided. I repine not on these accounts. I did my duty, to the Sicilifying of my conscience, and I am easy. . . . All I beg is that the just thing may be done immediately, and that I may have it permanent. I shall never again write an order about the estate."

As January and February 1804 wore out, in spectacular snow-storms, Nelson's anxiety to hear that Lady Hamilton had recovered from an unexplained illness became frantic. On February 10, in an unsigned letter, he told "My dearest friend", "I only hope our dearest friends are well, and happily past all danger." On the 25th he was "anxious in the extreme to hear that you are perfectly recovered from your late indisposition." On March 14, all he longed to hear was news of her health, and again "*perfectly* recovered" was the phrase employed. The *Royal Sovereign*, of 100 guns, joined the same evening, and he got letters dated January 15 and 28, which gave him "a raging fever all night". His postscript bade her "kiss dear Horatia for me, and the other, I approved of the name you intended". Four days later (again in a postscript) he described him-self as "very restless for these several days and nights past, and not likely to be relieved until I hear you are quite recovered". At the close of a couple of undated paragraphs on the same sheet he re-peated his injunction, "Kiss dear Horatia for me, and the other", and added, "call him what you please, if a girl, Emma."

At home, in the first week of February, Mrs. Matcham had

written to Lady Hamilton complaining of long silence, and hoping that illness was not the reason. On February 3, Dr. Este sat in Lady Hamilton's house in Clarges Street, watching while "the most noble creature living" wrote letters of introduction to be carried by another of his sons suddenly ordered to the Mediterranean. Nelson's anxiety was not relieved until the *Phœbe* joined the fleet on March 31, with a mail brought by the *Thisbe* to Gibraltar.

"I opened—opened—found none but December and early in January. I was in such an agitation! At last, I found one without a date, which, thank God! told my poor heart that you was recovering, but that dear little Emma was no more! and that Horatia had been so very ill—it all together upset me. But, it was just at bedtime, and I had time to reflect, and be thankful to God for sparing you and our dear Horatia. I am sure the loss of one—much more both—would have drove me mad. I was so agitated, as it was, that I was glad it was night, and that I could be by myself."

No suspicion of his private anxieties at this or any other time ever reached his officers. Indeed, the happily married young Captain of one of his ships-of-the-line gravely explained to his lady :

"Dear domestic happiness—my only boon—never abstracted his attention. He had not, or however did not, acknowledge of any incumbrances, such as I have. The rule he inculcated was that every man became a bachelor after he passed the Rock of Gibraltar, and he was not very tardy in showing that he practised what he preached."

6

Minor vexations, close under his eye, were not lacking as "a most terrible long winter" gave place to Mediterranean spring, and the tact and experience of a Chief singularly happy in his personal relations with subordinates were exercised, particularly in suggesting to young blood the most expedient way through, or around, or out of the "scrape". A wretched but still heated Lieutenant who had sent him a sad tale of wrongs was serenely advised :

"I have just received your letter, and I am truly sorry that any difference should arise between you and your Captain, who has the reputation of being one of the bright Officers of the Service, and yourself, a very young man and a very young Officer, who must naturally have much to learn. Therefore the chance is that you are perfectly wrong in the disagreement.

"However, as your present situation must be very disagreeable, I will certainly take an early opportunity of removing you, provided your conduct to your present Captain be such that another may not refuse to receive you."

Charles Connor, the young cousin of Lady Hamilton, was reminded, on receiving his commission :

"As you from this day start in the world as a man, I trust that your future conduct in life will prove you both an Officer and a Gentleman. Recollect that you must be a Seaman to be an Officer, and also that you cannot be a good Officer without being a Gentleman."

Charles, however, was to prove a source of nothing but distress. After Dr. Snipe, Physician to the Fleet, had examined him, it became necessary to apply to Lady Hamilton for information as to family history. Was there any record of insanity? While this trouble was dragging its course, Chevalier, the ideal steward supplied by Davison, sent to ask if he might speak privately with the Admiral. This interview was brief. "I beg pardon, my Lord, but I find myself so disagreeably situated in the Ship that I beg of your Lordship to send me to England by the first opportunity." "Certainly, Mr. Chevalier." Chevalier thought again, and was present in attendance upon his master in the cockpit of the *Victory* at Trafalgar, but Connor had another and more serious outbreak a few weeks later, and in March 1805 Captain Hillyer of the *Niger* had to write to Lady Hamilton, regretting that he had been obliged to leave her *protégé* in hospital at Plymouth, "with his hands bound, violently insane".

But in spite of "the same faces and almost the same conversation" day in and day out, variances in the Mediterranean fleet remained minor and rare, and the health record became unprecedented. The Chief, in despair of satisfying a tithe of his distinguished correspondents who wished to recommend a friend or relative, humorously explained that they had out here so far, "thank God! no Court-Martials", nobody asked to be sent home. "The Admiralty fill all vacancies except *death*, and nobody will die." He could not even get a ship for his dear Berry, whose face brought battles.

On St. George's Day, 1804, on a general promotion, Viscount Nelson was gazetted Vice-Admiral of the White (the highest rank he ever attained), but as communications were in the state so often deplored by him, he did not receive his commission until the last day of July. In the same week he, who had recently complained to Lady Hamilton, "Well, this is an odd War—not a battle!" read something in a French newspaper which surprised him greatly. As the weather grew warmer, La Touche Tréville, in command of the Toulon squadron, had begun to exercise his ships outside the harbour, as best he could, singly and in small groups. ("My friend Monsieur La Touche sometimes plays bo-peep in and out of Toulon, like a mouse at the edge of a hole.") "We are as usual", Nelson had told Hugh Elliot on June 8. "The French Fleet safe in Toulon; but upon the 14th Monsr. La Touche came out with eight Sail-of-the-Line and six Frigates, cut a caper off Sepet, and went in again. I was off with five Ships-of-the-Line, and brought to for his attack, although I did not believe that anything was meant serious, but merely a gasconade." His irritation was strong on August 3, when he discovered that La Touche had misrepresented the incident in a special despatch to Buonaparte as a refusal of the British Fleet to be brought to action, and that the letter had been given to the *Moniteur*, to be copied by the Press of Europe. "You will have seen", he wrote to Brother William, "Monsieur La Touche's letter of how he chased me, and how I *ran*. I keep it; and, by God, if I take him, he shall *Eat* it." La Touche was personally obnoxious to him, as an aristo who had turned republican, and professionally, as the officer who had attempted to bully the Neapolitan Court in 1793, and who had been in command of the Boulogne flotilla which had repelled his boat attack of August 1801. But he was not destined to settle accounts with this French Admiral, for on August 18 La Touche died, of sheer exhaustion, solemnly stated the French editors, from walking so often up to the signal post upon Sepet to watch for the English fleet. "I always pronounced that that would be his death", commented Nelson, mollified. The successor appointed by Buonaparte, after some delay, had also crossed Nelson's path before. Admiral Villeneuve had something of the same background as La Touche Tréville, but his promotion had been much more rapid. He had commanded the enemy rear at the Nile, and made his escape with two of the line and two frigates, to fight another day.

From two-months-old English newspapers which he got in July,

the Commander-in-Chief in the Mediterranean learnt that Mr.
Alexander Davison had been sentenced by the Court of King's
Bench to twelve months' imprisonment in the Marshalsea prison.
To Lady Hamilton he confessed that he was not surprised. "He
never would take a friend's caution, and he has been severely bit.
... After what passed in Parliament I did not expect so little. ...
He would only consult Lord Moira, and such clever folks, but an
ignoramus like me could only warn him not to touch boroughs.
He has, poor fellow, been completely duped, and who cares? Not
one of those great folks."

To Davison himself he wrote in much more sympathetic vein,
urging a man of mercurial temperament, "Keep up your spirits.
Do not take it to heart. It will soon pass away." At first he promised
to come to see his friend in the Marshalsea, but as months passed
without hope of his getting home, he was reduced to counting the
days until Davison would be at liberty again. "It is some comfort
that I shall be in England to shake you by the hand in St. James's
Square, where I hope you will live many years, and that I will often
breakfast with you. ... Before you receive this letter you will again,
thank God, be a free man." He never ceased to write, and never
ceased to suggest that no consideration should ever again tempt
Davison to dabble in politics—advice which was followed.

For the Mediterranean Fleet the summer of 1804 was boring. All
Europe was waiting breathlessly for Buonaparte's Invasion. In
England able-bodied males between the ages of fifteen and sixty
had been called upon to enrol in their parishes for Home Defence;
seventy-five Martello towers had been hastily erected, and the
beacons were ready for conflagration. "An awful and trying period
for us all", wrote Nelson's younger sister, whose family party now
sat down to dinner fifteen. "My neighbour Edwards", reported his
even more resolute elder sister, "sits at home and frightens himself
so much that he will not suffer any of his children to go to school."
To Nelson's disgust, early in April, the *Swift* cutter, bringing him
Admiralty despatches and a home mail, was captured by an enemy
privateer after her Captain had been killed in action. He sent Dr.
Scott down to Barcelona to try to buy back the private letters, but
they had, it appeared, already been forwarded to Paris, for Buona-

parte's delectation; and the Swedish and American Consuls told Lord Nelson's emissary on his arrival that their French *confrère* admired three portraits of Lady Hamilton too much to part with them, even to Buonaparte. Dr. Scott gathered that her ladyship's letters had been exhibited to at least one of these gentlemen.

On the night of June 3 the French fleet in Toulon fired a *feu de joie* in celebration of Buonaparte's assumption of the Imperial purple; next morning the British fleet exercised its great guns on the sixty-sixth anniversary of the birth of George III. Nelson meditated a lurid Naples rumour that the new Emperor was "to be divorced from Madame B. and married to a Blood Royal of Germany. Bravo! Corsican." English visitors to Paris during the Experimental Peace had learnt that Buonaparte kept a bust of Nelson on his dressing-room mantelpiece; but the admiration was unreciprocated. By Hugh Elliot's account, Acton was about to get his *congé* in order to satisfy "Napoleon". The gossip of Neapolitans on the subject of their Queen far surpassed any hints discreetly dropped, years past, by that perspicacious connoisseur, Sir William Hamilton. Maria Carolina was now credited with three lovers, all French *émigrés*. One was military (Lieut.-Col. St. Clair), another naval (Capitaine La Tour). "However, I never touch on these matters, for I care not how much she amuses herself." Lord Nelson's interest in a royal lady whose conduct seemed to provide a perfect illustration of the text "Put not your trust in Princes" was dying a lingering death. He could no longer doubt that her failure to respond to his repeated mentions of "your Emma" was deliberate.

Seventeen days of blowing weather in July decided him that he had better not attempt another winter at sea. He said that he was ready to die for his country, but could not see that allowing himself to degenerate into a helpless invalid would benefit anybody. "I can every month perceive a visible (if I may be allowed the expression) loss of sight." He observed his physician's injunctions to wear a green shade, but Mr. Beatty feared that such precautions were of little value while the Admiral persisted in spending most of his days on deck, in Mediterranean glare, staring through a telescope at a fleet which refused to be tempted out to an engagement. And as the summer began to wane, without bringing the Invasion, Nelson began to wonder whether the new Emperor might not, after all, be considering peace negotiations with a Ministry which he had heard —incorrectly—included Mr. Fox. In late August he ordered fires in his cabin ("The Mediterranean seems to have altered"), and wrote to the new First Lord, Viscount Melville, and to Mr. William Marsden, who had succeeded Sir Evan Nepean, asking for leave of absence for the re-establishment of his health. He told Lady Hamilton that he hoped to eat his Christmas dinner at Merton, and that "the moment I get home, I shall put it out of your power to spend dear Horatia's money. I shall settle it in trustees' hands and leave nothing to chance." Dr. Scott had succeeded in extracting one portrait from the French Consul at Barcelona, who had already had it framed. A cup bearing another likeness of Admiral Nelson's Famous Woman ("your dear phiz—but not the least like you") was never used except for ornamental purposes.

His "letters relative to my health" were no sooner irretrievably gone than he began to regret them. He considered who would be his successor, and decided upon Lord Keith as the most probable man. A few months' sick leave was all that he had asked, and he had mentioned that Bickerton was capable, under present conditions, of taking his place; but he was well aware that "there will be so many desirous of the Mediterranean Command that I cannot expect they will allow me to return to it. I may, very possibly, be laid on the shelf." And as he waited philosophically to hear his fate—telling himself, "Whatever arrangements are made about me by the Ministers, it is all settled by this time"; hoping against hope, "They will do the thing handsomely"; reflecting, "Once it is gone from me, I stand no chance of getting it back again"—he realised, as never before, how dear "my favourite Command" had become to him.

He sometimes fancifully pictured his battered fleet as a fine timepiece, ticking over gently in the worn palm of his single hand. The names, state and whereabouts of his ships, little and great, were engraved upon his memory, night and day :

> H.M.S. *Bittern, Arrow, Halcyon, Sophie*—Gibraltar.
>   ,,   *Morgiana, Termagant*—going to heave down.
>   ,,   *Seahorse, Childers*—between the fleet and Spain.
>   ,,   *Spider, Hirondelle, Cameleon*—gone to the Adriatic.

Their admired clockwork movement, however, was the result of infinite toil and deep forethought.

"If the *Maidstone* takes the Convoy, and when *Agincourt* arrives there is none for her and *Thisbe*, it puzzles me to know what orders to give them. If they chace the convoy to Gibraltar, the *Maidstone* may have gone on with it to England, and in that case, two ships, unless I begin to give a new arrangement, will either go home without convoy, or they must return, in contradiction to the Admiralty's orders to send them home."

And sometimes the Admiralty, diverting a ship without his knowledge, would temporarily stop the whole machine. Lord Elgin, from his French prison, was begging that a transport should call at Cerigo to remove to safety "some marble antiquities" collected during his happy years as Ambassador to the Porte. An Admiral "pulled to pieces" by the demands of merchants for convoy had written to beg for more frigates, "the Eyes of the Fleet", until he was tired, and noticed that their Lordships had given up answering those parts of his letters. On October 13 he received a piece of news that increased his growing unwillingness to go home. The *John Bull* cutter arrived with secret instructions which had been sent in duplicate to Cornwallis, blockading Brest, to detach two frigates to intercept the Monte Video treasure fleet, expected off Cadiz, bound for Ferrol. These orders could only mean that war with Spain was imminent. She had long been paying France an annual subsidy, and a French 74 had not been turned out of Cadiz. In order that the Spanish commander should need no justification for bloodless surrender, Nelson instantly sent an 80-gun ship, together with a further four frigates, to the spot. But the *Donegal* and her consorts arrived too late to avert disaster. Don Joseph Bustamente, finding himself detained by a force equal to his own, offered resistance. Within ten minutes one of his ships took fire and blew up, carrying with her to destruction thirteen ladies, passengers from South America. The other three ships soon surrendered. Spain issued orders for reprisals on British property, and Hookham Frere asked for his passport on November 5; but Spain did not formally declare war until December 12.

One of the Rev. Dr. Este's promising sons was at this time the Admiral's guest in the *Victory*. Lambton Este's foreign appointment had literally died upon him. He had come out as Secretary-Physician to Mr. Charles Lock's mission to the Levant, and having correctly diagnosed the dreadful malady with which his employer and two of the *suite* were presently stricken, he had resolutely immured himself with them in the *lazaretto* at Valetta until they had all died of the plague. He was now waiting a passage home in the *Superb*, in company with Lord Nelson. But on November 1 he was suddenly sent for to the Admiral's cabin, after breakfast, to be told a change of plans. "Oh! my good fellow! I have abandoned the idea of going to England for the present. I shall not go yet, and when I may go is quite uncertain—must depend on events, and upon my own precarious health. At the same time, I am doing you an evident injustice in detaining you here so long in uncertainty." The young doctor began to say that if he could be of any service, his wish would be to stay with Lord Nelson, but found himself somewhat terrifyingly cut short, and told that he was going to Lisbon without much delay, in the *Termagant* sloop, with Captain Pettet, an officer of humble origin but much merit, whom he would find a very worthy, agreeable companion. A signal was made for the sloop to move up to the *Victory*: Captain Pettet came on board to dine, and Lambton, entrusted with "the papers and state of the Fleet, which had been accumulating for some time, and the Admiral's despatches and letters", sailed forthwith. Off Cape St. Vincent the *Termagant* fell in with the *Swiftsure*, from England, flying the flag of Sir John Orde, and a young man who had become a confirmed "Nelsonite" during his weeks in the *Victory* noted gloomily that the Admiral sent out to take over the most lucrative portion of Lord Nelson's command was such a martyr to the gout that he had not quitted his cabin since leaving Portsmouth, and being at present absolutely confined to bed, could not receive either him or Pettet.

Nelson heard of Sir John Orde's appearance on his station on December 2, and supposing that his successor had come, sent some of his effects on board the *Superb*, and warned Captain Keats, "that treasure to the Service", to expect him at any moment. A fortnight passed before he received a notification from Orde himself of his appointment to the chief command of a squadron of five of the line to blockade Cadiz—obviously, in view of a Spanish war, the station for prize-money. "He is sent off Cadiz to reap the golden harvest, as Campbell was . . . to reap my sugar harvest. It's very odd, two Admiralties to treat me so: surely I have dreamt that I have 'done the State some Service'. But never mind. . . ." For another ten days he was left "in most total darkness". He did not even know whether his country was at war with Spain. He issued a General Order to his officers to detain all Spanish ships and vessels of war, as well as of trade, and, in his own words, "set the whole Mediterranean to work". Meanwhile, George Campbell, now one of his junior Admirals, had suddenly developed such unmistakable symptoms of nervous breakdown that there was no question but that he must be sent home immediately, and Capel was reporting from the *rendezvous* off Toulon that the French fleet was embarking troops, and seemed to be on the eve of coming out. At last, after dark on Christmas Day, the *Swiftsure* joined Nelson's fleet off Cape San Sebastian, bringing him letters from the Admiralty and Downing Street.

His permission to go home was come, and his suggestion that Bickerton should fill his place during his absence had been accepted; but, under the impression that he was about to quit it, his command had been reduced, as Orde had notified him. He kept the news of his leave having been granted a complete secret, and took the fleet to reconnoitre Toulon. The enemy force there, which now appeared to have increased to eleven of the line and eighteen frigates, was still in port, amusing itself with night signals, composed of "a quantity of rockets and blue lights", so after a week he went to Maddalena.

It was in Agincourt Sound, during the afternoon of January 19, 1805, a short winter's day of heavy gales from the north-west, that his look-out frigates H.M.S. *Active* and *Seahorse* came in sight, under a press of sail, flying the long-expected signal, "The Enemy is at sea."

ON the same morning that Lord Nelson was sending his wine to Captain Keats's battered old ship, off Toulon, in preparation for a passage home, Napoleon I was passing to his coronation in Notre-Dame.

Buonaparte's second attempt at pageantry on a great scale sounded very typical. His first—the Review of his Army for the Invasion of England, in his camp overlooking the Channel, on his birthday—had been marred by the persistent presence of English ships in the middle distance and an accident to a French squadron detailed to make an effective appearance towards the close of his distribution of Crosses of the Legion of Honour. Londoners read with mingled wrath and pity that the aged Pope, rudely summoned from Rome, had decked the conqueror's latest triumph, though only as a spectator. Buonaparte had, in the end, bestowed the Imperial wreath upon himself with his own hands. The royal procession of a new dynasty had taken an hour to pass from the Carrousel to the cathedral, and the salutes had been audible on the English coast. A large number of people believed him to set no store on the religious ceremony, but much on his claim to rank as the first crowned head of Europe. It might be that he was at work to distract the attention of his people from the fact that after all what Nelson called his "blustering and parading" at Boulogne, the invasion of England had not yet taken place. Nobody in London, or in the British Navy, knew for several months that the conquest of their country had indeed been prominent in his thoughts on that crowded day, and that, far from having abandoned hope of transporting his immense and fully equipped army across "the ruffled strip of salt", he was, at the moment, almost ready with a new stratagem to gain, for the few necessary days, naval control of the Straits of Dover.

His scheme, which received later modifications, was masterly in its simplicity. He had twenty ships in Brest, ten in Toulon, and five in Rochefort, to which he was soon to add the fleet of Spain, amounting to fifteen serviceable ships. All were under orders to evade the blockading British squadrons and, avoiding action, hasten to a *rendezvous* at the great French arsenal, Martinique. Having arrived, they were to proceed independently to deal havoc to the British possessions in that quarter, and then unite for an equally swift recrossing of the Atlantic and unexpected appearance in the English Channel. England would, he thought, send at least thirty ships-of-the-line in search of them. The Channel Fleet would be easily overpowered, or at least held in check, while an army corps was landed in Ireland and the main body disembarked on the English coast.

2

Dr. Scott had, upon one of his visits to Barcelona, been told by his employer to make a bid for a large store of church plate and vestments advertised in a Spanish newspaper. When the Mediterranean fleet quitted the Sardinian roadstead which had so often offered it friendly shelter, on the afternoon of January 19, 1805, the churches of many little towns along the coast were in possession of autograph letters and relics testifying to Admiral Nelson's gratitude. He left Agincourt Sound for the last time within three hours of hearing that the enemy were out. Darkness was falling and a fresh breeze was blowing from the W.N.W. It was impossible to leave the roadstead through the Straits of Bonifacio. The *Victory* led, with a light at her stern, through the narrow passage between the Biocian and Sardinian rocks. At 6.35 she burnt a blue light, followed after ten minutes by another. The whole fleet was clear of the Straits a quarter of an hour later. Nelson was about to attempt a feat as remarkable as his successful Actions—to summon a fleet of "crazy" ships, which had not been into port for twenty-two months, to follow him on a chase of 4,000 miles.

The enemy were reported as steering for the southern end of Sardinia, after which the wind was fair for Naples, Sicily, the Morea

NELSON'S SEARCH
in the
MEDITERRANEAN

January, 1805

Scale of Miles

Route of the Fleet ———
Frigates ....

Reproduced from *The Year of Trafalgar*, by Sir Henry Newbolt.
By kind permission of Messrs. John Murray

or Egypt. The *Seahorse* was sent ahead to the islands of San Pietro to look for them. The night was squally, and during the next afternoon, as the fleet drew out from under the lee of Sardinia, it encountered a gale from the S.S.W. At 9.25 on the morning of Sunday the 20th the *Victory* made the general signal "Prepare for Battle", and two hours later those for "Form the established Order of Sailing in two columns" and "Keep in close order". Throughout that night and next day there were very hard gales, and for most of the time the fleet was under storm staysails. Early on the morning of the 22nd the *Seahorse* came in sight. She made the signal that she had intelligence to communicate, and Captain Boyle came on board the Admiral to say that yesterday afternoon he had seen an enemy frigate off Pula. The weather had been so thick, giving an horizon of only three miles, that he had not been able to discover anything further. Nelson prayed for a fair wind, and that the Sardes might defend their capital, in which case he would be in time to save them. (The storm which had prevented him from getting farther to the southward had, in fact, scattered Villeneuve's squadron, which was already limping back to Toulon moderately damaged and much dispirited; but he was not to learn this for a month.) Satisfied that he lay in the path of any attempt upon Naples, he sent Boyle with an account of the situation to Acton, at Palermo, asking him to warn Naples. He also wrote to Ball at Malta, adding details of a dead foul wind and heavy sea; but the *Seahorse* had been his last frigate, so he had to keep this letter.

On the 25th the gale abated, and he stood into the Gulf of Cagliari, having "neither ate, drank or slept with any comfort" for five days. "I am in a fever! God send I may find them!" No enemy landing had been attempted there, but next morning information that an 80-gun ship, dismasted and crippled, had anchored in Ajaccio, led him to guess at the truth. Still, in spite of westerly gales, Villeneuve might have got round Sicily to the eastward.

"I considered the character of Buonaparte; and that the orders given by him, on the banks of the Seine, would not take into consideration winds or weather; nor indeed could the accident of three or four ships alter, in my opinion, the destination of importance; therefore such an accident did not weigh in my mind, and I went first to the Morea and then to Egypt."

Stromboli was burning very strongly as Nelson's fleet beat through the Straits of Messina on the last day of January—"a thing unprecedented in nautical history; but although the danger from the rapidity of the current was great, yet so was the object of my pursuit; and I relied with confidence on the zeal and ability of the Fleet". Seven frigates were now at his disposal, and he sent off half a dozen "in all directions, from Tunis to Toulon", following the seventh to Koroni, where, receiving no news, he went on to Alexandria. "Celerity in my movements may catch these fellows yet." The *Phœbe* rejoined without any tale of a French invasion, but equally certain reports that Egypt was practically defenceless. Cleopatra's Needle and Pompey's Pillar faded from view as the fleet instantly made sail with a fair wind for Candia. At Malta Nelson learnt, at last, that the enemy were back in Toulon. He trusted that their Lordships would approve of his having gone to Egypt in search of them. "I have consulted no man, therefore the whole blame of ignorance in forming my judgment must rest with me. I would allow no man to take from me an atom of my glory, had I fallen in with the French Fleet, nor do I desire any man to partake of any of the responsibility—all is mine, right or wrong." He prepared to regain his station as soon as possible, and to complete the victualling which had been cut short by the departure from Maddalena; for he did not neglect the possibility that Villeneuve, goaded by orders from the banks of the Seine, might, with the next favourable opportunity, put to sea again; and next time he was determined upon a battle. Reports of the flying artillery and number of saddles embarked, combined with the recently ascertained defencelessness of Alexandria, still led him to believe that Egypt had been the destination.

Plenty of news, all disagreeable, gradually dropped in to him in Palmas Bay, which he reached, after a weary struggle, on March 8; and even Lady Hamilton received her first, and only recorded, specimen of firm treatment. "When I see you are hurt at my non-arrival, I only wish that you would, for one moment, call your *good* sense before you, and see if it was possible. You know I never say a thing which I do not mean, and everybody knows that all my things are on board the *Superb*, and there they remain." Not a bulkhead had been up in his fleet since January 21. During his absence the *Raven* sloop, bringing despatches for Sir John Orde at Gibraltar and a mail for the Mediterranean, had been wrecked off Cadiz and fallen into Spanish hands. The *Arthur* cutter, with despatches for him and for Ball, had been intercepted by the French fleet returning to Toulon. Finally, a convoy homeward bound from Malta had been waylaid, and its escort, a sloop and bomb-ketch, captured. The convoy had scattered during a gallant little action; seventeen sail had reached Gibraltar, and he hoped some more might have got into Algiers; three, he knew, had been sunk. He unhesitatingly attributed this last of his mishaps ("I must not call them misfortunes") to the division of the command. "That would not have happened could I have ordered the Officer off Cadiz to send Ships to protect them." At such a moment it was additionally galling to be told by everyone that Sir John Orde, owing to the capture of the Spanish galleons within the limits of his station, was likely to become the richest Admiral that ever England saw. Lord Nelson, worse off than on the day he left Portsmouth, nearly two years past ("What a time!"), commented "Bravo!" and "Never mind!" But he still longed to settle a sufficient sum upon Horatia to protect her in case of his death, "or even anything foolish that I may do in my old age". Since, in every letter, he had pressed Lady Hamilton to have the child at Merton "*fixed*. Why not?" she had at last consented to do so, in spite of the comment that might result, and he had provided her with a not very convincing letter, suitable to be shown to enquiring neighbours, in which he explained "the extraordinary circumstances of a child being left to my care", and begged her to be its Guardian. Now he was told that the child's nurse was making difficulties. He sent instructions to Haslewood to pay a pension of £20 per annum to Miss Thompson's nurse on the clear understanding that she made no further attempt to keep or communicate with the child. Horatia, now old enough for a governess, should be entrusted to a Miss Connor, Lady Hamilton's cousin.

His young relative, Bolton, perhaps too easily and early promoted, knighted, married and "called Papa", was not giving satisfaction. Twice, when he had sent the *Childers* on a cruise which might have put her Captain in the way of prize-money, her long absence had made the Chief anxious. On both occasions the delay had been caused by nothing but lethargy. He set Hardy, "as good as ever", to talk to "Sir Billy", but feared that unless "that goose" mended his ways, their Lordships would be wishing Lord Nelson's recommendation at the devil.

Two other of his officers, to both of whom he was much attached, needed personal attention. Murray and Keats were having a nerve-racked altercation about the supply of hammocks to the *Superb*. The truth was that Captain Keats felt marital pangs, as his old ship was, he fancied, stinted, and Murray was dispersing a scanty store as equitably as possible. In the tactful but stately note which settled this misunderstanding, Lord Nelson remembered, "The situation of First Captain is certainly a very unthankful office."

Having heard that Sir John Orde had written to complain that ships under Lord Nelson's command had been frequently out of the Mediterranean, he had sent their Lordships a plain statement of fact which he trusted would produce a "trimmer". "I shall never enter into a paper war with him, or anyone else."

The loss of his private letters was painful, for he had heard nothing from home since November 2. The possibility that despatches might have fallen into enemy hands caused him greater uneasiness. Captain Layman swore that all had gone to the bottom, never to rise again, but as they had not been thrown overboard until the *Raven* struck the rocks, he kept on picturing them washing ashore. As usual in the case of a wreck, a court-martial was to be held. He had every confidence in Layman, who had never asked him for anything except to be detached on services of most danger and difficulty, and whose only outstanding fault was a tendency to talk and write too fast and too much. After seeing the narrative which the young man had prepared for the court he felt that his cup of misery was full. He read the Captain's "Orders for the Night", compared them with the result, and exclaimed, "If this is laid before the court they will hang the Officer of the Watch!" Layman willingly deleted his "severe reflections" upon this officer, and next day, to Nelson's dismay, the court severely reprimanded the Captain of the *Raven* for lack of caution in approaching the coast, and ordered his name to be put at the bottom of the list of Commanders.

The surprise was the greater to Nelson as the exertions of all officers and men to get the sloop into Cadiz had, by all accounts, been remarkable. Yesterday he had felt that his luck must change. "Much unhinged", he set himself to write to every possible person who might assist a young officer, very severely sentenced, of whose professional ability and generosity of heart he was convinced. He wrote at once to the First Lord.

"To Viscount Melville.
Victory at Sea,
10th March, 1805.

"My dear Lord,
"I inclose some remarks made by Captain Layman whilst he was in Spain, after the very unfortunate loss of that fine Sloop, which your Lordship was so good as to give him the command of. Your Lordship will find the remarks flow from a most intelligent and active mind, and may be useful should any expedition take place against Cadiz; and, my dear Lord, give me leave to recommend Captain Layman to your kind protection; for, notwithstanding the Court-Martial has thought him deserving of censure for running in with the land, yet, my Lord, allow me to say, that Captain Layman's misfortune was, perhaps, conceiving that other people's abilities were equal to his own, which, indeed, very few people's are.

"I own myself one of those who do not fear the shore, for hardly any great things are done in a small Ship by a man that does; therefore, I make very great allowances for him. Indeed, his station was intended never to be from the shore in the Straits; and if he did not every day risk his Sloop, he would be useless upon that station. Captain Layman has served with me in three Ships, and I am well acquainted with his bravery, zeal, judgment, and activity; nor do I regret the loss of the Raven compared to the value of Captain Layman's services, which are a National loss.

"You must, my dear Lord, forgive the warmth which I express for Captain Layman; but he is in adversity, and therefore, has the more claim to my attention and regard. If I had been censured every time I have run my Ship, or Fleets under my command, into great danger, I should long ago have been out of the Service, and never in the House of Peers.

"I am, my dear Lord, most faithfully,
your obedient servant,
Nelson and Brontë."

The result of all his efforts on behalf of "poor Captain Layman" was disappointing. That officer never recovered his place on the Commanders' List, and is dryly stated to have terminated his existence with his own hand in the year 1826. Nearly a quarter of a century later, however, upon "the perusal of this generous and characteristic letter", Sir Nicholas Harris Nicolas, G.C.M.G., conceived his *magnum opus*, and commenced editing the seven annotated, cross-referenced, conscientiously indexed volumes of Lord Viscount Nelson's Letters and Despatches, which remain to the present day the Bible of biographers of Nelson.

3

As soon as the wind served, Nelson left the Gulf of Palmas, and made a round, showing himself first off Toulon, and next at Barcelona, "in order to induce the enemy to believe I am fixed upon the Coast of Spain". The Rochefort squadron, which had sailed on the same day as that from Toulon, had not been seen since. Anchoring again at Palmas on March 26, he was still clearing his transports when he received his first pleasant surprise for many months. A frigate which saluted the *Victory* with thirteen guns during the dinner-hour proved to be H.M.S. *Ambuscade*, from Portsmouth, bringing him as replacement for Campbell, an old friend, an old "Crocodile". "The arrival of Admiral Louis will enable me to get a little rest, which I shall take as soon as I am satisfied in my own mind that the French will not put to sea."

About 10 a.m. five days after he wrote these comfortable lines, history repeated itself. The *Phœbe* was discovered in the offing as he beat against a head wind on the second day of a passage from Pula Bay to his *rendezvous* west of Toulon, and she was again flying the signal that the enemy was out. The *Victory* signalled the fleet to prepare for battle at 10.23. Capel, and Moubray of the *Active*, who joined four hours later, had first seen a French fleet of eleven of the line, seven frigates and two brigs at 8 a.m. on the morning of March 31, steering S.S.W. with a light breeze at N.E. and all sail set. They had kept company with the slow-moving flotilla all that day. The *Phœbe* had seen her last of it with sunset, when she had been detached to warn the Commander-in-Chief. The *Active* had stood upon a wind to the southward that night, but with dawn found herself alone.

Nelson heard nothing further for twelve days, when he got a second-hand report that the French fleet, or at least a fleet, had been seen on the 7th off Cap de Gatte, steering to the westward with a fresh easterly wind.

Villeneuve, much luckier, had on April 1 spoken a neutral who told him that Nelson was not (as he had supposed) off the Spanish coast, but nearing the southern tip of Sardinia. He had therefore kept away, at once, to the westward. The Spanish ships at Cartagena had declared themselves unready, so he had pressed on, and gone by the Rock on the 8th. Next day, off Cadiz, Orde had seen him, but believing him to be bound for Brest, had hurried north with his small squadron to join Lord Gardner's fleet. *L'Aigle* and six Spanish ships under the command of Admiral Gravina had joined Villeneuve the same night, and a Combined Fleet amounting to eighteen sail of the line had sailed for Martinique, where it had arrived on May 14.

Nelson's sufferings during the twelve days while he was "entirely adrift, by my Frigates losing sight of the French Fleet so soon after their coming out of Port", were so acute that he told Davison, "It cannot last long, what I feel." As in January, he had to weigh all the possibilities of Naples, Sicily, Sardinia, the Morea, or Egypt. He covered the channel from Barbary to Tunis with frigates and his fleet, and did what was most difficult for him, waited for information. He first took up a stationary position, between Sardinia and Galita. "I shall neither go to the eastward of Sicily or to the westward of Sardinia, until I know something positive." His fleet consisted of eleven of the line, four frigates and two corvettes. The *Amazon*, *Bittern*, *Phœbe*, *Moucheron* and *Ambuscade* had rejoined by the 6th, with nothing to tell him. He sent the *Moucheron* off again, to cruise between Galita and the shore and then go on to Tunis, the *Phœbe* to speak his look-out ship off Cape San Sebastian, and himself stretched across to Palermo. Three supply ships which had joined him on the preceding day transferred their stores at sea. On the 9th he started back from Palermo for Toulon. He had beaten against a head wind for a week, when he got an alarming rumour that the French fleet had passed the Rock. "If this account is true, much mischief may have happened." By the 18th he had made the momentous decision to follow them. "I am going out of the Mediterranean." But his good fortune seemed flown away. "I cannot", he mourned to Ball, "get a fair wind, or even a side-wind.

Dead foul!—dead foul!" He guessed, from the fact that the Spanish ships from Cadiz had joined Villeneuve, that their destination was probably not the West Indies, but Brest, or even Ireland, and he therefore warned both quarters, adding that should the assistance of his fleet be needed, "I have the pleasure to say that I shall bring with me, eleven as fine Ships of War, as ably commanded, and in as perfect order and health, as ever went to sea." Still, his progress was so slow that he began to believe that easterly winds had left the Mediterranean. "From March 26th, we have had nothing like a Levanter, except for the French fleet. . . . I never have been one week without one, until this very unfortunate moment. It has half killed me, but fretting is no use." Since fretting was no use, as he struggled down the Mediterranean he composed letters home, confidential and business, foreshadowing a long absence, and pleasant notes of invitation to Captains to come on board the *Victory* severally "for some conversation". In front of him as he wrote lay a letter from the Physician to the Fleet, "enforcing my return to England before the hot months", and all his heavy luggage was still in the *Superb*: but he had entirely put behind him the dream of Merton, and fixed his course to follow the enemy "to the East or West Indies". "What man can do shall be done. I have marked out for myself a decided line of conduct, and I shall follow it well up."

It was not until May 4 that he reached Mazari Bay, on the African coast, and as the wind was so adverse that he could not pass the Gut, he anchored to water his fleet and clear another transport. Here he was joined by the frigate *Decade*, from Gibraltar, and after hearing the latest rumours of the Rock, confided in Keats, "I am like to have a West India Trip." He still hoped that Orde had left behind him some small craft, with orders to dog the enemy and return to the mouth of the Straits with information.

"For I cannot very properly run to the West Indies, without something beyond mere surmise; and if I defer my departure, Jamaica may be lost. Indeed, as they have a month's start of me, I see no prospect of getting out time enough to prevent much mischief from being done. However, I shall take all matters into my most serious consideration, and shall do that which seemeth best under all circumstances."

Next day a breeze from the eastward enabled him to reach

Gibraltar, and he went into Rosia Bay to provision. The wind was foul for beating out of the Straits, and many officers and men gladly hastened ashore. The linen of the fleet was landed to be washed. Dr. Scott treasured the memory of an amusing incident of this evening.

"Lord Nelson, however, observing and weatherwise as he was, perceived an indication of a probable change of wind. Off went a gun from the *Victory*, and up went the Blue Peter, whilst the Admiral paced the deck in a hurry, with anxious steps and impatient of a moment's delay. The officers said, 'Here is one of Nelson's mad pranks.' But he was nevertheless right, the wind did become favourable, the linen was left on shore, the fleet cleared the Gut, and away they steered for the West Indies. This course Nelson pursued solely on his own responsibility, there being a variety of opinions as to the route the enemy had taken; some saying, 'They had gone to Ireland', some to this quarter, some to that."

Nelson told Scott, "If they are not gone to the West Indies, I shall be blamed. To be burnt in effigy, or Westminster Abbey is my alternative", and he had already drawn up instructions for Bickerton to assume the command in the Mediterranean with a small squadron; but as far as certain confirmation went, he was "as much in the dark as ever". He sadly pictured frigates sent by Orde, all captured. Three nights later, as he completed, in Lagos Bay, the victualling of his fleet for a five months' cruise, an unexpected old friend of Naples and Palermo days came alongside. That his decision had hardened after a private conversation with Rear-Admiral Donald Campbell of the Portuguese Navy was never mentioned by him, but the fact of this officer's call could not remain a secret, and within four months, at the instigation of the French Ambassador at Lisbon, Campbell lost his command, one of the two reasons given for his dismissal being his having gone on board H.M.S. *Victory* to give the English Admiral the destination of the Combined Fleets.

On the morning after the friendly entertainment so expensive to Admiral Campbell, Nelson wrote in farewell to Ball, "My lot is cast, and I am going to the West Indies, where, although I am late, yet chance may have given them a bad passage, and me a good one: I must hope the best." He despatched the *Martin* sloop to Barbados, to announce his approach and request that an embargo be laid on all vessels in port, to prevent the news reaching the enemy at

Martinique, or elsewhere. By 7 p.m. on the night of May 11 he was under full sail for the West Indies.

4

Villeneuve had crossed the Atlantic in thirty-four days. Nelson's fleet had a twenty-four days' passage. He hoped, "by exertions", to gain a fortnight on an enemy whom he now believed to be under orders to capture the Jamaicas. The prospect of coming to the rescue of islands so well known to him fired him. "I was bred, as you know, in the good old school, and taught to appreciate the value of our West India possessions, and neither in the Field, nor in the Senate, shall their just rights be infringed whilst I have an arm to fight in their defence or a tongue to launch my voice."

The *Superb*, overdue for repairs at home, was still with him. "My dear Keats, I am very much pleased with the cheerfulness with which you are determined to share the fate of the fleet. Perhaps none of us would wish for exactly a West India trip; but the call of our Country is far superior to any consideration of self." Keats asked for permission not to stop when the other ships did, and lashed his studding-sail booms to his yards. Still, the old *Superb* set the pace, slower than desire. The Admiral sent her Captain a considerate line. "I am fearful that you may think that the *Superb* does not go so fast as I could wish. However that may be, (For if we all went ten knots, I should not think it fast enough,) yet I would have you be assured that I know and feel that the *Superb* does all which is possible for a Ship to accomplish; and I desire that you will not fret upon the occasion."

The "severe affliction" which he had felt at the enemy's escape out of the Mediterranean faded, together with home thoughts, as he made what haste he could to a decisive action in the Antilles, if not before. He knew that all his home mail had gone up the Mediterranean in the *Nile* and *Avenger*, "and will never be received by me" . . . "but salt beef and the French Fleet, is far preferable to roast beef and champagne without them". The phrase "Self is out of the question" first began to appear in his letters written during these uneventful weeks of the Long Chase.

Blue days at sea succeeded one another, with hypnotic effect upon Dr. Scott. "I know not what to write—it is the old story. Nothing new—we must take it as it comes." On May 12, "Fourth Sunday after Easter", noted Dr. Scott, "Performed the Church service to the people." What the Admiral took to be an enemy privateer watched his fleet for two days, then disappeared. On the 15th the Chaplain beheld with interest the uninhabited islets heralding Madeira, and on the 17th the *Victory* spoke a Portuguese vessel. The friendly neutral had no news. She was bound for China, carrying a single priest "to convert the people there". Dr. Scott noticed that the weather was very fine and that he felt too lazy to read German. "We are going with a soft wind." The fleet was standing into the Trades, and during those days of slowest progress before reaching them Nelson transmitted to his officers his provisional plans for attack, in case he found the enemy at sea. He guessed them to be bound for Martinique, so he did not intend to anchor at Barbados, where he hoped to pick up some reinforcements. On May 22 "the usual Ceremonies on Crossing the Line were performed". On the 27th he calculated, "We shall be at Barbados the 3rd, or 4th, June. . . . Our passage, although not very quick, has been far from a bad one." On the morning of June 3 the *Amphion* spoke two English merchant vessels who declared that the French fleet was in the West Indies. Nelson arrived off Barbados with dawn of the following day (His Majesty's birthday), and Admiral Cochrane, whose flagship the *Northumberland* was lying in Carlisle Bay, came on board the *Victory* betimes attended by Sir William Myers, the Commander-in-Chief of the military at Barbados, and Governor of the Leeward Isles. What these gentlemen had to tell, disturbed and puzzled Nelson. On the previous night Sir William had received a letter from General Brereton, commanding the troops at Santa Lucia, which told him that an allied fleet, of twenty-eight sail, had passed Gros Islet going south, during the night of May 28-29. "Their destination, I should suppose, must be either Barbados or Trinidad." Brereton was an old acquaintance of Nelson. He had served as a Major at the sieges of Bastia and Calvi. Cochrane and Myers were unanimous that his information might be relied upon. Against his inclination, Nelson changed his plans. "There is not a doubt in the Admiral's or General's minds but that Tobago and Trinidad are the enemy's objects, and, although I am anxious in the extreme to get at their eighteen Sail-of-the-Line, yet, as Sir William Myers has offered to embark himself with 2,000 Troops, I cannot refuse such a handsome offer." Reviewing the situation seven weeks later, he explained, "I resisted the opinion of General Brereton's information till it would have been the height of presumption to have carried my disbelief further. I could not, in the face of Generals and Admirals, go N.W. when it was *apparently* clear that the enemy had gone South." He worked his fleet up to Carlisle Bay, and at 9.30 next morning weighed and made sail to the southward, having embarked the martial Myers and his troops. The *Victory* threw out the general signal "Prepare for Battle" at 2.15. Captain Bettesworth had been detached with the *Curieux* brig to look into Tobago; word had been sent to the Governor of Dominica; Colonel Shipley of the Engineers had been directed to communicate with the nearest post on Trinidad. The fleet arrived off Great Courland Bay with sunset on the 6th. Its salute was duly returned by Mud Fort, Tobago, and a schooner gave an even more welcome greeting. A deeply interested merchant of the island had sent off his head clerk in this vessel, with orders to stand towards the approaching fleet and let him know whether it was friend or enemy. By the most extraordinary coincidence of these days of misinformation, the clerk's signal for a friendly fleet was the same as that agreed upon between Admiral Cochrane and Colonel Shipley for the enemy being in Trinidad. There seemed no further reason to doubt the story of an American merchant captain, spoken earlier in the day by the *Curieux*, that he had been boarded by the French off Grenada; and next morning the distant view of troops abandoning Fort Abercrombie in flames seemed to settle the matter. A second Aboukir was confidently expected that evening in the Bay of Paria. Officers of the squadron could hardly believe their senses when, on entering the gulf, they found it calm and empty as a mountain tarn. No enemy was to be seen, and it was soon evident that none had ever been seen by the inhabitants of Trinidad.

Nelson received more certain news of a French fleet being in the West Indies next morning, as he came out of the gulf. Captain Maurice, her late commander, had to report with regret from

Barbados the loss of H.M. sloop *Diamond Rock*. (The pinnacled islet, so christened, standing out into the sea near the entrance to Fort Royal, had been a thorn in the side of the French of Martinique since it had been captured by a handful of bluejackets in February 1804.) Maurice believed that the enemy, who had still been in Martinique on June 2, intended to sail on the 4th for an attack on Grenada and Dominica, and a French Commodore had told him that the Ferrol squadron, consisting of six French and eight Spanish sail-of-the-line, had arrived safely. Nelson doubted the Ferrol story, since its source was tainted and it was unconfirmed from Fort Royal, but welcomed the possibility of matching his compact fleet against one so unwieldy, "and although a very pretty fiddle, I don't believe that either Gravina or Villeneuve know how to play upon it".

Next noon, having arrived in St. George's Bay with great expedition, he heard from the Governor of Dominica that all were safe at Grenada, St. Vincent and Santa Lucia, and that the enemy had not moved from Martinique on the 4th, "proving all our former information to be false". An hour later a letter from General Prevost was brought by Captain Champain of the *Jason*, who together with the General had been an eyewitness as an enemy fleet of eighteen of the line, six frigates and three brigs and schooners had passed Prince Rupert's Head on June 6. "In the evening, they were under the Saints, standing to the Northward." These authorities could not be doubted, and the last date and place mentioned enhanced Nelson's bitter disappointment.

"But for that false information, I should have been off Port Royal, as they were putting to sea; and our Battle, most probably, would have been fought on the spot where the brave Rodney beat De Grasse. I am rather inclined to believe that they are pushing for Europe, to get out of our way."

He had been "in a thousand fears for Jamaica", "for that is a blow which Buonaparte would be happy to give us". Now, he could only conclude that Villeneuve was on his return journey; but first he must satisfy himself that no attempt was being made upon Antigua or St. Kitts.

On June 12, in St. John Bay, Antigua, while the *Victory* echoed to the sound of the departure of Sir William Myers and staff, and all boats were employed transferring artillerymen to the *Northumber-*

land, Nelson began to piece together the available history of the enemy's operations in the West Indies. Villeneuve's unpractised fleet, carrying 3,000 French and 1,500 Spanish troops, had arrived at Martinique with three weeks' start of him, in very poor shape. The French had, on arrival, landed 1,000 sick, and had buried full that number during their stay. A frigate had certainly arrived from France on the 31st; "from that moment all was hurry". Nelson guessed that this ship was the mysterious stranger noticed by his squadron 200 leagues west of Madeira, and that she had given news of his approach to Gravina, "and probably hastened his movements".

Lord Nelson took his farewell with urbanity of a General to whose activity he could bear witness, and Sir William Myers left a famous man and ship happy in the knowledge that a letter was being sent to the Right Honourable Earl Camden recommending the very spirited, zealous and cheerful conduct of the Governor, the Leeward Isles, and the troops under his command. After the military were gone the *Victory* weighed promptly. All his former "affliction" at losing the French fleet in the Mediterranean returned as Nelson prepared to recross the Atlantic, again in haste.

"If either General Brereton could not have wrote, or his look-out man had been blind, nothing could have prevented my fighting them on June 6th. . . . So far from being infallible, like the Pope, I believe my opinions to be very fallible, and therefore I may be mistaken that the Enemy's fleet is gone to Europe, but I cannot bring myself to think otherwise."

He considered, "I flew to the West Indies without any orders, but I think the Ministry cannot be displeased." He had saved the Colonies and upwards of two hundred sugar-laden ships. He mournfully decided that if he failed to come up with Villeneuve before the mouth of the Straits, he would there leave the command with Bickerton "and take their Lordships' permission to go to England, to try and repair a very shattered constitution". General Brereton and "his damned intelligence" obsessed his thoughts as his fleet pursued its long return journey; but as he still did not despair of getting up with the enemy before they reached Cadiz or Toulon, and matching his eleven ships against twenty, he summoned his Captains on board the *Victory* whenever it was calm enough for boats to pass, to dine, and for consultation. Villeneuve had only five days' start of him this time, and he would carry every rag, night and day.

" I am thankful that the enemy has been driven from the West India islands with so little losses to our Country. I had made up my mind to great sacrifices; for I had determined, notwithstanding his vast superiority, to stop his career, and to put it out of his power to do further mischief. Yet, do not imagine I am one of those hot-brained people who fight at immense disadvantage without an adequate object. My object is partly gained. If we meet them we shall find them no less than eighteen, I rather think twenty Sail-of-the-Line, and therefore do not be surprised if I should not fall on them immediately: *we won't part without a battle*."

He discussed, in view of their actions, every possible order that could have been given to the Combined Fleets. He ruled out attacks on Barbados, St. Lucia, Grenada, Trinidad or Tobago. If Jamaica had been their object (with some 4,000 to 5,000 men) they should have steered direct from Martinique. The theory that they had been waiting to go to Puerto Rico, when reinforced, would not hold water. The season was past; nor, if they had been expecting a reinforcement of fifteen of the line, had they any reason to hide. "My opinion is firm as a rock, that some cause, *orders*, or *inability* to perform any service in these seas, has made them resolve to proceed direct for Europe."

He did not guess the truth: that they had fled, not from the face, but from the very name of Nelson. The Rochefort squadron, having waited the prescribed forty-five days at its Martinique *rendez-vous*, had returned without mishap. Villeneuve, whose original instructions had been to wait forty days for the Brest squadron, had, after a fortnight, received further Imperial demands to occupy his time, while waiting, in making some attempts upon British possessions. He had taken under his command two sail-of-the-line which he had found at Martinique, raising his force to twenty. He had captured the *Diamond Rock* and some sugar-laden vessels, which had most imprudently ventured out from St. John. But from them he had heard of Nelson's arrival, with fourteen of the line. He believed Cochrane at Barbados to have five more. He had landed a number of his military as garrisons for the French islands (where they remained until after Trafalgar, when they became prisoners-of-war) and had made off in haste for the safety of Ferrol. His orders to

THE CHASE TO THE WEST INDIES

May–June, 1805

Reproduced from *The Year of Trafalgar*, by Sir Henry Newbolt.
By kind permission of Messrs. John Murray

await Ganteaume for forty days had been reduced to thirty-five; but only twenty-six had elapsed.

Nelson had sailed for Europe on June 13. On the 17th a report from the *Sally*, of North Carolina, bound for Antigua, made him hope that he was hard upon the heels of the enemy, and on the 19th he sent off the *Decade* and *Martin*, one to the Mediterranean by Gibraltar, and the other to Lisbon and Ferrol. Three nights later he retired from his quarter-deck to write down in his private diary: "Midnight, nearly calm. Saw three planks which I think came from the French fleet. Very miserable, which is very foolish." He encouraged Keats: "I think the *Superb* has improved in her sailing." Another of his Captains was writing home, "We are all half-starved, and otherwise inconvenienced by being so long away from a port, but our full recompense is that we are with Nelson." On the last day of June, Sutton was detached with the *Amphion* to Tangier Bay, to discover if the enemy had entered the Mediterranean. He was given a *rendezvous* west of Cape Spartel, and told to keep the approach of Nelson's fleet as secret as possible. "Should you hear that I am gone to any other place after the Enemy, you will follow me, as I have not a single frigate with me." Sutton was also to rouse about the British Consul at Tangier, so that bullocks, onions, lemons and oranges in large numbers might be awaiting the fleet's arrival.

On July 8 Nelson chronicled in sombre mood, "Crawled 33 miles the last twenty-four hours. My only hope is that the Enemy's Fleet are near us, and in the same situation." On the 17th the story read more hopefully.

"Our whole run from Barbuda, day by day, was 3,459 miles; our run from Cape St. Vincent to Barbados was 3,227 miles; so that our run back was only 232 miles more than our run out. Allowance being made for the latitudes and longitudes of Barbados and Barbuda—average per day, thirty-four leagues, wanting nine miles."

With noon next day Cape Spartel was sighted, but no French fleet, nor any vessel bringing home news. He wrote to Collingwood, who had taken up his station off Cadiz, "I am, as you may suppose, miserable at not having fallen in with the Enemy's Fleet", and after telling his tale, which included fears that the enemy might have doubled back to Jamaica, he promised, the moment his ships were watered and provisioned, to pay his old messmate a visit, "Not, my dear friend, t› take your Command from you, (for I may probably add mine to you,) but to consult how we can best serve our Country, by detaching a part of this large force".

He anchored in Rosia Bay next evening, and acquainted the Secretary to the Admiralty that when he had provisioned his fleet for four months, and heard from Collingwood and Bickerton, he would, unless he heard that the enemy had gone for any ports in the Bay, join the squadrons off Ferrol or Ushant. That night he wrote in his diary, "I went on shore for the first time since the 16th of June, 1803; and from having my foot out of the *Victory*, two years, wanting ten days."

He went across to Tetuan again next morning, to receive the "refreshment" necessary to banish scurvy from a fleet which had, he thanked God, not lost an officer or man by sickness since he had left the Mediterranean. In the small hours of July 25, as he was passing the Straits with a fine easterly wind, he read in a Lisbon paper, brought from the Rock, of the arrival of Bettesworth in England, of the story brought by the *Curieux*, and the result. "I know it's true," he exclaimed, "from my words being repeated, therefore, I shall not lose a moment, after I have communicated with Admiral Collingwood, in getting to the northward." He scribbled a line to Parker of the *Amazon* to make haste to join him from Gibraltar, and the sloop which had brought the newspaper sailed instantly, carrying back to the Rock all his clean washing, "even to my last shirt". He had thought her from Lisbon.

As he pressed again into the Atlantic, Collingwood's division was sighted, some way to the leeward. "My dear Collingwood," he explained, "we are in a fresh Levanter; you have a westerly wind: therefore I must forgo the pleasure of taking you by the hand until October next, when, if I am well enough, I shall (if the Admiralty please,) resume the Command."

5

The *Curieux*, despatched home on June 12, had fallen in with Villeneuve 900 miles N.N.E. of St. John, Antigua, and kept company long enough to ascertain enemy numbers and course. Her Captain was in the presence of the First Lord before that personage had got his shaving-water or his breakfast on July 9, and the early midsummer interview in Whitehall was picturesque, for Captain Bettesworth, aged five and twenty, and the recipient of twenty-four wounds in action, was the most personable of "Nelsonian" officers, and Lord Barham, whose silver hair was thin, but whose eye was still bright, had been a frigate Captain in the West Indies when Nelson was three years old. The new First Lord was in his eightieth year, but he had long experience as Comptroller of the Navy. Within a few hours despatch vessels were under sail, with orders for the blockading squadrons off Rochefort and Ferrol to unite and take up a position 100 miles west of Cape Finisterre.

Sir Robert Calder's squadron of fifteen of the line met Villeneuve there on the cloudy morning of July 22. The action, which took place at long range, was indecisive. Two Spanish ships were captured. After four days Calder lost sight of the enemy, who first put in to Vigo, and, leaving three ships there, reached Ferrol on August 1. Calder, having sent five of his squadron to resume the Rochefort blockade, joined Cornwallis, twenty-five miles west of Ushant, a day before Nelson, who, delayed by northerly winds, had been three weeks making his passage from the Rock to the Channel Fleet. A frigate spoken on August 12 had told Nelson that, up to the 9th, there had been no tale of the enemy's arrival in the Bay of Biscay, or on the Irish coast. The *Victory* saluted the *Ville de Paris* at 6 p.m., and hove to, but was under sail again before 8. Cornwallis had excused him even the customary personal visit, and authorised him to go on to Portsmouth. He took with him only the *Superb*, and as there was little wind, Keats dined with him, on the last night of their long passage, and they discussed the large packet of English newspapers thoughtfully sent on board by Fremantle. From these they gathered that John Bull was howling for the recall and court-martial of Calder, and saying—quite unjustly so far as Nelson could judge—that Lord Nelson would have done better.

His last approaches towards home were tantalisingly leisurely. With daylight of the 17th he was abreast of Portland; at noon he saw the Isle of Wight, and at 1 that night the *Victory* and *Superb* anchored off the Princesses' Shoal. Having weighed with dawn they worked up to the Motherbank, and anchored again. Yellow fever had been devastating the ports of Spain and Portugal, and as his fleet had touched at Gibraltar, Nelson found himself, "for the first time in my life", in quarantine. He hastened to assure the Admiralty, the Port Admiral and the Collector of Customs that there had been no fever in the garrison at the Rock, that he was twenty-eight days out and that he had "not even an object for the hospital" in either his flagship or the *Superb*. Throughout his three weeks' struggle to join the Channel Fleet he had scarcely written a private letter. He had been entirely occupied with preparations for the battle which had, in the end, fallen to Calder. While he waited for permission to come ashore, on a wet Sunday, he sent short lines to Brother William and Davison, and a long screed (the third on the subject) to their Lordships, asking urgently that a volunteer pilot, whom he had in his haste borne away from Antigua, might be put in the way of a speedy and remunerative passage to his native Barbados. For the problem of the patriotic and ebullient Mr. James Marguette (a man of colour), alone in London, weighed upon his conscience.

He told his brother:

"I am but so-so, yet, what is very odd, the better for going to the West Indies, even with the anxiety. We must not talk of Sir Robert Calder's battle: I might not have done so much with my small force. If I had fallen in with them, you would probably have been a Lord before I wished; for I know they meant to make a dead set at the *Victory*."

To Lady Hamilton he sent two expresses, at twenty-four-hour intervals. He had not heard from her since April.

"I have brought home no honour for my Country, only a most faithful servant; nor any riches—that the Administration took care to give to others —but I have brought home a most faithful and honourable heart. . . . God send us a happy meeting as our parting was sorrowful."

His order of release came at 7 p.m. on the night of the 19th, and his welcome was the most enthusiastic that he had ever received. From the moment that his flag had been descried at Spithead, the ramparts, and every place that could command a view of the entrance to Portsmouth harbour, had been thronged, despite heavy showers, and as his barge pulled to the shore it was greeted with loud and reiterated huzzas. Taking Murray with him, he went first to make his bow to the Commander-in-Chief and the Commissioner. His intention had been to stay not as much as ten minutes, but he was obliged to drink tea with them. He ordered tea again as he sat waiting for a post-chaise at the "George", Portsmouth High Street, while rain dripped down. Nine o'clock of a very wet night saw him on the road for London. "His Lordship's movements here were in unison with his pursuit after the Combined Squadron, for he was not an hour in the town." He reached Merton at 6 a.m. on the morning of August 20, 1805.

Chapter XVIII

1805
(ætat. 46)

THE TWENTY-FIVE DAYS

I

INCREDIBLE though it may sound, a strange foreigner gained an interview with the great man, who had travelled throughout the night to his country retreat, on the very day of his arrival. The lucky intruder, who brought to his descriptions a quality of early-morning freshness, was a Mr. J. A. Andersen. He had sent several of his writings to Lord Nelson, and was now projecting a history of his native Denmark. In his *Excursions in England*, published two years later, he is quite distinct that his gracious reception took place on August 20, 1805. The visitor from London was

"charmed with the situation of Merton. Merton Place is not a large, but a very elegant structure. In the balconies I observed a number of ladies, who, I understood to be Lord Nelson's relations. Entering the house, I passed through a lobby which contained amongst a variety of paintings and other *objets d'art*, an excellent marble bust of the illustrious Admiral. Here I met the Rev. Dr. Nelson, the present Earl. I was then ushered into a magnificent apartment where Lady Hamilton sat at a window. I at first scarcely observed his Lordship, he having placed himself immediately at the entrance. The Admiral wore a uniform emblazoned with different Orders of Knighthood. He received me with the utmost condescension. Chairs being provided, he sat down between Lady Hamilton and myself, and having laid my account of the Battle of Copenhagen on his knee, a conversation ensued."

On his last birthday Nelson had recorded, "Forty-six years of toil and trouble". He had noticed vaguely that he seemed to be growing very thin. When animated, as his figure was light and he moved briskly, he did not look his age; but in repose he now looked more. Mr. Andersen found the lines of his face hard,

"but the penetration of his eye threw a kind of light upon his countenance, which tempered its severity, and rendered his harsh features in some measure agreeable. . . His aspect commanded the utmost veneration, especially when he looked upwards. Lord Nelson had not the least pride of rank; he combined with that degree of dignity which a man of quality should have, the most engaging address in his air and appearance."

That afternoon Nelson sat down at 3.30 to a scene upon which his pen had dwelt often during upwards of two years, "shut up in the Victory's cabin". Indeed, the dream of a lifetime was realised. He dined in his own country house, and offered hospitality to his own family—"people that do care for us". Looking down his table, he saw, in fact, at last, the rich gleam of Worcester china, decorated with oak-leaves and laurel and the coat-of-arms of Viscount Nelson, Duke of Brontë, the glitter of plate bearing his own monogram, the profiles of a brother and sister and their spouses, of Mrs. Cadogan and Miss Sarah Connor, a full-face view of Lady Hamilton, in her element, and the bright hair and rosy cheeks of four healthy young people, attacking festal fare. Horatia was four and a half now, and "uncommonly quick". She could write a letter, and was learning French and Italian and the piano, but had been frightened when told "how her dear, dear god-papa kill'd all the people".

Outside, as well as within, transformation had been wrought at Merton during the owner's long absence. The entrance had been successfully removed to the north front; the new drawing-room, bedrooms and kitchen were being employed, and he was lord of additional acres, on the opposite side of Merton High Road, in the parish of Wimbledon. The Merton Place coachman's cottage and stables had been across the road, and rented from a Mr. Bennett, an inconvenient arrangement. A spacious bricked tunnel now led under the road to his stables and new kitchen gardens, and Lady Hamilton had given orders for the construction of a walk, on which he might feel himself on his own quarter-deck, leading up to a rotund white summer-house, in fashionable classic style, christened "the Poop".

Cribb, who had been provided with twenty underlings to assist him in his delving and planting, certainly merited congratulation. With regard to the rebuilding, although he approved the result, the Admiral was not so happy. He had written painfully, when the new drawing-room was mooted, "I hardly know how to find the money; but if it is to be done this year it is begun before this time; it is too late to say a word."

He set out for London early on the morning after his happy return, and was dropped at the Admiralty by Lady Hamilton, who went on to her little house in Clarges Street, to await the arrival of the Misses Bolton from Norfolk, and write to summon the Matchams from Bath. ("What a day of rejoicing was yesterday at Merton! How happy he is to see us all!")

He was at the Admiralty by 9.45. "The public appearance in the streets of Lord Nelson, who in the short space of five weeks has viewed the four quarters of the Globe, attracted a concourse", and his movements of this day were chronicled in detail in next morning's gossip columns. After leaving Lord Barham he took a hackney down to Messrs. Marsh, Page and Creed, Navy Agents, of Norfolk Street, Strand, and on to the Navy Office, Somerset House, where he saw Sir Andrew Snape Hammond, Comptroller. By noon he was back in Whitehall, having made an expedition to Messrs. Salters, silversmiths, where he had chosen a child's set of knife, fork and spoon to be engraved with the name "Horatia", and a silver-gilt cup for which the inscription ordered was: "To my much-loved Horatia". He was wearing "plain uniform and a green shade over his left eye". A long interview with Mr. Pitt was his last engagement. He left Town at four, having collected two nieces at what reporters called "his house in Clarges Street".

His day had been surprisingly easy. Everywhere the name of Lord Nelson had acted as an open sesame to jealously guarded penetralia. Ministers now came treading rapidly down their soft carpets with outstretched hand and concerned enquiries for his health. Mr. Pitt had even spoken to Mr. Rose of riding over to Merton Place from Bowling Green House, Wimbledon. The moment seemed auspicious for the Admiral to mention to Rose that the widow of Sir William Hamilton had not yet received any acknowledgment of her patriotic services at the Court of the Two Sicilies, and he took the opportunity. At the Admiralty, Lord Barham, "an almost entire stranger", could not have been more forthcoming. The new Secretary of State wanted to see Lord Nelson without delay. . . . As he had worked his way up to Spithead, he had gathered from the newspapers sent on board by Fremantle, off Ushant, that far from being blamed for having missed the Combined Fleet, his dramatic dash "to save the West Indies only by a few days" had enhanced his reputation. Nevertheless, his agonies on that long passage had not been without reason. Lord Radstock, a stout admirer, who had a son in the *Victory*, had believed that "the loss of Jamaica would at once sink all his past services into oblivion", and miserably doubted whether, should any serious misfortune have overtaken him, their Lordships would do much for him. The Admiralty, perplexed and harassed by his long silence, had indeed been "out of humour with him". The alarm in the City upon the news of Villeneuve's escape out of the Mediterranean, and junction with Gravina, had been enormous. The alarm had been warm, and the relief at his re-appearance, having banished Villeneuve from the West Indies, corresponded. Still, he had not been quite prepared for the extreme civility of his official welcome. "Thank God, he is safe and well", wrote Miss Cecilia Connor, in a letter received by Lady Hamilton that morning.

"Timid widows and spinsters are terrified at his foot being on shore; yet this is the man that is to have a Sir R. Calder and a Sir J. Orde sent to intercept his well-earned advantages. I hope he may never quit his own house again."

That hope was quickly dissipated, and within two days he fully appreciated the reason for the extraordinary availability of Ministers. They were "full of the Enemy's Fleet". On the day of his first call at the Admiralty, the frigate *Iris* had brought the unwelcome tidings that Villeneuve had put to sea again on the evening of the 13th from Ferrol, with twenty-eight or nine of the line. Cornwallis had kept seventeen ships to confront the Brest squadron of twenty-one, and sent eighteen, under Calder, to look for Villeneuve.

A very poor Admiral, who wondered if his interest was yet sufficient to get a small post in the Customs Office for his brother-in-law, but was still so bad at asking favours that he preferred to send his request through his friend Rose to a Prime Minister whom he was seeing almost daily, was more amused than flattered at his situation. "I am now", he explained to Captain Keats, "set up for a *Conjuror*, and God knows they will soon find out I am far from one. I was asked my opinion, against my inclination, for if I make one wrong guess, the charm will be broken. But this I ventured without any fear—that if Calder got fairly alongside their twenty-seven or twenty-eight Sail, that by the time the Enemy had beat our Fleet soundly, they would do us no harm this year."

Ministers very new to office, however, had looked funereal when assured that Buonaparte's career might be checked at a cost which would be highly unpopular at home. Already the news from India was making a strong and unfavourable impression. It was whispered in the City that if the Combined Fleet fell in with the homeward-bound convoy daily expected, the India Company would be bank-rupt. They could not at such a moment lend an attentive ear to Admiral Nelson's opinions on the importance of Sardinia to their nation. Lord Castlereagh, privately written down by the Admiral as "a man who has only sat one solitary day in his Office, and of course knows but little of what is passed", hesitantly believed that he had not seen the despatches alluded to, addressed to his pre-decessors. But there was no escape. Lord Nelson offered, if they could not be found, to provide the whole series immediately. He had kept duplicates, with an index.

2

The accepted picture of Nelson, settled in peace during his last weeks at home, in a rustic retreat, alone with Lady Hamilton, is mistaken. He was in conference in London for at least part of four-teen of those twenty-five days, and within nine he had learnt beyond doubt from Pitt that "my services may be wanted". Nor even at Merton was there much peace to be had. A house with not more than fifteen bedrooms was accommodating never less than nine adults and seven children, in addition to a staff containing several foreigners. Still Lady Hamilton sounded trumpet-calls to the last of the Nelson family. "We have Room for you all, so Come as soon as you can. We shall be happy, most happy. Here are Sir Peter Parker, and God knows who, so Nelson has not time to say more than that he loves you, and shall rejoice to see you."

Captain Keats paced the quarter-deck at Merton together with his host, and the Admiral explained his Plan for Attack. "No day can be long enough to arrange a couple of Fleets, and fight a decisive Battle, according to the old system. When *we* meet them, (for meet them we shall,) I'll tell you how I shall fight them.

"I shall form the Fleet into three Divisions in three Lines. One Division shall be composed of twelve or fourteen of the fastest two-decked Ships, which I shall always keep to windward, or in a situation of advantage; and I shall put them under an Officer who, I am sure, will employ them in the manner I wish, if possible. I consider it will always be in my power to throw them into Battle in any part I may choose; but if circumstances prevent their being carried against the Enemy where I desire, I shall feel certain he will employ them effectually, and, perhaps, in a more advantageous manner than if he could have followed my orders."

He paused, and Keats, who hoped to be with him when the promised day came, wondered who was the officer intended for this distinguished service. But Nelson swept on:

"With the remaining part of the Fleet formed in two Lines, I shall go at them at once, if I can, about one-third of their Line from their leading Ship."

He broke off again, and then asked, "What do you think of it?"

While Keats considered, in silence, something so novel, he proceeded with vigour:

"I'll tell you what I think of it. I think it will surprise and confound the Enemy. They won't know what I am about. It will bring forward a pell-mell Battle, and that is what I want."

Lord Minto was detained by affairs in a capital which he found very empty, except of disagreeable rumour. (He was going to be offered the St. Petersburg Embassy, and was going to refuse.) On the first Saturday after his distinguished friend's return, he took his chance at Merton,

"and found Nelson just sitting down to dinner, surrounded by a family party, of his brother, the Dean, Mrs. Nelson, their children, and the children of a sister, Lady Hamilton at the head of the table and Mother Cadogan at the bottom. I had a hearty welcome. He looks remarkably well and full of spirits. His conversation is a cordial in these low times. Lady Hamilton has improved and added to the house and the place extremely well and without his knowing she was about it. She is a clever being after all: the passion is as hot as ever."

The conventions, however, were being as strictly observed as ever. "Nelson", wrote Lady Hamilton to his sister, "when he is in Town goes to a hotel." He never spent a night under the roof of 11, Clarges Street, which was her house. He booked rooms at Gordon's Hotel, 44, Albemarle Street, and it was there that he was at last tracked down on August 28, by old Lord Hood, who had been trying to get in touch with him from the moment he had landed. Lord Minto had been startled that morning to find the Victor of the Nile by his bedside before he was up, expatiating at top speed on his hopes "to see me Secretary of State, and so forth". Nelson, who could not sleep late, and bleakly headed letters from Gordon's Hotel "6 a.m.", had brought with him some papers concerning the Mediterranean, over which the ex-Viceroy of Corsica was begged to run his eye as he travelled to Merton to-morrow, where a further consignment would be awaiting him.

Sunday was a day of comparative peace at Merton Place, but the Admiral, although a clergyman's son, had no objection to Sunday travelling. When he called on Mr. Addington, now Lord Sid-mouth, on his second day in Town, he took that gentleman at an awkward moment. The ex-Prime Minister was without his coat, having just been bled. The caller, fresh from Downing Street, looked to a dejected statesman very well, and after an hour of comfortable conversation, offered to renew it next day, but stipulated that he must first attend morning service at Merton. The engagement was eventually transferred to a later date and country scene.

The summer of 1805 had been most disappointing; there had been much rain and wind, many deferred junketings and little call for muslins. A burst of seasonable heat coincided perversely with Nelson's mid-week stay at Gordon's Hotel, but opened in time for his first Sunday at home, when the whole Merton Place party attended the parish church of what he liked to call "our village". The relations of Merton Place with the Vicar had been cordial from the first. The Rev. Thomas Lancaster kept an academy, and had a younger son whom he hoped to send to sea, under the auspices of his most influential parishioner.

A daughter of Merton Vicarage, many years later, when she was a Victorian matron, tacitly supported her father's attitude towards

Merton Place, and volunteered to the editor of *Lord Nelson's Despatches*:

"In revered affection for the memory of that dear man, I cannot refrain from informing you of his unlimited charity and goodness during his residence at Merton. His frequently expressed desire was, that none in that place should want, or suffer affliction that he could alleviate, and this I know he did with a most liberal hand; always desiring that it should not be known from whence it came. His residence at Merton was a continued course of charity and goodness, setting such an example of propriety and regularity that there are few would not be benefited by following it."

Nelson missed church on his second Sunday morning at home. For two days he had been in anxious expectation of news from Calder of a victory. Otherwise he had no doubt that he would himself "be ordered to sea, *very very* soon". The *Victory* had received a signal not to go into port to undergo the very slight repairs necessary after the Long Chase. Hardy, who was on sick leave, was returning to her. On Saturday night, August 31, his brother-in-law seemed to Mr. Matcham unusually pensive, and he finally murmured, "They are mistaken! I will go myself and talk with Mr. Pitt." The fruit of his country musings, which he so urgently wished to communicate to the Minister, was that the missing Combined Fleet was probably destined, not for the West Indies again, as had been decided in Cabinet conclave, but for Cadiz and Toulon. "They will then have collected sixty or seventy sail-of-the-line, and then there will be a difficulty in overcoming them." Matcham, who saw him on his return from his flying Sunday afternoon visit to the capital, treasured the report of that interview. After long discussion, the Prime Minister became a convert to the Admiral's view, and they agreed upon the number of ships which must be sent to attack such a combination. Pitt's next question was abrupt: "Now, who is to take command?" "You cannot have a better man than the present one—Collingwood", replied a good friend, but this suggestion was brushed aside. "No. That won't do. You must take the command." Nelson's objections were overruled, and Pitt asked him to be ready to sail in three days, to which the answer was, "I am ready now."

When a post-chaise disturbed the drive of Merton Place at 5 a.m.

on the following morning, Captain the Hon. Henry Blackwood of H.M.S. *Euryalus*, with despatches from Admiral Collingwood for the Admiralty, found the master of the house, according to his custom, already up and dressed. Nelson exclaimed, "I am sure that you bring me news of the French and Spanish Fleets, and that I shall have to beat them yet." A young officer, with bronzed aquiline features, tersely expressed his hope of being present at the intended "drubbing", and then explained that, finding himself so near his Lordship's villa so early, on his road from Portsmouth to the Admiralty, he had seized the chance to inform him that the Combined Fleet had been traced to Cadiz harbour.

He set off for Whitehall as soon as he had delivered himself of his dramatic news, and Nelson followed. Harrison's romantic story that the Admiral was discovered by Lady Hamilton later in the day pacing the "quarter-deck" in his garden, in low spirits, and was persuaded by her to go to London and offer his services, must be discounted. He had known from the morning of his first call at the Admiralty that his services might be needed very soon; he had told George Matcham of the certainty of his speedy departure on the preceding evening. Mrs. Bolton had written from Merton to the Matchams, a week earlier, urging them not to delay their journey, as his length of stay was very uncertain, and he had himself repeated the phrase in a letter to Beckford, refusing an invitation to Fonthill. That Nelson, after revealing to Lady Hamilton the news brought by Blackwood, with all its implications, did utter the popular, "Brave Emma! good Emma! If there were more Emmas there would be more Nelsons", need not fall under the same suspicion. He had said very much the same, in other words, on several previous occasions, and it is clear from a note written by her, within two days, that she did accept the inevitable in heroic vein. "My dear Friend," she told Lady Bolton, "I am again broken hearted, as our dear Nelson is immediately going. It seems as though I have had a fortnight's dream, and am awoke to all the misery of this cruel separation. But what can I do? His powerful arm is of so much consequence to his Country." Nelson had always intended to go to Town on the day of Blackwood's call, and had made an appointment with Lord Minto, which he kept. Their main topic, however, was not, as had been threatened, Sardinia. During the week-end the Ministry had decided "to give its best hope a *carte blanche*". He told Minto, that morning, that there seemed no doubt that he would be going immediately to take command of Calder's fleet; and next morning, that he was going to resume the Mediterranean Command as soon as the *Victory* could be got ready, which would be within the week. When he had presented himself at the Admiralty, following Blackwood, Lord Barham had given into his hands the current list of the Royal Navy and begged him to choose his own officers. He had replied, "Choose yourself, my Lord, the same spirit actuates the whole profession; you cannot choose wrong", but the elderly First Lord, pottering out of the room, had insisted, "This is my Secretary; give your orders to him." Everything was now being done on the same handsome scale, and by September 6 the Press knew it. "Lord Nelson's new appointment is very extensive and in some degrees unlimited. Lord Nelson's new command comprehends not only the whole of the Mediterranean but extends also to Cadiz. His Lordship has the selection of his own favourite officers." The announcement was very popular, but could hardly increase public affection for a character whose every movement had been eagerly watched from the moment he had set foot on shore. A week earlier, Lord Minto, who possessed historic sense, had written to his wife:

"I met Nelson to-day in a mob in Piccadilly, and got hold of his arm, so that I was mobbed too. It is really quite affecting to see the wonder and admiration, and love and respect, of the whole world; and the genuine expression of all these sentiments at once, from gentle and simple, the moment he is seen. It is beyond anything represented in a play or a poem of fame."

Meanwhile, at Merton, over which the shadow of what was now inevitable had brooded heavily almost from the first, the *tempo* of daily existence, always confused and rapid, quickened. There was no cessation, rather the contrary, of large dinner-parties and sudden London journeys. It is possible to learn exactly what happened at Lord Nelson's villa, as observed by an ingenuous guest, from the very day of Blackwood's call. George Matcham, junior, was due to arrive that night from Somerset. He was nearly sixteen, but had never been to boarding-school, and would be set down by the Bath coach at the White Horse cellars, Piccadilly, at 10 p.m. His uncle, after a heavy day in London, had returned home to dine, with the ladies of the party, who had received at Clarges Street during the morning a hasty note warning them that his heavy luggage must be put on the road for Portsmouth within forty-eight hours. The invaluable Cribb was called to the rescue. George Matcham, junior, kept a diary.

3

The chaise hired by Cribb was an open one, and all the way down to Merton it rained. When the young traveller arrived at last in his noble uncle's Surrey villa, he found it utterly quiet and dark. Every soul in that overcrowded, tragic house, surrounded by sighing, weeping trees and shining waters, had gone to bed early, after a day which had opened with a summons at 5 a.m. But soon a door clicked, and a light of welcome appeared above. "Lady H. came out *en chemise*, and directed me to my cousin Tom's room, where I was to sleep. Had not seen him for ten years, soon made acquaintance."

Not a suspicion of the sword of Damocles troubled young George's receptive brain, as he proceeded, daily, from September 4 to 11, 1805, to enter in telegraphic form, in his compulsory journal, his impressions of the principal events and characters encountered on his historic "visit to see Lord N. my Uncle, before his departure".

On September 6, at 6 a.m., as the Admiral sat at his desk in his country study, a tremendous storm broke over southern England. It was still in progress when he set off for a council at Mr. Pitt's house. That morning's session in Downing Street did not leave him entirely satisfied. Government had decided that the Combined Fleets must be held in Cadiz, or forced to fight if they attempted to leave. If the blockade could be made sufficiently strict, they would probably be obliged to put out very soon, for Cadiz was already short of food. As it was not known that Villeneuve's course had been taken contrary to orders from Paris, the Mediterranean was naturally suspected to be his object. It had been settled that Nelson was to go out at once, in the *Victory*, and that other ships should be sent to him as soon as they were ready. He wanted to do what he called "the job" well. Half a victory would not content him or the nation; but he did not believe that the Admiralty could, at the moment, with the best will in the world, give him a force within two-thirds of that likely to be encountered. "And therefore, if every Ship took her opponent, we should have to contend with a fresh Fleet of fifteen or sixteen Sail-of-the-line." As the storm receded and the sunlight of a thunderous day broadened across a table in Downing Street, an expert who had come amongst them like a thunderbolt, and whose speech had a tumbling, boyish eagerness, explained to statesmen of very grave countenance that "annihilation" should be their object. "It is, as Mr. Pitt knows, annihilation that the Country wants—and not merely a splendid victory of twenty-three to thirty-six—honourable to the parties concerned, but absolutely useless in the extended scale, to bring Buonaparte to his marrow-bones. . . ."

He had not been much impressed by the new Secretary of State for War, though Lord Castlereagh was lending an unexpectedly sympathetic ear to his suggestion that neutrals likely to victual the enemy in Cadiz should be seized and sent into Gibraltar. He thought Mr. Canning, another stranger, attractively able, "a very clever, deep-headed man", but something in Canning seemed to arouse the baser competitive instincts. He believed that he had long out-grown his youthful hero-worship of Pitt, a great man who had never been of any use to him. A chance to dine at Walmer had been neglected four years past. Yet, when it came to deciding, in a dark hour, in an uneasy capital, what it was that the nation needed, Mr. Pitt, ah! Pitt, was, after all, the only man. George Matcham, junior, sharply noticed that when his uncle recounted to a family party in the drawing-room at Merton the incidents of his last interviews in London, he seemed to take particular pleasure in the fact that "the Minister", upon his rising, had himself escorted him out of the room and to his carriage. "I do not think he would have done so much for a Prince of the Blood."

George Rose, who was as close a friend as either man had, and combined that feat with complete avoidance of publicity, sometimes bewildered listeners by declaring that he had found Pitt and Nelson so much alike. They differed only, he would mournfully say, in one having been as highly educated as a man could be, and the other having been sent, like Mr. Rose himself, early to sea. In vain the burly, inexpressive President of the Board of Trade tried to explain, "These two great men died as they lived, for their Country." The phrase "Self is out of the question", which had begun to appear in Nelson's private letters during the "Long Chase", recurred noticeably, with the addition of the word "entirely", towards the end of the twenty-five days, when he was living at fever-heat, happier than ever before; and a sensitive, sickly young literary aspirant was touched by the flame which Rose could not communicate. Charles Lamb, who had been much prejudiced against Lord Nelson, saw him on an early September morning, after his new command had been announced, walking in Pall Mall, "looking just as a Hero should look", and confessed to having "followed him in fancy, ever since".

Rose's regrets that one sent early to sea could not enjoy cultural advantages were echoed by Nelson this week. "But", he said politely to the President of the Royal Academy, "there is one picture whose power I do feel. I never pass a print-shop where your 'Death of Wolfe' is in the window, without being stopped by it." He also asked the Rev. Mr. Este, who was what he called "a clever literary man", to supply some "old books" for his improvement during the forthcoming cruise. Mr. Este, apparently, complied tactfully, for a year later he wrote sadly to Charlotte Nelson, asking if just Boswell's *Life of Johnson* and the *Little Comedies of Foote* could be recovered from H.M.S. *Victory*.

On the following morning, from the Admiralty, Nelson scratched a few lines to be sent off in a brig to the squadron blockading Cadiz. "My dear Coll., I shall be with you in a very few days, and I hope you will remain Second-in-Command. You will change the *Dreadnought* for the *Royal Sovereign*, which I hope you will like. . . ."

Next day, being Sunday, the whole Merton Place party went again to church; later Admiral Sir Sidney Smith called. He did not neglect to refer to his famous defence of Acre, and young George thought him handsome. Time and chance had elected that Sidney

Smith was to be constantly in Nelson's company at the present crisis, for they met at the Admiralty next morning, and dined, with a company described as "rich and fashionable", at the "Ship", Greenwich.

On the forenoon of the 10th Nelson drove over to Richmond Park alone, in a shower, and Lord Sidmouth thereafter preserved "a little round study table" upon which his friend had shown him how he meant to attack the Combined Fleets if he should be so fortunate as to bring them to action. At dinner that day, at the London house of the wealthy Mr. James Crawford, the hero checked Lady Hamilton when she wished him to tell the company of his having been "mobbed and huzza'd in the City". "Why," said she, "you like to be applauded—you cannot deny it." His reply was, "I own it", but he went on to say that no man ought to be too much elated by popular applause. "It may be my turn to feel the tide set against me." He said that he hoped to be home for Christmas, and that nothing short of annihilation of the enemy's fleet would do any good. He reckoned that France and Spain together had a hundred ships-of-the-line at their disposal. Someone asked, "How many have we in all?" but the baffling reply of an Admiral in great good humour was, "Oh! I do not count our Ships."

Next morning the late Sir William Hamilton's connection, Mr. Beckford, presented himself at Merton. His invitations to stay at Fonthill having been refused, he had rushed up to London and taken rooms at an hotel sooner than miss Lord Nelson. Young George was unimpressed. "Mr. Beckford din'd here. Talkative. Praised his own composition. Play'd extempore on the Harpsichord. Sung. I thought it a very horrible noise."

The Boltons, taking with them all the nieces and nephews, were leaving for London the next morning. Nelson had asked his neighbours, the Perrys, and Lord Minto from Town to dine, mentioning that he expected to be at home all day. He had already been obliged to give up this hope, in deference to a request from Lords Castlereagh and Mulgrave. At a late hour a special messenger brought a letter, couched in most flowery terms, from a Colonel Macmahon, summoning him to Carlton House. "H.R.H. the Prince of Wales, who had come up from Weymouth specially, would feel miserable, etc." The command was unwelcome, but H.R.H. had graciously entreated Lord Nelson to name his own hour, however early. The Duke of Queensberry offered the loan of a carriage, and next morning Lady Hamilton accompanied the guest of royalty, though not to Carlton House. She waited at Clarges Street while Nelson was wished God-speed by a Prince whose (indiscreetly repeated) careless mention, "how Lady Hamilton had struck his fancy", had driven a jealous lover nearly crazy in the winter of 1800. No record exists of the farewell extended by an Heir to the Throne who could assume a fascinating grand manner to an officer whose attachment to the royal family was deeply rooted. The reason why the Admiral was late for dinner at Merton that day, however, is well documented.

As Lord Castlereagh was Secretary for War and the Colonies, the Colonial Office, Downing Street, was the *rendezvous* appointed by him, and on Nelson's arrival he was shown into a little waiting-room on the right of the hall, into which, presently, was ushered another gentleman. General the Hon. Sir Arthur Wellesley at once recognised Nelson, "from his likeness to his pictures, and the loss of an arm", but the Admiral saw in a high-nosed, haughty, curt military officer nothing but the embodiment of all he found unsympathetic in a Service of which he was critical. The officer of the Senior Service mentioned that the Cabinet had been sitting since 1 o'clock, discussing the instructions to be issued to him and to Sir Sidney Smith. "He entered at once into conversation with me", reported the General long afterwards. "If I can call it conversation, for it was almost all on his side, and all about himself, and in, really, a style so vain and silly as to surprise, and almost disgust me." Disgusted though Sir Arthur may have been, he took occasion to remark, with reference to Sir Robert Calder's recent action, "This measure of success won't do nowadays, for your Lordship has taught the public to expect something more brilliant." Nelson almost immediately left the room, evidently guessing "that I *was* somebody" and gone to inquire who, decided the General, whose story continues: "When he came back, he was altogether a different man, both in manner and matter." Having discovered that he was, by a lucky chance, alone with the Victor of Assaye, the

Admiral lost no time in proposing to a brilliant young General that he should lead the troops for an investment of Sardinia. Sir Arthur replied that he "would rather not", as he was only two days back from the East Indies, but during the long *tête-à-tête* which followed, entirely revised his opinion of Lord Nelson. "He talked like an officer and a statesman. The Secretary of State kept us long waiting, and certainly, for the last half or three quarters of an hour, I don't know that I ever had a conversation that interested me more. . . . He really was a very superior man."

At Merton, while an historic interview was taking place in a London waiting-room, Lord Nelson's guests also waited, but less enjoyably. The Perrys and Lord Minto, lacking a host and hostess, sat unintroduced. At length the welcome sound of wheels was heard, but their hopes were dashed by the entry of another lost soul, this time a large, odd clergyman. The Chaplain of the *Victory*, in good spirits, was able to tell them that he had just seen the Admiral, for a moment, after the council in Lord Mulgrave's office had broken up, and had been told by him to collect his luggage and get down to Merton. To young Dr. Lambton Este (who was going as one of the six secretaries with commissions from the Foreign Office to be carried in the *Victory*) his lordship had mentioned, "I have just settled your business with Lord Liverpool. I am now going to the Admiralty."

This sounded hopeless, but at last, two hours late, the master of the house walked into his drawing-room, and introduced his guests to one another, whereupon Lord Minto, in a flash, recollected, "Mr. Perry! Editor of *The Morning Chronicle*, whom I formerly sent to the King's Bench, or Newgate, I think for six months, for a libel on the House of Lords." A gentleman of the robe, a man of the world, hastened to say how glad he was "to have the opportunity of shaking hands on our old warfare", and an evening trembling on the brink of social disaster seemed about to recover, when tragedy re-entered in the person of Lady Hamilton. From her appearance it was at once clear that the last drive together had taken place. All Lord Minto's old aversion returned as he occupied the seat of honour next to a hostess who could not restrain large tears, "could not eat, and hardly drink, and near

swooning, and all at table". He stayed, however, until 10 o'clock
before taking his final leave of a very old friend whose attachment
to him was, he flattered himself, "little short of the other . . . and is
quite sincere".

Nelson's hours at Merton were now numbered. The last of the
dramatic high-tensioned twenty-five days was come. The summer
was waning. There was early mist, driven away by hot sun at
midday, and in the kitchens of Merton talk of mushroom ketchup.
On the morning of the 13th, when he presented himself for his
accustomed before-breakfast tour of his property, Thomas Cribb
made so bold as to impart "some private family news". The
Admiral congratulated an anxious dependant, and gave him an
extra tip, "to buy a Christening frock", adding his favourite, "If
it's a boy, call him Horatio, if a girl, Emma." Cribb's future son-
in-law, Hudson, with some of the garden lads, watched, with the
realisation that he was witnessing something he would remember
all his life, a post-chaise summoned from the "King's Head" dash
up to the front door, and the master embark, "To get his final
sailing orders from the Admiralty", the boy believed.

Nelson returned to dine with Lady Hamilton, and with the
Matchams, who had stayed to the last in a house suddenly and
noticeably quiet. Seated in the drawing-room, his relatives listened
to the arrival of the vehicle which was to carry the Admiral through
the night to Portsmouth. When they heard him coming downstairs
alone, George Matcham arose, and prepared to attend him, in
dreadful silence, to the front door. The heart of the accomplished
civilian was too full for words, but Nelson, up to the moment that
they grasped hands, was speaking cheerfully, only regretting that
he had not, so far, been able to repay the £4,000 which he had
borrowed from his brother-in-law, to buy Axe's field. George
Matcham found his voice, to reply, "My dear Lord, I have no other
wish than to see you return home in safety. As to myself, I am not
in want of anything."

One of Nelson's last acts before this scene had been a visit of
farewell to the bedside of Horatia. The country September night
was advanced; a child in its fifth year had been deeply asleep for
hours. Touched by a sight always awe-inspiring, even to a happy

parent, he fell upon his knees, and prayed that the life of Horatia might be happy. A prayer which he entered in his private diary, later that night, while horses were being changed, probably at Guildford, was copied by Dr. Scott.

"Friday night, at half-past ten, drove from dear, dear Merton, where I left all which I hold dear in this world, to go to serve my king and country. May the great God whom I adore, enable me to fulfill the expectations of my country; and if it is His good pleasure that I should return, my thanks will never cease being offered up to the throne of His mercy. If it is His good Providence to cut short my days upon earth, I bow with the greatest submission, relying that He will protect those so dear to me, that I may leave behind. His will be done. Amen. Amen. Amen."

Chapter XIX

1805
(ætat. 47)

TRAFALGAR

I

HE drank tea, by candlelight, at the "Anchor", Liphook, and arrived at the familiar "George", Portsmouth, at 6 a.m. on the morning of September 14. Outside its doors he saw the carriage of the Vicar of Merton, who had just parted with a fourteen-year-old-son, going as a volunteer, first-class, to the *Victory*, and Mr. Lancaster waited while the Admiral dashed off four lines, opening, "My dearest most beloved of Women, Nelson's Emma!" Within the hostelry he found visitors from London, come to see the last of him. George Rose was attended by Mr. Canning, almost a stranger, but newly appointed Treasurer to the Navy. George Murray, detained by business cares upon the death of a parent, had sent him a letter of deep regret and a haunch of venison. After breakfasting, he went to the Dockyard, to pay his formal call upon jolly old Commissioner Saxton. He learnt from the Captains of the *Royal Sovereign*, *Defiance* and *Agamemnon* that their ships were at Spithead, but not yet ready for sea, and as he hoped to sail with a fair wind that evening, he gave instructions that they were to follow him, with the greatest expedition possible, to a secret *rendezvous*. The Captains of two further ships-of-the-line, refitting at Plymouth, were sent orders to put to sea as soon as they were provisioned for six months. A frigate stationed off Cape St. Vincent should tell them where he was to be found. If after cruising twenty-four hours they failed to find her, they must call at Cape St. Mary's and Cadiz, approaching these places with the utmost caution.

Sir Isaac Coffin and Captain Conn accompanied him back to the inn in the High Street. Towards noon he had despatched all necessary business on shore. The day was a Saturday, and the streets, already full, were likely to become much fuller; indeed, since his arrival had become known, an expectant crowd had swelled outside the "George". He decided to embark from the beach at Southsea, at the place where the bathing-machines were drawn up, immediately behind the Assembly Rooms, and quitted the "George" inconspicuously by its narrow, stone-flagged back entrance. Even so, he was quickly recognised, and enthusiasts, running ahead, spread the news of his altered route and approach by Penny Street and Green Row. He pushed his way through a pressing multitude, in good vein, explaining that he was sorry he had not two arms, so that he could shake hands with more friends, and it was soon evident that his Portsmouth following felt more poignantly than the admirers who had mobbed him daily in London. As his figure came in sight, some people dropped to their knees in silence, uncovered and called out a blessing on him; tears ran down many faces. The crowd, encroaching upon the parapet to watch him embark, pushed aside the sentries and threatened to get out of hand: a military officer who gave orders for its repulse with bayonets was himself obliged to beat a retreat. After the Admiral's barge had pushed off, many persons swarmed into the water, and he acknowledged greetings by waving his hat. He turned to Hardy, as the regular dip of oars gained pre-eminence over Portsmouth cheers on an afternoon of flat calm, and said, "I had their huzzas before. I have their hearts now."

The *Victory*, lying at single anchor at St. Helen's, was the scene of much picturesque activity. As the wind had died, the politicians from London were invited to dine. George Rose, impressed by the ceremonious elegance of his entertainment, was surprised to hear that Lord Nelson was not a rich man, and departed muttering that "he would tell the whole". He had deemed the moment unsuitable for asking if his friend had found time to sit for a portrait by Edridge. He had been disconcerted by the almost testamentary urgency with which Nelson had recommended to his protection the cases of a brother-in-law, Mr. Bolton, and the Rev. Mr. Scott. Taking his statesman friend aside after the meal, Nelson had also entreated him again, with great earnestness, to approach the Prime Minister on the subject of Lady Hamilton's pension, and this Rose, having promised to do, did attempt within the next few days, though without conclusive result.

Next morning at 8 a.m. the *Victory* weighed, with light airs, and made sail to the S.S.E., having only Blackwood's frigate in company. There had been time for a boat to come off to the flagship and an express from Merton to be brought on board. Nelson replied:

> "Off Dunnose, Sept. 16th.
> 1805. 11 a.m.

"My beloved Emma,

"I cannot even read your letter. We have fair wind, and God will, I hope, soon grant us a happy meeting. The wind is quite fair and fresh. We go too swift for the boat. May Heaven bless you, and Horatia, with all those who hold us dear to them, for a short time, farewell,

> "Ever yours,
> "Nelson and Brontë."

2

The almost solitary progress of the *Victory* towards Cape Trafalgar was stately in pace. The Dorset and Devon coastline, in September weather, slowly altered. Such fashionable watering-places as Lyme and Torquay had suddenly filled. For some weeks there had been rumours that the army for the Invasion of England was going to be used against Austria. Already a great part of it had been set on the march to the Rhine. Buonaparte had broken up his camp at Boulogne.

Shortly after Nelson had scribbled his first note of the 16th, the wind came foul, and for an anxious hour he found himself likely to be blown into Weymouth. By dint of perseverance, Weymouth was avoided, and he was able to inform Davison, in a further private letter of that afternoon, dated "Off Portland", "My fate is fixed, and I am gone, and beating down Channel with a foul wind." (He had not been able, during the twenty-five days, to fulfil his often-made promise of taking Davison by the hand in St. James's Square. On his release from his year of detention, a temporarily extinguished man had fled to the solitudes of his Northumberland property, and there stayed; but up to a few days before Trafalgar, Nelson continued to send long confidential screeds to Swarland Park.) A Torbay boat got alongside during the nasty blowing night of the 16th and received a letter addressed to Lady Hamilton, and the lordly tip of half a guinea for putting it in the post. "I intreat, my dear Emma, that you will cheer up; and we will look forward to many, many happy years, and be surrounded by our children's children. God Almighty can, when He pleases, remove the impediment." At Plymouth, in very dirty weather, he signalled the two 74's waiting there to join him. He doubted their ability to obey, but they succeeded in doing so, off the Lizard, when it had fallen nearly calm. Two mornings later, thirty leagues S.W. of the Scillies, his glass showed him a frigate coming down to his little squadron. She was guessed to be the *Decade*, from the fleet off Cadiz, bringing home, sick, his old Second in the Mediterranean, and at 1.30 p.m. the *Victory* hove to, and Sir Richard Bickerton came on board, very unwell, but with the reassuring news that no battle had as yet been fought by Admiral Collingwood. After forty minutes the *Victory* made sail again, the *Decade* resumed her swift passage home, and the *Euryalus* was sent on ahead with letters to the British Consul at Lisbon, to Admiral Collingwood, and to Captain Sutton, urging them to secure every man possible, in every way, for the fleet, and on no account to mention Lord Nelson's approach or acknowledge his arrival. "I would not have you salute even if you are out of sight of land."

On the 25th, with sunset, the Captain of the *Constance*, steering for the mouth of the Tagus, took charge of a letter opening, "My dearest Emma,—We are now in sight of the Rock of Lisbon, and although we have very little wind, I hope to get round Cape St. Vincent to-morrow. We have had only one day's real fair wind, but by perseverance we have done much. I am anxious to join the fleet, for it would add to my grief if any other man was to give them the Nelson touch, which WE say is warranted never to fail."

His anxieties were brought to an end on the 28th. Dawn of that morning displayed a British bomb-ketch cruising. By noon the prospect included eighteen of the line. In a warmer dusk than he had recently experienced, with a breeze that carried the scent of orange-groves to sea, he "got fairly into the fleet", and could make out, in Cadiz harbour, thirty-six enemy men-of-war "looking me in the face; unfortunately there is a strip of land between us, but it is believed they will come to sea in a few days. The sooner the better." He could not communicate with Collingwood until the next morning. It was his birthday. He was forty-seven. He had been enthusiastically greeted before, when taking over a command, but on this occasion, in obedience to his orders, in silence; and the omission of customary salutes and hoisting of colours, at a moment when a fleet action was hourly expected, was recognised by all who took part as dramatic.

The rule of Collingwood had not been inspiring. Facing thirty enemy ships with twenty-two, he had imposed all the most dis- agreeable features of St. Vincent's iron *régime*. No visiting had been allowed, except on strict duty. Though country vessels from the North African coast came into his fleet often, the order was that no boats could be hoisted out, so no fresh food could be bought. "For Charity's sake", prayed Captain Edward Codrington of the *Orion*, who had never seen the hero, "send us Lord Nelson, ye men of power!" His first interview with the new Chief sealed the allegiance of this officer, for a much-hoped-for letter from Mrs. Codrington was produced with the courtly comment that as this had been entrusted by a lady, the messenger was making a point of delivering it personally. "The signal has been made this morning", wrote a correct young man whose domestic affairs were in good order, "for all of us who did not dine on board the *Victory* yesterday, to go there to-day. What our late Chief will think of this I do not know; but I well know what the Fleet will think of the difference; and even you, our good wives, who have some causes of disapprobation, will allow the superiority of Nelson in all these social arrangements which bind his captains to their Admiral. The signal is made that boats may be hoisted out to buy fruit, stock, or anything. This, I trust, will be a common signal hereafter, but it is the first day I have seen it made." Captain Pulteney Malcolm of the *Donegal*, who knew both Wellington and Nelson intimately, afterwards assured en- quirers that "Nelson was the man to *love*". Captain George Duff of the *Mars*, also writing to a good wife, reported on October 1, "Dined with his Lordship yesterday, and had a very merry dinner. He certainly is the pleasantest Admiral I ever served under", and three days before Trafalgar, "You ask me about Nelson, and how I like him. I have already answered that question as every person must do that ever served under him."

Fifteen commanding officers dined on board the *Victory* on the Admiral's birthday, and as many on the succeeding day. On the third night after his arrival, "my dear Coll.", now his second-in-command of a fleet "as perfect as could be expected", and Fremantle, another close personal friend, were tactfully entertained as sole guests. With Collingwood his line was, "Telegraph on all occasions, without ceremony. We are one, and I hope ever shall be. . . . Everybody in England admired your adroitness in not being forced unnecessarily into the Straits." To Fremantle he delivered a letter, asking first, "Would you have a Girl or a Boy?" The Captain of the *Neptune*, who already had two offspring of each sex, replied, "A girl", and was smilingly told to "be satisfied". The note from Mrs. Fremantle's sister announced the safe arrival of "Louisa". The dinner-party broke up at 8 o'clock, after which the guests were carried to witness a theatrical performance in the flagship, in which the seaman taking the chief female part (much dressed) was somewhat cruelly convincing. The night was very warm, and Fremantle retired to sleep with all windows and doors open, happy that he had been promised "my old place in the Line of Battle, which is *his second*". Nelson slept well until 4 a.m., when, to his disgust, he was woken by "one of my dreadful spasms". In vain he had recounted his symptoms to physicians of repute. Mr. Beatty, no courtier, diagnosed them as characteristic of nothing worse than indigestion, and the sufferer had to admit, "I had been writing seven hours, yesterday." His own impressions of an arrival described by Codrington as "causing a general joy in the Fleet" are available from two sources. Lady Hamilton was told on October 1:

"I believe my arrival was most welcome, not only to the Commander of the Fleet, but almost to every individual in it; and when I came to explain to them the '*Nelson touch*', it was like an electric shock. Some shed tears, all approved—'It was new—it was singular—it was simple!' and, from Admirals downwards, it was repeated—'It must succeed, if ever they will allow us to get at them! You are, my Lord, surrounded by friends, whom you inspire with confidence.' Some may be Judas's; but the majority are certainly much pleased with my commanding them."

A modestly anonymous officer afterwards communicated to *The Naval Chronicle* an historic note to him, dated October 3:

"The reception I met with on joining the Fleet caused the sweetest sensation of my life. The Officers who came on board to welcome my return, forgot my rank as Commander-in-Chief in the enthusiasm with which they greeted me. As soon as these emotions were past, I laid before them the Plan I had previously arranged for attacking the Enemy; and it was not only my pleasure to find it generally approved, but clearly perceived and understood."

The Plan of Attack expounded to his Captains at once on his arrival was formally issued to them in a secret memorandum on October 9, and in it are to be found the essential ideas eventually adapted to suit the conditions at Trafalgar.

3

"The whole system here is so completely changed", wrote Fremantle on October 6, "that it wears quite a different aspect. We are continually with something to change the scene, and know precisely how far we may go, which is very pleasant."

Nelson had found the fleet stationed some fifteen to twenty miles from Cadiz, and getting very short of water and provisions. As soon as possible he moved it to fifty miles west of the port, in order to give the enemy encouragement to come out (while remaining in ignorance how far he was being silently reinforced), and he ordered Admiral Louis, with six of the line, to Gibraltar and Tetuan. An old Crocodile departed reproachfully. "You are sending us away, my Lord—the Enemy will come out, and we shall have no share in the Battle." Nelson readily explained that he had no choice but to send his ships to water and provision in detachments, and, "I send you first, to insure your being here to help to beat them." But Louis had prophesied correctly.

An advanced squadron of fast-sailing 74's was thrown out, ten to twelve miles east of the fleet, and a squadron of frigates, under Blackwood, cruised indefatigably close to the harbour's mouth. Still the Chief was beset with fears that the enemy might slip out, in thick weather, and get into the Mediterranean. He dictated letters to the Secretary to the Admiralty, to Lord Barham, and to Lord Castlereagh asking for "more *eyes*. . . . The last Fleet was lost to me for want of Frigates: God forbid this should." He wrote confidentially to Rose, to ask if Mr. Pitt could be prevailed upon to drop a hint to the First Lord that the Prime Minister would be very uneasy until the necessary forces reached Lord Nelson. Meanwhile, he warned Blackwood: "Let me know every movement. I rely on you that we can't miss getting hold of them. Watch all points, and all winds and weather, for I shall depend upon you."

On the 5th he learnt that the enemy in Cadiz were getting their troops on board, and that the Spanish squadron of seven of the line at Cartagena had their topsails up, all of which sounded as if a junction was intended. Four days later all the Cadiz fleet but one had moved out of the Puerto Real and had bent their top-gallant sails. Nelson believed that Decrès, the Minister of Marine, was to take the command, but actually the tragic Villeneuve had received orders from Buonaparte, on September 28, to return to Toulon (after ranging along the Italian coast), and goaded by threats that he would be superseded if he did not put to sea, was preparing to do so. A report of the arrival of Louis's squadron at Gibraltar encouraged, and the news, on October 18, that his successor had reached Madrid, decided him. The Combined Fleet under his command consisted of fifteen Spaniards of the line, four of them three-deckers mounting 100 to 130 guns, four French 80-gun ships and fourteen 74's, five frigates and two gun-brigs, all French. Of Nelson's twenty-seven ships, seven were three-deckers, of 98 to 100 guns, one was an 80-gun ship, sixteen were 74's and three 64's. But at a council of war called by Villeneuve, a unanimous resolution had been passed to avoid an action if possible.

A delicate and unpleasant task entrusted to Nelson by the First Lord in London was tackled without delay. Rear-Admiral Sir Robert Calder had gone afloat when his present Chief was one year old, and was very generally believed to have been inimical to a brilliant junior since the Battle of St. Vincent. At an early stage during his first interview with Sir Robert, to whom he was empowered to communicate the deep dissatisfaction of H.M. Government with his conduct in the engagement with the Allied Fleets in July, Nelson found that Calder had already written home, in complete confidence, to ask for an enquiry which must in any case be ordered. When Sir Robert discovered that he was, by their Lordships' instructions, to be sent home in a fast frigate—"turned out of my Ship . . . in the face of the Fleet"—the scene became distressing. A highly indignant man, entirely ignorant of the popular clamour which had forced the hand of a Government new in office, broke down so pitiably that Nelson decided to depart from the letter of his instructions, and as soon as the *Royal Sovereign* (another three-decker) joined, allow Sir Robert to go home in his own ship. "He is in adversity, and if he has ever been my enemy, he now feels the pang of it, and finds me one of his best friends." A fortnight's inevitable harassing delay followed, and when the expected reinforcement did arrive, Nelson, sobered by the prospect of depriving his fleet of a 90-gun ship which might be essential in an action, reconsidered an offer made under the stress of emotion. But four letters marked "Private" from an afflicted brother-officer, all delivered within twenty-four hours, held him to his original resolution, and Sir Robert departed, a week before Trafalgar, taking with him H.M.S. *Prince of Wales* and the Captains of two other ships-of-the-line to give evidence on his behalf. A third officer, having discovered that the Admiralty order said that Captains were to go home only "if willing", was not willing, was wounded at Trafalgar, and as eventually the court-martial did not sit until Christmas week, 1805, was present to witness Sir Robert found guilty of an error of judgment and severely reprimanded.

Amongst other cares during the first days of October, a levanter was hindering Nelson from clearing his transports. "I am", he explained in a letter to Ball, "not come forth to find difficulties, but to remove them." At the head of his list of difficulties awaiting removal were the facts that his second-in-command did not fancy his new ship or his Flag-Captain. Collingwood had been promised that he would find the *Royal Sovereign* better than the *Victory*, but he knew that she was noted for her dull-sailing qualities, and had been christened by the Channel Fleet "the West Country Waggon". Upon making her acquaintance, however, he discovered that, as she had just been re-coppered, the nickname was now a libel. With regard to Captain Rotherham, he was simply reminded that "in the presence of the enemy, all Englishmen should be as brothers", and told "of course" to bring his Flag-Captain with him when asked to dine quietly with the Chief. To the officer commanding the look-out frigates, who was becoming touchy upon this wearing duty, Nelson sent two up-to-date newspapers ("I stole them for you") and the suggestion, "Do not, my dear Blackwood, be angry with anyone. It was only a laudable anxiety in Admiral Louis, and nothing like complaining." Admiral Knight, who (as grave witnesses were eager to attest) had "almost made us quarrel with the Moors of Barbary" at a most unsuitable moment, received a comradely reminder, "In our several stations, my dear Admiral, we must all put our shoulders to the wheel, and make the great machine of the Fleet intrusted to our charge, go on smoothly." By ill chance the Agent-Victualler at Gibraltar, inured to dealing with crafty Tetuan, was ill. The resourceful Mr. Ford, Agent-Victualler Afloat, was speedily despatched to a troublesome quarter towards which Louis's hungry squadron was fast approaching, and was amply provided "with money to put us right again" and private instructions "not to be *penny* wise and *pounds* foolish".

A strong letter must be sent to Lord Strangford, Minister at Lisbon, complaining of the hostile attitude of the Portuguese Government to H.M. ships. . . . The Sick and Hurt Department had forwarded returns which were clearly ridiculous; the Dispenser was asking for a survey, and the Surgeon had sent what Admiral Collingwood found "a very improper letter". . . . The troubles bred by young blood were also not absent, and a particularly painful case needed instant attention. The First Lieutenant of the *Hydra* was adrift in Italy, most probably in prison by now. He had bolted with a ballet-dancer from Valetta. The boy's father, an excellent officer, had offered to pay a trail of debts, supposed to be about £200 or £300. If a few more pounds were necessary, Lord Nelson would be answerable. "All we want is to save him from perdition. . . ." The Chief had just sat down to dinner on the 17th when a good digestive in the shape of a weighty packet from his second-in-command was delivered. The Consul at Lisbon and a Captain Dunbar had apparently long been conducting a violent correspondence on the subject of supplies to the fleet. Picking his way through the papers that night, it appeared to Lord Nelson that the Captain of the

Poulette had acted very incorrectly throughout and should be censured, and Mr. Gambier perfectly, until the moment that he lost his temper.

All the routine business of the Mediterranean Command remained to be dealt with by a man expecting a fleet action "every day, hour and moment". He sent a silky intimation of his appointment to his old antagonist, the Dey of Algiers ("I think your Highness will be glad to hear of my return to the command of His Majesty's Fleets in the Mediterranean"), and commiserated with her distressed Majesty of Naples, her now inveterate foe, Sir John Acton, and H.E. Hugh Elliot, whose recall was likely.

On the night of the 10th, as he concluded the dictation of the last of two dozen essential letters, heavy rain began to fall, to the irritation of many officers who had been engaged for the past week scraping their ships and repainting them *à la Nelson*, that is to say, in imitation of H.M.S. *Victory*, with black bands between the varnish-yellow of the gun-decks, and black ports, so that, with closed ports, the ship presented a chequered appearance. Five ships-of-the-line had now joined him from home, and one from Gibraltar. On the morning of the 13th, when H.M.S. *Agamemnon* and the frigate *Amiable* were signalled, he was noticed to rub his "fin" and exclaim: "Here comes Berry! Now we shall have a battle." Young Sir Edward, the stormy petrel of the Service, who had already seen seven general actions, had a tale to unfold. He had been chased, and all but taken, by the Rochefort squadron, when eight days out from Plymouth. He brought English newspapers, in one of which Lord Nelson found that General Mack was to be given the command of the Austrian forces in Germany. After reading this, he prophesied, "I know General Mack too well. He sold the King of Naples. If he is now intrusted with an important command, he will certainly betray the Austrian monarchy." His warning to the Duke of Clarence on the subject of this character, before he left England, had been in terms which would be appreciated by that blunt brother-officer. "If your Royal Highness has any communication with Government, let not General Mack be employed. For I knew him at Naples to be a rascal, a scoundrel and a coward."

That night he drew his Chief Surgeon apart and asked him "how long he thought it would be before Captain Hardy was perfectly recovered". Upon Mr. Beatty's reply, "he hoped not more than a fortnight", "Ah!" smiled his lordship, "before a fortnight, the Enemy will be at sea; the business will be done, and we shall be looking out for England." Actually, only six further days of waiting remained.

On the night of the 18th he noted in his private memorandum book, "Fine weather, wind easterly. The Combined Fleets cannot have finer weather to put to sea." Next morning he wrote to Collingwood, "What a beautiful day! Will you be tempted out of your Ship? If so, hoist the assent, and *Victory's* pendants." On the back of this sheet Collingwood afterwards added, "Before the answer to this letter had got to the *Victory*, the signal was made that the Enemy's fleet was coming out of Cadiz, and we chased immediately."

The Combined Fleets of France and Spain had begun to get under way at 7 a.m., but, from want of wind, only twelve ships effected their exits that day. A breeze from the W.N.W. sprang up during the afternoon, and they stood on the larboard tack to the northward, dogged by two British frigates. During the interval before the news raced from masthead to masthead, "The Enemy's Fleet is at sea", Nelson retired to his cabin to begin a letter.

"My Dearest beloved Emma, the dear friend of my bosom,
    "The Signal has been made that the Enemy's Combined fleet are coming out of Port. We have very little Wind, so that I have no hopes of seeing them before to-morrow. May the God of Battles crown my endeavours with success, at all events I will take care that my name shall ever be most dear to you and Horatia, both of whom I love as much as my own life, and as my last writing before the Battle will be to you, so I hope in God that I shall live to finish my letter after the Battle. May Heaven bless you prays your

                                                    "Nelson and Brontë."

A letter to Horatia, opening "My dearest Angel", and signed "your Father", was dated the same day. Other officers who had given hostages to fortune seized a last chance to set down home-thoughts. In the *Euryalus*, Blackwood was writing to his lady:

"What think you, my dearest love? At this moment the Enemy are coming out, and as if determined to have a fair fight. All night they have been making signals, and the morning showed them to us getting under sail. They have 34 Sail-of-the-Line, and five Frigates. Lord Nelson, I am sorry to say, has but 27 Sail-of-the-Line with him; the rest are at Gibraltar, getting water. . . . Within two hours, though our Fleet was at sixteen leagues off, I have let Lord N. know of their coming out. . . . At this moment we are within four miles of the Enemy, and talking to Lord Nelson by means of Sir H. Popham's signals. You see also, my Harriet, I have time to write to you and to assure you that to the last moment of my breath, I shall be as much attached to you as man can be. . . . It is very odd how I have been dreaming all night of my carrying home dispatches. God send so much good luck! The day is fine, the sight of course beautiful, though so distant.'

4

Daylight of October 20 found the British fleet close to the mouth of the Straits, in heavy rain and thick weather. These were the waters in which Howe, homeward bound after succouring the Rock, had encountered the fleet of Spain, in 1782, and nine years past Nelson had rescued Hardy. Through the sea-mist, at intervals, could be seen, upon the eastern horizon, the towering cliffs of Cape Trafalgar (which the learned and reverend Mr. Scott afterwards insisted should be pronounced with the accent on the third syllable, and when sharp Mr. Canning asked whether the same applied to Gibraltar, answered simply, "Yes").

There was no sign of the Combined Fleet on this Sunday morning of 1805, so the fleet made sail to the N.W., and presently a signal from the *Phœbe* told that the enemy still lay to the north. The *Victory* hove to, and Collingwood, with Captains Duff, Hope and Morris (all commanding swift-sailing 74's), came on board for an hour, after which the fleet made all sail to the N.W., and Nelson added a paragraph to his sheet of yesterday, saying that the wind had not come far enough to the westward to allow the enemy to weather the shoals of Cape Trafalgar, and he feared that they might return into Cadiz harbour. During the morning, however, the horizon cleared, the wind shifted, and Blackwood telegraphed that nineteen, twenty-five and at length thirty-four enemy sail were out of port. "The enemy appear determined to push to the westward." "That", wrote Nelson in his diary, "they shall not do, if in the power of Nelson and Brontë to prevent them", and he replied, "I rely on your keeping sight of the enemy."

He was continually on the *Victory's* poop while Blackwood was communicating, and mentioned to a group of midshipmen there assembled, "This day, or to-morrow, will be a fortunate one for you young gentlemen." At dinner he stated that he expected to capture twenty to twenty-two of the hostile fleet, and Dr. Scott heard him say, more than once, "The 21st will be our day", adding that it was the anniversary of a festival in his family.

It gradually became evident that October 20 was not to be the day. During the afternoon Nelson signalled two ships which had recently joined him from England to paint the hoops of their masts yellow. All his other ships were so painted, and black was, he knew, the colour used by the enemy. He issued his orders for signals during the hours of darkness. "If the Enemy are standing to the Southward, or towards the Straits, burn two blue lights together, every hour, in order to make the greater blaze. If the Enemy are standing to the Westward, three guns, quick, every hour." Blackwood, according to his instructions, was keeping two frigates in sight of the enemy, and a further couple between them and Hope's 74-gun ship. From the *Defence*, signals were repeated to the *Colossus*, stationed between the *Defence* and *Mars*, whence Duff communicated with the *Victory*. At 8 p.m. the British fleet wore, and stood to the S.W. At midnight the frigates closest to the enemy could see, upon one side, the glow of lamps from the stern-cabin windows of thirty-three men-of-war, on the other only scattered lights.

The date October 21 was written down, and a little before dawn the English fleet, hitherto sailing almost parallel to the enemy, though out of sight, again altered course. Nelson, considering that he had drawn his prey far enough out of Cadiz, had turned to the N.E. as a preliminary to attack.

Since the beautiful morning of the 19th the weather had broken. Throughout the night of the 20th there had been but light breezes, inclining to calm, and the same conditions, prevailing at daybreak, were to last the day; but there was also a heavy swell from the westward, which might herald a storm. At a chilly hour, Collingwood's steward, entering his master's cabin with a light, found him already up and dressing. The Admiral asked, in greeting, whether his servant had seen the enemy, and upon receiving a startled reply, advised him to take a look out. The man obeyed, and beheld with awe, through puffing mist, "a crowd of great ships" some ten miles to the leeward. But upon glancing from this array to Nelson's second-in-command, calmly continuing to shave his regular features, in mixed poor light, while murmuring that "In a short time we shall see a great deal more of them", he loyally decided that the spectacle in a British first-rate was the more inspiring. Alone of Collingwood's personal servants he was to survive this day. Collingwood, on the morning of a day when he was "to fight like an Angel", was distinguished by composure and terse speech. Upon the arrival of his First Lieutenant, he advised Mr. Clavell to follow his example, and change his boots for shoes and silk stockings—"so much more manageable for the surgeon". His Flag-Captain, north-country Captain Rotherham, who accompanied him as he visited the decks of the *Royal Sovereign*, was a dazzling sight in full-dress uniform. Rotherham said that he had always fought in his cocked hat, and always would.

Lord Nelson was observed upon the quarter-deck of the *Victory* with first daylight. He was wearing the same undress uniform coat which he had commonly worn since he left Portsmouth, and shoes and stockings as usual, but for the first time when expecting an action, no sword. His sword had been taken from its rack in his cabin, but left lying on a table. The coat was far from new, and its skirts were lined with white shalloon, not silk; but upon its left breast were embroidered the stars of the four Orders of Knighthood to which he was entitled. Mr. Beatty, representing several officers, expressed to the two Scotts the wish that someone might suggest to his lordship to cover his decorations with a handkerchief. The enemy were believed to have Tyrolean riflemen dispersed amongst their ships and were likely to have sharpshooters in their tops. Both the public and private secretary were certain that their employer would be highly displeased if anyone took the liberty of suggesting to him that he should make any alteration in his uniform on such an account, so Beatty took what he felt to be a duty upon himself, saying that he would make an opportunity when presenting his Sick Report for the day. He hung about, but the Admiral was at first closely engaged, giving instructions to his frigate Captains, and a few minutes before the enemy opened fire, ordered all persons not stationed on the quarter-deck or poop to get to their proper quarters. Hardy had been approached, however, and after the firing had begun, as he paced by Nelson's side, he mentioned that conspicuous decorations might draw enemy attention to the figure of the British Chief, and Nelson agreed that they might, but said, "it was now too late to be shifting a coat".

The signal guns, rockets and Bengal fires of the British fleet had made Villeneuve aware, overnight, of their immediate neighbourhood, and before daylight his five squadrons had received the order to form in close line of battle on the starboard tack. As the British advanced, in greater numbers than he had expected, and he saw that, in very light westerly breeze prevailing, it was impossible to avoid an action, he decided to lay his ships' heads in the direction of Cadiz, and at a little after 6 a.m. made the signals to wear all together and form line of battle on the port tack. This manœuvre was not accomplished until about 10 a.m., and then most irregularly, the ships, in some cases three abreast, drifting rather than sailing into a curve about five miles long, stretching from north to south.

The *Victory's* first general signal of the day, made at 6.40, to form the order of sailing in two columns, each ship to engage her opponent, was followed after ten minutes by "Bear up, and steer east". The Commander-in-Chief, leading the twelve ships of the northern or weather column, at once set the example, and Collingwood's southern or leeward division of fifteen ships fell into the wake of the *Royal Sovereign*. At 8 a.m. three junior frigate Captains came on board the *Victory*. Dr. Scott and Mr. Beatty at dawn had noticed that "his Lordship displayed excellent spirits". Blackwood, who as senior frigate Captain had been summoned before 6, found him "in calm but very good spirits". There is evidence from every eyewitness that he was in the taut, omniscient state common to him on such occasions. After receiving Blackwood's compliments on the approach of a long-looked-for hour, he briskly exclaimed, "I mean to-day to bleed the captains of the Frigates, as I shall keep you on board until the very last minute."

Five months previously, writing to Lady Hamilton on his homeward passage from the West Indies, he had told her: "I have sent two Codicils, in which you are deeply interested, to Mr. Haslewood, to be placed with my Will and other Codicils, for if I kept them on board ship they might be lost, and then you and Horatia would not get what I intend, which would embitter my last moments." After a few minutes' professional conversation with Blackwood, he now asked him, together with Hardy, to witness his signature. The long document in his own hand, which he had achieved after his view of the enemy with dawn, has always been styled his "last Codicil", though that word nowhere occurs in it.

"October the twenty-first, one thousand eight hundred and five, then in sight of the Combined Fleets of France and Spain, distant about ten miles.

"Whereas the eminent services of Emma Hamilton, widow of the Right Honourable Sir William Hamilton, have been of the very greatest service to our King and Country, to my knowledge, without her receiving any reward from either our King or Country;—first, that she obtained the King of Spain's letter, in 1796, to his brother, the King of Naples, acquainting him of his intention to declare War against England; from which letter the Ministry sent out orders to then Sir John Jervis, to strike a stroke, if opportunity offered, against either the Arsenals of Spain, or her Fleets. That neither of these was done is not the fault of Lady Hamilton. The opportunity might have been offered. Secondly, the British Fleet under my command, could never have returned the second time to Egypt, had not Lady Hamilton's influence with the Queen of Naples caused letters to be wrote to the Governor of Syracuse, that he was to encourage the Fleet being supplied with everything, should they put into any Port in Sicily. We put into Syracuse, and received every supply, went to Egypt, and destroyed the French Fleet.

"Could I have rewarded these services, I would not now call upon my Country; but as that has not been in my power, I leave Emma Lady Hamilton, therefore, a Legacy to my King and Country, that they will give her an ample provision to maintain her rank in life. I also leave to the beneficence of my Country my adopted daughter, Horatia Nelson Thompson; and I desire she will use in future the name of Nelson only.

"These are the only favours I ask of my King and Country at this moment when I am going to fight their Battle. May God Bless my King and Country, and all those who I hold dear. My relations it is needless to mention; they will of course be amply provided for.

"Nelson and Brontë."

The Captains signed their names, and Blackwood seized the chance, before his juniors arrived, to suggest that the Chief should shift his flag to the *Euryalus*, and conduct the battle from her; but "he would not hear of it, and gave as his reason the force of example". The only visible result of the suggestion was an order for more sail to be made upon the *Victory*. After receiving their instructions, the four frigate Captains stalked behind the Chief and his Flag-Captain as he went the rounds of the ship. The Admiral praised the manner in which the hawse holes had been barricaded, and reminded gun crews not to waste a shot. The word "Victory" was continually on his lips, and he appealed to Blackwood several times for an opinion as to the number of prizes they would take to-day, always adding that personally he would not be satisfied by anything less than twenty. Blackwood, in reply, was "careful not to hold the enemy light", and suggested that the capture of fourteen ships would be "a glorious result". A feature of the picture which did not surprise any contemporary was that the ship's company thus invoked included Frenchmen, Spaniards, Scandinavians, Hindus, Germans, Italians, Portuguese, Swiss, Dutch, Kanakas and Americans, and in spite of the efforts of press-gangs, the *Victory* was undermanned. On the other hand, the name of Nelson had brought to his flagship nearly two hundred volunteers.

At about 9.30, Blackwood, having failed to get Nelson to shift his flag to the *Euryalus*, suggested that one or two other ships might precede the *Victory* into action. "I ventured to give it as the joint opinion of Captain Hardy and myself how advantageous it would be for the Fleet for his Lordship to keep as long as possible out of the Battle." Nelson answered briefly, "Let them go", and Blackwood departed, allowed to hail the *Téméraire* to go ahead. "On returning to the *Victory*, I found him doing all he could to increase rather than diminish sail." Blackwood got the ear of Hardy, and pointed out that unless the swift-sailing *Victory* gave way, the labouring *Téméraire* could not pass, but Hardy would take no action, and when, half an hour before the *Victory* opened fire, the *Téméraire*, having been signalled at 12.15 to take her place astern, ranged up on the *Victory's* quarter, Nelson ("speaking as he always did, with a slight nasal intonation"), said, "I'll thank you, Captain Harvey, to keep in your proper station, which is astern of the *Victory*."

The approach to action was at a rate which promised a heavy

casualty list for the leading ships when the enemy opened fire. The advance of the British fleet, though all possible sail was set, fell from three knots to a mile and a half an hour. "About 10 o'clock, Lord Nelson's anxiety to close with the enemy became very apparent." He remarked again and again, "They put a good face upon it", always adding quickly, "I'll give them such a dressing as they never had before." A little before 11 he went below to his cabin for the last time.

Bulkheads throughout the fleet were down, and the Admiral's quarters were scarcely recognisable, having been cleared of all fixtures. Nearly all the furniture had gone into the hold, and Dr. Scott, while upon the poop, had heard him giving particular instructions to the men engaged in unhanging his pictures, using the words, "Take care of my Guardian Angel." His desk had been left with his pocket-book lying upon it, and he now added a paragraph to the few professional notes which he had entered earlier, under date "Monday, October 21st, 1805". His last writing was a prayer.

"May the Great God, whom I worship, grant to my Country, and for the benefit of Europe in general, a great and glorious Victory; and may no misconduct in anyone tarnish it; and may humanity after Victory be the predominant feature in the British Fleet. For myself, individually, I commit my life to Him who made me, and may His blessing light upon my endeavours for serving my Country faithfully. To Him I resign myself and the just cause which is entrusted to me to defend. Amen. Amen. Amen."

John Pasco, Signal Lieutenant, entering the cabin with a report, and finding the Admiral upon his knees, waited until he rose to deliver his message, and forebore from proceeding to a personal request. "I could not, at such a moment, disturb his mind with any grievances of mine." Nelson soon followed him to the poop. The distance between the contending fleets was still about three miles. Having telegraphed Collingwood, "I intend to pass through the van of the enemy's line, to prevent him getting into Cadiz", and changed the course of the *Victory* a little to the northward, Nelson could, for the moment, do nothing more. The sea was smooth, with a great ground-swell setting from the westward, and since the sky was now clear of cloud, the waters were richly dark blue in colour.

With the approach of noon, bands struck up on board the ships of the two British columns, rolling gently towards the enemy, and the first sunlight of the day broke through, picking up, according to eyewitnesses, "in a beautiful manner", a forest of masts with black hoops, and the freshly painted sides of a crescent-shaped formation of scarlet, black and yellow French and Spanish ships-of-the-line, which seemed to include a formidable number of three-deckers, amongst which Nelson's "old acquaintance", the *Santissima Trinidad*, glowing in vermilion and white, with a dazzlingly white figurehead, was prominent. A Second Lieutenant of Marines, sent below with orders in the *Ajax*, was surprised by the *sang-froid* of the bluejackets. Nearly all had stripped to the waist and bound their handkerchiefs round their heads. A number were performing an elaborate horn-pipe to the strains of the martial music which had just struck up. Veterans, engaged in sharpening their cutlasses or polishing their guns, as if an inspection instead of an action was momentarily expected, broke off occasionally to take a look out of the yawning gun-ports and differ as to the identity and previous records of the ships which they were about to engage. Someone remarked that this lot would make a fine sight as prizes at Spithead.

On the poop of the *Victory*, as the National Anthem was followed by "Rule, Britannia" and "Britons Strike Home", Nelson had asked Blackwood whether he did not think there was one more general signal wanting, adding: "I'll now amuse the Fleet". His conversation with his Signal Lieutenant had been, "Mr. Pasco, I wish to say to the Fleet, ENGLAND CONFIDES THAT EVERY MAN WILL DO HIS DUTY. You must be quick, for I have one more signal to make, which is for close action." Pasco begged leave to suggest the substitution of "expects" for "confides", as the first word was in the Signal Book and would save seven hoists, and to this the Admiral agreed. ("That will do; make it directly.") The response throughout the fleet, as the message passed down both lines, was, according to Blackwood, "truly sublime"; another witness says that "it was received with three cheers in every ship". "Number 16", the signal for close action, followed, and remained at the top-gallant masthead of the *Victory* until it was shot away. The log of Blackwood's frigate shows that it was preceded, by four minutes, by an order to be prepared to anchor after the close of the action. Nelson had foreseen the probability of a storm, and was anxious for the safety of his ships on a lee shore.

The *Royal Sovereign*, sailing well with her new copper, was in advance of her line, and rapidly closing with the enemy. Nelson struck his thigh and exclaimed, "See how that noble fellow Collingwood carries his ship into action!" and these were the last recorded words spoken by him without the background of gunfire, for by 11.40 Collingwood was under the direct fire of the huge, swarthy *Santa Ana* and the French *Fougueux*, and partially under that of four or five other ships. Collingwood broke the enemy line astern of the Spanish three-decker bearing the flag of Vice-Admiral de Álava. The *Belleisle* came into action next, and relieved the pressure on the *Royal Sovereign*. Within ten minutes the *Revenge*, ninth ship of the British lee division, was going through, between the fifth and sixth 74 of the enemy rear. A cloud of smoke closed over the division of the British second-in-command. Lieutenant Pasco, looking through his glass, exclaimed, "There is a top-gallant yard gone!" "Whose top-gallant yard is that gone?" asked the Commander-in-Chief sharply. "Is it the *Royal Sovereign*?" "No, my Lord, an enemy's." Lord Nelson smiled. "Collingwood is doing well." He pulled out his watch, and called to the officers about him to synchronise theirs by it.

The first shot at the *Victory* fell short of her. She was an almost stationary target, carried along by the long Atlantic swell and the remains of her own impetus. A second shot, fired after two or three minutes, fell alongside; a third passed over her. The last moment mentioned by Nelson had come, and he bade Blackwood and Captain Prowse of the *Sirius* to hurry on board their frigates, and on their way along the column tell the Captains of all line-of-battle ships to get into action immediately. "They might adopt whatever they thought best, provided it led them quickly and closely alongside an enemy." He ended his instructions with an urgent repetition of their dismissal, and Blackwood, as they shook hands in farewell, uttered a cheerful sentence expressive of his hopes, on a speedy return, of finding his lordship well and in possession of twenty prizes. But the young officer went over the *Victory*'s side "with a

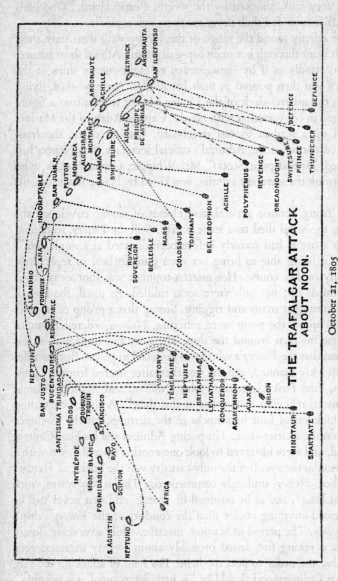

THE TRAFALGAR ATTACK
ABOUT NOON.

October 21, 1805

Reproduced from *The Year of Trafalgar*, by Sir Henry Newbolt.
By kind permission of Messrs. John Murray.

heart very sad", shocked by the words, clearly heard, "God bless you, Blackwood; I shall never speak to you again."

The enemy found the range of the *Victory* with their sixth shot, which went through her main top-gallant sail. After a short silence, as concertedly as if by signal, seven or eight enemy ships of the enemy van then poured in their broadsides. A round-shot, flying across the quarter-deck of the *Victory*, almost tore in two a figure engaged in conversation with Hardy. Captain Adair of the Marines called up a seaman to cast overboard, without delay, the fragmented corpse of the Admiral's official secretary, but Nelson had noticed. "Is that poor Scott?" Mr. Whipple, Captain's clerk, who undertook the secretary's duties, was killed by blast a few moments later.

As firing became general, and clouds of smoke enveloped the scene, the wind died to a mere breath. Still the *Victory*, sustaining "such a fire as had scarcely before been directed at a single ship", without being able to bring her own guns to bear in reply, held steadily on her course. Her mizzen-topmast was shot away about two-thirds up; her sails were soon riddled. As usual, the French were aiming at masts and rigging. Seeing that a group of marines drawn up on the poop were suffering, Nelson ordered Adair to disperse his men around the ship. The next and most serious loss yet was that the *Victory's* wheel was knocked to pieces. But the tiller was quickly manned, and she was thereafter steered from the gun-room, "the First Lieutenant, John Quilliam and Master, Thomas Atkinson, relieving each other at this duty". A shot, penetrating the thickness of four hammocks in the nettings, hit the forebrace bitts on the quarter-deck. The pacing Admiral and his Flag-Captain halted, and were observed to look one another up and down with a question in the eye. But the only casualty was the buckle of Hardy's left shoe. Nelson smilingly commented, "This is too warm work to last long", and as he resumed his march, said that never had he witnessed anything cooler than the conduct of the *Victory's* ship's company. The period of waiting, inactive, while advancing slowly under a raking fire, lasted probably about twenty minutes: then he gave the order to port the helm. His feint of attacking the van, so that Collingwood should be "as little interrupted as is possible", had served its purpose. The *Victory* opened fire with her larboard guns, "in a determined, cool and steady manner", as she hauled to starboard. She passed under the stern of a French three-decker, and fired into the cabin windows of the *Bucentaure*, first her forecastle carronade, and then, as she moved slowly ahead, a double-shotted broadside. Acrid smoke puffed back into the *Victory's* gun-ports, filling her lower decks, and a cloud of black dust and a shower of splinters descended upon her quarter-deck. Every glass there had long been scanning the enemy line in the fruitless attempt to discover the flag of the French Commander-in-Chief. The ship into which she had delivered her first, fatally-disabling counterstroke had, in fact, been Villeneuve's flagship, but close behind the *Bucentaure* lay the French 80-gun *Neptune*, and astern of her a French 74 in the act of ranging up. Hardy had gravely reported his regret that it would not be possible to cut through this line, "closed like a forest", without running on board one ship or the other. "I can't help it", had been Nelson's reply. "It does not signify which we run on board of—take your choice", whereupon Hardy had chosen the *Redoutable*. After the collision the *Victory* fell away at the rebound, but her yard-arm caught in the *Redoutable's* rigging, and the two ships hung together and so remained, locked in a death-grip, moving slowly before the wind to the S.S.E. While the *Victory's* starboard guns smashed in the *Redoutable's* sides, and her port guns continued to attack the *Santissima Trinidad*, lying ahead of the *Bucentaure*, men from the *Redoutable's* three tops attempted, with a deluge of langridge, musket-balls and hand-grenades, to clear the *Victory's* upper decks, and, under cover, a French boarding-party made ready.

Nelson had always been averse from the employment of small arms, or accumulation of explosives aloft, believing the danger of setting light to the sails to be greater than any possible gain, and the *Victory* had no guns mounted in her poop. The mizzen-mast of the *Redoutable*, a much smaller ship, rose midway between the *Victory's* mizzen and main, and the crouching Frenchmen, rising breast-high to fire, had the English Commander-in-Chief's quarter-deck not forty-five feet distant and immediately below them, though the lurching of both ships in the swell made accurate aim very difficult.

At the *Victory*'s last refit Nelson had ordered a large skylight over
his cabin to be removed and the space planked over, so as to give
him more room amidships. Here, clear of the ropes and guns, in
the centre of his quarter-deck, he had a walk twenty-one feet long,
from the wheel to the hatch-ladder leading to his cabin. At about
1.35, Hardy, who had turned at the wheel, and was advancing
towards the hatchway, realised that he had taken the last step in that
direction alone. Facing about, he saw the Admiral on his knees,
with the finger-tips of his left hand just touching the deck. The
single arm gave way, and Nelson fell on his left side, exactly on the
spot where his secretary had been killed an hour earlier. Sergeant-
major Secker of the Marines and two seamen were there in a
moment, raising him. As Hardy bent, he saw a smile, and heard
the words, "Hardy, I believe they have done it at last", or "They
have done for me at last." The large, consternated man muttered,
"I hope not", but the reply was, "Yes, my backbone is shot
through."

5

The shuffling party carrying an officer with a fractured spine
descended as quickly and quietly as possible from the light of day.
A background of white and gold paint, and buff and blue, gave
place to the half-lit glare of the universal red, chosen, it was said,
by Admiral Robert Blake for his middle and lower decks so that
seamen, accustomed to that colour, might not be distracted by
additions to it in the carnage of action. As the party prepared to
negotiate the last ladder leading to the cockpit, already thickly
bloodstained and very slippery, they encountered a panting clergyman. The Chaplain of the *Victory* had been so overcome by horror
and nausea as to be unable to continue his ministrations to the dying.
The incident of Lieutenant Ram, mortally wounded, defiantly
tearing off his bandages after the surgeon's mate had done with
him, had temporarily defeated Dr. Scott. He was hastening blindly
towards fresh air. Some hand, it was believed his own, had drawn a
handkerchief over the features and orders of the Commander-in-
Chief, so that the news of his fall might not spread and cause dis-
couragement. Scott either recognised garments, or learnt from the

bearers whom they were carrying. His love cast out fear, and he turned and followed the procession towards a scene which he soon afterwards shudderingly described, in answer to the direct question, "It was like a butcher's shambles." He never from that moment quitted his master, but as he never could be prevailed upon to write down or enlarge upon his experiences, the account of Mr. Beatty, Chief Surgeon, who had a record of twelve years in the Service, but who was often called away during the next three hours to attend other patients, is the principal source of information. Enquiries from Rose, begging to know what exactly had been the Admiral's last message to him, drew from Dr. Scott a letter, long and painstaking, but so obviously brought forth after mortal labour, and so rambling and repetitive, that it is to be doubted whether, could he have nerved himself to attempt anything fuller, he would have been able to produce much more. It is clear that throughout his hours of anguished constant attendance he scarcely thought; he could only feel. His description adds nothing to those of other eyewitnesses, except that at first Nelson, believing that he had only a few minutes to live, repeated in agitation that Rose must be told he had made a Will and left Lady Hamilton "to my Country". No regular prayers were said, although between bouts of pain Nelson rather led than followed short prayers with his Chaplain: and the last words heard by Scott were, "God and my Country!"

Beatty, a St. Andrews man, published two years later a detailed narrative, a model of clarity, expressed in terms worthy of the occasion.

On the arrival of yet another party, bringing down a silent figure with shrouded features, he directed the bearers to go far forward on the port side. He had already been presented with the dead bodies of two officers whom he believed to have drawn their last breaths during unskilful carriage below. He had over forty patients awaiting him. He gradually became aware that several of them were calling out, "Mr. Beatty! Lord Nelson is here!" "Mr. Beatty! the Admiral is wounded!" and turning, he saw a handkerchief falling from a pale but familiar countenance, and a coat with stars upon its breast. According to his custom, Lord Nelson had forbidden his attendants to distract the attention of surgeons from wounded of lesser rank.

Mr. Walter Burke, purser (a kinsman of the statesman), came running, and helped Beatty to remove the Admiral from the arms of seamen. On carrying him to one of the midshipmen's berths, they stumbled and almost fell. Beatty repeated his own name and that of the purser when the Admiral asked to whose arms he had been transferred. The easy business of stripping a one-armed man was quickly performed. Next to his skin Lord Nelson had been wearing a large miniature set as a locket. Its picture was that of Lady Hamilton as a Bacchante. He opened his eyes, and perceived the drooping figure of his Chaplain-Secretary, wringing his hands, and exclaiming, "Alas! Beatty, how prophetic you were!" He spoke to Scott, while Beatty was undressing him, saying, "Doctor, I told you so. Doctor, I am gone!" and after a short pause, in a lower voice, "I have to leave Lady Hamilton, and my adopted daughter, Horatia, as a legacy to my Country."

Another officer was at this moment brought in and laid by the Admiral's side, and a zealous assistant, seizing upon the first object to hand, rolled up the emblazoned coat deplored by Beatty and slipped it beneath the neck of Mr. Midshipman Westphal, who was suffering severe hæmorrhage from a head-wound. Beatty relinquished the Admiral's wrist, and turning down the sheet by which he had been covered, proceeded to an examination, keeping up a soothing monologue, in which it is noticeable that he already alluded with confidence to "a glorious victory". He satisfied himself that the musket-ball mentioned had gone deep into the chest, and probably lodged in the spine. He could perceive no external injuries to the back. He replaced the sheet, and asked if the patient would give him the full history of the occurrence, with all his sensations. Nelson answered that he had no sensation in the lower part of his body, and (which together with his pulse rate confirmed the surgeon's worst expectations) that he felt "a gush of blood every minute within his breast". Respiration was short and difficult, and he felt very acute pain about that part of the spine where he had been struck by the ball. "I felt it break my back."

Beatty, who had promised that he would not put his lordship to much pain, and had been quietly told, "You can do nothing for me", attempted nothing further. To the Chaplain, who was burning for employment, he suggested the administration of lemonade, which was in plentiful supply, and the construction of a paper fan. The cockpit, where three surgeons and their assistants were working with upturned sleeves and reddened forearms, by the light of candles in swaying horn lanterns, was below the water-line. The atmosphere during these hours of waiting was breathless. Burke and Scott spoke in turn, attempting to rouse the patient by hopes that he would live to carry the joyful news of his victory to his country. The purser was told, "It is nonsense, Mr. Burke, to suppose I can live: my sufferings are great but they will soon be over." To Scott, whose meaning phrase had been, "Your dear Country and Friends", his sadder reply was, "Ah, Doctor, it is all over—it is all over."

Once, as the minutes dragged past, the dreadful cry of "Fire!" penetrated, but died unexplained. From time to time the sound of cheers swelled. On one of these occasions the Admiral anxiously asked the cause, and Lieut. Pasco, lying at some distance, wounded in the right arm and thigh, raised himself on his left elbow to assure him that it meant another enemy ship had struck. The Chief's strongly expressed wish to see his Flag-Captain impelled the Principal Surgeon to send a succession of messengers to Captain Hardy, and after a long wait, during which the Admiral sighed, "Will no one bring Hardy to me? He must be killed", a bright-faced boy with a flesh-wound appeared, to state with due formality that, "Circumstances respecting the Fleet required Captain Hardy's presence on deck, but that he would avail himself of the first fav-ourable moment to visit his Lordship." The Admiral asked who had brought the message, and was told by the purser, "It is Mr. Bul-keley, my Lord." The name recalled to the dying man the visit of an old shipmate, the proud father of sons, to an invalid languish-ing in Bond Street lodgings, and the exhibition of a sea-officer's sword to a sea-struck boy. Dick Bulkeley heard and treasured the words, "It is his voice", and "Remember me to your father."

It was nearly three o'clock when the comfortable figure of Hardy came stooping into the cockpit, bringing reliable news. The *Victory* had been one of a group of four interlocked ships, of which the French *Fougueux* and *Redoutable* had now been beaten into silence.

Adair of the Marines had been killed while leading a small force to repel a French boarding-party. The fighting *Téméraire*, with a prize to either side, was still attacking the *Santissima Trinidad*. Half an hour before, a tremor, quite different from those caused by her guns in action, had passed through the *Victory*. She had worked herself free of the *Redoutable*, but to find herself threatened by five ships of Villeneuve's dismembered van. Not until he had signalled the *Spartiate* and *Minotaur* (also hitherto unengaged) had Hardy felt himself at liberty to quit the deck. The dialogue recorded by Beatty sounds the unmistakable note of high tragedy.

"Well, Hardy, how goes the battle? How goes the day with us?"

"Very well, my Lord. We have got twelve or fourteen of the enemy's Ships in our possession, but five of their van have tacked, and show an intention of bearing down upon the *Victory*. I have, therefore, called two or three of our fresh ships round us, and have no doubt of giving them a drubbing."

"I hope none of *our* ships have struck, Hardy?"

"No, my Lord. There is no fear of that."

"I am a dead man, Hardy. I am going fast; it will be all over with me soon. Come nearer to me...."

Mr. Burke, perceiving that something very intimate was to be disclosed, stirred. Together with Dr. Scott, he was supporting the Admiral in the semi-recumbent position which seemed the only one to bring him any relief. Burke's arm was behind the pillow. But he was desired not to move, and so, unwillingly, overheard the painfully achieved, low-spoken message. "Pray let dear Lady Hamilton have my hair, and all other things belonging to me."

Beatty, who had successfully concluded the amputation of a midshipman's leg, now returned to the bedside, and the Flag-Captain, greeting him, voiced hearty hopes that the Chief Surgeon might yet hold out some prospect of life. "Oh, no", murmured the patient. "It is impossible. My back is shot through. Beatty will tell you." Hardy shook hands, as he had done upon arrival, and departed in silence to send a warning message of the impending tragedy to Collingwood.

Beatty, on being begged not to waste his time on a hopeless case, explained that at present his assistants were doing all that was possible for the other wounded, but as the Admiral would not be gainsaid, he bowed and withdrew, the easier in his mind that two of his lordship's personal servants had now joined him. A few minutes later he was recalled to be told, "Ah! Mr. Beatty, I have sent for you to say, what I forgot to tell you before—that all power of motion and feeling below my breast are gone." Realising that he was being called upon to confirm the sentence pronounced upon himself by his patient from the first, the Surgeon began confusedly, "My Lord, you told me so before", and would have gone on to a futile examination of extremities, but was interrupted by the reminder that, "Scott and Burke have tried that already", and "You know that I am gone." Thus pressed, he summoned resolution to state heavily, "My Lord, unhappily for our Country, nothing further can be done for you", after which he found himself obliged to step aside to conceal his emotion. Nelson's voice followed him, saying, "I know. I feel something rising in my breast which tells me that I am gone," and softly, again and again, "God be praised I have done my duty."

Turning over in his mind the possibilities of palliatives, the Surgeon turned back again to enquire "if the pain was still very great", and was told, "it continued so very severe that he wished he was dead", with the yearning addition, scarcely audible, "Yet, one would like to live a little longer, too", and presently and feebler, "What would become of poor Lady Hamilton if she knew my situation ? . . ." As his wounded flagship roared her last broadside at the flying enemy van, causing violent concussion in the heated and dusky cavern in which he lay, he addressed her by name, "Oh! *Victory! Victory!* how you distract my poor brain!" He reflected, "How dear is life to all men!"

Three midshipmen, walking cases, and some more seamen were occupying the Chief Surgeon's attention when Hardy made his second entry.

The scene had now assumed the appearance made familiar to succeeding generations by the artist Devis, who came out to meet the *Victory* on her homeward passage, and stayed three weeks in her, making his sketches from life and upon the spot. On the left of the picture stood Lieutenant Yule and Mr. Midshipman Collingwood, their British bulk and complexions contrasting with those of the Admiral's wizened, whiskered Neapolitan valet. Dr. Scott, his hanging features fixed in a tragic mask, continued his office of "most tender nurse", gently rubbing any part of his master's body in which he admitted of pain. The arm of Burke (a man in his sixty-seventh year, who had been thirty years afloat) still propped the pillows. Hardy loomed above the group, looking down. The efficient steward, Chevalier, recommended by Davison, put a question to the kneeling Chief Surgeon. Beyond them crouched Lieutenant Bligh, dazed by a head-wound, and Neil Smith, Assistant Surgeon, at work. At a respectful distance, in the deepest shadow, hat in hand, lingered a bowed, homely, elderly figure, Mr. Bunce, Carpenter of the *Victory*, acclaimed by her master "an invaluable man".

Hardy's last interview with Nelson was noted by Beatty as occupying not more than eight minutes. As before, a formal handshake opened the dialogue, but this time a man of few words and no graces kept hold of the hand of a hero while he announced that he was come to congratulate him, even in the arms of death, "on a brilliant victory, which is complete". Hardy could not say for certain how many of the enemy were captured, as it was not yet possible for anyone to make out every ship distinctly. He could answer for fourteen or fifteen.

The reply was, "That is well, but I bargained for twenty", and then, with an access of energy, the order was given, "*Anchor*, Hardy, *anchor*." The Flag-Captain of a dying Commander-in-Chief hesitantly supposed that his Second would now take upon himself the direction of affairs, but such a suggestion brought Nelson almost upright in the arms of his attendants. "Not while I live, I hope!" Dropping back, he ordered, "No, do *you* anchor, Hardy."

"Shall we make the signal, sir?" asked the Flag-Captain, and was told, "Yes, for if I live, I'll anchor."

But he believed that he had only a few minutes more left, and his gaze pitifully outrunning his speech, he mentioned next:

"Don't throw me overboard, Hardy."

"Oh, no, certainly not," was the wretched answer.

The Scottish Chief Surgeon was amongst them, taking notes, and his decorous record approached a Biblical cadence.

"Then", replied his Lordship, "you know what to do. And take care of my dear Lady Hamilton, Hardy. Take care of poor Lady Hamilton. Kiss me, Hardy."

The Captain now knelt down and kissed his cheek, when his Lordship said: "Now I am satisfied; thank God, I have done my duty."

Captain Hardy stood a minute or two in silent contemplation. He knelt down again, and kissed his Lordship's forehead.

His Lordship said, "Who is that?"

The Captain answered: "It is Hardy", to which his Lordship replied, "God bless you, Hardy!"

He spoke very little more after Hardy's second withdrawal, and articulated with difficulty the orders for, "Fan—fan" or "Rub—rub". The *Victory* had ceased to fire some time past, and within the next few minutes even distant gunfire died away. When his *valet* turned him, at his request, upon his right side, he whispered breathlessly, "I wish I had not left the deck", and presently, to Scott, "I have not been a great sinner, doctor", followed by "*Remember* that I leave Lady Hamilton and my Daughter as a legacy to my Country —never forget Horatia."

Beatty, returning at increasingly short intervals, found him, upon a first inspection, whispering with evidently failing strength, "Thank God, I have done my duty", and upon the next, speechless, and with no discernible pulse at the wrist. At 4.30, about three hours after the Admiral had been hit, his steward, tiptoeing in search of the Chief Surgeon with the noiseless speed and speaking gesture of his calling, indicated something which brought that officer back with him quickly. They had to touch the shoulder of his lordship's private secretary, who was still mechanically chafing a cold breast.

6

With sunset, as the obsessing battle-noises ceased, and a comparative hush fell upon the scene, two junior officers in the dismasted *Belleisle* seized the chance to look about them, and, unknown to one another, recorded impressions of the aftermath of the greatest naval victory in history. Lieutenant Nicolas of the Marines, who could draw, jotted down colour notes of bottle-end green waters, amongst which appeared and reappeared fragments of timber surrounded by bent wet heads and clutching forearms. He saw, with the artist's eye, a central group which included a couple of boats putting off smartly, in indigo shadow, from the black and acid-yellow sides of the majestic *Royal Sovereign*, lying in an unmeant attitude of heroic exhaustion, with her sails as full of holes as if they had been powdered with confetti. His companion, who could only describe, but felt strongly that the "view of the Fleet at this period was highly interesting, and would have formed a beautiful subject for a painter", saw, "just under the setting rays", a dramatic huddle of five or six elaborately decorated enemy prizes, trailing severed rigging as they rose and fell helplessly on the Atlantic swell. A bank of lavender fog, produced by gunfire, drifted slowly towards the land, and a heavy scent, unmistakable to anyone who had taken part in a fleet action, burdened the air, and set hot men coughing. To the northward could be seen the full canvas of the enemy squadron flying for the security of Cadiz or Rota. About a mile distant, the *Achille*, with the tricolour upon her ensign staff still fluttering, was beginning to emit volumes of black smoke from her hull. "Our tenders and boats were using every effort to save the brave fellows who had so gloriously defended her; but only two hundred and fifty were rescued." This service was of no little difficulty or danger, as the *Achille's* guns began to go off, one by one. About five o'clock the flames reached her magazine, and she blew up with a tremendous explosion, sounding the last note of "the rout in Trafalgar's Bay".

Communication between the victorious ships was difficult, but the result of the day was obvious and appreciated. Not until darkness fell did a chilly whisper steal through the loudly triumphant fleet: "No Admiral's lights on board the *Victory*." Many contemporaries attest that when London newspapers appeared on November 6, with the heading "Glorious Victory over the Combined Fleets. Death of Lord Nelson", the instinctive comment of the British public was: "We have lost Nelson!" and strangers stopped one another in the street to repeat the news and shake hands to an accompaniment of tears. In the British fleet on the night of Trafalgar the feeling was the same. Officers of all ranks, writing home against time, gave their opening sentence to the victory, but the remainder of a long paragraph to a loss which was unanimously felt to be personal as well as national. From the lower deck arose the same note. "I never set eyes on him," explained a humble writer to a humble home, "for which I am both sorry and glad; for to be sure I should like to have seen him, but then, all the men in our ship who have seen him are such soft toads, they have done nothing but Blast their Eyes and cry ever since he was killed. God bless you! chaps that fought like the Devil, sit down and cry like a wench."

Nelson had spoken of "annihilation", and been disappointed to hear on his death-bed that only fourteen or fifteen of the thirty-three ships opposed to him that day had struck. But eighteen were accounted for on the day of battle, and eventually annihilation was the result of Trafalgar, though only four of the "beauties" watched by the men of the *Victory* as she drew slowly towards action were carried into Spithead as prizes. Dumanoir's squadron of four van ships was met and captured off Ortegal by Sir Richard Strachan on November 4, and of the eleven which succeeded in reaching Cadiz, none ever put to sea again, and those under the flag of Admiral Rosily surrendered to Spain in 1808.

Collingwood's list of the enemy flag-officers engaged, forwarded to England with his despatches, spoke for itself.

"Admiral Villeneuve, Commander-in-Chief. *Bucentaure*. Taken. Admiral Don Frederico Gravina. *Principe de Asturias*. Escaped; in Cadiz; wounded in the arm.

"Vice-Admiral Don Ignatio Maria D'Álava. *Santa Ana*. Wounded severely in the head; taken, but was driven back into Cadiz in the *Santa Ana*. Rear-Admiral Don Baltazar Hidalgo Cisneros. *Santissima Trinidad*. Taken.

"Rear-Admiral Magon. *Algeziras*. Killed.

"Rear-Admiral Dumanoir. *Formidable*. Escaped."

Collingwood did not anchor on the night of October 21, and during the following afternoon the gale foreseen by Nelson came on from the S.W., accompanied by torrential rain. Codrington of the *Orion* remarked, years later, that never had he been so glad to see the stars as after Trafalgar, as for four days following the death of the Chief no man in his fleet saw sun, moon or constellations.

While the shoals of Cape Trafalgar roared under the *Victory's* lee, her over-driven Chief Surgeon and his assistants did what they could for those departed this life. The body of Lord Nelson was stripped of the clothes in which it had been attired after death, with the exception of a shirt. The hair, for which Captain Hardy was asking, in accordance with his instructions, as a memento for Lady Hamilton, was secured. Beatty traced, with a probe, the course of the musket-ball from the spine, but stopped there for the present. A little before noon on the 24th the wounded ship, labouring deeply in the heavy seas, was taken in tow by the old *Polyphemus*, and managed to rig up jury topmasts and a mizzen. Next evening the *Polyphemus* was obliged to cut the towing hawser to prevent the *Victory* coming on board her, and in spite of burning blue lights, and searching to the best of her ability, she lost sight of the flagship for forty-eight hours. On the 26th the storm at last showed signs of abating, and Captain Fremantle, with H.M.S. *Neptune*, came to the aid of his old Chief. Next morning, although strong gales with thunder, lightning and downpour still prevailed, Dr. Scott was able to approach his first letter since the action. It was with a trembling pen that he addressed his sheet to "Mrs. Cadogan, Merton Place, Surrey", and began to trace the words:

"Hasten the very moment you receive this, to dear Lady Hamilton, and prepare her for the greatest of misfortunes."

Chapter XX

AFTERWARDS

I

TUESDAY, November 5, 1805, found London overwhelmed by the thickest fog known in the capital for many years. It extended for several miles outside town, blotting out hedgerows and cottages. In the City, shopkeepers, hopeless of doing any business, put up their shutters, to the distress of persons accustomed to certain lighted windows as landmarks on their homeward journey. In the streets, carriages proceeded at a footpace, and pedestrians, afraid of being run over, were halloing before they attempted crossings. Stage-coaches were hours late. By midnight Whitehall was almost deserted; but two post-chaises, which had been crawling up from the west, turned in at the Admiralty gates at the same moment, and two weary and crumpled officers who had last met in the Atlantic, in dirty weather, recognised one another with astonishment.

On October 26 Admiral Collingwood had taken advantage of the first abatement of the great storm following Trafalgar to send away the *Pickle* schooner with his despatches. Lieutenant Lapenotière, falling in with the *Nautilus* lugger, in the mouth of the Tagus, had communicated the news to Captain Sykes, who had hastened with it to Lisbon, where Mr. Gambier, British Consul, had only detained him while he wrote to London. Sykes had made the port of Plymouth a few hours later than Lapenotière, who had the longer land journey from Falmouth. The words "Despatches from Admiral Collingwood" brought the First Lord out of bed, to sit at his desk doing business with his staff till 5 a.m., by which time expresses had been sent off to His Majesty and all his ministers, and compositors were setting up the type for a *Gazette Extraordinary*. The Prime Minister, who was in residence at 10, Downing Street, confided in Lord Malmesbury next day that during an eventful career he had become accustomed to being knocked up at all hours by messengers bringing news of every description, but hitherto, be it good or bad, he had always been able to lay his head on his pillow and sink into a sound sleep again. On this occasion only had Mr. Pitt been unable to recover repose, and at length got up and dressed, although it was three in the morning. The image of Nelson in this quarter was too vivid, too recent.

A typical leading article of a daily paper published that morning opened with the words, "It is with mixed sensations of transport and anguish", and though the Park and Tower guns duly thundered, illuminations in London that night were described as "partial". Some days passed before officials, tradesmen and private residents had decided how best to express joy for a signal victory combined with a national loss. In St. James's Square, the mansion of the fabulously wealthy Mr. Goldsmid, a personal friend of Lord Nelson, exhibited but two small rows of plain lamps. Drury Lane blazed with an anchor and immense "L.N." wreathed with bays. "Nelson and Victory" was a popular form, and crowds paused appreciatively outside a well-known shop saying simply "Alas! Poor Nelson!"

Lord Mayor's Day was at hand, bringing poignant memories of an ardent and eloquent chief guest. His portrait was brought from the Council Chamber and hung above the Lord Mayor's seat in the Guildhall; his bust, garlanded with oak and laurel, presided over the Sheriff's table. On November 9 the *London Gazette* announced the first Trafalgar honours, and Vice-Admiral Collingwood (blockading Cadiz) was not much pleased when he discovered that his barony might not descend to his daughters, but the Rev. William Nelson was well satisfied to find that royal gratitude for the hitherto meagrely acknowledged services of Vice-Admiral Nelson had taken the extraordinary form of creating his elder brother an Earl. The body of Lord Nelson was being brought home in his own flagship, and it gradually became evident that "the last sad scene" pictured by the Matchams was to be much longer delayed and on a scale undreamt of by them when they had spoken of staying at Merton "till all is over".

At last, early on December 5, the day appointed for a National Thanksgiving, warning of the approach, from St. Helen's, of a large ship under low jury masts, which had been towed through the cheering Channel Fleet, drew to the sally port at Portsmouth, and the Blockhouse Fort opposite, crowds far exceeding in number those which had gathered on the same spot on a September day to watch Admiral Nelson wave farewell. The *Victory*, with his flag half-mast, anchored at Spithead, but the *Revenge* came into the harbour to be docked for repairs. "She bore marks of her bravery in the action, and the acclamations had a very pleasing effect."

During the week that the flagship lay at anchor at Spithead, the object of unceasing reverential attention, it was not possible to do anything, but directly she sailed for the Downs, Beatty, with his assistants, began an autopsy. To his relief, the body was in a perfect state of preservation, and death-masks (obtained either then or ten days later) represented features unchanged, except by an expression of profound repose. He was able, at last, to extract the fatal musket-ball, which he found lodged in the muscles of the back, a little below the right shoulder-blade, together with some gold lace and silk lining from an *epaulette* and a shred of navy blue cloth. The ball, after entering the left shoulder and breaking two ribs, had penetrated to the left lobe of the lungs and divided a large branch of the pulmonary artery, so the immediate cause of death, although on its further passage the ball had fractured the spine, had been, as he had expected, hæmorrhage from a vessel near the heart. He took the opportunity of examining the vital organs, and found that all were so healthy that they rather resembled those of a youth than a man in his forty-eighth year. These facts, taken together with his observations of his lordship's habits, led the Chief Surgeon of the *Victory* to suppose that Admiral Nelson might have survived to a great age, though, had he remained for longer than a few more years at sea, and overtaxing his remaining eye, he must almost certainly have become totally blind.

2

"He is to be buried in St. Paul's," wrote Mrs. Codrington to her Trafalgar Captain, "directly under the Cupola, which will be his *monument*, and may at the same moment remind *thousands* of spectators of his merits and his loss; and animate, in a last look at

London, the departing midshipman, lieutenant, captain and admiral to imitate his example."

Throughout the raw night of January 8–9 London could hardly be said to have slept. Thirty-one Admirals and a hundred Captains were up with their full-dress uniform. For days past country parties had been arriving to lodgings in the City and suburbs. "Town was never so full." A sudden hailstorm had drenched the capital as the coffin, brought in procession by water from Greenwich (on a day of brilliant sunshine, but impeded by a strong south-westerly wind), had been landed at Whitehall stairs.

The drums of the volunteer corps who were to line the streets beat to arms an hour before dawn on January 9. Young George Matcham's long day began at 6 a.m., when he rose at the Gloucester Coffee House by candlelight. St. James's Park, where the family joined the tail of the procession mustering to pass to Whitehall, was their first halt, and while they waited a weary while, young George saw the Duke of York talking much to his *aides-de-camp*, and many Admirals and Captains, in full-dress uniforms (but with black waistcoats), jangling with medals, and highly confused at not being able to find their carriages. In a coach well to the fore, ranked to precede those of the younger sons of Barons, sat a solemn trio bearing white staves: the Treasurer, Comptroller and Steward of the Household of the deceased. All had indeed known Nelson well: Alexander Davison, Esq., of St. James's Square and Swarland Park, William Haslewood, Esq., Senior Partner of Messrs. Booth & Haslewood, Attorneys, of Craven Street, Strand, and William Marsh, Esq., Senior Partner of Messrs. Marsh, Page & Creed, Navy Agents, of Norfolk Street, Strand.

Daylight broadened, and it became clear that Nelson's funeral was to be vouchsafed as dazzling a day as could be remembered in January London. Early sunlight beamed upon Portland stone and urban grass, from which the frost was passing. In the City the dome of St. Paul's rose against cloudless pale blue skies as if it had been cut out of pasteboard. The great bell of the cathedral began to toll at 8.30, by which time most ticket-holders were in their seats, and every window on the route from the Admiralty was filled; but the last part of the procession did not reach the Horse Guards, where it was to fall in behind the troops, until nearly noon. The military, under the command of the veteran Sir David Dundas, had been chosen chiefly from regiments which had served in the glorious campaigns amongst the sands of Egypt, after the Battle of the Nile (and were to serve under Wellington in the *sierras* of the Peninsula, and the wet woods and cobbles of Belgium).

At last the sound of fifes and muffled drums playing the Dead March in Saul gave notice that the procession was in motion. Minute guns boomed. At the Admiralty the coffin was borne out to the funeral car, which was fashioned to represent, in some sort, the Admiral's flagship, having a winged figure of Fame bearing a laurel wreath inclining from the prow, and upon the great lantern, above the stern windows, the inscription H.M.S. *Victory* in yellow block capitals.

The procession was so long that the Scots Greys leading it had reached the cathedral before the officers of both services, bringing up the rear, had left the Admiralty, but it was remarked that the only general sound made by an unusually orderly mob was one resembling a murmur of the sea, caused by a spontaneous movement to uncover as the funeral car came in sight. Two o'clock had sounded before the expectant silence was broken by words of command, the troops manœuvred to line and guard the entrance to the cathedral, and the coffin was taken from the car by twelve men of the *Victory*, to be met at the rails by six Admirals bearing a canopy.

The youngest relative, following his father, with bent head, up tremendous steps into darkness, thought the scene "the most aweful sight I ever saw. All the bands played." Sunlight and military music gave place to torchlight and the soaring voices of choristers. Simple words, very well known to a clergyman's son, swelled in the great dome. The first three anthems of a service which lasted four hours were, "I am the Resurrection and the Life", "I know that my Redeemer liveth" and "We brought nothing into this world". The Bishop of Chichester read the First Lesson. Young George found the Dean's voice heavy and monotonous. As the coffin was moved from the choir to the space beneath the dome, for interment, the Duke of Clarence, close behind his Royal kin, lumbered out of line to shake hands with Lord Nelson's brother-in-law and say in a stage whisper, "I am come to pay my last Duties here, and I hope you and I shall never meet on such a like occasion."

It had been foreseen that darkness must fall outside before the service ended. Within, the choir appeared but dimly lit, although many torches had been employed, but an effect of extraordinary brilliance had been achieved beneath the dome, and exactly above the bier, by the introduction of a temporary chandelier of a hundred and thirty lamps. The last stages of a State Funeral designed by the College of Arms arrived. Garter King at Arms lifted up his voice to proclaim the styles and titles of the departed. The officers of Lord Nelson's Household broke their white staves and handed them to Garter to be cast upon the coffin, about to be lowered by machinery into the crypt.

The final incident of Lord Nelson's funeral, found by many spectators the most impressive, was undisciplined and unrehearsed. It had been set down that the men of the *Victory* were to furl the shot-rent colours which they had borne in the procession and lay them upon the coffin; but when the moment came, they seized upon the ensign, largest of the *Victory's* three flags, and tearing a great piece off it, quickly managed so that every man transferred to his bosom a memorial of his great and favourite commander.

3

Most of the major characters of the Nelson drama lingered upon the stage long after his abrupt exit. He had been barely forty-seven. More than thirty years passed before the last of those who had known him best were quietly swept into the property box, all passion spent.

When his officers mourned the Nation's loss after Trafalgar, several added in despair that they had also lost their Patron. Codrington deemed the future of Hardy sunk in the grave together with his illustrious Chief. The voice was that of the eighteenth century, and they had under-estimated, amongst other things, the regard which immediately, and for all time, attached itself in the national mind to everyone and everything connected with the name of Nelson.

In 1810, when Lady Charlotte Nelson married Lord Hood's

grandson and namesake, Nelson's widow, flattered by a call from
the bridal couple, wrote of, "A Union of Names that will not easily
be forgotten". Lady Nelson, never strong and always on the move,
lived to be seventy-three. There is a shadowy glimpse of her "rather
prosy" in an hotel at Lyons, and a surprising one upon a boating
expedition on the Lake of Geneva, in company with her daughter-
in-law, an infant grandchild and nurse, and Lord Byron.

On May 12-14 in the year following Trafalgar, Parliament had
debated and finally voted a pension of £5,000 per annum to be
attached to the new Nelson peerage, £10,000 to enable the present
Earl to buy an estate, and £10,000 apiece to his sisters. A pension of
£2,000 per annum had already been granted to Viscountess Nelson
in February. There had been no mention of the woman and child
confidently entrusted by the Admiral to his King and Country,
"now I am going to fight their Battles".

Earl Nelson was still staying in Clarges Street with his wife and
daughter, and according to Lady Hamilton, on hearing at her
dinner-table of the splendid grant to his name and house, he produced the famous pocket-book containing the memorandum of
his brother's last wishes—"threw it to me, and said, with a very
coarse expression, that 'I might now do as I pleased with it'". A
violent scene between two very hot-tempered persons followed,
and though they were afterwards persuaded by well-wishers to
exchange conciliatory notes, and even visit one another, happy
relations were never resumed. The death of the Earl's heir, Horatio,
at the age of nineteen, upon which Tom Bolton became heir-
presumptive to the Nelson peerage, evoked no recorded comment from the guardian of slighted Horatia.

Lady Hamilton did her guest injustice in concluding that he had
deliberately suppressed the document explaining her claims until
his own future was assured, but there seems no doubt that he had
left her in ignorance of its persistently unlucky fate since it had
passed into his hands as executor. In fact, he had taken considerable
action, and it had not been in his power to suppress it even had he
so wished, for Rose had already seen it and undertaken to show it to
Pitt. But Rose was never able to perform his part, as by the next
time he saw Pitt, the Prime Minister was on his death-bed and the

doctors forbade all talk of business. On February 15, 1806, the luckless relic was taken on by the Earl to the new Prime Minister. This character was the "cold-hearted Grenville", whom Nelson had always prophesied would do nothing to help Lady Hamilton, and it is clear that on this occasion, and whenever afterwards approached on the same subject, his chilliness was remarkable.

Rose, with fainter hopes after the rebuff to Earl Nelson by Grenville, proceeded to tackle Canning relentlessly. The Prime Minister, who had been Foreign Secretary when Lady Hamilton had been Ambassadress at Naples, had not denied that her services deserved reward. But Canning, now Foreign Secretary, thought that Lord Grenville's letter, forwarded by Rose, "worded with the coldest caution", gave the Prime Minister the opportunity, as he evidently had the intention, of saying that the Foreign Secret Service Fund was not the appropriate source. Three Administrations had succeeded one another since the services mentioned by Lord Nelson as Lady Hamilton's sole claim for recognition had been performed, they had been performed by a lady at a foreign Court at which her husband was Ambassador, and far from having been kept secret, they had been made known to every person whom she had solicited, "and printed in extracts of a will registered in Doctors' Commons and accessible to all mankind".

On hearing the news of Trafalgar she had told Rose, "My heart and head are gone." A year later, a letter from William Hayley, who had known her in her spring-time in Romney's studio, had found her sitting in a stupor, in London, on a midsummer day, "leaning my cheek upon my hand, and very unhappy". "All seems gone like a dream." The old philosopher had told her that England would expect a heroic and serene bearing in the confidential friend of the immortal Nelson, and she had tried to assume it. "I did try and get a victory over myself and seem to be happy, alltho' miserable."

She might have pleaded that not all her debts had been selfishly incurred. She supported many poor relations, who requited her ill. The annuity of £500 left her by Nelson, charged upon his Brontë estate, produced nothing for three years, and after that was remitted irregularly. Cynics, who noticed that she went repeatedly to the theatre for the purpose of swooning when Braham sang "The Death of Nelson", would have been quick to record that Lady Hamilton was gambling again, and there is no such record. She did at a later date admit having been "dreadfully imposed upon for my good nature, in being bail for a person I thought honourable", but "my imprudence", stormy references to the machinations of "artful mercenary wretches", and Earl Nelson's meanness in throwing upon her the bills for the last improvements made at Merton were the only excuses ever offered by her for cumulative embarrassment. A meeting of what she called "my City friends" took place in London in November 1808, and her spirits soared. "They have rescued me from Destruction. . . . They are paying my debts. I live in retirement, and the City are going to put forward my claims. . . . *No power on earth* shall make me deviate from my present system." Abraham Goldsmid had given nearly £13,000 for Merton. She took lodgings in Bond Street. "The harp and viol were soon resounding from her lighted apartments, wilder extravagances than ever were committed." One by one she parted with her Nelson relics. Messrs. Salter received back the inscribed gift presented to Horatia during the twenty-five days, accompanied by an incoherent note that the child was "the daughter, the true and beloved daughter of Viscount Nelson. . . . *Her mother was too great to be mentioned*"—

a reference thought to point at the Queen of Naples. The death of shrewd old Mrs. Cadogan removed from her "the best of Mothers", and the last brake upon her irresponsibility. . . . The last reports of her in England are wholly pathetic. The New Year of 1813 found her, with "a fine snow scene" outside, huddled in ugly obscure rooms in the purlieus of the Temple, permitted to reside "within the rules of the King's Bench" on the condition that she made no attempt at escape.

All her effects left at her Bond Street lodgings had been seized and sold. She suffered a recurrence of jaundice, attended by the mental depression characteristic of the disease, and lay abed for weeks. Still she kept up a gallant pretence that her difficulties would soon be solved, and for a few months she did enjoy liberty again. She was re-arrested and back in "that vile Banco Regio" by July.

A City friend who had known Nelson since Jamaica days rescued her after she had endured a second bout of detention lasting nearly nine months. Alderman Joshua Jonathan Smith, senior partner of Messrs. Smith and Seiffe, sugar refiners, obtained her discharge from Lord Ellenborough in the first week of July 1814, and she sailed from Tower Wharf for France in a vessel called *The Little Tom*, with Horatia, and less than £50 in her pocket. Her few letters from the Calais district have the fragile charm of a contemporary water-colour.

Her health was mended by the simple regular round, the country air, the gentle exercise, the sensation of liberty, and above all the success of her last appearance in her favourite "Attitude", that of the English lady. "The Jaundice is leaving me, but my Broken Heart does not leave me." If her guardian could live to see Lord Nelson's child "well settled" she would "dye happy". Horatia takes up the story of the last four months, which is all darkness.

"At the time of her death she was in great distress, and had I not, unknown to her, written to Lord Nelson to ask the loan of £10, and to another kind friend of hers, who immediately sent her £20, she would not literally have had one shilling till her next allowance became due. Latterly she was scarcely sensible. I imagine that her illness originally began by being bled whilst labouring under an attack of jaundice whilst she lived at Richmond. From that time she was never well, and added to this, the baneful habit she had of taking wine and spirits to a fearful degree, brought on water on the chest. She died in January, 1815, and was buried in the burying ground attached to the town. That was a sad miserable time to me.

"The service was read over the body by a Roman Catholic priest who had attended her at her request during her illness. Lady H. had, ever since she had been in Calais, professed herself a Catholic.

"Latterly her mind became so irritable by drinking that I had written to Mr. Matcham, and he had desired that I would lose no time in getting some respectable person to take me over and that I was to come to them, where I should always find a home. After her death, as soon as he heard of it, he came to Dover to fetch me.

"With all Lady H.'s faults,—and she had *many*,—she had many fine qualities, which, had (she) been placed early in better hands, would have made her a very superior woman. It is but justice on my part to say that through *all her* difficulties, she *invariably* till the last few months, expended on my education etc., the whole of the *interest* of the sum left me by Lord Nelson, and which was left entirely at her control."

The Times recorded the marriage, at Burnham, on February 19, 1822, of Miss Nelson Nelson to the Rev. Philip Ward, M.A.

Nelson's prayer by the bedside of a sleeping infant at Merton was answered. The life of Horatia was happy, full and long. She settled to Victorian matronhood, bearing an annual child in rural peace, her only causes for anxiety, nursery epidemics (which included cholera) and, as the years slipped by, the number of fine boys for whom employment must be found. She never learnt her parentage. At fourteen she had been old enough to besiege her guardian with questions. "On her death-bed at Calais I earnestly prayed her to tell me who my mother was but she would not, influenced then, I think, by the fear that I might leave her."

As far as can be judged, Lord Nelson's Horatia inherited nothing from her mother except aptitude for languages and love of animals, and nothing from her father except his favourite "activity". But Nature had performed one of her celebrated tricks. Lady Hamilton's pupil was a perfect "throw-back" to the long-lived, country-rooted clerical Nelson stock of preceding generations. The child born on a winter's day in the year of Copenhagen, with whom Nelson had played on the carpet in Sloane Street lodgings (taken so that "I might be in an airy situation" after severe cow-pox following vaccination), lived to be eighty-one.

Six years after Mrs. Nelson-Ward had been laid to rest in Pinner churchyard under a tombstone inscribed, "the adopted daughter of Vice-Admiral Lord Nelson", a load of manuscripts rumbled up to the doors of the Pavilion, Fonthill, the old laundry quarters of the bizarre Wiltshire country seat in which Lord Nelson and Sir William and Lady Hamilton had spent the Christmas before her birth as guests of Beckford. The latest collection of holograph correspondence for which Mr. Alfred Morrison, the then owner of the Fonthill estate, had bid at Sotheby's had been put up to auction by a Mr. Joseph Mayer of Liverpool. It included hundreds of letters in the handwriting of Lord Nelson, addressed to Lady Hamilton, some of which, as they had been entrusted to private messengers, were completely unguarded. The correspondence was almost one-sided, as Lord Nelson had always burnt Lady Hamilton's replies, but Admiral Keats had returned to her, with the seals unbroken, two letters dated October 1805, beginning "My most dear" and "My dearest life", addressed to a Commander-in-Chief who had already fallen in action.

Parts of Mr. Morrison's purchase had already been quoted by Dr. Pettigrew, in his *Life of Nelson*, published in 1849, but as he had given no references, their authenticity had been questioned, and his taste censured. Sixteen months before he had chanced upon this tremendous *cache*, Mr. Morrison had secured, also at Sotheby's, from the executors of Mr. Finch-Hatton, grandson of Colonel Robert Greville, the private papers of Sir William Hamilton.

He caused the two complementary collections to be privately printed, in 1893–4, and any doubts as to Horatia being the child of Lord Nelson and Lady Hamilton were settled.

4

When Abraham Goldsmid bought Merton Place it seemed that the traditional silver lining had appeared in the noticeable cloud brooding over the house. The Dutch-Jewish financier who owned adjoining property announced his tactful intention of preserving some of the rooms as the Admiral had used and left them. Mrs. Bolton comforted herself and Lady Hamilton with prospects of driving down from London to take "a *melancholy pleasure* in tracing former times in those walks". For eighteen months the house became in effect what it had always unconsciously been, a Nelson museum. But on September 17, 1810, Sarah Connor, an uneducated but graphic correspondent, told Lady Hamilton that she had again waited in all day for a promised call from the banker. A trip to his business house had drawn from a clerk the disquieting intelligence that Mr. Goldsmid's attendances recently had been irregular. "It was feared he should lose a large sum of money. It would not ruin him, as he was so rich, but the sum was large." Eleven days later, Abraham Goldsmid wandered out alone into a part of the grounds called "The Wilderness", and there took his life. The house was never again a private residence, and the malediction upon it seemed to grow. Horatia well remembered hearing that Mr. Cribb, head gardener, had been assigned the dreadful duty of removing "Fatima, the black maid taken out of a slave ship, of whom Lady Hamilton was very fond, from Bear Lane Workhouse, where 10s. a week was being paid for her, to St. Luke's madhouse, where she died".

On Christmas Eve, 1863, James Hudson, son-in-law of Cribb, wrote to his son from Merton:

"When first we came to live here there were but three cottages on the Estate, and only eleven persons, three men, three women and five children. Now there are over two hundred houses, and nearly a thousand people. For nearly seven years after we came here, Nelson's beautiful mansion stood entire and furnished, as when he had left it to take command of the Channel Fleet, never to return. . . . But now, what a change has come over it! Of that mansion not so much as a stick or stone remains to mark the spot on which it stood. Those beautiful pleasure grounds and gardens all destroyed, the trees and shrubs all cut down, the birds have hied themselves to some more quiet and secluded spot . . . and if this is not sufficient to disfigure and transform the place, they are going to make a railroad right through the centre of it."

The evidence of Hudson that nothing remarkable was left of Merton Place within sixty years of Trafalgar is confirmed, with additions in the Ichabod vein, by every succeeding biographer of Nelson who made the due pilgrimage, but even the site of a hero's home holds attraction, and such pilgrimages, always touching, are seldom entirely unrewarding.

The extent of the estate can be judged with comparative accuracy from the advertisements preceding its sale, in 1808 and 1815. Large-scale maps of the district, published as late as 1817, show Morden Grove as the property of A. Goldsmid, Mr. Halfhide's smaller house, and Merton Place, still under the name of "— Greaves, Esq.", from whom Nelson bought it. A vicar of Merton has printed locally a booklet dealing with the environs, residence and circle of the most famous parishioner. In 1949, signposts on a by-pass, curving through Surrey water-meadows to avoid Kingston, talk promisingly and musically of Merton and Morden, recalling the well-known picture of the arrival of a frigate Captain, very early on an autumn morning, to the house where Lady Hamilton played at being a *châtelaine* and a *bergère*, and Nelson was never so happy. The railway anathematised by old Hudson, and in a form undreamt of by him—underground—carries the traveller from

London to either of two stations convenient for Merton Place in half the time proudly mentioned by the purchaser in 1802. In the vicinity of the stations crowds and noise and, what is worse than the "modern development" deplored by earlier biographers, mid-Victorian minor commercial architecture in decay, distract the imagination; but still a wider air than that of the City is noticeable at Merton—figures mostly walking and talking slower than in the Strand, and during the working-hours of the day, as in 1802, a preponderance of women and children, and dogs. The waters of the Wandle still run by the side of the High Street. "Hamilton", "Hardy", "Nelson" and "Victory" roads, filled with identical small dwellings, stretch, only slightly uphill, towards what was once "the Poop". In the vicinity of the church something of the old magic still lingers. There are chestnuts and hawthorns and lilacs and laburnums, fragments of warm red-brick wall, and buff lanes vanishing towards stiles. On a May day it is clear where Hudson's birds have betaken themselves. Within the church, high over the chancel arch, in very poor light, hang six heraldic paintings. One is the hatchment noticeable over the front door of Merton Place in engravings published in 1806, flowingly inscribed, "The Seat of the gallant Admiral Lord Nelson, who died in battle, Oct. 21, 1805". Time has struck a blow at the gold and silver paint and primitive oil colours, but the shapes can still be discerned of a palm tree *issuant* between a disabled first-rate and a battery in ruins, and a sailor, armed with a cutlass and a pair of pistols in his belt.

INDEX

INDEX